W9-ADO-743

HOOVER WAR LIBRARY PUBLICATIONS—No. 3

The Bolshevik Revolution
1917-1918

PUBLISHED UNDER THE AUTHORITY OF THE
DIRECTORS OF THE HOOVER WAR LIBRARY

HOOVER WAR LIBRARY PUBLICATIONS—No. 3

THE BOLSHEVIK REVOLUTION

1917-1918

DOCUMENTS AND MATERIALS

By

JAMES BUNYAN

and

H. H. FISHER

STANFORD UNIVERSITY PRESS
STANFORD, CALIFORNIA

STANFORD UNIVERSITY PRESS
STANFORD, CALIFORNIA

Library of Congress Catalog Card Number: 34-35285

Printed in the United States of America

First published, 1934
Second printing, 1961

PREFACE

THE MATERIALS of this book tell the story of how the Bolsheviks seized the power in Russia and kept it during the first six months of their rule. The story is told in the language of decrees, manifestos, and other public documents, in the words of participants and observers, and in the reports of the contemporary press. This volume follows chronologically the *Documents of Russian History, 1914–1917,* published by the late Professor Frank A. Golder, and constitutes a part of a collection of materials on the Russian Revolution planned by him and made possible through his initiative. It has been necessary to revise his original plan, but in carrying out this revision, I have attempted to reach the objectives which Mr. Golder had in mind. If, therefore, this and the other volumes now in preparation contribute to the knowledge and understanding of one of the great historical movements of this age, the credit belongs to him. While this volume has been in preparation materials have been selected and translated which relate to civil war, intervention, and war communism in European Russia; the revolution, civil war, and intervention in Siberia and the Russian Far East; the origins of the Third International; the revolution and the Communist régime in Hungary. These volumes are being prepared for the press along with certain memoirs and monographs dealing with the background of the Revolution and aspects of its development.

A considerable number of the documents of the present volume were selected and translated by Mr. Golder. The others, with a few exceptions, have been translated by Mr. James Bunyan, upon whom also has fallen the burden of the major part of the research involved in the preparation of the book. The materials relating to this time are exceedingly voluminous, and while there are many which would inevitably be included in a collection relating to this period there are many others included here for reasons less obvious or compelling. We have not made our selections for the purpose of upholding any theory of history in general or of the Bolshevik revolution in particular, beyond the general notion that it is not the first revolution in human history and possibly not the last. Nor have we had in mind the specialist who has access to the sources which we have used. There are others, who, presumably, do not have access to these materials but who have more than a controversial interest in the events described. For them we have tried to make selections which show the conditions of the time, how the various parties and leaders viewed them, what they proposed to do, the action that was taken, and the results as they appeared at the time. Because of the length of most of the materials quoted it has not been possible to give them in their entirety, but we hope that we have reproduced essential parts and have avoided any distortion of the meaning.

The Introduction, which relates to the March–October, 1917, period, is in no sense a history of those months but merely a résumé of the Bolshevik attitude toward the Provisional Government, the Soviets, the socialist parties, and the outstanding issues of the time. The editorial notes which accompany the documents of the following chapters are not interpretative. They are summaries of events described in the documents or of revelant materials which for one reason or another have not been included. Brief biographical notices are given in the Index. Wherever possible, citations are made to works in western European languages.

Mr. Bunyan and I desire to express our obligations to other members of the research staff of the Hoover War Library for the aid given by them in the preparation of this book, particularly to Dr. Merrill Spalding, Mrs. Xenia Joukoff, Mr. J. E. Wallace Sterling, and Miss Helene von Damm, whose contributions in labor and suggestions have been many and of the greatest value. Miss von Damm has also seen the book through the press and has prepared the index. We are also grateful to the administrative staff of the Library, especially to Miss Nina Almond, Librarian, Mr. Philip T. McLean, Reference Librarian, and Mr. Dimitry Krassovsky, bibliographer of the Slavic collections; and we are indebted to Professor William Hawley Davis, editor of the Stanford University Press, for his patience and helpfulness.

The International Publishers and the Appleton-Century Company have been kind enough to permit the inclusion in this volume of passages from the English edition of Lenin's *Works* and from Mr. Golder's *Documents of Russian History, 1914–1917,* for which I am greatly obliged.

H. H. Fisher *June 1934*

PREFACE TO THE SECOND PRINTING

The first printing of this volume was sold out in 1948. In view of the many requests for this publication, the Hoover Institution has accepted the suggestion of the Stanford University Press that the volume be reprinted. It must be emphasized, however, that this is not a new edition, but merely a reprint of the original edition, in which a few errata have been corrected and a few easily ascertained death dates added to the Index. We are aware that since 1934, when this volume was prepared for print, a number of new documents pertinent to the topics covered by this volume have become available. Unfortunately, it is not practicable to include them in this reprinting.

W. Glenn Campbell *March 1961*

CONTENTS

INTRODUCTION

THE BOLSHEVIKS AND THE PROVISIONAL GOVERNMENT

IN THE drab language of an official report written in the late autumn of 1916 an agent of the Petrograd Secret Police described for his superiors the material conditions and the state of mind of the Petrograd population and the activities of the revolutionary parties as they appeared to the police. The ordinary citizen, said the report, "doomed to semi-starvation" and without hope, had become peculiarly susceptible to revolutionary propaganda. The workers were in such deep despair that almost any signal might cause "elementary disorders." Moreover, "the suppression of workers' meetings, ... the suppression of labor organizations, the persecution of active participants in the shop-hospital funds, the suspension of labor press organs, etc., force the working masses, guided in their actions and sympathies by the most class-conscious elements, to show an acutely hostile attitude toward the governmental authorities and to protest in every way against a continuation of this war." "End the war, since you don't know how to fight" had become a popular slogan. Questionnaires sent out by some of the less radical leaders in the labor movement revealed that almost nine-tenths of the workers questioned were unable to maintain their pre-war standard of living despite wage increases of 100 to 300 per cent and only about one-fiftieth of the number considered their position tolerable. According to the authors of the questionnaire these conditions would inevitably lead to a general strike not later than January 1917, which would force the government to work for an immediate peace.

The Social-Democrats, the reporter for the police noted, were making the most of this situation. Among the many warring factions into which the socialist movement had split, there were two main groups: the defeatists, who were the most divided but the most popular; and the defensists, the supporters of a war of defense. Of the defeatists, the Bolsheviks were the most numerous and aggressive and as such had been the object of the solicitous attentions of the police in 1915 and 1916. Although the Bolsheviks had succeeded with considerable effort in re-establishing their organization after the raids and arrests, the police maintained, perhaps a shade too optimistically, that on the whole this party was leading a "pitiful existence, since their chief leaders are invariably arrested, while the masses of the people respond only weakly to the Social-Democratic propaganda and it is only hunger and the high cost of living that may drive them toward an open demonstration."[1]

In February the anticipated strikes began. Early in March, "hunger and the high cost of living" drove crowds of workers, men and women, into the streets in demonstrations which became, when the soldiers joined the demonstrators, a revolution. The Imperial régime fell and the task of establishing a new government was undertaken by the Provisional Committee of the State Duma in consultation with another improvised institution of very different origin and complexion—the Petrograd Soviet of Workers' and Soldiers' Deputies.

On March 12,[2] members of the State Duma met informally and authorized the Council of Elders to appoint a Provisional Committee. This committee of twelve members included representatives of the parties making up the Progressive bloc and of the Menshevik and Socialist-Revolutionist[3] deputies in the Duma. The party of the Right—the

[1] "Politicheskoe polozhenie Rossii nakanune Fevralskoi revoliutsii v zhandarmskom osveshchenii," in *Krasnyi Arkhiv,* XVII (1926), 1–35.

[2] This and all other dates in this book are according to the Western calendar.

[3] The Progressive bloc, which had constituted the principal opposition to the government in the last months of the old régime and which was most active in the

most conservative group—was not represented, nor were the Bolsheviks, whose deputies had been arrested and sent to Siberia in 1914. The Provisional Committee appointed commissars to the central government departments and then proceeded with the formation of a government, using as a basis of discussion lists which had been prepared several months before and circulated in the State Duma and various public bodies. The ten men chosen with Prince G. E. Lvov

organization of the first Provisional Government, included the deputies of two parties organized in 1905; the Union of the 17th of October (Octobrists) and the Constitutional Democrats ("Cadets"), with representatives of other Duma groups; Nationalists; Center; and Progressists. The Octobrists based their program on the Imperial Manifesto of October 17/30, 1905, by which, as is well known, Nicholas II promised a duma with legislative power and a share in the supervision of administration. The Cadets, also known as the Party of People's Freedom, stood at the extreme left of the bourgeois groups and advocated more extensive reforms than those granted in 1905, including wider powers to the State Duma, a responsible government, and the allotment to the peasants of state, monastery, and private lands, with compensation to the owners.

Of the parties and groups represented in the Soviets and the workers', soldiers', and peasants' congresses mentioned below, the Socialist-Revolutionist Party had been formed about the beginning of the present century by the union of groups of participants in the populist revolutionary movement of the preceding years. The party was by no means united on the issues of 1917 nor with respect to the Provisional Government, in which members with Right and Center tendencies participated. S.R.'s of the Left Wing opposed the government and, as will appear later, co-operated with the Bolsheviks in November.

In 1905, members of the then Right Wing of the S.R. Party had broken away and formed the Populist-Socialist Party, which in 1917 also supported the Provisional Government. The Labor group (Trudoviks) had been organized in 1906 in the First State Duma, mainly of peasant deputies. In March 1917 this group joined the Populist-Socialists to form a Labor-Populist-Socialist Party.

The Menshevik and Bolshevik wings of the Russian Social-Democratic Labor Party received their names at the time of the famous party split at the Second Congress of the party in 1903. Efforts during the following years to establish unity among Russian Marxists failed, and the movement was in a turmoil of struggle between Mensheviks and Bolsheviks and minor factional groups. In 1913 the Bolshevik deputies in the State Duma definitely broke with the Mensheviks, and during the war took a defeatest position with illegal, revolutionary tactics. As will appear, the Mensheviks supported the Provisional Government, as did the small Right-Wing group of Plekhanov. The Left-Wing groups of Menshevik-Internationalists and the United Social-Democratic Internationalists, still further to the left, opposed the Provisional Government as constructed, but did not support the Bolshevik revolutionary program. Still another group standing between the Mensheviks and the Bolsheviks were the Mezhraiontsy, who supported the program of the latter and formally united with them in August 1917. In this group were many who later held high places in the Soviet Government, among them, Trotsky, Joffe, Uritsky, Riazanov, Lunacharsky, Pokrovsky, and Karakhan.

as Prime Minister to constitute the First Provisional Government represented in general the same political tendencies as the Provisional Committee. A. F. Kerensky of the Socialist-Revolutionists became Minister of Justice, but N. S. Chkheidze, a Menshevik, declined to serve as Minister of Labor. The Provisional Government thus established succeeded nominally to the power of the Emperor, who had abdicated, to that of the Council of Ministers, which had been dismissed, to that of the State Council (the second legislative chamber), which took but little part in later events, and to that of the State Duma, which did not meet again but continued a shadowy existence, its members meeting informally to hear reports of individual ministers.[4]

The first steps in the organization of the Petrograd Soviet had been taken by members of the workers' section of the Central War Industries Committee, who were just released from jail and who with representatives of trade unions and co-operatives decided to form a Provisional Executive Committee of the Soviet of Workers' Deputies in the tradition of 1905. This Committee issued a call for the election of deputies to the Soviet on the basis of one for each company of troops and one for each thousand workers. On the evening of March 12 such deputies as had been hastily and informally elected, along with a number of Socialists who participated by invitation, met in the Taurida Palace under the chairmanship of Chkheidze. Here the Petrograd Soviet of Workers' and Soldiers' Deputies was organized with Chkheidze as President, Kerensky and M. I. Skobelev, a Menshevik, Vice-Presidents. This meeting also elected an Executive Committee of eleven. The Soviet subsequently

[4] English translations of materials relating to the March Revolution and the organization and policies of the Provisional Government and the Soviets are given in F. A. Golder, *Documents of Russian History, 1914–1917,* New York, 1927, chaps. 18–45. In the English edition of Lenin's works, *The Revolution of 1917,* 2 vols., New York, 1929, and *Toward the Seizure of Power,* 2 vols., New York, 1932, cover the same period and contain besides Lenin's writings much other information on the events of this time. For a discussion of sources for the study of this period, see Michael Karpovich's "The Russian Revolution of 1917," in *The Journal of Modern History,* II, No. 2, June 1930, 258–80.

declined to take part in the Provisional Government—an exception being made in the case of Kerensky—but voted to support the government in so far as it followed the Soviet program.

During the next few weeks Soviets of Workers' and Soldiers' Deputies sprang up throughout the country. Like their Petrograd prototype, they included representatives of workers, soldiers, and the various socialist parties. In order to co-ordinate their work, some four hundred representatives of these provincial Soviets held a conference in Petrograd, April 11–16. This conference, among other things, organized an All-Russian Central Executive Committee by adding to the Petrograd Executive Committee sixteen representatives from the provinces.

Those Bolshevik leaders who were on the scene took an active part in the organization of the Petrograd Soviet. They were, however, in a minority to the Mensheviks and Socialist-Revolutionists and, furthermore, they disagreed among themselves as to the attitude to be taken toward the Provisional Government and its program. Some of the party favored outright opposition to the government, but when in a meeting of the Soviet on March 15 they stated their position and moved the formation of a government by the Soviet they received only nineteen votes, with many party members voting against the motion.[5]

The party minority which favored outright opposition to the Provisional Government during these days was out of touch with and hence without the support of Lenin, who with Zinoviev, Sokolnikov, Bukharin, and others was abroad. Lenin in the meantime had expressed very strong opinions as to the tactics to be pursued by his party. To members of the party in Stockholm who were leaving for Russia, he telegraphed: "Our tactics consist in an absolute mistrust of the new government, in refusing to support it. Kerensky is especially suspicious. The arming of the proletariat would

[5] A. G. Shliapnikov, *Semnadtsatyi god,* 2 vols., Moscow, 1923–1925, I, 240.

be our only guaranty. . . . ."[6] In his "Letters from Afar" and in various other communications Lenin elaborated on his opposition to the Provisional Government, "the clerk of the billion-dollar 'firms' England and France," as incapable of making a democratic peace. He insisted that the Soviets be regarded as "organs of insurrection, as organs of revolutionary power"; that the existing state machinery must be destroyed and replaced; that the power must be transferred from the government of landowners and capitalists to a government of the workers and poorest peasants on the model of the Soviets. "We must tell the workers," he wrote in another letter, "that it is their duty to overthrow not only Wilhelm, but the English and Italian kings as well . . . . it is their duty to overthrow the bourgeois governments, and we must begin with Russia, because otherwise we shall never attain peace."[7]

When Lenin arrived in Petrograd on April 16 after his famous journey in a sealed train across Germany, he received a varied welcome. Many greeted him as a distinguished revolutionist whose words were worth listening to. Others, and this included some of the members of his own party, also welcomed him as a distinguished revolutionist but one who, unfortunately, had been so long abroad that he did not quite grasp the realities of the situation. To others he was now, as in the past, a disturbing element in the revolutionary movement, a narrow sectarian determined to continue his disruptive factionalism and break down the united revolutionary front. To still others who breathed a different political atmosphere he was an obscure agitator, an enemy of society, a madman whose ideas were so extreme that they could never gain any considerable following. Lenin lost no time after his arrival, defining his position in what were subsequently published and known as the "April

[6] V. Karpinsky, "Vladimir Ilich za granitsei v 1914–1917 g.g.," *Zapiski Instituta Lenina,* 3 vols. [Moscow], 1927, II, 91–93.

[7] This and other quotations from Lenin in this Introduction are from the volumes in the English edition of his *Works* referred to in note 4 above.

Theses." In this document he denounced the continuation of the war for the defense of the revolution or for any other reason so long as the Provisional Government remained in power, and advocated opposition and exposure of the real origins of this government, which he believed had been promoted by the Entente to insure Russia's continued participation in the war. He offered a program including the establishment of a Soviet rather than a parliamentary republic; the abolition of the existing police, army, and bureaucracy; the confiscation of all private lands; the immediate merger of all banks under Soviet control; the establishment of Soviet control of production and distribution of goods; the changing of the name of the party from Social-Democratic to Communist; and, lastly, the rebuilding of the Socialist International along revolutionary lines.

The April Theses evoked a hostile response both outside and inside the party. Plekhanov wrote an article "On Lenin's Theses and Why Deliriums Are Occasionally Interesting." The Bolshevik Petrograd Committee voted against Lenin's stand and the Moscow Committee followed suit. In *Pravda* (April 21) Kamenev observed that the theses were merely the personal opinion of Comrade Lenin and in opposition to the resolutions of the Central Committee and the party conference, which resolutions, he added, "remain our platform, which we'll defend both against the demoralizing influence of 'Revolutionary defensism' and against Comrade Lenin's criticism." Within a few weeks, however, sentiment within the party began to change, for events demonstrated the popularity of certain of Lenin's theses, particularly those on the war.

An opportunity to reveal the unpopularity of those who advocated a continuation of the war was offered when Miliukov, the Foreign Minister, issued on May 1 a note to the Allies affirming Russia's determination to continue the struggle until a decisive victory had been achieved. This declaration for a decisive victory aroused great popular opposition, and crowds of soldiers and civilians joined in demonstrations of protest. The Bolsheviks had not instigated the demonstration, but once it had started they helped on the good work by urging soldiers and workers into the streets. "We advocated peaceful demonstrations," said Lenin later, "but several comrades from the Petrograd Committee issued an entirely different slogan ['Down with the Provisional Government']. We decided against that slogan but had no time to prevent its use. . . . . All we wanted was a peaceful reconnoitering of the enemy's forces; we did not want to give battle." But battle was narrowly averted. Miliukov's supporters organized a counter demonstration, loyal troops were brought out, and finally the Soviet intervened to prevent civil strife by prohibiting street meetings and demonstrations for two days. On May 5, the Bolshevik Central Committee passed a resolution indorsing this order of the Soviet, condemning the slogan "Down with the Provisional Government" as premature, and declaring that the party would come out for "the transfer of power into the hands of the proletarians and semi-proletarians, only when the Soviets of Workers' and Soldiers' Deputies adopt our policy and are willing to take that power into their own hands."

Despite his advocacy of this assumption of power by the Soviets, Lenin does not appear to have taken much part in the activities of that institution. The mild and flexible Kamenev continued to be the Bolshevik spokesman in the Central Executive Committee, while Lenin threw himself into party affairs, developing its organization and striving to swing the majority to his program. In this he succeeded, and when the All-Russian Bolshevik Party Conference met in Petrograd, May 7–12, a majority of the 151 delegates representing 80,000 members voted resolutions in line with Lenin's position expressed in the April Theses and elsewhere. The Conference further declared it the duty of the party to develop the Soviets and bring them to adopt the "proletarian line," and to organize and arm the workers for the next stage of the revolution—the passing of state power to the Soviets or other organs expressing the will of the people.

In the meantime opposition in the Petrograd Soviet and elsewhere against the military and foreign policies of the Provisional Government produced the first of many government crises. Guchkov and Miliukov resigned and the Soviet took the important decision of approving the participation of Socialists in the formation of a new ministry. On May 18 the second Provisional Government, a bourgeois-socialist coalition, was formed. In this government Prince Lvov remained Prime Minister and Minister of the Interior; Kerensky succeeded Guchkov as Minister of War; and I. G. Tsereteli, a Menshevik, became Minister of Post and Telegraph, Skobelev Minister of Labor, and V. M. Chernov, a Socialist-Revolutionist, Minister of Agriculture.

During the period of the second Provisional Government, from the middle of May to the middle of July, four All-Russian congresses met in Petrograd. The votes of the delegates to these congresses undoubtedly reflected the general attitude of peasants, workers, and soldiers to the programs offered by the principal socialist parties. From May 17 to June 2 the first All-Russian Congress of Peasant Deputies was in session at People's House. Of the 1,115 delegates 537 were Socialist-Revolutionists, 465 non-partisan, and 103 Social-Democrats, including Mensheviks and Bolsheviks and smaller groups. The Socialist-Revolutionists controlled the Congress, elected N. D. Avxentiev chairman, and secured a majority of seats in the Executive Committee of thirty which was elected by the Congress and which was still in office during the November uprising. Although the deputies brought in no less than 242 recommendations concerning land, there was no dissent to the general resolution that the land should be turned over to the people, and only a few delegates, mostly Bolsheviks, opposed the Socialist-Revolutionist plan for the socialization of the soil to be put into effect after the meeting of the Constituent Assembly. In opposition to the Bolshevik program the Congress warned peasants against illegal seizures of the land, voted complete support of the Provisional Government, approved the war of defense until a peace without annexations and indemnities could be secured, and sanctioned the offensive then being prepared. With the same decisiveness with which it had approved the Socialist-Revolutionist resolutions, the Congress voted down Lenin's resolution on the agrarian question which proposed the immediate confiscation and seizure of church and private lands and the transfer of state power to the Soviets.

On the day following the adjournment of the Congress of Peasants' Deputies another congress met which revealed the popularity of the Bolshevik program among the workers. Since the overthrow of the Imperial régime there had been a tremendous growth of labor organizations; trade unions increased in number and membership; but even more remarkable was the spread of the factory-shop committees elected by the workers and other employees in a given industry without reference to crafts or categories. These committees had been sanctioned March 24 by the Petrograd Soviet in agreement with the Association of Factory Owners and Industrialists and later legalized by the Provisional Government. Naturally they were more responsive to the demands of unskilled labor than were the regularly organized craft unions. The Bolsheviks from the beginning had been active in this movement and they controlled the organization bureau which summoned the first conference of factory-shop committees on June 12–16. The conference, by 290 out of 421 votes, adopted a resolution drafted by Lenin which, along with the familiar demands for the transfer of power, the arming of the workers, exchange of products, etc., advocated the establishment of workers' control over the production and distribution of goods and over financial and banking operations; the transfer of the greater portion of the profits, income, and property of banking, financial, commercial, and industrial magnates to the hands of the people; and the introduction of universal labor duty. A resolution introduced by B. V. Avilov for state control of industry—according to the program of the Mensheviks and S.R.'s—was defeated.

On June 16 another congress met which enjoyed greater

prestige and had a wider representation than the meetings which had preceded it. The first All-Russian Congress of Soviets of Workers' and Soldiers' Deputies opened with 882 deputies having full voting rights. Of these 285 were Socialist-Revolutionists, 248 Mensheviks, and 105 Bolsheviks.[8] The Socialist-Revolutionist and Menshevik majorities carried a series of resolutions which touched the most serious problems of the moment but which offered less radical solutions than those of the Bolsheviks. On the questions of the composition of the government and the war the Congress approved the principle of participation of Socialists in the government in coalition with the bourgeois parties. It voted against a separate peace but urged that an attempt be made to persuade the Allies to accept the Soviet peace program and that, until the war was ended, the Russian army should be kept in combat condition.

Before its adjournment the First Congress of Soviets elected a new Central Executive Committee composed of 104 Mensheviks, 99 S.R.'s, 35 Bolsheviks, and 18 others. This C.E.C. remained in office until the November Revolution.

In the course of his speech before the Congress on the Provisional Government, Lenin, replying to a remark by Tsereteli, declared, "No party has a right to refuse power, and our party does not refuse it. Our party is ready at any moment to take all power into its hands." There was applause and laughter, and Lenin added, "You may laugh, but if the Citizen-Minister [Tsereteli] confronts us with this question . . . . he will receive the proper reply."

He accused the socialist parties supporting the government of being democratic in words only, of allowing the war to go on in the interests of the capitalists, who should be

[8] Of the 1,090 delegates attending the Congress, 268 had a consultative voice. Of the total, 777 definitely expressed their political views. In addition to the three major parties there were: Internationalists, 32; Socialists, not members of any party group, 73; United Social-Democrats, 10; S.R. sympathizers, 20; Menshevik sympathizers, 8; Bund (Jewish S.D.'s), 10; Plekhanov's group, "Edinstvo," 3; Populist-Socialists, 3; Trudoviks, 5; on the platform of the S.R. and S.D. parties, 2; Anarcho-Communist, 1. (*Pervyi Vserossiiskii Sezd Sovetov R.i.S.D.*, 2 vols., Moscow, 1930–1931, I, xxvii.)

put in jail instead of into the cabinet. "When we seize power," he said, "we shall curb the capitalists, then the war will be entirely *different* from the one now waged,—for the nature of a war is determined by the class that conducts it, and not by what is written on scraps of paper." In another speech at this Congress Lenin denied that his party favored a separate peace with Germany, but he also denounced "a separate peace with English and French imperialists. . . . . We must break with them forthwith, for this is a predatory alliance." As showing the only way out, Lenin quoted a letter from a peasant: "We must press the bourgeoisie harder, let it burst in all the seams. Then the war will be ended. But if we do not press the bourgeoisie hard enough, things will be bad."

A few days later, while the Congress was still in session, the Bolsheviks announced a demonstration on June 23 under the slogans "Down with the Capitalist Ministers" and "All Power to the Soviets." The announcement caused no little consternation in the Presidium of the Congress. Chkheidze urged action by the Congress to prevent bloodshed, and other speakers, seeing a connection between the demonstration and some of Lenin's statements in the Congress, charged the Bolsheviks with conspiring to overthrow the government. The Congress forbade all street demonstrations for three days, and, as in May, the Bolshevik Central Committee accepted this decision. On the 26th, *Pravda* denied the charge of conspiracy in an article on "The Truth about the Demonstration." The majority of the Congress did not press the issue, nor did the opponents of the Bolsheviks believe that *Pravda's* explanation was by any means the whole truth. On July 1, however, the Bolsheviks had the opportunity to display their slogans in a demonstration held under the auspices of the Soviet Congress.

Writing of these events some years later, and using information gathered in 1920, Sukhanov charges that the "smoke was not without fire" and that "Lenin's group was not going directly toward the seizure of power, but it was ready to take the power under favorable circumstances and was taking measures to bring about those circumstances." He alleges further that plans had been worked out to bring about the arrest of the ministers, whereupon the Bolshevik Central Committee would have been declared the government. "But," Sukhanov adds, "the plot was uncovered and the demonstration called off."[9] Trotsky ridicules Sukhanov's charges and explains that, although preparations for the demonstration were made secretly and some of the rasher spirits talked of the possibility of seizing the railroad stations, arsenals, banks, and post and telegraph offices, the real purpose was to put pressure on the Soviets to get rid of the capitalist ministers and not to set up a Bolshevik government.[10]

The Bolshevik program suffered another defeat, though by a narrower margin, in the Third All-Russian Conference of Trade Unions which met in Petrograd July 4–11.[11] Of the 220 delegates, representing 1,475,000 members of the trade unions, 120 were Mensheviks, S.R.'s, and their sympathizers; 80 supported the Bolsheviks, whose resolutions against conciliation or co-operation with the bourgeoisie, for immediate liquidation of the war by a mass struggle against the ruling classes, and for workers' control of industry were defeated. The Menshevik-S.R. majority passed their resolutions on centralization and state control of industry and elected a majority of the All-Russian Central Council of Trade Unions (16 Mensheviks, 3 S.R.'s, and 16 Bolsheviks) and of its Executive Committee (5 Mensheviks and 4 Bolsheviks), of which V. Grinevich, a Menshevik, was chairman.

The Bolsheviks had no reason to feel downhearted despite the rejection of their resolutions by all but one of the

[9] N. Sukhanov, *Zapiski o revoliutsii,* 7 vols., Berlin, Petrograd, Moscow, 1922–1923, IV, 317–22.

[10] L. Trotsky, *The History of the Russian Revolution,* 3 vols., New York, 1932, I, 438, 479–81.

[11] The first and second conferences were held in 1905 and 1906.

congresses of the various elements of the revolutionary democracy. In four months their organization had been greatly strengthened; their numbers had increased; their slogans, especially those on peace, increased more and more their popularity among the masses; and, as a party, they were more united in their aims than their principal socialist rivals. The Bolsheviks had their greatest strength in the industrial centers, but by July they had a considerable and growing following among the soldiers, as was shown in an All-Russian Conference of Bolshevik Military Organizations, June 29–July 7, in which there were 107 delegates representing 26,000 members. Meanwhile the Provisional Government, resting on a coalition of by no means friendly elements, had lost much of the wide popularity which had attended its formation.

The government had accomplished many things, but many things remained undone and these in the circumstances were vital for the retention of popular support. The government had restored the constitutional rights of Finland and had recognized the independence of Poland. It had promised to call a Constituent Assembly and had made plans for the elections. It had issued decrees providing for freedom of speech and assembly and inviolability of person; had set up the Central Land Committee, which had prepared agrarian reforms to be consummated by the Constituent Assembly; had proposed a law on local self-government on the basis of universal suffrage; had authorized workers' councils in industries; had introduced the eight-hour day; had given soldiers the rights of citizens; and had laid down the principle of transforming the Empire into a federation of free peoples. But these and other measures were not enough. The Finns and other nationalities demanded more self-government than had been conceded. The workers wanted a larger degree of control of industries. The peasants wanted immediate legalization of the seizure of the landowners' lands. Conditions of living grew worse instead of better; food and other necessities were scarce and expensive; and life for the masses of the people of the cities became steadily more difficult. Above all the Provisional Government had not brought peace.

While the Mensheviks, the S.R.'s, and the other parties which participated in the government shared the responsibility for what it had been unable to accomplish, the Bolsheviks did not. On the contrary they gave expression to the discontent of all the discontented groups and canalized that discontent against the government and the Socialist parties which supported it.

In mid-July, discontent, national issues, and party conflict brought on the most serious crisis that the government had yet experienced. At this time the Ukrainians' demand for a greater degree of autonomy was bringing to a head the long-standing differences between the Cadets and the Socialists in the Provisional Government. There was disaffection among the Petrograd troops, with the older reservists demanding immediate demobilization and units of the garrison in a ferment over rumors that they were to be sent to the front. On the night of July 15–16 the Cadet ministers resigned on the Ukrainian issue. Early in the morning of July 16 soldiers of the First Machine Gun Regiment, in which the Bolsheviks had great influence, began preparations for an armed demonstration against the Provisional Government. Delegates from the regiment came to the Bolshevik headquarters in the Kshesinskaia house to ask the party to lead the movement. The party officials refused on the ground that the attempt was premature. But preparations for the demonstration went on. In the evening the machine gunners and the Moscow and the Grenadier Regiments paraded under full equipment before the party headquarters carrying the banners which had been carried in the demonstration of July 1 with the Bolshevik slogans, "All Power to the Soviets" and "Down with the Capitalist Ministers."

Detachments of soldiers made casual and unsuccessful attempts to arrest some of the ministers, and crowds of soldiers and workers gathered near the Taurida Palace where the Central Executive Committees of the Soviets of Workers' and Peasants' Deputies were in joint session. During the night the Bolshevik Central Committee reversed the earlier decision and decided unanimously to call upon the soldiers and the people to take arms and join a peaceful demonstration. The workers' section of the Petrograd Soviet, in which the Bolsheviks had a majority, voted to take the power from the Provisional Government and appointed a committee of fifteen to direct this movement.

On the 17th, Lenin, who had been out of the city, returned. Great numbers of soldiers, workers, and sailors thronged the streets, and processions marched to Kshesinskaia's house to be greeted by Bolshevik leaders and then to the Taurida Palace to impress their demands on the Soviet. Sailors from Kronstadt occupied Peter and Paul Fortress. Here and there clashes occurred between the demonstrators and government troops and a number of people were killed.[12] Bolshevik speakers encouraged the demonstrators to demand "All power to the Soviets!" but the Menshevik and S.R. members of the Executive Committees refused to be moved and told the soldiers and workers to go back to their barracks and their factories and leave their affairs in the hands of the Soviet. This produced a situation which Lunacharsky later described in these words: "We are bound to admit that the party knew no way out of the difficulty. It was compelled to demand of the Mensheviks and Socialist-Revolutionists, through a demonstration, something they were organically unable to decide upon, and, meeting with the refusal the party had expected, it did not know how to

[12] The July demonstrations appeared quite differently to different persons. To the Bolsheviks they were a "spontaneous movement of protest . . . . guided into organized channels" by the Military Organizations of the party (S. E. Rabinovich, *Vserossiskaia voennaia konferentsiia bolshevikov 1917 goda*, Moscow, 1931, p. 87). But L. B. Krassin, who had been a Bolshevik and was later to accept high office in the Soviet Government, but at this time was the manager of an industrial establishment, saw the events in a different light. In a letter written at the time he wrote, "The so-called 'masses,' principally soldiers and a number of hooligans, loafed aimlessly about the streets for two days, firing at each other, often out of sheer fright, running away at the slightest alarm or fresh rumor, and without the slightest idea of what it was all about" (Lubov Krassin, *Leonid Krassin: His Life and Work,* London [1929], p. 50).

proceed further; it left the demonstrators around the Taurida Palace without a plan and gave the opposition time to organize its forces, while ours were breaking up, and consequently we went down to a temporary defeat with eyes quite open."[13]

On the 18th one of the newspapers carried the accusation that Lenin's actions and incidentally the demonstrations were directed by the German General Staff. Regiments that had been neutral shifted to the support of the Soviet, and pro-Bolshevik units edged back to neutrality. Toward evening, government troops and cadets from military schools occupied without difficulty strategic points in the city. Raids were made against the Bolsheviks, their newspaper offices were closed, and a number of their leaders were arrested. Warrants for the arrest of others were issued, but Lenin and Zinoviev escaped and went into hiding. Kamenev was arrested, and later Trotsky.

In connection with this affair Sukhanov again alleges, and the Bolsheviks deny, that there was a conspiracy to arrest the government and the Soviet Central Executive Committee, proclaim a new government composed of the most popular Bolsheviks, issue decrees on peace and land, and thus gain the support of the masses in the capital and the provinces. The plan failed, according to this version, when the troops on whom the Bolsheviks were relying went over to the Central Executive Committee.[14] It would perhaps be correct to say that on this occasion, as in June and May, the party Central Committee had formally sanctioned only a peaceful demonstration but some members of the party had hoped and worked to use the demonstrations to overthrow the government. The failure of the Bolsheviks to achieve the objectives proclaimed by their slogans and the

[13] Golder, *op. cit.*, p. 451.

[14] As the source of his information, Sukhanov names Lunacharsky, who, with Lenin and Trotsky, was allegedly actively involved in the conspiracy. Lunacharsky said that he had been misunderstood by Sukhanov, and Trotsky denied the whole story and added that of all people Lunacharsky was the least capable of entering a triumvirate for such a purpose. Sukhanov, *op. cit.*, IV, 511–15.

charges of German subordination checked temporarily the expanding influence of the party. But the July Days had their uses. Trotsky subscribes to Miliukov's statement that the events had shown the Bolsheviks "with what elements they had to deal, how to organize these elements, and finally what resistance could be put up by the government, the Soviet and the military units. . . . It was evident that when the time came for repeating the experiment, they would carry it out more systematically and consciously."[15]

During these disturbances the cabinet crisis remained unsolved. On July 20 Prince Lvov resigned and Kerensky became Prime Minister, retaining the portfolios of war and the navy. Great difficulty was experienced in selecting a new government, and while the inter-party negotiations were carried on, Chernov, Tereshchenko, Kerensky, and Nekrasov offered their resignations. Finally, on August 6, a new coalition ministry, the Third Provisional Government, was announced. Chernov, Tereshchenko, and Kerensky remained in office, the last-named as Prime Minister. The other portfolios were taken by S.R.'s, Mensheviks, Populist-Socialists, and Cadets.

In addition to promising to call the Constituent Assembly on September 30, to introduce local self-government, and to improve the conditions of labor and national economy, the new government announced its determination to continue the struggle against the foreign enemy and to safeguard the new state order from all monarchist and counter-revolutionary attempts. But in dealing with the party held responsible for the recent disorders the government acted less vigorously than many of its supporters desired. Its punitive measures did not seriously cripple the Bolsheviks' organizations, but only harassed them. Lenin and his friends did not lessen their efforts or abandon their plans to destroy the government; they merely acted a little more discreetly. A few days after the demonstrations Lenin wrote that there was no longer any hope of a peaceful development of the revolution;

[15] Trotsky, *The History of the Russian Revolution,* II, 84.

it was now a question of victory of a military dictatorship or victory of an armed uprising of the workers. But in order to have the article published in the legal press he substituted in his manuscript the words "decisive struggle" for "armed uprising."[16]

The Sixth Congress of the party, which met semi-legally in Petrograd, August 8–16, adopted Lenin's interpretation of the July Days as a victory for counter-revolution signalized by the surrender of the Mensheviks and S.R.'s to the bourgeoisie and the military, and by the persecution of the only party representing the real interests of the revolutionary proletariat. The resolutions stopped short of a definite commitment for an armed rising against the government and the Soviet majority. This, however, was implicit in the statement that since the painless transfer of power to the Soviets and the peaceful development of the revolution were no longer possible, the only correct slogan now was the complete liquidation of the dictatorship of the counter-revolutionary bourgeoisie. This could be accomplished only by the revolutionary workers with the aid of the poorest peasants. The task of these classes was to strain every effort to take state power into their own hands.

The Congress, which was attended by 175 delegates representing 112 organizations with a membership of 177,000, reflected the growth of the party since the May conference. It also showed a far greater degree of unity within the ranks than on the earlier occasion. A new Central Committee was elected, which remained in direction of party affairs until after the November overthrow. This committee included Lenin, Zinoviev, Kamenev, Trotsky, Nogin, Kollontai, Stalin, Sverdlov, Rykov, Bukharin, Artem (F. A. Sergeev), Joffe, Uritsky, Miliutin, and Lomov. Of these, Trotsky, Joffe, and Uritsky were members of the Mezh-

[16] According to the editors of Lenin's *Works,* in this article on "The Political Situation" written on July 23, Lenin raised for the first time since March the question of an armed uprising. *Toward the Seizure of Power,* I, 37, and note 18, p. 284.

raiontsy, who formally united with the Bolsheviks at this time.

In an attempt to restore discipline in the front and in the rear and to rally support for the government against external and internal enemies Kerensky called a state conference which met in the Bolshoi Theater at Moscow, August 25–28. The Bolsheviks loudly denounced the conference and expressed their opposition by organizing a one-day strike in Moscow on the day of the opening session. The conference accomplished little except to reveal the wide gulf which separated those like Generals Kornilov and Kaledin, who stood for the re-establishment of iron discipline and the suppression of all sorts of committees and Soviets, and of the moderate socialist leaders like Chkheidze and Tsereteli, who were exposed to a cross fire from both right and left.

Conversations begun behind the scenes while the conference was in session were continued after the adjournment at army headquarters between Kornilov, then the Commander-in-Chief, and representatives of Kerensky regarding the use of troops to support the government in case of a Bolshevik uprising. Kerensky interpreted Kornilov's conditions, which were presented through an intermediary, as amounting to the proclamation of a Kornilov dictatorship. He thereupon dismissed Kornilov from office and called upon the people to defend the government against the counter-revolutionists. The Soviets took an active part in preparations for defense, organizing military revolutionary committees to fight against counter-revolution, in which the Bolsheviks took active part. The arming of workmen was authorized on September 10, and the organization of the Red Guards was thus encouraged. The Kornilov movement collapsed by September 12, and the generals implicated were under arrest two days later.

Naturally the Bolsheviks profited greatly by these events. The Kornilov affair appeared as a fulfilment of their prophecies. Meanwhile the land question was still acute, and in the provinces the Bolsheviks were gaining headway as their slogans of immediate peace and immediate expropriation of the land were brought to the villages by soldiers returning from the front, where the conditions of service and the propaganda of the Bolshevik Military Organizations were steadily making converts to Lenin's program. The Constituent Assembly had been postponed, living conditions were worse, and above all the war still dragged on. Elections in September to the city Dumas and the shift of opinion in the Soviets and the soldiers' and sailors' committees reflected the decline in influence of the moderate parties. Particularly significant were the Bolshevik victories in the Soviets of the two capitals and certain other large towns.

The Kornilov affair made it necessary to reorganize the government. Disagreement as to whether or not the Cadets, some of whom had been compromised by the recent events, should be included in the new government prolonged the crisis, and on September 14 it was announced that pending the settlement of the cabinet question a Directory of Five (Kerensky, Tereshchenko, Verkhovsky, Verderevsky, and Nikitin) was responsible for the government of the state. On the same day Kerensky proclaimed Russia a republic. Two days later the Executive Committees of the Workers' and Soldiers' Deputies and of the All-Russian Congress of Peasants' Deputies issued a call for a Democratic Congress, which met in the Alexandrinsky Theater on September 27. At once the Conference, in which the Bolsheviks were a hostile minority, became entangled in the question whether or not to include bourgeois representatives in the government. By 766 to 688 the Conference voted for a coalition. Then it voted 595 to 493 to exclude the Cadets, the only bourgeois party of any importance. Thereupon many of the delegates changed their votes and a motion against coalition was carried by 813 to 183. The Conference then recessed to permit the party leaders to untangle the situation by negotiation. On October 3 a compromise motion was passed, 829 to 106, favoring coalition but omitting reference to the Cadets. After five days of negotiation the new cabinet, the third coalition, and the fourth and last Provisional Government, again headed by Kerensky, was announced. It contained three Socialist-Revolutionists (of the Right), three Mensheviks, four Cadets, four socialists not affiliated with any of the larger groups, and two non-party men. Meanwhile the Bolsheviks, who had opposed coalition in any form, had withdrawn from the Conference after demanding the adoption of a program including, among other things, turning over the land to the peasant committees, workers' control of industry, denunciation of secret treaties, an immediate peace offer, self-determination for the nationalities of Russia, and arming of the workers and organization of a Red Guard.

Before it disbanded, the Democratic Conference agreed to set up a Provisional Council of the Russian Republic to be composed of 555 delegates of the groups represented in the Democratic Conference and to serve as a preliminary parliament pending the meeting of the Constituent Assembly. The Provisional Council, also called the Pre-Parliament, held its first meeting in the Mariinsky Palace on October 20 and remained in session until dispersed by the events of November 7.

CHAPTER I

THE LAST DAYS OF THE PROVISIONAL GOVERNMENT

The Third Coalition Government began its brief term of office under conditions of exceptional difficulty. Reports from the front and from the cities and villages revealed the war weariness of the people, insubordination and "defeatism" at the front, hunger and want in the towns, and riots, looting, and incendiarism in the provinces. The government and the Pre-Parliament, which met on October 20, argued very heatedly as to what should be done: whether it was possible to go on with the war; how to restore the morale of the army, the navy, and the nation; what to do about the food shortage; how to satisfy the peasants. Discussion on most of these matters was still going on when this month ended. The government, however, refused to propose a separate peace and ordered that troops be used to maintain order in the rear.

The Bolsheviks, the most active and vocal opponents of the Provisional Government, were likewise involved in a heated discussion of how far that opposition should be pushed. Against the strong objection of certain party leaders the Bolshevik Central Committee voted on October 23, 1917, to prepare for an insurrection, and during the remaining days of the month secured the formation of a Military Revolutionary Committee in the Petrograd Soviet and made other preparations for the uprising. The Bolsheviks made no secret of their intentions. They intensified their agitation among the workers, and particularly among the soldiers of the Petrograd garrison, who had no desire to be sent to the front and were naturally receptive to the Bolshevik promise of an immediate peace.

A. "Peace, Bread, and Land"

During September and the first weeks of October, while the party leaders conferred, disagreed, and made compromises, the soldiers, workers, and peasants expressed their desire for "peace, bread, and land" in petitions and resolutions, and, more ominously, in acts of violence which the authorities were unable to prevent.

CONDITION OF THE TROOPS AT THE FRONT

[Army Intelligence Report for October 2–13, 1917][1]

Northern front.—The situation in the army has not changed and may be described as a complete lack of confidence in the officers and the higher commanding personnel. The belief is growing among the soldiers that they cannot be punished for what they do. . . . . The influence of Bolshevik ideas is spreading very rapidly. To this must be added a general weariness, an irritability, and a desire for peace at any price.

Any attempt on the part of the officers to regulate the life of the army . . . . is looked upon by the soldiers as counter-revolution . . . . and stigmatized as a "Kornilov" move. The soldiers seem to believe that the arrest of Kornilov made void all the orders which he issued reinstating discipline. The army committees are in most cases helpless to guide the mob and are often compelled to follow it so as not to lose completely the confidence of the masses. . . . .

The various peace resolutions that are being passed are interpreted by the soldiers in the rear as having the force of law. . . . . The Germans are very energetic in using newspapers and leaflets to advocate fraternization. . . . . Considerable numbers of soldiers . . . . feigning sickness are leaving the front for the hospital. . . . .

12th Army.— . . . . The press of the political parties is no longer influencing the soldier masses. Again and again one hears the orders of the Provisional Government severely criticized. The committee of the 95th Regiment . . . . declared Kerensky a traitor. . . . .

Apart from the Bolshevik not a single [political] movement has any popularity. Those who read moderate newspapers are looked upon as [followers of the] "bourgeoisie" and "counter-revolutionists." An intensive agitation is being conducted in favor of an immediate cessation of military operations on all fronts. Whenever a whole regiment or

[1] A copy of the original report is in the Hoover War Library, Stanford University, under the title *Belevsky Papers,* No. 7.

battalion refuses to carry out a military order, the fact is immediately made known to other parts of the army through special agitators. . . . .

Western front.— . . . . Because of general war weariness, bad nourishment, mistrust of officers, etc., there has developed an intense defeatist agitation accompanied by refusals to carry out orders, threats to the commanding personnel, and attempts to fraternize with Germans. Everywhere one hears voices calling for immediate peace, because, they say, no one will stay in the trenches during the winter. . . . . There is a deep-rooted conviction among the rank and file that fraternization with the enemy is a sure way of attaining peace. . . . .

The attitude of the soldiers is very definitely expressed in the army press. . . . . The question most frequently debated is the question of war and peace. The moderate newspapers . . . . try to warn their readers against entertaining false hopes, since the coalition of the Central Powers is not at all inclined to stretch a fraternal hand to the Russian proletariat. . . . .

In direct opposition to this are the newspapers *Izvestiia* (of the Minsk Soviet of Workers' and Soldiers' Deputies) and *Molot.* They openly advocate the immediate cessation of war, the transfer of political and military power to the proletariat, the immediate socialization of land, and a merciless struggle against capitalists and the bourgeoisie. Their method of argument is quite simple and comprehensible to the masses. It runs as follows: All the ministers of the Provisional Government are subservient to the bourgeoisie and are counter-revolutionists; they continue to wage war to please the Allied and the Russian capitalists; the government introduced the death penalty with the view of exterminating the soldiers, workers, and peasants. . . . .

Among the phenomena indicative of tendencies in the life in the rear of the Western front are the recent disturbances at the replacement depot in Gomel. On October 1 over eight thousand soldiers who were to be transferred to the front demanded to be sent home instead. . . . . Incited by agitators they stormed the armory, took some fifteen hundred suits of winter equipment, and assaulted the Assistant Commissar and a member of the front committee. Similar events . . . . have taken place in Smolensk. . . . .

Southwestern front.— . . . . Defeatist agitation is increasing and the disintegration of the army is in full swing. The Bolshevik wave is growing steadily, owing to general disintegration in the rear, the absence of strong power, and the lack of supplies and equipment. The dominant theme of conversation is peace at any price and under any condition. Every order, no matter what its source, is met with hostility. The dark soldier masses have become completely confused and lost in the midst of innumerable party slogans and programs, so that now they mistrust everyone and everything. Even their former leaders . . . .

—the committees—have lost their confidence. . . . . The commissars testify that the soldiers have lost all elementary notions of right, justice, and human worth. The position of the commanding personnel is very difficult. There have been instances of officers committing suicide. . . . .

The guard-cavalry corps of the 2d Army passed a resolution of no confidence in the majority of officers. The soldiers are engaging in organized armed invasions of the surrounding country estates, plundering provisions . . . . of which there is a scarcity in the army. Not a thing can be done to counteract this restlessness . . . . as there is no force which could be relied upon in any attempt to enforce order. The activity of the courts is paralyzed because of the hostile attitude of the soldiers. . . . .

The following general conclusions may be drawn from the reports of the commissars: The approaching winter campaign has accelerated the disintegration of the army and increased the longing for peace. It is necessary to leave nothing undone which might supply the soldiers with food, shoes, and winter clothing; to see that the army is reduced in numbers; to improve the discipline in the reserve regiments. Otherwise the ranks will be filled with such material as will lead to the complete demoralization and destruction of the army. . . . .

[The rest of the report deals with the Rumanian and Caucasian fronts, describing similar conditions.]

CONDITION OF THE TROOPS IN THE REAR

[Extracts from Official Reports of the Petrograd Telegraph Agency][2]

Helsingfors, September 14. Last night . . . . four officers of the battleship "Petropavlovsk" were shot by the sailors. . . . . The officers refused to give a pledge of loyalty to the Provisional Government. . . . . The provisional military section of the Central Executive Committee received information concerning what happened in Vyborg. . . . . A mob of soldiers removed from the guardhouse three generals and one colonel, who were kept there by the . . . . army committee of the 42d Corps for alleged participation in the Kornilov affair, and threw them from a bridge into the water. . . . . After that a number of other regimental commanders and officers were attacked and thrown into the water. Those who tried to save themselves were killed. In all, about fifteen officers were killed, though the exact number has not been established. . . . .

Elisavetgrad, September 21 . . . . A bloody encounter took place between a group of cadets and soldiers . . . . One cadet, one soldier, and three unknown persons were killed; twenty-one wounded . . . . The

[2] A. L. Popov, *Oktiabrskii perevorot: fakty i dokumenty,* Petrograd, 1918, pp. 85–88.

cadets were arrested. At the jail the soldiers attempted to lynch the cadets. One cadet committed suicide. . . . .

Stavka,[3] October 11. The Stavka received official news of the circumstances under which the departure of Generals Denikin, Elsner, Markov, and others took place from Berdichev to Bykhov. A mob of soldiers surrounded the building . . . . where the generals were kept and demanded that the prisoners go to the station on foot. To avoid complications the soldiers' demand was satisfied, but to safeguard the prisoners the Commander-in-Chief of the Southwestern Front, General Volodchenko, walked all the way to the station beside the prisoners. . . . . At the station the soldiers demanded that the generals be placed in a prisoners' car instead of a second-class railway car. As no prisoners' car was available, a freight car had to be used instead. . . . .

Active Army, October 5. On October 3 a group of soldiers . . . . destroyed the courthouse in the city of Dubno after a jury had condemned one of the instigators of a recent disturbance. Violence was done to the members of the jury and the court. . . . .

Irkutsk, October 5. [In view of recent disorders which took place in the city numerous arrests were made among the soldiers of the local garrison.] Yesterday morning . . . . regiments of sharpshooters led by agitators removed the rifles from the arsenal and refused to obey their commanders. The army commander, Lieutenant Krakovetsky, ... was placed under arrest. . . . . A detachment which remained loyal to the revolution succeeded . . . . in rescuing the commander. . . . . The rebels were disarmed and arrested. . . . .

Stavka, October 11. Official reports were received here of the disorders which took place in the Letichevsky Uezd. . . . . In the village of Markovtsy a wine distillery was stormed and then set on fire. . . . . In Brailovka the soldiers plundered an estate and broke into a liquor cellar. Drunken soldiers are rioting and shooting at their fellow soldiers who were placed on guard of the liquor cellars. In the town of Bari wine cellars were broken into. . . . . [The same in Karagievtsy.] In Letichevsky, Mogilevsky, and Ushitsky uezds of Podolsk Gubernia, soldiers are making unwarranted seizures of bread, fodder, horses, and oxen from large estates. . . . . No consideration is given to the property of manual workers. . . . .

Saratov, October 13. . . . . In Balashev the local garrison rebelled and seized the post and telegraph. Soldiers traveling on the Riazan-Uralsk railroad are engaged in violent seizure of flour and other supplies.

Feodosia [Crimea], October 26. In view of the disorderly conduct of the soldiers, Feodosia has been declared in a state of siege. . . . .

. . . . 20,000 vedros [of liquor] and 300 barrels of wine were destroyed [by the authorities]. . . . .

[3] The general headquarters of the army at Mogilev.

RESOLUTION OF THE ARMY COMMITTEE OF THE WESTERN FRONT[4]

[October 30, 1917]

In its session of October 30 the executive committee of the Western front adopted the following resolution: (1) All calamities that the country suffers are a direct consequence of the war which was started by the imperialists of all countries. (2) The continuation of the war is sure to destroy the revolution; the productive forces of the country lead revolutionary Russia to inevitable ruin.[5] (3) The army which has suffered for three years . . . . insistently demands peace. A movement is on foot which threatens to break up the front and to destroy the revolution. The indecisive policy of the government is accelerating the crisis.

The front committee, having deliberated on the state of affairs in the army and the country, resolved:

1. That the war must be stopped as soon as possible by the energetic efforts of the international and the Russian democracies in accordance with the program of the Russian Revolution which proclaimed a peace without annexations or indemnities, and on the basis of the self-determination of nations.

2. That the Russian democracy must take resolute measures toward a speedy realization of peace. The measures are as follows:

a) To demand categorically from the Provisional Government that it bring up the question of peace at the Paris conference. . . . .

b) To demand the issuing of passports to the socialists of the Allied countries in order that the Stockholm Socialist Conference may become a reality.[6]

c) To impress upon the democracies of the world that any delay on their part in the struggle for peace threatens to destroy the Russian Revolution and bring about the triumph of international reaction, and that the responsibility for the future of the Russian Revolution now lies with the democracies of the world.

[4] N. E. Kakurin, comp., *Razlozhenie armii v 1917 godu,* Moscow, 1925, pp. 147–48.

[5] This, whatever it may mean, is an exact rendering of the text.

[6] In May 1917 the Central Executive Committee of the Soviet of Workers' and Soldiers' Deputies issued a call for a world congress of socialists to be held in a neutral state to discuss war aims. Great Britain, France, and the United States refused passports to their socialists. The Bolsheviks also opposed the conference. No world congress was held, but during the summer various socialist groups from the Central Powers, from the subject nationalities, from neutral states, and from Russia went to Stockholm and issued memoranda on peace terms. A conference of Left socialists, the so-called 3d Zimmerwald Conference, met in Stockholm on September 5. A. Balabanoff, "Die Zimmerwalder Bewegung, 1914–1919," *Archiv für Geschichte des Sozialismus und des Arbeiterbewegung,* XII, 363–400.

1.[7] That, therefore, the democracies of the world must make every effort . . . . to bring about the Stockholm Conference so as to prevent a reactionary imperialistic peace. . . . .

3. In internal affairs the Russian democracy must secure a guaranty that the land reform will be accomplished without fail and must see to it that a decree is published transferring all privately owned large land estates to the state to be handed over to the land committees. (*Note:* The Socialist-Revolutionists maintain that all lands having agricultural value should be handed over to the land committees. They insist that the Constituent Assembly be convened at the time set and that until then the government should be responsible to the organs of the revolutionary democracy; that the death penalty be abolished, the army completely democratized, and its size reduced as much as possible.)

At the same time the front committee is of the opinion that the All-Russian democracy should undertake every means to supply the army with all necessities . . . . since the demobilization can proceed only gradually.

To accomplish the above measures . . . . it is necessary: (*a*) to elect representatives to make reports to all front committees and to the Central Executive Committee with the purpose of organizing an extensive peace campaign; (*b*) to propose that the Provisional Government accept the demands of the front; (*c*) to send a delegation to the Pre-Parliament to announce . . . . the resolutions of the front; (*d*) to appeal to the army explaining the ways of conducting an organized struggle for peace . . . . ; (*e*) to appeal to the country to support the front in its struggle for peace and to supply the front with necessities.

KOZHEVNIKOV
Chairman of Executive Committee
of the Western Front

FOOD RIOTS AND POGROMS

[Extracts from Official Reports of the Petrograd Telegraph Agency][8]

Zhitomir, September 15. As a result of the rise in the price of bread a tumult has arisen among the women. In view of the prevailing agitation, troops and a detachment of Cossacks were called out.

Kharkov, September 24. Information has been received about disorders in Bakhmut. On the evening of September 22 a wine storehouse was broken into and a large amount of liquor seized. The drunken

[7] A footnote to the Russian text states that the confusion of headings is in the original.

[8] A. L. Popov, *Oktiabrskii perevorot,* pp. 72–79.

crowds who took part in the destruction of the wine storehouse started to march through the streets singing and creating a disturbance. The population of the city is alarmed. The Jews have left the city. All stores are closed and the residents do not venture on the streets. Soldiers from the local garrison took part in the disturbance. A detachment of troops was sent from Kharkov to establish order and cadets were summoned from Chuguev. . . . .

Kharkov, October 11. During the past few days pillaging has been going on in the city. As a result of the shortage of staple goods and manufactured articles, rumors are abroad concerning the hiding of goods, and unauthorized searches are being conducted. Brigands plunder the goods and handle the proprietors roughly. It is in this way that . . . . an innocent artisan, the Jew, Morein, was killed.

During the night, the agitation for a pogrom has become stronger and the uprising has assumed a threatening character, being concentrated in the center of the city, on Pavlovsky Square. An instigation against Jews is being carried on in the city; on the fences are hung proclamations using monarchist slogans and calling for a pogrom and for a massacre of the Jews; a drygoods shop has been wrecked; many of the pogrom-makers wear soldiers' uniforms. . . . .

Simferopol,[9] October 13. From a number of rural communities of Melitopolsky and Dneprovsky uezds comes information that shops are being wrecked and unauthorized searches are in progress. The uezd and gubernia commissars have been sent there and troops will be dispatched. . . . .

Rostov-on-Don, October 10. In Azov, as a result of the dissatisfaction of the population with the rise in the price of bread and flour, disorder broke out. A crowd of residents marched to the city hall, broke into the food department, and attacked the government employees, who fled. When a member of the municipal government, Makarovsky, attempted to quiet the crowd, he was thrown down the stairs from the second floor, after which books, orders, and papers which were found in the department were flung about. Members of the Soviet of Workers' and Soldiers' Deputies who arrived at the place succeeded in pacifying the disorderly crowd. . . . .

Astrakhan, September 25. As a result of the reduction of the bread ration, a large crowd went to the opposite bank of the Volga where the gubernia food committee is located, and demanded an explanation from the chairman of the committee. They then broke into the commissariat, fell upon Sklabinsky, the gubernia commissar, and threw him into the street. Sklabinsky was wounded. With the arrival of the Cossacks and militia the crowd was quieted and dispersed. . . . .

[9] Popov, *Oktiabrskii perevorot,* p. 76.

Saratov, October 18. In Petrovsk, prisoners in jails and detention houses were released by the crowds.

Samara, October 26. In Bugulma, of Samara Gubernia, the wine storehouse, apothecary shops, and stores were demolished. The uezd commissar appealed to Samara and Simbirsk for help.

Kazan, September 27. As a result of the agitation against the grain monopoly, in the village of Bolshoi Sundur, Zapolsky, the chairman of the volost food administration, was tortured and then killed. . . . .

Ekaterinburg, October 21. In the village of Korabelsky, on account of the dissatisfaction with the grain monopoly, a crowd of peasants wrought havoc in the premises of the volost food committee and seized a member of the food administration. . . . .

Tiflis, October 17. According to information from Kutais, disorder began on October 15 with the destruction of one of the wine cellars, where eight barrels of wine were broken open and emptied. The drunken rioters, joined by ever increasing crowds, began to break into grocery and other shops and also into private quarters; in many places they started fires; the local chemical plant was burned and the freight station was robbed. On October 16 the riot was renewed, but upon the arrival of a military detachment sent from Tiflis, order was restored in the city. . . . .

Omsk, October 19. A military detachment has arrived from Petropavlovsk to put down the riot in the city. Before the arrival of the troops several shops and private homes were destroyed. Dimitriev, the chairman of the city food administration, was killed. . . . .

Tashkent, September 27. In connection with the aggravation of the provisions question, a number of soldiers decided to arrest the food manager . . . . and his two assistants. It was decided to transfer the business of provisions into the hands of the workers and soldiers and not to permit the shipment of manufactured goods to Bokhara. For this purpose a special guard was sent to the station. At the same time it was decided to conduct a general search through the entire city. On September 25, at a meeting attended by thousands of soldiers and workers, the resignation of the executive committee of the Soviet of Deputies was demanded. Speakers proclaimed Bolshevik slogans. A provisional revolutionary committee of fourteen was elected. . . . .

AGRARIAN DISTURBANCES

[Extracts from Official Reports of the Petrograd Telegraph Agency][10]

Kishinev, September 26. Local reports testify to the growth of agrarian disturbances in all uezds. Fear is expressed that the sowing will not be done in time or properly.

[10] *Ibid.*, pp. 81–83.

Tambov, September 27. Accurate information about the disorders in Kozlov Uezd has not been received up to the present time. It is definitely known that one estate has been pillaged and twenty-five have been burned. Besides, many peasants, living on separate farms,[11] have suffered.

Tambov, September 27. An expeditionary detachment despatched from Moscow arrived to quell the uprising. Representatives of the Moscow Soviet of Workers' and Soldiers' Deputies also arrived. According to information from them, the disturbance in Kozlov Uezd continues. At the moment of their departure from Kozlov, disorders broke out in a new place, forty versts from Kozlov. The village of Yaroslavka is burning.

Tambov, September 29. In Sofinskaia Volost, Kirsanov Uezd, agrarian disorders have started.

Taganrog, October 2. In the volosts of Taganrog Okrug[12] agrarian disturbances have arisen. Representatives of the okrug government and of the Soviet of Workers' and Soldiers' Deputies went to the okrug.

Saratov, October 8. In Serdobsky Uezd the estates of Baroness Cherkassov and of Azarevich have been destroyed by the peasants. The commander of the Serdobsky garrison has been instructed to move a detachment to the uezd to restore order.

Saratov, October 10. The agrarian disturbances in Serdobsky Uezd embrace a large district. Peasants are stealing cattle, dividing the land and forests, and carrying off the grain. The uezd officials appealed for the aid of troops. It is feared that a great store of government liquor will be pillaged. The uezd executive committee proposes to transfer all privately owned land to the land committees. The disorder has spread to Atkarsky Uezd.

Kishinev, October 10. Peasants of Megura village, Beletsky Uezd, influenced by propaganda, began to divide among themselves the land and pastures of the neighboring estates of Borchel and Slobodzei.

Odessa, October 12. Word has been received of the alarming situation in Akkerman and Orgeev, and also of the increased agitation of the ignorant elements in Berezovka. In Sorokovsky Uezd agrarian disturbances continue.

Zhitomir, October 12. A number of despatches have been received by the gubernia commissar about disturbances in the gubernia. Forests and crops are being destroyed. Troops have been sent to quell the disorders. . . . .

[11] Under the Agrarian Law of November 9, 1906, peasants who desired might demand their share of the communal land in the form of a permanent homestead free from re-allocation and independent of the village commune.

[12] Term used in Cossack areas in Southern Russia and Siberia for the administrative divisions corresponding to the uezd elsewhere.

Voronezh, October 20. In Zadonsky Uezd in the district of the village of Zhivotinsky, the estates of Chertkov and other landowners have been partially destroyed by the peasants. More than 60,000 puds of wheat and other grain have been burned. Valuable old furniture has been destroyed. . . . .

Zhitomir, October 23. After returning from a journey to Volhynia the assistant commissar gave a report on the situation. According to him, Volhynia is in a state of complete anarchy. In many uezds there is general destruction of the forests and seizure of privately owned land. In Staro-Konstantinovsky Uezd the Bolsheviks have seized power.

Nikolaevsk (Samara Gubernia), October 24. The executive committee, fearing that the numerous disorders in the uezd would destroy valuable estates, declared all privately owned estates public property and began their immediate confiscation. . . . .

Chernigov, October 26. Disorder in the gubernia continues. In the uezds of Sosnitsk and Surazhsk forests and crops are being destroyed.

Penza, October 26. In Novocherkassk Uezd eight estates have been destroyed. Cavalry has been sent to stop the disorder. In Krasnoslobodsky Uezd the estate of Madame Lebedev and in Insarsky Uezd the estate of Andronov have been pillaged.

Spassk, October 27. A wave of destruction swept over the whole uezd. Felling and stealing of trees is going on. The estate of Shreder has been pillaged and set on fire. The estate of Count Grabbe has been destroyed, including his valuable library.

Nizhni-Novgorod, November 1. According to the latest information the uprising has spread over six uezds, in which many estates have been pillaged and burned. The greatest disorder took place in Lukianovsky Uezd, where, according to the commissar, everything valuable is being ruthlessly destroyed. . . . .[13]

THE BOLSHEVIKS AND THE PEASANTS[14]

. . . . As volost commissar I received through the uezd Soviet of Workers' Deputies instructions from the Kerensky government to organize the volost committees. I called a general meeting in order to dis-

[13] An interesting attempt was made to measure the restlessness of the peasants by the number of their legal offenses registered by the Department of Militia of the Provisional Government for the months of March–September, 1917. The total of revolutionary actions reported are distributed as follows: March, 17; April, 204; May, 259; June, 577; July, 1,122; August, 691; September, 629. These offenses include cases of incendiarism, seizure of the gentry's land, grain, and agricultural machinery, cutting of timber, etc. See K. G. Kotelnikov and V. L. Meller (compilers), *Krestianskoe dvizhenie v 1917 godu,* Moscow, Leningrad, 1927.

[14] From Anton Mitrevich, "Vospominaniia o rabochem revoliutsionnom dvizhenii [1895–1919]," in *Proletarskaia Revoliutsiia,* 1922, No. 4, pp. 235–36.

cuss the matter and make my report. [The peasants] shouted at me: "What are you talking about a committee for? Better tell us about the land; can we take it away from the landlords? Never mind your committees."

I then told the gathering that my own party [Bolshevik] looks at the question in this way: "Take the land and be done with it! Don't be waiting for them to let you have it. Kerensky's flunkies are only saying they will give it to you, but actually they won't give you anything."

"And may we take the lake, too?"

That lake was surrounded by the fields and belonged to the Catholic bishop; one could not even bathe in it without paying for it.

"You may," I answered.

"Hear that, Uncle Mikhei? The chief says we can take everything right away."

"Go on," said the old man; "you might get us into trouble."

"What nonsense are you speaking, Uncle? The chief surely knows better. He is one of those Bolsheviks whose law is, take everything."

Then followed talk such as: "In our volost we have no landlord's estate, but here we do have the Bishop's lake. Well, let's chase off Theoktist Tarakanov, who has rented the lake, and then we'll all go fishing."

"Hey, boys! Who wants to go fishing?"

"And will those who live beyond the river, twelve versts away, get it too?" I heard some people asking.

"What do we care? Let them use the river, and, if they want to, let them fish here. We don't care; it's all the people's property; let all the people use it."

And so the rumor went out to all the volosts of the Rezhitsa Uezd that the Ruzhinskaia volost had resolved to confiscate the land, water, and forests from the landlords and monasteries, and that their chief had explained to them that there was such a law. In a mighty wave the excitement spread all over Latgalia, which consists of the three uezds of Rezhitsa, Dvinsk, and Liutsin, two-thirds inhabited by Letts and one-third by Old Believers. In some places there were armed clashes between the peasants and the government. . . .

B. The Provisional Government and Peace

The Pre-Parliament as constituted by the Democratic Conference consisted of 555 delegates, of whom 388 represented the democracy—i.e., the parties represented in the Soviets—and 167, the bourgeoisie, the Cossacks, the national minorities, and others. Kerensky opened the first session of the assembly in the Mariinsky Palace on October 20. Breshko-Breshkovskaia, as the oldest delegate present, made a brief speech, and N. D. Avxentiev, a Socialist-Revolutionist of the Right, was elected permanent chairman. Trotsky enlivened the proceedings with a fiery denunciation of Kerensky, his allies, and the bourgeoisie in general, whom he accused of intending to break up the Constituent Assembly. He excoriated the government for failing to make peace and concluded with the declaration that his party had nothing in common with this traitorous government. The Bolsheviks thereupon left the hall to the accompaniment of hoots, jeers, and advice to "get into the German railway cars."[15]

After the departure of the Bolsheviks, members of the government and the Pre-Parliament plunged into an acrimonious debate on the ability of the army to continue the war, the causes of its demoralization, and the general question of peace. The government, insistently assailed by the growing popular demand to take some step toward peace, was at the same time being pressed by the Entente Powers to carry on the war. On October 9 the British, French, and Italian Ambassadors had delivered a joint note warning that lack of confidence in Russia's ability to go on with the war might cause the Allies to discontinue furnishing arms and materials to Russia. To restore confidence, said the Ambassadors, Russia must revive discipline and military spirit and re-establish order at the front and in the rear.[16]

NATIONAL DEFENSE

[Debate at the Second Sitting of the Pre-Parliament, October 23, 1917][17]

a) [General A. I. Verkhovsky, Minister of War, spoke first]: I consider it my duty . . . . to tell the country the whole truth about the

[15] Golder, pp. 566–67.

[16] United States Department of State, *Papers Relating to the Foreign Relations of the United States, 1918, Russia,* 3 vols., Washington, D.C., 1931–32, I, 207–208. Hereafter cited as *U.S. Foreign Relations, 1918, Russia.*

[17] *Rech,* No. 239, October 24, 1917, pp. 3–4. An account of the first sitting is given in Golder, pp. 566–67.

army . . . . in order that the members of the Council [of the Republic][18] may be able to undertake measures to safeguard the existence of our country.

The enemy is using every opportunity to deliver us additional blows. . . . . The aim of these blows is not to achieve a decisive military victory . . . . which would enable the Germans to impose their will on us, ... but to produce on our people a psychological effect . . . . that will force us to make a dishonorable peace.

I must tell you that those who maintain that the Russian army is a nonentity do not know what they say. . . . . The Germans keep 130 divisions on our front . . . . that is how they evaluate the fighting strength of the Russian army. The Russian army still exists . . . . and will do its duty to the very end. (*Cheers on the Right.*) . . . .

At the same time I must say that disorders on the front and at the rear are growing steadily. . . . . This is due chiefly to the failure of the troops to understand our war aims. The Provisional Government and the Council [of the Republic] must, therefore, take all measures to see that every man clearly understands that we are not waging war for territorial conquests (*voices from the Left: "Bravo!"*) . . . . but for the salvation of our country. (*Applause on all benches.*) . . . .

The government's military program . . . . has been carried out in the most energetic manner. All the elements . . . . implicated in the Kornilov movement have been replaced by men who perceive the complexity of the situation. . . . . Gradually the commanders and the regimental committees are beginning to work amicably with the committees . . . . for the restoration of the combative power of the army . . . .

[The most urgent necessity is to restore discipline. In the name of the Provisional Government I shall submit to the Pre-Parliament an urgent bill providing for the establishment of qualified regimental disciplinary tribunals which will settle all cases within forty-eight hours. It is also intended to introduce a system of penalties by which whole regiments, if convicted of lack of discipline, will have their leaves and their allowances stopped and their rations considerably reduced. We need a definite decision of the Pre-Parliament as to whether or not it wishes that all disorders and anarchic manifestations be suppressed with a firm hand.]

b) [Statement of Admiral Verderevsky, Minister of Marine] : . . . . The Baltic Fleet which from the very beginning of the war shouldered the great responsibility of defending the approaches to our capital . . . . fulfilled its task conscientiously. . . . . So far the Baltic Fleet experienced no shortage of supplies. . . . . But now with the feeble productiveness of our factories . . . . it is doubtful whether it will be possible to make the necessary repairs on our ships. Let us hope that the recent

[18] The Pre-Parliament.

activities of the German fleet[19] will impress upon our workmen . . . . that every delay . . . . in work . . . . threatens to make the situation very grave. . . . .

[As to the relation between the officers and the sailors, it must be recognized as very critical indeed.] In the fleet the situation is even more tragic than in the army. It is possible to break up an insurgent regiment . . . ., but to disband the crew of a battleship . . . . is not so easy, as much training is required to attend to the complicated machinery [of a man-of-war]. We must, therefore, be lenient [with the sailors] . . . . and find the means . . . . of bringing about the desired co-operation between the officers and the sailors. Without . . . . this co-operation the fighting capacity of the fleet cannot be assured. . . . .

The restoration of discipline is as imperative in the fleet as in the army, but this will not be accomplished by threats and violence. Only the realization of individual responsibility . . . ., now dormant among the masses, but which is there none the less, [can save the situation by creating a self-imposed and voluntary discipline]. . . . .

c) [Statement of General M. V. Alexeev, former Commander-in-Chief] : Russia . . . . is passing through an extremely painful and difficult period . . . ., which is the result of the overpowering of the national spirit by the deadly idea that we are no longer capable of continuing the war and that we are in urgent need of an immediate peace. . . . .

The Russian people must first of all put squarely the question: is such a peace possible under present conditions . . . ., and is it likely to give to the world the things of which its advocates are dreaming . . . .? An impartial view of the situation will disclose that an immediate peace would be fatal for Russia, leading to her physical disintegration and an inevitable partition of her possessions. . . . . It would eliminate Russia from the Great Powers on which depends the solution of all European problems. . . . .

But what is the condition of our army? Our Minister of War has just been telling us that we still have an army. . . . . The Lord be praised for that! But in all frankness and courage let us open our eyes to the real condition [of that army] and not be carried away by alluring promises that the army will do its duty and defend the country. . . . . Our army is afflicted by grave ills, the most dangerous of which is the shattering of discipline. When once undermined, discipline is very difficult to restore, and of its own volition, it will, most assuredly, not come back. The masses [of soldiers] have tasted the sweets of insubordination . . . . and idleness. They are overwhelmed by the desire for personal safety, which creates longing for a speedy peace. Such an army is a real danger,

[19] In the Gulf of Riga, where the Germans occupied Dagö and Ösel islands during the first week of October.

and until those infirmities are overcome we shall not be able to say that our army is a healthy organization capable of continuing the struggle. . . . . Enthusiasm alone will not take the place of discipline, as the sad events of July have clearly demonstrated.[20] . . . .

d) [Martov, leader of the Menshevik Internationalists,[21] after a bitter polemic against General Alexeev, introduced the following resolution]:

The Provisional Council of the Republic hereby acknowledges the necessity of:

A radical purging of the commanding personnel with the object of removing all counter-revolutionary elements from the army and the Stavka;

The further democratization of the army command, to be accomplished by strengthening the army committees,[22] by giving them the right to remove undesirable commanders, and by further developing the institute of army commissars whose activity shall be controlled by the central organ of the revolutionary democracy;

The immediate abolition of the death penalty and restitution of their rights to all persons confined by sentence of the military tribunals for breach of discipline provided that the breach was committed for conscientious reasons;

A thoroughgoing investigation of the Kornilov affair and the arraignment of those found guilty in accordance with the laws governing offenses committed in the zone of military operations.

The Provisional Government should take the initiative and invite all the belligerent countries to undertake immediate negotiations leading to a general peace, declare an armistice on all fronts, and ask the Allied Governments to join the Russian Republic in that step.

e) [Statement of Prime Minister Kerensky]: . . . . General Alexeev said that the army in the trenches has lost its honor and sense of duty. As Supreme Commander of the army I deem it my duty to say that the army has not lost its honor and is ready to sacrifice itself for the country and for freedom. (*Applause on the Left and in the Center.*) . . . . I do not deny the disorganized condition of our armed forces . . . . but the army which the revolution inherited was already in a state of dissolution. . . . . The people were not aware of this fact, because the newspapers knew how to be silent. . . . .

[We are charged] with having delayed peace. . . . . But who delayed it . . . . ? Surely those who labored to undermine the fighting capacity of the army. . . . . I am obliged to bring back to your memory

20 The disastrous Russian offensive in July. See Golder, pp. 425–34.

21 The left-wing Mensheviks.

22 For the organization of the army committees, see Order No. 1, March 14, 1917, in Golder, pp. 386–90.

[the situation] when all true representatives of the democracy . . . . were fighting against those elements which owing to ignorance and lack of political perspective . . . . were encouraging [by their tactics] the further disintegration of the army. . . . .

It is also said that the June [July] offensive served as a prelude to the Kornilov affair. This is not true! Those who took part [in the offensive] will testify . . . . to the enthusiasm of the soldier masses. These were the days of the greatest triumph of the Russian Revolution, when the prestige of Russia was . . . . at its highest in the international concert, ... and I can tell everyone . . . . that if blind fanatics, assisted by a group of deliberate traitors, ... had not destroyed the fruits of the colossal effort of democracy, we should have had this Christmas a peace honorable for Russia and for her friends. (*Shouts of applause on the Right, Center, and part of the Left.*) . . . .

Now, I declare before the Russian people, before the bar of history and in the name of the democratic majority, whose interests I have ever championed, that we did everything we could and that we are not to blame if the prestige of the revolution has diminished. . . . .

The Provisional Government introduced revolutionary war tribunals and restored the death penalty, but it did so during the terrible pogroms in Galicia at the demand not only of the general staff and of the military commissars but also at the instance of the regimental committees. . . . .

I am glad to say that on all the fronts and in all the armies you will not find a single leader who is hostile to my system of military administration. . . . . What is important is to put an end once and for all to the legend that the majority of the officers are devoted to the cause of counter-revolution. . . . . This . . . . will enable us to undertake the necessary measures to stop the advance of the enemy. . . . . The ways to re-establish the fighting spirit of the army are not closed. . . . . All those who wish to hasten the conclusion of peace should remember that until our army is strong enough to inspire the respect of the enemy the prospects of peace will remain as remote as they are now. . . . .

The debates on national defense continued in the Pre-Parliament through October 25 with no prospect of arriving at any definite recommendation to the government. The moderate groups which favored a continuation of the war decided to draft a compromise resolution in the hope of uniting sufficient support for adoption by the Pre-Parliament. Negotiations between party leaders continued until October 31, when Chaikovsky introduced a resolution of the Center.

This resolution stated, among other things, that the first necessity was to concentrate all the material and moral forces of all groups, classes, and nationalities living in Russia to repel the enemy and defend the integrity and independence of the country; that only such a defense would make possible great agrarian reforms, especially the transfer of the land to the peasants; that the government should devote its strength to the establishment of democratic order at the front and in the country; and that the people should give their support in this plan for the safety of the fatherland.

The resolution was apparently adopted by 141 to 132, but when the Left groups demanded a second count it was lost by 135 to 130. Four other resolutions were voted on, but none received a majority, and the Pre-Parliament remained without any definite decision on this paramount question of going on with the war or concluding peace.[23] By this time (October 31) the Pre-Parliament had become involved in another debate over what is really the same question viewed in a different aspect, i.e., the problem of foreign policy.

DEBATE ON FOREIGN POLICY

[Tereshchenko's Speech][24]

[At the meeting of the Pre-Parliament on October 29, M. I. Tereshchenko, Minister of Foreign Affairs, delivered the long-expected statement on Russia's foreign policy.]

. . . . The practical interests of the state, quite apart from the question of honor and dignity, ... demand that Russia do not remain isolated and that the grouping of existing forces be left intact as corresponding perfectly to Russia's interests.

In Russia, as throughout the world, the desire for peace has become general, but no one in Russia could agree to a peace which would humiliate her or adversely affect her vital interests. (*Loud cheers from all benches, except the Internationalists.*) Such a peace would be a

[23] *Rech,* No. 246, November 1, 1917, p. 3; P. N. Miliukov, *Istoriia vtoroi russkoi revoliutsii,* 3 vols., Sofia, 1921–1923, I, Part 3, 142–48.

[24] *Rech,* No. 244, October 30, 1917, pp. 2, 3.

great historical blunder . . . . which would retard for many years and even for centuries the triumph of democratic principles throughout the world. (*Miliukov: "Right."*) Furthermore, such a peace would soon be followed by another war. These are the principles that have underlain Russia's foreign policy for the past few months, and the endeavors of the leaders of the department [of Foreign Affairs] have been directed to the carrying out of this program . . . . and to seeing that it was not altered under the influence of accidental occurrences. There is no domain where an accidental step is more likely to have a fatal repercussion than in that of foreign policy. . . . .

Our foreign policy, definitely formulated in May, still adheres to the essentials of that formulation. The renunciation of foreign conquests and indemnities imposed on the enemy and a similar repudiation on the part of our enemies . . . . is inseparably bound up with the self-determination of smaller nations. . . . . The Ministry of Foreign Affairs will insist that both . . . . aspects of that peace program shall be put into effect. . . . . To a dispassionate spectator Russia must appear as the most incomprehensible country. We have more men than any of the belligerent countries; we have also more supplies. . . . . Why have we, then, given so much cause for alarm? What we need is to create a state of mind and will that will give us the determination to offer all our resources in men and material to the defense of the state and the salvation of the country. And once more . . . . I tell you how important it is for us . . . . not to remain isolated [from our Allies]. . . . . The apprehensions that the Allies will take advantage of our disorganization to shift the whole burden of the war to our shoulders have absolutely no foundation. In this regard we have the most definite assurances of the Allied representatives. . . . .

Granted that we have got to go on with the war in coalition with the Allied Powers, it is reasonable to demand that a co-ordination of our views as to the aims of the war with those of our Allies . . . . should take place. That is why the question of an inter-allied conference has been raised. . . . . The purpose of the conference was clearly formulated by Lloyd George; its aims will be to . . . . co-ordinate questions of strategy with those of international policy . . . . and to devise means of bringing to a stop that terrible slaughter. . . . .[25] And I wish to tell you very definitely: . . . . Russia must come to that conference as one united whole (*applause in the Center and on the Right*) . . . . with a unity of purpose and point of view. . . . .

[25] Two days after Tereshchenko made this statement, it was stated in Parliament that the Paris conference would discuss not war aims but how to win the war. Cf. Sir George Buchanan, *My Mission to Russia,* 2 vols., London, 1923, II, 202.

[Miliukov's Speech][26]

. . . . Everyone seems to accept the fact that the most urgent task of the present is to defend the country and that there is only one way of achieving that task: We must restore discipline in the army and put an end to the anarchic conditions within the country. . . . . It is also becoming apparent that in order to accomplish this there must be a strong power, bold enough to dare, i.e., to act by constraint and not merely by those methods of persuasion and moral influence of which the Prime Minister spoke at the first session of the Pre-Parliament. And finally it is clear that such a power can function only in complete independence of the influence of private organizations, which are incapable of rising to a national point of view. There is one domain, however, into which these ideas penetrate very slowly and incompletely, and that is the domain of foreign politics. The root of all our evils—the disruption of the army, of the government, and of the country—boils down to the characteristic Russian point of view as to our aim in foreign politics, a view which passes as the Internationalist point of view . . . . but which in reality has been exported to the West from Russia so that in Germany and in Switzerland . . . . it is looked upon as a specifically Russian product. . . . .

The nobleman Lenin is merely repeating the nobleman Kireevsky or Khomiakov[27] when he maintains that from Russia will come the new Word which shall resuscitate the aged West, replacing the old banner of orthodox socialism by the new direct action method of the starving masses who will force the gates of the social paradise for a suffering humanity.

These men have been maintaining from the very beginning of the war . . . . that a revolution would come which would devour the war, that Russia would give the signal for the revolution which would start a universal conflagration in which the bourgeois world would perish forever. When the Russian Revolution did come, they thought that their predictions had come true. They began to look upon the Russian Revolution as the first step toward the realization of their prophecy and as a proof of their great prognostication. They were sincere in saying that the breakdown of Russia was the first step for them, a means through which the breakdown of Germany, France, England, and the rest of the bourgeois world would follow. The Russian Revolution for them was not an end in itself but only a means, a consideration which is important to bear in mind . . . . if we are to appraise justly the nature of their unconscious treachery. Because it is only on the basis of such a point of view that they could calmly urge the soldiers to leave the

[26] *Rech,* No. 245, November 1, 1917, pp. 3–4.

[27] Kireevsky (b. 1806) and Khomiakov (b. 1804) were active in the popular Slavophile movement in the time of Nicholas I.

trenches . . . . and fight their own capitalists and landlords instead of the external enemy. . . . .

I have mentioned the above considerations as a mitigating circumstance, to show that only a state of self-hypnotism could lead them to the supposition that the shortest way to peace is not victory but the insurrection of the laboring masses and a disintegration of the army, which they call democratization. The German Social-Democrats as well as the socialists of the Allied countries were well insured against this contagion and regarded these gentlemen with unconcealed contempt. But the [former] have decided *"gut für Russland"*—it will do for Russia—and sent us the apostles of the universal conflagration. (*Protests on the Left.*) . . . .

The formula of the Revolutionary Democracy is quite simple: No foreign politics, no diplomatic secrets, but an immediate, so-called democratic peace; and, in order to achieve it, all we need is to compel our Allies to adopt the points of view of Lenin and Trotsky and say with them: "We wish nothing; we have nothing to fight for." Then our enemies will repeat the same thing, and the brotherhood of nations will become an accomplished fact. . . . . Future generations will hardly believe that such madness was not merely the passing last word of human culture . . . . but became in a curtailed form the official foreign policy of a Russian Government. . . . .

[After a long and bitter criticism of the peace terms of the Revolutionary Democracy as formulated in the instructions to Skobelev,[28] Miliukov concluded his speech as follows]:

I will tell you this: Only those aims of foreign policy are real which can be backed by military force. Fortunately for us the aims of our Allies are of such a character, ... and from the sorrowful spectacle of what is going on on our front I should like to take you in imagination to those French and Flemish villages where the blood of our Allies is being shed, not in civil war but in the trenches. It is there, in the struggle with the enemy, that the foundations of justice and freedom of the world are being laid. Let us not plume ourselves on our democratic excellencies. It is not for us to give them [the Allies] lessons which they do not need. Let us better bow our heads in respectful admiration for those who, like England and France, are reaping on the battlefields the fruits of a three-years' long effort of their nations . . . . and [like] our new powerful ally, America, who is incessantly providing new supplies and new legions, by the aid of which, even if we should weaken completely, the cause of humanity and justice will prevail. (*Cheers on the Right and Center, passing into loud ovations for America.*) . . . .

[28] These instructions are given in Golder, pp. 646–48.

Long live the flower of humanity, the advanced democracies of the West, which have already covered a considerable part of the journey on which we are only embarking with faulty and shaky steps. Hail our glorious Allies! (*Loud applause for the Allies. Exclamations on the Left: "Long live the Revolution!" The Left section rises with applause.*)

[Dan's Speech][29]

. . . . This war has never been popular in Russia. . . . . We found ourselves in it as a result of the criminal adventures of tsarism seeking a refuge from the approaching revolutionary storm: . . . . It is natural, therefore, that for the vast masses of the people and the army our revolution was a revolt against the war in the name of a speedy conclusion of peace. But the dominant classes have shown a complete failure to understand the psychology of the masses when they took the revolution to be a means for a more efficient conduct of the war. It is not the weakness and the worn-out condition of the army that create the desire for peace, but the reverse; the unsatisfied striving for peace continues to work havoc in the army. And the phenomenon is not a specifically Russian one; it is going on in all armies of the belligerent countries. . . .

I declare that if . . . . we still have an army it is due to the efforts of the Revolutionary Democracy, which alone has been working for the organization of the army. It is all to the credit of the army committees. . . . .

Unfortunately . . . . we met but little encouragement from the government. It was Miliukov in particular who, in complete defiance of popular aspirations, obstinately continued a nationalistic and chauvinistic policy inherited from the old régime. It is this policy which, more than anything else, brought about the disorganization of the army and the anarchic conditions within the country. . . . . In May the Coalition Government proclaimed its intention of calling an Inter-Allied Conference to reconsider existing treaties and to restate the war aims in the spirit of the ideals which animated the Russian Revolution. We had no illusions as to the difficulties lying in the way of realizing such a peace policy and we cautioned the government that only by close cooperation with the democracy of its own country and the democracies of the rest of the world could such a policy be carried through successfully.

Has the Ministry of Foreign Affairs done everything to carry out the program to which it was committed? Has it created, to mention only one fact, a personnel suitable for the purpose? No! . . . .

[29] *Izvestiia,* No. 203, November 3, 1917, pp. 1–2. Dan was a Menshevik and a member of the Central Executive Committee of the Soviets of Workers' and Soldiers' Deputies.

The entire tsarist diplomatic personnel is left intact, and we can have no guaranty that the good intentions of the Ministry of Foreign Affairs can reach a point where policy is converted into practice. . . . .

We have failed to perceive in the speech of the Minister of Foreign Affairs that revolutionary and democratic assertiveness which alone is able to guarantee to Russia success in her peace policy. . . . . Instead, Russia, in Miliukov's representation, is pictured as a poor relative living on charity and ungrateful to its benefactors. (*Applause on the Left.*) . . . . But revolutionary Russia has her assets. . . . . Our first asset is our enormous army on the front holding an enormous army of Germany and Austria. Our second asset is the future of our country, which has thrown off the fetters of tsarism. . . . . And, finally, we have the third colossal asset and that is the moral prestige of our revolution. History is moving to a point where peoples themselves will dispose of their fortunes and in that movement the Russian Revolution is looked upon as the advance guard and the standard bearer. (*Applause on the Left.*) The democracy of the world is aware of these assets and that is why it is exercising pressure on the governments of the possessing classes to move closer and closer toward peace. . . . .

THE ARMY AND PEACE

[Statement of the Minister of War Delivered at the Secret Conference of the Committees on Foreign Affairs and National Defense, November 3, 1917]

a) *Preliminaries of the Session.*—A Conference of the Committees on Foreign Affairs and National Defense was called for November 3, 1917, at 9:00 P.M. Intense interest centered around the conference, which everyone expected to be sensational. All important secrets of state were going to be revealed. Members of the Pre-Parliament were not allowed to be present. Ministers Verkhovsky and Tereshchenko were to make statements.[30]

Before making his statement Verkhovsky decided to acquaint the different political factions with its main content. He requested and was granted the opportunity to meet privately a few responsible leaders of the Party of People's Freedom.[31] He told them that he saw only one way to arrest the disintegration of the army and that was to promise an immediate peace. In this way he hoped to infuse some enthusiasm into

[30] Sukhanov, *Zapiski o revoliutsii,* VI, 292.

[31] Otherwise known as the Constitutional Democrats or, for short, the Cadets. The meeting took place at the home of Nabokov. See his memoir on the Provisional Government in *Arkhiv Russkoi Revoliutsii,* I, 81; also Sukhanov, *op. cit.,* VI, 293–94. (The *Arkhiv Russkoi Revoliutsii* will hereafter be cited as *A.R.R.*)

the troops. A change in the attitude of the soldiers was, moreover, vital from the point of view of internal policy. He had succeeded once in preventing a Bolshevik rising, but a second time he might fail. . . . .[32]

b) *Verkhovsky's declaration.*—1. An army of nine and one-half million men cannot be supported by the country. . . . . According to the data of the Minister of Food . . . . the utmost we are able to support is seven million. These figures are indisputable. On the Northern front famine conditions are already in evidence and the soldiers' rations have been reduced to one and one-half pounds. Furthermore, we can neither shoe nor clothe that army. On account of the decrease in the productivity of labor after the revolution and the lack of raw material the output of footwear has fallen off to one-half of the output of 1916, and there is less than one-half of the warm clothing necessary. Having discharged some six hundred thousand to seven hundred thousand men, the Stavka categorically declared that not one more soldier would be released. The Stavka, having charge of the matter and knowing what the conditions of the country are, considers a further reduction of the army to be dangerous from the point of view of the country's defense. . . . . We shall remain in that blind alley until the men who are now guiding the defense of the country are replaced by others capable of finding a way out. Without such a change [of command] there is no solution but to conclude peace.

2. Our expenditures have reached the sum of sixty-five million rubles a day, of which only eight go for the needs of the state. . . . . But according to the report of the Minister of Finance, we live without any income—solely by the printing machine. . . . . In this way by the first of January 1918 we shall face a deficit of eight billion rubles. We can change this by radically reducing our war expenditures, but since the Stavka refuses to reduce the army, we are in another blind alley.

3. The Bolsheviks are demoralizing the army . . . . by undermining the very foundations of its organization—the relation to the commanding personnel. But there is no way to fight Bolshevism, since by its promise of peace it is winning over the masses. We, on the other hand, have done nothing to bring peace closer, to take advantage, that is, of the only factor that is capable of changing the psychology of the masses and giving us the support of the forces of the army. Shall we hope to check the Bolshevik movement in some other way? No—those hopes are in vain. We shall be driven out because of our alleged incapacity to conclude peace, and those who take our place will unscrupulously conclude peace at any price. This once more is a terrifying blind alley from which there is but one escape. We must compel our Allies to negotiate peace, otherwise they themselves will suffer incalculable injury.

[32] P. N. Miliukov, *Istoriia vtoroi russkoi revoliutsii,* I, Part 3, 172.

4. An army can function only when it can lean upon the commanding personnel. But under present conditions this is impossible. The officers require [their soldiers] to fulfil their duty, to give their lives for the salvation of the country. But the soldiers, misled by propaganda, do not understand what it is for which they are asked to die. Thus a chasm between officer and soldier is created, making impossible the normal functioning of the army. Little is done to enlighten the people, and the result is that the soldier continues to look upon the officer as his enemy forcing him into irrational sacrifices. We shall not improve the situation unless we adopt radical measures. . . . .[33]

The objective data furnished above lead to the inevitable conclusion that we cannot go on with the war. . . . . We have already received news that several detachments have decided to leave the trenches before winter comes. The Congress of Soviets is to assemble in the near future and there is no doubt that it will intensify the tendency toward peace. Until now it was only the threat of the front that kept the Bolsheviks from seizing the power. But who will guarantee that five days hence the threat will retain its force and that the Bolsheviks will not come out? We must not forget also that Germany is strongly supporting the peace propaganda; the *Minister is quite certain that two newspapers published here are financed by the enemy.* The only possible method of combating these subversive influences is to take away their ammunition and to raise the question of peace ourselves. We can take our stand in the first place on the fact . . . . that we keep tied up on our front 130 divisions of the enemy troops, and, secondly, that we owe our Allies some twenty billions. Such arguments will prove quite sufficient to induce our Allies to bring to an end this devastating war, the continuation of which is important only to them but has lost all purpose for us. There is no doubt that the news of a speedy peace will infuse into the army a regenerating spirit which will make it possible to suppress anarchy at the front and in the rear. It will surely be some time before peace is concluded. During that time the combative power of the army will be restored, which, in its turn, will favorably affect the terms of peace.[34]

c) *Opposition to Verkhovsky.*— . . . . The Minister of Foreign Affairs was to make his report [to the conference] next. . . . . But the members of the Party of People's Freedom protested, and in this protest they were supported not only by the representatives of the co-operatives

[33] A. I. Verkhovsky, *Rossiia na Golgofe* (*Iz pokhodnago dnevnika 1914–1918 g.*), Petrograd, 1918, pp. 135–36. Hereafter cited as Verkhovsky, *Rossiia na Golgofe*.

[34] "Nakanune oktiabrskago perevorota. Vopros o voine i mire. Otchety o sekretnykh zasedaniiakh Vremennago Soveta Rossiiskoi Respubliki," in *Byloe*, 1918, No. 12, pp. 33–34.

but also by certain members of the Left. They pointed out that the conclusions of the Minister of War cannot be taken as final and absolute, and that before proceeding to a consideration of foreign policy which must be largely based on those conclusions, the latter must be subjected to a preliminary scrutiny. . . . . To everyone's surprise Tereshchenko, Minister of Foreign Affairs, came out first as Verkhovsky's opponent. . . .[35]

Tereshchenko requested the Minister of War to state definitely, in connection with the question of provisioning the army, whether the figure of nine million, which according to Verkhovsky constitutes the numerical strength of our army, is reliable. . . . Further, he said it was important to know how the provisioning of the army was carried out last year. As regards the general conclusion of the Minister of War one cannot help asking the question: Does the Minister of War consider it possible to combat German peace propaganda by bringing about those very ends at which the propaganda is aiming? . . . .

Martynov wished to know whether the conclusions of the Minister of War came up for discussion in the Provisional Government. If so, what was the government's attitude? The Minister of Foreign Affairs declared that the views of the Minister of War had never come up before the Provisional Government and that they were being presented for the first time. . . . .

Malevsky wished to know what would happen if the Allies should refuse to accept our proposal to conclude peace.

The Minister of War replied that being under certain obligations we should have to submit to fate, i.e., to go through such trials as a Bolshevik insurrection . . . . anarchy with all its consequences. . . . .

The Minister of Foreign Affairs said that he now found it impossible to make a report in the name of the government in view of the unexpected disagreement with the Minister of War, whose conclusions were in radical opposition to the previous policy of the government. . . . .

Yu. Tsederbaum [Martov] inquired whether the proposal of the Minister of War to suppress anarchy must be interpreted in the sense of establishing a dictatorship.

The Minister of War replied that, no matter what name we use, a strong unified government is needed for the suppression of anarchy no less than for the command of an army. In that sense the government in question might be called a dictatorship. . . .[36]

[35] Miliukov, *op. cit.*, I, Part 3, 173–74. Miliukov was a member of the conference.

[36] *Byloe, op. cit.*, pp. 34–40.

On the next day Burtzev published the statement that Verkhovsky had proposed a separate peace. This was officially denied, but Kerensky ordered Burtzev's paper closed and himself took over Verkhovsky's duties. It was publicly announced that Verkhovsky was going on leave because of illness. Verkhovsky states that his

Along with the question of peace the government discussed the equally pressing problems of bread and land. In the face of the continuing disorders the Minister of the Interior on November 3 authorized the gubernia commissars to call upon the troops to maintain public order.

FOOD SUPPLIES OF THE ARMY AND THE CAPITAL

[Statement by the Minister of Supplies, Prokopovich, before the Pre-Parliament, October 29, 1917][37]

. . . . I have the following telegram . . . . from the Northern front: "The most terrific autocrat—hunger—is menacing the army. A number of bakeries have had to stop working and in two or three days the rest will close because of lack of flour. Not an hour must be lost. . . . . Passenger traffic must be cut in half at once and flour rushed on the trains." And here is a telegram from General Cheremisov:[38] "The food situation at the front is catastrophic. Horses are perishing for lack of forage. Bakeries stop working because there is no flour. The last reserves of hardtack are now being consumed. [When these are finished] an epidemic of starvation will break out with all its consequences. Every hour of delay . . . . threatens to ruin the army." Such is the situation in spite of the increased purchase of supplies. The reason for it is that between the base of supplies and the army there lies a vast area submerged by anarchy which defeats every regulated effort to supply the army and the population. . . . .

I come now to Petrograd. Bread supplies in the capital on October 27 consisted of 152 carloads, with an average daily arrival of twenty to twenty-two cars and a daily consumption of forty cars. . . . . We are thus provided for the next seven or eight days, and the rations will continue as before, three-fourths of a pound per day. . . . . In Petrograd we have to face the very disturbing fact that the bread already purchased is not being delivered. . . . . Out of the 400,000 puds shipped to Petrograd by way of the Mariinsky Canal . . . . 200,000 puds were either detained or stolen on the way. . . . . Here is a telegram from Cherepovetz: "Shipments of bread are being plundered by peasants of Novgorod and Olonetsk gubernias. . . . . Soldiers escorting [the transports] cannot stop [the peasants]. Please take immediate measures to save [the bread]." [Here is] a telegram from Rybinsk: "This is the

offered resignation was not accepted, as it might be interpreted that the government was opposed to peace. (*A.R.R.*, VII, 281; Verkhovsky, *Rossiia na Golgofe*, p. 137.)

[37] *Rech*, No. 244, October 30, 1917, p. 3.

[38] Commander at the Northern front.

second time that [our] barge has been stopped . . . . by armed peasants who plundered some 120,000 puds of flour. The soldiers who were sent after them refused to bring it back. . . . ." A telegram from Petrozavodsk: "The soldiers refuse to escort the cargo. In Vytegorsky and Lodeinoplsky uezds lawless seizures have begun. Similar disturbances are also occurring in other places. . . . ." Under such conditions there can be no certainty that we shall emerge successfully from the crisis in which we find ourselves. . . . .

Ordinarily the peasants are forced to sell their grain by economic needs. No such need exists at present, and special measures have to be taken to get the grain [from the peasants]. . . . . [The peasants] refuse to give bread not only for the cities but for the army as well. . . . . At times army delegates who were sent to the villages in the capacity of agitators [to urge the peasants to sell bread] would begin their speeches as follows: "Brother peasants. Stop giving food and the war will have to come to an end." . . . .

The minister then read telegrams from Saratov, Samara, and Voronezh. [These telegrams] state that plundering of food trains is very common. . . . . Railway employees are being compelled, under threat of lynching, to give up freight cars. In Saratov . . . . the number of starving people and of speculators is growing larger every day, becoming more and more menacing. The local committee and the Soviet of Workers' and Soldiers' Deputies are helpless to cope with the situation. . . . . In this way, along with actual starvation we have a widely developing wave of speculation. It is known that in some places a pud of grain costs between 20 and 25 rubles. Local representatives of the committees [of supply] and railroad employees are especially endangered. The violence of the mob is often directed against them, and they are wholly helpless to offer resistance. . . . .

LAND REFORM

[October 30, 1917]

The Provisional Government at its meeting yesterday discussed a project of the Minister of Agriculture, S. L. Maslov, on the subject of transferring the land to the land committees.

[According to that project] all farm land, pending the final settlement of the land question by the Constituent Assembly, is to be placed with the local land committees, whose duty it will be to take account of the land, to see that the farms are not depreciated in value by their owners or tenants, and to devise ways and means of alleviating extreme cases of land starvation among local farmers by creating for that purpose a provisional land fund. . . . .[39]

[39] *Novaia Zhizn,* No. 156, October 31, 1917, p. 2.

Deliberations by the Provisional Government on Maslov's project proposing the transfer of all land to the land committees are proceeding very slowly. Out of some hundred articles of the project only four were considered at the session of November 2. The project is meeting with great opposition by a considerable number of ministers.[40]

THE GOVERNMENT DECIDES TO USE TROOPS TO MAINTAIN ORDER

[Circular of the Ministry of the Interior, November 3, 1917][41]

To all Gubernia, Regional, and City Commissars:

The uninterrupted growth of anarchy threatening to disrupt the internal life of the country, and the necessity of handling in a decisive and effective manner every disorder that infringes upon the safety of social life makes it imperative for the gubernia commissars, as the local representatives of the Provisional Government, to call for military assistance.

Orders have accordingly been issued by the Minister of War to all army commanders to place cavalry units from reserve cavalry regiments at the disposal of the gubernia commissars.

In bringing the above to the notice of the gubernia commissars the Ministry of the Interior considers it its duty to point out that every precaution must be taken in the exercise of that duty, that local conditions be taken into consideration, and, above all, that the need to act promptly and decisively in the suppression of disorders be kept in mind.

Placing at the disposal of the gubernia commissars this extraordinary measure called forth by the grave internal conditions of the Republic, the Ministry of the Interior expresses its hope that with the co-operation of all healthy elements of the population, especially the organs of local self-government, the gubernia commissars will make every effort in the struggle against anarchy.

[A. M.] NIKITIN
Minister of the Interior

[40] *Ibid.*, No. 160, November 4, 1917, p. 3. Lenin described the project as "a complete betrayal of the peasants by the Socialist-Revolutionary Party." "Let the peasants know," he wrote, "how the Socialist-Revolutionary Party has betrayed them, how it has delivered them to the landowners. Let the peasants know that only the *workers' party*, only the *Bolsheviks* are firmly and irrevocably *against* the capitalists, *against* the landowners, for the interests of the poorest peasantry and *all* the toilers." (*Rabochii Put*, No. 44, November 6, 1917, translated in Lenin, *Toward the Seizure of Power*, II, 138–43.)

[41] *Krestianskoe dvizhenie v 1917 godu*, p. 427.

C. Preparation for an Uprising

The Bolsheviks, like the other parties, had their dissensions and wavering during the tense September and October days. They had taken part with the other elements of the revolutionary democracy in opposing the Kornilov movement, and more than any other party they profited by that counter-revolutionary fiasco and the political crisis that followed. They were not, however, able to agree on the tactics to be adopted in the new situation. Lenin, who was still in hiding, warned his comrades against being led to support Kerensky in their campaign against Kornilov. "We will fight," he wrote, "we are fighting against Kornilov, even *as Kerensky's troops do,* but we do not support Kerensky. *On the contrary,* we expose his weakness."[42] Lenin believed that this weakness was so manifest after the defeat of Kornilov that it offered an opportunity for a peaceful development of the revolution on the basis of the replacement of Kerensky by a government of Socialist-Revolutionists and Mensheviks responsible to the Soviets. In such a government the Bolsheviks would not participate, but they would "refrain from immediately advancing the demand for the passing of power to the proletariat and the poorest peasants [and] from revolutionary methods of struggle for the realization of this demand." They would, however, insist on full freedom of propaganda and on the summoning of the Constituent Assembly.[43]

The Mensheviks and Socialist-Revolutionists did not take to this idea and made their compromise with Kerensky and the Cadets. When the Democratic Conference met, Lenin turned from all thought of a "peaceful development" and began to press his associates to prepare to seize power. "What matters," he wrote on September 25–27, "is that we must make the *task* clear to the party, place on the order of

[42] "To the Central Committee of the Russian Social-Democratic Labour Party," written September 12, 1917; in Lenin, *Toward the Seizure of Power,* I, 137.

[43] *Ibid.,* I, 153, in an article "On Compromises" written September 14–16.

the day the *armed uprising* in Petrograd and Moscow (including their regions), the conquest of power, the overthrow of the government. We must think of *how* to make propaganda in favor of this without committing ourselves in the press. . . . . It is just the miserable vacillations of the Democratic Conference that must and will cause the patience of the workers of Petrograd and Moscow to end in a violent outburst! History will not forgive us if we do not assume power now."[44] This letter Lenin followed with an even more forceful demand for decision and action by the party. He argued that as a result of the events of July and August and particularly of the Kornilov affair in September, the proletariat was now definitely behind the Bolshevik program and there was a "general revolutionary upsurge of the people" in the provinces. At the same time there were "enormous" vacillations among the democratic parties and the Allied imperialists; in short, he concluded, "We have before us all the objective prerequisites for a successful uprising."

Having recognized the absolute necessity of an uprising of the workers of Petrograd and Moscow for the sake of saving the revolution and of saving Russia from being divided among the imperialists, Lenin continued, the party should adopt tactics looking toward the accomplishment of the uprising which should be treated according to Marxian precept as an art. To achieve this he proposed that the following steps be taken: the consolidation of the Bolshevik group in the Democratic Conference; the issuance by the group of a short declaration condemning speech-making, demanding action, insisting upon breaking with the bourgeoisie, severing all relations with the Mensheviks and Socialist-Revolutionists, ousting the Kerensky government, severing relations with the Anglo-French imperialists by proposing an immediate peace, and the assumption of power by the revolutionary democracy headed by the proletariat.

[44] *Ibid.*, I, 222, "The Bolsheviks Must Assume Power," a letter to the Central Committee and the Petrograd and Moscow committees of the party.

Having made this declaration the Bolsheviks should turn from speeches in the Democratic Conference to speeches in the factories and barracks, clarifying the party program. At the same time the party must organize a staff for the insurrection, designate the forces, place loyal units at strategic points, surround the Alexandrinsky Theater where the Democratic Conference was in session, occupy Peter and Paul Fortress, arrest the general staff and the government, move against the military cadets and other hostile units, mobilize the armed workers, occupy the telegraph and telephone offices, install the insurrectionary staff in the central telephone exchange, and establish wire connections with the factories, all regiments, and all points of attack.[45]

Lenin's proposal staggered and bewildered the party leaders. After considering the matter the Central Committee decided to reject the proposal and to burn the letter that contained it.[46] Equally significant of the reluctance of the leaders to adopt the revolutionary course was the decision by a vote of seventy-seven to fifty to participate in the Pre-Parliament. This leaning toward parliamentarism, this tendency to put off preparations to seize power, and the alternative plan of waiting for the forthcoming Congress of Soviets were to Lenin idiocy and treason to the revolution. In an article on this theme written on October 12 he expressed his opinion of the party leaders and delivered an ultimatum:

> To refrain from seizing power at present, to "wait," to "chatter" in the Central Committee, to confine ourselves to "fighting for the organ" (of the Soviet), to "fighting for the Congress," means to *ruin the revolution.*
>
> Seeing that the Central Committee has left *even without an answer*

[45] Lenin, *Toward the Seizure of Power,* I, 224–29, "Marxism and Uprising," a letter to the Central Committee of the party, September 26–27. Neither this nor the letter previously cited was published until 1921.

[46] Bukharin, "Iz rechi t. Bukharina na vechere vospominanii v 1921 g.," in *Proletarskaia Revoliutsiia,* 1922, No. 10, p. 316. Cf. Trotsky, *The History of the Russian Revolution,* 3 vols., New York [1932], III, 133–34.

my writings insisting on such a policy since the beginning of the Democratic Conference, that the Central Organ *is deleting* from my articles references to such glaring errors of the Bolsheviks as the shameful decision to participate in the Pre-Parliament, as giving seats to the Mensheviks in the Presidium of the Soviets, etc., etc.—seeing all that, I am compelled to recognise here a "gentle" hint as to the unwillingness of the Central Committee even to consider this question, a gentle hint at gagging me and at suggesting that I retire.

I am compelled to tender *my resignation from the Central Committee* which I hereby do, leaving myself the freedom of propaganda *in the lower ranks* of the party and at the Party Congress.

For it is my deepest conviction that if we "await" the Congress of Soviets and let the present moment pass, we ruin the revolution.[47]

Lenin did not leave the Central Committee but pushed his campaign in the press and by letters to party workers. Supporters of his program in the military organization and among the workers intensified their agitation in the barracks and factories. On October 18 all the Bolshevik members of the Pre-Parliament except Kamenev voted to make a demonstrative withdrawal from that body. This decision, as has been seen, was carried out at the first session on October 20. On the 21st Lenin addressed letters to the Central Committee and to members of the party participating in the Congress of Soviets of the Northern Region in which he reiterated his arguments for action, and urged the party to take the offensive by moving units of the Baltic fleet and of neighboring garrisons against the capitals. "Only the immediate movement of the Baltic fleet, of the Finnish troops, of Reval and Kronstadt against the Kornilovist troops near Petrograd, is capable of saving the Russian and the world revolution. . . . . Delay means death."[48] The revolutionary troops did not move at once, but on October 23 the Central Committee accepted Lenin's resolution that the party organization should definitely prepare for an armed insurrection to seize power in the name of the Soviets.

[47] Lenin, *Toward the Seizure of Power,* I, 278.

[48] *Ibid.,* II, 104.

MEETING OF THE BOLSHEVIK CENTRAL COMMITTEE

[Minutes of the Sessions, October 23, 1917][49]

Present: Lenin, Zinoviev, Kamenev, Trotsky, Stalin, Sverdlov, Uritsky, Dzerzhinsky, Kollontai, Bubnov, Sokolnikov, Lomov.

Chairman: Sverdlov.

Order of Business: 1. Rumanian front. 2. Lithuanians. 3. Minsk and northern front. 4. Present situation. 5. Regional congress. 6. Evacuation of troops.

1. Rumanian Front

Report submitted by *Sverdlov.* On the Rumanian front a conference of Social-Democrats of all shades took place. A mixed list was prepared. Submitted to the Central Committee (united). Was approved. They ask what the attitude of our Central Committee is on this. Out of 20 candidates 4 Bolsheviks were put up.

Decided: taking into consideration the decision of the Congress, no blocs are permitted.

2. Lithuanians

Report by *Sverdlov.*

The Lithuanians had a conference in Minsk, where, it appeared, defensists frequently speak in the name of the party. In order to counteract this practice, it was decided to elect a temporary centre which is to put itself, as well as the entire conference, under the banner of the Bolsheviks. This centre should be confirmed.

Comrade Lomov thinks it should be confirmed. But attention should be called to the fact that defensist organisations were also present.

The temporary bureau is approved.

3. Minsk and Northern Front

Report by *Sverdlov.*

Representatives of several armies of the northern front came and stated that on that front some shady affair is being prepared with regard to the evacuation of the troops into the interior.

It is reported from Minsk that a new Kornilov affair is in preparation there. Because of the character of the garrison Minsk is surrounded by Cossack detachments. There are some negotiations of a suspicious nature going on between the staff and headquarters. Agitation is being conducted among the Osetians and several parts of the army against the Bolsheviks. At the front, however, sentiment is for the Bolsheviks. They will follow them against Kerensky. There are no

[49] From the archives of the Central Committee, translated in Lenin, *Toward the Seizure of Power,* II, 326–28.

documents at all. They can be obtained by seizing the staff, which is technically altogether possible in Minsk; in that case the local garrison can disarm all the troops around. All the artillery has been driven into the Pinsk marshes. A corps can be sent from Minsk to Petrograd.

4. Present Situation

Lenin takes the floor.

He states that since the beginning of September a certain indifference toward the question of uprising has been noted. He says that this is inadmissible, if we earnestly raise the slogan of seizure of power by the Soviets. It is, therefore, high time to turn attention to the technical side of the question. Much time has obviously been lost.

Nevertheless the question is very urgent and the decisive moment is near.

The international situation is such that we must take the initiative.

What is being planned, surrendering as far as Narva and even as far as Petrograd, compels us still more to take decisive action.

The political situation is also effectively working in this direction. On July 16–18, decisive action on our part would have been defeated because we had no majority with us. Since then, our upsurge has been making gigantic strides.

The absenteeism and the indifference of the masses can be explained by the fact that the masses are tired of words and resolutions.

The majority is now with us. Politically, the situation has become entirely ripe for the transfer of power.

The agrarian movement also goes in this direction, for it is clear that enormous efforts are needed to subdue this movement. The slogan of transferring the entire land has become the general slogan of the peasants. The political background is thus ready. It is necessary to speak of the technical side. This is the whole matter. Meanwhile we, together with the defensists, are inclined to consider a systematic preparation for an uprising as something like a political sin.

To wait for the Constituent Assembly, which will obviously not be for us, is senseless, because it would make our task more complex.

We must utilise the regional congress and the proposal from Minsk to begin decisive action.

Comrade Lomov takes the floor, giving information concerning the attitude of the Moscow Regional Bureau and the Moscow Committee, as well as about the situation in Moscow in general.

Comrade Uritsky states that we are weak not only in a technical sense but also in all other spheres of our work. We have carried a mass of resolutions. Actions, none whatever. The Petrograd Soviet is disorganised, few meetings, etc.

On what forces do we base ourselves?

The workers in Petrograd have 40,000 rifles, but this will not decide the issue; this is nothing.

The garrison after the July days cannot inspire great hopes. However, in any case, if the course is held for an uprising, then it is really necessary to do something in that direction. We must *make up our mind* with regard to definite action.

Comrade Sverdlov gives information concerning what he knows about the state of affairs throughout Russia.

Comrade Dzerzhinsky proposes that for the purpose of political guidance during the immediate future, a Political Bureau be created, composed of members of the C.C. [Central Committee].

After an exchange of opinion, the proposal is carried. A Political Bureau of 7 is created (the editors + two + Bubnov).

A resolution was accepted, reading as follows [see below.—Ed.].

Ten express themselves for it, and two against.

The question is then raised of establishing a Political Bureau of the C.C. It is decided to form a bureau of 7: Lenin, Zinoviev, Kamenev, Trotsky, Stalin, Sokolnikov, Bubnov.

Resolution[50]

The Central Committee recognises that the international situation of the Russian Revolution (the mutiny in the navy in Germany as the extreme manifestation of the growth in all of Europe of the world-wide Socialist revolution; the threat of a peace between the imperialists with the aim of crushing the revolution in Russia) as well as the military situation (the undoubted decision of the Russian bourgeoisie and of Kerensky and Co. to surrender Petrograd to the Germans) and the fact that the proletarian parties have gained a majority in the Soviets; all this, coupled with the peasant uprising and with a shift of the people's confidence towards our party (elections in Moscow); finally, the obvious preparation for a second Kornilov affair (the withdrawal of troops from Petrograd; the bringing of Cossacks to Petrograd; the surrounding of Minsk by Cossacks, etc.)—places the armed uprising on the order of the day.

Recognising thus that an armed uprising is inevitable and the time perfectly ripe, the Central Committee proposes to all the organisations of the party to act accordingly and to discuss and decide from this point of view all the practical questions (the Congress of the Soviets of the northern region, the withdrawal of troops from Petrograd, the actions in Moscow and in Minsk, etc.).

[50] Lenin, *Toward the Seizure of Power,* II, 107.

ZINOVIEV AND KAMENEV OPPOSE THE CENTRAL COMMITTEE

[Extracts from a Letter to the Petrograd, Moscow, Moscow Regional, and Finnish Regional Committees of the R.S.-D.L.P., the Bolshevik Group of the C.E.C. of the Soviets of Workers' and Soldiers' Deputies, the Bolshevik Group of the Congress of the Soviets of the Northern Region, written October 24, 1917][51]

On the Present Situation

In connection with the political situation, the withdrawal of the Bolsheviks from the Pre-Parliament put before our party the question: What next?

In labour circles there is developing and growing a current of thought which sees the only outcome in the immediate declaration of an armed uprising. The interaction of all the conditions at present is such that if we are to speak of such an uprising a definite date must be set for it, and that within the next few days. . . . .

We are deeply convinced that to call at present for an armed uprising means to stake on one card not only the fate of our party, but also the fate of the Russian and international revolution.

There is no doubt that there are historical situations when an oppressed class must recognise that it is better to go forward to defeat than to give up without a battle. Does the Russian working class find itself at present in such a situation? *No,* and *a thousand times no!!!*

As a result of the immense growth of the influence of our party in the cities, and particularly in the army, there has come about at present a situation such that it is becoming more and more impossible for the bourgeoisie to obstruct the Constituent Assembly. Through the army, through the workers, we hold a revolver at the temple of the bourgeoisie: the bourgeoisie is put in such a position that if it should undertake now to attempt to obstruct the Constituent Assembly, it would again push the petty-bourgeois parties to one side, and the revolver would go off.

The chances of our party in the elections to the Constituent Assembly are excellent. The talk that the influence of Bolshevism is beginning to wane, etc., we consider to have absolutely no foundation. In the mouths of our political opponents this assertion is simply a move in the political game, having as its purpose this very thing, to provoke an uprising of the Bolsheviks under conditions favourable to our enemies. The influence of the Bolsheviks is increasing. . . . .

[51] *Ibid.*, II, 328–32.

The Constituent Assembly, by itself, cannot of course abolish the present camouflaging of these interrelations. The Soviets, which have become rooted in life, can not be destroyed. The Constituent Assembly will be able to find support for its revolutionary work only in the Soviets. The Constituent Assembly plus the Soviets—this is the combined type of state institutions toward which we are going. It is on this political basis that our party is acquiring enormous chances for a real victory.

We have never said that the Russian working class *alone,* by its own forces, would be able to bring the present revolution to a victorious conclusion. We have not forgotten, must not forget even now, that between us and the bourgeoisie there stands a huge third camp: the petty bourgeoisie. This camp joined us during the days of the Kornilov affair and gave us victory. It will join us many times more. We must not permit ourselves to be hypnotised by what is the case at the present moment. Undoubtedly, at present this camp is much nearer to the bourgeoisie than to us. But the present situation is not eternal, nor even durable. And only by a careless step, by some hasty action which will make the whole fate of the revolution dependent upon an immediate uprising, will the proletarian party push the petty bourgeoisie into the arms of Milyukov. . . . .

We are told: (1) that the majority of the people of Russia is already with us, and (2) that the majority of the international proletariat is with us. Alas!—neither the one nor the other is true, and this is the crux of the entire situation. . . . .

In what perspective then does the immediate future present itself to us? Here is our answer.

It stands to reason that our path does not depend upon ourselves alone. The enemy *may compel* us to accept decisive battle before the elections to the Constituent Assembly. Attempts at a new Kornilov affair will of course not leave us even the elections. We will then, of course, be unanimous in the only possible decision. But at that time a substantial part of the petty-bourgeois camp too will surely support us again. The flight of the government to Moscow will push the masses of the petty bourgeoisie over to us. . . . .

But in so far as the choice depends upon us, we can and we must limit ourselves to a *defensive position.* The Provisional Government is often powerless to carry into execution its counter-revolutionary intentions. . . . . The strength of the soldiers and workers is sufficient to prevent the realisation of such steps by Kerensky and Company. The peasant movement has only just begun. The mass suppression of the peasant movement by the Cadets cannot succeed with the sentiment of the army as it now is. The Provisional Government is powerless to fix up the elections to the Constituent Assembly. Sympathy with our party will grow. The bloc of the Cadets, the Mensheviks, and the S.-R.'s will fall apart. In the Constituent Assembly we shall be such a strong opposition party that in a country of universal suffrage our opponents will be compelled to make concessions to us at every step, or we will form, together with the Left S.-R.'s, non-party peasants, etc., a ruling bloc which will fundamentally have to carry out our programme. This is our opinion.

Before history, before the international proletariat, before the Russian Revolution and the Russian working class, we have no right to stake the whole future on the card of an armed uprising. It would be a mistake to think that such action now would, if it were unsuccessful, lead only to such consequences as did July 16–18. Now it is a question of something more. It is a question of decisive battle, and defeat in *that* battle would spell defeat to the revolution.

This is the general situation. But everyone who does not want merely to talk about uprising must carefully weigh its chances. And here we consider it our duty to say that at the present moment it would be most harmful to underestimate the forces of our opponent and overestimate our own forces. The forces of the opponent are greater than they appear. Petrograd is decisive, and in Petrograd the enemies of the proletarian party have accumulated substantial forces: 5,000 military cadets, *excellently* armed, *organised, anxious,* . . . . and able to fight, also the staff, shock troops, Cossacks, a substantial part of the garrison, and very considerable artillery, which has taken up a position in fan-like formation around Petrograd. Then our adversaries will undoubtedly attempt, with the aid of the C.E.C., to bring troops from the front. The proletarian party at the present time would have to fight under an entirely different interrelationship of forces than in the days of the Kornilov affair. At that time we fought together with the S.-R.'s, the Mensheviks, and to some extent even with the adherents of Kerensky. Now, however, the proletarian party would have to fight against the Black Hundreds, plus the Cadets, plus Kerensky and the Provisional Government, plus the C.E.C. (S.-R.'s and Mensheviks).

The forces of the proletarian party are, of course, very substantial, but the decisive question is, is the sentiment among the workers and soldiers of the capital really such that they see salvation only in street fighting, that they are impatient to go into the streets? No. There is no such sentiment. Even those in favour of the uprising state that the sentiment of the masses of workers and soldiers is not at all even like their sentiments upon the eve of July 16. If among the great masses of the poor of the capital there were a militant sentiment burning to go into the streets, it might have served as a guarantee that an uprising initiated by them would draw in the biggest organisations (railroad unions, unions of postoffice and telegraph workers, etc.), where the influence of our party is weak. But since there is no such sentiment even in the factories and barracks, it would be self-deception to build any plans on it.

We are told: but the railroad workers and the postoffice and telegraph employees are starving, are crushed by poverty, are exasperated with the Provisional Government. All this is so, of course. But all this is still no guarantee that they will support an uprising against the government, in spite of the S.-R.'s and Mensheviks. The railroad workers and employees were crushed by poverty also in 1906, even as they are now in Germany and France. . . . . If all these people who are crushed by poverty were always ready to support the armed uprising of the Socialists, we would have won Socialism long ago.

This emphasises our immediate task. The Congress of Soviets has been called for November 2. It must be convened, no matter what the cost. It must organisationally consolidate the growing influence of the proletarian party. It must become the centre of the consolidation around the Soviets of all proletarian and semi-proletarian organisations, such as those same railroad unions, unions of postoffice and telegraph employees, bank employees, etc. As yet there is no firm organisational connection between these organisations and the Soviets. This cannot be considered as other than a symptom of the organisational weakness of the proletarian party. But such a connection is in any case a preliminary condition for the actual carrying out of the slogan, "All power to the Soviets." For any given moment this slogan naturally signifies the most decisive resistance to the slightest encroachment on the rights of the Soviets and organisations created by them, on the part of the government.

Under these conditions it would be a serious historical untruth to formulate the question of the transfer of power into the hands of the proletarian party in the terms: either now or never. . . . . The party of the proletariat will grow. Its programme will become known to broader and broader masses. It will have the opportunity to continue on an even larger scale the merciless exposure of the policy of the Mensheviks and S.-R.'s who stand in the way of actual transfer of the power into the hands of the majority of the people. And there is only one way in which the proletarian party can interrupt its successes, and that is if under present conditions it take upon itself to initiate an uprising and thus expose the proletariat to the blows of the entire consolidated counter-revolution, supported by the petty-bourgeois democracy.

Against this perilous policy we raise our voice in warning.

G. Zinoviev
U. Kamenev

LENIN'S REPLY TO ZINOVIEV AND KAMENEV

[Extracts from His "Letter to the Comrades"][52]

It is not easy to discover an explanation for such shameful vacillations [of the comrades Zinoviev and Kamenev]. . . . . The revolutionary party has no right to tolerate vacillations in such a serious question, as this little pair of comrades, who have scattered their principles to the winds, might cause a certain confusion of mind, it is necessary to analyse their arguments, to expose their vacillations, to show how shameful they are. . . . . [They say]

"We have no majority among the people, and without this condition the uprising is hopeless. . . . ."

Men capable of saying this are either distorters of the truth or pedants who at all events, without taking the least account of the real circumstances of the revolution, wish to secure an advance guarantee that the Bolshevik Party has received throughout the whole country no more nor less than one-half of the votes plus one. Such a guarantee history has never proffered, and is absolutely in no position to proffer in any revolution. To advance such a demand means to mock one's audience, and is nothing but a cover to hide one's own *flight* from reality.

For reality shows us palpably that it was after the July days that the majority of the people began quickly to go over to the side of the Bolsheviks. This was demonstrated first by the September 2 elections in Petrograd,[53] even before the Kornilov affair, when the Bolshevik vote rose from 20 to 33 per cent in the city not including the suburbs, and also by the elections to the borough councils in Moscow in September, when the Bolshevik vote rose from 11 to 49⅓ per cent. . . . . It was proven by the fact that a majority of the peasant Soviets, ... has expressed itself *against* the coalition. To be against the coalition means *in practice* to follow the Bolsheviks. . . . .

Last, but not least, the most outstanding fact in the present situation is *the revolt of the peasantry*. Here is an objective passing over of the people to the side of the Bolsheviks, shown not by words but by deeds. For, notwithstanding the lies of the bourgeois press and its miserable henchmen . . . . and their wails about pogroms and anarchy, the fact is there. The movement of the peasants in Tambov province was an uprising both in the material and political sense, an uprising that has yielded such splendid political results as, in the first place, permission to give the land to the peasants. . . . .

This is a fact. Facts are stubborn things. And such a factual "argu-

[52] This letter, written October 29–30, was published in three installments in the Bolshevik paper *Rabochii Put,* Nos. 40, 41, 42, November 1, 2, 3, 1917. The full translated text is in Lenin, *Toward the Seizure of Power,* II, 111–28.

[53] See Golder, p. 577.

ment" in *favour* of an uprising is stronger than thousands of "pessimistic" evasions on the part of confused and frightened politicians.

If the peasant uprising were not an event of nation-wide political import, the S.-R. lackeys from the pre-parliament would not be shouting about the necessity of giving over the land to the peasants. . . . .

"We are not strong enough to seize power, and the bourgeoisie is not strong enough to hinder the calling of the Constituent Assembly."

The first part of this argument is a simple paraphrase of the preceding argument. It does not gain in strength and convincing power, when the confusion of its authors and their fear of the bourgeoisie is expressed in terms of pessimism concerning the workers and optimism concerning the bourgeoisie. If the military cadets and the Cossacks say that they will fight against the Bolsheviks to the last drop of their blood, this deserves full credence; if, however, the workers and soldiers at hundreds of meetings express full confidence in the Bolsheviks and affirm their readiness to stand fast for the passing of power to the Soviets, then it is "timely" to recall that voting is one thing and fighting another! . . . .

Look at the facts. . . . . We have said thousands of times that the Soviets of Workers' and Soldiers' Deputies are the power, that they are the vanguard of the revolution. . . . .

And what has the Kornilov affair proven? It has proven that the Soviets are a real power.

And, now, after this has been proven by experience, by facts, we shall repudiate Bolshevism, deny ourselves, and say: we are not strong enough. . . . . Are these not shameful vacillations? . . . .

How can it be proven that the bourgeoisie is not sufficiently strong to hinder the calling of the Constituent Assembly?

If the Soviets *have not the power* to overthrow the bourgeoisie, this *means* that the latter is strong enough to hinder the calling of the Constituent Assembly, for there is nobody to prevent it from doing this. To trust the promises of Kerensky and Co., to trust the resolutions of the pre-parliament lackeys—is this worthy of a member of a proletarian party and a revolutionist?

Not only has the bourgeoisie power to hinder the calling of the Constituent Assembly, if the present government is not overthrown, but it can also *indirectly* achieve this result by surrendering Petrograd to the Germans, by laying the front open. . . . . It has been proven by facts that, to a certain extent, the bourgeoisie has already been doing all this. That means that it is capable of doing all this *to the full extent,* if the workers and soldiers do not overthrow it. . . . .

"The bourgeoisie cannot surrender Petrograd to the Germans, although Rodzyanko wants to, for the fighting is done not by the bourgeoisie, but by our heroic sailors."

This argument again reduces itself to the same "optimism" *concerning the bourgeoisie* which is fatally manifested at every step by those who are pessimistic regarding the revolutionary forces and capabilities of the proletariat.

The fighting is done by the heroic sailors, *but* this did not prevent *two* admirals from disappearing before the capture of Esel [Ösel]!

This is a fact. Facts are stubborn things. The facts prove that the admirals are capable of treachery no less than Kornilov. That General Headquarters has not been reformed, and that the commanding staff is Kornilovist, are undisputed facts.

If the Kornilovists (with Kerensky at their head, for he is also a Kornilovist) want to surrender Petrograd, they can do it in two or even in three ways.

First, they can, by an act of treachery of the Kornilovist commanding staff, open the northern land front.

Second, they can "agree" concerning freedom of action for the entire German fleet, which is *stronger* than we are; they can agree both with the German and with the English imperialists. Moreover, the admirals who have disappeared may also have delivered the *plans* to the Germans.

Third, they can, by means of lockouts, and by sabotaging the delivery of foodstuffs, bring our troops to complete desperation and impotence. . . . . The facts have proven that the bourgeois-Cossack party of Russia has already knocked at all three of these doors, that it has tried to open all of them.

What follows? It follows that we have no right to *wait* until the bourgeoisie strangles the revolution. . . . .

It follows that to vacillate in the question of an uprising as the only means to save the revolution means to sink into that half-Liberdan,[54] S.-R. – Menshevik cowardly confidence toward the bourgeoisie, half "peasant-like" unquestioning confidence, against which the Bolsheviks have been battling most of all. . . . .

"We are becoming stronger every day. We can enter the Constituent Assembly as a strong opposition; why should we stake everything?"

This is the argument of a philistine who has "read" that the Constituent Assembly is being called, and who confidently acquiesces in the most legal, most loyal, most constitutional course.

It is only a pity that by *waiting* for the Constituent Assembly one can solve neither the question of famine nor the question of surrendering Petrograd. This "trifle" is forgotten by the naïve or the confused or those who have allowed themselves to be frightened.

The famine will not wait. The peasant uprising did not wait.

[54] Lieber and Dan, two Menshevik leaders.

The war will not wait. The admirals who have disappeared did not wait. . . . .

"There is really nothing in the international situation that would oblige us to act immediately; rather would we damage the cause of a Socialist revolution in the West, if we were to allow ourselves to be shot."

This argument is truly magnificent: Scheidemann "himself," Renaudel "himself" would not be able to "manipulate" more cleverly the sympathies of the workers for the international Socialist revolution!

Just think of it: under devilishly difficult conditions, having but *one* Liebknecht (and at hard labour at that), without newspapers, without freedom of assembly, without Soviets, with *all* classes of the population, including every well-to-do peasant, incredibly hostile to the idea of internationalism, with the imperialist big, middle, and petty bourgeoisie splendidly organised—the Germans, i.e., the German revolutionary internationalists, the German workers dressed in sailors' jackets, started a mutiny in the navy with one chance of winning out of a hundred.

But we, with dozens of papers at our disposal, freedom of assembly, a majority in the Soviets, we proletarian internationalists, situated best in the whole world, should refuse to support the German revolutionists by our uprising. We should reason like the Scheidemanns and Renaudels, that it is most prudent not to revolt, for if we are shot, then the world will lose such excellent, reasonable, ideal internationalists! . . . .

"There is enough bread in Petrograd for two or three days. Can we give bread to the insurrectionists?"

One of a thousand skeptical remarks (the skeptics can *always* "doubt," and cannot be refuted by anything but experience). . . . .

It is Rodzyanko and Co., it is precisely the bourgeoisie that is preparing the famine and speculating on strangling the revolution by famine. There is no escaping the famine and *there can be none* outside of an uprising of the peasants against the landowners in the village and a victory of the workers over the capitalists in the cities and in the centre. Outside of this it is *impossible* . . . . to get grain from the rich. . . . .

The longer the proletarian revolution is delayed, ... the more victims it will cost and the more difficult it will be to *organise* the transportation and distribution of foodstuffs.

"Delaying the uprising means death"—this is what we have to answer to those having the sad "courage" to look at the growing economic ruin, at the approaching famine, and still *dissuade* the workers from the uprising. . . . .

The opposition of Kamenev and Zinoviev created excitement not only within the party but outside, where it was interpreted as evidence of an internal conflict which would prevent united action. Outside the party organizations the Bolshevik program was approved by the unofficial Congress of Soviets of the Northern Region which met in Petrograd under Bolshevik auspices October 24,[55] and by the All-Russian Congress of Factory-Shop Committees which met in the capital a week later.[56] Of more practical, immediate importance was the fact that the Bolsheviks controlled the Petrograd Soviet and Trotsky was its president. Over the opposition of the Mensheviks and Socialist-Revolutionists the Petrograd Soviet on October 25–26 organized a Military Revolutionary Committee ostensibly to prepare for the revolutionary defense of the capital and actually to take control of the garrison out of the hands of the Provisional Government's local military command. The Mensheviks openly accused the Bolsheviks of having formed the Military Revolutionary Committee in order to seize the power.[57]

The open intentions of the Bolsheviks encountered the opposition of the moderate socialists not only in the Petrograd Soviet but elsewhere. The All-Russian Central Executive Committee of Workers' and Soldiers' Deputies on October 27 voted down the Bolshevik resolution to transfer all power to the Soviets and appealed to workers, soldiers, and peasants to oppose an uprising of any kind.[58] Four days later the Central Executive Committee postponed the meeting of the Second All-Russian Congress of Soviets from November 2 to November 7 and ordered that no arms be given to any organization without the Committee's authori-

[55] L. Trotsky, *Sochineniia*, III, 1917, Book 2, *Ot oktiabria do Bresta*, Moscow [1924], 11–13. S. Oldenbourg, *Le coup d'état bolcheviste, 20 octobre–decembre 1917, recueil des documents relatifs à la prise du pouvoir par les bolchevistes, traduits et annotés*, Paris, 1929, p. 43.

[56] *Rabochii Put*, No. 42, November 3, 1917, p. 3. A translation of the resolution is given by John Reed in *Ten Days that Shook the World*, New York, 1919, pp. 43, 330–33.

[57] Golder, pp. 589–90.

[58] *Izvestiia*, No. 198, October 28, 1917, p. 3; Oldenbourg, pp. 56–63. This Central Executive Committee had been appointed by the First All-Russian Congress of Soviets in June 1917 in which the Bolsheviks were a minority.

zation. The following day the Committee urged representatives of the garrison not to take part in the uprising that was being prepared.[59]

For its part on October 28 the Provisional Government discussed informally the reports that the Bolsheviks had been urging soldiers and workers to revolt and decided to take energetic action[60] which for the time being consisted of an order of the Commander of the District to officers and men not to become involved in "uprisings."

THE ORIGIN OF THE MILITARY REVOLUTIONARY COMMITTEE

[Trotsky's Account][61]

I begin my recollections with a meeting of the Soldiers' Section [of the Petrograd Soviet]. . . . . There we learned that the Staff of the [Petrograd] Military District had ordered about one-third of the regiments of the Petrograd garrison to go to the front. . . . . As soon as we heard this . . . . we understood that the idea back of it was to remove the Bolshevik and the more revolutionary troops from the capital. It occurred to some of us that we might use the occasion to bring about the armed uprising which had already been decided upon. We said that we should agree to the order if it could be shown that it was a military necessity. We suggested that it was important, first of all, to determine whether this was or was not a Kornilov move. We decided to call for some kind of an organization to investigate the matter. . . . . At this meeting there was a man by the name of Lazimir, a Socialist-Revolutionist of the Left . . . . who supported us and we made use of him. Thus the demand for the establishment of a Military Revolutionary Committee appeared to come from a Left S.R. and not from us. . . . . Whether he perceived that this was a question of a conspiracy or simply expressed the formless revolutionary mood of the Left S.R.'s, I don't know. . . . . At any rate he agreed to do it, while other Left S.R.'s were suspicious. . . . . When he produced his project we polished it up, masking as much as possible the revolutionary insurrectionist nature of the plan. Next evening the plan was put before the Petersburg Soviet and accepted. . . . .

59 Golder, pp. 604, 612; Oldenbourg, pp. 89–90.

60 Golder, p. 611.

61 "Vospominaniia ob oktiabrskom perevorote," in *Proletarskaia Revoliutsiia*, 1922, No. 10, pp. 52 ff.

THE ORGANIZATION OF THE MILITARY REVOLUTIONARY COMMITTEE

[Discussions and Resolutions in the Petrograd Soviet, October 23–26][62]

Yesterday [October 22] there was a meeting of the Executive Committee of the Petrograd Soviet. . . . . The question of the protection of Petrograd and the need of taking part of the garrison out of the city to defend the approaches to the capital called forth a warm debate. Though admitting the strategic necessity of taking part of the garrison, the Bolsheviks claimed that they had no confidence in the Provisional Government and its military leaders, and therefore proposed the organization of a revolutionary staff of their own. . . . . A resolution was introduced to the effect that the Soviet could assume no responsibility for the strategy of the Provisional Government and that the only way to save Petrograd was to hand over the government to the Soviets, to declare an armistice immediately, etc. The Mensheviks and Socialist-Revolutionists pointed out that to form a military staff alongside the Government's meant dual authority and a serious menace to the defense of the city. The following resolution was adopted: . . . .

1. To appeal to the garrison to strengthen its fighting capacity . . . . to make energetic preparations, in case it should be necessary, to call out a part of the garrison from Petrograd to defend its approaches.

2. To form a collegium of representatives of the Petrograd Soviet . . . . the Central Executive Committee . . . . and the "Tsentroflot" [Central Committee of the Fleet] to function alongside the commander of troops of the Petrograd Military District. No part of the garrison is to be moved without first notifying this collegium.

3. To take steps to reorganize the militia.

4. To take extra measures to clean out the commanding personnel.

5. In addition, the Petrograd Soviet authorizes the Executive Committee, together with the presidium of the soldiers' section [of Soviet] and representatives of the Petrograd garrison, to organize a committee of revolutionary defense. This body is to make a study of the question of the defense of Petrograd and its approaches and work out a plan for the protection of the city with the active support of the working class.

REPORTS FROM THE RANK AND FILE OF THE BOLSHEVIK PARTY

[Secret Session of the Petrograd Committee and Active Leaders of the Bolshevik Party held October 28, 1917][63]

Comrade Bubnov made [the following] report: At the present moment the whole situation may be summed up as follows: We are

[62] *Izvestiia*, No. 193, October 23, 1917, p. 7; in Golder, pp. 587–88.

[63] *Krasnaia Letopis*, Nos. 2–3, 1922, pp. 324–32.

approaching a climax, the crisis has fully developed, and events are beginning to unfold themselves. We are being drawn into a struggle with forces directed against us. We are on the eve of an insurrection. Rodzianko claims that he will surrender Petersburg in order to strangle the revolution. Everything is against us. Kerensky is bringing into play diplomatic cunning; he is attempting to remove the troops from Petersburg. . . . . Six months of the revolution have brought us to the brink of ruin. As a consequence the masses are beginning to denounce everybody and everything. We must give this situation our most concentrated attention. In order to organize these elementary forces and to save the revolution we must take the reins of power into our own hands. In the international situation [we have] the attempt to conclude a separate peace, which is the plan of the imperialistic bourgeoisie, and is directed against the proletariat. The internal situation is thus closely bound up with the external. We have arrived at a moment when the seizure of power will give us the means of leading the revolution and the country toward creative ends. Upon seizing the power we shall be forced to bring our slogans into life, [and] to realize our program immediately. We must organize everything. When in power we shall have to carry on wholesale terror. The general situation is such that an armed insurrection is inevitable, and our whole problem is to get ready for it. . . . . We face a very essential problem—to have all mass propaganda focused on the conditions of the [present] moment. We must call together all agitators . . . . and tell them how to conduct the agitation. Steps must be taken to conduct our agitation in accordance with a definite plan. The Executive Committee has worked out a number of theses which are herewith presented to the assembly. The external conditions of the country must first be characterized, then the internal. We must break up the illusions about the Constituent Assembly. We must tell the masses that the strength and power of the Constituent Assembly are the strength and power of one class or another. And if we want the Constituent Assembly to be ours, we must first take power into our hands. It may well happen that we shall not succeed in taking the power; in that case the elemental wave of excitement will roll over our heads. To prevent this we must take the power into our hands. In our agitation we must emphasize that the collision is inevitable. We are facing the most critical hour of civil war—the armed struggle of two hostile classes. To save the revolution our policies must be not only defensive but also offensive. . . . . We must calculate the moment when it is best for the offensive to begin. . . . . These are the salient points. . . . .

Nevsky: As a representative of the military organization I must call your attention to a number of difficulties confronting us. The military organization suddenly began to move to the Right. We must distinguish two questions: those of (1) fundamental principles, and (2) their practical realization. With reference to the resolution of the Central Committee[64] the military organization pointed out that this resolution has left unconsidered a number of conditions, namely, that the poor peasants are also taking a part in the revolution. Instead of the village turning away from us it has only begun to come to us. We receive information from numerous places that the Bolsheviks are beginning to become popular. The decisive factor in the revolution is, of course, the working class. . . . . But we must not on that account neglect the spirit of the peasant masses; if we do we shall not win the victory. In quite a number of gubernias . . . . the peasants say that in case of an insurrection they will not give us any bread. Absolutely nothing has been done to stir up the village. An armed uprising of the proletariat here in Petersburg is a feasible thing. The whole garrison will come out at the call of the Soviet. . . . . But we cannot confine the insurrection to Petersburg. How will Moscow and the provinces react to this? Can the Central Committee give us the assurance that Russia as a whole will support us? We all realize that the moment is ripe. But are we ready? Have we the majority which will guarantee freedom? From the report it is quite clear that we are not ready, and the question stands thus: If we should come out, we shall find ourselves isolated from the rest of Russia. We have no data concerning the situation on the railroads. And are you sure that the 5th Army will not be sent against us? . . . . Neither the military organization nor the Central Committee has this assurance. . . . . The military organization will come out [for us] any time, but I cannot tell what this will accomplish. . . . . The resolution of the Central Committee which raised the question [of insurrection] with such an urgency should have considered the other question of the preparedness of the masses. The Petrograd Committee must call the attention of the Central Committee to the necessity of preparing the provinces. . . . .

Fenigstein moved that reports be made on conditions in the different districts. The motion was carried. . . . .

Kharitonov: . . . . The joint session of the Petrograd Committee, the Central Committee, the district committee, and the Moscow district [disclosed] that there is a general lack of enthusiasm. In Krasnoe Selo, where we have a large organization of some 50,000 members, only 500 may be expected to come here [Petrograd]; the rest will remain in Krasnoe Selo undecided. Krasnoe Selo is living through a mood of depression. Drunkenness is prevalent even among our comrades. From a military point of view the sailors are a very poor lot. A good many of them have been sent back from the front because they did not know

[64] Resolution of October 23.

how to handle arms. As for the post and telegraph employees, we have in our organization from 140 to 150 members. . . . . The telegraph operators are mostly Cadets and have very little sympathy with us. At a decisive moment there may be sufficient force to occupy the telegraph and other important positions.

Slutskaia:[65] Regarding the military situation in our district, I can say that military instruction is being given in the factories and industrial plants. There is not much desire to take part in the insurrection.

Latsis (Viborg district): A serious concentration of interest in events is observable among the masses. In addition to the district committees a new central organization grew up from the bottom. . . . . The masses will support us.

Kalinin (Lesnovsky sub-district): We have decided to investigate the conditions; as yet the business is badly managed. We have decided to get in contact with the army units. We receive telegrams from Finland and from the front protesting against the uprising of the Bolsheviks. On the other hand, over the head of the army organization, delegates are arriving from the front, and their demands clearly indicate a militant frame of mind. It proves that the army committees are not with us, and that they do not express the wishes of the masses. We have a Red Guard; only 84 rifles.

Naumov (Viborg district): There is a marked dissatisfaction among the masses . . . . and a feeling of suppressed indignation in connection with the evacuation [of Petrograd] and the paying off of the workmen.

Menzhinskaia:[66] With regard to arms, conditions are very bad. In the committee there are only 6 rifles, in one factory 100, in another 20. It is difficult to estimate the spirit of the workers.

Pakhomov (second city district): The frame of mind is better than it was on July 16 to 18. The Red Guard is badly organized. We have 50 rifles, 3,000 cartridges. From 60 to 80 are receiving [military] instruction. . . . .

Ravich (Moscow district): In the factories there is a turbulent state of feeling. The masses will rise only at the call of the Soviet, but very few will respond to the call of our party. The organs created during the Kornilov days are still intact. . . . .

Hessen (Narva district): In general, there is no desire to rise. Where our influence is strong, the spirit is cheerful and eager. Among the backward masses there is an indifference to politics. But our party has not lost its authority. . . . . We have several hundred rifles, but there is no concentration point and our military forces are scattered. . . . .

[65] Woman representative of the Vasilevsky Ostrov district.

[66] Woman representative of the first city district.

Vinokurov (Neva district): The state of mind is in our favor. The masses are alert. We have no Red Guard. . . . .

Comrade from the Obukhov factory: Previously the Obukhov factory stood for the defensists. But now there is a break in our favor. The attendance at our mass meetings is from five to seven thousand . . . . we have 2,000 in the Red Guard, 500 rifles, 1 machine gun, and 1 armored car. . . . . We have organized a revolutionary committee. The factory will no doubt respond to the call of the Petrograd Soviet.

Pervukhin (Okhtensky district): There is no desire among the workers to rise. In the factories the Black Hundreds have raised their heads.

Prokhorov (Petersburg district): Where our influence is strong the attitude is one of watchfulness—otherwise the masses are apathetic. . . . . Generally there is a complete disorganization in the district. Even if the Soviet should issue a call for an uprising, certain factories (ours for example) will not respond.

Axelrod (Rozhdestvensky district): The attitude is one of watchfulness. In case of an offensive on the part of the counter-revolution we shall offer resistance, but to a call to insurrection the workers will hardly respond. There is discouragement due to the paying off of workers in connection with the evacuation of factories.[67] The influence of the anarchists is considerably on the increase.

Porokhovskoi district: . . . . Before the Kornilov events the Mensheviks and the Socialist-Revolutionists predominated. But now the feeling is in our favor. . . . . The committee in the factory is quite ready to lead the masses if there should come a call for the uprising. . . . .

Schlüsselburg district: Our district is small; two hundred members in all. But the majority of the masses will go with us. A Red Guard has been organized, but the enlistment is not popular. The workers have taken upon themselves the defense of the factories. The masses will come out at the call of the Soviet.

Railroad section: Dissatisfaction with the Provisional Government is manifest. . . . . Our propaganda does not go outside the limits of Petersburg. Now we have connections with Moscow. . . . . We have sent thirteen comrades into the provinces to establish connections with railroad workers there. Some of them have come back with reports that political conditions are not so good. . . . .

Trade unions: There are no signs of an aggressive spirit among the masses. If there should be an offensive of the counter-revolution, resistance would be offered, but the masses by themselves will not take the offensive. The masses might respond to the call of the Soviet.

[67] This refers to the evacuation of certain Petrograd munitions factories to prevent their capture by the Germans.

Rakhia (Finnish district): The Finns all feel that the sooner the better. . . . .

[A discussion of general principles followed.]

Kalinin: The resolution of the Central Committee is the best it has ever passed. That resolution summons our organization to direct political action. We are confronted with an armed insurrection but our stumbling-block is the practical aspect of the situation. When that insurrection will take place, we cannot say—possibly in a year's time. . . . .

Toward the end of the session Latsis announced that a new conspirative center had just been organized in connection with the [Petrograd] Soviet whose membership is not exclusively Bolshevik. . . . .

THE GENERAL SITUATION AND PARTY POLICY

[Extracts from the Report of a Meeting of the Central Committee, the Executive Commission of the Petrograd Committee, Military Organization, Petrograd Soviet, Trade Unions, Factory Committees, Railroad Workers, Petrograd Regional Committee, October 29, 1917][68]

Chairman: Comrade Sverdlov.

Comrade Sverdlov proposes the order of business: 1. Report on last session of C.C. 2. Brief reports by representatives. 3. Present situation.

1. *Report on Last Session of C.C.*

Comrade L[enin] reads the resolution that was adopted by the Central Committee at the previous session. He says that the resolution was adopted with two voting against. If the comrades who disagree wish to express themselves, he says, discussion may be opened; in the meantime, however, he gives the reasons for this resolution.

Had the Menshevik and the Socialist-Revolutionary Parties broken with conciliationism, it would have been possible to offer them a compromise. This offer was made; it is obvious, however, that this compromise has been rejected by the above-named parties. On the other hand it has become clear at this period that the masses are following us. It was so even before the Kornilov affair; he proves it by statistics of the elections in Petrograd and in Moscow. The Kornilov affair has pushed the masses still closer to us. Interrelation of forces at the Democratic Conference. Situation is clearly either a dictatorship of Kornilov, or a dictatorship of the proletariat and the poorest strata of the peasantry. Sentiment cannot serve as guide, since it is changeable and cannot be measured; we must be guided by an objective analysis and an appraisal of the revolution. The masses have expressed confidence in

[68] From Archives of the Central Committee in Lenin, *Toward the Seizure of Power,* II, 332–41.

the Bolsheviks and they demand of them not words, but deeds, a decisive policy both in the struggle against the war and in the struggle against economic ruin. If we make our basis a political analysis of the revolution, it will become perfectly clear that this is now being proven even by anarchistic actions.

He analyses further the situation in Europe and proves that a revolution there is still more difficult than here. If, in a country like Germany, there has been a mutiny in the navy, this proves that things there have gone very far. The international situation gives us a good deal of objective data showing that if we act now, we will have on our side all of proletarian Europe. He proves that the bourgeoisie wishes to surrender Petrograd. We can save ourselves from this only by taking Petrograd into our hands. The conclusion from all this is clear, namely, that the armed uprising of which the Central Committee resolution speaks is on the order of the day.

As to practical conclusions from the resolution, it is more convenient to make them after listening to the reports of the representatives of the centres.

From a political analysis of the class struggle, both in Russia and in Europe, follows the necessity of a most decisive, most active policy, which can be only an armed uprising. . . .

[In the name of the Secretariat of the Central Committee, Sverdlov reported that the party had grown rapidly and that it included at least 400,000 members. Others reported on the sentiment in the different regions in the army and in the trade unions. There followed a long debate on whether in the present situation the party could or should attempt to carry out the resolution of October 23. Kamenev and Zinoviev led the opposition against Lenin. Several speakers favored preparing for the uprising but opposed precipitate action. Zinoviev's resolution, "Without delaying the reconnoitering preparatory steps, it is considered that such uprisings are inadmissible until a conference with the Bolshevik part of the forthcoming Congress of Soviets," was rejected 15 to 6 with 3 abstaining. The meeting then adopted the following resolution by Lenin by a vote of 19 to 2 with 4 abstaining.]

The meeting heartily greets and fully supports the resolution of the Central Committee. It calls upon all the organizations and all the workers and soldiers to prepare the armed uprising most energetically, in every way, to support the organ which the Central Committee is creating for this purpose, and expresses full confidence that the Central Committee and the Soviet will in due time indicate the favourable moment and the most expedient methods for an offensive.[69]

[The Central Committee then adopted the following decision]:

[69] *Ibid.*, II, 110.

The C.C. organizes a military revolutionary center of the following composition: Sverdlov, Stalin, Bubnov, Uritsky, and Dzerzhinsky. This center becomes a part of the revolutionary committee of the Soviet.[70]

On October 31 Kamenev and Zinoviev carried their opposition to the party policy into the open by publishing in Gorky's paper, *Novaia Zhizn,* a declaration that they and other "practical comrades" were against any attempt to take the initiative in an armed uprising which would be fatal for the party, the proletariat, and the revolution. Lenin immediately replied in two letters to the party, severely condemning the recalcitrants for their timidity and the violation of party discipline.[71] Kamenev resigned from the Central Committee and his resignation was accepted on November 2. Kamenev and Zinoviev were ordered to make no further statements against the Committee's decisions, and a further resolution was passed that no member of the Committee should have the right to speak against its decisions.[72]

POLKOVNIKOV'S ORDER TO THE MILITARY DISTRICT OF PETROGRAD

[October 30, 1917][73]

Again armed uprisings of irresponsible persons are being prepared in the streets of Petrograd.

These uprisings are a symptom of anarchy; they will lead certainly to useless suffering and bring the fatherland to the edge of ruin.

He who is capable, at this time, of calling the masses to a civil war is either insane or a conscious tool of the Emperor William.

I order all units under my command, all officers and soldiers, not to allow themselves to become involved in uprisings.

Soldiers and officers, bear in mind the great responsibility which you carry before the entire democracy and free Russia.

COLONEL POLKOVNIKOV
Commander-in-Chief of the Military District

70 Lenin, *Toward the Seizure of Power,* II, 341.

71 "Letter to the Members of the Bolshevik Party" and "Letter to the Central Committee of the R.S.–D.L. Party," written on October 21 and November 1, and translated in Lenin, *Toward the Seizure of Power,* II, 129–37.

72 "Protokoly tsentralnogo komiteta R.S.D.R.P. (b) (sentiabr-oktiabr 1917 g.)," in *Proletarskaia Revoliutsiia,* 1927, No. 10 (69), p. 288.

73 *Rech,* No. 244, October 30, 1917, p. 5.

THE PETROGRAD GARRISON AND AN UPRISING

[From a Statement by Captain Kuzmin, Assistant Commander of the Petrograd Troops, October 30, 1917][74]

As regards the probability of an uprising, the assistant commander states that the impressions he has received in visiting different units of the garrison are indefinite. There are some units which accept entirely the platform of the Petrograd Soviet; but there are others, apparently a majority, which, upholding the platform of the . . . . Central Executive Committees of the Soviets of Workers' and Soldiers' Deputies and of the Executive Committee of the Soviets of Peasants' Deputies, disapprove formally of the uprising projected by the Bolsheviks. . . . .

A. I. Kuzmin is sure that the Provisional Government and the . . . . Petrograd military authorities have sufficient military forces at their disposal not only to prevent the uprising but even to suppress it if it breaks out. . . . . The assistant commander therefore does not believe that the uprising conceived by the Bolsheviks will succeed.

In concluding, A. I. Kuzmin emphasized again that he was convinced that the existing forces were sufficient for the struggle against anarchistic disturbances.

[Ambassador Francis to the Secretary of State, October 30, 1917][75]

Beginning to think Bolsheviki will make no demonstration; if so, shall regret as believe sentiment turning against them and time opportune moment for giving them wholesome lesson. . . . .

[74] *Ibid.*, No. 245, October 31, 1917, pp. 4–5; cf. Oldenbourg, pp. 69–71.
[75] *U.S. Foreign Relations, 1918, Russia,* I, 216.

CHAPTER II

THE SEIZURE OF POWER

(November 3–November 8, 1917)

After November 1 each day produced its crop of rumors and speculation about the plans to launch a revolt against the Provisional Government. The newspapers discussed it, orators debated it in the barracks, in the factories, and on street corners, and the general public speculated on the success of the uprising. Although the date of the revolt had not been set, the tension increased as the day of the opening of the Second Congress of Soviets (November 7) drew near. On November 3, representatives of the garrison publicly declared their support of the Bolshevik program. Thereupon the Military Revolutionary Committee directly challenged the Provisional Government, demanding the control of the Petrograd Military Staff. Efforts of moderate socialists to effect a compromise failed, and when, on the 6th, the Provisional Government began to make defensive preparations, forces of the Military Revolutionary Committee seized public buildings and strategic points in the city without meeting serious opposition. When the Second Congress of Soviets met on November 7, the Bolsheviks were in control of practically all sections of the capital except the Winter Palace. Late that night the palace was occupied and the ministers, except Kerensky, who had escaped, were arrested. The Second Congress of Soviets then assumed power, passed decrees on peace and land, and elected a Soviet of People's Commissars as head of the new Provisional Workers' and Peasants' Government. Mensheviks and other groups, deserting the Congress, formed a Committee to Save the Country and the Revolution. Others merely demanded a socialist coalition.

A. The Provisional Government and the Military Revolutionary Committee

On November 3, at a meeting at Smolny called by the Petrograd Soviet, representatives of the garrison adopted, on Trotsky's motion, the following resolutions adhering to the Bolshevik program. The Petrograd Soviet also issued an appeal to the Cossacks, whose attitude was uncertain.

RESOLUTIONS OF THE PETROGRAD GARRISON

[In Support of the Military Revolutionary Committee][1]

The Petrograd Garrison welcomes the formation of a Military Revolutionary Committee in connection with the Petrograd Soviet of Workers' and Soldiers' Deputies. The Petrograd Garrison will support the Military Revolutionary Committee in all its undertakings. . . . .

[On Transferring the Power to the Soviets][2]

Welcoming all the decisions of the Petrograd Soviet the Petrograd Garrison hereby declares:

The time for words is past. The country is on the verge of ruin. The army demands peace, the peasants land, and the workers bread and work. The Coalition Government is against the people. It became the tool of the enemies of the people. The time for words is past. The All-Russian Congress of Soviets must take the power into its own hands in order to give to the people peace, land, and bread. Only thus can the safety of the revolution and of the people be insured.

All power to the Soviets!
An immediate armistice on all fronts!
The land to the peasants!
An honest and prompt convocation of the Constituent Assembly.

The Petrograd Garrison gives its solemn promise to place at the disposal of the All-Russian Congress its entire strength even to the last man.

You may count on us—you who are the legitimate representatives of the soldiers, workers, and peasants. We are all at our posts ready *to conquer or to die!*[3]

[1] *Izvestiia,* No. 204, November 4, 1917, p. 3.

[2] L. Trotsky, *Sochineniia,* III, *1917,* Book 2, "Ot oktiabria do Bresta," Moscow, 1924, 37.

[3] A third resolution set November 4, "Soviet Day," as the occasion for a review of the forces of the workers and soldiers of Petrograd. The Cossacks, who had planned a religious procession for that day, were urged to participate in the Soviet demonstration and were warned not to be led astray by provocateurs. (*Izvestiia,* No. 204, November 4, 1917, p. 4; Oldenbourg, *op. cit.,* p. 116.)

THE PETROGRAD SOVIET APPEALS TO THE COSSACKS[4]

[November 3, 1917]

Brother Cossacks!

The Petrograd Soviet addresses you as follows:

Attempts are being made to incite you, Cossacks, against us, the workers and soldiers. This work of Cain is done by our common enemies—nobles, bankers, landlords, former bureaucrats, and servants of the Tsar. They always maintained their power by setting the people against each other, inciting the soldiers against the workers. And now they are instigating the Cossacks against the soldiers.

By what means do they achieve their purpose? Through abuse and calumny, of course. Cossacks, soldiers, sailors, workers, and peasants are all brothers; are all alike in that they have to work hard, are poor, are living from hand to mouth, and are suffering from the same war, which has taken everything from them.

Who wants this war? Who started it? Certainly not the Cossacks or the soldiers, not the workers or the peasants! It is the generals and the bankers, the Tsars, and the landlords who want the war! Upon it they build their power, their might, and their riches. . . . .

The people want peace. The soldiers and workers of every country are thirsting for peace. The Petrograd Soviet demands of the bourgeoisie and the generals: "Get out of the way, you tyrants! Let the power pass into the hands of the people and the people will at once conclude an honest peace!"

Are we not right, Comrade Cossacks? We have no doubt that you will say yes. But it is just for this reason that we are hated by the rich, the profiteers, the princes, the nobles, and the generals, including your own Cossack generals. They are ready at any moment to destroy the Petrograd Soviet, to strangle the revolution and to enchain the people as in the days of the Tsar. To accomplish this they spread lies about us. . . . . They tell you that the Soviet intends to start an insurrection on November 4, to enter a fight with you and to prepare a massacre. Those who tell you this are scamps and traitors. You may tell them so! For November 4 the Soviet is arranging peaceful gatherings . . . . where workers, soldiers, sailors, and peasants may come together and listen to speeches about peace and war and the welfare of the people. You too are invited to attend these peaceful meetings. You will be cordially welcomed, Brother Cossacks!

Let those of you who are still in doubt come to Smolny where the Soviet is located. You will find there many soldiers and Cossacks who will explain to you what the Soviet stands for and by what means it

[4] Trotsky, *Sochineniia,* III, Book 2, 38–40.

attains its ends. Was it not for just that very purpose of enabling you to discuss freely your needs and to take your destinies into your own hands that the people overthrew the Tsar? You too, Cossacks, should remove from your eyes the cover by which the enemies of the toiling Cossacks, the Kaledins, Bardizhis, and Karaulovs, are trying to blindfold you. . . . .

THE PETROGRAD SOVIET OF WORKERS' AND SOLDIERS' DEPUTIES

During the night of November 3–4 the Military Revolutionary Committee, fortified with the resolutions of the representatives of the garrison, sent commissars to the District Military Command demanding the right to control the acts of the District Military Staff. Polkovnikov refused to consider this demand. The Military Revolutionary Committee thereupon called a special meeting of the garrison representatives at Smolny and sent out the following order to the units of the garrison, an open challenge to the authority of the Provisional Government:

THE MILITARY REVOLUTIONARY COMMITTEE TO THE GARRISON

[November 4][5]

At its meeting on November 3 the revolutionary garrison of Petrograd gathered around the Military Revolutionary Committee of the Petrograd Soviet of Workers' and Soldiers' Deputies as its directive organ.

In spite of this the staff of the Petrograd Military District refused, during the night preceding November 4, to acknowledge the Military Revolutionary Committee, declining to transact business with the representatives of the soldiers' section of the Soviet. By this act the [military] staff has broken off relations with the revolutionary garrison as well as with the Petrograd Soviet. Having broken off relations with the organized garrison of the capital, the staff thereby becomes the tool of counter-revolutionary forces.

The Military Revolutionary Committee is thus released from all responsibility for the acts of the staff of the Petrograd Military District.

Soldiers of Petrograd! It is for you, under the direction of the

[5] N. Podvoisky, "Voennaia organizatsiia Ts. K.R.S.-D.R.P. (Bolshevikov) i voenno-revoliutsionnyi komitet 1917 g.," in *Krasnaia Letopis,* No. 8, 1923, p. 17.

Military Revolutionary Committee, to defend the revolutionary order against counter-revolution. Orders not signed by this committee are void. Every soldier should be on guard and maintain strict discipline. The revolution is in danger! Long live the revolutionary garrison!

On November 4, Polkovnikov also called a meeting of representatives of the garrison and of the Central Executive Committee. A delegation from the soldiers headed by Dashkevich appeared at the District Military Headquarters and declared that only orders countersigned by the Military Revolutionary Committee would be obeyed. Dashkevich refused to negotiate. In the evening the government learned of the M.R. Committee's open defiance of the District Military Command. Kerensky and other members of the government favored immediate action but were dissuaded by members of the Central Executive Committee, who proposed to settle the affair by negotiating with the Petrograd Soviet. In the meantime various peaceful demonstrations had taken place in the streets celebrating "Soviet Day." In the evening there was a great mass meeting in the People's House.

ROUSING THE MASSES

["Soviet Day," November 4, 1917][6]

. . . . The colossal building of the People's House was packed with a vast throng . . . . mostly workers and soldiers . . . . all waiting in grave silence. . . . .

A warm, if fitful, applause greeted Trotsky as he appeared. The crowd was at once curious and impatient: What would he say? Using to the utmost his skill and brilliancy, Trotsky at once began to create a favorable atmosphere. I [Sukhanov] remember with what vividness and force he depicted the soldiers' sufferings in the trenches. For a moment I thought that this part of his speech was disproportionately long. But Trotsky knew what he was doing. The important thing was to create an atmosphere. The political inferences were already known. They could, therefore, be summed up at the end. . . . .

And Trotsky did it with great vividness. The Soviet Government would not only do away with the suffering in the trenches; it would also give the land to the people and cure all ills. Again he repeated the familiar remedy against famine: a soldier, a sailor, and a woman worker requisi-

[6] N. Sukhanov, *Zapiski o revoliutsii,* Book 7, 89–92.

tioning bread from the rich and sending it free of charge to the cities and the front. . . . . He went even further: The Soviet power in fact would hand over everything in the country to the poor and the soldiers. . . . .

"You, bourgeois, have two fur coats; give one to the soldier who is cold in the trenches. You have warm boots. You may sit at home . . . . the worker needs your boots."

Those were good and just ideas. They could not but awaken the enthusiasm of a mob brought up under the tsarist whip. . . . . However that may be, I am bound as a witness to testify that those were the very words spoken on that memorable day. The masses were in a state of ecstasy . . . . ready to join in a religious hymn. . . . . Trotsky announced a brief resolution—something to the effect that "we shall all stand by the cause of the workers and peasants till the last drop of our blood."

"Who is for it?"

Thousands, as one man, raised their hands. I could see the eyes of men and women burning with enthusiasm. Was it the fever of spiritual exaltation? Or, perhaps, they caught a glimpse of the promised land? Were they imbued with the consciousness of the importance of the political moment under the influence of a political speech by a socialist?

Do not ask me these questions! I am merely stating the facts.

As the mob stood there with hands upraised, Trotsky continued, choosing every word: "This resolution of yours shall be your solemn pledge to support with all your might the Soviet which has taken upon itself the great burden of bringing the revolution to a triumphant end . . . .!"

In an effort to avert an open conflict the Central Executive Committee urged the garrison to obey the orders of the Petrograd Military Command and offered the Military Revolutionary Committee (M.R.C.) an increased representation on the District Military Staff in return for the recall of the M.R.C.'s order inciting the troops to insubordination. The M.R.C. refused the offer and issued a new declaration defying the authority of the government. During the day of the 5th the Pre-Parliament continued its debate on foreign policy, while the government and the staff discussed measures to be taken against the Bolsheviks. Later the government decided to break off all negotiations with the M.R.C. and Colonel Polkovnikov ordered the closing of two Bolshevik papers and two organs of the extreme Right.[7]

[7] *Novaia Zhizn,* No. 162, November 7, 1917, p. 3.

THE MILITARY REVOLUTIONARY COMMITTEE TO THE PEOPLE[8]

[November 5]

To the Population of Petrograd:

In order to safeguard the conquests of the revolution against the counter-revolutionary attempts, commissars have been appointed to the different units of the garrison located in the most important districts of the capital and its environs. No military orders are effective until they have the sanction of the duly appointed commissars. As the representatives of the Soviets, the commissars are unimpeachable. Resistance to the commissars will be considered as opposition to the Soviet of Workers' and Soldiers' Deputies. The Soviet has taken every measure to defend the revolutionary order against counter-revolution. All citizens are urged to give every assistance to our commissars. In case of disorders they are expected to inform the commissars of the Military Revolutionary Committee at the nearest military post.

THE PETROGRAD SOVIET ACCLAIMS THE MILITARY REVOLUTIONARY COMMITTEE

[Resolution of November 5, 1917][9]

The Petrograd Soviet, having heard the report of the Military Revolutionary Committee, hereby approves all the measures taken by the latter for the purpose of safeguarding the conquests of the revolution and hopes that it will continue its resolute activity along the same lines. The Petrograd Soviet is bound to state that owing to the efforts of the Military Revolutionary Committee the ties between the Petrograd Soviet and the revolutionary garrison have become firmly established . . . . which circumstance will serve as a guaranty that the work of the Second Congress of Soviets will be unobstructed. . . . .

B. THE PROVISIONAL GOVERNMENT AND THE PRE-PARLIAMENT

In the morning of the 6th Polkovnikov issued proclamations to the garrison and the citizens, loyal troops were ordered to strategic points, cadets were summoned from

[8] *Rabochii Put,* No. 45, November 7, 1917, p. 3. This bill was posted in the streets of Petrograd on November 5.

[9] *Ibid.*

the suburbs, Oranienbaum, Pavlovsk, and Tsarskoe Selo, and the government decided to take legal measures against the Military Revolutionary Committee and to arrest the Bolsheviks guilty of promoting the revolt. The M.R.C. replied with proclamations to the troops to be prepared to defend the Petrograd Soviet and to reopen the closed printing establishments.

ORDER OF THE COMMANDER OF THE PETROGRAD MILITARY DISTRICT[10]

[November 6, 1917]

In view of the fact that a number of unlawful acts have been committed by the representatives of the Petrograd Soviet acting as commissars of the said Soviet, I herewith order all units, institutions, and departments of the army: (1) to remove all commissars appointed by the Petrograd Soviet pending their appointment by the government commissar of the Petrograd Military District; (2) to start judicial investigations of all unlawful acts committed (by the said commissars) for the purpose of instituting legal proceedings against them; (3) to report to me promptly the names of the commissars responsible for those unlawful acts.

COLONEL POLKOVNIKOV
Commander-in-Chief

THE PROVISIONAL GOVERNMENT ACTS[11]

[November 6, 1917]

On the morning of November 6 the government began active operations. The cadets took over the patrolling of the Winter Palace. The Women's Battalion came to demonstrate its loyalty to the government. At 2:00 P.M. all bridges were occupied by cadets and by 3:00 P.M. all traffic across the bridges had stopped. The [draw] bridges were opened at 4:00 P.M.; at the same time cadet detachments occupied the electric power station, all railroad stations, and government institutions. Pickets were placed at the corners of all principal streets. . . . .

Kerensky is said to be personally in charge of the movements of the cadets. . . . .

[10] *Rech,* No. 251, November 7, 1917, p. 3. Polkovnikov also ordered all soldiers and officers to remain in barracks until further orders.

[11] *Novaia Zhizn,* No. 162, November 7, 1917, p. 4.

ORDER TO THE PETROGRAD GARRISON[12]

[November 6, 1917]

The Petrograd Soviet of Workers' and Soldiers' Deputies is in danger. During the night counter-revolutionary plotters have attempted to bring cadets and shock troops from the suburbs. The papers *Soldat* and *Rabochii Put* have been closed.

You are hereby ordered to hold every regiment in readiness and await further orders. Any delay or failure to obey this order will be considered a betrayal of the Revolution.

PODVOISKY, Chairman
ANTONOV, Secretary

ORDER TO REOPEN SUPPRESSED PAPERS[13]

[November 6, 1917]

Two revolutionary papers, *Rabochii Put* and *Soldat,* have been closed by the plotters from the General Staff. The Soviet will not tolerate the strangling of free speech. The people engaged in repelling the attacks of dark forces must be guaranteed an honest press. The Military Revolutionary Committee hereby resolves: (1) to reopen the printing shops of the closed revolutionary papers; (2) to urge the editorial staff and the printers to continue their work; (3) that the honorary duty of guarding the revolutionary printing shops against counter-revolutionary attempts is to be borne by the brave soldiers of the Lettish regiment and of the 6th Sapper Battalion.

Chairman [PODVOISKY]
Secretary [ANTONOV]

The Pre-Parliament opened its session on November 6 between 11:00 and 12:00 A.M. Kerensky asked for the floor in order to deliver an urgent communication.

PETROGRAD PROCLAIMED IN A STATE OF INSURRECTION

[Kerensky's Speech in the Pre-Parliament, November 6, 1917][14]

The Provisional Government has authorized me to make the following statement:

[12] A. L. Popov, *Oktiabrskii perevorot,* p. 170.

[13] *Rabochii Put,* No. 45, November 7, 1917, p. 3.

[14] *Rech,* No. 251, November 7, 1917, p. 2. Kerensky's account of the occasion is given in *The Catastrophe,* New York, 1927, pp. 325–26. See also F. Dan, "K istorii poslednikh dnei Vremennogo Pravitelstva," in *Letopis Revoliutsii,* 1923, I, 171.

Of late, the nearer we come to the day for the convening of the Constituent Assembly, which will establish forever a free democratic régime in Russia, ... the more persistent and insolent become the attempts of the two extreme wings of political opinion to block the convening of this assembly. At the same time we are witnessing a persistent and growing endeavor to disorganize our country's defense and to betray the liberty and independence of Russia into the hands of a cruel and relentless enemy who is advancing on our capital.

Hitherto the Provisional Government . . . . has considered it its duty to safeguard the freedom of every citizen in the exercise of his political and civil rights and has remained indifferent to the violent criticism and abuse to which it has been subjected in the press and at public meetings. . . . . Throughout Russia, especially in the capital, an irresponsible section of the revolutionary democracy is instigating open insurrection, ... while another section . . . . [to the Right] is urging the immediate supplanting of the Provisional Government by a dictatorship. . . . .

That you may not think my statement unfounded and that the Provisional Government may not be reproached for wrongly accusing or maliciously libeling any party, I . . . . shall cite here a few passages from a number of proclamations published in the paper *Rabochii Put* by the much-wanted offender against the state, Ulianov-Lenin, who is now in hiding. [Then follow quotations from "Letters to the Comrades."][15]

Simultaneously with these appeals other Bolshevik leaders at public meetings . . . . advocated an immediate armed uprising. Especially noteworthy is the speech made by the President of the Soviet of Workers' and Soldiers' Deputies in Petersburg, Bronstein-Trotsky, and the public declarations of other organizers of the uprising. Similar proclamations and appeals inciting the soldiers to disobey the military authorities appeared in *Soldat,* another Bolshevik publication intended especially for the soldiers, ... I am not going to cite the newspapers of the opposite camp which also were suppressed by my order last night. I merely wish to stress . . . . the very definite . . . . connection between the attacks and preparations of the two wings. . . . .

To the Provisional Government it is quite immaterial whether these are being made deliberately or inadvertently. Fully aware of my responsibility I proclaim, from this platform, that such actions of a Russian political party are treason and betrayal of the Russian State. (*Voices from the Right: "Name the plotters." Noises and exclamations at the Left: "They are in your midst."*) . . . .

And, now, after these open preparations . . . . for the uprising, the groups which call themselves Bolsheviks have come to the point of carrying their propaganda into action. For instance, three days ago the troops

[15] See pp. 63–66 above.

of the Petrograd district received orders not to obey their commanders or any military authorities unless the orders were countersigned by the commissars of the Petrograd Revolutionary Staff. . . . .

Although there was every reason for immediate, decisive, and energetic action, the military authorities, following my suggestion, believed it necessary first to give these people the opportunity of acknowledging their . . . . errors (*cries from the Right: "That is what's wrong!"*) and to allow them time to retract, ... especially since their order had no appreciable results during the first few days after it was issued. Generally I prefer that the authorities should act more slowly but more surely, and, when necessary, more resolutely. . . . .

Not until 3:00 A.M. were we informed that the . . . . ultimatum of the military authorities was acceptable in principle. Thus at 3:00 A.M. the instigators of the insurrection were compelled to admit formally that they had committed an unlawful act, which they now wished to retract. (*Miliukov, from his seat: "How beautiful!"*) But as I expected, in fact as I knew positively from the preceding tactics of these men, this was but another case of their usual delay and deliberate deceit. (*Cries from the Right: "At last you have learned that much!"*) At this moment the period of grace has expired, but we have not yet received the declaration which (as we insisted) should be made [by the Revolutionary Staff] to the regiments. On the contrary, there has been an unauthorized distribution of ammunition and arms, and two companies have been called out to the aid of the Revolutionary Staff. Thus I am obliged to inform the Provisional Council that a state of open insurrection exists among a certain part of the population of Petersburg. (*Voice from the Right: "That's what it has come to!"*) From a legal point of view it can be so termed, and I have proposed an immediate judicial investigation (*noise from the Left*) and ordered arrests to be made. (*Protests from the Left.*) Yes, Yes! Listen—because when the state is imperiled by deliberate or undesigned treachery and is at the brink of ruin, the Provisional Government, myself included, prefers to go down to destruction rather than to betray the life, the honor, and the independence of the state. (*Applause, loud noise. All members of the Pre-Parliament except the Internationalists . . . . rise from their seats. . . . .*)

Adzhemov (*from his place*): Give us a photograph of them sitting. (*Loud exclamation on the Left.*)

Chairman: I call the meeting to order. . . . .

The Provisional Government may be reproached for its weakness and excessive patience, but no one has the right to say that the . . . . government, while I have been at its head or even before, has had recourse to any measures of coercion unless some immediate menace threatened the state. (*Loud applause in the Center and on the Right.*) . . . . I think that our aim, which is the strengthening of the cause of freedom . . . . gives us the right . . . . to demand that the country shall support our decisive measures, since no one can suggest that these measures are being undertaken for reasons other than the safety of the state. (*Loud applause in the Center.*) I must tell you that the attitude of the front to the events taking place in the rear, and especially in Petersburg, is a definite one. The front clearly perceives that the activities of certain political groups are nothing but attempts to play on the darkness and ignorance of the masses, and their unwillingness to fulfil their duty on the front. (*Loud applause in the Center and on the Right.*)

I shall not burden you with all the telegrams, appeals, and resolutions which the Provisional Government and the Central Committee of the Soviets have received from army committees at the front. I deem it my duty, however, to make known to you the resolution of the All-Army Committee at the Stavka: "The army . . . . calls upon every citizen of the Russian Republic to endure every possible sacrifice in the cause of a peace which will bring justice to the toilers of the world and well-being to all nations. [The army] insists . . . . on a steadfast adherence to the will of the organized majority of the people. It calls upon the Provisional Government together with the Provisional Council of the Republic and the All-Russian Central [Executive] Committee [of the Soviets] to put a stop to the mad military pogroms in the cities and in the villages, and to suppress resolutely and energetically every form of excess and license. In exercising pressure upon these conspirators against the integrity of the country the authorities may rely upon the support of the army as though they were fighting the enemies of the people." (*Loud applause on all benches with the exception of the Internationalists.*)

[At this point A. Konovalov[16] approached the platform and handed a note to Kerensky. After glancing at it Kerensky continued]: I have in my hands a copy of a document which is being circulated among the regiments. It says: "The Petrograd Soviet is in danger. . . . . I hereby order the regiments to be in complete readiness for action and to wait further instruction. Every delay or failure to carry out this order will be considered a betrayal of the revolution. [Signed] Podvoisky and Antonov."[17] (*Cries from the Right: "Traitors!"*)

You see, now, that at present a situation exists in the capital which in the language of the law . . . . is called a state of insurrection. . . . . It is an attempt to incite the rabble against the existing order, to prevent the convening of the Constituent Assembly, ... and to expose the front to the serried ranks of Wilhelm's mailed fist. (*Exclamations from the Center and the Right: "Correct"; noise on the Left and cries:*

[16] Minister of Commerce and Vice-Premier of the Third Coalition Government.

[17] See above, p. 86, for the authentic text of this order.

"Enough!") I say deliberately—"rabble"—because the intelligent part of the democracy, the Central Executive Committee [of the Soviets], all army organizations and all that free Russia is justly proud of—the reason, conscience, and honor of the great Russian democracy—all protest against it, ... (*storm of applause on all benches except the Internationalists*) . . . . realizing that the real danger of the demonstration lies not at all in the possibility of the local garrison seizing the government but in the fact that the insurrection will be a signal to the Germans, as in the month of July, to deliver a new blow on our borders which will call forth a new [counter-revolutionary] attempt, even more serious than the attempt of General Kornilov. . . . .

[Turning to the Internationalists Kerensky continued] : I believe that at this moment everyone should place himself either on the side of the Republic, of Freedom and of Democracy, or against them. (*Long applause on all benches except the Internationalists.*) And if there are those who believe that truth is on the other side, let them courageously and actively support that cause and not be mere obstructionists. (*Violent applause on the Right and Center; noise on the Left.*)

I have come to plead with you, members of the Provisional Council . . . . not with the intention of disturbing your peace of mind . . . . I have come to ask you to be vigilant, to come out for the defense of the liberty won by the blood and lives of many generations of Russian people. I have come here not to make requests of you, but with the conviction that the Provisional Government, which is now defending this newly acquired liberty, the new Russian state born for a glorious future, will win the unanimous support of everyone except those who have not the courage of their convictions—to tell the truth openly. . . . . (*Loud applause on all benches except Internationalists.*)

I was authorized by the Provisional Government to declare from this platform: The Provisional Government has never violated the right of Russian citizens to exercise their political privileges. Because of its point of view on the general state of affairs, the Provisional Government considered itself bound, as far as possible, not to create any disturbance until the Constituent Assembly is convened. Now, however, fully realizing its responsibility to the state and to the future of the country, the Provisional Government makes the following declaration: All the elements of Russian society, those groups and those parties which have dared to raise a hand against the free will of the Russian people, threatening at the same time to open the front to Germany, should be immediately, decisively, and forever liquidated. (*Loud applause from the Center and partly Left. Laughter among the Internationalists.*) Let the populace of Petrograd know that they will meet a resolute power, and, it may be, that at the last hour or even the last minute reason, conscience, and honor will conquer in the hearts of those to whom these things still have meaning. . . . . I request, and, may the Provisional Council of the Republic forgive me, I demand that this very day, ... the Provisional Government receive your answer as to whether or not it has the assurance of the support of this high gathering in the fulfilment of its duty.

A recess was declared to enable the party groups to define their attitudes toward Kerensky's statement. At 6:00 P.M. the session was resumed. Leaders of the Left groups attacked the position of the Premier and the government and insisted that civil war could be avoided only by more revolutionary and democratic policies, particularly in respect to peace and land.[18] The session was again interrupted for inter-party negotiations. Two resolutions were presented when the session was resumed, the first by the Menshevik-Internationalists and Socialist-Revolutionists, the second by the Cadets and the representatives of the Co-operatives.

RESOLUTIONS OF THE PRE-PARLIAMENT

[Session of November 6, 1917][19]

[Resolution No. 1.] The attempt at insurrections, for which preparations have recently been made, and which has for its purpose the seizure of power, threatens to bring about civil war, creates conditions favorable to pogroms and to the rise of the Black Hundred counter-revolutionary forces. It must inevitably lead to the breaking up of the elections to the Constituent Assembly, to a new military catastrophe, and to the downfall of the revolution in the midst of economic paralysis and a complete disruption of the country. The success of the agitation [in favor of an uprising] is due not merely to the objective conditions of war and general disorganization but also to the delay in carrying out measures which the country most urgently needs. Therefore, it is necessary, first of all, to pass immediately a decree transferring the land to the land committees and to take a decisive stand in foreign policy proposing to the Allies that they announce the conditions of peace and begin peace negotiations. In order to combat active outbursts of anarchy and pogroms it is necessary to take immediate measures for their termination and to create for that purpose in Petrograd a Committee of Public Safety comprised of repre-

[18] *Rech,* No. 251, November 7, 1917, p. 2; Oldenbourg, pp. 138–43.

[19] *Rech,* No. 251, November 7, 1917, p. 2.

sentatives of municipal corporations and the organs of the revolutionary democracy, acting in concert with the Provisional Government.

[Resolution No. 2.] The Provisional Council of the Russian Republic, having heard the communication of the Prime Minister, declares that, in the cause of the revolution and in the struggle against the traitors to the country who, in the face of the enemy and on the eve of the Constituent Assembly, have organized an open insurrection in the capital, the Provisional Council will give its full support to the government, and demands that most resolute measures be taken to suppress the rebellion.[20] . . . . .

The first motion received 123 votes; 102 voted against it; and 26 did not vote. . . . . The session closed at 8: 30 P.M.

While the debate went on in the Pre-Parliament, Kerensky discussed military measures with the Petrograd command, and telegrams were sent to General Headquarters at Mogilev to stand by for orders. The City Duma passed a resolution protesting against an armed uprising.[21] On learning that the Pre-Parliament had passed the resolution of the Left groups, Kerensky proposed that the government resign.[22] Leaders of the Left, unwilling to form a government, went to the Winter Palace to convince Kerensky that this resolution was not an expression of lack of confidence and to urge him to remain in office and adopt the measures proposed as the only way of averting an insurrection.

THE PROPOSAL OF DAN, GOTZ, AND AVXENTIEV

[Extracts from Dan's Account of Kerensky's Refusal to Act on the Resolution Voted by the Pre-Parliament][23]

With the adoption of the resolution it was a question of what to do next. Time was precious, and there was not a moment to lose.

[20] The Cossack section supported the second motion but made a separate declaration criticizing the Provisional Government for weakness and demanding that it put an end to the Bolshevik movement. The text is given by Mrs. Ariadna Tyrkóva-Williams, *From Liberty to Brest-Litovsk*, London, 1919, p. 246. Also in Oldenbourg, pp. 144–45.

[21] Oldenbourg, pp. 146, 151.

[22] *Rech*, No. 251, November 7, 1917, p. 3; *Novaia Zhizn*, No. 162, 1917, p. 4.

[23] F. Dan, "K istorii poslednikh dnei Vremennogo Pravitelstva," in *Letopis Revoliutsii*, 1923, I, 172–75. Dan was a Menshevik; Gotz and Avxentiev were Right Socialist-Revolutionists.

I conceived the idea of going immediately to the session of the Provisional Government and demanding in the name of the majority of the Council of the Republic that the following declaration of the Provisional Government be printed immediately and copies of it be posted throughout the city during the night: (1) that the Allied Powers have been requested to make an offer to all belligerents to stop military operations and begin negotiations for a general peace; (2) that orders have been sent by telegraph authorizing the transfer of land . . . . to the local land committees; (3) that the date for the convening of the Constituent Assembly has been advanced. . . . .

Gotz, to whom I communicated my idea, seized upon it. We decided to ask Avxentiev, the Chairman of the Council of the Republic, to join us. . . . .

The Provisional Government was in session. . . . . At our request the officer on duty called Kerensky, who, with obvious displeasure, led us into one of the adjacent rooms. . . . . We informed Kerensky of the text of the resolution, to which he replied irritably with a philippic. . . . .[24] We tried to suppress our own indignation. . . . .

[We told him] that we had a definite and concrete proposal to make to the Provisional Government: that resolutions on the question of peace, land, and the Constituent Assembly should be passed at once and made known to the population by means of telegraph and by posting bills [in the city]. We insisted that this must be done that very night in order that every soldier and every worker might know of the decisions of the Provisional Government by the next morning. . . . .

[We told him] that he was being misled by the "reactionary staff" . . . . which in its own self-deception, was deceiving the government, assuring it that the staff had "loyal troops" sufficient to overcome the Bolsheviks in an open battle . . . . [we told him] that the resolution of the Council of the Republic might prove beneficial . . . . in that the acceptance of its terms by the government was certain to change abruptly the attitude of the masses . . . . and to reduce greatly the influence of Bolshevik propaganda. . . . . We stressed the fact . . . . that there was considerable vacillation among the Bolsheviks themselves, that the rank and file of the Bolshevik Party were afraid and did not want an insurrection, and that the acceptance of our proposal would strengthen the group which is against the insurrection. Finally we criticized very sharply "the measures for suppressing the insurrection" in so far as they were of a purely military character and had no solid political foundation behind them. . . . . We pleaded . . . . with Kerensky that even from a purely military point of view the struggle against the Bolsheviks would have a chance of

[24] Kerensky's version is in *The Catastrophe,* pp. 326–28.

success only if the peasant-soldiers knew that they were defending peace and land against the Bolsheviks. . . . .

Our conversation did not last very long. Kerensky gave the impression of a man completely enervated and worn out. To every argument he replied with irritation, saying finally with disdain that the government did not need any of our advice, that this was not the time to talk but to act. . . . .

NIGHT SESSION OF THE PROVISIONAL GOVERNMENT, NOVEMBER 6[25]

The concluding part of last night's session of the Provisional Government was devoted principally to a discussion of the uprising of the Military Revolutionary Committee. The Prime Minister, who was supported by a majority of the Cabinet, insisted that decisive measures be taken against the members of the Committee. The commander [of the district] said that he had issued orders for the arrest of the Committee.

The Minister of Justice tried to persuade the Prime Minister not to employ such stern measures. He said that it was his intention to initiate judicial proceedings at once against the members of the Military Revolutionary Committee. The members of the Provisional Government agreed with Maliantovich (Minister of Justice), and Kerensky proposed to the commander that the order for the arrest of the Committee be revoked.

In the meantime the Bolsheviks were going forward with their plans to transfer the power to the Soviets. At a meeting of the Petrograd Soviet at 7:00 P.M. on November 6, Trotsky reported on the preparations made to check the measures taken by the Provisional Government which, he said, "We regard . . . . as nothing more than a pitiful, helpless, half-government, which waits the motion of a historical broom to sweep it off. . . . . But if the government wishes to make use of the hours—24, 48, or 72—which it still has to live, and comes out against us, then we will meet it with a counter-attack, blow for blow, steel for iron. . . . ."[26]

The M.R. Committee, in order to prevent the cadets summoned from the suburbs from coming to the aid of the government, sent troops to occupy the Baltic station. Red

[25] *Izvestiia*, No. 206, November 7, 1917, p. 7.

[26] Golder, pp. 616–17.

Guards, under Bolshevik orders, prevented the raising of the Neva bridges. Lenin, still in hiding, issued another appeal to his party to seize power at once.

DECLARATIONS OF THE MILITARY REVOLUTIONARY COMMITTEE

[November 6, 1917]

In spite of all sorts of reports and rumors, the Military Revolutionary Committee hereby declares that it exists not to make preparations to seize power but solely to defend the interests of the Petrograd garrison and the democracy against counter-revolution and pogroms.[27]

Citizens:

Counter-revolution is raising its head. The Kornilovists are mobilizing their forces to crush the All-Russian Congress of Soviets and to defeat the Constituent Assembly. At the same time pogrom-makers are waiting for a chance to instigate disorders and massacres.

The Petrograd Soviet of Workers' and Soldiers' Deputies assumes the defense of the revolutionary order against counter-revolution and pogroms.

The garrison of Petrograd will not allow any violence or disturbance. The population is requested to detain all hooligans and Black Hundred agitators, and bring them to the nearest military post. . . . .

Citizens! We call upon you to maintain complete calm and self-control. The cause of order and of the revolution is in safe hands![28]

MILITARY REVOLUTIONARY COMMITTEE
OF THE PETROGRAD SOVIET OF
WORKERS' AND SOLDIERS' DEPUTIES

LENIN URGES THE IMMEDIATE SEIZURE OF POWER

[Letter of November 6, 1917][29]

COMRADES:

I am writing these lines on the evening of the 6th. The situation is extremely critical. It is as clear as can be that delaying the uprising now really means death.

With all my power I wish to persuade the comrades that now everything hangs on a hair, that on the order of the day are questions that are not solved by conferences, by congresses (even by Congresses of So-

[27] *Novaia Zhizn,* No. 162, November 7, 1917, p. 3.

[28] *Izvestiia,* No. 208, November 9, 1917, p. 3.

[29] Lenin, *Toward the Seizure of Power,* II, 144–45.

viets), but only by the people, by the masses, by the struggle of armed masses.

The bourgeois onslaught of the Kornilovists, the removal of Verkhovsky show that we must not wait. We must at any price, this evening, tonight, arrest the Ministers, having disarmed (defeated if they offer resistance) the military cadets, etc.

We must not wait! We may lose everything!

The immediate gain from the seizure of power at present is defence of *the people* (not the congress, but the people, in the first place, the army and the peasants) against the Kornilovist government which has driven out Verkhovsky and has hatched a second Kornilov plot.

Who should seize power?

At present this is not important. Let the Military Revolutionary Committee seize it, or "some other institution" which declares that it will relinquish the power only to the real representatives of the interests of the people, the interests of the army (immediate offer of peace), the interests of the peasants (take the land immediately, abolish private property), the interests of the hungry.

It is necessary that all the boroughs, all regiments, all forces should be mobilised and should immediately send delegations to the Military Revolutionary Committee, to the Central Committee of the Bolsheviks, insistently demanding that under no circumstances is power to be left in the hands of Kerensky and Co. until the 7th, by no means!—but that the matter must absolutely be decided this evening or tonight.

History will not forgive delay by revolutionists who could be victorious today (and will surely be victorious today) while they risk losing much tomorrow, they risk losing all.

If we seize power today, we seize it not against the Soviets but for them.

Seizure of power is the point of the uprising; its political task will be clarified after the seizure.

It would be a disaster or formalism to wait for the uncertain voting of November 7. The people have a right and a duty to decide such questions not by voting but by force; the people have a right and duty in critical moments of a revolution to give directions to their representatives, even their best representatives, and not to wait for them.

This has been proven by the history of all revolutions and the crime of revolutionists would be limitless if they let go the proper moment, knowing that upon them depends the *saving of the revolution,* the offer of peace, the saving of Petrograd, the saving from starvation, the transfer of the land to the peasants.

The government is tottering. We must *deal it the deathblow* at any cost.

To delay action is the same as death.

C. The Military Revolutionary Committee Acts

Throughout the night detachments of the Military Revolutionary Committee were active. Without meeting any resistance they occupied the railway stations, the telephone exchange, the telegraph office, and the State Bank, so that by dawn of the 7th the Committee held all the important strategic places of the city except the Winter Palace and the district military headquarters, and these were commanded by the guns of the "Aurora" and of the Peter and Paul Fortress. During the same hours there was a meeting at Smolny of the Central Executive Committee and the Central Committee of Peasants' Deputies. To this session Mensheviks and S.R.'s brought the resolution that had passed the Pre-Parliament a few hours earlier, as a basis of compromise with the Bolsheviks. The Bolsheviks were not interested in compromises and went on with the uprising. The C.E.C. remained in session and passed a resolution of warning and censure against the Bolsheviks. Kerensky, meanwhile, had called out the Cossack regiments in Petrograd, and summoned troops from the front.

KERENSKY SUMMONS AID FROM THE FRONT

[Communication by Direct Wire to the Stavka,[30] 2:20 A.M., November 7][31]

To the Commander of the Northern Front. Copy to the Commander of the 42d Corps, Copy to the Commander of the 5th Caucasian Division:

You are hereby ordered to assemble all regiments of the Fifth Caucasian Cossack Division, together with its artillery, the 23d Don Cossack Regiment, and all other Cossack units stationed in Finland, to dispatch them by train to Petrograd (Nikolaevsky Railroad Station) under the general command of the Commander of the Fifth Caucasian Cossack Division, and to place them at the disposition of the Chief Commander of the Petrograd [Military] District, Colonel Polkovnikov. Report to me at once by ciphered telegram stating the time of the departure of the

[30] General Headquarters.

[31] *A.R.R.*, VII (1922), 286–87.

troops. Should the dispatch of said troops by rail become impossible, send them on foot. No. 11687.

A. KERENSKY
Supreme Commander-in-Chief
CAPTAIN PONOCHEVNY
Commissar of the Union of Cossack Voiskos

[At the same time the Commander of the Northern Front was ordered to send the First Don Cossack Division to Petrograd and to hasten the movement of the troops previously ordered.]

THE GOVERNMENT APPEALS TO THE COSSACKS[32]

[November 7, about 4:00 A.M.]

The Supreme Commander-in-Chief herewith orders the 1st, 4th, and 14th Don Cossack regiments to come to the rescue of the Central Executive Committee of Soviets, the Provisional Government, and the revolutionary democracy. The honor and freedom of the fatherland are at stake.

MAJOR-GENERAL BAGRATUNI
MALEVSKY, Commissar of the Central Executive Committee

PROGRESS OF THE INSURRECTION

[Levitsky to Dukhonin by Direct Wire, Morning, November 7][33]

[Levitsky]: . . . . Part of the Petrograd garrison . . . . joined the Bolsheviks; sailors arrived from Kronstadt. . . . . The whole city is covered with pickets, who at present manifest no activity of any kind. The telephone exchange is in the hands of the insurgent troops. The units stationed at the Winter Palace are only seemingly on guard, as they have decided not to fight for the government. One has the feeling that the Provisional Government is in the capital of an enemy which has just completed mobilization but has not yet begun military operations. This lack of resoluteness on the part of the Bolsheviks, who for some time have had it in their power to make an end of us all, gives me assurance that they will not dare to go against the will of the entire army on the front. . . . .

[32] *Rech,* No. 252, November 8, 1917, p. 2.

[33] *A.R.R.,* VII (1922), 290. General Levitsky was aide-de-camp to Kerensky; General Dukhonin, Chief of Staff of the Army.

[Polkovnikov to the Stavka by Direct Wire Sent at 10:15 A.M., November 7][34]

The situation in Petrograd is menacing. There are no street disorders, but a systematic seizure of government buildings and railway stations is going on. None of my orders is obeyed. The cadets surrender their posts almost without resistance, and the Cossacks, who were repeatedly ordered to come out [to defend the government], refused to do so. . . . . I must report, conscious of my responsibility to the country, that the Provisional Government is in danger. There is no guaranty that the insurrectionists will not next attempt to arrest the Provisional Government.

COLONEL POLKOVNIKOV
Commander-in-Chief of the Petrograd District

The Cossack regiments in Petrograd, which Kerensky regarded as absolutely loyal, after long debates and frequent reports that they were about to saddle their horses, finally decided to remain neutral.[35] The troops summoned from the front did not appear and Kerensky decided to go to Gatchina, a suburb, in the hope of meeting loyal troops there. After sending a message urging the Allies not to recognize the Bolsheviks, Kerensky left the capital in a motor car about 11:30 A.M., November 7.[36] In the meantime the M.R. Committee proclaimed that the Provisional Government had been deposed and that Petrograd was in the hands of the M.R. Committee as the representative of the Petrograd Soviet and garrison. The *Izvestiia,* still controlled by the C.E.C. of the First Congress, condemned the Bolshevik uprising and

[34] "Oktiabr na fronte," in *Krasnyi Arkhiv,* XXIII (1927), 149; also *A.R.R.,* VII (1922), 286, which gives the time as 12:15 A.M.

[35] Oldenbourg, pp. 181–82.

[36] *Rabochaia Gazeta,* No. 196, November 8, 1917, p. 2. Kerensky's own account of his last hours in Petrograd is given in *The Catastrophe,* pp. 329–38. He says, among other things, that the British and American embassies, having learned of his proposed departure, sent representatives to insist that he be accompanied by a car with the United States flag. Kerensky gave in to this insistence, but left in his own car followed at a respectful distance by a member of his staff in the American car flying the United States flag. Sheldon Whitehouse, Secretary of the American Embassy, says that his car was commandeered by one of Kerensky's officers who refused to remove the American flag. (D. R. Francis, *Russia from the American Embassy, April 1916–November 1918,* New York, 1922, pp. 179–80.)

prophesied famine, civil war, and surrender to the Emperor William.[37]

"THE PROVISIONAL GOVERNMENT IS DEPOSED"

[Proclamation of the Military Revolutionary Committee, 10:00 A.M., November 7][38]

The Provisional Government is deposed. All state authority has passed into the hands of the Military Revolutionary Committee, the organ of the Petrograd Soviet of Workers' and Soldiers' Deputies acting in the name of the Petrograd proletariat and the garrison.

The causes for which the people were struggling—immediate democratic peace, abolition of the *pomeshchik's* [landlord] right to the land, labor control of industry, and a Soviet form of government—are now all guaranteed.

Long live the revolution of Workers, Soldiers, and Peasants!

"THE REVOLUTION HAS TRIUMPHED"

[Proclamation of the Military Revolutionary Committee, November 7][39]

All railroad stations and the telephone, post, and telegraph offices are occupied. The telephones of the Winter Palace and the [District Military] Staff Headquarters are disconnected. The State Bank is in our hands. The Winter Palace and the [military] Staff have surrendered. The shock troops are dispersed, the cadets paralyzed. The armored cars have sided with the Revolutionary Committee. The Cossacks refused to obey the government. The Provisional Government is deposed. Power is in the hands of the Revolutionary Committee of the Petrograd Soviet of Workers' and Soldiers' Deputies.

"PETROGRAD IS IN THE HANDS OF THE MILITARY REVOLUTIONARY COMMITTEE"

[Radiogram of the Military Revolutionary Committee to the Soldiers, November 7][40]

Petrograd is in the hands of the Military Revolutionary Committee of the Petrograd Soviet. In a unanimous effort the workers and soldiers obtained a victory almost without bloodshed. Kerensky's govern-

[37] Golder, pp. 614–16.

[38] *Novaia Zhizn,* No. 163, November 8, 1917, p. 1.

[39] *Novoe Vremia,* No. 14907, November 8, 1917, p. 2.

[40] *Novaia Zhizn,* No. 163, November 8, 1917, p. 1.

ment is deposed. The Committee appeals to the front and the rear to pay no heed to provocation, and to support the Petrograd Soviet and the new revolutionary government which is going to offer at once a just peace, to transfer the land to the peasants, and to summon the Constituent Assembly.

Local authority is transferred to the Soviet of Workers', Soldiers, and Peasants' Deputies.

MILITARY REVOLUTIONARY COMMITTEE
OF THE PETROGRAD SOVIET

After Kerensky's departure the Provisional Government, in session at the Winter Palace, designated Konovalov, a Cadet, acting Prime Minister and appointed Kishkin, also a Cadet, as plenipotentiary of the government for the re-establishment of order, with Palchinsky and Rutenberg as his assistants. Kishkin immediately removed Polkovnikov and appointed General Bagratuni as commander of the Petrograd Military District.[41] The Bolsheviks had failed to cut off completely the telephone and telegraph connections of the palace, and the government remained in communication with various organizations in the city and with the front. Konovalov issued appeals to the people and the army to support the government.

APPEALS OF THE PROVISIONAL GOVERNMENT

[November 7][42]

TO THE PEOPLE

Citizens! Save the fatherland, the republic, and freedom! Maniacs have raised a revolt against the only governmental power chosen by the people—the Provisional Government.

The members of the Provisional Government, faithful to duty, will remain at their posts and continue to work for the good of the fatherland, the re-establishment of order, and the convocation of the Constituent Assembly, the future sovereign of Russia and of the peoples inhabiting it.

Citizens, you must help the Provisional Government. You must strengthen its authority. You must oppose these maniacs, with whom are

[41] *Izvestiia,* No. 207, November 8, 1917, p. 3.
[42] *Ibid.*

joined all enemies of liberty and order including the followers of the old régime whose purpose is to destroy all conquests of the revolution and the future of our dear fatherland.

Citizens, rally around the Provisional Government for the defense of its provisional authority in the name of order and the welfare of every people of our great fatherland. . . . .

To the Army

[Direct Wire to the Stavka, 7:00 P.M., November 7][43]

The Petrograd Soviet of Workers' and Soldiers' Deputies has declared the Provisional Government deposed and demands the transfer of power under the threat of bombarding the Winter Palace from the Peter and Paul Fortress and the cruiser "Aurora." The government will surrender its power only to the Constituent Assembly. It has decided not to yield and appeals to the nation and the army for protection. Rush the dispatch of troops.

A. Konovalov
Acting Prime Minister

At the Mariinsky Palace, members of the Pre-Parliament gathered and exchanged news while waiting for a quorum. About 1:00 P.M. soldiers and sailors in armored cars surrounded the palace and representatives of the Military Revolutionary Committee demanded that the members of the Pre-Parliament leave at once. Members of the Council of Elders discussed whether to submit or to leave only when actually forced to do so. A majority favored submission, and a resolution was passed protesting against the criminal attack on the rights of the people and proclaiming the sessions to have been temporarily interrupted by violence.[44] Thereupon the Bolsheviks occupied the palace and members of the other parties gathered at the City Duma, where a Committee of Public Safety was being organized by the non-Bolshevik groups.[45]

At Smolny, meanwhile, where delegates to the Second

[43] *A.R.R.,* VII (1922), 294.

[44] *Rabochaia Gazeta,* No. 196, November 8, 1917, p. 1.

[45] Oldenbourg, p. 166.

Congress of Soviets were already gathering, a special session of the Petrograd Soviet opened at 2:35 P.M. In the name of the M.R. Committee Trotsky declared that the Provisional Government was no more, that some of the ministers had already been arrested[46] and the others soon would be, that the garrison under the M.R. Committee had dispersed the Pre-Parliament, that the administrative offices had been occupied, and that the Winter Palace would soon be taken. While he was speaking, Lenin entered the room and received a noisy ovation. Trotsky continued: "In our midst is Vladimir Ilich Lenin, who, by force of circumstances, has not been able to be with us all this time. . . . . Hail the return of Lenin!" Lenin spoke of the significance of the revolution and of the new Soviet government to be created by the oppressed masses which would bring an end to the war, secure a just peace, win over the peasants by wiping out the landlord's property, set up workers' control of production, and lead the proletariat to world revolution.[47]

Trotsky then proposed that revolutionary commissars be sent to the front and throughout the country to announce the successfully accomplished revolution. To a remark from the audience that this was anticipating the will of the Second Congress of Soviets, Trotsky replied: "The will of the Second Congress of Soviets has already been predetermined by the significant fact of the insurrection of the Petrograd workers and soldiers. Our immediate task is to extend and develop the victory."[48] After further speeches the Soviet passed a resolution hailing the revolution and predicting the formation of a Soviet government based on the program of the Bolsheviks.[49] The M.R. Committee sent a message to the soldiers ordering them to watch their officers and arrest those who came out against the revolution.

[46] Only Prokopovich was under arrest at that time. Kartashev had been arrested and released.

[47] Golder, pp. 617–18.

[48] *Izvestiia*, No. 207, November 8, 1917, p. 7; Oldenbourg, pp. 170–71.

[49] Oldenbourg, pp. 172–73.

ORDER OF THE MILITARY REVOLUTIONARY COMMITTEE TO THE ARMY

[November 7, 1917][50]

To All Army Committees in the Active Army. To All Soviets of Soldiers' Deputies:

The Petrograd garrison and proletariat have overthrown Kerensky's government, which had come out against the revolution and the people. The overthrow of the Provisional Government was bloodless. The Petrograd Soviet of Workers' and Soldiers' Deputies hailed the overthrow and recognized the authority of the Military Revolutionary Committee until the formation of a government of Soviets. In announcing this to the army at the front and rear, the Military Revolutionary Committee calls on the revolutionary soldiers to watch carefully the behavior of their officers. Those who refuse to come out openly for the revolution that has just taken place should be arrested immediately as enemies.

The program of the new government of the Petrograd Soviet consists in offering immediately a democratic peace, in transferring immediately the land of the large landowners to the peasants, in handing over all power to the Soviets, and in having an honest summoning of the Constituent Assembly.

The people's revolutionary army should not permit the sending of unreliable military units from the front to Petrograd. Use persuasion and, if that fails, do not hesitate to use force. This order should be read to all soldiers. Any attempt to conceal it from the soldier masses will be regarded as a revolutionary crime and punished with all the severity of the revolutionary law. Soldiers! Fight for peace, bread, land, and popular government!

MILITARY REVOLUTIONARY COMMITTEE

BOLSHEVIK SUCCESSES IN THE CAPITAL

[Stankevich to Dukhonin by Direct Wire, Afternoon, November 7][51]

. . . . The situation is growing more difficult every moment. The Mariinsky Palace has been taken by the Bolsheviks. . . . . The attempt of our patrol . . . . to recapture the telephone exchange[52] failed completely, as our cadets were met by armored cars. The government holds the cen-

50 *Rabochii Put,* No. 46, November 8, 1917, p. 1.

51 *A.R.R.,* VII (1922), 292. Stankevich was chief army commissar of the Provisional Government.

52 Stankevich personally led the cadets in that venture. *See* his *Vospominaniia 1914–1919 g.,* Berlin, 1920, pp. 262–64; also Alexander Sinegub, "Zashchita Zimniago Dvortsa. (25 oktiabria–7 noiabria 1917 g.)," in *A.R.R.,* IV (1922), 138–50.

tral part of the city including the Winter Palace and the General Staff. The government forces consist of two and one-half schools of cadets and one battery of the Mikhailovsky school and two armored cars. These forces are sufficient to hold on for forty-eight hours, but no longer. Without outside help there is no possibility of taking any active step. . . . .

PETROGRAD ON NOVEMBER 7[53]

Petrograd looked as usual during the course of the day. Street-cars ran almost as usual. Here and there their routes were changed, owing to the opening of the Nikolaevsky Bridge to let warships pass. As usual they were overcrowded. . . . . [Soldiers] from every part of the garrison are on guard and on picket duty . . . . to preserve order. . . . . The Military Revolutionary Committee . . . . has also issued appeals to the people [to keep order]. . . . .

With an exception here and there, there were few reports of disorders on the street in the course of the day. . . . .

All the streets leading to the Mariinsky Palace were barricaded, but this should not be taken too seriously. These barricades were nothing more than piles of wood . . . . across the street. . . . . In some parts of the streets automobiles were stationed . . . . to stop traffic. . . . . By evening traffic on the streets was reduced to a minimum. . . . .

According to information in possession of Smolny there was a general meeting of the 1st, 4th, and 14th Cossack regiments at which it was decided not to obey the orders of the Provisional Government but at the same time not to come out against it. . . . .

During the day news of the events in Petrograd reached other cities. In Kiev a conference of Cossacks of the front passed a resolution against the Bolsheviks. The Moscow City Duma passed a similar resolution and decided to form a Committee of Public Safety. The Moscow Soviet, however, adopted a Bolshevik resolution to form a Military Revolutionary Committee. In Petrograd the Central Executive Committee of the All-Russian Union of Railwaymen (Vikzhel)[54] resolved to support the existing Central Executive Committee of Soviets. The Stavka reported that the detachments of loyal troops ordered to Petrograd were moving but some had been delayed about seventy versts from the city.[55]

[53] *Delo Naroda,* No. 189, November 8, 1917, p. 2.

[54] Vserossiiskii Ispolnitelnyi Komitet Zheleznodorozhnikov.

[55] Oldenbourg, pp. 178–83.

In the meantime the Bolshevik plans for the capture of the Winter Palace were encountering obstacles. According to the accounts of Antonov and Podvoisky,[56] who, with Chudnovsky, were responsible for the plan and its execution, units of the garrison had been ordered to surround the palace at noon. A thousand sailors from Kronstadt were to arrive as re-enforcements at 2:00 P.M. An ultimatum had been drawn up and, in case the ministers refused to surrender, it had been arranged for the guns of Peter and Paul Fortress to open fire. The "Aurora" was to fire blank charges from six-inch guns, but the fort and other ships were to use real ammunition. The sailors were five hours late, there were too many commanders to co-ordinate the units engaged, and it was not until after nightfall that the Bolshevik forces actually began to close in on the defenders of the government. About 7:30, without meeting opposition, they occupied the headquarters of the military district and arrested General Bagratuni. The forces guarding the palace began to melt away. By a ruse the cadet artillery was led out of the palace yard and disarmed and the Women's Battalion of Death marched out and surrendered. About 8:30 Antonov sent his ultimatum to Kishkin. The ministers refused to surrender and the Peter and Paul Fortress and the "Aurora" were ordered to open fire. The firing lasted for an hour, and made a great deal of noise but did very little damage. After an hour's lull, firing began again at 11:00. The Bolsheviks at the District Headquarters learned that a Military Revolutionary Committee had been formed at Pskov (Headquarters of the Northern Front) to prevent the sending of troops to rescue the Provisional Government and that the Commander of the Northern Front, General Cheremisov, was well disposed toward this committee.[57]

[56] These are translated in E. A. Ross, *The Russian Bolshevik Revolution,* New York, 1921, pp. 270, 276–78.

[57] Oldenbourg, pp. 186–87. Cheremisov had countermanded Kerensky's order for this advance. See below, p. 140.

THE ACTION OF THE CRUISER "AURORA"

[Report of the Commissar of the Cruiser][58]

The cruiser "Aurora" had been under repairs at the Franco-Russian yards and was supposed to leave Petrograd on November 4 to try out its new machinery. But in view of the approaching Second Congress of Soviets, the Tsentrobalt[59] issued an order postponing our departure indefinitely. The sailors of the "Aurora" were told that they would have to take an active part in the defense of the Soviet Congress, and, possibly, in an uprising. On November 6 the Military Revolutionary Committee appointed me commissar of the cruiser "Aurora." A special meeting of the [sailors'] committee was called in the presence of the commander and other officers. I briefly explained the instructions I had received, saying that I was going to execute all orders of the Military Revolutionary Committee . . . . regardless of the views of the commanding officers. In the evening [November 6] instructions were received from the Military Revolutionary Committee to reopen traffic on the Nikolaevsky Bridge. . . . . It was necessary to move the ship closer to the bridge, and I gave orders to get up steam . . . . and weigh anchor. . . . .

The commander refused to pilot the ship on the pretext that the "Aurora" would not be able to move on the Neva. I gave orders to take soundings in the channel of the Neva, which showed that the cruiser could pass quite easily. . . . .

At 3:30 A.M. the ship cast anchor near the Nikolaevsky Bridge. We worked all day, November 7, to bring the ship in fighting order. . . . . Toward evening we received orders from the Military Revolutionary Committee to fire a few blank shots upon receiving a signal from Peter and Paul Fortress and, if necessary, to shell [the Winter Palace] with shrapnel. There was no occasion, however, for the latter, as the Winter Palace soon surrendered. . . . .

The only immediate answer to the government's appeals for support came from the City Duma where, toward midnight, the members decided to march to the Winter Palace and take their places beside the besieged ministers. Each member made a solemn personal declaration that he was "ready to go and die for the government." The Menshevik-Internationalists abstained from making the declaration and

[58] B. Elov, "Rol petrogradskogo garnizona v oktiabrskie dni (Po doneseniiam komissarov Voenno-Revoliutsionnogo Komiteta)," in *Krasnaia Letopis,* No. 6, 1923, p. 120.

[59] Central Committee of the Baltic fleet.

the Bolsheviks said they were "ready to go and die with the Second Congress of Soviets at Smolny."[60]

IN THE CITY DUMA

[November 7, 1917]

Before the opening of the Duma on November 7 the Assistant Minister of the Interior, V. V. Khizhniakov, visited the Mayor to request that the City Duma . . . . come to the defense of the Provisional Government. . . . .[61] During the session of the City Duma the Mayor announced that the bombardment of the Winter Palace would begin in a few seconds and that the Provisional Government would surely perish in its ruins. "It is our duty," he said, "to prevent bloodshed."

The Duma decided to send delegations to the cruiser "Aurora," to the Winter Palace, and to the Petrograd Soviet of Workers' and Soldiers' Deputies. . . . .

The delegation to the "Aurora" was detained on its way by a commissar of the Military Revolutionary Committee. The delegation to the Winter Palace was also unable to pass the sentries.

When this became known in the City Duma, Bykhovsky, a member of the Duma and a Socialist-Revolutionist, said: "We have sent our comrades to the Provisional Government, thus placing on their shoulders a tremendous burden. The Provisional Government has made many mistakes, but we are partly responsible for them. It is our duty to go and die with the Provisional Government. . . . ."

The entire Duma decided to go to the Winter Palace. Similar decisions were made by the Executive Committee of the All-Russian Soviet of Peasants' Deputies, the Mensheviks, and the Socialist-Revolutionists of the Central Executive Committee [of Soviets].

The Duma succeeded in getting in touch with the Provisional Government by telephone. The Winter Palace was under fire of the cruiser "Aurora."

Members of the Duma together with representatives of organizations marching with them to the Winter Palace reached the first line of sentries. There they were stopped while the sentry went to look for the commissar of the Military Revolutionary Committee. After half an hour's waiting they were informed that they would not be allowed to go to the Winter Palace. The procession went back to the Duma and resumed the session.[62]

[60] *Rech,* No. 252, November 8, 1917, p. 3.

[61] *Ibid.*

[62] *Izvestiia,* No. 207, November 8, 1917, p. 4.

Another account is given in English by P. Sorokin, *Leaves from a Russian Diary,* New York [1921], pp. 101–102. Sorokin took part in this affair. Still

D. The Second Congress of Soviets and the Capture of the Winter Palace

At Smolny they were waiting for news of the capture of the Winter Palace. The delegates to the Second Congress of Soviets, which was scheduled to open at 3:00 P.M., were impatiently waiting for the session to begin. Lenin, who wished to confront the Congress with an accomplished fact and secure its sanction for a new government, was furious over the delay in occupying the palace and, according to Podvoisky, threatened to shoot the members of the Military Revolutionary Committee for failing to deliver the final blow.[63] Finally, under pressure from the delegates, particularly those who were hostile to the Bolsheviks, the session opened at about eleven o'clock. Lenin, however, refused to attend.

THE OPENING OF THE SECOND CONGRESS OF SOVIETS[64]

[Session of November 7, 1917]

The Congress was opened at 11:00 P.M. At the presiding table were Dan, Gotz, Filipovsky, Bogdanov. From the chair Dan made the following statement:

The Second All-Russian Congress of Soviets meets at an unusual moment and under most extraordinary circumstances. You will understand, therefore, why I consider it untimely to open the Congress with a political speech. You will understand this especially if you know that at this very moment, while I am addressing you, my party comrades who were sent to the Winter Palace to fulfil their duty are being bombarded (those words made a deep impression). Without saying anything further

another is by John Reed, who witnessed the procession and who says there were between three and four hundred persons from the Duma. (*Ten Days That Shook the World,* pp. 97–98.)

[63] *Krasnaia Letopis,* No. 8, 1923, pp. 38–39. Trotsky's accounts are given in *Lenin,* pp. 98–102; *My Life, An Attempt at an Autobiography,* New York, 1930, pp. 327–28; and *The History of the Russian Revolution,* III, chaps. viii–x.

[64] This account is derived from the following sources: (1) *Novaia Zhizn,* No. 163, November 8, 1917, p. 3; (2) *Izvestiia,* No. 208, November 9, 1917, p. 4; (3) the text of the Tsentrarkhiv publication entitled *Vtoroi Vserossiiskii Sezd Sovetov R. i S.D.,* Moscow, Leningrad, 1928; (4) N. Sukhanov, *Zapiski o revoliutsii,* Book 7, 197–204, and *Pravda,* No. 170, November 9, 1917, p. 2.

I declare the session of the Congress open and propose that we proceed to the election of presiding officers.

Avanesov, on behalf of the Bolsheviks, ... moved that a presidium be elected on the principle of proportional representation[65] as follows: Bolsheviks, 14; Socialist-Revolutionists, 7; Mensheviks, 3; and Internationalists, 1.[66] He then proposed the following names for the Bolshevik ticket: Lenin, Zinoviev, Trotsky, Kamenev, Rykov, Skliansky, Nogin, Krylenko, Madame Kollontai, Antonov, Riazanov, Muralov,[67] Lunacharsky, and Stuchka.[68]

The representatives of the Socialist-Revolutionists of the Right and the Social-Democrats (Mensheviks) declared that they would not take part in the election of the Presidium. The Internationalists made a similar announcement. . . . . As elected the Presidium was made up only of Bolsheviks and Socialist-Revolutionists of the Left. . . . .

Kamenev announced the following program for the day: (1) the organization of a government; (2) the question of war and peace; (3) the Constituent Assembly.[69]

Martov, on behalf of the Internationalists, insisted that before any other question was taken up the question of a peaceful settlement of the political crisis should be considered. . . . . At a time when the question of power is being solved by a conspiracy of one revolutionary party and when all other revolutionary parties are confronted with an accomplished fact, it is imperative that we consider first of all the question of how to avert the civil war which is imminent. . . . . A peaceful solution is possible

[65] The total membership and the party composition of the Second Congress of Soviets can only be approximately determined. Papers of the period give the number of delegates as 517 of whom 250 were Bolsheviks, 159 Socialist-Revolutionists (Right and Left), 6 Ukrainian Socialist-Revolutionists, 60 Mensheviks, 14 Internationalists, 3 Anarchists, 22 non-party men, and 3 Independent Socialists. A preliminary count by officials of the Congress gives a total of 670 members distributed as follows: Bolsheviks, 300; Socialist-Revolutionists (Right and Left), 193; Ukrainian Socialists, 7; Mensheviks, 68; Internationalists, 14; Bund [Jewish S.D.], 10; Anarchists, 3; non-party, 36; Indefinite, 22; Socialist-Zionists, 10; Socialist-Nationalists, 3; Latvian Socialists, 4. Party committees give the following numbers: Bolsheviks, 390; Socialist-Revolutionists (Right and Left), 160; Ukrainian Socialists, 7; Mensheviks, 72; Menshevik-Internationalists, 6; Internationalists, 14; making a total of 649. (*Vtoroi Vserossiiskii Sezd Sovetov R. i S.D.*, p. 171.) Apparently fewer of the local Soviets were represented in the historic session of November 7 than in the earlier and later Congresses. At the First Congress (July 1917) there were 1,090 delegates; at the Third Congress (January 1918), 942; at the Fourth (March 1918), 1,204.

[66] *Novaia Zhizn,* No. 163, November 8, 1917, p. 3.

[67] Trotsky gives Muranov, not Muralov, as Bolshevik candidate for membership in the Presidium, *History of the Russian Revolution,* III, 305.

[68] *Pravda,* No. 170, November 9, 1917, p. 2.

[69] *Novaia Zhizn,* No. 163, November 8, 1917, p. 3.

and that solution lies in the formation of a uniformly democratic power. We should elect a delegation to negotiate with other socialist parties and organizations with the purpose of putting an end to the strife. . . . . Blood is already flowing on the streets of Petrograd. (*Cries: "What a shame!"*)

Martov's proposal was supported by the Socialist-Revolutionists of the Left, United Social-Democrats (Internationalists), and representatives from the front. . . . .

Lunacharsky said that the Bolsheviks had nothing against Martov's proposal. On the contrary they [the Bolsheviks] were anxious that each party should state its attitude toward the events that were taking place and its opinion as to the best way out of the situation.

Martov's proposal was . . . . accepted unanimously.[70]

On behalf of the 12th Army, Kharash made the following statement: While proposals are being made here to settle peacefully the question of power, a struggle is in progress on the streets of Petrograd. The Winter Palace is under fire, and the specter of civil war is at hand.[71] Owing to the duplicity of the Bolsheviks, a criminal adventure is being staged behind the back of the All-Russian Congress of Soviets.[72] The Mensheviks and the Socialist-Revolutionists refuse to be involved in that adventure and are ready to gather all forces to resist this seizure of power.[73] . . . .

On behalf of the Mensheviks, Khinchuk said the only possible way to a peaceful solution is to begin negotiations with the Provisional Government with the purpose of forming a new cabinet supported by all strata [of society]. (*Loud noise.*) We disclaim all responsibility for what is happening and withdraw from the Congress, inviting other parties to do the same. He then read the declaration of his party.[74]

THE MODERATE SOCIALISTS LEAVE THE CONGRESS[75]

[Party Declarations]

Whereas, (1) the military conspiracy was organized and executed by the Bolshevik Party in the name of the Soviets and behind the backs of all other parties and groups represented in the Soviets,

(2) The seizure of power by the Petrograd Soviet just before the Congress assembled is a distortion and a violation of the principle of

[70] *Vtoroi Vserossiiskii Sezd Sovetov R. i S.D.*, pp. 34–35.

[71] *Izvestiia*, No. 208, November 9, 1917. The account given in *Izvestiia* of November 8, when it was still edited by the Mensheviks, says that Kharash spoke in behalf of the Mensheviks and Socialist-Revolutionists of the Right.

[72] *Vtoroi Vserossiiskii Sezd Sovetov R. i S.D.*, p. 35.

[73] *Izvestiia*, No. 208, November 9, 1917.

[74] *Ibid.*

[75] *Vtoroi Vserossiiskii Sezd Sovetov R. i S.D.*, pp. 37–40.

Soviet organization, tending to undermine the value of the Congress as a plenipotentiary representative of the revolutionary democracy,

(3) The said conspiracy throws the country into civil war, hinders the convocation of the Constituent Assembly, threatens a military catastrophe, and leads to the triumph of a counter-revolution,

(4) The only possible way out of the situation is to begin negotiations with the Provisional Government with the purpose of forming a government that can win the support of the whole democracy,

(5) The Social-Democratic Labor Party (United) considers it its duty to the working class not only to disclaim all responsibility for the activities of the Bolsheviks, who shield themselves under the banner of the Soviet, but also to warn the workers and the soldiers of the pernicious effects upon the country and the revolution of a policy of adventure—the Russian Social-Democratic Labor Party (United) is leaving the Congress and is inviting other groups which are likewise unwilling to assume the responsibility for the activities of the Bolsheviks, to come together at once for the purpose of considering the present situation. . . .

[On behalf of the Socialist-Revolutionists, Hendelman made a similar declaration.]

. . . . Erlich . . . . "On behalf of the Bund[76] group I deem it my duty to say that a great calamity has occurred in Petrograd. Our duty to the Jewish proletariat and the proletariat of the whole country is to say this: . . . .

"By way of protest we call upon all those who disapprove of the bloodshed to leave [the Congress]. It may be that our going will bring these madmen and criminals to reason." . . . .

After that statement the Socialist-Revolutionists, the Mensheviks, and the Bund groups left the assembly hall amid the clamor of the Bolsheviks. . . . .

THE MENSHEVIK-INTERNATIONALISTS' RESOLUTION

[First Session of the Second Congress of Soviets][77]

[On behalf of the Menshevik-Internationalists, L. A. Martov introduced the following resolution]:

In view of the fact (1) that the coup d'état, which placed all authority in Petrograd in the hands of the Military Revolutionary Committee on the eve of the opening of the Congress, was accomplished by the Bolshevik Party alone and by means of a military conspiracy; (2) that this coup d'état threatens to produce bloodshed, civil war, and the triumph of

[76] Jewish Social-Democratic Party.

[77] *Novaia Zhizn*, No. 163, November 8, 1917.

a counter-revolution which is likely to drown in blood the proletarian movement together with all the conquests of the revolution; (3) that the sole remedy which might still prevent the outbreak of civil war is an agreement between the insurgent part of the democracy and the remaining democratic organizations, having in view the formation of a democratic government acceptable to the whole revolutionary democracy and to whom the Provisional Government might hand over its authority without a struggle—the Menshevik group calls upon the Congress to resolve that it is absolutely necessary to end the crisis in a peaceful manner, by forming a government composed of representatives of all the democratic elements.

With this in view, the Menshevik-Internationalist group invites the Congress to appoint a delegation to enter into negotiations with the other organs of democracy and with all the Socialist parties.

Pending the report of that delegation . . . . the Congress is to be adjourned.

TROTSKY'S REPLY

The insurrection of the masses stands in no need of justification. What is taking place is not a conspiracy but an insurrection. We molded the revolutionary will of the Petrograd workers and soldiers. . . . . The masses gathered under our banner, and our insurrection was victorious. But what do they [the other socialists] offer us? . . . . To give up our victory, to compromise, and to negotiate—with whom? With whom shall we negotiate? With those miserable cliques which have left the Congress or with those who still remain? But we saw how strong those cliques were! There is no one left in Russia to follow them. And millions of workers and peasants are asked to negotiate with them on equal terms. No, an agreement will not do now. To those who have left us and to those proposing negotiations we must say: You are a mere handful, miserable, bankrupt; your rôle is finished, and you may go where you belong—to the garbage heap of history![78]

In conclusion Trotsky read the following resolution:

The Second All-Russian Congress of Soviets is bound to state that the departure of the Mensheviks and the Socialist-Revolutionists is a hopeless and criminal attempt to break up the representative assembly of the workers and soldiers at a moment when the advance guard of the masses is attempting to defend the revolution against the attacks of counter-revolution. The parties who stand for agreement [with the bourgeoisie] have in the past lowered the prestige of the revolution and have hopelessly compromised themselves in the eyes of workers, soldiers, and peasants.

[78] N. Sukhanov, *Zapiski o revoliutsii,* Book 7, 203.

The compromisers have initiated and sanctioned the disastrous July offensive which brought the army and the country to the verge of ruin.

The compromisers supported a government which introduced the death penalty and betrayed the people . . . . which broke up revolutionary organizations . . . . and helped the bourgeoisie to starve millions of toilers.

Having lost the confidence of the masses, as a result of their previous policies . . . . the compromisers have been making every effort to prevent the [meeting of the] Congress of Soviets. Having failed in this . . . . they are now resorting to their last measure and are breaking with the Soviets. . . . . Their departure, however, does not weaken the Soviets. On the contrary, it gives the latter additional strength by removing from . . . . revolution the counter-revolutionary admixture. . . . . The Second All-Russian Congress, therefore, resolves to continue its work the object of which was predetermined by the will of the working people and its insurrection of November 6–7. . . . .[79]

THE PEASANT DEPUTIES LEAVE THE CONGRESS[80]

Comrade Gurevich, member of the Executive Committee of Peasants' Deputies, declared:

I came here to urge you in the name of the Executive Committee of the All-Russian Soviet of Peasants' Deputies to leave the Congress which was called against the wishes of the majority of provincial soviets. (*Loud noises.*)

Today we made a proposal to the Military Revolutionary Committee to do something to prevent bloodshed. The Military Revolutionary Committee replied that it will not accept our proposal.

The Winter Palace is under fire. Representatives of the democracy, including three members of the Executive Committee of Peasants' Deputies . . . . are in the palace. We decided to go there and die with those who were sent there to do our will.

The Peasant delegates left the hall.

[At 2:40 A.M. an intermission was announced.]

At the Winter Palace, meanwhile, the defending forces had dwindled by 1:00 A.M. to a few weak units of cadets, some of whom stood on guard near the room where the ministers were waiting. At 2:00 A.M. the Bolsheviks entered

[79] *Pravda,* No. 170, November 9, 1917, p. 2.

[80] *Vtoroi Vserossiiskii Sezd Sovetov R. i S.D.,* p. 44.

the palace, arrested the ministers, and marched them off to Peter and Paul Fortress.[81]

PETROGRAD ON THE NIGHT OF NOVEMBER 8

[The Ministry of War to the Stavka by Direct Wire, November 8, 1917][82]

[Stavka]: Can you give us a statement of the situation in Petrograd at the present moment?

[Ministry of War]: The situation is as follows: The Nevsky [Prospect] down to the Moika is open for traffic, but from the Moika to the Winter Palace it is occupied by soldiers and sailors . . . . who are gradually closing in on the palace from the right and the left. All other streets are open. . . . . The railway stations are occupied by the insurrectionists, and their pickets patrol the streets, detaining everyone who has not the proper credentials. Around the Smolny Institute, where the staff of the insurgents is located, armored cars . . . . are on guard. Generally the streets are quiet; the day passed without any encounter, and the crowds . . . . are amazingly indifferent to what is going on. In the [City] Duma a "Committee to Save the Revolution" is in session. [The committee] consists of representatives of the Duma, and of that part of the Central Committee [of the Soviets] which left the Smolny Institute, after having broken with the Bolsheviks.[83] The insurrectionists maintain order in the city; there have been no disorders or pogroms of any kind. . . . .

The plan of the insurrection was undoubtedly worked out beforehand and is being executed with great precision and resoluteness. The Committee to Save the Revolution has at present no forces to rely upon, but puts its hopes on the troops coming from the front. . . . .

In the beginning the insurrectionists showed no determination, and only later, when they saw there was no resistance.[84] . . . .

[Stavka]: Where are the members of the Provisional Government now?

[Ministry of War]: They were in the Winter Palace an hour ago and are now under arrest. . . . .

[81] Cf. Danilevich's account in "Oktiabr na fronte," in *Krasnyi Arkhiv,* XXIII (1927), 157–60, and in Oldenbourg, pp. 227–30. Accounts in English of the seizure of the Winter Palace are given by John Reed, *op. cit.,* pp. 99–106; Louise Bryant, *Six Red Months in Russia,* New York [1918], pp. 79–88; and A. R. Williams, *Through the Russian Revolution,* London, 1923, pp. 105–16.

[82] *A.R.R.,* VII (1922), 303–304. The *A.R.R.* gives the time as 1:00 A.M.; 3:00 A.M. is more in accordance with the situation.

[83] See below, pp. 118–19.

[84] Sentence not finished.

THE TAKING OF THE WINTER PALACE

[Statement of S. L. Maslov, Minister of Agriculture][85]

On Tuesday [November 6] I attended as usual the meeting of the Provisional Government at the Winter Palace. All the ministers were present and Kerensky presided.

After several minor matters were attended to we took up the land law. The first and second articles were accepted without change. While we were at work, Kerensky received several reports about the uprising which the Bolsheviks were preparing. It was decided to lay the land law on the table temporarily and to take up current affairs.

The matter of the resolution of the Pre-Parliament was discussed, and then we turned to the question of the defense of Petrograd. About one in the morning the meeting came to a close.

On Wednesday morning at half-past eleven I was summoned by telephone to a special meeting of the Provisional Government. It was reported to us that the Bolsheviks had seized the Petrograd news agency, the State Bank, the post and telegraph. It was agreed that Polkovnikov, the man in charge of the defense, had not acted with decision, and N. M. Kishkin was appointed in his place, with two assistants, Palchinsky and Rutenberg. Kishkin left for the office of the General Staff. After this an appeal to the population was drawn up and approved. It was decided that the Provisional Government should remain in continuous session. While at work, reports of Bolshevik success reached us.

At seven in the evening, Kishkin, who was at the General Staff, was handed a note signed by Antonov demanding the surrender of the Provisional Government and the disarming of the guard. The note called attention to the fact that all the guns of the "Aurora" and Peter and Paul Fortress were trained on the Winter Palace. Kishkin was given twenty minutes in which to decide. When the ministers learned of this demand they decided that only the Constituent Assembly and not a self-appointed organization could take over their powers.

The guard of the Winter Palace was made up of some cadets, part of the Engineering School, two companies of Cossacks, and a small number of the Women's Battalion.

At 10:00 [P.M.] a shot was fired in the palace, followed by cries and shots from the cadets. On investigation it appeared that two sailors had climbed to the upper story of the palace and had thrown down two hand grenades. The bombs wounded two cadets, who were quickly attended to by N. M. Kishkin.

The sailors were arrested and disarmed. A search was made throughout the building and about fifty hostile sailors and soldiers were arrested

[85] *Delo Naroda,* No. 193, November 11, 1917, pp. 1–2.

and disarmed. In the meantime more and more sailors and soldiers arrived, until the guard seemed helpless. Outside the palace, rifles, machine guns, and even cannon were being fired. About two in the morning [November 7–8] there was a loud noise at the entrance to the palace. The insurrectionists were trying to break in and thirty of the cadets were trying to hold them back. Members of the Provisional Government took a hand and stopped [further] trouble. The armed mob of soldiers, sailors, and civilians, led by Antonov, broke in. They shouted threats and made jokes. Antonov arrested everybody in the name of the Revolutionary Committee and proceeded to take the names of all present. He began with Konovalov, then Kishkin, and then the others. He inquired for Kerensky, but he was no longer in the palace.

We were placed under arrest, and told that we would be taken to Peter and Paul Fortress. We picked up our coats, but Kishkin's was gone. Someone had stolen it. He was given a soldier's coat. A discussion started between Antonov, the soldiers, and the sailors as to whether the ministers should be taken to their destination in automobiles or on foot. It was decided to make them walk.

Each of us was guarded by two men. As we walked through the palace it seemed as if it were filled with the insurrectionists, some of whom were drunk. When we came out on the street we were surrounded by a mob, shouting, threatening, ... and demanding Kerensky. The mob seemed determined to take the law into its own hands and one of the ministers was jostled a bit. Just then a shot was fired and the mob quieted down. We moved on by the palace, past the Hermitage . . . . to the Troitsky Bridge. At the Troitsky Bridge the mob recovered its voice and shouted, "Throw them into the river!" The calls were becoming louder and louder. Just then a machine gun opened fire from the other side of us. We threw ourselves down, while some of the mob ran, and with them one of the arrested officers. . . . .

From this point to the fort we proceeded without further excitement. . . . . Each of us was placed in a separate cell . . . . which was cold and damp. In this manner I spent the night. In the morning I was given some hot water and a piece of bread, at noon some kind of a soup. It was only at nine in the evening that I got something to eat, two cutlets and some potatoes. Nothing happened during the day. I was given a catalogue of books and a piece of paper on which to write down things I needed for tomorrow. At three in the morning I was awakened by the entrance of several military men. They informed me that according to the decision of the Second Congress of Soviets Salazkin and I were placed under house arrest. They took me to the office; Salazkin was also there. . . . . They asked me to promise on my word of honor not to leave the house. I declined and said that I was not obliged to make any promises to jail guards. Salazkin replied in the same manner. We were then informed that Red Guards would be placed in our homes. When I explained that I was living in the building occupied by the Central Executive Committee of the All-Russian Soviet of Peasants' Deputies, they were a bit confused. . . . . Another attempt was made to persuade me to make a promise, but I refused.

Following this conversation a member of the Revolutionary Committee and I got into a car, and we went without any other guard to the [building] of the Executive Committee. As we entered, ... he said: "You are free, but you should know that by refusing to give me your word of honor, you expose me to the danger of being placed under arrest."

The news of the arrest of the Provisional Government reached the City Duma at about 3:00 A.M. Members of the Duma and the groups that had bolted the Second Congress of Soviets decided to form a Committee to Save the Country and the Revolution in order to preserve the continuity of legal authority pending the re-establishment of the Provisional Government.

FORMATION OF THE COMMITTEE TO SAVE THE COUNTRY AND THE REVOLUTION[86]

[November 8, 1917]

A meeting of all organizations opposed to the Bolshevik adventure took place in the City Duma at 3:00 A.M. . . . . It was decided to form a "Committee to Save the Country and the Revolution." On this committee the following named groups were represented: the City Duma, the Central Executive Committee of the Soviets of Workers' and Soldiers' Deputies,[87] and the Executive Committee of Peasants' Deputies, the groups of the Socialist-Revolutionists and Mensheviks who left the Congress of Soviets,[88] the railwaymen's union, the post and telegraph union, the central committees of the Socialist-Revolutionists and Mensheviks, the Council of the Russian Republic, and organizations at the front.

The committee issued the following appeal to the citizens of the Russian Republic:

"On November 7 the Petrograd Bolsheviks, defying the will of the Russian people, arrested some of the members of the Provisional Gov-

[86] *Delo Naroda,* No. 190, November 9, 1917, p. 2.

[87] Of the First All-Russian Congress.

[88] Second All-Russian Congress.

ernment, dispersed the Council of the Russian Republic, and proclaimed an illegal government.

"The use of force against the government of revolutionary Russia at a moment when we are threatened by one of the greatest dangers from the foreign enemy is an unheard-of crime against the country.

"The conspiracy of the Bolsheviks deals a mortal blow to the cause of the country's defense and puts the desired peace a long way off.

"The civil war begun by the Bolsheviks threatens to drag the country into indescribable horrors of anarchy and counter-revolution, to prevent the convening of the Constituent Assembly, whose purpose is to consolidate the republican form of government, and to transfer the land to the people.

"Endeavoring to preserve the continuity of the only legal authority, the All-Russian Committee to Save the Country and the Revolution has taken upon itself the task of re-establishing the Provisional Government, which, resting upon the strength of the democracy, will lead the country to the Constituent Assembly and save it from counter-revolution and anarchy.

"The All-Russian Committee to Save the Country and the Revolution calls on you citizens: Do not recognize the authority of violence! Do not carry out the orders of such an authority. Stand up in defense of the country and the revolution! Give your support to the All-Russian Committee to Save the Country and the Revolution!"

[Signatures of the above-mentioned groups and organizations follow]

E. The Second Congress of Soviets Assumes Power

News of the capture of the Winter Palace soon reached Smolny. Antonov telephoned his official report. The delegates to the Congress rushed back into the assembly hall, and the session was resumed at 3:10 A.M.

ANTONOV'S REPORT OF THE ARREST OF THE PROVISIONAL GOVERNMENT[89]

On this day, November 7, at 2:10 A.M.,[90] Antonov, a member of the Military Revolutionary Committee of the Executive Committee of Soviets of Workers' and Soldiers' Deputies, at the order of the Committee,

[89] *Vtoroi Vserossiiskii Sezd Sovetov R. i S.D.*, p. 48.

[90] An error of twenty-four hours.

arrested [the following]: Verderevsky, Vice-Admiral; Kishkin, Minister of Social Welfare; Konovalov, Minister of Commerce; Maslov, Minister of Agriculture; Liverovsky, Minister of Communications; General Manikovsky, in charge of the Ministry of War; Gvozdev, Minister of Labor; Maliantovich, Minister of Justice; Tretiakov, Chairman of the Economic Council; Borisov, General; Smirnov, State Comptroller; Salazkin, Minister of Education; Bernatsky, Minister of Finance; Tereshchenko, Minister of Foreign Affairs; Rutenberg and Palchinsky, Assistants to the Minister Plenipotentiary of the Provisional Government; Nikitin, Minister of Post and Telegraph and the Interior; Kartashev, Minister of Cults.

All officers and cadets were disarmed and set free . . . .; Comrade Chudnovsky, member of the Second All-Russian Congress of Soviets and private of the Preobrazhensky regiment, was appointed commandant of the Winter Palace. All ministers were sent to Peter and Paul Fortress.

RESUMED SESSION OF THE SECOND CONGRESS OF SOVIETS[91]

When the session was resumed Kamenev declared: News has just been received that the chiefs of the counter-revolution, assembled at the Winter Palace with the recently named dictator, Kishkin, at their head, have been arrested by the revolutionary garrison of Petrograd. (*Applause.*) The Third Battalion of Cyclists, ordered against Petrograd by the ex-Supreme Commander-in-Chief, Kerensky, has gone over to the side of the revolutionary people. (*Shouts of applause.*)

[A representative of the Socialist-Revolutionists protested the arrest of socialist ministers.[92] A commission from Tsarskoe Selo announced that the garrison of that suburb was guarding the approaches to Petrograd. To the accompaniment of much applause a representative of the Third Cyclist Battalion told how his comrades had decided to support the Congress of Soviets instead of the Provisional Government. Kapelinsky, in the name of the Menshevik-Internationalists, spoke again

[91] *Izvestiia,* No. 209, November 10, 1917, p. 4.

[92] John Reed, pp. 107–108, writes: "A big peasant, his bearded face convulsed with rage, mounted the platform and pounded with his fist on the presidium table. 'We, Socialist Revolutionaries, insist upon the immediate release of the Socialist Ministers arrested in the Winter Palace! Comrades! Do you know that four comrades, who risked their lives and their freedom fighting against tyranny of the Tsar, have been flung into Peter-Paul prison—the historical tomb of Liberty?' In the uproar he pounded and yelled. Another delegate climbed up beside him and pointed at the presidium. 'Are the representatives of the revolutionary masses going to sit quietly here while the *Okhrana* of the Bolsheviki tortures their leaders?'" Cf. *Novaia Zhizn,* No. 163, November 8, 1917, p. 3.

of a peaceful solution, insisted on an immediate election of a delegation to treat with the other socialists, and declared that because their proposal was not approved by the meeting, the members of his group had decided to withdraw.]

Comrade Kamenev stated [in reply] that the Congress had unanimously decided to take up the question of which the Menshevik-Internationalists spoke insistently, but that unanimous decision of the Congress could not be carried out because the attention of the Congress was occupied by all sorts of declarations. Taking into consideration the necessity of discussing more thoroughly the departure of the Mensheviks and the S.R.'s, Comrade Kamenev proposed to postpone the vote on Trotsky's resolution and to discuss an appeal to the workers, soldiers, and peasants of Russia.

[Krylenko read a telegram from the newly formed Military Revolutionary Committee of the Northern front. Kamenev proposed to send the greetings of the Congress to the M.R. Committee of the Northern front. Lunacharsky read the proposed appeal to the workers, soldiers, and peasants. Representatives of the Menshevik-Internationalists and of the Jewish Socialists refused to vote because the Congress was not representative and not the responsible power. The Ukrainian socialists insisted that the resolutions should mention Ukrainian autonomy if they were to support the Soviet Government. After some unimportant amendments the appeal was adopted with only two opposing votes and twelve abstentions. The Polish Socialists of the Left declared that they would remain in the Congress. The Congress decided to give representation to local peasant societies with one delegate for every twenty-five thousand. The session closed between 5:00 and 6:00 A.M., November 8.]

PROCLAMATION OF THE CONGRESS ON THE ASSUMPTION OF POWER[93]

To All Workers, Soldiers, and Peasants:

The Second All-Russian Congress of Soviets of Workers' and Soldiers' Deputies has opened. It represents the great majority of the Soviets, including a number of deputies of peasant Soviets. The prerogatives of the Central Executive Committee of the compromisers are ended.

Supported by an overwhelming majority of the workers, soldiers, and peasants, and basing itself on the victorious insurrection of the workers and the garrison of Petrograd, the Congress hereby resolves to take governmental power into its own hands.

The Provisional Government is deposed and most of its members are under arrest.

[93] *Vtoroi Vserossiiskii Sezd Sovetov R. i S.D.*, pp. 93–94.

The Soviet authority will at once propose a democratic peace to all nations and an immediate armistice on all fronts. It will safeguard the transfer without compensation of all land—landlord, udel,[94] and monastery—to the peasant committees; it will defend the soldiers' rights, introducing a complete democratization of the army, it will establish workers' control over industry, it will insure the convocation of the Constituent Assembly on the date set, it will supply the cities with bread and the villages with articles of first necessity, and it will secure to all nationalities inhabiting Russia the right of self-determination.

The Congress resolves that all local authority shall be transferred to the Soviets of Workers', Soldiers', and Peasants' Deputies, which are charged with the task of enforcing revolutionary order.

The Congress calls upon the soldiers in the trenches to be watchful and steadfast. The Congress of Soviets is confident that the revolutionary army will know how to defend the revolution against all imperialistic attempts until the new government has concluded a democratic peace which it is proposing directly to all nations.

The new government will take every measure to provide the revolutionary army with all necessities, by means of a determined policy of requisition from and taxation of the propertied classes. Care will be taken to improve the position of the soldiers' families.

The Kornilovists—Kerensky, Kaledin, and others—are endeavoring to lead troops against Petrograd. Several regiments, deceived by Kerensky, have already joined the insurgents.

Soldiers! Resist Kerensky, who is a Kornilovist! Be on guard!

Railwaymen! Stop all echelons sent by Kerensky against Petrograd!

Soldiers, Workers, Employees! The fate of the Revolution and democratic peace is in your hands!

Long live the Revolution!

THE ALL-RUSSIAN CONGRESS OF SOVIETS OF WORKERS' AND SOLDIERS' DEPUTIES
DELEGATES FROM THE PEASANTS' SOVIETS[95]

While these events were taking place at the Winter Palace and Smolny, Kerensky was striving to organize on the Northern front a force loyal to the Provisional Government and willing to march against the Bolsheviks. His efforts, which began on the 7th and continued for several days, are described in the following chapter. At Moscow the Bolshe-

[94] For an explanation of this term, see p. 129, n. 108.

[95] In *Izvestiia*, No. 208, November 9, 1917, p. 3, this decree appears over the signature of the Military Revolutionary Committee.

viks had closed the principal bourgeois newspapers and little news from Petrograd appeared even in the Socialist organs. A decision of the Moscow telegraph workers to hold up all messages from the capital not only deprived the city of authentic news but cut off the local Bolsheviks from communication with the Central Committee of the party. The Moscow M.R. Committee occupied the arsenal and the Kremlin, and the latter was surrounded by the forces of the anti-Bolshevik Committee of Public Safety. Proclamations were issued that power was in the hands of this committee. A telegram from the Don region said that Kaledin, Ataman of the Don Cossacks, had assumed power pending the re-establishment of the Provisional Government.[96]

In Petrograd, November 8 passed quietly with patrols of the M.R. Committee circulating in the streets. With a few exceptions the morning papers appeared, all of which except the Bolshevik organs criticized or violently condemned the seizure of power.[97] The Menshevik Central Committee issued a protest against the seizure of power and the old Central Executive Committee declared that the acts of the Second Congress of Soviets were illegal.[98] The opponents of the Bolsheviks met at the City Duma where it was decided to establish house committees authorized to resist with arms any invasion of the premises. During the day there was a session of the Bolshevik Central Committee which discussed the composition of the government and relations with the Socialist groups, and at 8:00 P.M. the second and last session of the Second Congress of Soviets opened at Smolny. Kamenev read the following decrees issued in the name of the Congress:

[96] See below, p. 404.

[97] *Izvestiia,* appearing for the last time under the control of the old Central Executive Committee of the Soviets, again characterized the Bolshevik success as a "mad adventure." The following day the Bolsheviks were in control of *Izvestiia* in the name of the new Central Executive Committee. (Golder, p. 619; cf. Reed, pp. 112–16.)

[98] A. G. Shliapnikov, "Oktiabrskii perevorot i stavka," in *Krasnyi Arkhiv,* VIII (1925), 154; Oldenbourg, pp. 223–24.

ABOLITION OF CAPITAL PUNISHMENT[99]

[November 8, 1917]

Capital punishment, restored by Kerensky on the front, is hereby abolished. Fullest freedom of agitation on the front is restored. All soldiers and revolutionary officers who are now under arrest charged with a so-called "political crime" are to be released immediately.[100]

TRANSFER OF AUTHORITY IN THE PROVINCES TO THE SOVIETS[101]

[November 8, 1917]

By decree of the All-Russian Congress of Soviets all members of land committees under arrest are hereby set free. The commissars who arrested them are subject to arrest.

Henceforth all authority belongs to the Soviets. The commissars of the [Provisional] Government are removed. All chairmen of the Soviets are to communicate directly with the revolutionary government.

All-Russian Congress of Soviets

After representatives of the Menshevik-Internationalists and other groups had stated their reasons for leaving the Congress or remaining in it, Lenin was given the floor to speak on the peace declaration.

LENIN'S SPEECH ON THE PEACE DECLARATION

The question of peace is a burning question, the most pressing question of the present day. Much has been said and written [about it] and

99 *Vtoroi Vserossiiskii Sezd Sovetov R. i S.D.*, p. 94.

100 ". . . . When he [Lenin] learned of this first legislative act his anger knew no bounds. 'This is madness,' he repeated. 'How can we accomplish a revolution without shooting? Do you think you can settle with your enemies if you disarm? What repressive measures have you then? Imprisonment? Who pays any attention to that in a time of bourgeois war when every party hopes for victory?' Kamenief [Kamenev] tried to show that it was only a question of the repeal of the death penalty that Kerensky had introduced especially for deserting soldiers. But Lenin was not to be appeased. . . . . 'It is a mistake,' he repeated, 'an inadmissible weakness. Pacifist illusion. . . . .' He proposed changing the decree at once. We told him this would make an extraordinarily unfavorable impression. Finally someone said: 'The best thing is to resort to shooting only when there is no other way.' And it was left at that." Trotsky, *Lenin*, New York, 1925, pp. 133–34.

101 *Vtoroi Vserossiiskii Sezd Sovetov R. i S.D.*, p. 95.

all of you have probably considered it not a little. Allow me, therefore, to proceed at once to the reading of the declaration which the government you have chosen is going to issue.[102]

[PROCLAMATION]

The Workers' and Peasants' Government, created by the revolution of November 6–7, and drawing its strength from the Soviets of Workers', Soldiers', and Peasants' Deputies, proposes to all warring peoples and their governments to begin at once negotiations leading to a just democratic peace.

A just and democratic peace for which the great majority of wearied, tormented, and war-exhausted toilers and laboring classes of all belligerent countries are thirsting, a peace which the Russian workers and peasants have so loudly and insistently demanded since the overthrow of the Tsar's monarchy, such a peace the government considers to be an immediate peace without annexations (i.e., without the seizure of foreign territory and the forcible annexation of foreign nationalities) and without indemnities.

The Russian Government proposes to all warring peoples that this kind of peace be concluded at once; it also expresses its readiness to take immediately, without the least delay, all decisive steps pending the final confirmation of all the terms of such a peace by the plenipotentiary assemblies of all countries and all nations.

By annexation or seizure of foreign territory the government, in accordance with the legal concepts of democracy in general and of the working class in particular, understands any incorporation of a small and weak nationality by a large and powerful state without a clear, definite, and voluntary expression of agreement and desire by the weak nationality, regardless of the time when such forcible incorporation took place, regardless also of how developed or how backward is the nation forcibly attached or forcibly detained within the frontiers of the [larger] state, and, finally, regardless whether or not this large nation is located in Europe or in distant lands beyond the seas.

If any nation whatsoever is detained by force within the boundaries of a certain state, and if [that nation], contrary to its expressed desire—whether such desire is made manifest in the press, national assemblies, party relations, or in protests and uprisings against national oppression—is not given the right to determine the form of its state life by free voting and completely free from the presence of the troops of the annexing or stronger state and without the least pressure, then the adjoining of that nation by the stronger state is annexation, i.e., seizure by force and violence.

[102] *Vtoroi Vserossiiskii Sezd Sovetov R. i S.D.*, p. 59.

The government considers that to continue this war simply to decide how to divide the weak nationalities among the powerful and rich nations which had seized them would be the greatest crime against humanity, and it solemnly announces its readiness to sign at once the terms of peace which will end this war on the indicated conditions, equally just for all nationalities without exception.

At the same time the government declares that it does not regard the conditions of peace mentioned above as an ultimatum; that is, it is ready to consider any other conditions, insisting, however, that such be proposed by any of the belligerents as soon as possible, and that they be expressed in the clearest terms, without ambiguity or secrecy.

The government abolishes secret diplomacy, expressing, for its part, the firm determination to carry on all negotiations absolutely openly and in view of all the people. It will proceed at once to publish all secret treaties ratified or concluded by the government of landlords and capitalists from March to November 7, 1917. All the provisions of these secret treaties, in so far as they have for their object the securing of benefits and privileges to the Russian landlords and capitalists—which was true in a majority of cases—and retaining or increasing the annexation by the Great Russians, the government declares absolutely and immediately annulled.

While addressing to the governments and peoples of all countries the proposal to begin at once open peace negotiations, the government, for its part, expresses its readiness to carry on these negotiations by written communications, by telegraph, by parleys of the representatives of different countries, or at a conference of such representatives. To facilitate such negotiations the government appoints its plenipotentiary representative to neutral countries.

The government proposes to all governments and peoples of all belligerent countries to conclude an armistice at once; at the same time it considers it desirable that this armistice should be concluded for a period of not less than three months—that is, a period during which it would be entirely possible to complete the negotiations for peace with the participation of representatives of all peoples and nationalities which were drawn into the war or forced to take part in it, as well as to call the plenipotentiary assemblies of people's representatives in every country for the final ratification of the peace terms.

In making these peace proposals to the government and peoples of all warring countries, the Provisional Government of Workers and Peasants of Russia appeals particularly to the class-conscious workers of the three most advanced nations of mankind, who are also the largest states participating in the present war—England, France, and Germany. The workers of these countries have rendered the greatest possible service to the cause of progress and socialism by the great example of the Chartist movement in England, several revolutions of universal historic significance accomplished by the French proletariat, and, finally, the heroic struggle against the Law of Exceptions in Germany, a struggle which was prolonged, stubborn, and disciplined, which could be held up as an example for the workers of the whole world, and which aimed at the creation of proletarian mass organizations in Germany.[103] All these examples of proletarian heroism and historic achievement serve us as a guaranty that the workers of these three countries will understand the tasks which lie before them by way of liberating humanity from the horrors of war and its consequences, and that by their resolute, unselfishly energetic efforts in various directions these workers will help us to bring to a successful end the cause of peace, and, together with this, the cause of the liberation of the toiling and exploited masses from all forms of slavery and all exploitation.[104]

The Workers' and Peasants' Government created by the revolution of November 6–7 and drawing its strength from the Soviets of Workers', Soldiers', and Peasants' Deputies must begin peace negotiations at once. Our appeal must be directed to the governments as well as to the peoples. We cannot ignore the governments, because this would delay the conclusion of peace, a thing which a people's government does not dare to do, but at the same time we have no right not to appeal to the peoples. Everywhere governments and peoples are at arm's length; we must, therefore, help the peoples to take a hand in [settling] the question of peace and war. We shall of course stand by our program of peace without annexations and without indemnities. We shall not relinquish [that program], but we must deprive our enemies of the possibility of saying that their conditions are different and that they do not wish, therefore, to enter into negotiations with us. No, we must dislodge them from that advantageous position by not presenting them our conditions in the form of an ultimatum. For this reason we have included a statement to the effect that we are ready to consider any condition of peace, in fact, every proposal. Consideration, of course, does not necessarily mean acceptance. We shall submit [the proposals] for consideration to the Constituent Assembly, which will then decide, officially, what can and what cannot be granted. We have to fight against the hypocrisy of the governments, which, while talking about peace and justice, actually carry on wars of conquest and plunder. Not one single government will tell you what it really means. But we are opposed to secret diplomacy and can afford to act openly before all people. We do not now close nor have we ever closed our eyes to the difficulties.

[103] In *Sobranie Uzakonenii i Rasporiazhenii Rabochego i Krestianskogo Pravitelstva,* 1917, No. 1, p. 3 (second edition), the construction of the last two sentences has been altered. (This publication will hereafter be cited as *S.U.R.*)

[104] *Izvestiia,* No. 208, November 9, 1917, p. 1.

Wars cannot be ended by a refusal [to fight]; they cannot be ended by one side alone. We are proposing an armistice for three months—though we are not rejecting a shorter period—[in the hope] that this will give the suffering army at least a breathing spell and will make possible the calling of popular meetings in all civilized countries to discuss the conditions [of peace].[105]

Representatives of the Socialist-Revolutionists of the Left, the Internationalists, and other groups supported the resolution which after some debate the Assembly passed unanimously to the accompaniment of loud cheers. The delegates then sang the "International" and gave Lenin a great ovation. After the chanting of the funeral march in honor of the victims of the struggle, Lenin took the floor to speak on the land decree.[106]

LENIN'S SPEECH ON THE LAND DECREE

[November 8, 1917, 2:00 A.M.]

The revolution has conclusively demonstrated how important it is to formulate clearly the land question. The armed insurrection of the Second (November) Revolution has clearly shown us that the land must be turned over to the peasants. A crime was committed by the government that has just been overthrown and by the parties of compromisers, the Mensheviks and the Socialist-Revolutionists, who, under various pretexts, postponed the solution of the land question and brought the country to the verge of ruin and a peasant uprising. How false and basely deceitful their words sounded when they talked about pogroms and anarchy in the village! Where and when did intelligent policies produce pogroms and anarchy? If the government had proceeded intelligently and if its measures had aimed to meet the needs of the poorest peasants, would there have been any uprising of the peasant masses? But all the measures of the government, approved by the soviets led by men like Avxentiev and Dan, have been opposed to the interests of the peasants and have forced them to rebel.

Having provoked the insurrection, they [supporters of the Provisional Government] began to howl about pogroms and anarchy which they themselves had brought about. They wanted to quell [anarchy] with blood and iron, but instead they themselves were overthrown by the armed insurrection of the revolutionary soldiers, sailors, and workers. The gov-

105 *Vtoroi Vserossiiskii Sezd Sovetov R. i S.D.*, p. 62.

106 Oldenbourg, pp. 236–42; cf. Reed, pp. 130–33.

ernment of the workers' and peasants' revolution must first of all solve the question of land—the solution of which will pacify and make content immense masses of poor peasants. I shall read to you the points of the decree which your Soviet Government is about to proclaim. One of the sections of that decree includes the Land Mandate to the land committees based on two hundred and forty-two petitions of local Soviets of Peasants' Deputies.[107]

The Land Decree

1. The landlord's right to the land is hereby abolished without compensation.

2. All landlords' estates, all lands, udel,[108] monastery and church—with all their live stock and inventory, and all buildings with all their accessories are transferred to the volost land committees and the uezd Soviets of Peasants' Deputies until the Constituent Assembly meets.

3. Any damage done to the confiscated property which henceforth belongs to the whole people shall be considered a grave offense punishable by the revolutionary tribunals. The uezd Soviets of Peasants' Deputies shall take all necessary measures to preserve the strictest order during the confiscation of the landlords' estates; they shall determine what estates are liable to confiscation as well as the extent of that liability; they shall draw up a detailed inventory of the confiscated property and guard all the farming property on the land, including all buildings, implements, cattle, supplies, etc.

4. The following Land Mandate drawn up by the editorial board of the *Izvestiia* of the All-Russian Soviet of Peasants' Deputies on the basis of two hundred and forty-two peasant petitions and published in the *Izvestiia,* No. 88, September 1, 1917, shall everywhere regulate the realization of the great land reforms until their final solution by the Constituent Assembly.[109]

Concerning the Land

The land question in its full scope is to be settled by the All-Russian Constituent Assembly.

The most equitable settlement is as follows:

1. The right of private ownership of land is abolished forever. Land cannot be sold, bought, leased, mortgaged, or alienated in any manner whatsoever. All lands—state, udel, cabinet,[110] monastery, church, pos-

107 *Vtoroi Vserossiiskii Sezd Sovetov R. i S.D.,* p. 69.

108 Lands used for the support of members of the imperial family except the immediate family of the Emperor.

109 This mandate reflected S.R. rather than Bolshevik agrarian policy.

110 Lands used for the support of the immediate family of the Emperor.

sessional,[111] seigniorial, private, communal, peasant, etc.—are alienated without compensation, become the property of the people, and are turned over for the use of those who till them.

Persons who have suffered from the loss of property are entitled to public aid only during the time necessary for their readjustment to the changed conditions of existence.

2. All the underground resources, minerals, petroleum, coal, salt, etc., as well as forests and water of national importance, are transferred to the state for its exclusive use. All small streams, lakes, forests, etc., are transferred to the communes for their use on condition that they be administered by the organs of local self-government.

3. Intensively cultivated holdings — orchards, plantations, gardens, nurseries, greenhouses, etc.—are to be not divided but turned into model farms and, depending upon their size and importance, handed over to the state or the commune.

Small private estates and city and village land in fruit or truck gardens remain in the possession of their present owners, but the size of these holdings and the amount of tax to be paid on them shall be determined by law.

4. Stud farms, state and private farms for breeding thoroughbred stock, poultry, etc., are confiscated, nationalized, and, depending upon their size and importance, turned over for the exclusive use of either the state or the commune. The question of indemnification is to be settled by the Constituent Assembly.

5. The entire inventory and live stock of confiscated lands, depending upon size and importance, is turned over without indemnification for the exclusive use of the state or the commune. The confiscation of the equipment does not apply to small landholding peasants.

6. All Russian citizens (irrespective of sex) who are willing to till the land, either by themselves or with the assistance of their families or in collective groups, are entitled to the use of the land, as long as they are able to cultivate it. Hired labor is not permitted. In case a member of a rural commune is accidentally incapacitated for a period of two years it becomes the duty of the rural commune to help him until he recovers, by collectively tilling his land. Farmers who, on account of old age or invalidism, have lost forever the capacity to till the soil lose their right to its use but receive instead a state pension.

7. The use of the land is to follow the principle of equality, i.e., the land is to be divided among the toilers in accordance with the consump-

[111] From the Russian "possessionnaia," which has reference to land granted by the state to private individuals for the purpose of building industrial establishments especially in the mining industry. Such land could not be sold by the owner.

tion-labor standard[112] and in relation to local conditions. The form of land utilization is entirely optional and each village and hamlet is free to decide whether land shall be held collectively or as homesteads, in the form of artels or separate farms.

8. All the alienated land goes into one national land fund. Its distribution among the toilers is in charge of the local and central self-governing bodies, beginning with the democratically organized village and city communities and ending with the central regional institutions.

The land fund is subject to periodical redistribution, conditioned upon the rise in population, the increase in production, and the improvement in the rural economy.

In changing the boundaries of land allotments, the original nuclei of the allotments [made after the emancipation of the serfs] shall not be disturbed.

The land of members passing out of the community reverts to the land fund, but the preferential right to receive the holdings of those who passed out goes to the nearest relatives and persons designated by the departed.

When the land reverts to the land fund, there shall be compensation for the fertilization and improvements (fundamental improvements) made on it in so far as these improvements have not yet yielded returns.

If in certain localities the available land fund is inadequate to supply the needs of the whole local population, the surplus population must emigrate.

The state shall take upon itself the organization of the emigration as well as the expenses connected with such emigration, including supplying of settlers with implements. The settlers shall be taken in the following order: landless peasants volunteering to go, undesirable members of the commune, army deserters *et al.*, and, lastly, those chosen by lot or who agree to go.

All that has been stated in this mandate, being the expression of the absolute will of an overwhelming majority of the intelligent peasants of Russia, is proclaimed a provisional law, which, pending the meeting of the Constituent Assembly, is to be enacted at once except as regards those parts which require time and which are left to the discretion of uezd Soviets of Peasants' Deputies.

The lands of peasants and Cossacks of average means shall not be confiscated.[113]

I hear voices raised here declaring that both the decree and the land mandate were drafted by the Socialist-Revolutionists. Well, suppose

[112] For an explanation of the term "consumption-labor standard," see below, p. 676.

[113] *Izvestiia,* No. 209, November 10, 1917, p. 1.

they were? What does it matter who drafted them! As a democratic government we cannot ignore the resolutions of the lower strata of the people, even though we may not be in sympathy with them. In actual practice the peasants will find out for themselves where the truth lies. And even if the peasants should continue to follow the Socialist-Revolutionists and give that party a majority in the Constituent Assembly, we shall say to them: Good and well! Life is the best teacher; it will show in the long run who is right. Let the peasants from their end proceed to solve that question; we shall proceed similarly and life will force us to approach each other in the common stream of revolutionary creative activity. In the forging of new institutions, we must follow in the footsteps of life, allowing complete creative freedom to the masses. . . . . We do not go into detail now because what we are concerned with is a decree and not a program of action. Russia is vast, and local conditions vary considerably; we trust that the peasantry, when left to itself, will know better how to solve the question. Whether it be according to our ideas or in the direction of the Socialist-Revolutionist program does not matter. The essential point is to give the peasantry a firm conviction that there are no more *pomeshchiks* in the villages, and that it is now for the peasants themselves to solve all questions and to build their own life.[114]

Members of the Central Executive Committee of the Peasants' Deputies and a representative of the 3d Army protested against the arrest of the Socialist members of the Provisional Government. A peasant from Tver justified their arrest and declared that all the members of the Peasant Executive Committee should be arrested. Trotsky also defended the actions of the M.R. Committee in making the arrests. The session then recessed for an hour. About 2:00 A.M. the session was resumed. There were four or five brief statements from the floor on the peace and land questions, and then the chairman put the land decree to a vote. There were eight abstentions and only one vote in opposition. Next on the order of business was the organization of the government. Kamenev briefly explained the plan and presented the following proposal for a Provisional Workers' and Peasants' Government:[115]

[114] *Vtoroi Vserossisskii Sezd Sovetov R. i S.D.*, pp. 72–73.

[115] *Ibid.*, pp. 73–79; Oldenbourg, pp. 244–47; Reed, pp. 134–38.

THE SOVIET OF PEOPLE'S COMMISSARS (SOVNARKOM)[116]

By decree of the All-Russian Congress of Soviets a Provisional Workers' and Peasants' Government, to be known as the Soviet of People's Commissars, is formed to govern the country until the meeting of the Constituent Assembly.

The administration of the different departments of state shall be intrusted to special commissions, whose membership will insure the realization of the program of the Congress in close co-operation with the organized masses of workers, soldiers, sailors, peasants, and other employees. Government power shall be vested in a collegium of chairmen of those commissions, i.e., the Soviet of People's Commissars.

Control over the acts of the People's Commissars and the right of recall belong to the All-Russian Congress of Soviets of Workers', Soldiers', and Peasants' Deputies and its Central Executive Committee.

For the present the Soviet of People's Commissars is made up of the following persons: *President of the Soviet,* Vladimir Ulianov (Lenin); *Commissar of the Interior,* A. I. Rykov; *Commissar of Agriculture,* V. P. Miliutin; *Commissar of Labor,* A. G. Shliapnikov; *Commissar of War and Navy,* Committee made up of V. A. Ovseenko (Antonov), N. V. Krylenko, and P. E. Dybenko; *Commissar of Commerce and Industry,* V. P. Nogin; *Commissar of Education,* A. V. Lunacharsky; *Commissar of Finance,* I. I. Skvortsov (Stepanov); *Commissar of Foreign Affairs,* L. D. Bronstein (Trotsky)[117]; *Commissar of Justice,* G. I. Oppokov (Lomov); *Commissar of Food,* I. A. Teodorovich; *Commissar of Post and Telegraph,* N. P. Avilov (Glebov); *Chairman for Nationalities,* I. V. Dzhugashvili (Stalin); *Commissar of Railways* (not named for the time being).

[116] *Vtoroi Vserossiiskii Sezd Sovetov R. i S.D.,* pp. 79–80. Trotsky traces the origin of the name of the new government to the following conversation between Lenin and himself: "The power in Petersburg was won. Therefore it was a question of forming the government. 'What name shall we use?' Lenin considered aloud. 'Not minister, that is a repulsive, worn-out designation.' 'We might say commissars,' I suggested, 'but there are too many commissars now. Perhaps chief commissar. . . . . No, "chief" sounds bad. What about people's commissars?' . . . . 'People's Commissars? As for me, I like it. And the government as a whole?' 'Council of People's Commissars?' 'Council of People's Commissars,' Lenin repeated. 'That is splendid. That smells of revolution.'" (Trotsky, *Lenin,* p. 132.)

[117] ". . . . at the meeting of the Central Committee of the party, he [Lenin] proposed that I be elected chairman of the Soviet of People's Commissaries. I sprang to my feet, protesting—the proposal seemed to me so unexpected and inappropriate. 'Why not?' Lenin insisted. 'You were at the head of the Petrograd Soviet that seized the power.' I moved to reject his proposal without debating it. The motion was carried." (Trotsky, *My Life,* p. 339.)

AVILOV PROPOSES A SOCIALIST COALITION[118]

The fate of our revolution is being sealed at this very moment and it is only proper that we should ask ourselves calmly and without emotion where we are going and what is happening around us.

The ease with which the Coalition Government was overthrown is not to be explained by the strength of the Left [wing] of the democracy but solely by the fact that the government was incapable of giving the people bread and peace. Similarly the Left wing of the democracy will be in a position to maintain itself in power only if it can solve these problems. . . . . But the new government cannot give the people bread, since bread is very scarce. Whatever bread is left in the country is concentrated in the hands of the rich and middle peasantry, and you can get that bread . . . . only in two ways: either you must give the village what it needs . . . . or you must secure the active support of the strata of the peasantry mentioned above . . . . we can count on the support of the well-to-do peasantry . . . . only if the latter are made to feel that the new authority is their own and that the aims of the new government correspond to their own interests.

It is necessary [therefore] to form a government which will be supported by the peasantry as a whole. . . . . The solution of the land question by itself will not make certain the government's success; the poor peasants without implements cannot advantageously use the land.

As for peace, that will be even more difficult. The Allied governments refuse to enter into relations with the new government and will never accept the proposal to negotiate peace. The [Allied] ambassadors are getting ready to leave; this means a break with the Allied Powers. The new government will find itself isolated and its proposals will remain hanging in mid-air. It is impossible to count on the effective support of the proletariat and the democracy of the enemy or the Allied countries because they are far from being revolutionary in spirit and have even proved incapable of calling the Stockholm Conference. The representatives of the Left wing of the German Social-Democrats very plainly say that a revolution in Germany is impossible during the war.

As a result of the isolation which is confronting Russia, we shall have either a defeat of the Russian army by the Germans and the patching up of a peace between the Austro-German and Anglo-French coalitions at Russia's expense, or a separate peace between Russia and Germany. In either case the conditions of peace will be most intolerable for Russia; nor is peace likely to come soon, unless we are willing to surrender completely to the will of the German victors.

[118] *Vtoroi Vserossiiskii Sezd Sovetov R. i S.D.*, pp. 80–82. Avilov spoke for the United Social-Democrat Internationalists and the Menshevik-Internationalists who had not left the Congress.

To overcome these great difficulties, to give bread and peace to the country, and to safeguard the conquests of the revolution we need the united effort of the majority of the people. But for the present the leading democratic groups have split into two camps—the Left wing remaining at the Congress of Soviets at the Smolny and the Right wing concentrating in the City Duma under the banner of the Committee to Save the Country and the Revolution. At the same time the reactionary Kornilov-Kaledin forces are assuming the offensive. In order to save the revolution it is imperative to form at once a government drawing its support from the whole, or at least the majority of the revolutionary democracy.

[On behalf of the Social-Democrats (Internationalists) Avilov introduced a resolution to appoint a provisional executive committee to form a government by an agreement with those groups of the revolutionary democracy that were represented in the Congress. This resolution was not passed. Karelin, speaking for the Socialist-Revolutionists of the Left, opposed a one-party government and explained the refusal of his party to enter the government on the ground that it could thus act more effectively in mediating between the Bolsheviks and the other groups. Trotsky took the floor to reply to Avilov and Karelin.]

TROTSKY OPPOSES COALITION[119]

[November 8, 1917]

. . . . A few days ago when the question of the uprising was raised, we were told that we were isolating ourselves, that we were drifting on the rocks. . . . . Against us were the counter-revolutionary bands and the different moderate groups. One part of the Socialist-Revolutionists of the Left worked with us . . . . but the other took a position of waiting neutrality. Nevertheless the revolution . . . . gained an almost bloodless victory. If it had been really true that we were isolated, how did it happen that we conquered so easily? No [it is not true]. Not we but the [Provisional] Government and the democracy, or rather the quasi-democracy, ... were isolated from the masses. By their hesitations and compromises they lost contact with the real democracy. It is our great virtue as a party that we have a coalition with the [masses] . . . . with the workers, soldiers, and poorest peasants.

Political combinations come and go, but the fundamental interests of the classes remain, and the victory goes to the political party that understands and satisfies these fundamental interests. . . . . If a coalition is necessary, it must be a coalition with our garrison, especially with the peasants and working classes. Of this kind of a coalition we can be proud. It has stood the test of fire. . . . .

[119] *Vtoroi Vserossiiskii Sezd Sovetov R. i S.D.*, pp. 84–87.

Comrade Avilov spoke of the enormous problems before us, and as a solution he proposed a coalition government. He did not, however, make it clear just what kind of a coalition he had in mind. . . . . A coalition with Dan and Lieber . . . . would weaken rather than strengthen the revolution. . . . . Comrade Avilov spoke of [a coalition with] the peasants. Which peasants? . . . . Today we heard a peasant request . . . . the arrest of Avxentiev. We shall have to decide whether to form a coalition with the peasant . . . . who asks for the arrest of Avxentiev or with Avxentiev himself, who filled the prisons with members of the land committees.

A coalition with the "Kulak" [wealthy peasant] we refuse . . . . in the name of the workers and poorest peasants. If the revolution has taught us anything, it has taught us that only through a coalition with the workers and poorest peasants can we succeed. Those who follow the phantom of coalition will in the end lose touch with real life. . . . .

Notwithstanding the fact that the defensists [moderate Socialists] of all shades used every means in their struggle against us, we did not turn against them. We proposed that the Congress as a whole should assume authority. . . . . Our party held out its hand, with the gunpowder still in it, and said: "Come, let's seize the power together"; but instead they [moderate Socialists] ran to the City Duma to join the counter-revolutionists. What are these men but betrayers of the revolution? We shall never form a union with them.

Comrade Avilov said that peace can be attained only through a coalition. . . . . There are two ways of obtaining peace. One is to bring the Allied and enemy countries face to face with the material and spiritual forces of the revolution, and the other is to form a union with Skobelev and . . . . Tereshchenko, which amounts to a complete submission to imperialism. It has been said that in our peace decree we address at the same time both the governments and the people. . . . . Of course, we have no hope of having any influence . . . . on the imperialistic governments, but so long as they exist we cannot ignore them. Our whole hope is that our revolution will kindle a European revolution. If the rising of the people does not crush imperialism, then we will surely be crushed. There is no doubt about that. The Russian Revolution will either cause a revolution in the West, or the capitalists of all countries will strangle our [revolution]. (*"There is still a third!" shouts someone.*) The third—that's the course of the Central Executive Committee which holds out one hand to the workers of Western Europe and the other to the Kishkins and Konovalovs. It is the course of falsehood and hypocrisy which we will never adopt.

We do not say peace will be concluded on the day when the European workers rise. It is possible that the bourgeoisie, frightened by the approaching revolution . . . . will hasten to conclude peace. The day and hour of the rising are not known. . . . . The important thing is to decide on a course of action. Its underlying principles are the same whether used in foreign or domestic policies. It is this: The Union of the Oppressed Everywhere. That is our course.

The Second Congress of Soviets has worked out a program to be carried through. To all those who really desire to help carry out that program . . . . we say: "Dear comrades, we are brothers-in-arms, we shall be with you to the end." (*Loud applause.*)

Before the question of the composition of the government could be put to a vote, a representative of the All-Russian Central Committee of the Union of Railway Workers (Vikzhel) demanded the floor. Kamenev, the chairman, refused to recognize him. This caused great commotion in the meeting; some demanded that the railwaymen be given the floor, others opposed. Finally the Vikzhel representative was allowed to speak to explain his vote. After reviewing the services of the railway union to the revolution and its support of the Soviets, he stated that, at a meeting on November 8, Vikzhel, in view of the doubtful legality of the Congress of Soviets, and in the absence of a central authority, had decided that it was opposed to the seizure of power by a single party; that the power ought to be socialist and revolutionary and responsible to the whole revolutionary democracy; that, pending the formation of such a government, Vikzhel would take over the activities of the Ministry of Communications and the supervision and economic management of the railways. The representative of Vikzhel concluded by declaring that the Union would not permit the transportation of troops except when authorized by the Central Executive Committee (which had opposed the seizure of power) or by the plenipotentiary body to be formed by the City Duma and the other revolutionary organizations. If measures of repression were taken against the railway men, they would cut off the food supplies of Petrograd. Kamenev defended the legality of the Second Congress. Other representatives of railway workers charged that Vikzhel no longer represented the workers who had long since repudiated it.

The debate was closed, the question of the composition of the government was put to a vote, and, overwhelmingly, the Congress approved the Bolsheviks' list of People's Commissars.[120]

The Second Congress then proceeded to the formation of a new Central Executive Committee to replace the old committee elected by the First All-Russian Congress in June 1917. A partial list of the members of the new C.E.C. was announced and was published in *Izvestiia* on the 16th. The 110 members were divided among the parties as follows: Bolsheviks, 61; Socialist - Revolutionists of the Left, 29; United Social-Democrats (Internationalists), 6; Ukrainian Socialists, 3; Peasant representatives, 5; Navy, 2; trade unions, 1; United Socialists, 1; others, 2. As the question of the participation of other Socialists was unsettled, the organization of the committee was only tentative.

At 5:15 A.M. Kamenev declared the Second Congress closed. The delegates cheered the revolution and socialism and quickly dispersed.

[120] Oldenbourg, pp. 255–58; cf. Reed, pp. 143–44.

CHAPTER III

THE COUNTER-ATTACK

The events of November 7 in Petrograd were a tremendous victory for the Bolsheviks, but that victory was by no means conclusive. During the week of November 7–15 they faced the active though divided opposition of a majority of the leaders of other political groups, of Vikzhel and of the unions of employees in government offices. They had to meet an uprising of the cadets from the military schools and to defend the capital against the movement of troops which Kerensky was trying to organize and which got under way while the Second Congress of Soviets was still in session. During this week also Moscow Bolsheviks gained control of the ancient capital. Elsewhere events recorded Bolshevik victories in many industrial centers; in some regions coalitions reigned; in others representatives of the nationalities and the Cossacks assumed the power. In general it was recognized that the Provisional Government was no more, but there was by no means a general acceptance of the new order proclaimed in Petrograd.

A. Kerensky at the Northern Front

Kerensky had left Petrograd at midday on the 7th in the expectation of meeting near the city the troops he had ordered from the front. At Gatchina, thirty miles south of Petrograd, the Prime Minister found no troops from the front but, instead, a decidedly hostile atmosphere. He left at once, barely escaping arrest by the local Military Revolutionary Committee, and drove on to Pskov, the headquarters of the Northern front, where he arrived about ten that evening. At Pskov he learned that a Military Revolutionary Committee hostile to the Provisional Government had been formed and that it was in close contact with Cheremisov, the general commanding on this front.[1] He learned also that the General had countermanded the orders for the dispatch of troops to the capital and could not or would not aid the government. Cheremisov further advised Kerensky to leave Pskov, where his arrest was inevitable. During the evening Kerensky issued an order suggesting the possibility of a reorganization of the Provisional Government and urging all military and naval units to remain at their posts and obey orders.[2]

During the night of November 7–8 Krasnov, commander of the Third Cavalry Corps, arrived at Pskov to clear up the contradictory orders concerning the advance against the Bolsheviks. He found Kerensky and with him left for Ostrov.[3]

CHEREMISOV COUNTERMANDS KERENSKY'S ORDERS

[Conversation of General Dukhonin by Direct Wire with the Headquarters of the Northern Front, Night of November 7–8, 1917][4]

General Lukirsky, Chief-of-Staff of the Northern Front, is at the apparatus: . . . . At ten o'clock this evening the Glavkosev [Commander-in-Chief of the Northern Front, General Cheremisov] countermanded all orders of the Supreme Commander-in-Chief relative to the movement of troops to Petrograd. Copies of these last instructions have been forwarded to you. I do not know for what reasons the change has been made. . . . . The army units affected by the order have either been detained at their points of entrainment or turned back. The commander of the Third Cavalry Corps[5] . . . . is perplexed by this new order. In his communication to me he says that he had direct instructions from the Supreme Commander-in-Chief to lead the 1st Don [Cossack Division]

[1] In the course of the evening this committee had reported to the M.R. Committee in Petrograd that the army would not send troops to support the Provisional Government and that Cheremisov was well disposed toward the committee. Oldenbourg, pp. 186–87.

[2] *Ibid.*, pp. 195–96.

[3] Kerensky, *The Catastrophe*, pp. 340–43; P. N. Krasnov, "Na vnutrennem fronte," in *A.R.R.*, I (1922), 149–51.

[4] *A.R.R.*, VII (1922), 297–98; also "Oktiabr na fronte," in *Krasnyi Arkhiv*, XXIII (1927), 160–61.

[5] General Krasnov.

to Petrograd. We decided that he should come to Pskov at one o'clock tonight to see the Glavkosev. . . . .

[Dukhonin]: I cannot understand the reasons for such a change. I shall wait for the Glavkosev to clear up the matter. Where are the cyclist battalions now? . . . .

[Cheremisov coming to the wire.]

[Cheremisov]: Greetings, Nikolai Nikolaevich! What were you saying?

[Dukhonin]: General Lukirsky informed me just now that you have countermanded the order for the dispatch of troops to Petrograd. . . . . What were your reasons for so doing?

[Cheremisov]: This was done with the consent of the Supreme Commander-in-Chief. . . . . Have you been informed of the situation in Petrograd?

[Dukhonin]: Please tell me in detail what the situation is and where is the Supreme Commander-in-Chief at present?

[Cheremisov]: The former Provisional Government no longer exists; the government is in the hands of the Revolutionary Committee; the Cossack regiments remained passive . . . . while the armored car squad went over to the Revolutionary Committee. Tonight someone . . . . appointed Kishkin governor-general of Petrograd. Kishkin's adherence to the Cadet Party is known here on the front, and his appointment created a sharp break [in the attitude] of the army organizations at the front, not in favor of the Provisional Government. . . . . Kerensky relinquished his post and expressed the desire to hand over the office of Supreme Commander-in-Chief to me. The question, in all probability, will be settled today. Be so kind as to countermand the sending of all troops to Petrograd from other fronts. The Supreme Commander-in-Chief is with me. Is there anything you wish to tell him?

[Dukhonin]: Is it possible to call him to the wire?

[Cheremisov]: Impossible. In his own interest. . . . .

CHEREMISOV ORDERS KRASNOV TO REMAIN AT OSTROV

[Extracts from General Krasnov's Story][6]

[November 7–8, 1917]

Having issued all necessary orders . . . . I left [for the railway station of Ostrov] arriving there at 11:00 P.M. [November 7].

"Are the horses loaded?" I inquired.

"Yes," replied Colonel Popov.

"So we can start now?"

"No."

[6] P. N. Krasnov, "Na vnutrennem fronte," in *A.R.R.*, I (1922), 146–48.

"Why not? Our troop train was to leave at 11:00 P.M. . . . ."

"Not a single troop train has left yet."

"How so? What about the 9th Regiment?" . . . .

"The station-master says that he has no permission to let the troop trains through."

I went to the station-master. He was very much embarrassed and confused.

"I don't understand a thing," he said. "A telegram was received just now to detrain the troops and detain them in Ostrov."

"Whose order was it?"

"The Chief of Military Communications."

I called up Pskov. Colonel Karamyshev must have been waiting for me at the wire.

"What is it all about?"

"The Commander-in-Chief of the Northern Front gave orders to detrain the division and to detain it in Ostrov."

"But you know the order of the Supreme Commander-in-Chief to rush troops to Petrograd?"

"I do."

"Which order then shall we follow?" . . . .

There was utter confusion. It was necessary to clear up the situation. . . . . I sent for an automobile and together with Popov drove to Pskov. I arrived there late at night. . . . .

I went to the Commander-in-Chief. The upper story of his house . . . . was brilliantly lighted. . . . .

"The Commander-in-Chief is busy at the Soviet," the officer on duty informed me. "He cannot be bothered now."

"I must insist that you notify the Commander. My business cannot wait until tomorrow." . . . .

I was led to the office of the Commander-in-Chief. After waiting for some ten minutes . . . . the door opened and in came Cheremisov. His face looked gray from fatigue. His eyes were dim and he avoided looking at me. He was yawning, sometimes nervously, sometimes ostensibly, as if wishing to convey the impression of the utter triviality of the things I was about to tell him.

"The Provisional Government is in danger," I said. "We gave an oath to the Provisional Government and our duty . . . ."

Cheremisov looked at me. "The Provisional Government no longer exists," he said . . . . with emphasis as if he were trying to convince me.

"How so?" I exclaimed.

Cheremisov was silent. Then he said in a low and weary voice: "I order you to detrain your troops and remain in Ostrov. This is quite sufficient for you. Anyway, you will not be able to do a thing."

"Give me a written order, then," I said.

Cheremisov looked at me sadly, shrugged his shoulders, and stretching out his hand to me said: "My sincere advice to you is to remain in Ostrov and not to undertake anything. Believe me, that is the best thing."

Then he left.

THE SITUATION IN THE ARMIES ON THE NORTHERN FRONT

[Communication by Direct Wire from General Lukirsky, Chief-of-Staff of the Northern Front, to General Dukhonin in the Morning of November 8][7]

[Lukirsky]: .... After the orders had been issued to discontinue the dispatch of troops to Petrograd, Alexander Fedorovich [Kerensky] arrived here. He disapproved of the decision of the Commander-in-Chief of the Northern Front to stop the movement of troops to Petrograd. But it was impossible [to reissue the original order] as the telegraph station was guarded by special sentries of the Revolutionary Committee which had just come into existence in Pskov.

At 5:30 A.M., November 8, Alexander Fedorovich left for Ostrov together with the Commander of the Third Cavalry Corps [General Krasnov]. The latter had arrived here at 3:00 A.M. ....

We are in receipt of the following telegraphic communications: (1) a resolution of the .... Cossack Congress[8] violently condemning the Bolshevik uprising and calling upon all Cossacks .... to come out in defense of the country; (2) an appeal of the united organizations comprising the Socialist-Revolutionists, Social-Democrats, the Tsentroflot,[9] the army organizations of Petrograd, and the Central Executive Committee of Soviets to the same effect.

On our [front] the situation is as follows: The 12th Army has come out definitely and decisively against the Bolsheviks, declaring that it will make every effort to suppress the rebellious gang of Bolsheviks. The 1st and 5th Armies have announced that they will not defend the Provisional Government but will support the Petrograd Soviet. ....

KERENSKY ORDERS THE ADVANCE ON PETROGRAD RESUMED

[Telegram from Voitinsky, Commissar of the Provisional Government for the Northern Front, to the Stavka, November 8, 1917][10]

I wish to transmit a copy of the order issued by the Supreme Commander-in-Chief to the Commander-in-Chief of the Northern Front ....:

[7] *A.R.R.*, VII (1922), 310.

[8] In Kiev.

[9] Central Committee of the Fleet.

[10] *A.R.R.*, VII (1922), 309.

"You are hereby ordered to resume the movement of the Third Cavalry Corps to Petrograd. Supreme Commander-in-Chief Kerensky. November 8, 5:30 A.M."

In the morning of November 9, Kerensky and Krasnov with a detachment of some seven hundred Cossacks arrived in the vicinity of Gatchina. The local garrison, though Bolshevik in sympathy, offered no resistance and the town was occupied without bloodshed. Kerensky established his headquarters in the Gatchina Palace, appointed Krasnov commander of all the troops in the Petrograd district, and issued orders to the Petrograd garrison and the Commander of the Northern Front to send reinforcements.

ORDER TO THE PETROGRAD GARRISON[11]

[November 9]

I, Prime Minister of the Provisional Government and Supreme Commander-in-Chief of All the Armed Forces of the Russian Republic, have today taken charge of the loyal troops at the front.

I order all the units of the Petrograd Military District who, through ignorance or error, have joined that gang of betrayers of the country and of the revolution, to resume their duties without an hour's delay.

This order is to be read in all companies, platoons, and squadrons.

A. KERENSKY
Prime Minister of the Provisional Government
and Supreme Commander-in-Chief

KERENSKY TO THE COMMANDER OF THE NORTHERN FRONT

[Telegram of November 9, 1917][12]

Gatchina was occupied by the troops loyal to the government without any bloodshed. The Kronstadt, Semenovsky, and Izmailovsky regiments and the sailors surrendered their arms without resistance and joined the government forces. You are ordered to hasten the dispatch of troops. The soldiers of the Military Revolutionary Committee have received orders to retreat.

KERENSKY

[11] S. A. Piontkovsky, *Khrestomatiia po istorii oktiabrskoi revoliutsii,* Moscow, 1924, pp. 254–55.

[12] *Rabochaia Gazeta,* No. 198, November 19, 1917, p. 1.

CHEREMISOV URGES THE TROOPS TO REMAIN NEUTRAL

[Telegram, November 9, 1917][13]

To the Commanders of the 1st, 5th, 12th Armies, the 42d Corps, the Committee of the Fleet, and the Chief of the General Staff:

We must see to it that the army is kept out of the political struggle now going on in Petrograd. Our aim must remain as before, to hold our positions, preserving order and discipline.

CHEREMISOV

B. BOLSHEVIKS AND THEIR OPPONENTS IN PETROGRAD

The news of the taking of Gatchina reached Petrograd in the early afternoon of the 9th, stimulating the Bolsheviks to more intensive preparation for defense and encouraging their opponents. Lenin called for aid from the Russian troops in Finland and from the sailors of the Baltic fleet, the hostile press was ordered closed, and the people and the soldiers were summoned to fight Kerensky. The anti-Bolshevik organizations participating in the Committee to Save the Country and the Revolution made plans to unite the elements opposed to the new government. The union of employees in government institutions declared a strike in all administrative departments.[14]

LENIN SUMMONS AID FROM KRONSTADT AND HELSINGFORS

[Extracts from Conversation by Direct Wire with the Regional Committee of Finland and the Tsentrobalt on November 9, 1917][15]

[Lenin]: Can you send at once to Petrograd a great number of torpedo boats and other armed vessels?

The chairman of the Tsentrobalt will come to the wire directly. . . . . What news is there in Petrograd?

[Lenin]: We have received information that Kerensky's forces have taken Gatchina. In view of the fact that the Petrograd soldiers are tired we need a strong reinforcement at once.

What other news have you?

[13] "Oktiabr na fronte," in *Krasnyi Arkhiv,* XXIII (1927), 176.

[14] Materials on this strike are given in chapter iv, pp. 224–31.

[15] Lenin, *Sochineniia,* XXII, 27–29.

[Lenin]: Instead of your question "what other news have you," I expected you to say that you were ready to come and fight. . . . .

Mikhailov, chairman of the Regional Committee . . . . is at the wire. . . . .

[Mikhailov]: How many bayonets do you need?

[Lenin]: We need as many as you have, but the men must be reliable and willing to fight. How many can you send?

[Mikhailov]: We can send some 5,000, and they are sure to fight. . . . . Vice-Chairman of the Tsentrobalt is at the wire. . . . .

[Lenin]: How many torpedo boats and other armed vessels can you send?

We can send one battleship, the "Republic," and two torpedo boats. . . . .

[Lenin]: How soon?

It will take about eighteen hours. Is there an immediate urgency?

[Lenin]: Yes. The government is absolutely convinced of the necessity of the battleship coming at once and casting its anchor in the Morskoi Channel and close to shore. . . . .

MEETING OF THE COMMITTEE TO SAVE THE COUNTRY AND THE REVOLUTION

[November 9, 1917][16]

A meeting of all organizations which compose the Committee to Save the Country and the Revolution took place in the City Duma. . . . . The meeting was opened by Filipovsky, member of the Central Executive Committee. Comrade Skobelev was the principal speaker. He dealt chiefly with the measures which he thought the revolutionary democracy should adopt in order to save the country and the revolution which are being seriously menaced. . . . . It should be clear to all by now [he said] that the Soviet power is nothing but a dictatorship [directed] against the will of the proletariat and that counter-revolution can come not only from the Right but also from the Left. It is therefore necessary to unite all forces of the revolutionary democracy; the united effort of which has already resulted in the formation of the [Committee] to Save the Country and the Revolution. Skobelev then enumerated all the organizations which took part in the organization of the Committee . . . . and proceeded to define its aims.

First of all it is necessary to unite all the forces of the revolutionary democracy and to secure the calling of the Constituent Assembly at the time set. Then there is the important work of bringing about a democratic peace as soon as possible.

[16] *Delo Naroda,* No. 191, November 10, 1917, p. 2.

To accomplish these tasks it is necessary that the deputies who left the [second] Congress of Soviets should go to the provinces and organize the people. It is necessary . . . . to organize everywhere Committees to Save the Country and the Revolution . . . . especially among those organizations which control the railway transportation, the post and telegraph, and other branches of state administration. It is important, however, in doing this to exercise great caution. Already rumors are in circulation that certain generals wish to take advantage of the situation. They will first declare themselves our allies and march under our banners in order that they may overthrow us afterward. . . . .

Comrade Nikanorov, a delegate from the city of Luga, declared that he had been sent by the military committee of the Luga Soviet of Workers' and Soldiers' Deputies . . . . notwithstanding the intensive propaganda of the Bolsheviks the [Luga] Soviet had condemned the Bolshevik adventure as a criminal act. . . . . The Luga garrison had resolved to take orders only from the Central Executive Committee [of the First Congress]. At the same time the garrison demanded that the questions of peace and land be attended to immediately. Under these conditions, the garrison of Luga, which has thirty thousand men and several batteries of artillery, is ready to defend the country and the revolution. . . . .

[Comrade Weinstein of the C.E.C. argued that it was necessary to work out a detailed program before taking any action. He proposed that the meeting adjourn while the party groups held caucuses to formulate their proposals. The meeting was abruptly ended when a detachment of Red Guards and sailors invaded the premises of the Duma about 3:30 P.M.]

PROCLAMATION OF THE SOCIALIST-REVOLUTIONISTS OF THE RIGHT[17]

[November 9, 1917]

The Bolsheviks are doing everything in their power to bring about a bloody civil war. They seized power with the aid of guns, and they now perceive that only by means of guns can they retain power for any length of time.

Today they have declared that the press is "as dangerous as guns, bombs, and machine guns." They arrested the Central Committee of the Socialist-Revolutionist Party. . . . .

Their power is short-lived. They are knights of an hour. Their creation is a soap bubble. . . . . They say that their government is the government of the Soviets. *This is not true.*

[17] *Delo Naroda,* No. 192, November 10, 1917, p. 1, Evening Edition, p. 19.

The Soviets of Workers, Soldiers, and Peasants have not yet expressed their opinion. . . . .

The great Russian Revolution is bigger, more sublime, and on a wider scale than the Petrograd adventure of the Bolsheviks. Our revolution is a national revolution. . . . . The Socialist-Revolutionist Party, representing the toiling peasants, has turned away from the Bolsheviks. It is true that the Bolsheviks have painted themselves in the colors of the Socialist-Revolutionists; they have taken over our land program. But that will not help them much, because the peasants will go only with those whom they *know* and *trust*.

The toiling masses of Russia *will* secure land, peace, and freedom. . . . . But to do this there must be no civil war. The Bolshevik adventure must be brought to an end in a *peaceful manner*. There should be no shedding of blood! Their venture will die of itself. . . . .

A general strike against the Bolsheviks! Boycott them!

We should form at once a homogeneous Socialist ministry, without Bolsheviks, without the propertied classes, and with this program:

1. Liquidate the Bolshevik adventure, which, like a soap bubble, will burst at the first contact with hard facts.

2. Hand over all agricultural land to the land committees.

3. Work energetically for an early peace on the basis of no annexation, no indemnity, and self-determination.

4. Undelayed summoning of the Constituent Assembly.

Only a government such as this has a chance to prevent civil war, to gather about itself the toiling democracy not blinded by Bolshevik demagogy and capable of evaluating at its true worth the Bolshevik promises.

CALL TO THE WORKERS TO SUPPORT THE ARMY AND THE RED GUARD[18]

The Kornilovist bands of Kerensky threaten the approaches of the capital. All the necessary orders have been given to crush without mercy the counter-revolutionary attempt against the people and its revolutionary conquests.

The army and Red Guard need the immediate support of the workers.

We call on the regional Soviets and the factory committees:

1. To send a large number of workmen to dig trenches, to erect barricades, defenses, and wire obstructions.

2. To do this even if it should be necessary to close the factories.

3. To collect all the wire, barbed and smooth, and all tools necessary for digging trenches and erecting barricades.

[18] *Izvestiia,* No. 211, November 11, 1917, p. 2.

4. Those having guns to carry them.

5. To preserve the strictest discipline and to be ready to come to the aid of the army and the revolution with all your means.[19]

LEV TROTSKY
Chairman of the Petrograd Soviet of Workers' and Soldiers' Deputies and People's Commissar

NIKOLAI PODVOISKY
Chairman of the Military Revolutionary Committee, Commander of the [Petrograd] Area

The Committee to Save the Country and the Revolution replied with an appeal to the soldiers not to obey the M.R. Committee and not to oppose the advancing troops.[20] Meanwhile Krasnov's Cossacks had advanced on Tsarskoe Selo, which they occupied in the evening of the 10th almost without resistance.

PROGRESS OF THE STRUGGLE

[Bulletins of the Military Revolutionary Committee, November 10]

The ex-minister Kerensky is broadcasting reports of his victories in Gatchina. Their sole purpose is to demoralize our troops. According to our most reliable information Kerensky has only five thousand deluded Cossacks. . . . . One-half of that number refuses to advance on Petrograd, while the other is vacillating. . . . .

MILITARY REVOLUTIONARY COMMITTEE[21]

1. A battle is in progress in Tsarskoe Selo. Two of our regiments fought heroically but were compelled under pressure of superior forces to retreat to new positions . . . . near Kolpino.

2. There is fighting in the sector of Krasnoe Selo–Gatchina. The situation is favorable. Our troops are engaged in a flanking movement. Red Guards were dispatched to the aid of our troops. . . . .

3. Kerensky is making use of traitors . . . . to spread false rumors about his victories. This encouraged the counter-revolutionists to attempt the disarming of the Red Guard. There was shooting on the

[19] Trotsky says in *The History of the Russian Revolution to Brest-Litovsk*, London, [1919], p. 100, that the disorganization of the military units and their unwillingness to take part in the campaign led to the decision to appeal directly to the workers, who promptly responded.

[20] Oldenbourg, p. 282.

[21] Popov, *Oktiabrskii perevorot*, p. 224.

Nevsky Prospect yesterday at 2:00 P.M., resulting in a number of fatalities.

4. Manikovsky, former Minister of War, was set free. He consented to take charge of the technical work of the War Department under the supervision of Commissar Krylenko.[22]

THE ADVANCE ON TSARSKOE SELO

[From Krasnov's Recollections][23]

Toward the evening of November 9 I had at my disposal three platoons of the 9th, two platoons of the 10th, and one platoon of the 13th Don Regiments, eight machine guns, and sixteen pieces of mounted artillery. . . . . There were 480 Cossacks in all. . . . .

To go with such forces to Tsarskoe Selo, the garrison of which consisted of some 16,000 soldiers, and then to Petrograd, which numbered 200,000 . . . . was sheer madness. But civil war is not real war. . . . . Besides, I knew too well the habits of the Petrograd garrison. Until late at night they would have a good time in the saloons and cinemas, with the result that you could not awaken them in the morning. We had, therefore, a good chance to take Tsarskoe Selo before dawn when the strength of my army could not be revealed. . . . .[24]

While Kerensky and his tiny force waited at Tsarskoe Selo for reinforcements, the anti-Bolshevik groups in Petrograd attempted to liquidate the "Bolshevik adventure." The Committee to Save the Country and the Revolution organized a rising of the cadets of the military schools timed to coincide with the approach of the Kerensky forces. Blagonravov, the Bolshevik Commissar at Peter and Paul Fortress, accidentally discovered the plan of the uprising, and during the night of the 10th–11th the Bolsheviks began to disarm the cadets. Fighting broke out and continued throughout the day.[25]

[22] *Izvestiia,* No. 210, November 11, 1917, p. 2.

[23] P. N. Krasnov, "Na vnutrennem fronte," in *A.R.R.,* I (1922), 158–59.

[24] "The government forces entered Tsarskoe Selo in the evening of November 10." (*Volia Naroda,* No. 158, November 12, 1917, p. 3.)

[25] *Novaia Zhizn,* No. 167, November 12, 1917, p. 3; cf. Oldenbourg, pp. 294–95. Other accounts in English of this uprising are given by John Reed, *op. cit.,* pp. 193–207; A. R. Williams, *Through the Russian Revolution,* pp. 119–49; Bessie Beatty, *The Red Heart of Russia,* New York, 1919, pp. 225–43; Krassin, *Leonid Krassin: His Life and Work,* London, 1929, p. 62; Meriel Buchanan (Mrs. Knowling), *The Dissolution of an Empire,* pp. 252–53.

ORDER OF THE COMMITTEE TO SAVE THE COUNTRY AND THE REVOLUTION[26]

[November 11, 8:30 A.M.]

To the People and the Soldiers of Petrograd:

The troops of the Committee to Save the Country and the Revolution have succeeded in freeing all cadet schools. . . . . They occupy the telephone building, and forces are being gathered . . . . to capture Peter and Paul Fortress and Smolny, the last stronghold of the Bolsheviks. You are hereby urged . . . . to assist in every way the commissars and the officers who carry out the orders of Colonel Polkovnikov, Commander of the armies of the Committee to Save the Country and the Revolution . . . . and to arrest all commissars of the so-called Military Revolutionary Committee. All military units . . . . are hereby ordered to assemble at the Nikolaevsky Engineering School.

Every delay will be considered a betrayal of the revolution and will lead to serious consequences for the offenders.

President of the Pre-Parliament
AVXENTIEV
President of the Committee to Save the Country and the Revolution
GOTZ[27]

BULLETIN OF THE COMMITTEE TO SAVE THE COUNTRY AND THE REVOLUTION[28]

[November 11, 1917]

9:30 A.M. The director of the telephone exchange reports that the Petrograd telephone station is occupied by the troops of the Committee to Save the Country and the Revolution.

9:40 A.M. Telegram of A. F. Kerensky. Gatchina, November 10, 9:25 P.M. "You are hereby advised not to take any orders from individuals calling themselves People's Commissars or Commissars of the Military-Revolutionary Committee, nor to enter into any relations with them, and to keep them out of all government institutions."

9:40. Fighting is going on between Red Guards and the cadets of the Vladimir School at the corner of Grebetskaia Street and the Grand Prospect.

[26] *Novaia Zhizn,* No. 167, November 12, 1917, p. 3.

[27] On the following day Avxentiev and Gotz published statements in *Delo Naroda,* No. 195, p. 2, denying that they had ever signed this order.

[28] *Delo Naroda,* No. 194, November 12, 1917, p. 2.

10:10 A.M. The Vladimir School is being bombarded from armored cars and light artillery. The school is besieged. . . . .

10:55. The Vladimir School is asking for aid.

11:00 A.M. A report from the Vladimir School states that one of the armored cars was damaged by the cadets. . . . . The cadets appeal for help. . . . .

1:30 P.M. The bombardment of the school continues. There are many wounded among the besieged.

12:25 P.M. Martianov the commissar of the Engineering Castle reports that the Pavlovsky regiment is about to begin the siege of the castle. . . . .

2:00 P.M. A small armed vessel made its way through the Moika and stopped opposite the School of Law, the headquarters of the Central Executive Committee of Soviets of Peasants' Deputies.

3:00 P.M. The bombardment of the Vladimir School continues. The Bolsheviks sent delegates with proposals to surrender, but the cadets flatly refused and opened fire on the delegates. . . . .

PROGRAM OF THE COMMITTEE TO SAVE THE COUNTRY AND THE REVOLUTION[29]

[Published November 12, 1917]

In order to bring about revolutionary order and to prevent the fratricidal civil war, the All-Russian Committee to Save the Country and the Revolution has resolved:

1. To start conversations with the Provisional Council of the Russian Republic and the central committees of the Socialist parties . . . . on the subject of forming a democratic government with the following program: (*a*) To liquidate quickly the Bolshevik adventure in such a way as will safeguard the interests of the democracy. (*b*) To crush energetically all counter-revolutionary attempts and pogroms. (*c*) To do everything possible to have the Constituent Assembly meet on time. (*d*) To pursue a vigorous foreign policy by informing the Allies of the government's readiness to commence at once conversations leading to the kind of peace that will not fasten economic or political chains on any of the belligerent countries, and to defend the country as long as the foreign foe threatens it. (*e*) To put into force a law that will hand over the landlords' estates to the land committees.

2. To demand that the Military Revolutionary Committee should immediately lay down its arms, give up the power seized, and call on the troops under its command to submit to the authority of the Committee to Save the Country and the Revolution.

[29] *Delo Naroda*, No. 194, November 12, 1917, p. 2.

TROTSKY ON THE CADET UPRISING

[Extracts from Speech at the Petrograd Soviet, November 11, 1917][30]

In Petrograd we won easily, thanks to propaganda. . . . . We must bear in mind, however, that . . . . the dominant classes . . . . never relinquish their power without a bitter struggle. They have already begun to gather their forces, and are assuming the offensive.

In Petrograd they captured the telephone exchange, the Mikhailovsky Manège . . . . the Engineering School. . . . . Our commissar of the Peter and Paul Fortress arrested an officer on whom documents were found disclosing a military conspiracy against us. Colonel Polkovnikov, commander of the troops of the so-called Committee to Save [the Country and the Revolution] appointed commissars to the different military units. . . . . [The documents] were signed by Gotz, former member of the Central Executive Committee. . . . .

[Against this] we had to take decisive steps. . . . . The Pavlovsky Cadet School is destroyed; the cadets are disarmed . . . . and will be sent to Kronstadt. The Second Cadet School has also surrendered. We hold the cadets as prisoners and hostages. If our men fall into the hands of the enemy, let him know that for every worker and for every soldier we shall demand five cadets. We have demonstrated today that . . . . we are not joking. . . . . We remember how they [the capitalists] treated rebellious soldiers, workers, and peasants. . . . . They thought that we would be passive, but we showed them that we can be merciless when it is a question of holding on to the conquests of the revolution. . . . . Measures taken in the defense of the interests of the masses need no justification. . . . . Let our enemies know that they will pay dearly for the life of every worker and soldier. . . . .

C. Intervention of Vikzhel and the Left Socialists

While the fighting was still going on, the Left Socialists who had remained in the Second Congress undertook to stop the civil war and bring about the formation of a Socialist coalition government. They found support in Vikzhel,[31]

[30] *Izvestiia*, No. 211, November 12, 1917, p. 2.

[31] Vikzhel contained about forty members, with the following party affiliations: Socialist-Populist, 3; Right S.R., 4; Pro-Right S.R. Independent, 1; Menshevik, 6; Menshevik Internationalist, 1; Mezhraiontsy, 2; Left S.R., 9; Bolshevik, 2; Pro-Bolshevik Independent, 1; Non-Party (many of whom were said to have supported the Cadets), 11. P. Vompe, *Dni oktiabrskoi revoliutsii i zheleznodorozhniki,* Moscow, 1924, p. 10; A. Taniaev, *Ocherki dvizheniia zheleznodorozhnikov v revoliutsiiu 1917 g. (fevral-oktiabr)*, Moscow, 1925, p. 91.

which issued an ultimatum threatening to call a railway strike in case civil strife was not brought to an end. At 5:00 P.M. the Central Executive Committee, elected by the Second Congress of Soviets, discussed Vikzhel's ultimatum and agreed to take part in negotiations with the Socialist groups. Kamenev, Riazanov, Rykov, and Sokolnikov were sent to parley with the other Socialists, while Lenin and Trotsky went to the meeting of the Petrograd garrison to make sure of the support of the soldiers.

THE LEFT-WING SOCIALISTS APPEAL FOR A UNITED REVOLUTIONARY FRONT[32]

[November 11]

WORKERS, SOLDIERS, AND PEASANTS! THE REVOLUTION IS IN DANGER!

The government established by a section of the Congress of Soviets after the coup d'état in Petrograd is a purely Bolshevik government; it cannot have the support of the entire democracy when recognized by one party only. . . . .

The split within the ranks of the democracy is pushing the reactionary elements . . . . into an alliance with the propertied classes. This will facilitate the work of the counter-revolution, which, under the pretext of suppressing the Bolshevik insurrection, is mobilizing its forces to strangle the revolution. The civil war which is threatening the country with an unparalleled cataclysm and bloodshed is certain to reduce the strength of the democracy and lead to the destruction of the revolution. . . . .

We address this energetic appeal to the two camps of the revolutionary democracy to find a way to an agreement and to establish a uniformly democratic power capable of resisting the counter-revolutionary coalition of the propertied classes.

We appeal to the two camps of the democracy to re-establish the unity of the revolutionary front in order that the revolution may not be submerged in the blood of soldiers, workers, and peasants.

[*Signed*] Menshevik-Internationalists
Socialist-Revolutionists of the Left
United Social-Democrats-Internationalists
Polish Socialist Party
Jewish Social-Democratic Labor Party (Poalei Zion)

[32] *Novaia Zhizn,* No. 166, November 11, 1917, p. 1.

VIKZHEL'S ULTIMATUM TO END THE CIVIL WAR AND FORM A SOCIALIST COALITION GOVERNMENT

[Circular Telegram, November 11, 1917][33]

To All Railroad Unions; Soviets of Soldiers', Workers', and Peasants' Deputies; Moscow Vikzhel; Petrograd Sovnarkom; Central Executive Committee of Soviets of Workers', Soldiers', and Peasants' Deputies; Tsentroflot; Tsentrobalt; Central Committees of Political Parties; Central Committee of Postal-Telegraph Unions; Central Council of the All-Russian Trade Unions; Military Revolutionary Committees; All Army Organizations and Committees; To All, All, All!

The country is without an organized government, and a bitter struggle for power is in progress. Each of the contending parties is trying to create a government by means of force, and [as a result] brother is killing brother. At the very time when the foreign foe threatens the freedom of the people, the democracy settles internal quarrels with blood and iron. The Provisional Government with Kerensky at its head has proved itself too weak to retain the reins of power. The government of the Soviet of People's Commissars, formed at Petrograd by one party only, cannot expect to be recognized or supported by the country as a whole. It is, therefore, necessary to form a government that will have the confidence of the democracy as a whole and have enough prestige to retain the power until the meeting of the Constituent Assembly. Such a government can be formed only by common consent of the democracy but never by force. Civil war never has and never can create a government that has the backing of the whole country. A people that is opposed to the death penalty as a means of justice, and is rejecting war as a method of settling international disputes, cannot accept civil war as a means to end internal quarrels. Every civil war leads straight to counter-revolution and is advantageous only to the enemy of the people. In order to guard the liberty of the country and to save the revolution, the Central Committee of the All-Russian Union of Railwaymen has, from the very beginning of this civil strife, assumed a strictly neutral attitude and has declared that the only way to obtain internal peace is by forming a homogeneous ministry, made up of the Socialist parties, from the Bolsheviks to the Socialists-Populists inclusive. Our stand has been accepted and approved by many public organizations and parties in Petrograd and Moscow. The Central Executive Committee [of the Railwaymen's Union] has repeatedly declared and declares once more that it will place the whole railway service at the disposal of those who accept

[33] *Novaia Zhizn*, No. 167, November 12, 1917, p. 2.

its platform. The Central Executive Committee makes clear its determined position to all citizens, workers, soldiers, and peasants and categorically demands that the civil war be ended and that a homogeneous revolutionary-socialist government be formed. The Railwaymen's Union gives notice that it will make use of every means at its disposal, even to complete stoppage of all train movements, to carry out its decision. Train service will be suspended at midnight today, November 11–12, if by that time the fighting in Petrograd and Moscow has not ceased. All railwaymen's organizations are to take the necessary steps to strike and to appoint strike committees. The Railwaymen's Union denounces as enemies of democracy and as traitors to the country all those who continue to settle internal quarrels by means of force.

MALITSKY
Chairman of the Central Executive Committee
of the All-Russian Railwaymen's Union

THE CENTRAL EXECUTIVE COMMITTEE DISCUSSES VIKZHEL'S ULTIMATUM

[Meeting of November 11, 5:00 P.M.][34]

. . . . A representative of the All-Russian Railwaymen's Union made the following declaration:

"The All-Russian Railwaymen's Union had no intention to mix into the political strife of the parties, but the recent news from Moscow[35] made it necessary to do something. We received information that civil war is raging in Moscow; that two liquor stores were broken into during the night of November 10 and drunken mobs are plundering the city. . . . ." [He then read the Vikzhel ultimatum and continued]: "I must declare . . . . that though Moscow is surrounded by government troops, ... we shall not allow the latter to enter either Moscow or Petrograd. We are sending just now a delegation to Kerensky to let him know our decision, and even if Kerensky should succeed in entering Petrograd he would have to surrender, otherwise the railway union will block all the roads leading to Petrograd. . . . ."

Replying to the representative of the Vikzhel, Kamenev declared that he welcomed the fact that in its resolution the Railwaymen's Union acknowledged the bankruptcy of the Coalition Government. . . . . The important thing in organizing an all-Socialist government was not so much the question of the composition of that government . . . . as the acceptance of the basic principles adopted by the [second] Congress of Soviets.

[34] *Novaia Zhizn*, No. 167, November 12, 1917, p. 3.

[35] The Moscow events are given below, pp. 174–80.

We are willing to attend a conference [with other Socialist parties]. .... I move, therefore, that we accept without further discussion the Vikzhel invitation to send our delegates to that conference.

Kamenev's proposal is accepted. ....

MEETING OF THE PETROGRAD GARRISON[36]

[November 11]

.... The meeting was opened by Comrade Chudnovsky. ....

Comrade Lenin, President of the Soviet of Commissars, spoke.

There is no need [he said] to dwell on the political situation since the latter reduces itself to the military. It is quite clear that Kerensky is basing himself on the followers of Kornilov, for he cannot rely on anybody else. .... The army is against Kerensky. Even the vacillating elements, Vikzhel, for example, are in favor of the land and peace decrees. For these are not the policies of the Bolsheviks, ... but of the workers, the soldiers, and the peasants. .... We invited everybody to take part in the government .... and everybody knows that the Socialist-Revolutionists and the Mensheviks left [the Congress] because they were in a minority. The Petrograd garrison knows that we wanted a Soviet coalition government. We excluded no one from the Soviet. They refused to co-operate with us, and they are to be blamed. ....

Kerensky's attempt is as pitiful an adventure as the attempt of Kornilov. But the moment is a very difficult one. ....

We cannot tolerate victory by Kerensky. If [Kerensky] wins there will be neither peace, nor land, nor liberty. I have no doubt that the Petrograd soldiers and workers who accomplished a triumphant insurrection will be able to put down the Kornilovists. .... We should organize a [military] staff at once, and .... we shall triumph in a few days. ....

[Trotsky]: Comrades. .... The hatred against the old government has reached its peak, and the news of the passing of power to the Soviet has roused a delirious enthusiasm. .... As for the coalition ministry, that is a question of program and not of persons. Even many of those who hesitate, as Comrade Lenin has just said, come out for the program of peace and the land decree. On the other side there are the Kornilov-socialists. I wonder whether you know that last night a plot was uncovered to overthrow the Soviet Government. We have all the documents. .... In a distorted fashion [the Committee to Save the Country and the Revolution] intended to follow our own plan [of insurrection] .... with the difference, however, that while we acted openly .... they act in secret. From Polkovnikov's orders it is clear that important events

[36] *Izvestiia*, No. 212, November 13, 1917, pp. 7–8.

were to take place last night. All military orders were signed by Gotz. Soldiers of the cyclist regiment were to take over the guard of the Peter and Paul Fortress and free the ministers. [Two of their men] were arrested and the execution of the plan was frustrated. The events of this morning[37] are only part of a general scheme. . . . . Now, is it possible to form a coalition with these gentlemen? . . . .

[Representatives of the various units deliver reports which in general indicate that the soldiers are ready to defend the new government.]

THE VIKZHEL CONFERENCE[38]

[November 11–12, 1917]

At 8: 30 P.M. a conference of all Socialist parties called by Vikzhel took place.

Vikzhel outlined a program for an agreement between the representatives of all parties. Its essential points were as follows: the formation of a government including all Socialist parties, the speediest conclusion of peace, the calling of the Constituent Assembly on time, the transfer of land to the peasants, et cetera.

Upon the announcement of this program there followed an exchange of points of view.

Speech of Comrade Hendelman: As a member of the Central Committee of the Socialist-Revolutionists I must say . . . . that I was sent here not to negotiate a detailed agreement with the Bolsheviks . . . . but solely to tell our comrades the railwaymen what we think is the best way of solving the conflict. . . . . Comrades, railwaymen! The fate of the revolution hangs on your decision. The future historian will most likely say "the railwaymen saved the revolution" or "the railwaymen ruined the revolution." We think that the railwaymen are right in their description of the horrors of the civil war brought about by the seizure of power by the Bolsheviks; we also think that there is only one way out, and that is to form an all-revolutionary democratic government. But [the railwaymen] are mistaken if they suppose that [the two camps of] the revolutionary democracy can come to an agreement. The Bolsheviks have adopted a method of solving political questions by force of arms and I anticipate that they will so continue in the future. The masses, to be sure, will abandon them very soon.

An all-revolutionary government must be formed, for the present at least, without the Bolsheviks. And this for two reasons. In the first place, after what has happened, the country will not recognize a gov-

[37] The cadet uprising.

[38] *Delo Naroda,* No. 195, November 13, 1917, pp. 1–2.

ernment with Bolsheviks in it. The country will not forgive them the blood that has been shed. In the second place, no matter what agreements the Bolsheviks may enter into, they will continue to impose their will by force and overthrow governments as they did the other day. It follows that, as a beginning, the Bolshevik adventure must be liquidated . . . . and that the railwaymen have no right to remain neutral in that task. . . . .

The railwaymen should start negotiations with Kerensky and if he promises that after the Bolshevik adventure is settled . . . . he will surrender his prerogatives to an all-revolutionary democratic government, then the railwaymen should side with those parties which undertake the liquidation of the Bolshevik adventure.

The representatives of the Committee to Save the Country and the Revolution and the Mensheviks supported that point of view.

The Bolsheviks declared that they accepted the Vikzhel program to form a coalition. . . . .

[About 10:00 P.M. a recess was declared to permit the party groups to discuss the composition of the ministry. The session reopened at 3:00 A.M., November 12.]

The Mensheviks and the S.R.'s proposed the following conditions for an agreement: The Red Guard is to be disarmed; the City Duma shall take charge of the Petrograd garrison; all military operations are to cease. At the same time a guaranty will be given that upon entering Petrograd Kerensky's troops will not fire a single shot. . . . . After the armistice is concluded it will be possible to form an all-Socialist government, composed of all Socialist parties . . . . but excluding the Bolsheviks. . . . .

The Socialist-Revolutionists proposed . . . . that a three-day armistice be concluded at once. . . . . The Bolsheviks opposed the idea of an immediate armistice, insisting on their program.[39] . . . .

VIKZHEL DELEGATION TO KERENSKY[40]

[November 11, 1917]

On November 11 Vikzhel sent a delegation to Kerensky . . . . to propose that he should take no aggressive measures against the Petrograd garrison and to ask him to form a coalition government. Kerensky

[39] The account in *Delo Naroda* is very incomplete, as it does not report the speakers of the groups other than the S.R.'s. *Izvestiia* gives no account of the conference, and *Pravda* for that date could not be consulted. *Novaia Zhizn* gives only a brief summary of the points of view advanced at the conference. A fuller account given below (pp. 166–70) is by An-sky, a representative of the City Duma to that conference.

[40] *Delo Naroda,* No. 195, November 13, 1917, p. 2.

received the delegation, assured it that his purpose was not aggressive and that in case an agreement between the Socialist representatives was reached he would pursue no repressive measures. . . . .

[A somewhat different account is given in *Novaia Zhizn,* No. 168, November 13, 1917, p. 2.]

. . . . The delegates communicated the Vikzhel decision to Kerensky and explained the reasons why Vikzhel adopted a position of neutrality in the civil strife. . . . . The delegates further pointed out that quite a number of the democratic organizations share the Vikzhel point of view. In conclusion the delegates pointed out that by midnight, in case their ultimatum is not accepted, the railwaymen will go on strike. Kerensky declared that Vikzhel placed him in a difficult position presenting this ultimatum within two hours of the strike. He asked that there be sent to him a few representatives of the parties composing the Committee to Save the Country and the Revolution . . . . in order that he might consider the question with them. The delegates replied that they would report this to Vikzhel, though they could not guarantee that his request would be satisfied. . . . .

D. Defeat of the Counter-attack

At Tsarskoe Selo only insignificant reinforcements joined the Krasnov detachment. Kerensky sent out more appeals for aid, to which no one responded, and gave orders for the arrest of General Cheremisov, which no one obeyed. In Petrograd the Vikzhel negotiations dragged on and the Cossack Council urged Krasnov to push on to the capital to save the cadets of the military school from massacre.[41] During the afternoon Red Guards, now reinforced by sailors, checked the advance of Krasnov's troops on the heights of Pulkovo. There followed a noisy but not very damaging artillery duel. Renewed agitation against Kerensky broke out in the barracks of Tsarskoe Selo. Despairing of further aid from the front, Krasnov in the evening ordered a retreat; Tsarskoe Selo was abandoned, and the Kerensky forces fell back on Gatchina.

[41] P. N. Krasnov, "Na vnutrennem fronte," in *A.R.R.*, I (1922), 177; cf. Oldenbourg, p. 324.

THE SOVIET COMMANDER-IN-CHIEF TO THE PRESIDENT OF THE SOVNARKOM

[Telegram of November 12, 1917][42]

Our revolutionary soldiers captured and occupied Tsarskoe Selo. Kerensky's troops retreated in the direction of Pavlovsk (second) and Gatchina.

Long live the Revolution!

COLONEL MURAVEV
Commander-in-Chief of the Petrograd
Military District

PULKOVO, November 12, 11:50 P.M.

DEFEAT OF KRASNOV'S FORCES AT PULKOVO

[Miller's Telegram from Gatchina to the Stavka, November 13, 1917, 4:30 P.M.][43]

. . . . Today a great battle took place in the region of Tsarskoe Selo, Alexandrovskaia, and Pulkovo. The enemy turned out to be numerically superior. At first the fire of our artillery and an attack of two Cossack troops . . . . forced the enemy to retreat, but owing to shortage of ammunition we were compelled to reduce the fire to a minimum. The enemy took advantage of this . . . . assumed the offensive, trying by flanking movements to surround our small force. We decided to retreat to Tsarskoe Selo under cover of an armored train. We soon learned that the enemy was concentrating at Kolpino to attack us in the rear. In view of this General Krasnov retreated further to Gatchina. . . . .[44]

THE BOLSHEVIKS' MILITARY ACTION AGAINST KERENSKY

[Trotsky's Recollections][45]

. . . . The military operations, on both sides, were hidden in a fog. No one could give us an idea of the forces that were being moved against us. . . . .

[42] Popov, *Oktiabrskii perevorot,* p. 227.

[43] "Oktiabr na fronte," in *Krasnyi Arkhiv,* XXIV (1927), 87. Miller was Kerensky's aide-de-camp.

[44] By midnight the Bolsheviks had recovered Tsarskoe Selo, and at 2:10 A.M. on the 13th Trotsky sent out news of the victory from the Tsarskoe Selo radio station. The text of this message is given in Trotsky's *The History of the Russian Revolution to Brest-Litovsk,* pp. 103–104.

[45] L. Trotsky, *Sochineniia,* III, Book 2, 86–89.

We had a considerable force . . . . but it lacked discipline . . . . and officers. . . . . We had a Red Guard, but its fighting capacity [was of a dubious nature]. . . . . We had no idea where to get supplies. . . . . . A conference of the garrison was called at Smolny. . . . . [Some of the officers came.] . . . . They had little reason for liking Kerensky and even less reason for loving the Soviet régime. There was as yet no organized counter-revolutionary camp. . . . . No one, however, wished to assume the post of chief command . . . . not knowing what the final outcome might be. . . . . In the end . . . . Colonel Muravev was selected for the post. . . . . He was a born adventurer. He called himself a Socialist-Revolutionist of the Left. . . . . He had certain military qualifications . . . . he knew how to get along with soldiers. . . . . During the Kerensky régime . . . . he organized . . . . detachments . . . . to fight the Bolsheviks; now he desired to lead the Soviet troops [against Krasnov]. After much hesitation . . . . he was selected. . . . . Five men, soldiers and sailors, ... were set to watch him, with orders to get rid of him on the first signs of betrayal. . . . . It was unnecessary, for he was loyal and ardent. . . . .

The Petrograd proletariat took the struggle more seriously than the soldiers. . . . . The issue of the battle was decided by the artillery. . . . . The Cossacks fought without the least enthusiasm. . . . . They decided to talk things over with our men, and when it came to talking they were no match for us. They retreated. . . . . Kerensky ran . . . . the November Revolution was saved. . . . .

Another of our officers was Colonel Walden,[46] who commanded at Pulkovo Hill. He surrounded Krasnov with large forces and put an end to Kerensky's offensive.

Walden was an old soldier and carried the scars of many battles. We were under no illusions as to his feeling for us. . . . . Apparently the only reason why he sided with us was his great hatred of Kerensky.

CONDITIONS ON THE FRONTS

[Dukhonin to Baranovsky, November 13, 2:00 A.M.][47]

To the Supreme Commander-in-Chief (Confidential):

On November 11 the situation on the fronts was as follows: In the north, in the 12th Army the Letts abandoned their positions and retreated in the direction of Walk, Wolmar, and Wenden. There were no disorders in Reval, but the 13th and 15th Don Regiments could not be sent to Petrograd,[48] as the Bolsheviks threatened to prevent by force

[46] "Vospominaniia ob oktiabrskom perevorote," in *Proletarskaia Revoliutsiia,* 1922, No. 10, pp. 61–62.

[47] "Oktiabr na fronte," in *Krasnyi Arkhiv,* XXIV (1927), 83–85.

[48] The regiments in question were parts of the 1st Don Cossack Division ordered by Kerensky to Petrograd on November 7.

the use of the railroad for that purpose. The regiments themselves . . . . had not the courage to break through to the nearest railroad station and entrain outside the region of Reval. The Committees of the 5th Army were in favor of sending troops to Petrograd to aid the Bolsheviks, and the Committees of the 1st Army adopted a neutral attitude. . . . . On the whole the attitude of the army units on this front . . . . is rather passive, ... showing no desire to support actively the government in its struggle against the increasing influence of the Bolsheviks. . . . .

On the Western front . . . . the whole situation is in the hands of the Minsk Committee to Save the Revolution, and no army unit can be moved without its sanction. . . . . In most cities adjoining the front as well as in the important railroad junctions the influence of the Bolsheviks is in the ascendant. . . . .

On the Southwestern front the situation is in favor of the government, but a few encounters have occurred resulting in bloodshed. Heavy fighting has taken place in Vinnitsa, in which armored cars and airplanes took part. . . . .

In Moscow the situation is very serious. . . . .

Kharkov, Voronezh, and Kursk . . . . are in the hands of the Bolsheviks. . . . .

The wave of Bolshevism is rapidly moving from the rear to the front and I am obliged to state that if the crisis lasts two or three days longer it will be difficult to maintain order at the [front]. . . . .

DUKHONIN

Back at Gatchina Kerensky issued new orders to all army committees and commanding officers to hurry the dispatch of troops. These orders, like the earlier ones, could not be executed because of the action of the various soldiers' committees. The failure of reinforcements to arrive from any direction naturally affected the morale of Krasnov's Cossacks. Kerensky, still hopeful, called a council of war of Krasnov, Popov, Kuzmin, Savinkov, Stankevich, and another officer. Unmoved by the arguments of Kerensky and Savinkov, a majority favored opening negotiations with the Bolsheviks for an armistice. Stankevich left for Petrograd to get in touch with the Committee to Save the Country and the Revolution, and Savinkov started for the Stavka in search of reinforcements.[49]

[49] Krasnov, "Na vnutrennem fronte," in *A.R.R.*, I (1922), 170–77; Kerensky, *The Catastrophe*, New York, 1927, pp. 361–62.

CONDITIONS DELAYING THE MOVEMENT OF TROOPS FROM THE FRONT

[Conversation by Direct Wire of Generals Maliavin, Walter, and Dietrichs, November 13][50]

[Maliavin]: According to our information Orsha is occupied by the Bolsheviks, who are obstructing the movement of troop trains going to Petrograd and to the Stavka. . . . . The sending of armored cars to Moscow is . . . . being prevented by the Minsk Committee to Save [the Country] and the Revolution. For the same reason we were unable to send reinforcements to Viazma, which fell into the hands of the Bolsheviks, and now all trains are stopped there. . . . .

All our activities are virtually paralyzed by the Army and Front Committees to Save [the Country and] the Revolution. Until something is done . . . . to restrain [these committees] we are helpless to carry out the orders of the Stavka. . . . .

[Walter]: . . . . I should like to describe the local Committee to Save [the Country and] the Revolution. It is composed partly of loyal elements and partly of Bolsheviks. This peculiar alliance came about as a result of the fact that the Socialist-Revolutionists and the Social-Democrats, who are on the whole well-meaning, were not sure that the military men would actively support them against . . . . the Bolsheviks. There was further the uncertainty as to the outcome of the struggle in Petrograd. Hence fearing for their own lives they refrain from asserting their policy in the Committee. They also fear that any decisive measure against [the Bolsheviks] will cause outbursts of violence at the front and that bloodshed will lead to anarchy, pogroms, and the plundering of Minsk. The Bolsheviks [on the other hand] are very resolute in carrying out their line of action. . . . . Everyone is singing in tune with Petrograd. As soon as the tangle in Petrograd is resolved in favor of the Provisional Government the influence of . . . . the Bolsheviks will disappear as a matter of course. There is, in addition, an entire lack of sympathy for Kerensky. When all is put together [we can see why there is] the fear to help Petrograd and Moscow openly. . . . . Just now the sending of reinforcements is opposed on the ground that the Railwaymen's Committee has presented an ultimatum to both sides in Petrograd . . . . requiring them to come to an agreement and to form a government acceptable to both. . . . .

[Dietrichs]: . . . . The difficulties of which you speak are not peculiar to your front; they are the same throughout Russia. Tactical con-

[50] "Oktiabr na fronte," in *Krasnyi Arkhiv,* XXIII (1927), 173–75. Maliavin and Walter spoke from Minsk, the headquarters of the Western front; Dietrichs was in Mogilev.

siderations of the present require that we should overcome all difficulties so that the infantry may appear on the fields of Gatchina. . . . .

KRASNOV'S PEACE PROPOSALS

[Telegram to the Military Revolutionary Committee, November 13 (?), 1917][51]

The conference called by the Central Executive Committee of the All-Russian Railway Union of representatives of the Central Executive Committee of the All-Russian Soviet of Workers' and Soldiers' Deputies, the Committee to Save the Country and the Revolution, the Petrograd City Duma, the Central Committee of the Social-Democrats (Mensheviks), the Central Bureau of the Social-Democrats (Internationalists), the Central Committee of the Social-Democrats (Bolsheviks), the Central Committee of the Socialist-Revolutionists, the Petrograd Conference of the Socialist-Revolutionists of the Left, the Jewish Socialist Labor Party, the Polish Socialist Party, the United Jewish Socialist Party, the All-Russian Central Soviet of the army organization . . . . and Vikzhel, having considered the question of bringing to an end the armed conflict between the troops and the workers, resolved that in order to arrive at a final understanding as to the form and construction of the new government it is necessary to conclude an immediate armistice and to stop bloodshed and armed conflicts.

The Supreme Commander-in-Chief, wishing to avoid useless bloodshed, gave his consent to the beginning of negotiations and to the resumption of normal relations between the troops of the government and the rebels.[52] In view of this I hereby propose to the staff of the rebels to recall its troops to Petrograd and to fix a neutral zone along the lines Pulkovo-Kolpino, leaving the government troops to patrol Tsarskoe Selo. An answer to this proposal must be transmitted not later than November 14, 8:00 P.M.

MAJOR-GENERAL KRASNOV

[51] *Krasnyi Arkhiv,* XXIV (1927), 207–208. The document bears no date; was sent in all probability November 13, 1917.

[52] The following telegram was received by Vikzhel during the night of November 13–14: "Petrograd Committee to Save the Country and the Revolution and Vikzhel: In accordance with the proposal of the Committee and all democratic organizations associated with it, I have stopped all movements against the rebellious troops and sent my representative Stankevich, commissar attached to the Commander-in-Chief, to open negotiations. Take the necessary steps to stop the useless shedding of blood. Kerensky." (*Delo Naroda,* No. 197, November 15, 1917, p. 2.)

THE CITY DUMA AND INTER-PARTY NEGOTIATIONS

[S. An-sky's Account of the Negotiations to Form a Socialist Coalition Government, November 10–14, 1917][53]

. . . . The most interesting question was what was happening at the front. The front stretched from Tsarskoe Selo to Pulkovo. There were plenty of contradictory reports: that Vikzhel had given notice that it would not transport the troops of Kerensky or the Bolsheviks; that it insisted that both camps should come to an agreement. In the anti-Bolshevik camp it was believed that Vikzhel was on the side of the Bolsheviks, who had their troops in Petrograd and did not need transportation, and that under the guise of neutrality it was preparing to strike . . . . Kerensky. The representative of Vikzhel offered all Socialist parties and the Duma to bring the two political camps together in the hope that they would agree and thus put an end to the civil war.

The Socialist parties, namely, the Socialist-Revolutionists, Mensheviks, and Internationalists, accepted the offer; the more moderate Socialist-Populists and the Plekhanov group either were not invited or turned down the offer. The question whether to accept or decline the invitation was warmly debated. . . . . In the end the Duma decided to send . . . . Chikhachev (Socialist-Revolutionist) and me as delegates. We were given the following instructions:

1. To urge the calling of a new Pre-Parliament made up of representatives of Socialist parties and of the City Dumas. At least one-third of the membership of this Pre-Parliament should be from the [City Dumas].

2. Out of this Pre-Parliament a cabinet is to be chosen. The Bolsheviks are not to be taken into the cabinet and, under no circumstances, Lenin and Trotsky.

3. [To insist that] the Bolsheviks must free all arrested persons, especially the ministers, before entering into any kind of conversations. . . . .

When we reached the place of meeting, the quarters of the Railwaymen's Union, there were about forty people present. I learned that in order to save time the assembly had asked the delegates of the more important groups to get together in a caucus and come to some provisional agreement. [The caucus] included delegates of Socialist-Revolutionists, Mensheviks, Railwaymen's Union, and Dumas.

When we entered the room where this [caucus] was taking place, we saw the following named delegates: Kamenev and Riazanov (Bolsheviks), Martov (Internationalist), Lieber (Menshevik), Rakitnikov

[53] S. An-sky (Rapoport), "Posle perevorota 25-go oktiabria 1917 g.," in *A.R.R.*, VIII (1923), 45–54.

(Socialist-Revolutionist). The Railwaymen's Union was represented by its chairman (whose name I do not remember);[54] in addition there was someone by the name of Krushinsky. . . . .

The conference dragged on until eight in the morning [and then adjourned] until five in the afternoon.

At the City Duma the results of the conference were awaited with impatience. My report of what had taken place . . . . raised a storm. The moderate elements, even the moderate Socialist-Revolutionists, were greatly shocked by the insolence of the Bolsheviks. They shouted that it was criminal and humiliating to attend a conference with the Bolsheviks. Shingarev, in particular, was very much excited. . . . .

The second inter-party conference began very late . . . . close to midnight [November 12]. After long debates we agreed on the necessity of having a Pre-Parliament and a new council of ministers [but could not agree as to their composition]. . . . .

About three in the morning, as we were about to break up, a very interesting incident took place. The doorkeeper announced that a delegation of workers from Putilov's works[55] was persistently demanding to be admitted. They had something important to say to us. The conference was against admitting them . . . . but the delegation was insistent and threatened that if it were not admitted it would come in by force. Under the circumstances it was admitted. There were about fifteen of them, young and old, looking very thoughtful. One of them, a young workman, with an . . . . intelligent face and clear, cold eyes, stepped forward and spoke with a great deal of emotion as if sounding a warning:

"Already for a week the two revolutionary camps have been shedding each other's blood in this criminal civil war. We demand that this be brought to an end! We have had enough of it! You have been here for two days trying to come to an understanding, and it seems as if you were in no hurry. We will not allow this civil war to go on. To hell with Lenin and Chernov! Hang them both! . . . . We are telling you to put an end to this situation, otherwise we will make you pay!"[56]

[54] Malitsky was chairman of Vikzhel and the meeting.

[55] In his report on the Conference to the City Duma on November 16, 1917, An-sky stated that the delegation in question came from the Obukhov factories. *Delo Naroda*, No. 197, November 15, 1917, p. 3.

[56] "The workers of the munition factories having met and considered the present state of affairs have come to the conclusion that for these trying times party strife has gone beyond all limits, that it is having a bad influence on the attitude and psychology of the laboring class, and that the revolution is about to go under owing to this dirty political fight. We regard this as an intolerable situation and demand that all political parties should come together at once on the question of a government made up of all Socialist parties that are represented in the Soviet of Workers', Soldiers', and Peasants' Deputies. Those parties that refuse to come to an understanding we denounce as enemies of the revolution and the toiling masses.

This speech and the threat . . . . made a deep impression on all, especially on Riazanov. He jumped up . . . . shouting: "You are perfectly right! We Bolsheviks have been ready to come to an understanding from the very first. We are making all kinds of concessions, but the Socialist-Revolutionists, the Mensheviks, and, in particular, the representatives of the City Duma are blocking us and stand in the way of an agreement. Go to them, to the central committees of these parties and to the Duma, and demand that the civil war be brought to an end."

"Very well," cried the workmen, "we will go there and drag them here!"

Riazanov's speech . . . . aroused us all. I pointed out to the workmen how Riazanov distorted the facts and explained the differences in our points of view.

"The devil alone knows who among you is right or wrong," said one of the workmen. "You insult the earth by walking on it. If we could hang all of you on one tree the country would enjoy peace. . . . . Let's go, men. We have nothing to gain from talking to this gang."

They went.

This incident was not without some good. When we assembled the next day, November 12,[57] there was a greater desire to co-operate. The speeches were shorter. The Mensheviks proposed an armistice, and the Socialist-Revolutionists supported it. They reported having received authority from Kerensky to conclude a peace or an armistice with the Bolsheviks on such terms as the Central Committee should find acceptable and that Kerensky promised to live up to the agreement. As representative of the City Duma, I also came out in favor of the proposal of an armistice. Kamenev, however . . . . would not listen to it. He said that the Executive Committee of the Soviet of Workers' and Soldiers' Deputies would have nothing to do with armistices until the anti-Bolsheviks offered definite guaranties.

"To conclude an armistice now," said Kamenev, "means giving Kerensky the chance to organize a new army."

In any case . . . . the question of an armistice is for the [military] staff at the front to settle and not for Kamenev and Riazanov. . . . .

Further debate brought out the fact that the two Bolshevik delegates had no plenipotentiary power to conclude anything definite. It seemed that they had come merely to get information but would not admit it. They argued that they had definite but limited power. No matter how much we tried we could not find out just how much author-

---

The shedding of blood must stop and we shall hold responsible those who take an uncompromising position." A resolution adopted November 13, *Delo Naroda*, No. 196, November 14, 1917, p. 1; see also *Delo Naroda*, No. 197, November 15, 1917, p. 2.

[57] November 13.

ity they had. It seemed to us anti-Bolsheviks that the Bolsheviks came to the conference in order to gain the good will of the Railwaymen's Union, and, particularly, to gain time until the outcome of the struggle near Petrograd and Moscow was known.

Under the circumstances the armistice was dropped, and we took up the question of forming a provisional national Soviet. After long and heated debates, which dragged on through November 12 and 13, we finally came to an agreement. The new . . . . Soviet was to be made up of 100 members from the Soviet of Workers' Deputies, 75 from the Peasants' Soviet, 100 from the Petrograd and Moscow dumas, and 50 from All-Russian trade unions. . . . .

The next question was the composition of the ministry, and that was settled quickly. It was the consensus that only Socialists should be admitted. The difficult point was to balance the ministry in such a way that neither the Bolsheviks nor their opponents should have a majority. There was also the question of personalities. The Socialist-Revolutionists, the Mensheviks, and the City Duma insisted that Lenin and Trotsky should not be included, while the Bolsheviks crossed out the name of Kerensky, and, if I am not mistaken, Avxentiev. An agreement was finally reached . . . . calling for a government of specialists. The names of Lenin, Trotsky, and Kerensky were not mentioned. . . . .

This understanding was reached late in the night of November 13. . . . . As soon as that was accomplished, the question of armistice was brought forward once more. The Bolshevik delegates declared that the agreement must be provisionally approved by the Central Executive Committee of the Soviet of Workers' Deputies. We anti-Bolsheviks insisted that there must be an end to bloodshed, and Kamenev gave in. He gave assurance that the Soviet . . . . would approve the agreement, and was ready to take steps to stop fighting on the Petrograd front.

A protocol of the agreement was quickly drawn up, and it was decided to send this protocol with letters from the conference to the two general staffs. . . . . These letters pointed out the necessity of concluding an armistice.

To get to the front it was necessary to get a pass from the Petrograd military staff at Smolny.

A representative of Vikzhel and I were delegated to go to the front. The Bolshevik delegates gave us a letter to Smolny recommending that we be given a pass to go to the front. It was already after two in the morning when the two of us got into an automobile . . . . and started for Smolny, intending to go on from there to the front. . . . .

Notwithstanding the lateness of the hour, Smolny was very much alive. . . . . I ran into an old acquaintance, Bonch-Bruevich, a former disciple of Tolstoy and a recent convert to Bolshevism. . . . .

He led us past the guards [to the office of the military staff]. We walked into a large, well-lighted room where several girls were typing. . . . . This room led into another, where three young men were seated at a long table. . . . .

"We must see the chief-of-staff," said I.

One of the young men looked me over from head to foot. "What do you need him for?"

I explained my business.

He listened to me rather indifferently and ironically and then said: . . . . "I cannot let you go to the front."

I tried to explain to him the importance of the mission, the need of stopping the flow of blood.

He stretched out in his chair, yawned, looked at me contemptuously and remarked with a cold self-confidence: "It is not worth your while to go to the front. . . . . It is a bit late to enter into any kind of understandings with counter-revolutionists. . . . ."

"Why?"

"Because Kerensky's band has been knocked in the head. The Cossacks have surrendered and Kerensky is surrounded. At this moment he is probably a prisoner, and will be here in a few hours. You are, it would seem, a bit late with your agreement." . . . .

When on the day following my visit to Smolny I reported to the Duma the results of my conversation with the Bolshevik military staff, it became quite evident that nothing would come out of the inter-party conference with the Bolsheviks. The negotiations, however, did not come to an end. . . . .

The Duma remained optimistic, even when the news of Kerensky's defeat and flight were confirmed. It was believed that the Bolsheviks could not hold on very long; . . . . that Moscow would come to the rescue; that the whole of Russia was against the Bolsheviks.

At the time of the conversations with the Bolsheviks the mayor of the city, Schreider, telegraphed to all the cities in the Petrograd and Moscow gubernias to send representatives for a congress.[58] Much was expected from this gathering. But owing to the bad telegraph and the even worse railway service only about ten people came . . . . of whom one was from Moscow. They met for about two days, made speeches, and went home without having accomplished anything. . . . .

[58] The City Duma sent out the following special telegram: "The present insurrection has put a stop to the calling of the Constituent Assembly. In order to establish a government and public order in the country until the meeting of the Constituent Assembly, the Petrograd Duma has resolved to assemble representatives of the city dumas, zemstvos, executive committees of the Soviets of Peasants', Workers', and Soldiers' Deputies. These representatives are to be elected by universal, direct, equal, and secret ballot, and are to reach Petrograd on November 20. Please reply. Chairman of the Duma, Isaev; Mayor of the City, G. Schreider." (*Delo Naroda,* No. 197, November 15, 1917, p. 4.)

In the evening of November 13, Zinoviev reported to the Petrograd Soviet on the victory over Kerensky and the intention of the M.R. Committee to negotiate not with Kerensky but with the Cossacks on condition that they lay down their arms, recognize the Soviets as the source of power, recognize the decisions of the Second Congress, accept the decrees on peace and land, put an end to hostilities and agree to return to their units, and consent to the arrest of Kerensky, Krasnov, and Savinkov.[59] The Bolshevik armistice offer to the Cossacks was presented by Dybenko, who proposed among other things to hand over Lenin in exchange for Kerensky.

The Cossacks were still debating among themselves when delegates arrived from the 5th Army, who, according to Dybenko, said that if the Cossacks marched against the revolution, the whole army on the front would march against the Cossacks. "This argument produced a strong impression on the Don Cossacks. They declared their desire to end the civil war."[60]

An agreement was reached during the morning which provided for the liberation of the arrested cadets and members of the Cossack Council, the freedom of Cossacks to leave Petrograd with their families, the reopening of railway service, the exclusion of Lenin and Trotsky from the government pending proof of their innocence of treason, and the placing of Kerensky in the hands of the Military Revolutionary Committee for trial before a court of the people.[61]

The news of these negotiations soon reached Kerensky. He discussed the situation with Krasnov, who gave him to understand that his position was hopeless.[62] Presently, how-

[59] *Izvestiia,* November 14, 1917; cf. Oldenbourg, pp. 342–44.

[60] Dybenko gave his report to the Petrograd Soviet on November 15. *Izvestiia,* No. 159, November 16, 1917; cf. Oldenbourg, pp. 384–87.

[61] *Novaia Zhizn,* No. 173, November 18, 1917, p. 4; cf. Oldenbourg, pp. 350–52.

[62] There are at least three versions of this conversation, two by Krasnov which differ considerably, and a third, still different, by Kerensky. The latter is given in *The Catastrophe,* pp. 364–65. One of Krasnov's versions is quoted by Trotsky in *The Russian Revolution to Brest-Litovsk,* pp. 105–109, and the other is in the *A.R.R.,* I (1922), 173–74.

ever, a soldier and a sailor appeared in Kerensky's quarters bringing a sailor's cloak and hat and automobile goggles. Thus disguised, and accompanied by the sailor, Kerensky walked out of the palace and made his way to one of the city gates where an automobile was waiting in which he drove off toward Luga. Krasnov and Voitinsky were arrested and the latter was forced to send out a telegram countermanding the movement of troops against Petrograd.

In the meantime, unaware of the events at Gatchina, Chernov informed Dukhonin of the plan to form a new government with Avxentiev as Prime Minister.

REMOVAL OF KERENSKY

[Telegram of the Chief Commissar of the Northern Front to Headquarters of the Northern Front][63]

THIRD CAVALRY CORPS, November 14

An agreement has been reached between the [government] troops concentrated near Petrograd and the representatives of the Petrograd garrison on condition of Kerensky's removal. Stop at once the movement of all echelons going to Petrograd and bring to an end all preparations for the Kerensky expeditionary force.

VOITINSKY

KERENSKY'S DISAPPEARANCE

[Lukirsky to Dukhonin, November 14][64]

. . . . Kerensky disappeared about 1:00 P.M. The negotiations with the Bolsheviks included provision for his arrest. To this the Cossacks apparently gave their consent. . . . .

PLANS FOR A NEW GOVERNMENT

[Direct Wire Communication to Dukhonin, November 14][65]

Members of the Committee to Save the Country and the Revolution (Chernov, Feit, and Kharash) at the apparatus: We wish to give you the [following] information: . . . . Kerensky is about to give up his authority. You will be appointed Supreme Commander-in-Chief and

63 "Oktiabr na fronte," in *Krasnyi Arkhiv,* XXIV (1927), 90.

64 *Ibid.,* p. 92.

65 *Ibid.,* pp. 97–98.

Avxentiev, chairman of the Pre-Parliament, will become Prime Minister.[66] On your part it will be necessary to remove Cheremisov at once by sending him an urgent call to come to the Stavka and then appointing his successor. . . . . Cheremisov's removal is absolutely essential as it will give us a free hand in Pskov for further operations. . . . .

There is a possibility of a peaceful settlement of the crisis in Petrograd . . . . provided you hurry up considerable reinforcements. . . . .

DUKHONIN STOPS MOVEMENT OF TROOPS AGAINST PETROGRAD

[Radiotelegram from the Stavka][67]

To All, All, All:

In order to stop the bloodshed of civil war the troops of General Krasnov, gathered near Gatchina, today, November 14, concluded an armistice with the [Petrograd] garrison.

According to General Krasnov, the Supreme Commander-in-Chief, Kerensky, has left the troops and his whereabouts are unknown. In view of this and in conformity with the regulations of the field army administration I have temporarily taken upon myself the duties of the Supreme Commander-in-Chief and have given orders not to send more troops against Petrograd.

At the present moment negotiations are being carried on between the various political parties for the purpose of forming a Provisional Government. While waiting for the final settlement of the crisis, I call upon the troops at the front to remain quietly at their posts and do their duty to the country so that the external foe may not take advantage of our internal troubles to advance farther into the interior.

DUKHONIN

Dukhonin's order could not of course immediately reach all the units which were actually en route to Gatchina in accordance with earlier orders. As a result there were near Luga considerable forces which Savinkov, who was also at Luga, believed to be sufficiently reliable to make a successful attack on the Bolsheviks. He attempted to persuade Dukhonin to order the advance resumed. Dukhonin hesitated. The

[66] On the evening of the 12th Kerensky had written a letter to Avxentiev transferring to him "in the event of 'possible necessity'" the rights and duties of premier of the Provisional Government. (Kerensky, *op. cit.*, p. 359.)

[67] *Delo Naroda,* No. 198, November 16, 1917, p. 2.

army committees at Pskov and Minsk continued to oppose aiding either side, Savinkov again appealed to the Stavka, but finally on the 17th Dukhonin confirmed his order to stop the concentration of troops. This order reached Luga on the following day and the troops began to return to their former positions.[68]

E. The Moscow Uprising

While Kerensky and Krasnov were unsuccessfully attempting to make an effective counter-attack against the Bolsheviks in Petrograd, the supporters of the Provisional Government in Moscow were engaged in a costly struggle to prevent the Bolsheviks from gaining control of the ancient capital. There had been rumors of a Bolshevik uprising planned for October 28 and again for November 2, to which the Bolsheviks had replied that when they were ready to act they would announce it.[69] This they did on November 7 when news was received of the insurrection in Petrograd. On that day the Moscow Soviet, against considerable opposition, voted to establish a Revolutionary Committee "for the purpose of giving full support to the revolutionary committee of the Petrograd Soviet."[70] The Moscow City Duma, on the

[68] Cf. Oldenbourg, pp. 395–97, 409–13, 416–17.

[69] Statement by the Bolshevik regional and city committees, November 1. Oldenbourg, p. 89.

[70] *Oktiabrskoe vosstanie v Moskve,* Moscow, 1922, p. 22. Relatively few documentary materials are available for the study of events in Moscow during this week. Most of the documents of the Bolshevik side were destroyed by the Bolsheviks themselves and the bourgeois newspapers were closed. There remain chiefly reminiscences of participants in the struggle. Bolshevik reminiscences in the press in 1917–18 were republished by Ovsiannikov in 1919 in *Moskva v Oktiabre 1917.* Another collection of reminiscences, *Oktiabrskoe vosstanie v Moskve,* appeared in 1922, as did *Oktiabrskie dni v Moskve i raionakh* (Moscow, 1922), published by the Moscow Committee of the Russian Communist Party. *Krasnyi Arkhiv,* LIV–LV, 80–132, published an itemized list of "transactions" of the Moscow Military Revolutionary Committee for the period November 13–23. It lists 1,027 resolutions and orders, of which only a few have been preserved in the Arkhiv Oktiabrskoi Revoliutsii. The rest were destroyed during the fighting. Accounts of the struggle as it was observed by Americans who were in Moscow are given by Arthur Bullard, *The Russian Pendulum,* New York, 1919, pp. 84–85; by Consul-General Summers in David R. Francis, *Russia from the American Embassy,* pp. 190–93; by the same in *U.S. Foreign Relations, 1918, Russia,* I, 234–35; and by O. M. Sayler in *Russia White or Red,* Boston, 1919, pp. 19–37.

same day, passed a resolution condemning an uprising and called on the population to support the Provisional Government and the sovereignty of the people under the old revolutionary banners. The Duma also decided to form a Committee of Public Safety.[71]

One of the first acts of the Revolutionary Committee was to call a general strike and close the bourgeois newspapers. On the 8th, troops of the Committee occupied the arsenal and the Kremlin. The following day the Committee of Public Safety announced that only the orders which it issued were legal and appealed for support.[72] On the 9th there were proclamations from both sides.

PROCLAMATION OF THE MOSCOW MILITARY REVOLUTIONARY COMMITTEE[73]

[November 9]

The revolutionary workers and soldiers of Petrograd led by the Petrograd Soviet of Workers' and Soldiers' Deputies have entered into a decisive struggle with the Provisional Government which had betrayed the revolution. It is the duty of the Moscow workers and soldiers to support their Petrograd comrades in that struggle. For that reason the Moscow Soviet of Workers' and Soldiers' Deputies has organized a Military Revolutionary Committee which has already taken charge of the movement.

The Military Revolutionary Committee herewith declares: (1) The entire garrison of Moscow must put itself in complete readiness for action. Every military unit must be ready to come out at the first call of the Military Revolutionary Committee. (2) All orders not coming from the Military Revolutionary Committee or countersigned by it are declared void.

APPEAL OF THE COMMITTEE OF PUBLIC SAFETY TO THE MOSCOW GARRISON[74]

[November 9]

Comrades—Soldiers! At this difficult moment a Committee of Public Safety has been organized in Moscow to preserve order and safeguard the revolution. The Committee is working in complete co-ordi-

[71] Oldenbourg, p. 183.
[72] *Ibid.*, pp. 274–75.
[73] *Oktiabrskoe vosstanie v Moskve*, pp. 182–83.
[74] *Ibid.*, p. 183.

nation with the Central Executive Committee of the Soviet of Workers' and Soldiers' Deputies and the All-Russian Soviet. In these circumstances the Committee of Public Safety urges the regimental . . . . and company committees to inform all army units of the Moscow garrison that all orders of the staff of the Moscow Military District must be carried out without questions. The orders of the Bolshevik Military Revolutionary Committee, as a self-appointed organization, must not be obeyed, since they are contrary to law and aim to create dissension and rebellion in the ranks of the soldiers. Comrades—Soldiers! Remember that in this difficult hour we must all rally around the Committee of Public Safety and help bring the country out of the state of chaos which the Bolsheviks created. We must help to convene the Constituent Assembly on time. Similar appeals have been made by the Supreme Commander-in-Chief and by all army committees on the front. Remember that only in close contact with democratic organizations will our salvation and the salvation of Russia be found.

In the meantime cadets from the military schools and officer detachments under orders of the Committee of Public Safety had surrounded the Kremlin, cutting off the Bolshevik forces there and preventing the delivery of ammunition to them from the arsenal. During this siege Colonel Riabtsov, the District Commander, was inside the Kremlin attempting to negotiate a peaceful settlement with the Bolsheviks. There were rumors that he was being held as a hostage and when he ordered the cadet cordon withdrawn, the cadets refused to obey. On the evening of the 9th Riabtsov returned to the City Duma, where he learned of Kerensky's success at Gatchina. Encouraged by this and the determination of the Duma leaders he telephoned an ultimatum to the Revolutionary Committee, giving them ten minutes to agree (1) to disband the Military Revolutionary Committee, (2) to remove all troops from the Kremlin, and (3) to return all arms removed from the Kremlin arsenals.[75]

The Bolsheviks refused to yield and sent about 300 men from the Dvina regiment to raise the siege of the Kremlin. When the soldiers reached the Red Square opposite one of the Kremlin gates they were met by the fire of the cadets

[75] *Oktiabrskoe vosstanie v Moskve,* p. 199.

and were forced to retreat, leaving forty-five dead.[76] The failure of the relief expedition and rumors that their enemies were gaining strength and that the Revolutionary Committee had capitulated caused the Bolsheviks in the Kremlin to lose hope, and Ensign Berzin, their commander, decided to surrender. On the morning of the 10th his men were disarmed, but a number were shot by the cadets as they left the Kremlin.[77] Appalled by the loss of life and the destruction caused by the fighting, the Soldiers' Soviet (dominated by Mensheviks and S.R.'s) and Moscow Menshevik Committee issued appeals to end hostilities. The Committee of Safety proposed peace on the basis of surrender of arms, the reestablishment of the status quo before the insurrection, and the submission of the Revolutionary Committee to judiciary authority.[78] The Revolutionary Committee declared these terms unacceptable, and the fighting continued until the evening of the 11th, when the Vikzhel ultimatum was received in Moscow and the Moscow division of the Railwaymen's Union and the Mensheviks induced the belligerents to start peace negotiations. Riabtsov ordered his men to cease firing at 6:30 P.M.[79]

PROGRESS OF THE MOSCOW INSURRECTION

[Moscow District Headquarters to the Stavka, November 10][80]

Rovny.—With the surrender of the Kremlin the movements of the Bolsheviks are becoming disorganized. The situation at present is as follows: The central part of the city, with the exception of the section in the vicinity of the [former] residence of the governor-general, is in our hands. The suburbs are in the hands of the Red Guards and the insurgent part of the soldiers. The region beyond the Moscow

[76] These soldiers of the Dvina regiment had been arrested in August 1917 and since confined in the Butyrki prison in Moscow by order of the Provisional Government. In September the soldiers had been released by the Moscow Soviet, and when the fighting broke out in November they were among the first to come out for the Revolutionary Committee.

[77] *Oktiabrskoe vosstanie v Moskve,* p. 227.

[78] Oldenbourg, pp. 286–88. [79] *Ibid.,* p. 310.

[80] A. G. Shliapnikov, "Oktiabrskii perevorot i stavka," in *Krasnyi Arkhiv,* VIII (1925), 158–59.

River is outside the sphere of our influence. The Bolsheviks do their shooting mostly from the roofs, using machine guns and rifles. The majority of the troops remained in their barracks. . . . . Our liaison officers report that whole companies of drunken soldiers and workers wander about the streets. Moscow is seriously threatened with pogroms, since the masses are armed . . . . and are already out of control. None of the public buildings has as yet been taken by the Bolsheviks, though the Kursky and Alexandrovsky railway stations are occupied by Red Guards. Because of the lack . . . . of troops loyal to the government there appears to be little hope of suppressing the insurrection in Moscow within a short time. We have just received information that a battalion of Red Guards is moving toward Moscow from Ivanovo-Voznesensk . . . . where the Bolsheviks appear to be in power. . . . .

NEGOTIATIONS BETWEEN THE COMMITTEE OF PUBLIC SAFETY AND THE MILITARY REVOLUTIONARY COMMITTEE[81]

[November 11–12]

The Military Revolutionary Committee entered into negotiations with the Committee of Public Safety. The Committee of Public Safety proposed the following conditions: (1) To disarm the Red and White guards. The Bolsheviks to return the arms removed [from the arsenals]. (2) To dissolve the Military Revolutionary Committee and the Committee of Public Safety. (3) To hand over to justice all those found guilty [of starting the fight]. (4) To fix a neutral zone where the disarming can take place. (5) The truce to last twenty-four hours, during which time conditions of surrender will be formulated. (6) All units of the garrison which took part in the fighting must return to their barracks. The Commander of the Moscow Military District assumes control over the garrison.

Provision was also made for the formation of a general democratic organ. . . . . The official truce lasted from midnight, November 11, until midnight, November 12. . . . .

November 12

. . . . The Bolsheviks took advantage of the truce to rearrange the position of their artillery and bring reinforcements to a number of points.[82]

[81] *Russkoe Slovo,* No. 245, November 21, 1917, p. 3.

[82] The Bolsheviks claim that their opponents used the truce to improve their positions. (*Oktiabrskie dni v Moskve i raionakh,* p. 22.)

The negotiations of November 12 ended in a complete break between the Committee of Public Safety and the Bolsheviks. The latter, when they realized that the superiority was on their side, began to insist on the transfer of power to the Soviets.

The fighting continued for two days more. Both sides received reinforcements, but the advantage lay with the Bolsheviks, whose artillery caused considerable damage to the Kremlin and other public buildings. The Council of the Russian Church exhorted the combatants to end the bloodshed and to save the Kremlin from destruction.[83] When the news of the bombardment reached Petrograd, Lunacharsky in protest resigned as Commissar of Education but withdrew his resignation the next day.[84] On the 15th the Committee of Public Safety decided to surrender and the terms of capitulation were signed at 5:00 P.M.

THE COMMITTEE OF PUBLIC SAFETY DECIDES TO SURRENDER

[Statement, November 15][85]

The artillery fire directed on the Kremlin and the rest of Moscow is not causing any damage to our troops but is destroying monuments and sacred places and is bringing death to peaceful citizens. Conflagrations and famine are already in progress. The Committee of Public Safety in the interest of the population of Moscow puts the following question to the Military Revolutionary Committee: On what concrete conditions will the Military Revolutionary Committee immediately cease military operations? For its own part the Committee of Public Safety considers it imperative under existing conditions to end the armed struggle against the political system initiated by the Moscow Military Revolutionary Committee and to adopt purely political methods of struggle, leaving to the future the solution, on an All-Russian scale, of the question of the construction of government both central and local.

[83] Oldenbourg, pp. 376–77.

[84] *Delo Naroda,* No. 198, November 16, 1917, p. 3. As an expression of grief over the destruction of the holy and artistic monuments in Moscow, the actors of the Petrograd theaters decided to close the playhouses for three days (*Delo Naroda,* No. 201, November 19, 1917, p. 2). Similar action was taken by the Moscow actors (*Russkiia Vedomosti,* No. 245, November 21, 1917, p. 3).

[85] *Oktiabrskoe vosstanie v Moskve,* pp. 97–98.

CONDITIONS OF SURRENDER

[Agreement between the Military Revolutionary Committee and the Committee of Public Safety, November 15, 5 P.M.][86]

(1) The Committee of Public Safety is to end its existence.

(2) The White Guards are to surrender their arms and disband. The cadet military schools are to be allowed to retain whatever arms are needed for instruction; the rest must be given up. The Military Revolutionary Committee is to guarantee freedom and inviolability to everyone.

(3) A special commission is to be organized to disarm the White Guards, as stipulated in Section 2; the committee to consist of representatives of the Military Revolutionary Committee, of the commanding personnel, and of organizations that took part in the negotiations.

(4) All military operations must cease from the moment of signing of the peace agreement.

(5) All prisoners taken by either side are to be set free immediately after the agreement has been signed.

Representatives of the Military Revolutionary Committee: V. SMIRNOV, I. SMIDOVICH
Representatives of the Committee of Public Safety: V. RUDNEV, I. SOROKIN, S. STUDENETSKY
Representative of the Troops Loyal to the Government: YAKULOV
Representatives of the Moscow Organization of the Social Democratic Party (Internationalists): V. VOLGIN, A. PLESKOV

Provincial towns and villages responded in various ways to the news of the overturn in Petrograd. In some of the larger towns with an industrial population events followed very much the Petrograd pattern. Elsewhere, as a rule, local Soviets took control in some cases under Bolshevik domination, in others under the S.R.'s, and often as a socialist coalition. Here and there the zemstvos and institutions and appointees of the Provisional Government continued to function for weeks or even months after the overturn in the capital. Regions inhabited by the Cossacks and by non-Russian nationalities in general refused to recognize the Bolshevik régime and, having set up their own governing institutions, proclaimed their intention to become autonomous units in a

[86] *Oktiabrskoe vosstanie v Moskve,* pp. 236–37.

future Russian Federal Republic. The following materials are illustrative of what took place in Great Russia. Events in the areas of the Cossacks and non-Russian nationalities are discussed in chapter viii.

THE NOVEMBER UPRISING IN SARATOV[87]

. . . . The so-called October [November] revolution, i.e., when the power passed into the hands of the Soviet of Workers and Peasants in which the Bolsheviks formed a majority, took place in Saratov on November 8–10, 1917. On November 8, at one o'clock in the morning, at a meeting of the Soviet, it was decided to help the Petrograd workers who had risen against the Provisional Government. The Socialists of the Right, the Socialist-Revolutionists, and the Mensheviks, left the Soviet and decided, together with the representatives of the bourgeoisie, to seize the power at the City Duma. But the garrison was with the Soviet. The City Duma was defended only by students of the officers' school, by officers, and by the hurriedly formed troops of college and high-school students. The Duma called the Cossacks from Balanda Station and Penza to help them, hoping to hold their own with the small force they had till help arrived. But there was a sufficient number of followers of the Soviet, especially among the railway employees, to breed dissatisfaction among the Cossacks, and to delay their arrival. Meanwhile the Duma got no satisfactory news from Petrograd, and on November 10, after some shooting, the Duma surrendered, and the Soviet took control in Saratov into their hands. Meanwhile, the Cossacks were approaching Saratov and the Soviet began to build trenches around the city. At the same time the city and uezd organs of administration were undergoing radical reconstruction. The negotiations with the Cossacks continued for a week. During that time the Communistic propaganda among the Cossacks unsettled their ranks and the Cossack officers had to agree to peace. After this the employees of the different organizations went on strike, and only by the strict and sometimes severe administration of the Bolshevik commissars, who were appointed in all organizations, did the government succeed in getting the work into some sort of order.

[87] From *Civil War in Saratov Gubernia and in the Region of the Volga.* A manuscript in the Hoover War Library, by a citizen of Saratov.

THE NOVEMBER REVOLUTION IN THE VILLAGES

[Extracts from a Peasant's Recollection of Events in a Village of Kaluga Gubernia][88]

With the coming of October more than half of the peasants joined the soldiers, who already called themselves Bolsheviks. Those who joined the Bolsheviks belonged chiefly to the poor and middle peasantry. However, they did not dare as yet to annihilate the rights of pomeshchiks and only eagerly awaited the news of another revolution of which soldiers said that "soon Bolsheviks will rise and will give everything to the workers and peasants, sending all soldiers home and ending war forever."

These days came. The number of Bolsheviks in the village grew from day to day. The peasants became tired of the terrible war, every village had many wounded and killed workers. This was one of the reasons that made the peasantry join the Bolsheviks, i.e., for the sake of quick cessation of war. . . . .

No force could stop the peasants headed by the soldiers from the seizure of land and estates from pomeshchiks. The population of the entire villages and sometimes several villages set off for the pomeshchiks' estates in carts and on horseback armed with whatever they had. . . . .

Some pomeshchiks only begged to have their lives spared. . . . .

Having looted the pomeshchiks' property, the peasants proceeded immediately to divide the land, to fell the trees, and to repair their own houses.

The Kulak peasants, watching this, began to hide under the ground all their property, such as food supplies, clothing, valuable furniture, china, as well as money, fearing that this property would be confiscated. All this hidden treasure perished: 75 per cent was destroyed completely and 25 per cent came to be unfit for use. That is what was taking place in our village until December 1917.

YA. NAUMCHENKOV

[In Tver Gubernia][89]

The news of the November Revolution soon spread over Russia and on the third day our volost knew that the authority passed to the Soviets headed by the Soviet of People's Commissars with Lenin at the head.

Local Socialist-Revolutionists and other critics of the Bolsheviks

[88] I. V. Igritsky, *1917 god v derevne. Vospominaniia krestian*, Moscow, 1929, pp. 206–208.

[89] *Ibid.*, pp. 227–28.

declared at the meetings that "the Bolsheviks seized power because they deceived the soldiers, the poor, and the peasants. . . . . This, however, will not last long because the soldiers at the front are for the Provisional Government and, therefore, the usurpers' power will soon vanish."

However, the soldiers who spoke at these meetings definitely stated that the soldiers at the front were against the government and for the Soviets. They also described the plans of the Soviet government. These men were very active in carrying out into life the new government's program. The village began to be divided into two hostile camps: the poor for the Soviets, and the rich against them.

The work in the volost zemstvo proceeded slowly. The population paid less and less attention and followed less and less the orders of land committees. Seizures of land took place in different volosts. . . . . In the beginning of November during the session of uezd zemstvo, information was received regarding the passing of Kerensky's troops near Petrograd to the Bolsheviks. . . . . In spite of the fact that in a number of neighboring uezds the authority passed to the Soviets in November, in our Vesegonsky Uezd this change took place only in January with the help of a detachment of revolutionary soldiers, specially sent, while in our volost the transfer of the authority actually took place only in March 1918 with the help of the sailors from Kronstadt who happened to be on leave. . . . .

A. Vorobev

CHAPTER IV

THE BOLSHEVIKS AND THE SOCIALIST OPPOSITION

The defeat of the Kerensky expedition and their victories in Moscow and elsewhere strengthened the Bolsheviks not only by removing the immediate menace of an armed counter-attack but also by weakening the position of the Socialists, who demanded that the Bolsheviks share the power in the new government with representatives of other groups of the revolutionary democracy. During the remaining three weeks of November the Bolsheviks defeated the attempts made to bring them to agree to a Socialist coalition government, despite a revolt of some of their own leaders. They did, however, give a minority position in the government to the Left Socialist-Revolutionists, who accepted the Bolshevik program, and they gained the support of a special congress of peasant delegates. Further they imposed new restrictions on the opposition press and successfully met the strike of the employees in state offices. Finally, during this period they issued a number of important decrees in their social and economic program and succeeded in opening armistice negotiations with the Germans. These matters are treated in chapters v and vi.

A. THE BOLSHEVIK PROGRAM IN THE SOVNARKOM AND CENTRAL EXECUTIVE COMMITTEE

It will be recalled that just before it adjourned the Second Congress of Soviets voted to establish a Soviet of People's Commissars (Sovnarkom) as the executive organ of the new government; the Sovnarkom was to be subject to the control of the All-Russian Congress of Workers', Soldiers', and

Peasants' Deputies and its Central Executive Committee. The members of the Sovnarkom, chosen by the Bolshevik Central Committee, were approved by the Congress and a list of members of the new C.E.C. was announced.[1] For the time being the duties of the C.E.C. were largely perfunctory, since policies were determined by the Bolshevik Central Committee and executed by the Sovnarkom. Opposition to some of the acts of the Sovnarkom was voiced in the Central Executive Committee, but the attempt to give the Central Executive Committee the power of a legislative chamber—to debate, approve, or reject the acts of the Sovnarkom—failed. Many of the decrees issued by the Sovnarkom were of a fundamental character, for, as Trotsky says,[2] ". . . . Lenin was eagerly impatient to answer all problems of economic, political, administrative, and cultural life by decrees. In this he was guided . . . . by a desire to unfold the party's program in the language of power. . . . . Lenin was in a hurry to tell the people what the new power was, what it was after, and how it intended to accomplish its aims."

THE FIRST DAYS OF THE SOVNARKOM

[Larin's Recollections (Extract)][3]

During the first days of its existence the Sovnarkom met in room No. 36 in the Smolny Institute. The room was small and dirty. During these days the Sovnarkom and the party Central Committee were not clearly differentiated.[4] . . . .

The first law was published in No. 1 of the *Gazeta Vremennogo*

[1] The new Central Executive Committee met for the first time on November 9 and elected Kamenev provisional chairman.

[2] *My Life*, p. 342.

[3] Yu. Larin, "U kolybeli," in *Narodnoe Khoziaistvo*, No. 11, November 1918, pp. 16–17. Larin was chief of the Bureau of Legislation of the Sovnarkom.

[4] A member of the staff of *Novaia Zhizn* who visited Smolny during the first days of the Bolshevik régime makes the following remarks: "In one room Lenin and Trotsky act in the capacity of people's commissars. In the next room they become the Central Committee of the Bolsheviks. In still another room they are the Central Executive Committee of the Soviets. . . . . In one room they propose resolutions which the Central Executive Committee ordinarily approves without discussion. In the next room they write decrees which are looked upon as laws." (*Novaia Zhizn*, No. 180, November 27, 1917, p. 2; cf. Trotsky, *My Life*, p. 343.)

Rabochego i Krestianskogo Pravitelstva [*Gazette of the Provisional Workers' and Peasants' Government*] . . . . It authorized the local organs of administration . . . . to requisition warehouses, stores, restaurants, and other trading and industrial establishments. . . . . This decree was the only legal basis for the numerous requisitions which local "Sovdeps"[5] afterwards undertook. . . . . The government held no regular sessions at that time. The first decree of the Sovnarkom was drafted by Kamenev, Stalin, and myself. . . . . There was much talk how to sign it, "Lenin," "Ulianov," or both. Stalin signed "Vladimir Ulianov-Lenin" and sent it to the press. . . . .

Of the first fifteen decrees which are found in No. 1 of the Collection of Laws [*Sobranie Uzakonenii i Rasporiazhenii Rabochego i Krestianskogo Pravitelstva*] only two were actually considered by the Sovnarkom. . . . . I remember Lenin's astonishment when he first saw . . . . the decree No. 12, under his signature, which conferred legislative powers on the Sovnarkom (the Congress of Soviets granted only executive powers) and gave the Central Executive Committee the right to annul the decisions of the government. (The Congress had given the Central Executive Committee only the right of recall and of supervision.) . . . .

[Pestkovsky's Recollections][6]

[Pestkovsky relates that he visited Smolny in search of a job in the government. After visiting Trotsky and Lenin, he entered the room opposite Lenin's office.]

The room was rather large. In one corner the Secretary of the Sovnarkom, Comrade N. P. Gorbunov, was working at a small table. . . . . Farther on, Comrade Menzhinsky, looking very tired, was lounging on a sofa . . . . over [which] was the sign: "The People's Commissariat of Finance."

I sat down near Menzhinsky and began to talk with him. In the most innocent way he started to question me about my earlier career and became curious in regard to my past studies.

I answered . . . . that I had worked at the University of London, where, among other subjects, I had studied finance.

Menzhinsky suddenly arose, fixed his eyes upon me, and categorically declared: In that case we shall make you the director of the State Bank.

I was frightened and answered . . . . that I had no desire to hold this position, since it was entirely "outside my line." Saying nothing, Menzhinsky asked me to wait, and left the room.

He was gone for some time, and then returned with a paper signed

[5] Soviets of Deputies.

[6] "Ob oktiabrskikh dniakh v Pitere," in *Proletarskaia Revoliutsiia,* 1922, No. 10, pp. 99–100.

by Ilich [Lenin] on which it was stated that I was the director of the State Bank.

I became even more dumfounded, and began to beg Menzhinsky to revoke the appointment, but he remained inflexible on this point.[7]

THE RIGHT TO ISSUE LAWS

[Decree of the Sovnarkom, November 12, 1917][8]

1. From now on until the convocation of the Constituent Assembly the preparation and drafting of laws shall be carried out by the Provisional Government of Workers and Peasants elected by the All-Russian Congress of Soviets of Workers', Soldiers', and Peasants' Deputies in the order set forth in the present regulations.

2. Each law project is to be submitted to the government by the respective Commissariat concerned, over the signature of the corresponding People's Commissar; or it may be submitted by the Bureau of Legislative Projects attached to the government over the signature of the chief of the department.

3. After it has passed the government, the decree in its final wording is to be signed in the name of the Russian Republic by the President of the Soviet of People's Commissars or, acting in his stead, by the People's Commissar who submitted the said decree for the consideration of the government; it will then be published for general information.

4. The day of its publication in the official Gazette of the Provisional Workers' and Peasants' Government will be the day on which a decree is recognized as having come into force as a law.

5. Other conditions by which it may come into force may be especially mentioned, or it may become effective by telegraph, in which case it will be considered as having come into force whenever and wherever such telegrams are published.

6. The publication of government decrees by the State Senate is suspended. The Bureau of Legislative Projects attached to the Soviet of People's Commissars is to publish periodically digests of those decrees and ordinances of the government which have become laws.

7. The Central Executive Committee of the Soviet of Workers', Soldiers', and Peasants' Deputies has a right to defer, modify, or annul any decisions of the government.[9]

V. ULIANOV (LENIN)
President of the Soviet of People's Commissars

[7] "Stanislav Pestkovsky is hereby appointed director of the State Bank," *Izvestiia*, No. 225, November 27, 1917, p. 6.

[8] *S.U.R.*, 1917, No. 1, pp. 10–11.

[9] W. R. Batsell, *Soviet Rule in Russia*, New York, 1929, pp. 77–79, gives a translation of a plan of organization of the Central Executive Committee dated

The practice of the Sovnarkom of issuing decrees without referring them to the Central Executive Committee brought objections from the Socialist-Revolutionists of the Left, who as yet had no place in the executive body. This objection was promptly voted down in the C.E.C. by the Bolshevik majority, but two weeks later, after the Bolsheviks and Left S.R.'s had come to an agreement,[10] the relation of the two organs was more precisely defined with an apparent extension of the authority of the C.E.C.

THE SOCIALIST-REVOLUTIONISTS OBJECT TO THE PROCEDURE OF THE SOVNARKOM

[Meeting of the Central Executive Committee, November 17, 1917][11]

The group of the Socialist-Revolutionists of the Left recommends that the Central Executive Committee ask the President of the Soviet of Commissars, Ulianov-Lenin, the following questions:

At the Second Congress of Soviets of Workers' and Soldiers' Deputies it was determined that the government was to be responsible to the Central Executive Committee . . . . and yet during the last days a number of decrees have been published in the name of the government which were not submitted to the Central Executive Committee for consideration and approval. In this way government measures were introduced which abolished all civil liberties. We wish that the President of the Soviet of Commissars would explain:

1. Why decrees or other [official] acts are not submitted to the Central Executive Committee and

2. If the government intends to give up this arbitrarily constituted and altogether illegal procedure of issuing decrees.

V. KARELIN, V. SAPIRO, A. SCHREIDER
V. DMITRIEVSKY-ALEXANDROVICH
I. NESTEROV, S. KOTLIAREVSKY
I. V. BALASHEV, PETR BUKHARTSEV
A. PROSHIAN, S. ZAK, GR. ZAKS

November 15, 1917. The plan provided for large and small sessions, for a presidium, and for eleven departments or commissions.

[10] See below, p. 215.

[11] L. Trotsky, *Sochineniia,* III, Book 2, 43.

THE CENTRAL EXECUTIVE COMMITTEE APPROVES THE PROCEDURE OF THE SOVNARKOM

[Resolution, November 17, 1917][12]

In reply to the questions raised the Central Executive Committee resolves that:

1. The Soviet parliament of the toiling masses has nothing in common with the procedure of bourgeois parliaments where different classes and divergent interests meet and where the representatives of the ruling class use rules of procedure for the purpose of parliamentary obstruction.

2. The Soviet parliament cannot deny the Soviet of People's Commissars the right to issue decrees of immediate necessity in the spirit of the general program of the All-Russian Congress of Soviets without first submitting them to the C.E.C.

3. The C.E.C. has general control over all the acts of the Soviet of People's Commissars with the power to recall the government or any member of it.

4. The C.E.C. expresses its regret that the representatives of the Socialist-Revolutionists of the Left whose members raised the question did not find it possible to associate themselves with the government in the drafting of all the decrees of immediate necessity.

RELATION OF THE CENTRAL EXECUTIVE COMMITTEE TO THE SOVNARKOM

[Resolution of the C.E.C., November 30, 1917][13]

1. In accordance with the decision of the Second All-Russian Congress, the Soviet of People's Commissars is wholly responsible to the Central Executive Committee.

2. All legislative acts and important ordinances of a general political character are to be submitted to the Central Executive Committee for examination and ratification.

3. Measures relating to the fight against counter-revolution may be taken directly by the Soviet of People's Commissars with the reservation of its responsibility to the Central Executive Committee.

4. Once a week each of the People's Commissars will give an account of his acts to the Central Executive Committee.

5. An immediate reply will be given to interpellations made by the Central Executive Committee. An interpellation, in order to be valid, must be presented by at least fifteen members of the Central Executive Committee.

[12] L. Trotsky, *Sochineniia,* III, Book 2, 108–109.

[13] Popov, *Oktiabrskii perevorot,* p. 292.

B. Inter-Party Negotiations

The question of the composition of the government raised by non-Bolshevik groups immediately after the uprising of November 7 remained a critical issue even after the Bolshevik victories at Pulkovo and Moscow. The Vikzhel ultimatum of November 11 had, as we already know, brought together representatives of the parties and of the City Duma in a conference at the headquarters of the Railwaymen's Union. After three days of almost continuous session this conference had worked out a tentative plan of a new government responsible to an assembly made up of representatives of various existing organs such as the old and new Central Executive Committees, the army committees, the Moscow and Petrograd dumas, trade unions, et cetera. The conference adjourned about 2:00 A.M., November 14, and the delegates reported to their organizations on the results of the Vikzhel conferences.

REPORT ON THE VIKZHEL CONFERENCE AT THE PETROGRAD SOVIET[14]

[November 14]

. . . . Comrade Sokolnikov reported on the negotiations with the Socialist parties. . . . . When the Railwaymen's Union proposed coming together for the purpose of reaching an agreement the Bolsheviks and Socialist-Revolutionists of the Left were the first to accept. The Mensheviks said that one should talk to the Bolsheviks with guns and declined to come; and the Central Committee of the Socialist-Revolutionists was against an agreement with the Bolsheviks. A little later the Socialist-Revolutionists abandoned their position and declared that although they refused to negotiate with the Bolsheviks as a party they had no objections to having individual Bolsheviks in the ministry. The Central Committee of the Mensheviks also gave in and declared that although the Mensheviks would not go into the ministry they would support a ministry which included Bolsheviks. Later the Mensheviks agreed to enter the government. From today's discussion it is quite evident that in coming to this decision they [the Mensheviks] intended to propose conditions that would make an agreement impossible.

[14] *Izvestiia,* No. 215, November 16, 1917, p. 5.

At yesterday's conference two questions were considered: (1) the formation of a body to which the government should be responsible, and (2) the Bolshevik proposal that the government should be responsible to the Central Executive Committee of the All-Russian Congress [second].

The Mensheviks favored a new institution—National Soviet—to which the new government should be responsible. The composition of this new National Soviet was to be as follows: (*a*) 100 men from the old and new Central Executive Committees as they may agree among themselves; (*b*) representatives of the Central Executive Committee of the Soviet of Peasants' Deputies as it is made up at present (the Bolsheviks opposed this on the ground that the present Central Executive Committee of the Peasants' Deputies no longer represented the peasant masses but only the Avxentievs); (*c*) 100 representatives of city dumas; (*d*) 80 representatives of the army and navy, that is, army committees; (*e*) 40 representatives of railway, post, and telegraph unions.

Altogether there were to be 420 representatives in the National Soviet.

Out of this number the Central Executive Committee of the Soviet of Workers' and Soldiers' Deputies would have 100, which would include representatives of the old Central Executive Committee. This would give the new Central Executive Committee only about one-sixth of the total [420] places. This National Soviet would be no other than our old acquaintance, the Pre-Parliament, and it would give a majority to the followers of Kerensky. . . . . We said no, no, and again, no. . . . . The Mensheviks and Socialist-Revolutionists proposed to exclude Lenin and Trotsky. (*Exclamations: "This will never happen."*) . . . .

The question before us is whether to come to an agreement on such terms or to go on with the fight. To agree means to put a cross over the grave of the revolution and to admit that all our sacrifices have been in vain. We are on the way to victory. Kerensky's shameful attempt has failed miserably. . . . . We are offered an agreement and an armistice so as to win time to bring up military assistance for Kerensky. . . . . Let's fight on to victory, to the point where the will of the All-Russian Congress will be recognized. (*Loud applause.*)

REPORT ON THE VIKZHEL CONFERENCE AT THE CITY DUMA

[November 14, 1917]

Shirsky reported on the Vikzhel conference. . . . . The reporter presided over the conference when the question of the composition of the future government came up. . . . . On this question it was agreed

[15] *Delo Naroda,* No. 197, November 15, 1917, pp. 3–4. The first speaker was An-sky (Rapoport). The substance of his report is contained in the statement quoted in chapter iii, pp. 166–70.

that for the present it should be considered from a general point of view, leaving the determination of details to a future date.

N. D. Avxentiev and V. M. Chernov were proposed as candidates for the post of prime minister. The Bolsheviks objected to Avxentiev; as for Chernov, it was pointed out that he would be unacceptable to the foreign powers. . . . . The Bolsheviks were then asked if they had a candidate of their own for the post of prime minister, to which they replied that their cabinet already had a prime minister. This reply, however, was hardly made in earnest, as the Bolsheviks did not insist on Lenin's candidacy. . . . .

For the post of minister of foreign affairs the following candidates were proposed: Avxentiev, Trotsky, Skobelev, and Pokrovsky. The last-named is professor of history at the University of Moscow, and shares, according to the Bolsheviks, their point of view. Skobelev's candidacy was rejected by mutual agreement, while that of Trotsky was vetoed by the Right wing of the conference. Verkhovsky was proposed for the post of minister of war; Verderevsky as minister of the navy; Lunacharsky and Salazkin, education; Maliantovich and Sokolov, justice; Professor Rozhkov of the University of Moscow, Skvortsov, and Kuzovkov, finance; Maslov, agriculture; Krasikov,[16] industry and commerce. The latter is a Bolshevik and an engineer in charge of a large industrial concern. . . . .

After long debate the Duma passed the following resolution:

"The City Duma hereby reaffirms its stand on the rôle of the city government in the civil war which is now in progress. It instructs its delegates to the Vikzhel [conference] to use every means to stop the bloodshed.

"At the same time the City Duma considers it advisable to take part in the Democratic Soviet which [the conference] proposes to organize."

THE BOLSHEVIKS DISCUSS THE VIKZHEL COMPROMISE

[Meeting of the Bolshevik Central Committee, November 14, 1917][17]

Comrade Kamenev made a report on the negotiations with the representatives of the [Socialist] parties, Vikzhel and others, ... on the question of forming an organ to which the government would be responsible. . . . .

Comrade Trotsky said the report gave him the impression that the parties who took no part in the uprising were trying to snatch the power from those who overthrew it [Kerensky's government]. "It was hardly

[16] It was probably Krasin and not Krasikov who was mentioned for the post of Minister of Commerce.

[17] *Proletarskaia Revoliutsiia,* 1922, No. 10, pp. 465–70.

worth while to organize the uprising if we cannot have a majority. If they [opponents] do not agree to this it means that they are against our program. We should have 75 per cent. We cannot allow [our opponents] to remove members of the government [viz., Lenin and Trotsky] or to prevent Lenin from being the president of the government. We could agree to admit representatives of the Duma if these bodies would have a re-election in the course of a week." . . . .

Comrade Lunacharsky thought that the Central Committee could not reconsider its decision. It had decided that the Bolsheviks must insist on a majority in the Central Executive Committee, a majority in the government, and the [acceptance of the] Bolshevik program. It was not necessary to reconsider the question. The delegation had enough instruction on these points. Lunacharsky, on the other hand, protested against the idea that the Bolsheviks must have 75 per cent; such a decision had not been taken. . . . .

Comrade Lenin said that it was time to put an end to Kamenev's politics; that it was not worth while to negotiate with Vikzhel. The thing to do was to send soldiers to Moscow. . . . .

The negotiations should be regarded as a diplomatic move to conceal war plans. . . . . It is necessary to send help to Moscow and the victory will be complete. . . . .

Comrade Rykov said . . . . that he took the negotiations seriously. If they were discontinued, the Bolsheviks would alienate those groups that support them, and would not then be in a position to retain power. Kamenev acted quite properly. . . . .

Comrade Zinoviev was of the opinion that it was very important for the party to come to an agreement; but it was not necessary to accept the proposed conditions. We lay down two conditions: our program and the responsibility of the government to the Soviets, as the source of all authority. If Vikzhel which has so far been neutral comes out against us, it is not likely that it can be brought into line by military force. It will take several weeks to settle the strike [of railwaymen] and in the meantime [the fight] will be lost. He called attention to the delegation from the Obukhov[18] factories, Kaledin, etc. . . . . I am for agreement; but that does not mean that I am for accepting all the proposals.

Comrade Lenin: . . . . It is time to put an end to delegations. It is clear to me that Vikzhel is on the side of the Kaledins and Kornilovs. This is no time for hesitation. The majority of workers and peasants in the army are with us. No one has yet proved that the lower classes are against us. [We must side] either with the agents of Kaledin or with the lower masses. We should lean upon the masses, send agitators to the villages. We have asked Vikzhel to transport troops to Moscow and

[18] See p. 167, above.

Vikzhel has refused. Let's appeal to the masses and they will overthrow it [Vikzhel].

Comrade Sverdlov argued that the negotiations should not be discontinued but changed. . . . .

The question of breaking up the negotiation was then put to vote. Four were in favor, ten voted against. . . . .

[The following resolution was adopted]:

"In view of the fact that all previous negotiations have fully demonstrated that the compromisers are not aiming to form a unified Soviet Government but are trying to split the ranks of the workers and soldiers, to disrupt the Soviet Government, and to win over the Socialist-Revolutionists of the Left to the camp of the bourgeoisie, the Central Committee resolved to allow party members to attend today's negotiations in which for the last time the Socialist-Revolutionists of the Left will make a final attempt to form a so-called uniform [Socialist] government. [The Bolshevik delegates] must try to show the impossibility of such an attempt and the futility of further negotiations on the subject of forming a coalition government."

[Meeting of the Bolshevik Petrograd Committee, November 14, 1918][19]

Ya. G. Fenigstein: . . . . It is a question of co-ordinating our work with that of the Mensheviks and the Socialist-Revolutionists . . . . to find an agreement with other Socialist parties. The considerations that "blood is flowing," that the workers are exhausted, should not be given much weight. A political party which wishes to make history cannot stop before these [considerations].

Lenin: . . . . It is a question of a party crisis which has now come out in the open. . . . . Those who watched the development of the party are familiar with the polemics which I conducted in the *Rabochii Put* against Kamenev and Zinoviev. . . . . When the question of an insurrection was raised at the meeting of the Central Committee on October 14 . . . . a few old members of the Central Committee were in opposition. This chagrined me very much . . . . for how could we give up [the insurrection] just because Zinoviev and Kamenev disagreed? . . . . I appealed then to the Central Committee, urging their expulsion from the party. . . . . Now that the victory is won I would not like to be too severe with them and [at first] I rather favored Kamenev's attempts to reach an agreement [with the other Socialists]. . . . . But when the Socialist-Revolutionists refused to take part in the government I understood that they did this because of the armed resistance which Kerensky raised . . . . and [because] of the delay in the seizure of power in Moscow. Our right-wingers became despondent . . . . and

[19] L. Trotsky, *Stalinskaia shkola falsifikatsii,* Berlin, 1932, pp. 116–24.

raised the question of an agreement. . . . . During the fight in Moscow the cadets committed many atrocities . . . . while the Bolsheviks showed themselves too kind-hearted. Had the bourgeoisie won they would have behaved very much as they did in 1848 or 1871. Who ever thought that we should encounter no sabotage on the part of the bourgeoisie? Even an infant could anticipate that. What we have to do is to apply force: to arrest the bank directors, etc. . . . . By themselves they [bank directors] cannot fight. Their sole concern is to retain their soft jobs. In Paris the guillotine was used, while [all we do] is to deprive them of food cards. . . . . It is our duty to do this.

We are now threatened with a split [in the party]. Zinoviev and Kamenev say that we cannot gain control over the country as a whole. I cannot listen calmly to this talk. It is betrayal. What do they want? That there should be a fight of all against all? Only the proletariat can save the country. . . . . As for an agreement, I cannot even speak about that seriously. Trotsky said long ago that a union was impossible. Trotsky understood this, and from that time on there has been no better Bolshevik.[20]

Zinoviev says that we [alone] cannot form a Soviet government, that we are only [one party], that there are also Socialist-Revolutionists and Mensheviks who withdrew, etc. But it was not our fault that they left. We were elected by the Congress of Soviets . . . . an organization . . . . which united those who wished to fight. . . . .

We are told that we should stop [our policies]. But this is impossible. . . . . If you wish a split, go ahead. If you get the majority, take the power in the Central Executive Committee and carry on. We'll go to the sailors. . . . . We are told that we cannot maintain ourselves in power alone, etc. But we are not alone. The whole of Europe is with us. We have got to make a beginning. Only a Socialist revolution can succeed now. All those doubts . . . . are nonsense. When I spoke at a people's meeting [and said] that we should take away the bread cards from [the bourgeoisie] the sailors' faces glowed with enthusiasm. . . . . The peasant delegate from Tver said at the [Second] Congress of Soviets: "Arrest them all." . . . . Here is a man who grasped the meaning of the dictatorship of the proletariat! Our present slogan is: No compromise! A homogeneous Bolshevik government.

Lunacharsky: . . . . I was surprised to hear Vladimir Ilich [Lenin] say that Kamenev was not for a Socialist revolution. . . . . Our influence grows. The peasants are coming to our side. . . . . Our land decree is

[20] Trotsky alleges that these words of Lenin were removed from the records of the Bureau of Party History as "obviously" incorrect, but he implies that the real cause for their removal was a part of the Stalin campaign to minimize his part in the revolution and to conceal Lenin's commendation. (*The Real Situation in Russia,* New York [1928], pp. 226–27.)

based on the resolution of the Socialist-Revolutionists. [We should give them, therefore, a place in the government.] The Right opposition insisted [during the negotiations with the other Socialists]on a homogeneous Socialist government. . . . . We further demanded workers' control and the regulation of industry by factory-shop committees. The other parties accept [these demands]. . . . . This is our program plus the Soviet [form] of government. Does it mean that we have to repudiate the city dumas? Are not our men sitting there? Should the dumas attempt to seize power, then we shall demolish them. . . . . [As things stand] we should give the dumas representation in the Soviet Government. Or shall we go on with the civil war just on account of this? No, this we will not do. . . . . We have already been in power eight days, but have we the assurance that the people have heard about the peace decree? . . . . The bourgeois and petty bourgeois technical personnel is against us. . . . . Famine is in sight. . . . . If the technical personnel continues to oppose us our foreign propaganda will fail. . . . . Of course, we can use terror, but what good will it do? . . . .

We seem to have acquired a great love for war, as if we were not workers but soldiers, a military party. We should be creating something positive, but instead we engage in polemics. It looks as though polemics will go on until one man remains—a dictator. . . . .

Trotsky: They tell us that we are incapable of creative work. In that case why do we not surrender the power to those . . . . who fight against us. . . . . They tell us that bayonets alone would not do. But we cannot go on without bayonets. We need bayonets *there* to sit [in safety] *here*. . . . . We must be ready for a merciless class war in the future. That mediocre riffraff which is incapable of taking sides is bound to join us as soon as they find out that force is on our side. . . . . The petty bourgeois masses will be only too glad to submit to a force after they know that there is one. He who cannot understand that understands nothing in the world, and least of all in political matters. As far back as 1871 Karl Marx said that a new class cannot make use of the old [state] machinery. That machinery has to be broken up. . . . .

The Bolshevik Central Committee then formulated the conditions given below which Volodarsky offered at the meeting of the C.E.C. which was held immediately. Against the opposition of the Socialist-Revolutionists of the Left and the Social-Democrat Internationalists, the Bolshevik resolution carried, 38 to 29.[21] The Social-Democrat Inter-

[21] *Revoliutsiia 1917 goda.* (*Khronika sobytii*) 6 vols., Moscow, 1923–1930. Vol. VI by I. N. Liubimov, *Oktiabr-dekabr,* p. 48. (Hereafter Vol. VI will be cited as Liubimov, *Revoliutsiia 1917 goda.*)

nationalists resigned from the C.E.C. as a protest against the resolution. The Left S.R.'s remained and raised the question again at the next session of the C.E.C., November 15–16, when another resolution on the negotiations was adopted.

BOLSHEVIK CONDITIONS OF AGREEMENT WITH THE OTHER SOCIALISTS[22]

[November 14, 1917]

Agreement with other Socialist parties is desirable . . . . on the following terms:

1. Acceptance of the program of the Soviet Government as expressed in the decrees of land and peace and the two projects on workers' control.
2. Unrelenting war against counter-revolution (Kerensky, Kornilov, Kaledin).
3. Acceptance of the Second All-Russian Congress of Soviets of Workers' and Soldiers' Deputies with the participation of peasants as the only source of authority.
4. The government to be responsible to the Central Executive Committee.
5. No admission into the Central Executive Committee of organizations not represented in the Soviet.
6. To enlarge the Central Executive Committee by admitting the following organizations: Soviets of Workers', Soldiers', and Peasants' Deputies (not yet represented); All-Russian trade union organizations, such as the Council of Trade Unions, Soviet of Factory-Shop Committees; Vikzhel and Post-Telegraph Union; All-Russian Soviet of Peasants' Deputies, on condition of and only after there has been a new election. [The same is to apply to] all those army organizations that have held no elections in the course of the last three months.

THE CENTRAL EXECUTIVE COMMITTEE AUTHORIZES CONTINUATION OF NEGOTIATIONS[23]

[November 15–16, 1917]

The Central Executive Committee is of the opinion that it is necessary to have in the government representatives of the Socialist parties that are in the Soviets of Workers', Soldiers', and Peasants' Deputies and which accept the conquests of the November 6–7 revolution; the

[22] *Izvestiia,* No. 214, November 15, 1917, p. 5.

[23] *Ibid.,* No. 216, November 17, 1917, p. 5.

decrees of land and peace, workers' control, and the arming of workmen. In view of that the Central Executive Committee authorizes the continuation of conversations relative to [the formation of] a government with the Soviet parties, but insists on the following conditions:

The government is to be responsible to the Central Executive Committee. . . . .

At least half of the ministerial posts . . . . [including] the ministries of Labor, Interior, and Foreign Affairs, shall go to the Bolsheviks. The command of the troops in the Petrograd and Moscow military districts shall be in the hands of representatives of the Petrograd and Moscow Soviets of Workers' and Soldiers' Deputies.

The government will set for itself the task of arming the workers all over Russia.

The candidacy of Lenin and Trotsky [for ministerial posts] should be insisted upon.

RESOLUTIONS OF THE CENTRAL COMMITTEE OF THE SOCIALIST-REVOLUTIONIST PARTY TO BREAK OFF NEGOTIATIONS[24]

[November 15, 1917]

The Socialist-Revolutionist Party has always been definitely opposed to the plans of the Bolsheviks, which led the country to civil war, to the disruption of the Constituent Assembly, to the disorganization of economic life and the army supply, to the general demoralization of the army and to the ruin of the country.

When, within a month of the Constituent Assembly and on the eve of the Congress of Soviets, the Bolsheviks, by means of a military insurrection, seized the government and shamelessly violated the will of democracy, the Central Committee of the Socialist-Revolutionist Party decided to leave the conspirators to their own fate, to recall their [Socialist-Revolutionist] members from the Military Revolutionary Committee, the Central Executive Committee, and all political organizations on which the Bolsheviks lean, and to organize the entire democracy against them in a Socialist government (excluding Bolsheviks). The program of this government was to be: prompt liquidation of the Bolshevik adventure, a law for the transfer of the land to the land committees, energetic measures to bring about an early conclusion of peace, and the calling of the Constituent Assembly on time.

But when civil war broke out all over the country and . . . . brother killed brother, the Central Committee of the Socialist-Revolutionist Party accepted the proposal of the All-Russian Union of Railwaymen

[24] *Delo Naroda,* No. 198, November 16, 1917, p. 1.

and, together with other parties and organizations, entered into conversations with the Bolsheviks. As a condition of these conversations, the Central Committee insisted on an immediate armistice and a cessation of all hostile acts. As a basis for discussion, it proposed the following:

1. The new government shall not be bound up with the Bolshevik coup d'état.

2. The new government shall be made up of the Socialists without Bolshevik representatives.

3. In selecting ministers there should be kept in mind the personality of the candidates and the aim of the government, especially the need of stopping the civil war, which is likely to spread all over the country.

In entering on these negotiations the Central Committee had but little hope that an agreement with the Bolsheviks was possible, but was determined to make use of every available means to avoid civil war. . . . .

The Bolsheviks, however, not only refused an armistice but continued the civil war. In Moscow they violated the armistice in order to turn that city into an arena for fratricide, and now, at the last meeting of the C.E.C., they passed a resolution . . . . that will not stop but will prolong the civil war. In view of that . . . .

The Central Committee of the Socialist-Revolutionist Party has come to the conclusion that an agreement with the Bolsheviks is impossible, and has decided to discontinue conversations and to recall its delegates from the conference called by the All-Russian Union of Railwaymen.

RESOLUTION OF THE CENTRAL COMMITTEE OF THE MENSHEVIKS ON CONDITIONS OF AGREEMENT[25]

[November 15, 1917]

In view of the fact that throughout the negotiations for an agreement the Bolsheviks stubbornly refused to yield to the demand for an immediate truce, to stop the system of political terror and revoke the orders for the arrest . . . . of members of the parties and organizations with which they were negotiating, and considering the resolutions of new Central Executive Committee and the Bolshevik Central Committee of November 14. . . . .

The Central Committee of the Russian Social Democratic Labor Party (United) feels bound to state that an agreement with the Bolsheviks is impossible and that the responsibility for all future consequences lies with the Bolsheviks.

The Central Committee . . . . however, is determined to make every effort in the future to stop civil war . . . . and is ready to resume nego-

[25] *Rabochaia Gazeta,* No. 202, November 16, 1917, p. 1.

tiations . . . . provided the Bolsheviks accept the following preliminary conditions . . . .:

1. To free all political prisoners. . . . .

2. To stop the system of political terror by restoring the freedom of the press, speech, assembly, association, strikes, and the inviolability of persons and domicile.

3. To declare a truce wherever civil war is going on.

4. To place at the disposal of the city municipality sufficient military force for the maintenance of order. . . . .

The Mensheviks and the Socialist-Revolutionists of the Right were not the only ones who believed that the Bolshevik domination of the government would result in a party dictatorship maintained by political terror. Within the Bolshevik ranks an influential minority, which favored a Socialist coalition, actively opposed the tactics of the majority led by Lenin. On November 16 Lenin attempted to silence the opposition by a threat of party discipline. But the opponents would not submit and the next day at the session of the Central Executive Committee moved that the Press Decree of November 9 be repealed. In this they were supported by the Socialist-Revolutionists of the Left, who were also opposed to a single-party dictatorship. The motion, however, was defeated and the Bolshevik minority resigned from the Sovnarkom and the Central Committee of the party. Likewise the Socialist-Revolutionists of the Left announced their withdrawal from the Military Revolutionary Committee and the Military Staff.

LENIN SERVES NOTICE ON THE MINORITY OPPOSITION

[Declaration of the Majority Group of the Bolshevik Central Committee, November 16, 1917][26]

The majority of the Central Committee of the R.S.D.L.P. (Bolshevik), which fully accepts the policy which the Soviet of People's Commissars has hitherto been following, finds it necessary to present to the minority of the Central Committee the following categorical notice:

[26] Lenin, *Sochineniia,* XXII, Moscow, 1929, pp. 38–39. A. S. Bubnov, a member of the Bolshevik Central Committee, gives the following account of the origin of the document. "On November 16, Lenin composed the text of the declaration

The present policy of our party is determined by the resolution introduced by Comrade Lenin and accepted by the Central Committee yesterday, November 15. This resolution makes it treason to the proletarian cause to attempt to force our party to relinquish power when the All-Russian Congress of Soviets handed over that power in the name of millions of workers, soldiers, and peasants to the representatives of our party on the basis of our party program. This fundamental aim of our tactics, which is a sequel to our whole struggle against the Kerensky government, forms at present the revolutionary essence of Bolshevism, and, having been accepted by the Central Committee, it is unconditionally binding on every member of the party and especially on the minority of the Central Committee.

Meanwhile the minority representatives, both prior to and after yesterday's session of the Central Committee, were engaged in a policy which is clearly directed against the fundamental aim of our policy and which demoralizes our ranks by sowing dissension at a moment when the greatest firmness and resolution are necessary. Thus, at yesterday's session of the C.E.C., the Bolshevik group, which includes members of the Central Committee belonging to the minority, openly voted against the resolution of the Central Committee (on the question of what number and what individuals should represent our party in the government).

Such an unheard-of infraction of discipline by members of the Central Committee behind the back of the Central Committee, after long hours of debate in the Central Committee initiated by the same opposition members, makes it quite evident that the opposition intends to capture the party institutions by starving out [the majority], by sabotaging the work of the party at a moment when the future of the party and of the revolution are at stake.

We cannot and will not assume the responsibility for this state of affairs. In presenting this notice to the minority of the Central Committee we demand a categorically written answer to the following question: Does the minority intend to submit to party discipline and to support the policy which was formulated in Comrade Lenin's resolution, and which was adopted by the Central Committee?

In case of a negative or indefinite answer to this question we shall appeal at once to the Petrograd and Moscow Committees [of the Bolshevik Party], to the Bolshevik group of the C.E.C., to the Petrograd [party] Conference, and to a special party congress with the following

. . . . and invited every member of the Central Committee to come to his private office one at a time. There he read them the text of the declaration, asking them to sign it" (*Izvestiia*, No. 256, November 6–7, 1927, p. 9). In this way he got nine signatures, including full members and candidates. The following affixed their names: Lenin, Trotsky, Stalin, Sverdlov, Uritsky, Dzerzhinsky, Joffé, Bubnov, Sokolnikov, and Muranov (Lenin, *Sochineniia,* XXII, 580).

alternative propositions: either the party will delegate the present opposition to form a new government with their present allies for whose sake the opposition is sabotaging our work, in which case we shall consider ourselves entirely free in regard to this new government which cannot bring anything but vacillation, weakness, and chaos, or—and this will no doubt happen—the party will approve the only possible revolutionary line expressed in yesterday's decision of the Central Committee, in which case the party must emphatically tell the representatives of the opposition to transfer their disorganizing activity outside the limits of our party organization. There is no other way out. It is beyond question that a split would be a regrettable thing. But just now an honest and open split is much better than sabotage, the undermining of one's own decisions, disorganization, and prostration. At any rate, we have not a moment's doubt that when our disagreements are referred to the judgment of the masses our policy will receive the unconditional and self-sacrificing support of the revolutionary workers, soldiers, and peasants, while the opposition will promptly be condemned to an impotent isolation.

BOLSHEVIK RESIGNATIONS FROM THE SOVNARKOM

[Statement Read in the Central Executive Committee, November 17, 1917][27]

We take the stand that it is necessary to form a Socialist government of all parties in the Soviet. We believe that only such a government can preserve the fruits of the heroic war won by the working class and the revolutionary army in the October–November days. The alternative is —a purely Bolshevik government which can maintain itself only by means of political terror. It is this last-named alternative which the Soviet of People's Commissars has chosen.[28] We cannot and will not accept it, for it is certain to alienate the proletarian masses and cause their withdrawal from political leadership; it will lead to the establishment of an irresponsible régime and to the ruin of the revolution and the country. We cannot assume responsibility for such a policy, and, therefore, we give up the name of People's Commissars.[29]

V. Nogin, People's Commissar of Commerce and Industry; A. Rykov, People's Commissar of Interior; V. Miliutin, People's Commissar of Agriculture; I. Teodorovich, People's Commissar

[27] *Novaia Zhizn,* No. 173, November 18, 1917, p. 3. This statement was made at the conclusion of the discussion of the decree on the press which is given below, pp. 221–22.

[28] It is interesting in this connection to note that the Soviet of People's Commissars consisted of only fourteen members, of whom five signed this document.

[29] In the debate following this announcement Trotsky retorted: "Let the weaklings go. Reduced in quantity but strengthened in quality we shall march on with

of Food; A. SHLIAPNIKOV,[30] People's Commissar of Labor; D. RIAZANOV, Commissar of Railways; N. DERBYSHEV, Commissar of the Press; I. ARBUZOV, Commissar of the State Printing Office; YURENEV,[30] Commissar of the Red Guard; G. FEDOROV, Chief of the Section of Conflicts in the Commissariat of Labor; YU. LARIN, Chief of Section of Legislation

RESIGNATION OF THE LEFT SOCIALIST-REVOLUTIONISTS

[Statement Read in the Central Executive Committee, November 17, 1917][31]

The resolution on the press just passed by the majority of the Central Executive Committee is a clear and sharp expression of the system of political terror and a kindling of civil war. The Socialist-Revolutionists who remain in the Central Executive Committee . . . . to protect the interest of the workers and peasants . . . . refuse to assume responsibility for the baneful system of terror and recall their representatives from the Military Revolutionary Committee, the Staff, and other responsible posts.

RESIGNATIONS FROM THE BOLSHEVIK CENTRAL COMMITTEE[32]

[November 17, 1917]

The resolution of the Central Committee of the Bolsheviks on November 14 practically amounts to a refusal to come to an understanding with the parties that make up the Soviet of Workers' and Soldiers' Deputies on the question of forming a Socialist Soviet Government. We believe that only by an agreement along the lines indicated by us will it be possible for the proletariat and the revolutionary army to strengthen their hold on the conquests of the November Revolution, to fortify their new positions, and to gather strength for continuing the struggle for socialism.

We believe that the formation of such a government is necessary to put a stop to the further shedding of blood, to halt the approaching famine, to crush Kaledin, to call the Constituent Assembly on time, and

our heads erect. You speak of the disruption of the government! No, this is not a disruption but a purification. Those of us who remain are determined not to make a single concession to the bourgeoisie and the intelligentsia groups who stand for agreement." (*Izvestiia,* No. 218, November 20, 1917, p. 4.)

30 "I agree with the above estimate of the political situation . . . . but do not feel it is right to resign."

31 Trotsky, *Sochineniia,* III, Book 2, 402.

32 *Delo Naroda,* No. 201, November 19, 1917, p. 1.

to put into life the program of peace passed by the Second All-Russian Congress of Soviets of Workers' and Soldiers' Deputies.

After unprecedented efforts we succeeded in having the decision of the Central Executive Committee reconsidered and in bringing forward a new resolution which could be used as a basis for forming a Soviet Government. But this new resolution has called forth such a series of measures on the part of the leading group of the Central Committee that it is quite clear that that group is determined not to permit the formation of a government of the parties in the Soviet and to insist on a purely Bolshevik government regardless of the sacrifices to the workers and soldiers.

We cannot assume responsibility for this ruinous policy of the Central Committee, carried out against the will of a large part of the proletariat and soldiers who are most eager for an early cessation of blood-shedding by the different wings of the democracy.

We resign from membership in the Central Committee so that we may be free to speak openly to the workers and soldiers and to ask them to support our slogan: Long live the government of the parties in the Soviet and an immediate understanding on these terms!

We leave the Central Committee at the moment of victory, at the moment when our party is dominant, but we do so because we cannot quietly look on while the leading group in the Central Committee wastes the fruit of this victory and leads the proletariat to ruin.

By remaining in the ranks of the proletarian party we hope that the proletariat will surmount all obstacles and will perceive that our actions were inspired by our feeling of duty and responsibility before the Socialist proletariat.

YU. KAMENEV G. ZINOVIEV
A. I. RYKOV V. NOGIN
V. MILIUTIN

LOZOVSKY'S CRITICISM OF PARTY POLICY

[A Letter to the Bolshevik Group in the Central Executive Committee, November 17, 1917][33]

DEAR COMRADES:

In view of the fact that the question of the day is group and party discipline, I deem it my duty to make the following statement:

I cannot, in the name of party discipline, be silent . . . . when I feel with all my soul that the tactics of the Central Committee are leading to the isolation of the advance guard of the proletariat, to civil war within the working class, and to the defeat of the great revolution.

[33] *Novaia Zhizn,* No. 172, November 17, 1917, pp. 1–2.

I cannot, in the name of party discipline, pass over the administrative zeal of the representatives of the Military Revolutionary Committee, such as the order issued by Colonel Muravev about taking the law into one's hand,[34] confiscation of enterprises. . . .

I cannot, in the name of party discipline, be silent when I see what is being done with the press; when I see before me houndings and persecutions, searches and arrests—all of which arouse the masses and lead them to think that the dictatorship of the proletariat which the socialists have preached for decades is the same as the old régime of the club and saber.

I cannot, in the name of party discipline, be silent when one of the People's Commissars threatens to remove the striking officials from the military exemption list and send them to the front; when the postal and telegraph employees are threatened with the loss of their food cards.

I cannot, in the name of party discipline, be silent when such acts and proclamations sweep away the right of combination won by the toilers in a bloody struggle. This right will undoubtedly continue in a socialist state just as the right to strike, in order to enforce political and economic demands.

I cannot, in the name of party discipline, be silent and thereby assume political and moral responsibility when the responsible leaders of the party proclaim that for every one of our men we will kill five of our opponents. This proclamation is similar to the one made by Hindenburg that he would burn three Russian villages for one Prussian.

I cannot, in the name of party discipline, remain silent when the Military Revolutionary Committee does as it pleases with the country, when it issues fantastic decrees about extraordinary tribunals, when it exceeds its military sphere and takes upon itself the civil administration of the country.

I cannot, in the name of party discipline, pass over in silence the discontent of the toiling masses that fought for a Soviet government only to discover that for reasons not clear to them this government has turned out to be a purely Bolshevik one.

I cannot, in the name of party discipline, be silent when Marxists . . . . refuse to look facts in the face and decline an agreement with all

[34] The order in question appeared on November 14 and ran as follows: "For the purpose of immediately restoring normal order in Petrograd and its environs, I order that the following be carried out to the letter:

(1) I intrust to the soldiers, sailors, and Red Guards and the whole revolutionary proletariat the maintenance of internal order in the capital. . . .

I order soldiers, sailors, and Red Guards to take the law into their own hands against representatives of the criminal element and to destroy them unsparingly, as soon as their participation in crimes against the lives, health, or property of citizens has been proved beyond doubt. . . ." (Popov, *Oktiabrskii perevorot*, p. 289.)

Socialist parties which would immediately end the war within the revolutionary democracy and which would unite all forces against Kaledin.

I cannot, in the name of party discipline, become a hero-worshiper and insist that this or that person must be a member of the government when our basic terms are accepted and when every minute of delay in coming to an agreement with all the Socialist parties means shedding of blood.

Finally, I cannot, in the name of party discipline, be silent when every day of war within the revolutionary democracy deepens the chasm in the working class, makes more difficult the fight against counter-revolution, and leads the revolution and Russia to an inevitable crash.

In view of all this I declare that I shall denounce in party meetings, in the C.E.C. and in labor circles the wrong and destructive (both for the party and working classes) tactics pursued by the Central Committee, that I shall mobilize party, labor, and public opinion to persuade the Central Committee to follow a better line and to call in the near future a congress of the party to decide: whether the Russian Social-Democratic Labor Party (Bolshevik), shall remain Marxist and the party of the working class or shall follow a course that has nothing in common with revolutionary Marxism.

With fraternal greetings,

A. Lozovsky[35]

LENIN THREATENS THE MINORITY OPPOSITION WITH EXPULSION FROM THE PARTY

[Ultimatum of November 18, 1917][36]

The Central Committee has already presented an ultimatum to the leading advocates of your policy (Kamenev and Zinoviev) requiring them to submit unconditionally to the decisions of the Central Committee and its program, to desist from sabotaging the work of the Committee, and to refrain from subversive activity of any kind.

Although they have broken with the Central Committee, the advocates of your program have remained within the ranks of the party and, by so doing, have assumed the obligation of submitting to the decision of the Central Committee. Meanwhile you are not content to spread criticism within the party but are causing disorganization in the ranks of those who fight for a cause which has not yet achieved its final aim; in violation of party discipline, you continue to undermine the decisions

[35] Lozovsky continued to protest against other actions of the Bolshevik majority and was excluded from the party on January 11, 1918. See pp. 637–38, below.

[36] Lenin, *Sochineniia,* XXII, 57.

of the Central Committee outside the limits of the party—in the Soviets, municipal institutions, trade unions, etc.—thus putting a brake on the work of the Central Committee.

In view of all this the Central Committee is forced to repeat its ultimatum and propose that you either give a written guaranty that you will submit to the Central Committee and adhere to its program or give up all public and party activities and relinquish all responsible posts in the labor movement until the party congress meets.

Failure to give either of the two assurances will make it necessary for the Central Committee to consider the question of your immediate expulsion from the party.[37]

While the Bolsheviks were publicly airing their family quarrel the inter-party negotiations came to a complete deadlock.

RESOLUTION OF THE VIKZHEL-SOCIALIST CONFERENCE ON NEGOTIATIONS WITH THE BOLSHEVIKS[38]

[November 18, 1917]

The conference of Socialist parties called by Vikzhel for November 17 did not take place because of the absence of the Bolsheviks, ... who had a long session last night at Smolny.

The resolution of Smolny regarding the press makes an agreement practically impossible. After the representatives of all the Socialist parties and Vikzhel had discussed this question, they passed the following resolution:

"The conference of the representatives of all the Socialist parties, called on the initiative of Vikzhel, had agreed to form an all-democratic government with the object of peacefully ending the political crisis. . . . . But the conference had to discontinue its efforts when it learned that the Central Executive Committee of the Soviet of Workers' and Soldiers' Deputies had decided, by an insignificant majority, to adopt measures that make agreements of any kind practically impossible, and

[37] Zinoviev was the first to announce his recantation (*Izvestiia,* No. 219, November 21, 1917, pp. 2–3), and he was readmitted to the Central Committee. On this same day Kamenev was replaced by Sverdlov as chairman of the Central Executive Committee. Kamenev, Miliutin, Nogin, and Rykov petitioned for readmission on December 12, but Lenin did not consider their repentance sufficiently complete and refused to reinstate them (Lenin, *Sochineniia,* XXII, 107). Later, however, their recantations were accepted and they were given places of responsibility in the government.

[38] *Delo Naroda,* No. 201, November 19, 1917, p. 2.

had refused to put a stop to its policy of terror against that part of the population that disagrees with it.

"The conference has resolved: (1) to demand an immediate cessation of civil war; (2) to protest against political terror and encroachment on political and civil liberties; (3) to insist on the formation of an All-Socialist government, composed of representatives of all parties, from the Socialist-Populists to the Bolsheviks inclusive. This government shall be responsible to an organ of government, representing all wings of the democracy. The immediate task of such a government shall be to bring about peace between all the belligerent nations, to hand over immediately the land to the land committees, and to call the Constituent Assembly as soon as possible."

ANOTHER ATTEMPT TO COME TO AN AGREEMENT[39]

[November 19–20, 1917]

On November 19, at midnight, representatives of the various parties met at Vikzhel for the purpose of coming to an agreement.

Comrade Krushinsky . . . . read the resolution of the Central Committee of the Mensheviks which favored the formation of a committee of representatives of all Socialist parties that believe in the formation of a homogeneous Socialist government. . . . .

The representative of the Executive Committee of Peasants' Deputies announced that he was unable to take part in the discussion on the formation of a government until such time as there was freedom of the press, when all those arrested were freed, and when the Military Revolutionary Committee has been dissolved. He also pointed out that one of the preliminary conditions to the discussion should be that no Bolsheviks should be allowed to enter the ministry.

Zinoviev stated that if no agreement were reached at this meeting the Bolsheviks would drop the subject.

An adjournment was declared until the representatives of the Socialist-Revolutionists and Mensheviks came. At two in the morning [November 20] the meeting came to order. . . . .

Comrade Erlich said that it was quite impossible to form a government as long as the people were not sure of their liberty and safety. . . . . The Mensheviks were ready to come to an agreement, but now that the C.E.C. refused to accept their conditions they have no common ground with the Bolsheviks. . . . .

[The meeting came to an end at 4:00 A.M. without reaching any definite conclusion.]

[39] *Delo Naroda*, No. 203, November 21, 1917, p. 4.

While the different Socialist groups were engaged in a vain endeavor to form a coalition government at Petrograd the All-Army Committee at the Stavka was also trying to form a national government. V. M. Chernov, who was designated as minister-president of that government, describes the project in a manuscript article entitled "Tsentralnyi Komitet Partii Sotsialistov Revoliutsionerov na rubezhe dvukh revoliutsii."[40] According to this account Chernov was summoned to the Stavka by the chairman of the All-Army Committee, where he was told that in view of the failure of the several Socialist groups to reach an agreement the All-Army Committee had decided to take the initiative in forming a government and asked Chernov to be the president of this government. Representatives of Vikzhel, who arrived at the Stavka at the same time, concurred in the plan and offered the free use of the railroads to the new government. Chernov communicated the proposal by direct wire to the Central Committee of the Socialist-Revolutionists. The latter agreed to the plan, Chernov proceeded with the selection of a cabinet, and the All-Army Committee called for support of the new government on a program of restoration of civil liberties, transfer of land to the land committees, and immediate peace negotiations.[41]

Meanwhile Gotz and Avxentiev arrived at the Stavka and they at once took a hostile attitude toward the whole affair and Chernov was forced to drop the undertaking. Chernov claims that Avxentiev's opposition was due to the fact that he had been previously designated to form a new government and carried with him a letter from Kerensky conferring on Avxentiev the rights and duties of the Prime Minister.[42]

C. The Peasant Congresses and the Formation of a Socialist Coalition

The breakdown of the Vikzhel inter-party conference did not end the negotiations for a Socialist coalition government,

[40] The manuscript is in the Hoover War Library.

[41] Popov, *Oktiabrskii perevorot*, p. 413.

[42] See above, pp. 172–73.

for this question became the principal issue at the Special Congress of Peasant Soviets which met in Petrograd, November 23 to December 8. This congress had been called by the Left wing of the Socialist-Revolutionists against the will of the Executive Committee of the First Congress of Peasant Soviets, which had been elected in June 1917 and which was dominated by the moderate elements of that party. When it became clear that the special peasant congress was going to take place the Executive Committee attempted to have the sessions held at Mogilev, the army headquarters, where efforts were being made to form a new government headed by V. M. Chernov.[43] This attempt failed and the congress met in Petrograd on the 23d. Its membership included 195 Socialist-Revolutionists of the Left, 65 of the Right, and 37 Bolsheviks.

In the early sessions of this congress the majority of the delegates undoubtedly favored the formula of a coalition government "composed of all Socialist parties from the Bolsheviks to the Socialist-Populists inclusive." Presently, however, the Right and Center sections of the Socialist-Revolutionists became hopelessly at odds with the Left over the proposal to elect a new Executive Committee to be fused with the Central Executive Committee. The Left S.R.'s began negotiations with the Bolsheviks, whose general position had been strengthened by victories in the Petrograd elections for the Constituent Assembly and by their aggressive peace policy.[44] An agreement was reached on November 28 by which the S.R.'s entered the government. Vikzhel likewise came to an understanding with the Bolsheviks, and one of its members took over the post of Commissar of Ways and Communications.

[43] *Delo Naroda,* No. 204, November 22, 1917, p. 3.

[44] The results of the elections to the Constituent Assembly are given in chapter vii, pp. 347–48, 350, and the preliminaries of the armistice negotiations in chapter v.

SESSIONS OF THE CONGRESS OF PEASANTS' DEPUTIES

[November 23–28, 1917]

November 23. The Congress of Soviets of Peasants' Deputies which assembled on November 23 . . . . had a stormy time. . . . . One group was in favor of giving the right to vote to all representatives . . . . of declaring the present gathering a Special Congress, and of proceeding with the formation of a government that would unite all the revolutionary democracy. Another group took the stand that since the All-Russian Congress had been called for December 13 and since only representatives of gubernia Soviets of Peasants' Deputies and army organizations had been invited, and since the present representation was incomplete, this gathering was nothing more than a conference and could not be regarded as authoritative. . . . .

After a long and warm debate which dragged on into the night the motion to give the right to vote to the representatives of the army and uezd Soviets was carried. . . . .

November 24. The meeting on the night of [November 23–24] ended in a split. The Socialist-Revolutionists [Right] moved that the presidium of the Executive Committee[45] [of the First Congress] be continued and supplemented by representatives of the parties. . . . . The Socialist-Revolutionists [Left] and the Bolsheviks, who looked upon this conference as an All-Russian Congress, opposed the motion and proposed a new presidium of fifteen, proportionately divided among the parties. The motion of the Socialist-Revolutionists [to keep the old presidium] was lost by a vote of 155 to 84. After the vote . . . . the Socialist-Revolutionists [Right] left the meeting . . . . and were followed by others, peasant delegates from [twenty-one] gubernias . . . . and from four armies. . . . . When they had gone, the conference declared itself a "Special Congress."[46] . . . .

After the Socialist-Revolutionists and some of the representatives of the [old] Central Committee had departed . . . . the Congress was able to proceed with its work. Maria Alexandrovna Spiridonova was made chairman. . . . . A new presidium of fifteen was elected.[47]

November 25. The meeting opened at ten o'clock in the morning. Comrade Ustinov declared that the Socialist-Revolutionists of the Right and Center had drifted away from the masses. The question of the

[45] The chairman of this committee was Avxentiev.

[46] *Delo Naroda,* No. 207, November 24, 1917, p. 4. "It is important to note that at the First All-Russian Congress [which met in May–June] there were 1,453 delegates and that at this so-called 'Special Congress' there are only 202, and some of these have left the meeting" (*loc. cit.*)

[47] Chairman, Spiridonova; vice-chairmen: Nathanson, Kolegaev, Kamkov, Stashkov, Ustinov, Zinoviev, Nikitin; secretaries: Polov, Malkin, Ivashchenko, Proshian, Miliutin, Nevsky.

moment was to form a coalition of the internationalist elements capable of opposing the coalition of the bourgeois elements. . . . .

Comrade Zinoviev: . . . . I was one of those who favored an agreement with the Socialist parties. But the defensists and compromisers, by their preliminary conditions to allow the publication of bourgeois papers and to free the arrested ministers . . . . destroyed all chances of agreement. It is they who, while pretending to come to an agreement with us, issued leaflets calling on the people to oppose the new government; it is they who approved the sabotage of the employees. An agreement with them is out of the question. But we welcome all those who are ready to carry out the program of the Second All-Russian Congress.

[After a recess the session was opened by Comrade Kolegaev.]

Comrade Surokin of the 3d Army: . . . . In their resolutions the masses had made it clear that a coalition [with the bourgeoisie] is a thing of the past. . . . . We demand that all power be given to the Soviets and that the government be composed of all the Socialist parties from the Bolsheviks to the Socialist-Populists inclusive. . . . .

Krushinsky, representative of Vikzhel: Argues for a Soviet government. . . . . The representative organs of the revolutionary democracy should be the source of [such a] government. The Second Congress is not authoritative enough. The Central Executive Committee should be supplemented by representatives of the peasants, the army, trade unions, and city governments. We shall join the Central Executive Committee if the peasant congress decides to join. . . . .

Comrade Nevsky, in the name of the Bolsheviks, proposed that a report of the Soviet of People's Commissars be heard. This was opposed . . . . on the ground that it would be interpreted as a committal on the question of government. The Bolshevik proposal was voted down. . . . .

The chairman announced that the Socialist-Revolutionists of the Center, headed by Chernov, had returned to collaborate with the Congress and proposed that Chernov be given special permission to speak. Citizen Chernov replied that he would rather not do so until he had learned the attitude of the Congress. . . . .

The chairman moved that Chernov be made honorary chairman. . . . .

Zinoviev: This motion . . . . carries important political implications. . . . . Before electing citizen Chernov honorary chairman, it might not be a bad thing to have him explain why he was at the Headquarters of General Dukhonin at the time of the workers' and peasants' revolution. . . . . We appeal to our comrades, the Socialist-Revolutionists of the Left, and say: the revolutionary democracy of Russia has followed your lead not because of your former relations with the defensists but because of your new revolutionary policy. You . . . . must decide once and for all whether you are with us and with the revolutionary workers, soldiers, and peasants or against us. We Bolsheviks protest most vigorously against electing as honorary chairman a man who once dispersed the Diet of Finland.

In his reply . . . . Chernov declared that the charges against him were unfounded,[48] that he had just returned from the army congress at Mogilev where the question of putting an end to the civil war was discussed, and concluded by saying that he was ready to give an explanation at any time. [Noise and excitement became so great that the session was suspended. *Delo Naroda,* No. 209, November 27, 1917, p. 4.]

After the recess the Socialist-Revolutionists of the Left announced that they could not support Chernov's candidacy for honorary chairman. The Bolsheviks [made a similar declaration]. Before putting this question to a vote . . . . another was raised whether members of the old Executive Committee had a deciding or merely a consultative voice. . . . .

[When the vote was taken, 155 expressed themselves against a deciding vote, 137 for it, and 6 refused to vote.] . . . .

Gurevich . . . . protested against the decision of the Congress. Bykhovsky announced the threatening telegram of the agents of the Allied Powers, stating that Russia violated the agreements of 1914, and that this would lead to grave consequences.[49] [Owing to the commotion another recess was declared.]

During the recess representatives of the army and navy were in private session and decided (1) that there must be an end to [mere] talking, (2) that the question of government must be decided at once . . . ., (3) that a committee of three be sent to notify all the parties of this decision and to get them to approve it . . . ., and (5) that if the Congress should refuse to accept these demands the army and navy delegates would withdraw and settle the question by themselves. . . . .

When the meeting came to order the presidium introduced a motion . . . . to proceed with the organization of a government. A representative of the army read the resolution of the army [and navy] and added: "At the front conditions are terrible, and here we do nothing but talk and quarrel. . . . ." He was followed by a delegate from the fleet [who said]: "The fleet has neither food nor fuel. We and the soldiers agree. If you do not settle the question of government, we will, and it will be a government with a fist." (These words made a deep impression.)[50]

[48] "Comrades, I do not know in what paper the speaker [Zinoviev] read that I was with the Tsar's generals. No doubt in the papers in which he writes" (*Delo Naroda,* No. 209, November 27, 1917, p. 4). "In reply to Chernov's question in what paper I read that he was with the troops marching on Petrograd, I should like to call his attention to page 1, No. 149 (November 12) of the *Izvestiia,* where it says, 'V. M. Chernov is with the troops moving on Petrograd'" (*Izvestiia,* No. 225, November 27, 1917, p. 5). Zinoviev was at this time an editor of *Izvestiia.*

[49] See p. 245, below.

[50] *Izvestiia,* No. 225, November 27, 1917, p. 4.

Before voting on the resolutions on government, members of the [old] Executive Committee announced that in view of the importance of the question, they would not leave the meeting. The Bolsheviks, Maximalists, and Socialist-Revolutionists of the Left introduced resolutions; the first received 45, the second 5, and the third 123 votes. At half-past five the meeting adjourned.

November 26. The meeting opened with the following declaration of the Socialist-Revolutionists of the Left: "Having considered the situation brought about by denying the vote to members of the Executive Committee, be it resolved that the Executive Committee lay down its power and become a part of the Special Congress." With the participation of the Executive Committee a new provisional Executive Committee of 108 members will be chosen. The old Executive Committee will take part in the proceedings with the right to vote. The Bolsheviks and representatives of the fleet protested against this action. . . . . The declaration of the Socialist-Revolutionists of the Left was accepted by a large majority.

Ustinov then announced in its final form the resolution [on the subject of organizing a government] adopted the previous day:

1. The Executive Committees, elected by the Special Congress of Peasants' Deputies and by the Second Congress of Soviets of Workers' and Soldiers' Deputies are to be joined on an equal footing into one body.

2. The new government to be organized by the Executive Committee of the Soviets of Workers', Soldiers', and Peasants' Deputies is to be made up [of Socialists] from the Socialist-Populists to the Bolsheviks inclusive.

3. In case any one of the parties refuses to join, the government is to be made up of those parties that accept the platform of the joint Executive Committees of the Soviets of Workers', Soldiers', and Peasants' Deputies.

4. The government is to be responsible to the Executive Committee of the Soviets of Workers', Soldiers', and Peasants' Deputies and is to carry out the legislation of the Second Congress of Soviets of Workers' and Soldiers' Deputies, namely, to summon the Constituent Assembly on time, to give the land to the people, to work for an early peace, and to bring about workers' control in industry.

Before voting Kharitonov, a Bolshevik, announced that his party would vote against the resolution as a whole. The resolution was approved by a vote of 175 to 22, with six not voting.

The next topic for discussion was the question of the selection of the 108 members of the Executive Committee. . . . .[51]

[51] *Delo Naroda,* No. 209, November 27, 1917, p. 4.

November 27. The meeting that had been adjourned in order to discuss the question of the return of the Executive Committee to the work of the conference was resumed at two in the morning.

G. A. Martiushin said that he spoke in behalf of 155 members of the Executive Committee and representatives of gubernia and uezd Soviets of peasants and declared in their name that the motion of the Socialist-Revolutionists of the Left to fuse the Executive Committee with the conference and to elect a new provisional Executive Committee was a violation of the rights of the Executive Committee chosen by the First All-Russian Congress of Soviets of Peasants' Deputies.

The Executive Committee was of the opinion that it could hand over its power only to the Second All-Russian Congress, which would be called soon. Until then the Executive Committee regarded itself as responsible to the Russian peasants who elected it and no other than the Second Congress had a right to remove it. . . . .

On the motion of the chairman, the conference proceeded with current questions. Martiushin and members of the Executive Committee [of the First Congress] left the meeting.[52]

November 28. The meeting opened at 4:00 P.M. Ustinov [in the chair] announced that an agreement had been reached between the provisional Excutive Committee of the Special Peasant Congress and the Central Executive Committee of the Soviets of Workers' and Soldiers' Deputies.[53] An agreement was also reached between the Bolsheviks, Socialist-Revolutionists [Left], and Social-Democrats [Internationalists] (united). Vikzhel and the Post-Telegraph Union approved the agreement. The organizations named are engaged in the formation of a government. . . . .

[A delegation from Smolny arrived to congratulate the Congress. After a number of speeches the whole company proceeded to Smolny to demonstrate to the union of workers and peasants.][54]

In Smolny

. . . . About seven o'clock in the evening Zinoviev appeared at the meeting of the Petrograd Soviet of Workers' and Soldiers' Deputies and announced that . . . . the first [joint] session of the Central Exec-

[52] *Delo Naroda,* No. 210, November 28, 1917, p. 2.

[53] At a meeting of the Central Executive Committee, November 28, 1:00 P.M., the chairman announced the following text of agreements between the Bolsheviks and the Socialist-Revolutionists of the Left: "The Central Executive Committee is to be formed on the following basis: The Central Executive Committee of the Soviets of Workers' and Soldiers' Deputies and the [special] Peasant Congress shall have 108 representatives each; the Army and Navy, 100; trade unions, 35; Vikzhel, 10; Post and Telegraph, 5." (*Izvestiia,* No. 227, November 29, 1917, p. 1.)

[54] *Novaia Zhizn,* No. 182, November 29, 1917, p. 3.

utive Committee and the [Executive Committee] of the Peasants' Deputies would take place today. After relating the history of the great event he said that an agreement has been reached between the two presidia. . . . .

This coalition is a sure sign of the victory of the revolution. . . . . Our slogan, "All Power to the Soviets of Workers', Soldiers', and Peasants' Deputies," is becoming a reality for the first time.[55]

Half an hour after Zinoviev's announcement the peasant deputies arrived and were met with stormy applause. . . . . The presidium table was taken by the presidia of the Central Executive Committee and the Peasant Congress. . . . . [Speeches were made by Spiridonova, Trotsky, Krylenko, Krushinsky, and Lunacharsky, and a resolution was adopted as follows]:

"The All-Russian Central Executive Committee of the Soviets of Workers' and Soldiers' Deputies together with the All-Russian Special Congress of Peasants and the Petrograd Soviet accept the land and peace decrees passed by the Second Congress of Soviets of Workers' and Soldiers' Deputies, as well as the decree of Workers' Control passed by the All-Russian Central Executive Committee.

"The Central Executive Committee and the All-Russian Peasants' Congress, meeting in a body, express their firm conviction that this union of workers, soldiers, and peasants, this fraternal union of all toilers and exploited people will strengthen the power of the state, which will take all revolutionary measures to hasten the transfer of authority to the laboring masses in the more advanced countries and in this way bring about a just peace and advance the cause of socialism. Long live the revolutionary alliance of workers, soldiers, and peasants!"[56]

THE EXECUTIVE COMMITTEE OF PEASANTS' DEPUTIES REPUDIATES THE CONGRESS

[An Address to the Russian Peasantry, November 28, 1917][57]

Comrades:

At the very time we called a conference of the gubernia Soviets there was summoned, with the consent of the Bolsheviks, another similar conference by a group calling itself "Socialist-Revolutionists of the Left." They invited representatives of uezds and [army] divisions.

[55] *Izvestiia,* No. 227, November 29, 1917, p. 2.

[56] *Novaia Zhizn,* No. 182, November 29, 1917, p. 3. On December 10, 1917, the Socialist-Revolutionists of the Left approved the entrance of members of their party in the Soviet of People's Commissars. (*Izvestiia,* No. 250, December 13, 1917, p. 8.)

[57] *Delo Naroda,* No. 210, November 28, 1917, p. 2. This appeal was issued by the Executive Committee of the First Peasant Congress and others who left the meeting on the 24th.

Notwithstanding the fact that those whom they invited represented unequally the country and the army, notwithstanding the fact that they were political partisans, leaning toward the Bolsheviks and "Left" Socialist-Revolutionists, we made every attempt to co-operate with them so as to avoid a division of the peasantry. . . . . We hoped that the other side would also see the necessity of coming together and would strive to bring about friendly co-operation. But our expectations have not been realized. In reply to our patient attitude in verifying mandates . . . . the other side took unheard-of liberties and denied the right to vote to the Executive Committee—the committee that had been in part elected by the First All-Russian Congress of Soviets of Peasants' Deputies and in part delegated by the gubernia congresses of Soviets, the very committee that had called the present conference. . . . .

By taking away the vote from those elected by the All-Russian Congress and the gubernia congresses the Conference usurped the rights belonging only to the Second All-Russian Congress. Not wishing to submit to an illegal authority we members of the Executive Committee, together with representatives of the gubernia Soviets, armies and front, certain divisions, and a few uezd Soviets, about 150 men in all, left the joint meeting. Those who remained, about 175 members . . . . went on with this high-handed work and proceeded to take away from the Executive Committee all the machinery of the Soviet peasant organization. They next decided to join the Bolshevik Executive Committee of Soldiers' and Workers' Deputies and with them to form a government.

The All-Russian Conference made up of representatives of gubernia Soviets, armies, divisions, and uezds, together with the [old] Executive Committee, continued its sessions separately.

In calling these facts to the attention of the Russian peasantry we protest most vigorously against the violence of the Bolsheviks and "Left" Socialist-Revolutionists. We denounce their actions and opinions as falsifications of the opinions of the peasantry. . . . .

We should like also to call to the attention of the peasantry that, in view of the serious situation, the Second All-Russian Congress of Soviets of Peasants' Deputies will open on December 8.[58] Delegates to the Congress should set out for Petrograd as soon as they receive the inclosed instructions. . . . .

Representatives of Soviets of Peasants' Deputies, gubernia, army, several uezds, and members of the Executive Committee of the All-Russian Soviet of Peasants' Deputies at the All-Russian [Peasants] Conference

[58] At the Congress of the Socialist-Revolutionists of the Left on December 3, it was voted that the Executive Committee had no right to call a congress. (*Izvestiia*, No. 232, December 5, 1917, p. 6.)

The controversies and the disturbances which were evoked in the Special Congress of Peasants were repeated with very much the same results in the Second Congress of Soviets of Peasants' Deputies which met in Petrograd, December 9–25, 1917. Attending this Congress were about eight hundred representatives about half of whom sided with the Socialist-Revolutionists of the Right and Center and half with the Bolsheviks and the Socialist-Revolutionists of the Left. The sessions were first disturbed when the Socialist-Revolutionists of the Right introduced a resolution condemning the policy of the Sovnarkom with respect to the Constituent Assembly. The resolution carried by a vote of 360 to 321. When the Bolsheviks attempted to have the resolution reconsidered on the following day, the S.R.'s of the Right strenuously objected. At this moment Trotsky appeared in the meeting and was greeted with cries: "Down with the violator, executioner! Down with the usurper! etc." Thereupon Trotsky, followed by the Bolsheviks and Left S.R.'s, walked out of the meeting and began a rump session in the Nikolaevsky Hall of the City Duma building.

Later the joint sessions were renewed, but a commotion again broke out over the election of a new presidium. Feeling ran so high that the delegates were on the point of starting a general fist fight. Again a part of the Congress withdrew. This time it was the Right S.R.'s who established their headquarters in the Museum building on the Fontanka. Thereafter the two groups continued to meet separately until the Congress adjourned. The Bolsheviks and the Left S.R.'s, having already reached an agreement in the Special Congress, had no difficulty in finding a common language. They indorsed the policies of the Soviet Government, proclaimed themselves to be the only plenipotentiary Congress, and passed a resolution of non-confidence in the old Executive Committee of Soviets of Peasants' Delegates. On December 20 they elected a new Executive Committee and appointed a special technical commission to take over the affairs of the old Executive Committee.

The S.R.'s of the Right and Center continued to criticize Bolshevik policies, passed a resolution condemning the Sovnarkom's declaration of war against the Ukrainian Rada (given below) and reaffirmed their pledge to support the Constituent Assembly. On December 23 they issued a circular letter to the Russian peasantry in which they blamed their radical opponents for the split which had occurred in the ranks of the peasantry. They then elected a provisional executive committee to call a third congress of peasants' deputies to re-establish the unity of the peasants.

Meanwhile the Bolsheviks and Left S.R.'s proceeded to take the control of the peasant organizations into their own hands. With the aid of soldiers they occupied the building of the Soviet of Peasants' Deputies, excluded the moderate members of the Congress from the dormitories, and deprived them of their food rations.[58a]

D. The Bolsheviks and the Opposition Press

The Bolsheviks had never supported the democratic idea of freedom of the press. It is true that before November 1917 they had protested against the suppression of their papers by the Provisional Government, but at the same time they had quite openly declared their intention to close the bourgeois press, once they were in power. On November 10, while the Kerensky counter-attacking forces were still undefeated, the Sovnarkom issued a decree closing all hostile newspapers.

Hostile papers, however, continued to appear, and on November 17 the Central Executive Committee passed the Bolshevik resolution to confiscate all private printing presses and stocks of paper. This aroused wide opposition even among the Bolsheviks. The resolution was not immediately put into effect, but the government continued to harass the opposition press, Socialist as well as bourgeois.

As a new weapon of attack the Sovnarkom decreed ad-

[58a] *Delo Naroda,* Nos. 220–31, December 13–26, 1917. *Izvestiia,* Nos. 238–49, December 11–25, 1917.

vertising a state monopoly. This provoked a new controversy over the freedom of the press. On December 1 all the non-Bolshevik papers in Petrograd except *Delo Naroda* and *Novaia Zhizn* were suspended for publishing an appeal of the former ministers of the Provisional Government.[59] The plant of the *Novoe Vremia,* which had been appearing under the name *Utro,* was confiscated. Playing cat and mouse with the Bolsheviks, some of the opposition papers continued for several weeks to appear irregularly and under various names.[60]

SUPPRESSION OF HOSTILE NEWSPAPERS

[Extract from Decree of the Sovnarkom, November 9, 1917][61]

Everyone knows that the bourgeois press is one of the mighty weapons of the bourgeoisie. In a critical time like this, when the new Workers' and Peasants' Government is just getting started, it is not possible to leave in the hands of the enemy a weapon no less dangerous than bombs and machine guns. This is why temporary and special measures were taken to stop the flow of mud and lies from the green and yellow press which would have drowned the young victory of the people. . . . . The Soviet of the People's Commissars decrees that:

1. Those organs of the press will be closed which (*a*) call for open opposition or disobedience to the Workers' and Peasants' Government; (*b*) sow sedition by a frankly slanderous perversion of facts; (*c*) encourage deeds of a manifestly criminal character. . . . .

2. The closing of the press, provisionally or permanently, can come into effect only upon the resolution of the Soviet of People's Commissars.

3. The above regulations are of a temporary nature and will be removed by a special decree just as soon as normal conditions are reestablished.

VLADIMIR ULIANOV (LENIN)
President of the Soviet of People's Commissars

59 See below, p. 263.

60 P. Sorokin, a Socialist-Revolutionist of the Right and an editor of the *Volia Naroda,* gives a lively account of this newspaper war in *Leaves from a Russian Diary,* pp. 105–106.

61 *Izvestiia,* No. 209, November 10, 1917, p. 2.

THE CENTRAL EXECUTIVE COMMITTEE DISCUSSES THE DECREE ON THE PRESS

[November 17, 1917]

[Larin's resolution]: "To do away with the decree of the press and to create a revolutionary tribunal [composed of representatives of all parties in the Central Executive Committee] to deal with all cases of suppression and punishment."[62]

[Bolshevik resolution]: "The closing of the bourgeois press was necessitated not only as a war measure . . . . but also as a means of bringing about a new régime . . . . that will prevent the capitalists, owners of printing presses and paper, from becoming autocratic makers of public opinion. The next step will be the confiscating of private printing presses and stocks of paper and handing them over to the Soviet authorities, both central and local, for the use of political parties and groups in proportion . . . . to the number of their adherents. To restore the so-called freedom of the press (that is to say, to return the printing presses and paper to the capitalists who poison the minds of the people) is to capitulate to capitalism and to abandon one of the strongholds of the revolution." . . . .[63]

Debates on the Resolution

Trotsky [said]: . . . . that to do away with suppression . . . . is to demand an end of the civil war, a demand which only the enemies of the proletariat can make. . . . . In time of civil war suppression of the press is considered legitimate.[64] . . . .

We ought to confiscate all printing presses and paper . . . . and make them public property. . . . .

The *Novoe Vremia* which has not one vote [in the Soviet] should have not one word of type or one sheet of paper. As long as the *Russkaia Volia* is an organ of the banks, it has no right to exist. . . . . Can we allow [the *Novoe Vremia*] to spread its poison at the time of the elections to the Constituent Assembly. . . . .

You say that we demanded freedom of the press for *Pravda*.[65] At that time we were in a position where we could demand only a minimum

[62] *Izvestiia*, No. 217, November 18, 1917, p. 4.

[63] *Delo Naroda*, No. 200, November 18, 1917, p. 2.

[64] *Novaia Zhizn*, No. 173, November 18, 1917, p. 2, gives this version of this portion of Trotsky's speech: "The right to oppress belongs only to the oppressed. But when this right is employed by the oppressors it becomes immoral. (*From the S.R. benches a voice is heard, 'Hottentot.'*)"

[65] Bolshevik paper which appeared March 18, 1917, and was closed by the Provisional Government July 18, after the July uprising.

program, but now we ask for a maximum. . . . . I have no doubt that the workers and peasants are on my side. (*Applause. Exclamations: "Demagogy."*) . . . .[66]

Karelin [remarked that Trotsky's speech suggested] a Hottentot code of ethics according to which it is wrong to steal my wife but right to steal the other man's. . . . .

Lenin: . . . . Trotsky was right. In the name of the freedom of the press there was a rising of the cadets and an outbreak of war in Petrograd and Moscow. . . . . We are against civil war, but if it is forced on us, what can we do? . . . . How can we discontinue measures of precaution against an enemy which continues to be hostile? . . . . The *Rech* is an organ of Kaledin. . . . . The firmer you soldiers and workers are the more certain you are to succeed. . . . . We have said before that if we ever got into power we would close bourgeois papers. To tolerate them means to cease being Socialist. He who is for allowing the bourgeois papers to appear does not understand that we are going full steam ahead toward socialism. . . . . The bourgeoisie has come out for liberty, equality, and fraternity. But the workmen say: we are not interested in that. . . . . It is said that our resolution is something new and unheard of. Of course, it is something new, for we are on the road to socialism. . . . .

Comrade Malkin: . . . . We positively refuse to accept the point of view which says that socialism has to be introduced by force. . . . . We shall succeed not because we close the bourgeois papers but because we serve the interests of the laboring masses. . . . .[67]

[At the end of the debate a vote was taken. The Bolshevik resolution carried by a vote of 34 to 24, one not voting.]

ADVERTISING A STATE MONOPOLY

[Decree of the Sovnarkom, November 20, 1917][68]

1. Paid advertisements in periodical publications, booklets, posters, advertisements in news-stands, bureaus, etc., are declared to be a state monopoly.

2. Such advertisements may be printed only in the publications of the Provisional Workers' and Peasants' Government at Petrograd and in the publications of the local Soviets of Workers', Soldiers', and Peasants' Deputies. Publications inserting advertisements without authority are to be closed.

[66] *Izvestiia*, No. 217, November 18, 1917, p. 4.

[67] *Ibid.*, No. 218, November 20, 1917, p. 3.

[68] *Ibid.*, No. 219, November 21, 1917, p. 3.

3. Until it [advertising] is taken over by the state newspaper owners, managers of advertising offices and all employees in such or similar offices are required to remain at their work, will be held responsible for its order and continuation of business, for the turning over to Soviet publications of all private advertisements, and of all money collected for advertising, and for a full documentary account.

4. In order to organize more efficiently and properly the business of private advertising in Soviet publications as well as to draw up better regulations for the benefit of the public in advertising, all those in charge of offices that accept advertisements for money, as well as their employees and workers, should meet in their cities and join first the city unions and later the All-Russian Unions.

5. Persons guilty of concealing documents or money and of disregarding sections 3 and 4 above are punishable by confiscation of property and three years in prison.

6. Paid advertisements in private publications in the form of accounts, articles, or other disguises are punishable in the manner [indicated in section 5].

7. The government is confiscating advertising offices and is ready in case of need to compensate the owners by temporary help. Small owners, depositors, and stockholders of confiscated offices are to be compensated in full for what they have invested.

8. All publishing houses, offices, and, in general, all business undertakings dealing with advertisements must furnish at once to the Soviets of Workers' and Soldiers' Deputies accurate information as to their location, and must proceed to hand over their affairs. Those failing to do so will be punished as indicated in section 5.

V. Ulianov (Lenin)
President of the Soviet of People's Commissars

A. Lunacharsky
People's Commissar of Education

DELO NARODA DEFIES THE SOVNARKOM[69]

In May 1906 the *Delo Naroda,* organ of the Central Committee of the Socialist-Revolutionists, was closed by the Tsar's government.

History repeats itself . . . . autocracy has come back and is trying to suppress freedom of speech. On the night of December 6 an armed gang of Red Guards came to our printing office and ordered us to close the *Delo Naroda* because it did not submit to the authority of the people's commissars.

[69] *Delo Naroda,* No. 218, December 7, 1917, p. 4.

Force had its way. *Delo Naroda* did not appear on December 6 [217]. What does this prove? That we are broken, that we submit? Not in the least. We did not recognize, do not recognize, and will not recognize authority seized by force. We will continue as before to fight for the conquests of the revolution and for freedom.

We protest with all our might against this attempt . . . . to drown out our voice, which the new government has good reason to fear. To your threats we say: We shall remain at our post as guardians of the revolution. *Delo Naroda* cannot die. History has set before us the task of continuing to defend the people's cause. We remain at our post.

EDITORIAL STAFF

ADVERTISEMENTS AND THE SOCIALIST PRESS[70]

Comrades and Readers:

We have looked upon the Bolshevik decree on advertising in the press . . . . as a violation of the freedom of speech. After the appearance of this decree many of the Socialist papers, a majority of which never carried advertisements, regarded it as their duty to put in advertisements as a protest against this measure.

The Bolsheviks took advantage of these protests to destroy the independent press. They have closed almost all the Socialist papers. The attempt to open them under a new name has been opposed by physical force.

Realizing how important it is at the present time . . . . to keep the public properly informed and to fight for the Constituent Assembly . . . . the following papers will appear *without advertisements:*

Rabochaia Gazeta
Delo Naroda
Narodnoe Slovo
Novaia Zhizn
Prostaia Gazeta
Izvestiia Vserossiiskogo Soveta Krestianskikh Deputatov

E. STRIKES OF STATE EMPLOYEES

Besides all their other troubles the Bolsheviks had to fight a strike of state employees declared by the Union of Unions of State Employees on November 9 as a part of the action

[70] *Delo Naroda,* No. 220, December 13, 1917, p. 1. A similar statement was issued by the All-Russian Society of Editors in *Nash Vek,* No. 1, December 13, 1917.

organized under the Committee to Save the Country and the Revolution against the Bolshevik seizure of power. The strike continued for several weeks with diminishing effectiveness. Some employees immediately resumed work, others under the threats of the Military Revolutionary Committee returned to their places, and still others were replaced by new appointees; and so the strike ended. Opponents of Bolsheviks in the state service thereafter expressed their opposition by sabotage rather than by open defiance of the Soviet power.

STRIKE OF THE STATE EMPLOYEES OF PETROGRAD

[Decree of Union of Unions of State Employees of Petrograd][71]

The committee of the Union of Unions of the State Employees at Petrograd, having discussed with the delegates of the central committees of the All-Russian Union of State Employees the question of the usurpation of power by the Bolshevik group in the Petrograd Soviet a month before the convocation of the Constituent Assembly, and considering that that criminal act threatens the destruction of Russia and all the conquests of the revolution, in accord with the All-Russian Committee to Save the Country and the Revolution, composed of delegates of the [Petrograd] Central Duma, the Provisional Council of the Republic, the Central Executive Committee of the Soviets of Workers' and Soldiers' Deputies, the C.E.C. of the Peasants' Soviets, groups of the front and representatives of the Socialist-Revolutionist, Social-Democrat (Menshevik), Socialist-Populist and "Edinstvo" groups of the Second Congress of Soviets of Workers' and Soldiers' Deputies and other social and political organizations which are concerned with the safety and honor of the fatherland, resolved that:

1. Work in all the administrative departments of the state shall cease immediately;

2. The question of food supply for the army and the population, as well as the activity of the institutions which are concerned with the maintenance of public order, are to be decided by the Committee to Save [the Country and the Revolution] in co-operation with the committees of the Union of Unions;

3. The action of the administrative departments which have already ceased their work is approved.

COMMITTEE OF THE UNION OF UNIONS
OF STATE EMPLOYEES OF PETROGRAD

[71] *Volia Naroda*, No. 156, November 10, 1917, p. 3.

THE SPREAD OF THE STRIKE OF STATE EMPLOYEES[72]

[November 10, 1917]

Yesterday the new "minister," Trotsky, came to the Ministry of Foreign Affairs. After calling together all the officials, he said, "I am the new Minister of Foreign Affairs, Trotsky." He was greeted with ironic laughter. To this he paid no attention and told them to go back to their work. They went, ... but to their homes with the intention of not returning to the office as long as Trotsky was at the head of the ministry.[73] . . . .

The Central Committee of the All-Russian Union of Railwaymen has decided not to take orders from the Military Revolutionary Committee. The question was raised of declaring a railway strike as a means of fighting the Bolshevik usurpers, but in view of the fact that such a strike would affect the food supply, it was given up. . . . .

In all the ministries the employees have passed resolutions of protest against the seizure of power by the Bolsheviks and their "people's commissars." The employees of the Ministry of Agriculture after pointing out that the Bolsheviks have already done away with a number of conquests of the revolution, such as freedom of the press, assembly, and speech, have resolved not to recognize the organs of government set up by the Bolsheviks but to rally around the Committee to Save the Country and the Revolution and to work only under the direction of members of the Provisional Government. . . . .

The employees of the Ministry of Education, being unable to work under the threat of a club, have resolved to quit work and not to resume it until a legal government is formed.

The employees of the Ministry of Food have refused to acknowledge the authority of the commissar and have declared that they recognize no government but the Provisional Government.

In the Ministry of Finance, the employees have declined to have anything to do with the power-snatchers and have decided to go on strike until the organization of a national government.

REASONS FOR THE STRIKE

[Extract from Statement of the Union of Unions of State Employees, November 21, 1917][74]

When the March Revolution, which gave liberty to the people, occurred, we greeted the . . . . Provisional Government. We wish to be

[72] *Delo Naroda,* No. 191, November 10, 1917, p. 3.

[73] Russian diplomatic missions in Western Europe agreed not to recognize the Bolshevik government or to carry out its instructions. Cf. *U.S. Foreign Relations, 1918, Russia,* I, 230.

[74] *Delo Naroda,* No. 203, November 21, 1917, p. 3.

and still are true servants of the people. We ceased work in state institutions not because of a desire to improve our material condition . . . . our . . . . union takes no sides in politics. . . . . We are ready to work for any government which is recognized by the people as a whole.

The Bolsheviks, making use of brute force, have declared themselves at the head of the government. Both capitals are reddened with the blood of fratricidal war, the lives and freedom of citizens have been brutally violated, and holy places have been ruined. Now, the Bolsheviks are aiming to get control . . . . of the entire machinery of government.

We are working in close co-operation with the All-Russian Committee to Save the Country and the Revolution.[75] We defy the threats [of the Bolsheviks], and refuse to offer our experience and knowledge, the very machinery of government to men who have violated the will of the people. [If we were to do so] we would help them in the fight against the other parties. . . . .

While pursuing this extreme measure—cessation of regular work—we shall not stop for a minute in our work for the defense and [army] supply . . . .

FIGHTING THE STRIKE

In the Commissariat of Foreign Affairs

[Trotsky's Recollections][76]

In connection with the Commissariat of Foreign Affairs I should like to say something about Comrade Markin who, to a certain extent, organized the Ministry. Markin was a sailor in the Baltic fleet and a member of the Central Executive Committee of the Second Congress. . . . . I came to know him through my boys about two or three weeks before the revolution. He offered his services . . . . and when I went into the Ministry he came with me. . . . .

When I arrived [at the Ministry] . . . . some kind of prince named Tatishchev told me that there was no one there. . . . . I demanded that the officials be summoned . . . . quite a crowd appeared. . . . .

After I left, Markin arrested and locked up Tatishchev and Taube. . . . . About two days later Markin sent for me, and I found Tatishchev ready to show us about. . . . . Markin got hold of the secret documents and proceeded to publish them.[77] . . . . He was helped by an armless

[75] The Military Revolutionary Committee ordered the dissolution of the Committee and the arrest of its members on November 22, 1917. (Liubimov, *Revoliutsiia 1917 goda*, p. 108.)

[76] "Vospominaniia ob oktiabrskom perevorote," in *Proletarskaia Revoliutsiia*, 1922, No. 10, pp. 59–61. Trotsky describes this incident again in *My Life*, p. 293.

[77] They began to appear in the *Izvestiia*, November 23, 1917. See below, pp. 242–44.

young man of about twenty-five. . . . . He was a hard drinker and there were rumors that he was taking bribes. . . . . He was discharged for that. . . . .

Markin was . . . . an intelligent man with strong will power. . . . . But could not write without making many mistakes. . . . . Later on he commanded our flotilla on the Volga and there lost his life.

In the Commissariat of Labor[78]

[November 9, 1917]

Having assumed, in accordance with the will of the Congress of Soviets of Workers' and Soldiers' Deputies, the direction of the Ministry of Labor, I request all employees to resume their work at once. In these days when the revolution is being threatened, the work of the ministry must not stop. All employees must be at their places tomorrow, November 10, at the usual hour. Those who fail to appear will be regarded as having resigned. All heads of departments and former assistants of the Minister of Labor are requested to appear tomorrow, November 10, at noon, to hand over their affairs.

Alexander Shliapnikov
People's Commissar of Labor

In the Commissariat of Finance[79]

[November 12, 1917]

The acting commissar of the Ministry of Finance calls to the attention of the inhabitants of Petrograd that the employees of the treasury and savings banks are upsetting the work of the banks in utter neglect of the interest of the poor and the population in general.

We cannot permit a strike of these employees. Tomorrow, November 13, work must go on as usual. If the strike should continue in any of the institutions of the Ministry of Finance, the officials . . . . will be arrested.

V. R. Menzhinsky
Acting Commissar in the Ministry of Finance

Warning to Strikers

[Proclamation of the Military Revolutionary Committee, November 20, 1917][80]

To All Citizens!

The wealthy classes are offering resistance to the Soviet Government, the government of the workers, soldiers, and peasants. The parti-

[78] *Izvestiia,* No. 209, November 10, 1917, p. 3.
[79] *Ibid.,* No. 212, November 13, 1917, p. 5.
[80] *Ibid.,* No. 218, November 20, 1917, p. 2.

sans [of the wealthy classes] brought about a strike of state and municipal employees; they are calling out the employees of the banks; and they are trying to stop the railway, telegraph, and postal service, etc.

We warn them . . . . they are playing with fire. The country and the army are threatened with famine. To fight the famine it is necessary to execute most carefully all work in food institutions, railways, banks, and postoffices. The Workers' and Peasants' Government is taking the necessary measures to supply the country with its needs. *Opposition to these measures is a crime against the people.* We warn the wealthy classes and their partisans that if they do not cease their sabotage and if it leads to the cessation of the transport of food products, *they will be the first to feel the effects of their acts. The wealthy classes and their partisans will be deprived of the right to receive food. Whatever supplies they have on hand will be taken from them. The property of the more guilty will be confiscated.*

We have done our duty; we have warned them not to play with fire.

We are certain that if it becomes necessary to carry out these threats, we will have the fullest support of all those loyal to the revolution, all workers, soldiers, and peasants.

THE MILITARY REVOLUTIONARY COMMITTEE OF THE ALL-RUSSIAN CENTRAL COMMITTEE OF THE SOVIETS OF WORKERS' AND SOLDIERS' DEPUTIES

ORDER OF THE COMMISSAR OF POSTS AND TELEGRAPH[81]

[November 27, 1917]

All employees and officials who work in the Ministry of Posts and Telegraph and do not recognize the authority of the Soviet of People's Commissars and my authority as the head of the Ministry are dismissed from service from the moment this order is published and are deprived of their pensions.

All of military age are removed from the exemption list.

Dismissed officials who occupy state dwellings must vacate them within two days after the publication of this order. These vacated quarters are to be placed at the disposal . . . . of those who remain in the service and others who join it.

Employees and officials who wish to continue their work must wholly submit to the Revolutionary Government of the Soviet of People's Commissars.

N. AVILOV, People's Commissar in the Ministry of Posts and Telegraph

[81] *Izvestiia,* No. 225, November 27, 1917, p. 6. Similar orders were issued by the other commissariats.

Strikers Declared Outlaws

[Proclamation of the Military Revolutionary Committee, December 8, 1917][82]

Officials of state and public institutions who went on strike . . . . are declared enemies of the people. Their names will appear from now on in all the Soviet publications and . . . . will be posted in all public places.

People who increase the economic disorganization and interfere with the food supplies of the army and the country are nothing but outlaws and have no right to protection. They are outside the pale of society. Soviets of Workers', Soldiers', and Peasants' Deputies, trade unions, co-operatives, and all people's organizations in general should keep their eyes on these counter-revolutionary officials. . . . . These outlaws are not entitled to any kind of support. He who will not work with the people has no place in the ranks of the people.

Blacklist all saboteurs!

Boycott the criminals who are also the tools of Capitalism!

Military Revolutionary Committee

On the Railways

[December 21–22, 1917]

A representative of the Military Revolutionary Committee with a company of soldiers took possession of the railway telegraph and all the entrances to the Ministry of Railways and refused to admit members of the Vikzhel. . . . . From now on admittance to the ministry will be only by a pass from the Bolshevik Commissar. . . . .

After December 21 only those will be admitted who sign a card that they "submit wholly to the Soviet of People's Commissars and to no other authority." Those who refuse to sign are asked "not to trouble themselves to come." . . . . [83]

Yesterday [December 21] the Commissar of Railways sent out telegrams ordering all the railway committees . . . . to take railways under their control. . . . . He threatened to hand over to the revolutionary tribunal those who decided to strike.[84]

THE END OF THE STRIKE

Yesterday [January 26] there was a meeting of the Executive Committee of the Union of Unions to take up the question of ending the

[82] Trotsky, *Sochineniia,* III, Bk. 2, 120.

[83] *Delo Naroda,* No. 227, December 21, 1917, p. 2.

[84] *Ibid.,* No. 228, December 22, 1917, p. 4.

political strike. . . . . It was moved to call off the political strike and confine it to economic questions. The economic demands to be: back pay for the time of the strike; dismissal of strike-breakers; assurances that the strikers will not be prosecuted. . . . . The motion was voted down . . . . and it was decided to refer the question to the local unions. . . . .

[The employees of the Ministry of Agriculture have called off the strike.[85]]

At a meeting of the post-telegraph employees it was decided by a vote of 141 to 32 to call off the strike. . . . . [86]

The Soviet of People's Commissars has voted not to have any negotiations with the saboteurs. Each commissariat may employ such individual saboteurs as are needed and are willing to submit and support the Soviet Government. . . . .[87]

The Executive Committee of the Commissariat of Food has resolved: " . . . . under no circumstances to take back the saboteurs . . . . and that all vacancies in the Commissariat are to be filled by honest laborers from the free proletariat."[88]

85 *Novaia Zhizn,* No. 10, January 27, 1918, p. 4.

86 *Ibid.,* No. 18, February 7, 1918, p. 3.

87 *Pravda,* No. 25, February 14, 1918, p. 3.

88 *Novaia Zhizn,* No. 26, February 16, 1918, p. 3.

CHAPTER V

THE ARMISTICE

The declaration of the Second Congress of Soviets on November 8 proposing an armistice of three months for the negotiation of a general peace without annexations or indemnities evoked no response from either enemies or allies. On November 21, therefore, the Bolsheviks made new moves. They ordered General Dukhonin to begin direct negotiations with the Germans, and Trotsky invited the Allies and the United States to consider the declaration of November 8 a formal offer of an armistice on all fronts and of general peace negotiations. Dukhonin's refusal to carry out the order precipitated a conflict with Smolny which ended in the Bolshevik occupation of the Stavka on December 3. The protests of Allied military missions against separate negotiations, Trotsky's publication of the Entente secret treaties on November 22 and the opening of negotiations with the Germans further embittered relations between the Soviet Government and its nominal allies. The Central Powers, however, were willing to negotiate, and an armistice was signed at Brest-Litovsk on December 15.

A. The Bolsheviks and the Stavka

The Sovnarkom replied to Dukhonin's refusal to open negotiations with the Central Powers by dismissing him and appointing Krylenko Commander-in-Chief and by ordering the regiments at the front to open negotiations. The Socialists of the All-Army Committee condemned the Sovnarkom's policy as a failure and urged the troops to support an All-Socialist government. Lenin's tactics were also criticized by Bolshevik members of the Central Executive Committee.

ORDER TO DUKHONIN TO OPEN ARMISTICE NEGOTIATIONS

[Radiogram from the Sovnarkom, November 21, 1917][1]

Citizen Supreme Commander-in-Chief!

In accordance with instructions from the All-Russian Congress of Soviets of Workers' and Soldiers' Deputies, the Soviet of People's Commissars has assumed the authority, as well as the obligation of proposing to all warring nations and their governments an immediate truce on all fronts and an immediate opening of negotiations with the object of [making] peace on democratic principles.

At present, with the Soviet power firmly established at all the most important points throughout the country, the Soviet of People's Commissars finds it necessary to make at once formal proposals for an armistice to all the warring nations, allied and enemy. A note to this effect has been dispatched by the People's Commissariat of Foreign Affairs to all the plenipotentiary envoys of the Allied countries in Petrograd.

Immediately after the receipt of this communication you, Citizen Supreme Commander-in-Chief, are ordered by the Soviet of People's Commissars, in compliance with the resolution of the All-Russian Congress of Soviets of Workers' and Soldiers' Deputies, to address yourself to the military authorities of the enemy armies with the proposal of an immediate cessation of hostilities for the purpose of starting peace negotiations. In intrusting you with the conduct of these preliminary pourparlers, the Soviet of People's Commissars orders you: *First,* to keep the Soviet constantly informed by direct wire of the progress of your pourparlers with the representatives of the enemy armies, and, *secondly,* to sign a truce only after obtaining the consent of the Soviet of People's Commissars.

V. ULIANOV (LENIN), President of the Soviet of People's Commissars
L. TROTSKY, Commissar of Foreign Affairs
KRYLENKO, Commissar of War

DUKHONIN DECLINES TO OPEN ARMISTICE NEGOTIATIONS

[Conversation by Direct Wire with Lenin, Stalin, and Krylenko, 2:00 A.M., November 22, 1917][2]

[Stavka]: General Dietrichs, Supreme Commander-in-Chief [*sic*] is at the apparatus.

[1] Piontkovsky, *Khrestomatiia po istorii oktiabrskoi revoliutsii,* p. 265. The message was sent at 4:00 A.M., November 21, and received at the Stavka at 5:05 A.M.

[2] *Delo Naroda,* No. 205, November 23, 1917, p. 2.

[Commissars]: Be so kind as to ask the acting commander-in-chief, General Dukhonin [to the apparatus]. . . . . So far as we know he has not yet given up his post.

Stavka: General Dukhonin waited for you until one o'clock. He is now asleep. The telegraph was not working and later it was used by Headquarters for conversation with the Quartermaster-General.

[Commissars]: Can you tell us whether you received a radiogram sent out about four o'clock by the Soviet of People's Commissars and if so what was done to carry out the orders contained therein?

Stavka: A telegram of state importance was received, but as it had neither number nor date General Dukhonin asked General Manikovsky to give him the necessary assurances that the telegram was genuine.

[Commissars]: What did General Manikovsky reply? When and how was this request made, by radio, telegraph, or telephone?

Stavka: We have as yet no reply, and about an hour ago we sent a request to hurry with an answer.

[Commissars]: Please tell us the exact hour, and how the first telegram was sent? Is it possible to hurry a bit?

Stavka: The telegram was sent . . . . by radio and telegraph . . . . about 19: 50 o'clock.

[Commissars]: Why was not I, Commissar of War, asked for this information? The Supreme Commander-in-Chief knows . . . . that General Manikovsky occupies himself exclusively with the technical questions of food and supplies, while I am responsible for the political supervision of the Ministry of War.

Stavka: I have nothing to say.

[Commissars]: We wish to declare very emphatically that we hold General Dukhonin responsible for the delay in executing such important state matters. We demand categorically that (1) plenipotentiaries be sent [to open armistice negotiations] and that (2) General Dukhonin be at the telegraph tomorrow morning exactly at eleven o'clock. If the delay leads to famine, collapse, defeat, or riots, we shall hold you responsible and shall report it to the soldiers.

Stavka: I shall report this to General Dukhonin.

[Commissars]: When will you report? If immediately, we will wait for him.

Stavka: I shall call him at once.

General Dukhonin . . . . is now at the apparatus.

Stavka: From the telegraph tape of conversation with you, which has just been handed to me, I feel sure that you sent me the telegram before there was a clear understanding on certain essentials. I request, therefore, to have definite information on the following points: (1) Has the Soviet of People's Commissars received any kind of reply to its appeal to the belligerents regarding the decree of peace? (2) What is to be done with the Rumanian Army which is a part of our front? (3) Is it the intention to open negotiations for a separate truce? If so, with whom? Only with the Germans, or also with the Turks, or is it to be a general armistice?

[Commissars]: The telegram which was sent to you was absolutely clear and precise. It said to begin immediate negotiations with all belligerents. You have no right to delay such an important matter by such preliminary questions. We insist that you send at once plenipotentiaries and keep us hourly informed of the course of the armistice negotiations.

Stavka: My questions are purely technical, and it is impossible to proceed with the negotiations until they are answered.

[Commissars]: You know as well as we do that numerous technical and detailed questions will come up and we shall answer them as they are raised. . . . . We again insist that you open at once official negotiations for an armistice between all belligerents, allied as well as enemy. Be so kind as to give a definite reply.

Stavka: I understand that it is difficult for you to carry on direct negotiations with the Powers. It is even more difficult for me to do so in your name. Only a government . . . . supported by the army and the country can have sufficient weight to impress the enemy . . . . and to get any results. I too am of the opinion that an early general peace is for the best interests of Russia.

[Commissars]: Do you refuse to give us a straight answer and to carry out our orders?

Stavka: I have given you a clear answer of the reason why I cannot execute the orders in your telegram, and I repeat again that the peace which Russia needs can be given to her only by a central government [recognized by all the people].

[Commissars]: In the name of the Government of the Russian Republic and by the authority conferred upon us by the Soviet of People's Commissars we dismiss you from your post for refusing to carry out the orders of the government and for pursuing a course that will bring incredible misery to the toilers of all countries, especially for the armies. We order you, on pain of being handed over to the military courts, to continue your duties until relieved by a new commander-in-chief or by someone authorized to take over your affairs. Ensign Krylenko is appointed Commander-in-Chief.

[*Signed*] LENIN, STALIN, KRYLENKO

LENIN URGES THE SOLDIERS TO NEGOTIATE WITH THE ENEMY

[Proclamation to Soldiers and Sailors, November 22, 1917][3]

To All Regimental, Divisional, Corps, Army and Other Committees, to All Soldiers of the Revolutionary Army and Sailors of the Revolutionary Navy:

During the night of November 20 the Soviet of People's Commissars dispatched a wireless message to Commander-in-Chief Dukhonin, ordering him to propose immediately and officially an armistice to all belligerent nations, allied as well as enemy.

This wireless message was received at the Stavka at 5:05 in the morning of November 21. . . . . Simultaneously the same proposal—that of an armistice—was made officially to all the plenipotentiary representatives of the Allied countries in Petrograd.[4]

Failing to obtain an answer from Dukhonin up to the evening of November 21, the Soviet of People's Commissars authorized Lenin, Stalin, and Krylenko to inquire of Dukhonin by direct wire the reason for this delay. The conversations were carried on from 2:00 till 4:30 in the morning of November 22. Dukhonin made many attempts to evade an explanation of his action and [failed] to give a clear answer concerning the government order. When he was told that he must begin at once official negotiations for an armistice, he refused to obey. Thereupon Dukhonin was informed in the name of the Government of the Russian Republic, by order of the Soviet of People's Commissars, that he was dismissed from his post for disobeying the orders of the government and for acting in a manner that was bound to lead to great calamities for the toiling masses of all countries, especially for the armies. . . . .

Soldiers, the cause of peace rests in your hands! You will not permit counter-revolutionary generals to frustrate the great cause of peace. You will surround them with guards, so as to avoid lynchings unworthy of revolutionary armies and to prevent these generals from escaping the judgment that is in store for them. You will maintain the strictest revolutionary and military discipline.

Let the regiments at the front immediately elect representatives to open formal truce negotiations with the enemy. The Soviet of People's Commissars gives you this authority. In every possible way keep us informed of each step in the pourparlers, but sign no final agreement for an armistice. This can be done only by the Soviet of People's Commissars.

[3] *Izvestiia,* No. 221, November 23, 1917, p. 2.

[4] See p. 243, below.

Soldiers, the peace is in your hands! Watchfulness, patience, energetic action—and the cause of peace will triumph!

In the name of the Government of the Russian Republic,

V. ULIANOV (LENIN)
President of the Sovnarkom

N. KRYLENKO
People's Commissar of War and
Supreme Commander-in-Chief

THE MINISTRY OF WAR AND THE STAVKA

[From Conversation by Direct Wire, November 23, 1917][5]

[Marushevsky]: . . . . Can you suggest some way out of our difficulties? It seems to me that inasmuch as fraternization has been going on for weeks, and since the proposal for an immediate armistice . . . . has penetrated the soldier masses, it will be most difficult to do anything. I should like to know the attitude of the commanders-in-chief of the different fronts regarding recent events and whether [they think] the army will accept the new Supreme Commander [Krylenko]. I cannot tell whether Headquarters is a mere island, separated from the rest of the army, or whether the army as a whole is in favor of an immediate armistice notwithstanding all the grave consequences contained in the note of protest which the Allies handed to you.

[Dukhonin]: Peace is desirable, but it must be approached in the right way . . . . with the Allies . . . . [Without them] the consequences may be very serious. . . . . The consequences of the radiogram of November 22, ... calling on different units of the army to open armistice negotiations . . . . may also be very serious. Such a procedure will not bring real peace. . . . . It may open the front and bring on . . . . civil war. . . . . Headquarters is not yet an island of personal opinions. . . . . I believe that it still represents the majority of the army. . . . .

[Marushevsky]: General Manikovsky had a meeting today of representatives of officers and soldiers. . . . . It resolved to work together for the needs of the army . . . . to work under the orders of General Manikovsky, and not to allow the Commissars to interfere in the Ministry of War. This means that the great mass of employees does not recognize the government, which is ruling exclusively by the aid of bullets and bayonets. It is doubtful if we can actually live up to our resolution. . . . . These are some of the problems which the administration of the Ministry of War is facing. We know little of the political life of the

[5] *Krasnyi Arkhiv,* XXIII (1927), 203–207.

army and the country. All we know is that the troops who came to establish order in Petrograd soon became an idle mob. . . . . So far as I could personally observe, the sailors and armed workmen did all the fighting. . . . . The soldiers on reserve were apathetic and apparently avoided active fighting in order to be on the safe side. . . . . It should be said in justice to Krylenko and Podvoisky, who were present at the Manikovsky meeting, ... that they are ready to come to some understanding in order to save the country and the army from anarchy. It seems that the Commissars are hesitating to go to the Stavka. Krylenko did not go today as I hoped he would. By an exchange of opinion between you, your staff, and the Commissars some way out . . . . might be found. It seemed to me that the Commissars were in a hurry to force the issue when they talked with you . . . . or when they appointed a new supreme commander. It would be better for you to remain at your post or, with your advice, to appoint someone else from the front. In that case I should suggest General Shcherbachev.[6]

[Dukhonin]: My attitude toward armistice and peace is not influenced by the question who is supreme commander. I believe with all my heart that a question [armistice] of such importance to the state can be handled only upon agreement between the central governments [of Russia and the Allies]. But in view of our present complicated situation I might perhaps be willing to assume . . . . the responsibility and attempt . . . . to bring peace to Russia if an agreement could be reached with the Allies and the enemies. . . . . [But to attempt to do this] without even a preliminary understanding with the Allies is dishonorable. . . . . Therein lies the root of all complications. In order to get out of this blind alley . . . . the proposal [of an armistice] must come from a government which is recognized, at least temporarily, by a majority of the country. . . . . This is all I have to say.

[Marushevsky]: . . . . I still do not know what the attitude of the Ministry of War . . . . of General Manikovsky . . . . should be. . . . . Is it desirable that the Commissar [Krylenko] should go to the front? I am afraid that if the Commissars appeal directly to the masses at the front . . . . it will be the last blow to the administration of the army and will create an intolerable situation.

[Dukhonin]: I am in full agreement with the position taken by the Ministry of War in its resolution of today. . . . . I prefer to deal only with General Manikovsky. I regard him . . . . as the representative of the highest military authority and . . . . as an intermediary of a government that is being formed but not yet formed. . . . . I am not interested in the political complexion of the government. The important thing now is

[6] Commander of the armies on the Rumanian front.

to have a government. . . . . I do not think it desirable to have the Commissars come to the front. . . . .

[Marushevsky]: In principle I fully agree with you. . . . . We cannot wait . . . . we must find a way out. . . . . What shall we do with the representatives of the Allies? I . . . . have tried my best to keep them from making an open protest. I was successful as long as no public peace proposal was made. Is it not possible to make them see that Russia must have an armistice, if only for a short time, say, until the Constituent Assembly meets? . . . . Perhaps there is still time to ask them to . . . . talk things over either through General Manikovsky or directly with the People's Commissar. We cannot remain in a state of passivity any longer. A delay of a day or two may be fatal to the state.

[Dukhonin]: . . . . I am not at all anxious to be in authority. All I desire is to be useful to my country. [It might be better to have General Shcherbachev assume the Supreme Command] . . . . if that will help General Manikovsky . . . . provided General Shcherbachev is allowed to carry out his duties . . . . in accordance with our obligation to the Allies, and provided also that I myself hand over my authority to him, something I have been wishing to do for several days. . . . .

[Marushevsky]: . . . . I shall report to General Manikovsky and then communicate with you. . . . .

[Dukhonin]: I would like to add that it would take General Shcherbachev four or five days to reach Mogilev after being summoned. . . . .

[Marushevsky]: Have you anything else to say?

[Dukhonin]: The armies are in urgent need of money to pay the soldiers and laborers. . . . .

KRYLENKO LEAVES FOR THE FRONT

[Order No. 1 to the Army and Navy, November 24, 1917][7]

In the name of the Revolution.

In view of the refusal of General Dukhonin to carry out the instructions of the government to begin negotiations for an armistice, I have been appointed Supreme Commander-in-Chief by decree of the Soviet of People's Commissars.

I am leaving for the front.

The general direction of affairs of the Ministry of War is left to Comrade Podvoisky; all officers and department heads will take this as an official announcement of the fact.

Pending the final surrender of his duties, General Dukhonin is to remain in charge of all operations against the enemy.

[7] Popov, *Oktiabrskii perevorot*, pp. 245–46.

Comrades! Soldiers of the Revolutionary Army! The struggle for peace is now in your hands. Misery, sickness, privation, hunger, and death stand in your way.

Comrades! We must be victorious in the struggle for peace.

All hail immediate peace.

KRYLENKO
Supreme Commander-in-Chief
People's Commissar of War

APPEAL OF THE ALL-ARMY COMMITTEE TO THE SOLDIERS

[Radiogram, November 21, 1917][8]

All! All! All!

Comrades! You observe that in the present difficult situation the only obstacle in the way of peace is the government of Lenin and Trotsky. That which had been foreseen by some of the best minds in the democracy has come to pass. Those who shouted the loudest for peace are the least capable of bringing it about. Lenin has taken charge of the government; for two weeks he has waited in vain for an answer to his appeal, until now he is finally obliged to admit that the Powers refuse to talk to him. Being unwilling to acknowledge this bitter truth to the soldiers and workers whom he had deceived and desiring to throw the blame for this failure on someone else he asked the Supreme Commander-in-Chief to open armistice negotiations. Inasmuch as they refused to negotiate with Lenin's government, it is obvious that the Powers will be even less willing to talk to General Dukhonin, as a representative of that government. Lenin and Trotsky understand this very well, but their chief object, judging by their own statements in the Central Executive Committee, is to spread a fratricidal civil war, and their conversation with General Dukhonin is a step in that direction.

Comrades! It is in your power to put an end to this juggling with the fate of the country. Declare firmly and immediately that the army needs a government that will give it real peace and not merely high-sounding talk about peace. Demand the immediate formation of an All-Socialist government and the stepping aside of the gang of usurpers led by Lenin who have been disowned by some of their own followers. [An All-Socialist] government will be accepted by the country, recognized by the Powers, and will proceed at once with peace negotiations.

Comrades! Concentrate all your efforts toward a real peace and trust the realization of it to the new government with Victor Mikhailovich Chernov at its head. This is the only way to save the country, the only way to put an end to three years of suffering.

THE ALL-ARMY COMMITTEE

[8] *Krasnyi Arkhiv,* XXIII (1927), 196.

CRITICISM OF LENIN'S PROCLAMATION TO THE SOLDIERS

[Meeting of the Central Executive Committee, November 23, 1917]

. . . . Lenin said that the Soviet of People's Commissars did not authorize Dukhonin to conclude an armistice. He resented the talk that the Soviet had proposed a separate armistice. The armistice is for all countries.

"Our party," continued Lenin, *"never promised that we would give peace immediately. What we said was that we would immediately offer an armistice and publish the secret treaties. This we have done. Now commences the revolutionary struggle for peace.* Our success is assured. We will bring about the armistice in a revolutionary way."[9]

Chudnovsky thought that it was not right to leave the question of peace in the hands of the soldiers. Suppose one [Russian] regiment concluded peace with a neighboring [German] regiment, what was there . . . . to prevent a second German regiment from firing on other Russian regiments? We have always been against a "shameful" peace. What Comrade Lenin has just done has made it impossible for our army to go on with the war if the German Government should refuse to enter into peace negotiations. . . . .

Kamenev said that Chudnovsky's speech showed that the proclamation of the People's Commissars to the soldiers to start armistice negotiations laid itself open to wrong interpretations. . . . . The Central Executive Committee should issue a new proclamation to rectify the mistake of the . . . . Commissars. The proclamation should make clear (1) that . . . . the conclusion of an armistice was a government matter and included Russia as a whole, and that (2) one of the stipulations of the armistice should be a guaranty that the Germans would not move troops from the Russian to the French or Italian fronts. This condition is necessary in order not to leave the impression with the French, English, and Italian workmen that we have abandoned them. . . . .

Lenin [in reply to the criticisms of Chudnovsky said]: "When we negotiated with Dukhonin we knew that we had to do with an enemy. . . . . We have dismissed Dukhonin, but we are not legalists . . . . and perceive that mere dismissal is insufficient. He came out against us, and we roused the soldier masses against him. We gave them the right to open but not to conclude armistice negotiations. . . . . I believe that almost any of the regiments is sufficiently organized to uphold revolutionary and military order. If advantage is taken of the armistice discussions to betray the cause of peace, if at the time of fraternization an attack is made, then it will be the duty of the soldiers to shoot the traitors without any formalities. To say that we have weakened our

[9] *Delo Naroda,* No. 206, November 24, 1917, p. 3.

front in case the Germans should attack is monstrous. As long as Dukhonin was . . . . at his post the army had no confidence that it could do anything to bring about an international peace. This confidence the army now has. The only way to deal with Dukhonin is to urge the soldiers to direct action against him. Peace cannot come only from above; it must come also from below. We have not the least confidence in the German generals, but we do have confidence in the German people. Peace concluded by the generals without the active participation of the soldiers will be of short duration. I am opposed to Kamenev's motion . . . . because it does not go far enough . . . ."[10]

[The Socialist-Revolutionists of the Left supported Kamenev's motion, which, however, was voted down.]

B. The Bolsheviks and the Allies

On November 23, the day on which Trotsky's note inviting the Allies and the United States to consider the peace decree as a formal offer for an armistice was made public, *Izvestiia* and *Pravda* began to publish selections from the diplomatic correspondence of Russia and the Entente which the Bolsheviks had found in the archives of the Ministry of Foreign Affairs. Trotsky prefaced the publication with the statement given below. The revelations included the territorial compensation promised Italy for joining the Allies, the territorial offers to Rumania and Greece, the plans of the Entente to partition Turkey and the allocation of Constantinople and the Straits to Russia, the Franco-Russian understanding regarding the changes in the eastern and western frontiers of Germany, a report of a secret conference of French, British, and German bankers who were alleged to have a plan to compensate Germany with Russian territories for losses in the west, and the pressure of France, Italy, and Great Britain on the Provisional Government to continue the war.[11]

[10] *Izvestiia,* No. 223, November 25, 1917, pp. 4–5.

[11] In the United States these materials were published by Oswald Garrison Villard in the New York *Evening Post* in January 1918 and reprinted in a pamphlet under the title: *Full Texts of Secret Treaties as Revealed at Petrograd. The sensational "secret diplomacy" disclosures made by Trotsky when the Bolsheviki came into possession of the Russian archives.* The terms of the secret treaties are given by Seymour Cocks in *The Secret Treaties and Understandings, Text of the Available Documents,* London, 1918.

TROTSKY TO THE FRENCH AMBASSADOR[12]

[November 21, 1917]

I herewith have the honor to inform you, Mr. Ambassador, that the All-Russian Congress of Soviets of Workers' and Soldiers' Deputies organized on November 8 a new Government of the Russian Republic, the Soviet of People's Commissars. The President of this government is Vladimir Ilich Lenin, and the direction of foreign policy has been intrusted to me in the capacity of People's Commissar of Foreign Affairs.

In calling to your attention the text of the proposed armistice and democratic peace without annexations and indemnities on the basis of national self-determination, which was approved by the All-Russian Congress of Soviets of Workers' and Soldiers' Deputies, I have the honor to request you to consider the document referred to above as a formal offer for an armistice on all fronts and an immediate opening of peace negotiations—an offer which the plenipotentiary Government of the Russian Republic is addressing simultaneously to all the belligerent nations and their governments.

Accept the assurances, Mr. Ambassador, of the profound respect of the Soviet Government for the people of France, who are as eager for peace as are all the other peoples exhausted and bled by this unparalleled slaughter.

(*Signed*) L. TROTSKY
People's Commissar of Foreign Affairs

PUBLICATION OF THE "SECRET TREATIES"

[Trotsky on Secret Diplomacy, November 22, 1917][13]

In undertaking the publication of the secret diplomatic documents relating to the foreign diplomacy of the tsarist and the bourgeois-coalition governments, ... we fulfil an obligation which our party assumed when it was the party of opposition.

Secret diplomacy is a necessary weapon in the hands of the propertied minority which is compelled to deceive the majority in order to

[12] *Izvestiia,* No. 221, November 23, 1917, p. 2. Identic notes were sent to the British, American, Italian, Belgian, and Serbian representatives.

At a meeting on November 22 the Allied diplomatic representatives made a "unanimous and emphatic" agreement to ignore this note and to request their governments not to direct them to reply, as the "pretended government [had been] established by force and [was] not recognized by Russian people." (*U.S. Foreign Relations, 1918, Russia,* I, 245.)

[13] *Izvestiia,* No. 221, November 23, 1917, p. 4.

make the latter serve its interests. Imperialism, with its world-wide plans of annexation, its rapacious alliances and machinations, has developed the system of secret diplomacy to the highest degree. . . . . The Russian people as well as the other peoples of Europe and those of the rest of the world should be given the documentary evidence of the plans which the financiers and industrialists, together with their parliamentary and diplomatic agents, were secretly scheming. . . . .

Abolition of secret diplomacy is the first essential of an honorable, popular, and really democratic foreign policy. The Soviet Government has undertaken to carry out such a policy, and that is why, having offered to all belligerents an immediate armistice, it at the same time publishes the treaties and agreements which are no longer binding on the Russian workmen, soldiers, and peasants. . . . .

The bourgeois politicians and newspapers of Germany and Austria-Hungary will no doubt seize upon the published documents and will try to represent the diplomatic work of the Central Empires in a favorable light. Such an attempt is foredoomed to failure; and this for two reasons: In the first place, we intend in a short time to present at the bar of public opinion a series of secret documents which amply illustrate the diplomatic methods of the Central Empires. In the second place—and this is most important—the methods of secret diplomacy are as international as those of imperialistic plunder. When the German proletariat, by revolutionary means, gets access to the secrets of the chancelleries of its government it will discover documents in them of just the same character as those we are about to publish. It is to be hoped that this will happen at an early date.

The government of workers and peasants abolished secret diplomacy with its intrigues, ciphers, and lies. We have nothing to hide. Our program expresses the ardent desires of millions of workers, soldiers, and peasants. We desire a speedy peace on the basis of honest relations with and the full co-operation of all nations. We desire a speedy abolition of the supremacy of capital. In revealing to the whole world the work of the governing classes as it is expressed in the secret documents of diplomacy, we offer to the workers the slogan which will always form the basis of our foreign policy: "Proletarians of all countries, unite!"

L. Trotsky
People's Commissar of Foreign Affairs

PROTEST OF THE ALLIED MILITARY MISSIONS AGAINST SEPARATE NEGOTIATIONS

[Letter to Dukhonin, November 23, 1917][14]

YOUR EXCELLENCY:

The undersigned chiefs of the military missions accredited to the Russian Supreme Command, in accordance with formal instructions received from their respective governments by their ambassadors in Petrograd, have the honor to protest to the Russian Supreme Command in the most energetic manner against the violation of the treaty signed by the Allied Powers of the Entente on September 5, 1914, by which the Allied Powers, including Russia, solemnly engaged not to conclude either a separate armistice or a [separate] suspension of hostilities.

The undersigned chiefs of military missions consider it their duty to inform Your Excellency that the violation of that treaty will entail the gravest consequences.[15]

The undersigned chiefs of military missions beg Your Excellency to acknowledge in writing the receipt of their note and to accept the assurances of their deep respect.

[Signatures]

TROTSKY'S REPLY

[November 24, 1917][16]

To All Regimental, Divisional, Corps, and Army Committees, to All Soviets of Workers', Soldiers', and Peasants' Deputies. All, All, All!

The former Commander-in-Chief Dukhonin has circulated throughout the army the note of the representatives of the Allies at headquarters. . . . .

I feel it my duty to make a statement to the army and the country on the subject of this note to General Dukhonin. The sending of such a note by the representatives of the Allies to General Dukhonin, an officer who had been dismissed for refusing to carry out the orders of the government, is technically a flagrant interference in the domestic affairs of

[14] *Krasnyi Arkhiv,* XXIII (1927), 201. The note was signed by the chiefs of the British, Rumanian, Italian, Japanese, French, and Serbian military missions at the Stavka.

[15] This was interpreted in certain places as a threat that Japan would be called on to invade Russia. See Buchanan, II, 224; *Novaia Zhizn,* No. 180, November 27, 1917, p. 1.

[16] *Izvestiia,* No. 223, November 25, 1917, p. 5.

our country with the object of bringing about civil war. If this diplomatic note is genuine, it means that the Allied representatives are trying to intimidate the Russian people and army, to go on with the war and to carry out the treaties concluded by the Tsar and accepted by the governments of Miliukov—Kerensky—Tereshchenko.

As soon as it came into existence the Soviet of People's Commissars declared publicly that Russia was not bound by the old treaties which had been concluded behind the backs of the people for the benefit of the bourgeois classes of Russia and the Allied countries. Any attempt to bring pressure on the revolutionary Soviet Government by means of dead . . . . treaties is bound to fail miserably. Leaving aside the threats which can not divert us from the struggle for an honest democratic peace, we should like to say that the republican government represented by the Soviet of People's Commissars proposes not a separate but a general peace, and in doing so it feels that it expresses the true interests and desires not only of the Russian masses but of all the belligerent countries.

Soldiers! Workers! Peasants! Your Soviet Government will not allow the foreign bourgeoisie to wield a club over your head and drive you into the slaughter again. Do not be afraid of them. The exhausted nations of Europe are on our side. They are all asking for an immediate peace and our armistice call is like music to their ears. The peoples of Europe will not allow their imperialist governments to harm the Russian people who are guilty of no crime but the desire to have peace and to assert the brotherhood of man. Let all know that the soldiers, workers, and peasants of Russia did not overthrow the governments of the Tsar and Kerensky just to become cannon fodder for the Allied imperialists.

Soldiers, continue in your fight for an immediate armistice. Elect your delegates for the negotiations. Your Commander-in-Chief, Ensign Krylenko, starts for the front today to take charge of the armistice negotiations.

Down with the old secret treaties and diplomatic intrigues!

Hail the honest and open struggle for a universal peace!

L. Trotsky

People's Commissar of Foreign Affairs in the name of the Soviet of People's Commissars

Smolny, 6:00 a.m.

THE ALLIES URGE DUKHONIN TO ASK THE PARTIES TO CEASE DEMORALIZING AGITATION ON THE FRONT

[Allied Military Missions to Dukhonin, November 24, 1917][17]

EXCELLENCY:

As the reports received from the front during the last few days indicate that the political crisis has the effect of increasing disorder in the army and that increasing demoralization constitutes a grave danger to the security of the Russian front, the Chiefs of Military Mission accredited to the High Command of the Russian Armies believe it their duty respectfully to insist that Your Excellency ask all the representatives of the different political parties to refrain from all speech and action which will aggravate the very dangerous situation which exists at this time on the front, vis-à-vis the enemy.

In view of the real and brotherly alliance of the Entente Powers with Russia, in view of the sacrifices that these powers have made to bring aid to Russia at the moment for her conquest of liberty, in view of the disastrous consequences for Russia and the Allied cause that will follow the weakening of the Russian front, the undersigned military representatives feel justified in their urgent request that Your Excellency do everything possible to make clear, by an appeal to all political parties as well as to the army, that honor and patriotism require them to make every effort to preserve and consolidate order and discipline on the front.

[Signed by the Chiefs of the Belgian, Rumanian, British, Italian. Japanese, French, and Serbian Missions.]

FRANCE DEMANDS THE REPUDIATION OF SEPARATE PEACE NEGOTIATIONS

[General Berthelot to General Shcherbachev][18]

JASSY, November 25, 1917

GENERAL:

I have the honor to bring to your knowledge a telegram which I received from the President of the Council of Ministers and the War Minister:

[17] *Krasnyi Arkhiv,* XXIII (1927), 211–12. The original of this letter, it is stated, bears a note from Dukhonin directing the Quartermaster-General to prepare the draft of an appeal. Dukhonin's appeals to the army and the parties are given below, pp. 253–54.

[18] *Izvestiia,* No. 225, November 27, 1917, p. 2. Shcherbachev forwarded this note to General Dukhonin. On the same day Lavergne informed Dukhonin by

"In the communication from Russian Headquarters of November 21 (new style) nothing is said about the situation at the front but it does contain an order of the Soviet of People's Commissars which commands the Supreme Commander-in-Chief to begin negotiations with the military authorities of the enemy for the immediate cessation of hostilities and to start peace negotiations.

"I request you to inform the Russian Supreme Command to which you are attached that France does not recognize the Government of the Soviet of People's Commissars, and, believing in the loyality of the Russian Supreme Command, expects that the latter will categorically repudiate all criminal negotiations, and will hold the Russian Army at the front facing the common enemy.

"France considers herself bound to Russia by previous military agreements. She has stated before and now once more definitely states that she will not recognize any government in Russia which deigns to enter into an agreement with the enemy."

I beg you to accept, General, assurances of my high regard and consideration.

Berthelot

The representatives of the United States were as strongly opposed to the separate peace negotiations as were the representatives of the Allies, but that opposition could not be based on the London Treaty of September 5, 1914, of which the United States was not a signatory. The Americans could object only on the ground that a separate peace would be injurious to Russia and disloyal to the democracies at war with German imperialism. On November 19, before Trotsky made his formal proposal for a general armistice, Ambassador Francis issued a long address "To the People of Russia." He deplored the civil war and warned the Russian people against attempting to secure peace from a government "not only imperialistic in form but the greatest enemy of democracy." He indicated his attitude toward a separate peace in these words: "My country has no secret treaties in connection with this war. We are bound to our Allies in a league

---

letter that France did not recognize the Soviet Government, that the armistice was an affair of governments and could not be taken up without consultation with the Allies, and that the "criminal pourparlers" should be repudiated by the Supreme Command. (*Krasnyi Arkhiv,* XXIII (1927), 214–15; Oldenbourg, p. 459.)

of honor. Our forefathers . . . . warned us against entangling alliances with foreign powers, but they also taught us that a government which fails to fulfil its obligations to live up to its agreements, cannot command the respect of civilization and neither merit nor receive the loyal support of its own citizens, and consequently cannot survive."[19] On November 20, in a report to the State Department, Francis said among other things: "I have a strong suspicion that Lenin and Trotsky are working in the interests of Germany, but whether that suspicion is correct or not, their success will unquestionably result in Germany's gain."[20] On the following day he reported his belief that "German headquarters" had been established in Petrograd and Moscow where their work was becoming more open daily.[21]

This assumption that the Bolsheviks were playing into the hands of Germany, deliberately or otherwise, was doubtless responsible for the statement which appeared in the American press on November 21[22] and is the subject of General Judson's letter given below.

THREAT OF AN AMERICAN EMBARGO ON CREDIT AND SUPPLIES FOR RUSSIA

[General Judson to Russian Chief-of-Staff, November 25, 1917][23]

To the Chief of the Russian General Staff, Petrograd

EXCELLENCY:

There has been brought to my attention the following press communication from the United States:

"The American Government has announced that no shipments of military supplies and provisions to Russia will be effected until the situation of this country will be established. The government before permitting the export of American products wants to know into whose

[19] Francis, *op. cit.*, pp. 173–77.

[20] *Ibid.*, p. 185.

[21] *U.S. Foreign Relations, 1918, Russia,* I, 243.

[22] The statement appeared in the *New York Times,* of this date.

[23] *Izvestiia,* No. 225, November 27, 1917, p. 2. The text is that sent by General Judson to the War Department, *U.S. Foreign Relations, 1918, Russia,* I, 266–67.

hands they will get in Russia. The exports to Russia will be resumed only after the formation of a stable government which can be recognized by the United States; but if the Bolsheviks will remain in power and will put through their program of making peace with Germany, the present embargo on exports to Russia will remain in force. The credits of the Provisional Russian Government amount at the present day to 325 million dollars, of which 191 millions have already been appropriated; the larger part of this money has already been spent for the purchase of supplies, which are ready for loading. The ships allotted by America for the carrying of this freight are ready for sailing, but do not receive permission to leave the ports and they will be refused coal."

It occurs to me that it is but fair to convey to Your Excellency the circumstance that neither I nor the American Ambassador has as yet received from the United States of America instructions or information similar to that contained in the press report above quoted. Nevertheless, it seems but fair to express to Your Excellency the opinion that the press report correctly states the attitude of the Government of the United States. We are in daily expectation of receiving information similar to that conveyed by the above-mentioned press report.

Before sending you this communication I have submitted it to the American Ambassador who concurs in the expressions contained in it.

I avail myself of this opportunity to renew to Your Excellency the assurance of my high consideration.

W. V. Judson
Brig.-Genl. U.S. Army, American Military Attaché,
Chief of American Military Mission to Russia

IZVESTIIA'S COMMENT ON THE FRENCH AND AMERICAN NOTES[24]

The equivocal note of the American General . . . . that the United States has declared a kind of boycott against us goes hand in hand with the telegram of General Berthelot. It would seem that the North American plutocrats are ready to trade locomotives for the heads of Russian soldiers. This is rather a high price and does not harmonize with the November Revolution. The Russian people are interested in having economic and political relations with the Allies, but they are not willing to pay for them with blood to the satisfaction of Clemenceau and the New York kings of war industry.

In politics we have to face facts, both pleasant and unpleasant. The Allies cannot dodge them. Russia has a government of the people crea-

[24] *Izvestiia,* No. 225, November 27, 1917, p. 2.

ted by the All-Russian Congress of the Soviet of Workers' and Soldiers' Deputies. This government does not need Mr. Clemenceau's recognition to be a fully empowered organ of the Russian soldiers, workers, and peasants. The Soviet of People's Commissars is leading the country to peace. Do the governments of the Allies wish to make this peace general? Do they wish to enter at once into an exchange of opinion on this subject? Do they or do they not? This is the only question which interests the people of the belligerent countries. The threats of the Allied diplomats are not going to change our policy. We do not doubt for a moment that these contemptible threats will be disowned by the peoples in the Allied countries.

We are on the way to peace, and we will reach our goal in spite of all obstacles.

C. The Beginning of Negotiations with the Germans

On his arrival on the sector of the front held by the Russian 5th Army, Krylenko arrested General Boldyrev, the Army Commander, and sent a delegation across the lines with an offer to the Germans to negotiate an armistice. The Germans promptly accepted and Trotsky formally notified the Allies of this fact and again asked them if they would participate in the negotiations.

KRYLENKO ARRIVES AT DVINSK

[Boldyrev to Dukhonin, November 24, 1917][25]

Boldyrev: . . . . I have been informed that Ensign Krylenko is to arrive at Dvinsk by special train today, November 24. The Army Committee has received instructions from Petrograd to provide for his personal safety and to select comrades who know the German language. This announcement, together with the radiograms, leads me to think that Krylenko's journey means an attempt to open peace discussions. In view of the fact that all army committees . . . . have the Bolshevik point of view and the soldier masses are strong for an immediate peace, I take it for granted that Krylenko will be warmly received. Not having any real power behind me I can do nothing to stop him. . . . .

[Boldyrev to Levitsky, November 25][26]

Boldyrev: Please make this report to General Dukhonin. Krylenko arrived at Dvinsk about nine o'clock. About noon I had a telephone call

[25] *Krasnyi Arkhiv,* XXIII (1927), 208.

[26] *Ibid.,* pp. 222–23.

to come to his car. I said nothing and, of course, did not go. I had left word yesterday with the Army Committee for him to come to see me to talk over certain important matters—the note of the Allies. At 15:30 o'clock I received another invitation, this time from the Army Committee to be present at its meeting at which the Supreme Commander-in-Chief, Ensign Krylenko, would be present. I replied that I could not come. Later I had a report . . . . of Krylenko's speech on that occasion. He said that he had come to Dvinsk to open a fight on three foes. The first—the foreign [foe]—was not dangerous; the second—famine—was being handled by the government of the People's Commissars; the third—the counter-revolutionary commanding staff of Dukhonin, who is a Kornilovist. He went on to say that the masses would attain peace over the dead bodies of the counter-revolutionary commanding staff; that he would open his guns today on the Stavka, where all hostile elements are gathered; and that he would commence peace discussions with the enemy. When asked . . . . about the note of the Allies, Krylenko said that he was not afraid of them; that it was the old game of bluff. . . . . Krylenko has a guard of fifty sailors from the "Aurora," soldiers and Red Guards. I assume that Dvinsk will become for the time being the headquarters of Krylenko. I have not the means to interfere. The Socialist-Revolutionists in the Army Committee have declared that they do not recognize Krylenko as Supreme Commander, but these men have not much support in the army and can do little. Under the present circumstances my position is very difficult. . . . .

DUKHONIN ORDERS KRYLENKO'S GUARD STOPPED AT ORSHA

[Order to the Finland Division, November 25, 1917][27]

In case the train with Krylenko and his guard of fifty-nine men on board shall start from Dvinsk for Mogilev, you are ordered to do the following:

(1) At the stations Orsha and Shklov his train will be met by representatives of the Army Commissar of the Northern Front and the All-Army Committee. They will tell Krylenko either to return to Petrograd or to proceed to Mogilev alone, leaving his armed guard at that place [station] or sending it to Petrograd. (2) If necessary you are to make use of force to prevent Krylenko's armed guard from proceeding to Mogilev. . . . .

DUKHONIN

PEREKRESTOV, Chairman of the All-Army Committee

[27] *Krasnyi Arkhiv,* XXIII (1927), 223.

DUKHONIN'S APPEAL TO THE PEOPLE AND THE ARMY

[November 25, 1917][28]

Russians:

This is the fourth year that the Russian army has stood in the trenches guarding the country against a cunning foreign foe. This is the fourth year that the army has carried the full weight of this terrible war, enduring sickness, wounds, hunger, and cold, and longing for peace that it might return home. But fate has brought it new trials. Insurrection has broken out in our land; [the country is being] ruined for lack of government; and the army is suffering from want of food and from anarchy introduced into its midst by evil-minded people leading Russia to ruin.

The army turns to you, representatives of the Russian democracy, the zemstvos, and the peasants, imploring you to come to an agreement . . . . and give to suffering Russia a government—an all-national government, a government based on the principle of freedom for all Russian citizens, freedom from violence, blood, and clubs. The army awaits your answer! . . . .

Soldier-Citizens!

You are troubled because you desire peace and our Allies do not. For that reason you are advised to break the treaties made with them in the time of the Tsar. Those who would lead you to peace with the imperialistic government of Germany fail to tell you that it is almost the same kind of autocratic government [as that] from which the revolution has freed Russia and given her her liberty. You are urged to take a counter-revolutionary step and deprive yourself of all the conquests of a free democracy which has just commenced to form and organize itself in Russia.

Who is it that is so anxious to deprive you and the Russian people of this freedom? The imperialistic Germans, of course, and not the Allies. From the moment that Russia became free they [the Allies] have done their best to help us with arms, money, and supplies to enable us to defend the freedom won, the democratic form of government achieved. It is not true that the Allies are opposed to peace. They have never been asked by the Russian Government, for the simple reason that no such legal government exists in Russia at present. Such a government must be formed. Our trouble is not that we have to live up to the agreement with the Allies . . . . but that in breaking the agreement Russia deprives herself of defenders of democracy and becomes a slave of imperialistic Germany where justice, freedom, and conscience yield to

[28] *Krasnyi Arkhiv,* XXIII (1927), 218–20.

force, trickery, and deceit. Soldiers, do not let yourselves be lured by external promises and do not be in a hurry to fall into the arms of William. Give the true Russian democracy time to form a government, and this government, together with the Allies, will immediately give you a lasting peace.

Rapprochement with the Germans means new war in the near future. The Germans will not endure a free democratic Russian people on their borders.

THE ARMY AND THE NEGOTIATIONS

[Cheremisov to Dukhonin, November 26, 1917][29]

[Cheremisov]: . . . . The commanding staff of the Northern front is in an awkward situation . . . . the soldiers are doing pretty much as they like. At present the Germans are inactive, but should they make a move a catastrophe on a grand scale is inevitable. We are out of food. . . . . The 13th Don Regiment . . . . went somewhere and has left no trail behind. This is also true of [other army units]. . . . . Krylenko was here yesterday. He ordered me to meet him; when he arrived he invited me, through his adjutant, to see him; later he sent his adjutant to me. I did not go but invited him to come to see me . . . . but he did not come. He went to Dvinsk and is now with the 19th Corps. . . . . Under present conditions . . . . I am helpless to prevent the collapse of the front. . . . . Perhaps someone else could do better . . . . and therefore I ask you . . . . to put someone else in my place. . . . .

[Dukhonin]: . . . . I fully understand your position and the unfortunate situation . . . . but I believe that the only way to get through these difficulties is to hold on to the command, even if only nominally. You are the only one on your front who can handle the situation . . . . and I cannot agree to your leaving. I beseech you in the name of our country to stay at your post. As to food . . . . [a number] of cars and trains are on the way to you. . . . .

[Cheremisov]: Food trains never reach us; they are held up on the way. . . . .

I don't fit in with the political situation. . . . . Tomorrow or the day after tomorrow I shall be asked to make peace with the enemy on the front, and if I do not do so, then my authority will slip out of my hands. I feel that it is useless for me to remain here any longer. There is no likelihood that any military operations will take place other than running away from the front. . . . .

[Dukhonin]: I find it difficult to grant your request . . . . and I beg you not to leave your post. . . . . There are others in the same

[29] *Krasnyi Arkhiv,* XXIII (1927), 224–26.

difficult position . . . . this is not the time to quit. . . . . I believe that [Krylenko's] efforts are bound to fail; the Germans will hardly enter into serious conversations with him. The Allies have quite definitely stated that . . . . the commanding personnel has no right to start [peace] negotiations. Their threats, in case [we conclude] a separate armistice, are really menacing. . . . . Krylenko is recognized only by the dark and ignorant masses, who desire peace at any cost. Krylenko's ambition to conclude an armistice will not go much beyond fraternization, on a much larger scale, to be sure. Judging from conversations with our soldiers they have not much faith in such a peace. They say quite openly that only the Constituent Assembly can conclude such a peace; nor will the Germans accept such a peace. . . . .

[Cheremisov]: You are mistaken in supposing that Krylenko has the masses behind him. . . . . He has with him the Committees which, given the inertia of the masses, are all powerful. Theoretically the Allies may be in the right, but . . . . I am sure that they have not the least conception of the material conditions or the morale of our army. We are quite incapable of waging a defensive war to say nothing of [undertaking] an offensive. The Germans know it quite well, and they can move as many troops as they like from our front. An attack on their part would lead to a catastrophe. It seems to me that we should open the eyes of the Allies to these facts so that they may not face us with demands which cannot be fulfilled.

[Dukhonin]: I am always telling them. They see our situation and understand, but refuse to admit that we can start separatc armistice negotiations. So far as I can understand them, they would not oppose the conclusion of a peace if they could participate—but no separate peace. . . . .[30]

FIRST NEGOTIATIONS WITH THE GERMANS

[Krylenko's Armistice Commission, November 26, 1917][31]

This [November 26] morning at eleven o'clock the Commander-in-Chief sent out a delegation vested with the following powers: "In the

[30] It appears that Cheremisov left Pskov the next day, November 27. Upon his arrival in Petrograd he was arrested by the Bolsheviks and locked up in the Peter and Paul Fortress (*Utro Rossii,* No. 263, November 29, 1917, p. 3). At the headquarters of the Western front a similar situation existed. On the 25th the Military Revolutionary Committee had ordered General Baluev to open armistice negotiations or resign his command. He resigned. Dukhonin was unable to persuade Baluev, Walter, Danilov, or Dowbor-Musnicki, commander of a Polish unit, to assume the position of Commander of the Group of Armies or to attempt to oppose the overwhelming forces supporting the M.R. Committee (Oldenbourg, pp. 460–64).

[31] *Izvestiia,* No. 226, November 28, 1917, p. 2.

name of the Russian Republic and by the authority conferred upon me by the Soviet of People's Commissars, I, People's Commissar of War and Navy and Supreme Commander-in-Chief of the armies of the Russian Republic, authorize you—Lieutenant Vladimir Schneur of the Ninth Kiev Hussars, ... Michael Sagalovich and George Meren, ... to proceed to the designated place and to ask the Commander-in-Chief of the German army . . . . whether he is ready to send his plenipotentiaries to open immediate negotiations looking toward an armistice on all fronts to be followed by peace discussions. In the event of an affirmative answer . . . . arrange the time and place at which the plenipotentiaries of both sides can meet."

N. Krylenko
People's Commissar of War and Navy
and Supreme Commander-in-Chief

[Krylenko's Order No. 2, November 26, 1917][32]

The plenipotentiaries crossed the German trenches in the region of the 5th Army. An answer is expected tomorrow, the 27th, at 20 o'clock. Comrades, peace is at hand and in our hands. Stand firm in these last days; muster all your strength and hold the front in spite of hunger. Success depends on your revolutionary tenacity. Treat with contempt the lies and the false appeals of General Dukhonin's gang, and of his bourgeois pseudo-Socialist flunkies who are gathered at headquarters. For eight months they have fed the Russian people with false promises of peace. They have brought misery to the country, famine and exhaustion to the army through their criminal attempts to oppose the government of the Soviet of People's Commissars created by the All-Russian Congress of Soviets. For failure to obey my written order to appear before me I dismissed General Cheremisov, Commander of the Northern Front. Until his successor is appointed he is to continue at his post under the control of Comrade Pozern, Commissar of the Northern Front. Commissar Shibin of the former government is to be arrested for refusing to give up his post. For failure to appear before me, General Boldyrev, Commander of the 5th Army, is dismissed, and his temporary successor is General Antipov of the 19th Corps. General Boldyrev is to be arrested and tried for disobeying a war order.[33] The commander of the 27th Corps is removed from his post for disobeying

[32] *Izvestiia,* No. 226, November 28, 1917, pp. 2–3.

[33] General Boldyrev, a man of the people, was a popular officer. One of his defenders at his trial was a soldier, a member of the Army Committee. Boldyrev was sentenced to three years imprisonment. He did not serve out the term and later took part in events in Siberia. Boldyrev's account of these events is given in his work: *Direktoriia, Kolchak, Interventy,* Novonikolaevsk, 1925.

the order to appear [before me]. His place is to be taken by someone appointed by the Commissar of the Corps and the corps committee. I pronounce the former Supreme Commander-in-Chief, General Dukhonin, an enemy of the people, for his stubborn refusal to obey the order of dismissal and for his criminal acts which gave a new impetus to civil war. All those who support Dukhonin are to be arrested regardless of their social position, party affiliations, and past record. These people will be arrested by someone especially appointed for that purpose. General Manikovsky is to take the steps necessary to effect the above orders and changes in the status of the above-mentioned persons.

KRYLENKO
Supreme Commander-in-Chief

[When the Soviet's armistice proposal reached the German command on the Eastern front, it was immediately forwarded by direct wire to German General Headquarters. Ludendorff promptly telephoned to the Chief-of-Staff on the Eastern front: "Is it possible to negotiate with these people?" Hoffmann replied: "Yes, it is possible to negotiate with them. His Excellency requires troops and these are the first that can come."][34]

[The Germans Agree to Negotiate][35]

1. The German Commander-in-Chief of the Eastern Front is ready to enter into negotiations with the Russian Supreme Commander-in-Chief.

2. The German Commander-in-Chief is authorized by the German High Command to conclude an armistice.

3. If the Russian Supreme Commander-in-Chief is prepared to carry on negotiations with the German Commander-in-Chief of the Eastern Front, he should send a plenipotentiary commission with the necessary written credentials to the headquarters of the German Commander-in-Chief of the Eastern Front.

4. The German Commander-in-Chief of the Eastern Front will likewise appoint a special plenipotentiary commission.

5. The day and hour of the meeting of the two commissions may be set by the Russian Commander-in-Chief. The German Commander-in-Chief of the Eastern Front should be given due notice so as to have ready a special train. It is also necessary to indicate at what point the Russian Commission will cross the front.

6. The Commander-in-Chief of the German Front will provide the necessary telegraph apparatus so as to make possible direct communica-

[34] General von Hoffmann, *The War of Lost Opportunities,* London, 1924, p. 195.

[35] *Izvestiia,* No. 227, November 29, 1917, p. 1.

tion between the commission and the Russian chief command. The commission may bring with it a Hughes apparatus.

[LEOPOLD, Prince of Bavaria]
Commander-in-Chief of the German Eastern Front

VON HOFMEISTER
Accurate. Lieutenant-General and Commander of a Division

[Krylenko's Order No. 3, November 27, 1917, 16:15 o'clock][36]

Our delegation has returned with an official reply from the German Commander-in-Chief. . . . . The next meeting of the plenipotentiaries is to take place on December 2. Without any more formalities I turn over to the local revolutionary tribunals of the regimental committees all those who conceal or hinder the dissemination of this order. I command an immediate cessation of firing and fraternization on all fronts. It is necessary to keep a more watchful eye on the enemy. Make no military move unless it is to counteract a move of the enemy. Everyone at his post! Only the strong man gets what he wants.

Hail an early peace!

KRYLENKO
Supreme Commander-in-Chief

The above telegram is to be broadcast to all, all, all.

THE SOVNARKOM TO THE PEOPLE OF THE BELLIGERENT COUNTRIES

[Radiogram, November 27, 1917][37]

In reply to our proposal for an immediate armistice on all fronts . . . . the German High Command agreed to the conduct of peace negotiations. Ensign Krylenko, Commander-in-Chief of the Armies of the Republic, proposed to postpone armistice negotiations for five days . . . . in order once more to invite the Allied Governments to state their attitude toward peace negotiations. Military operations on the Russian front are suspended by mutual agreement. It is understood, of course, that no transfer of troops is to take place on either side during these five days.

The decisive step has been taken. The triumphant revolution of the workers and peasants of Russia has brought the question of peace into the foreground. . . . . Now all governments, all classes, all parties of the belligerent countries are called upon to give a plain answer to the

[36] *Izvestiia,* No. 226, November 28, 1917, p. 2.

[37] *Pravda,* No. 190, November 28, 1917, p. 1.

question: Do they agree to join us on December 1 [*sic*] in the negotiations for an immediate armistice and a general peace?

Do they or do they not?

On their answer to this question depends whether there shall be a new winter campaign with all its horrors and miseries for the toilers in the factories and fields, whether Europe shall go on bleeding.

We, the Soviet of People's Commissars, address this question to the governments of our Allies: France, Great Britain, Italy, the United States, Belgium, Serbia, Rumania, Japan, and China. We ask them in the face of their own people, in the face of the whole world: Do they agree to join us in the peace negotiations on December 1? We . . . . ask the allied people and, first and foremost, the toiling masses: Will they consent to go on with this endless and aimless slaughter and go blindly to the ruin of the whole European culture? We demand that the workers' parties of the allied countries give an immediate answer to the question: Do they wish that peace negotiations should open on December 1? A plain question has been put. Soldiers, proletarians, toilers, peasants! Do you wish to take with us a decisive step toward a people's peace?

We . . . . appeal to the toiling masses of Germany, Austria-Hungary, Turkey, and Bulgaria. The peace which we propose must be a people's peace. . . . . Such a peace can be concluded only by means of a direct and courageous struggle of the revolutionary masses against all imperialist plans and annexationist aspirations. . . . .

To our proposals the official representatives of the ruling classes of the Allied countries replied by a refusal to recognize the Soviet Government. . . . . The government of the victorious revolution stands in no need of recognition from the technicians of capitalist diplomacy, but we do ask the people: Does reactionary diplomacy express their thoughts and aspirations? Will they allow such diplomacy to pass by the great opportunity for peace offered by the Russian Revolution? The answer to these questions must be given at once and it must be answered in deeds and not in words only. The Russian army and the Russian people cannot and will not wait any longer. . . . . We want a general peace, but if the bourgeoisie of the Allied countries force us to conclude a separate peace, the responsibility will be theirs. . . . .

L. TROTSKY
Commissar of Foreign Affairs

V. ULIANOV (LENIN)
President of the Sovnarkom

Although the American and British officials were less openly hostile toward the Bolsheviks than were the French, they were no less firm in their refusal to recognize the Soviet Government or to participate in the armistice negotiations. In Washington, where Bakhmetev, the ambassador appointed by the Provisional Government, had repudiated the Bolsheviks, the State Department announced on November 24 that it would continue to regard him as the representative of Russia.[38]

On the 27th, Lieutenant-Colonel Kerth, American Military Representative at the Stavka, sent to General Dukhonin a protest against a separate armistice. There followed a second note from General Judson to the "Chief of the Russian General Staff" stating that "Americans . . . . do not wish to interfere except helpfully in the solution of any Russian problem. . . . . Their representatives here are now informed that no important fraction of the Russian people desires an immediate separate peace or armistice. And it is certainly within the rights of Russia . . . . to bring up the question of a general peace."[39] At a meeting of the Petrograd Soviet on November 30, Trotsky interpreted Judson's conciliatory gesture as meaning that the Americans "have become convinced that since they cannot control the Russian revolution, it would be best to play the friend, hoping thereby to put themselves in a position to compete after the war with German and especially English capitalists." And he added, "We snap our fingers at the opinion of all the imperialists, Allied or enemy . . . ."[40] Trotsky followed this with a warning in *Izvestiia,* December 1, that Kerth's and Lavergne's notes constituted interference in the internal affairs of Russia which, if repeated, would "entail the most serious consequences, the responsibility for which the Soviet of People's Commissars refuses beforehand to accept."[41] On this same

[38] *New York Times,* November 11 and 25, 1917.

[39] These notes are given in Cumming and Pettit (eds.), *Russian-American Relations, March 1917–March 1920. Documents and Papers,* New York, 1920, pp. 48–49, 53–54. Hereafter cited as *R.A.R.* See also Edgar Sisson, *One Hundred Red Days,* New Haven, 1931, pp. 72–75.

[40] *Izvestiia,* No. 229, December 1, 1917, p. 3.

[41] *Ibid.,* p. 6. Full text in *R.A.R.,* p. 54.

day, having been privately informed that further communications would not be unwelcome, Judson visited Trotsky to urge that the armistice, if made, should be of long duration and contain strict clauses against the transfer of German troops from the Russian front. Trotsky was "responsive" and suggested that Judson cable the United States that in the negotiations Trotsky would observe and endeavor to protect the interests of Russia's allies. Trotsky's report of the interview in *Izvestiia* did not refer to this part of the conversation but quoted Judson as having said that "the time of protests and threats addressed to the Soviet Government has passed, if that time ever existed." In view of this statement Trotsky considered the incident of the Kerth note closed.[42] Trotsky's account of the Judson interview aroused wide comment and considerable criticism in Entente and neutral circles, with the result that Secretary Lansing directed American representatives to "withhold all direct communication with Bolshevik government."[43]

In Paris, meanwhile, on November 30, the Allied Supreme War Council had discussed the Bolshevik armistice proposals. The immediate occasion was Balfour's reading of Buchanan's dispatch to the Foreign Office of November 27 in which the Ambassador had said: "In my opinion the only safe course left to us is to give Russia back her word and tell her people that, realizing how worn out they are by the war and the disorganization inseparable from the great revolution, we leave it to them to decide whether they will purchase peace on Germany's terms or fight on with the Allies, who are determined not to lay down their arms till binding guarantees for the world's peace have been secured."[44]

According to Colonel House, this proposal ". . . . brought violent opposition from Sonnino and a somewhat milder

[42] *Izvestiia*, No. 230, December 2, 1917, p. 1; *R.A.R.*, p. 55; *U.S. Foreign Relations, 1918, Russia*, I, 279; cf. Sisson, *op. cit.*, pp. 79–83.

[43] *U.S. Foreign Relations, 1918, Russia*, I, 289.

[44] Buchanan, II, 225.

objection from Clemenceau. We finally sent for the Russian Ambassador[45] here and asked his opinion. He decided against such a reply as the British Ambassador at Petrograd suggested, but recommended practically what I had proposed." House's proposal was that "The Allies and the United States declare that they are not waging war for the purpose of aggression or indemnity. The sacrifices they are making are in order that militarism shall not continue to cast its shadow over the world, and that nations shall have the right to lead their lives in the way that seems to them best for the development of their general welfare."[46]

At the meeting of the Supreme War Council on the following day (December 1), the Russian question again came up, but no agreement could be reached on the text of a communication to be sent to Russia. Finally it was decided that each government should separately instruct its ambassador at Petrograd to state that "the Allies were willing to reconsider their war aims in conjunction with Russia as soon as she had a stable government with whom they could act."[47]

While these discussions were going on in Paris, Buchanan in Petrograd was endeavoring to explain why the Allied representatives had not replied to the Sovnarkom's armistice note and the reason for Lord Robert Cecil's statement that while it was necessary to have certain dealings with the Bolsheviks there was "no intention of recognizing such a government."[48] Buchanan's statement published on November 30 and *Izvestiia*'s reply the next day[49] did not help

[45] Maklakov, who had been appointed by the Provisional Government just before its fall. On November 30, Trotsky dismissed Maklakov from his post and warned him that his participation in the Inter-Allied Conference would constitute "an offense against the state entailing grave consequences." (*Izvestiia,* No. 228, November 30, 1917, p. 6.)

[46] Charles Seymour, *The Intimate Papers of Colonel House,* 4 vols., Boston and New York, 1926–1928, III, 282–83. Hereafter cited as Seymour.

[47] House to President Wilson, December 2, 1917, Seymour, p. 285. Seymour says that at this meeting Clemenceau urged on House the desirability of asking the Japanese to land troops in Siberia. This House opposed. (*Ibid.,* p. 387; cf. *U.S. Foreign Relations, 1918, Russia,* I, 255.)

[48] *The Manchester Guardian,* November 24, 1917.

[49] Both are given in *R.A.R.,* pp. 51–53.

the situation, which was further aggravated by Trotsky's attempt to secure the release of Chicherin (Ornatsky) and Petrov, then interned in England, by refusing to allow British subjects to leave Russia,[50] and by Trotsky's statement to Sadoul, of the French Mission, that he intended to arrest Buchanan for aiding the counter-revolutionists, a statement duly reported to the Ambassador by General Niessel.[51]

Various Russian anti-Bolshevik groups took a hand in the affair. On November 29, several former members of the Provisional Government made a declaration warning against the disastrous consequences of a separate peace and maintaining that "the acts of the insurrectionists can under no circumstances be considered as governmental acts or as expressing the will of the people."[52] Similar declarations were made by the Central Committees of the Cadets, the Mensheviks, the S.R.'s of the Right, the Council of the Russian Church, and the Petrograd and Moscow City Dumas.

The Central Powers, naturally, had received the armistice offer in a different spirit than the Allies. On November 29 Count Hertling, the German Chancellor, and Count Czernin, the Austro-Hungarian Foreign Minister, stated that they considered the Soviet proposals a suitable basis for opening negotiations. Kühlmann, the German Foreign Minister, and Dr. Seidler, the Austrian Premier, elaborated these statements on November 30.[53] On November 29 Trotsky again asked the Allies if they intended to participate in the armistice negotiations.

[50] An order to this effect appeared in *Izvestiia,* No. 228, November 30, 1917, p. 6.

[51] J. Sadoul, *Notes sur la révolution bolchevique,* Octobre 1917–Janvier 1919, Paris, 1919, p. 124; Buchanan, *op. cit.,* II, 227; Trotsky, *My Life,* p. 348.

[52] *Nasha Rech,* No. 2, November 30, 1917, p. 3. The M.R. Committee on December 2 ordered that those who had signed this declaration be detained "in order to prevent public violence against them arising out of the just indignation of the revolutionary workers and soldiers of Petrograd" (*Pravda,* No. 194, December 2, 1917, p. 2). A translation is given in Oldenbourg, pp. 478–83.

[53] *Die Friedensverhandlungen in Brest-Litowsk und der Friede mit Russland, Authentische Berichtung,* Leipzig [1918], pp. 1–5. The Bulgarian and Turkish governments announced on December 1 and 6 their willingness to participate in the negotiations.

TROTSKY INVITES THE ALLIES TO JOIN THE ARMISTICE NEGOTIATIONS[54]

[November 29, 1917]

In reply to a formal proposal of the Soviet of People's Commissars to open negotiations for an immediate armistice on all fronts, aiming to bring about a democratic peace without annexations and indemnities and with the right of all nations to self-determination, the German Supreme Command replied affirmatively. All documents and facts concerning this matter were published by me in the *Izvestiia Tsentralnago Ispolnitelnago Komiteta Sovetov Rabochikh i Soldatskikh Deputatov.*

Hostilities on the Russian front have ceased. Preliminary negotiations will start on December 2. The Soviet of People's Commissars was and is of the opinion that it is necessary to carry on negotiations simultaneously with the Allies in the hope of attaining a speedy armistice on all fronts and concluding a general democratic peace.

The Allied Governments and their diplomatic representatives in Russia are kindly asked to reply whether they wish to take part in the negotiations which are to begin at five o'clock in the afternoon of December 2.

L. TROTSKY
People's Commissar of Foreign Affairs

D. THE BOLSHEVIK OCCUPATION OF THE STAVKA

That it would be futile to attempt to defend the Stavka was apparent even to Dukhonin before Krylenko's contingents of sailors and soldiers reached Mogilev. The idea of armed resistance was therefore abandoned and the All-Army Committee attempted to negotiate with Krylenko.[55] Another plan to move the Stavka from Mogilev to Kiev or Jassy, headquarters of the Rumanian front, was vetoed by the troops guarding the Stavka.[56] On December 2 the Military Revolutionary Committee at Mogilev took over the control of the Stavka, dissolved the All-Army Committee, and arrested Dukhonin. Krylenko arrived at Mogilev on the 3d and a few hours later Dukhonin was murdered.

[54] *Izvestiia,* No. 228, November 30, 1917, p. 6.

[55] Lelevich, *Oktiabr v Stavke,* Gomel, 1922, p. 76.

[56] Oldenbourg, *op. cit.,* pp. 491–93.

RESOLUTION OF THE ALL-ARMY COMMITTEE[57]

[December 1, 1917]

1. The Stavka in view of its great importance should be left in the hands of the present officers.

2. For that purpose the Stavka should be transferred to Kiev.

3. Negotiations with the Sovnarkom should be started so as to prevent a clash.

4. As a means of enforcing the demands it was decided that the threat of armed force should be used, but

5. The actual use [of force] should under no circumstances be permitted.

6. The Supreme Command is to be appointed by mutual agreement between the All-Army Committee and the All-Russian Central Executive Committee.

7. Krylenko is to be removed from the post of Supreme Commander-in-Chief.

8. The questions of peace and armistice should remain outside the competence of the Stavka.

9. Krylenko's echelons should return to Petrograd immediately.

REPORT THAT THE ALLIES CONSENT TO SEPARATE ARMISTICE

[Dukhonin to Shcherbachev, December 1, 1917][58]

Dukhonin: . . . . Since yesterday the situation has changed as follows: The [Ukrainian] Rada has not yet replied to the [suggested] plan of moving [Headquarters] to Kiev. We have nevertheless made preparations. . . . . The foreign missions were ready to go with me. At that moment the Italian military representative, General Romei, received a telegram from his embassy at Petrograd, saying that the Allies had decided to free Russia from her obligations and to make it possible for her to conclude a separate peace . . . . and for the time being an armistice on the following bases: the troops to remain where they are, no exchange of prisoners, Russia not to furnish bread or raw material to the Germans. This telegram has not yet been officially confirmed. This circumstance may radically change the whole armistice question. . . . .[59] [Dukhonin further states that the armies on the North

[57] Liubimov, *Revoliutsiia 1917 goda,* pp. 166–67.

[58] *Krasnyi Arkhiv,* XXIII (1927), 236–38.

[59] Sadoul wrote on November 18 that Trotsky had told him of receiving a proposition from the Americans to the effect that if Russia was definitely unable

and West fronts are virtually in the hands of the Bolsheviks, and refers to the decision of the All-Army Committee and to proposals to turn over the command to General Bonch-Bruevich.]

[Shcherbachev to Dukhonin, December 2, 1917][60]

General Berthelot is positive that the telegram received by the Italian military attaché is a fake. . . . . He added that under no circumstances could the Allies agree to Russia's concluding a separate peace or truce. He says that . . . . the telegram should not stand in the way of the immediate transfer of Headquarters to Kiev. . . . .

1: 55 o'clock.

ORDER OF THE MOGILEV MILITARY REVOLUTIONARY COMMITTEE[61]

[December 2, 1917]

1. The Mogilev Military Revolutionary Committee accepts Ensign Krylenko as the only lawful commander of the Russian Army. . . . .
2. The ex-commander, General Dukhonin . . . . is placed under house arrest.
3. Stankevich, the Commissar of the deposed bourgeois-coalition government at the Stavka, is removed from his post. . . . .
4. General Vyrubov, Assistant to the Chief-of-Staff, ... is placed under house arrest.
5. The All-Army Committee is dissolved. . . . . The Military Revolutionary Committee assumes provisionally the functions of the All-Army Committee. . . . .
6. The Mogilev Military Revolutionary Committee has appointed commissars to control the activities of the Stavka and no order may be carried out without their signature.
7. The Military Revolutionary Committee has appointed commissars to take charge of the garages, and no automobile may be used without their permission.

---

to go on with the war without aggravating internal conditions, the United States would not consider it an unfriendly act if Russia signed a separate armistice with Germany on condition that Russia agreed to give no aid of any kind and not to resume commercial relations with the Central Powers until the conclusion of a general peace (Sadoul, p. 92).

This opinion was undoubtedly held by several American officials, not including the Ambassador, and a message to this effect was sent to Washington (cf. Sisson, *op. cit.*, pp. 87–90).

[60] *Krasnyi Arkhiv,* XXIII (1927), 241.

[61] Liubimov, *Revoliutsiia 1917 goda,* pp. 462–63.

THE BOLSHEVIKS TAKE CONTROL OF THE STAVKA

[Krylenko's Proclamation to the Soldiers, December 3, 1917][62]

Comrades!

I have this day entered Mogilev at the head of the revolutionary forces. Surrounded on all sides, Headquarters surrendered without fighting. The last obstacle to peace is removed. I cannot pass over the tragic lynching of the former Supreme Commander-in-Chief, General Dukhonin. The hatred of the masses boiled over. Notwithstanding all efforts to save him, he was dragged from his car at the Mogilev station and killed. Kornilov's escape on the eve of the fall of Headquarters is responsible for this excess.[63]

Comrades! I cannot permit the banner of the revolution to be stained. Such acts should be severely condemned. Be worthy of the newly won liberty! Don't disgrace the government of the people! The revolutionary people should be fierce in war but magnanimous in victory.

Comrades! With the fall of Headquarters the struggle for peace receives a new impetus. In the name of the Revolution and Freedom I call on you for revolutionary union and revolutionary discipline.

Long live the government of the Soviets of Workers', Soldiers', and Peasants' Deputies!

KRYLENKO
Supreme Commander-in-Chief

THE MURDER OF GENERAL DUKHONIN

[Extracts from Krylenko's Report to the Sovnarkom][64]

I arrived at Mogilev about noon on December 3. . . . . Soon afterward I was informed that General Dukhonin, accompanied by Pavlov, a midshipman, was in my train and in my dining car. Pavlov explained that while the guard was being changed he learned of a plot . . . . to get rid of Dukhonin and for that reason brought him to my train. I went at once to the dining car, where I saw the general and spent about an hour with him discussing military and political matters. . . . . I offered to take him with me to Headquarters or to leave him in the car.

62 *Izvestiia,* No. 231, December 4, 1917, p. 1.

63 On December 2 Generals Kornilov, Denikin, Lukomsky, Romanovsky, Markov, and other officers arrested after the Kornilov affair made their escape from Bykov where they had been confined. Kornilov left at the head of a detachment of loyal troops; the others left in disguise and with fake papers. Eventually they reached the Don to take part in organizing the Volunteer Army. See below, p. 406, and A. Lukomsky, *Memoirs of the Russian Revolution,* London [1922], pp. 128–29.

64 *Novaia Zhizn,* No. 189, December 13, 1917, p. 3.

He chose the latter as the safer [alternative]. Before leaving I gave orders . . . . to strengthen the guard, to station sailors at the very door of my compartment, and to protect the car even by using machine guns. . . . . In the meantime a large crowd gathered. At first it asked to see the general. When I firmly refused this request, the crowd clamored for his shoulder-straps. . . . . I went into the compartment and asked . . . . the general for them. He hesitated for a time, then offered to face the mob; but this I would not allow. Upon receiving the straps the mob dispersed. . . . .

[Half an hour later the mob was back again. Krylenko and Roshal tried to block the way into the car.] Two or three sailors stood on the lower steps and pulled my hands so that I could not get my revolver. Then I heard shouts from the other side of the car and realized that it was too late. The sailors carried me off the platform as if I were a child, saying, "Don't be afraid. Nothing is going to happen to you . . . . !" I looked around and saw Dukhonin dragged out of the car. . . . . He was surrounded by a mob and beaten. . . . . He fell on the ground face downward, but the beating continued. Finally one of the sailors fired two shots into his body. The crowd gave a cheer and scattered. . . . .[65]

E. The Armistice

At midday on December 3 the Russian armistice delegation consisting of the following members arrived at Brest-Litovsk: Joffe (Krymsky), Chairman; Kamenev; Sokolnikov; Madam Bitsenko; Mstislavsky; Obukhov, a worker; Stashkov-Romanov, a peasant; Olich, a sailor; Beliakov, a soldier; and Karakhan, secretary. The military advisers were: Rear Admiral Altvater; Captain Dolivo-Dobrovolsky; and six officers of the General Staff—Shishkin, Stanislavsky, Bereng, Morozov, Sukhov, Fuke.[66] For the Central Powers general instructions on the terms of the armistice had been

[65] Another account is given by the military correspondent of *Russkoe Slovo,* an eyewitness, who wrote: "Krylenko, who had himself incited the soldiers to lynch law, who encouraged the Red Guards' wolfish ferocity, endeavored to prevent the crime by speech. But by speech only. Dukhonin could have been saved. Ensign Krylenko had a numerous suite. Not all the sailors were inclined to the lynching. Dukhonin might have been locked up in the car and the train started. But apparently Krylenko counted the cost. Passions were excited to such a pitch that any intervention on his part might mean death to him also. He only clutched at his head and sat for a long time with his face buried in his hands." (*Russkoe Slovo,* December 6, 1917; quoted by Mrs. Tyrkóva-Williams, *op. cit.,* pp. 311–12.)

[66] *Izvestiia,* No. 231, December 4, 1917, p. 1.

given to Crown Prince Leopold of Bavaria, the General Commanding the Eastern Front, who placed the conduct of negotiations in the hands of General Hoffmann. Assisting Hoffmann were Rosenberg of the German Foreign Office. Lieutenant-Colonel Pokorny, Adjutant-General Zekke, and Colonel Gantchev represented the General Staffs of Austria-Hungary, Turkey, and Bulgaria. As practically all the buildings in Brest-Litovsk had been destroyed, the Soviet delegates were housed in some of the huts in the Citadel and took their meals in the German staff-officers' mess. At four o'clock, December 3, Prince Leopold opened the negotiations with a short speech of welcome.[67]

THE SOVIET DELEGATION LEAVES FOR BREST-LITOVSK

[Telegram from Dvinsk, December 3, 1917][68]

On December 2 at eleven o'clock the Peace Delegation of the Soviet of People's Commissars arrived at Dvinsk. The delegation was invited to attend the Extraordinary Congress of the 5th Army . . . . and was given a noisy ovation. The Congress gave a most solemn promise to wipe out all counter-revolutionary nests that stand in the way of peace, and to attack at once the group at Mogilev, including Dukhonin, Gotz, Avxentiev, and other traitors of the revolution. At 14 o'clock the Army Congress escorted the delegates to the train. . . . .

SKLIANSKY
President of the Congress of the 5th Army
and the Army Committee

FIRST NEGOTIATIONS AT BREST

[Joffe Proposes a General Armistice, December 3, 1917][69]

. . . . In accordance with the principles . . . . laid down in the decree of the [Second] All-Russian Congress of Soviets . . . . our aim is the speediest possible conclusion of a general peace without annexations and without indemnities, with a guaranty of national self-determination.

[67] Hoffmann, *op. cit.*, pp. 196–97; *Der Friedensverhandlungen in Brest-Litowsk und der Friede mit Russland,* p. 13.

[68] *Izvestiia,* No. 231, December 4, 1917, p. 1.

[69] *Ibid.,* No. 236, December 9, 1917, p. 2.

That we may secure this general peace we are authorized to negotiate armistice conditions on all fronts. . . . .

We therefore propose that an appeal be made to all belligerent nations not represented here, inviting them to take part in the negotiations. . . . .

[Hoffmann Proposes a Separate Armistice, December 3, 1917][70]

General Hoffmann . . . . asked whether or not the Russian delegation was authorized to speak in the name of the Allies.

Joffe replied that the Russian Government had addressed the Allies proposing that they should take part in the negotiations but as yet had received no definite answer. . . . .

Hoffmann declared that he had no authority to enter into peace negotiations with the absent Allies of Russia. . . . .

Germany was there represented by military men only, who are competent to negotiate the military questions relating to an armistice and nothing else. . . . .

[Movement of Troops from the East to the West Front. From Kamenev's Report to the C.E.C., December 7, 1917][71]

. . . . We insisted that all [German] forces on the Russian front remain where they are. Not one soldier, not one cannon must be transferred to other fronts. . . . . To this the Germans finally agreed. . . . . This gives you an indication of the extent to which Germany is willing to go to meet our demands. . . . .[72]

[Propaganda. From a Speech by Trotsky, December 21, 1917][73]

We did not yield even to the Germans' demand that we stop spreading propaganda among their troops. We replied that we came to Brest to negotiate with the German generals on the subject of putting an end to military operations, but in regard to other matters, particularly revolutionary propaganda, we had nothing to say to them. Our real negotiations were with the German workers and peasants dressed in soldiers' uniforms. . . . .[74]

[70] *Izvestiia, loc. cit.;* also Hoffmann, *op. cit.,* p. 198.

[71] L. B. Kamenev, *Borba za mir,* Petrograd, 1918, p. 13.

[72] Hoffmann explains (*op. cit.,* p. 199) that orders had already been issued to send the bulk of the Eastern Army to the Western front and it was therefore not difficult to agree not to send away from the Eastern front any troops beyond those already being moved or under orders to go.

[73] L. Trotsky, *Sochineniia,* III, Pt. 2, 215–16.

[74] The Soviet delegation, according to Hoffmann, demanded the right to send out by telegraph and wireless a verbatim report of each session, but accepted the German counter proposal that the minutes be drawn up by a joint commission and

Other proposals by the Soviet delegation were for the German evacuation of the Moon Sound Islands and for a six months' armistice. The Germans flatly refused to consider the evacuation of the Islands and proposed an armistice of twenty-eight days. A draft treaty for an armistice following the German rather than the Soviet proposals was finally agreed upon. On the 5th Joffe announced that he must return to Petrograd to secure authority to sign. The negotiations were thereupon suspended for one week (to December 12), and the suspension of hostilities was extended until December 17.[75]

TROTSKY'S INVITATION TO THE ALLIES

[Note on Joining the Negotiations, December 6, 1917][76]

The negotiations between the delegates of Germany, Austria-Hungary, Turkey, and Bulgaria, on the one hand, and the Russian delegates, on the other, have been suspended for a week in order to inform the Allied nations and governments that such negotiations are taking place as well as to indicate the direction of those negotiations.

On behalf of Russia it was proposed that the intended armistice should have for its object the conclusion of a democratic peace on the basis of the declaration of the All-Russian Congress of Soviets of Workers' and Soldiers' Deputies, that during armistice negotiations there should be no transfer of troops from one front to another, and that the Moon Sound Islands should be evacuated.

On the question of war aims the enemy delegates refrained from any definite statement on the ground that they were under limited orders to regulate the military side of the armistice only. Likewise on the question of a general armistice the enemy delegates insisted that they had no authority to discuss armistice conditions with countries whose delegates took no part in the negotiations. . . . .

issued for publication after being approved by both sides. To the Russian proposal that fraternization between the two armies be unhindered, Hoffmann objected and agreed that intercourse be permitted at certain places, where, as he believed, it would be possible to control it and to intercept the greater part of the propaganda literature. Hoffmann refused the demand that Bolshevik literature be freely admitted into Germany, but added he would be glad to assist its export to France and England. (Hoffmann, *op. cit.*, pp. 198–200.)

[75] *Izvestiia,* No. 236, December 9, 1917, p. 3; also *Die Friedensverhandlungen in Brest-Litowsk,* pp. 13–14.

[76] *Izvestiia,* No. 234, December 7, 1917, pp. 1–2; *U.S. Foreign Relations, 1918, Russia,* I, 258.

In view of the unwillingness of our delegation to sign a formal armistice at this stage of the negotiations the period of suspension of military activities has been extended for one week, and armistice negotiations will be postponed for that period.

Thus a period of more than one month will have elapsed between the first peace decree of the Soviet Government (November 8) and the resumption of peace negotiations (December 12). This interval . . . . affords ample time to the Allies to set forth their attitude toward the peace negotiations, i.e., to say whether they will accept or decline [the opportunity of] taking part in the armistice and peace negotiations, and, in case of refusal, to state clearly and definitely before all humanity, for what causes the nations of Europe must continue shedding their blood during the fourth year of war.

L. TROTSKY
People's Commissar of Foreign Affairs

There was no reply to Trotsky's note, but on December 8 Buchanan gave to the Russian press a statement, based on instructions from London, in which he pointed out that the separate negotiations with the Germans constituted a violation of the agreement of September 5, 1914. He warned that the Germans would impose an imperialistic peace. The Allies could not take part in the negotiations but were ready "as soon as a stable government has been constituted that is recognized by the Russian people as a whole" to discuss war aims and peace terms. He further complained that "hardly a day passes without some bitter attack being made on my country by what are now the official organs of the [Russian] Press," and objected especially to Lenin's appeal to the Moslems, inciting British Indian subjects to rebellion.[77]

On December 9 the Central Committees of the Socialist parties in Petrograd issued an address "To All Citizens" in which it is stated that "the separate armistice concluded by the Bolsheviks must be considered as the act of one party only . . . . and is not binding on Russia . . . . until the Constituent Assembly makes its decision."[78]

[77] Buchanan, II, 233–37; *Russkiia Vedomosti,* No. 259, December 9, 1917, p. 4. The appeal to the Moslems is given below, pp. 467–69.

[78] *Delo Naroda,* No. 219, December 9, 1917, p. 2.

The same day the Russian and Rumanian troops on the Rumanian front signed an armistice with Austria-Hungary, Bulgaria, and Turkey at Focsani.[79]

On December 13 Trotsky announced that the Russian delegation had returned to Brest to resume negotiations. "The armistice," he said, "is thus assuming the character of a separate agreement. . . . . The responsibility for this falls wholly upon those governments which up to the present time have refused to state their conditions. . . . ."[80] The agreement was signed on the 15th.

Article I provided that the armistice should come in force at noon on the 17th, to remain in force until January 14, 1918, being continued thereafter automatically until terminated on seven days' notice.

Article II stated that the armistice applied to the Russo-Turkish theaters of war in Asia as well as on the European front. Both parties agreed not to regroup their troops and not to transfer the troops excepting those already under orders.

Article III provided for the lines of demarcation.

Article IV stated the conditions for intercourse across the neutral zone between the front lines.

Article V provided discontinuance of naval and aërial operations.

Article VI prevented infantry and artillery practice firing and aërial operations near the front.

Article VII established armistice commissions at Riga, Dvinsk, Brest-Litovsk, Berdichev, Koloszvar, and Focsani.

According to Article VIII the present agreement superseded all previous armistice agreements.

By Article IX the contracting parties agreed to enter peace negotiations immediately after signing the present agreement.

By Article X the Turks and Russians agreed to withdraw their troops from Persia.

[79] Liubimov, *Revoliutsiia 1917 goda*, p. 215.

[80] *Izvestiia*, No. 240, December 13, 1917, p. 2.

Article XI provided for the exchange of signed copies of the agreement.[81]

After the signing of the armistice, Trotsky on December 19 sent out another appeal to the "Toiling, Oppressed, and Exhausted Peoples of Europe" in which he declared that the Soviets did not "consider existing capitalist governments capable of a democratic peace . . . . [the full realization of which can be guaranteed only] by the victorious proletarian revolution in all capitalist countries. The Soviet of People's Commissars . . . . has never for a moment turned from the path of social revolution. . . . . In negotiating for peace the Soviet Government has set itself a double task: first, to achieve the speediest possible cessation of the shameful and criminal slaughter which is laying Europe waste; and, second, to assist with all means at our disposal the working class in all lands to overthrow the sway of capital and seize state power in order to effect a democratic and socialist reconstruction of Europe and the whole of humanity." Trotsky urged the workers of Germany and her allies to oppose the imperialistic program of their ruling classes. He declared that the capitalist governments of the Allies and the United States "are masking their treacherous and venal calculations under phrases about eternal justice and the future society of nations." The crimes of the ruling classes "shriek for revolutionary revenge." The governments opposing peace "must be swept away." The proletarians of all countries must close up their ranks "under the flag of peace and the social revolution."[82]

On this same day, the 19th, Trotsky called on the French Ambassador, Noulens, to protest against the presence of

[81] On the same day a supplement to the Armistice was signed providing for a mixed commission to meet in Petrograd to settle the details regarding the exchange of civilian and war prisoners, repatriation of women and children, and the re-establishment of commercial and postal intercourse. (*Deutscher Reichsanzeiger*, No. 299, December 18, 1917 [p. 2]). The agreement is given in *Texts of the Russian "Peace,"* U.S. Government Printing Office, Washington, 1918, pp. 1–7; R. H. Lutz, *The Fall of the German Empire, 1914–1917*, 2 vols., Stanford University, 1932, II, 768–70.

[82] Trotsky, *Sochineniia*, III, Book 2, 206–208. This has been translated in *The Soviet Union and Peace*, New York [1929], pp. 30–33.

French officers at the Ukrainian Rada at Kiev. This and other matters were discussed and then, according to one account, Noulens inquired about the armistice negotiations. Trotsky said that the Soviet Government would continue them on the basis of the right of self-determination. In case the Germans refused to negotiate on that basis Trotsky was in favor of resuming the war, but as public opinion was opposed to this he would break off negotiations and refer the whole matter to the Constituent Assembly for its decision.[83]

[83] Claude Anet, *La révolution russe,* 4 vols., Paris, 1919, III, 162–64. Trotsky says that this conference had no results and it did not raise his "opinion of the rulers of human destiny" (*My Life,* p. 346). Sadoul, who was present, says that the interview was cordial and Noulens and Trotsky separated very satisfied with each other (Sadoul, *op. cit.,* p. 158). Noulens gives the 18th as the date of this interview which, he says, Trotsky forced upon him, and which affected Clemenceau, when he heard of it, like a kick in the stomach. (*Mon ambassade en Russie soviétique, 1917–1919,* 2 vols., Paris, 1933, I, 70–76.)

CHAPTER VI

TOWARD THE DICTATORSHIP

As a result of their victory of November 7 the Bolsheviks decreed the transfer of power to the Soviets and the establishment of a Provisional Workers' and Peasants' Government. The adjective "provisional" was retained until the Third Congress of Soviets, which met after the dissolution of the Constituent Assembly in January 1918. But during the "provisional" period the new rulers proceeded to apply the orthodox Marxian theory that all government is class rule, an organized violence by which one class imposes its will on all other classes. Having overthrown the bourgeois government it was then the duty of the workers to destroy the old state apparatus and create a new one by means of which the proletariat should exercise the dictatorship during the period of transition from capitalism to socialism. "The state," said Lenin, "is simply the weapon with which the proletariat wages its class war. A special sort of bludgeon *rien de plus!*" The class war under the dictatorship, Lenin explained,[1] had five tasks to carry out: (1) suppression of the exploiters' resistance (i.e., suppression of plots, strikes, sabotage, efforts to influence the lower middle class); (2) transformation of the imperialist war into a civil war, the extermination of the non-proletarian parties by terror and war; (3) neutralization of the lower middle class and in particular the peasants "by satisfying in a revolutionary manner their essential economic needs at the cost of the expropriation of the landed proprietors and the bourgeoisie";[2] (4) "exploitation" of the bourgeoisie not only by crushing their resistance and compelling their neutrality but by their com-

[1] *Leninskii Sbornik,* No. 3, 1926, pp. 493–518.

[2] *The Dictatorship of the Proletariat and the Elections to the Constituent Assembly,* New York, 1920, p. 18.

pulsory service for the proletariat; (5) education to a new discipline by means of the dictatorship of the proletariat and the trade unions.

The materials of the present chapter relate to the efforts of the Bolsheviks during the first two months of their rule to fashion the institutions of the new government apparatus to the purposes of the dictatorship, to utilize that apparatus in the economic sphere and satisfy the essential needs of the masses by expropriation of the bourgeoisie and to establish workers' control of industry and trade. During these two months, it should be borne in mind, the Bolsheviks were in conflict with their democratic opponents over the fate of the Constituent Assembly and their troops were engaged in wars against the Ukrainians, the Cossacks, and various other nationalists and regionalists.

A. The Transfer of Power to the Workers

Even in those regions which recognized the new régime as the successor of the Provisional Government the direction of local affairs did not always pass immediately into the hands of Soviets. In many places the old institutions like the zemstvos continued to function in the absence of Soviets or in rivalry with them. In many cases where Soviets were established they were dominated by elements hostile to the Bolsheviks or by coalitions. The central Soviet authorities were concerned, therefore, during these first two months with supplanting the old institutions with the new, eradicating the influence of the bourgeoisie, and installing in power workers and peasants sympathetic to as much of the new program as they were able to understand.

TRANSFER OF POWER AND THE MEANS OF PRODUCTION TO THE TOILERS

[Decree of the Sovnarkom, November 18, 1917][3]

Comrades—Workers, Soldiers, Peasants, All Toilers!

The workers' and peasants' revolution has won a decisive victory in Petrograd, having scattered and arrested the last remnants of a small

[3] *S.U.R.*, 1917, No. 2, pp. 27–28.

number of Cossacks deceived by Kerensky. The revolution has triumphed in Moscow . . . . the cadets and other Kornilov supporters have signed peace. They are now disarmed, and the Committee [of Public Safety] has been dismissed. An overwhelming majority of soldiers in the trenches and peasants in the villages are supporting the new government in its peace decree and its decree to hand over immediately the land to the peasants. The victory of the workers' and peasants' revolution is assured; the majority of the people are for it.

It is easy to understand why the landowners, the capitalists, and the higher state officials who are closely bound up with the bourgeoisie—in one word, all the rich and those who held out their hands to the rich—should assume a hostile attitude toward the new revolution, should stand in its way, and should threaten to close the banks and to stop or to sabotage, directly or indirectly, the work of various institutions.

Every class-conscious worker knows full well that this opposition is inevitable, that the higher officials were selected to oppress the people, and that they are not going to give up their place without a struggle. The laboring classes will not allow themselves to be frightened, even for a minute, by the threats and strikes of these partisans of the bourgeoisie. The majority of the people are with us. With us are the majority of the toilers, and the oppressed of the world. Right is on our side. Our victory is certain. The opposition of the capitalists and higher officials will be broken. We will not deprive a single person of his property otherwise than by a special government law concerning the nationalization of banks and trusts. This law is now in preparation. Not a single laborer and toiler will lose one kopek; on the contrary, he will be helped. The government will impose no new taxes now and will aim at an open and strict accounting and control over the taxes heretofore levied.

In the name of these just demands the great majority of the people has rallied around the Provisional Workers' and Peasants' Government.

Comrade Toilers! Remember that you yourself are now running the government. Unless you get together and take all affairs of the government into your own hands, no one will do it for you. Your Soviets are from now on all-powerful and all-decisive organs of government. Rally around your Soviets. Strengthen them. Take matters into your hands and don't wait for anyone [to tell you what to do]. Insist on the strictest revolutionary order. Crush mercilessly all anarchistic disturbances by drunkards, rowdies, counter-revolutionary cadets, Kornilovists, and their like.

Organize strict control over production and accountability for the products. Bring before the revolutionary tribunal everyone who dares to harm the cause of the people by sabotaging (spoiling, hindering, destroying) in industry, concealing grain and produce, interfering with transportation of grain, tearing up rail, post, and telegraph lines, or in other ways opposing the great cause of peace, of transferring the land to the peasants, and of assuming workers' control over production and distribution.

Comrade workers, soldiers, peasants, and all toilers! Take all local power into your own hands. Take and guard as the apple of your eye the grain, factories, implements, products, and transport—all these are from now on wholly yours; they are public property.

Gradually, with the approval and agreement of the majority of the peasants, guided by their practical experience and that of the workers, we shall move on firmly and resolutely to the victory of socialism, a victory which the advance guard of the workers of the more civilized countries will make secure and which is bound to give the people a lasting peace and freedom from all oppression and exploitation.

V. ULIANOV (LENIN)
President of the Soviet of People's Commissars

ABOLITION OF CLASS DISTINCTIONS AND CIVIL RANKS

[Decree Confirmed by the C.E.C., November 23, 1917][4]

1. All classes and class distinctions which have hitherto existed in Russia, class privileges and class limitations, class organizations and institutions, as well as all civil ranks are abolished.

2. All estates (noble, merchant, commoner, peasant, etc.), titles (prince, count, etc.), and designations of civil ranks (privy councilor, state councilor, etc.) are abolished, and in their places the inhabitants of Russia are to have one name common to all—citizens of the Russian Republic.

3. Property of the nobility[5] is to be transferred at once to the corresponding zemstvo institutions.

4. Properties of merchants' and commoners' associations are to be transferred at once to the municipalities.

5. All class institutions, transactions, records, and archives are to be transferred at once to the municipal and zemstvo institutions.

6. All laws [relating to class institutions] are repealed.

7. The present decree is to go into effect on the day of its publication and to be put into effect at once by the local Soviets of Workers', Soldiers', and Peasants' Deputies.

[4] *S.U.R.*, 1917, No. 3, pp. 35–36.

[5] Of the nobility as a class, such as schools, clubs, etc.

The present decree has been confirmed by the Central Executive Committee of the Soviets of Workers' and Soldiers' Deputies at its meeting of November 23, 1917.

YA. SVERDLOV
President of the Central Executive Committee

V. ULIANOV (LENIN)
President of the Soviet of People's Commissars

ON THE RIGHTS AND DUTIES OF SOVIETS

[Decree of the Sovnarkom, January 7, 1918][6]

1. Soviets of workers', soldiers', and peasants' deputies, being local organs, are quite independent in regard to questions of a local character, but must always act in accord with the decrees and decisions of the Central Soviet Government as well as of the larger bodies (uezd, gubernia, and regional Soviets) of which they form a part.

2. Upon the Soviets, as organs of government, devolve the tasks of administration and service in every sphere of local life, viz., administrative, economic, financial, and educational.

3. In the field of administration the Soviets must carry out all decrees and decisions of the central government, undertake to give to the people the widest information about those decisions, issue obligatory ordinances, make requisitions and confiscations, impose fines, suppress counter-revolutionary organs of the press, make arrests, and dissolve public organizations which incite active opposition or the overthrow of the Soviet Government.

Note: The Soviets must report to the Central Soviet Government regarding all measures undertaken by them and concerning most important local events.

4. The Soviets elect from their number an executive organ (executive committee, presidium) which is charged with the duty of carrying out their decisions and the performance of all current business of administration.

Note 1: The Military Revolutionary Committees as fighting organs, which came into existence during the coup d'état, are abolished.

Note 2: As a temporary measure commissars may be appointed in those provinces where the power of the Soviet is not sufficiently well established or where the Soviet Government is not exclusively recognized. . . . .

[6] *S.U.R.*, 1917, No. 12, p. 189.

THE ZEMSTVO AND THE SOVIETS

[An Account of the Transfer of Power in a Village of Tver Gubernia][7]

Officially the volost zemstvo lasted in our village [Tver Gubernia] until January 12, 1918, when a last session of the Goritskoe zemstvo took place. After the report of the chairman on the situation in the gubernia the following resolution was taken: "To charge the local volost Uprava [board] immediately to organize a local Soviet of peasants' deputies and to transfer to the Executive Committee elected by this Soviet, together with the Inspection Commission, all property and duties of the volost zemstvo."

Thus our volost zemstvo had lasted officially as long as the beginning of 1918, but in actual fact since the end of November and beginning of December 1917 our zemstvo officials were helpless both to carry out their work and to display their authority. The influence in the volost had passed to the group which sympathized with the Bolsheviks.

Since March [1917] the peasants of our volost followed the lead of the Socialist-Revolutionists; some did it more or less consciously, others were carried away by the slogan, "Land and Freedom." In November and December, however, the village began to be crowded with the soldiers from the front and the rear who brought with them the slogan: "Away with the war." The sympathy of the great majority of the population was transferred to them because our people considered war senseless. They were tired of losing their relatives and longed for the return of the members of their families with whose help they greatly hoped to restore their husbandry shattered by the war. Therefore, all sympathies of the population were now with the Bolsheviks, who had proclaimed: "Away with the war."

The supporters of Bolsheviks began to call volost meetings. At these meetings all current questions were settled. The zemstvo was left at the side and it lost connection with the population of the volost.

Only nominal clerical work continued to be carried on in the volost zemstvo Uprava. . . . .

The Bolsheviks had always supported the movement for the self-determination of national minorities as a step to promote the disintegration of imperial states. They severely criticized the Provisional Government for its refusal to grant national minorities in Russia full rights of self-determination and they had promised to concede this right if and

[7] A. M. Bolshakov, *Derevnia 1917–1927*, Moscow, 1927, pp. 218–19.

when they achieved power. This they did by the decree of November 15. This encouragement of separatism contributed not a little to the break-up of the old state organization, and, as will appear later, to a division among the opponents of the dictatorship. The limitations which the Bolsheviks imposed on self-determination became apparent later.

Bolshevik ideas on the necessity of an international struggle against capital were given expression in the appropriation of funds by the Soviet Government to support the international revolution. At this time there was no attempt to distinguish between the Soviet Government and the Bolshevik Party in the support of world revolution.[8]

RIGHTS OF THE PEOPLES OF RUSSIA TO SELF-DETERMINATION

[Decree of the Sovnarkom, November 15, 1917][9]

The November revolution of the workers and peasants began under the common banner of emancipation.

The peasants are being emancipated from the power of the landlords, for the landlord no longer has any property right in the land—that right has been abolished. The soldiers and sailors are being emancipated from the power of autocratic generals, for henceforth generals will be elective and subject to recall. The workers are being emancipated from the whims and arbitrary will of the capitalists, for henceforth workers' control will be established over mills and factories. Everything living and viable is being emancipated from hateful shackles.

There remain now only the peoples of Russia who have suffered and are suffering under an arbitrary yoke. Their emancipation must be considered at once and their liberation effected with resoluteness and finality.

During the tsarist times the peoples of Russia were systematically incited against one another. The results of this policy are well known: massacres and pogroms on the one hand, slavery and bondage on the other.

There can be and there must be no return to this shameful policy of provocation. Henceforth it must be replaced by a policy of voluntary and honest co-operation of the peoples of Russia.

[8] See chapters vii and viii.

[9] *Izvestiia,* No. 215, November 16, 1917, p. 4.

During the period of imperialism, after the March Revolution, when the government passed into the hands of Cadet bourgeoisie the unconcealed policy of instigation gave way to one of cowardly distrust of the peoples of Russia, of caviling and provocation camouflaged by verbal declarations about the "freedom" and "equality" of peoples. The results of this policy, too, are well known—the growth of national enmity, the impairment of mutual trust.

An end must be made to this unworthy policy of falsehood and distrust, of cavil and provocation. Henceforth it must be replaced by an open and honest policy leading to complete mutual confidence among the peoples of Russia.

Only as the result of such a confidence can an honest and lasting union of the peoples of Russia be formed.

Only as the result of such a union can the workers and peasants of the peoples of Russia be welded into a revolutionary force capable of resisting all [counter-revolutionary] attempts on the part of the imperialist-annexationist bourgeoisie.

The Congress of Soviets, in June of this year, proclaimed the right of the peoples of Russia to free self-determination.

The Second Congress of Soviets, in November of this year, reaffirmed this inalienable right of the peoples of Russia more decisively and definitely.

In compliance with the will of these Congresses, the Soviet of People's Commissars has resolved to adopt as the basis of its activity on the problem of nationalities in Russia the following principles:

1. Equality and sovereignty of the peoples of Russia.
2. The right to free self-determination of peoples even to the point of separating and forming independent states.
3. Abolition of each and every privilege or limitation based on nationality or religion.
4. Free development of national minorities and ethnographic groups inhabiting Russian territory.

All concrete measures appertaining to the above declaration are to be decreed immediately upon the formation of a special commission for nationalities.

IOSIF DZHUGASHVILI (STALIN)
Commissar for Nationalities

V. ULIANOV (LENIN)
President of Soviet of People's Commissars

ON THE NATIONAL QUESTION IN THE SOVIET REPUBLIC

[Extract from Speech by Lenin at the All-Russian Navy Congress, December 5, 1917][10]

. . . . Turning our attention to the national question we must note particularly the motley national composition of Russia, where the Great Russians form only 40 per cent [of the population] while the remaining majority consists of other nationalities. During the tsarist régime the oppression of these nationalities, unprecedented in its cruelty and absurdity, succeeded in accumulating a tremendous hatred for the monarchs among the oppressed peoples. It is not surprising, therefore, that the hatred against those who prohibited even the usage of the native tongue, thus condemning the masses of population to illiteracy, was transferred against all Great Russians. It was thought that the Great Russians, as the privileged nation, wished to retain the privileges which both Nicholas and Kerensky faithfully guarded for them.

We are told that Russia will be divided, will split into separate republics. We should not be afraid of this. No matter how many separate republics are created we shall not be frightened by it. It is not the state frontiers that count with us but a union of toilers of all nations ready to fight the bourgeoisie of any nation.

If the Finnish bourgeoisie brings arms from Germany to use them against their workers, we offer to the latter a union with the Russian toilers. Let the bourgeoisie carry on a contemptible and petty brawl and bargain over the question of frontiers; the workers of all countries will not quarrel on that score. We are now—I am using a bad word—"conquering Finland," but not in the way in which the international plunderers-capitalists do it. We are conquering Finland by the fact that while letting her live in a union with us or others we at the same time support the toilers of all nationalities against the international bourgeoisie. This union is based not on treaties but on the solidarity of the exploited against their exploiters. We are witnessing at present a national movement in the Ukraine and we say: We are unquestionably for a complete and absolute freedom of the Ukrainian people. We must break the old bloody and dirty past, when Russia was dominated by capitalist-oppressors and played the rôle of executioner to other peoples. We shall wipe out this past and we shall not leave a stone of this past untouched. We shall say to the Ukrainians: As Ukrainians you may organize your life as you wish, but we shall stretch our brotherly hand to the Ukrainian workers saying: Let us fight together against our common [enemy the] bourgeoisie. Only a Socialist union of the toilers of all countries will clear away the ground of the national quarrels and enmities. . . . .

[10] *Sochineniia,* XXII, 100–101.

AN APPROPRIATION FOR THE SUPPORT OF WORLD REVOLUTION

[Decree of the Sovnarkom, December 26, 1917][11]

Taking into consideration the fact that Soviet power bases itself on principles of international solidarity of the proletariat and on the brotherhood of the toilers of all countries; that the struggle against war and imperialism can lead toward complete victory only if waged on an international scale, the Soviet of People's Commissars considers it necessary to offer assistance by all possible means, including money, to the left international wing of the labor movement of all countries, regardless of whether these countries are at war or in alliance with Russia or are neutral.

For this reason the Soviet of People's Commissars decides to grant two million rubles for the needs of the revolutionary international movement and to put it at the disposal of the foreign representatives of the Commissariat of Foreign Affairs.

V. ULIANOV (LENIN)
President of the Soviet of People's Commissars

L. TROTSKY
People's Commissar of Foreign Affairs

As with other government institutions the personnel of the judicial bodies was in the main hostile to the Bolsheviks, who on their part intended not to reorganize the administration of justice but to uproot the old system and set up a new one on entirely different foundations. This proceeded slowly, and in the meantime improvised people's courts appeared here and there to deal with complaints in the localities in which those courts functioned.

HOW THE FIRST COURTS WERE ORGANIZED

[From Koslovsky's Recollections][12]

. . . . We had much work to do as far as the old law courts were concerned, but we were unable to accomplish anything as long as the

[11] *S.U.R.*, 1917, No. 8, p. 119.

[12] "Vospominaniia ob oktiabrskom perevorote," in *Proletarskaia Revoliutsiia*, No. 10, 1922, pp. 64–67.

revolutionary operations continued in the streets before the Winter Palace.

The Committee of Inquiry had its office in Smolny; most of those arrested were military men whom we kept prisoners in the [Smolny] cellar. A sailor, Alexeevsky, was in charge of this Committee. When I joined the Committee, he appeared to combine the duties of chairman, member, and . . . . secretary. The Committee occupied one small room on the third floor; the conditions of work were appalling. Bread and sheepskin coats were scattered on the floor, the latter producing a terrible odor. One table and several chairs were in the room. We wrote on our knees. Countless civilians and soldiers passed before us. The examination of the arrested proceeded in a classical disorder, ... but the work was interesting. The Committee continued to function in this way for about a week and a half. A great many state officials and clerks, particularly those of the State Bank, who proved to be particularly obstinate, were arrested.

When the first days [of the revolution] were over, it became necessary to plan the organization of the [new] judicial institutions. We were confronted with the following picture: The district courts, especially the department for criminal offenses, which had not functioned at all under the Provisional Government and had not held any sessions, suddenly started work. We were obliged to send commissars and several soldiers to these courts in order to deal with them. The sessions were interrupted, and the judges left peacefully for home.

It was necessary to deal in some manner with the . . . . State Senate, which enjoyed great authority among the jurists [as well as the public].[13] Many of our comrades were worried by questions of what would happen if we destroyed old laws and were left without any organs of justice. Some believed that it was necessary to retain them, and it was suggested merely that commissars should be appointed for these institutions and should participate in the examination of every case question. We solved the problem in a revolutionary manner. The Military Revolutionary Committee gave us some soldiers, and they dispersed the Senate; the Senators offered no resistance, and in half an hour the Senate was liquidated.

There now remained the office of the Justices of the Peace, who were very popular in the judicial institutions as well as among the public. They continued to carry on their duties for a while as revolutionary courts. During Kerensky's period, perhaps the only revolutionary meas-

[13] The Senate, established in 1711 by Peter the Great, was the High Court of the Empire. It was also charged with the promulgation of laws. The Senate had six departments, two of which were Courts of Cassation. The Minister of Justice presided over the plenary session of the Senate.

ure that was actually taken in the domain of justice was the appointment of a soldier and a workman in the capacity of commissars attached to [each] Justice of the Peace. These commissars carried on their duties for about a month and a half. Kerensky found that such measures were too revolutionary. He abolished the office of commissars, and in this way Justices of the Peace were left to carry on their work alone once more.

The latter sent their representative to me, a much respected Justice of the Peace, Davydov, who came and insistently requested an interview. I had lots of soldiers and arrested men around me and was terribly busy, so I was not in a great hurry to see him. But the soldiers who had, as it seemed, a certain respect for the Justices of the Peace, came to me and insisted that he should be seen: "He is Justice of the Peace" [they said]. "You must see him." I was obliged to do so, and Davydov requested me officially and in the name of the Congress of Justices of the Peace to allow him to examine places of detention in Petersburg. According to paragraph nine [of the Code], he said, Justices of the Peace were allowed to do so. . . . .

I sent him away without giving him satisfaction, saying that at the present time we were applying the paragraphs of the revolutionary code and not of the peace-time code. . . . . However, this incident forced me to issue next day an order in the name of the Committee of Inquiry to close all institutions of the Justices of the Peace.

As far as the office of the examining magistrates was concerned, the matter was settled much more simply. We ordered the magistrates to hand over their work to us, and this was done. When at last we went to the offices of the Ministry [of Justice] with Stuchka, we found there about twelve messengers and one official. This official—I think his name was Kolosov—was a member of the Union of Russian People[14] and at one time secretary to the Minister of Justice, Shcheglovitov, etc. He expressed a desire to work for us and actually did so. On the same day when we entered the splendid room of Shcheglovitov and were wondering how to start work, the messengers came to us demanding their salaries. . . . . With the help of the official we wrote an order for money, and upon the receipt of it we paid the wages to the messengers. They cheered us and were very much pleased. However, it was necessary to create official courts. We had to have some sort of official organs where we could investigate cases and deal justice. We created the revolutionary tribunals. This is how we did it: We appointed three comrades (Comrade Zhuk was made chairman) and two additional comrade workmen. The Tribunal started functioning in the palace of Nikolai Nikolaevich, a gloomy building with no windows.

[14] A monarchist organization.

The first case which the Tribunal was to examine was that of Panina.[15] The beginning was difficult. The spectators were hostile. The hall was full of lawyers, intelligentsia, who tried to interrupt the session. The judges acted with indecision. The public kept on jumping up and rushing to the judges' table.

It was necessary to interrupt the session and to remove some individuals. This had to be done with some caution, because Panina was very popular. However, on the whole, everything ended satisfactorily. The sentence passed was approved by our adherents among the public. Panina was charged with the appropriation of government money to the amount of 150,000 rubles for the purpose of preventing us from using it. She was sentenced to arrest until she returned the money. Of course she was well able to do this, but she refused to comply with the judgment on principle and therefore remained under arrest for a month and a half. Later some professors collected this money for her and she was released. That was how the Tribunal started to function. Later courts began to spring up in Petersburg, spontaneously. We were too busy to think of them and, besides, we were short of people. Three Bolsheviks—Krasikov, Stuchka, and I—had to do all the work.

We were far off as yet from the organization of popular courts in which we could examine crimes of general character. They too came to exist spontaneously. The first court, unique in its character, sprang up in the Vyborg ward [of Petrograd]. . . . .

Later, according to a plan, courts presided over by delegates of the Petersburg Soviet began to function, with jurors from the people and in accord with the lists of workshop committees. In this way judicial institutions were established which remained in their fundamentals until the present day.

It is interesting to recall how we got control of prisons. When we came to the prisons the old officials offered no opposition; on the contrary, they appeared to be sympathetic and congratulated us on the assumption of power. The criminal offenders (the political ones were released at once) asked permission to gather together in order to greet the Soviet authorities. They elected delegates and promised to behave properly. Many of them were released by us because they had lived under very bad conditions for a long time.

We found among them many cases of scurvy and so forth. Of course many of those who were released were soon back in prison. The personnel of prisons was not replaced. Only special commissars were appointed [to assist the personnel], and the machinery began to function well.

[15] Accounts in English of this trial are given by Bessie Beatty, *op. cit.*, pp. 294 ff., and by Mrs. Tyrkóva-Williams, *op. cit.*, pp. 384 ff.

IN A PEOPLE'S COURT[16]

It was the first meeting of the revolutionary tribunal of the Viborg city ward [in Petrograd]. The . . . . hall was filled with spectators . . . . eager to know what kind of a court it was going to be. . . . . Everybody was convinced that now there would be real justice and not as before, because now all were equal before the law.

The judges, consisting of workmen and soldiers, took their places. One could see that they were excited, for they recognized their responsibility.

The defendants were brought in. A member of the Red Guard showed them politely to their seats and offered them cigarettes. They smoked and chatted. How different from the old court!

One of the judges . . . . addressed the assembly, explained . . . . the underlying ideas of the court, and invited those present to help the judges. . . . . Then the chief judge . . . . said: "The procedure [of the court] will be as follows: Each side will state its case, then the audience will be allowed to take a hand, two for and two against conviction." . . . .

The first man up [for trial] was the soldier-militiaman, Beliaev, accused of firing off his rifle while intoxicated. When asked to explain, he . . . . said: "Comrades, it is true that I was drunk, and it is possible that I fired the gun, but I do not know. I swear it will never happen again."

The chairman called for someone in the audience to say something for the prosecution. After a pause two men came forward and pointed out the harm that a man can do with a gun in these exciting days and demanded that the accused be punished.

When the judge asked for someone to come to the defense of the accused, no one offered his services. . . . . But finally one workman asked to be permitted to say a word. . . . . He argued that "the misfortune of the poor soldier might come to any of us" . . . . and recommended that he be acquitted but be dismissed from the militia. The audience approved with exclamations of "That's right; that's fair!" After a brief consultation the chairman announced that Beliaev was to be set free and dismissed from the militia, but he warned the soldier that if he ever did that again he would be severely punished. After hearing the decision of the judge, Beliaev turned to the public and said, "Thank you humbly, comrades," and walked out. . . . .

Great interest was aroused by the case of a thief called Vaska, the

[16] *Izvestiia,* No. 219, November 21, 1917, p. 2. For a fuller description of the revolutionary court, see Bessie Beatty, *The Red Heart of Russia,* chapter xvi.

Red-haired. He was caught with a burglar's outfit and seven keys—"One to my trunk, one to mother's, and . . . . from other trunks." . . . .

"You have served a term before?"

"Yes, for stealing."

There was a titter in the audience, but Vaska paid no attention and proceeded: "I stole until the revolution but since—never."

It was a clear case. One of the judges recommended forced labor. . . . . The audience approved and suggested a full year. Vaska was not without friends. Someone urged a milder sentence, but this did not meet with public favor. . . . . In the end he was sentenced to hard labor for a year with the understanding that if he behaved himself his term might be shortened. . . . .

The next case was that of two waiters in a hotel . . . . who concealed and sold strong drink. They were fined three hundred rubles each, the money to go to a fund for those who suffered in the war against Kerensky. It was also decided to close the hotel and bring the hotel-keeper before the court. . . . .

[In the Provinces][17]

The following "penal code" was formulated in the village of Lubny, Lebediansky Uezd, Tambov Gubernia:

"If one strikes another fellow, the sufferer shall strike the offender ten times. If one strikes another fellow causing thereby a wound or a broken bone, the offender shall be deprived of life. If one commits theft or receives stolen articles he shall be deprived of life. If one commits arson and is caught, he shall be deprived of life."

Such is the brief code of law. For its enforcement a revolutionary court was elected. Soon two thieves were brought to trial. They were condemned to death. One was killed outright. They broke his head . . . . and ribs . . . . and threw him naked on the highway. . . . . The other thief began to cry aloud and implore that a priest be sent to him for confession and communion. The priest and the reader who arrived on the scene pleaded with the mob and secured a pardon for the condemned. The death sentence was commuted and twenty-five blows by a rod were substituted. (*Novoe Slovo,* No. 20, February 21, 1918.)

The Volost Committee of the village of Studenets, Sviazhsky Uezd, condemned four peasants suspected of robbery to death by burning. Among the condemned was a woman in the last stage of pregnancy. (*Ufimskii Vestnik,* No. 38, March 19, 1918.) . . . .

In Sarapulsky Uezd a peasant woman, aided by her paramour, killed her husband. The people's court sentenced the man to death and the woman to be buried alive. A grave was dug; the body of the dead

[17] *Svoboda Rossii,* No. 38, May 30, 1918, p. 1.

paramour was placed in first and on top they put the woman bound and alive. An arshin of earth was already on her but she still continued to cry, "Help, little fathers." (*Delo Naroda,* No. 29, April 26, 1918.)

Voronezh. The peasants are quite explicit in their declarations against sending criminals to jail. They think it is too great an honor to the criminals and a waste of public money to feed them. The peasants decided to close all detention houses. (*Zaria Rossii,* No. 10, April 28, 1918.)

ABOLITION OF EXISTING LEGAL INSTITUTIONS

[Decree of the Sovnarkom, December 7, 1917][18]

The Soviet of People's Commissars herewith resolves:

1. To abolish all existing general legal institutions, such as district courts, courts of appeal, and the Senate with all its departments, military and naval courts of all grades, and commercial courts; to replace all these institutions with courts established on the basis of democratic elections. . . . .

2. To abolish the existing institution of Justices of the Peace and to replace the Justices of the Peace, heretofore elected by indirect vote, by local courts represented by a permanent local judge and two jurors summoned for each session from a special list of jurors. Local judges are henceforth to be elected on the basis of direct democratic elections, and until these elections have been held they shall be provisionally appointed by district and volost Soviets, or, in the absence of such, by uezd, city, or gubernia Soviets of Workers', Soldiers', and Peasants' Deputies. . . . .

3. To abolish the existing institutions of investigating magistrates, the procurator's office, ... counselors-at-law, and private attorneys.

Pending the reformation of the entire system of legal procedure, preliminary investigations in criminal cases will be made by local judges singly, but his orders of detention and indictment must be confirmed by the decision of the entire local court.

The functions of prosecutors and counsels for the defense, which may begin even with the preliminary investigation, ... may be performed by all citizens of moral integrity, regardless of sex, who enjoy civil rights. . . . .

5. Local courts will try cases in the name of the Russian Republic and will be guided in their rulings and verdicts by the laws of the deposed governments only in so far as those laws have not been annulled by the revolution and do not contradict the revolutionary conscience and the revolutionary conceptions of right.

[18] *S.U.R.*, 1917, No. 4, pp. 49–51.

Note: All those laws shall be considered void which contradict either the decrees of the Central Executive Committee of Soviets of Workers', Soldiers', and Peasants' Deputies and the Workers' and Peasants' Government, or the minimum program of the Russian Social-Democratic Labor Party and the party of Socialist-Revolutionists.

6. In all disputed civil and criminal cases the parties may resort to the arbitration court. The procedure of the arbitration court will be determined by a special decree.

7. The right of pardon and the restitution of rights of persons convicted in criminal cases will belong henceforth to judicial authorities.

8. In order to fight counter-revolution . . . . as well as to try cases against profiteering, speculation, sabotage, and other abuses of merchants, manufacturers, officials, and other persons, revolutionary tribunals of workmen and peasants are hereby established. [These tribunals will] consist of a chairman and six jurors, which are to serve in turn and are to be elected by the gubernia and uezd Soviets of Workers', Soldiers', and Peasants' Deputies.

For the conduct of the preliminary investigation of such cases, special investigating commissions will be formed under the above Soviets.[19] . . . .

V. ULIANOV (LENIN), President of the Sovnarkom
A. SCHLICHTER, L. TROTSKY, A. SHLIAPNIKOV,
I. DZHUGASHVILI (STALIN), N. AVILOV (GLEBOV),
P. STUCHKA, Commissars

INSTITUTIONS FOR INVESTIGATION AND ARREST

[Decree of the People's Commissar of Justice, December 29, 1917][20]

From the moment of the publication of this decree all arrests, searches, seizure of documents, and other actions of investigation are to be carried on according to the order of the following institutions:

(1) The Committee of Inquiry of the Petrograd Soviet of Workers' and Peasants' Deputies.

(2) The organs of inquiry of the regional Soviets of Workers' and Soldiers' Deputies.

(3) The Revolutionary Tribunals of all newly organized judicial offices.

(4) Special Committees of Inquiry: (*a*) All-Russian Commission to Fight Counter-Revolution and Sabotage, attached to the Soviet of

[19] A more detailed decree on the subject of the People's Court was published by the Central Executive Committee on March 7, 1918, in *S.U.R.*, 1918, No. 26, pp. 401–404.

[20] *S.U.R.*, 1917, No. 9, pp. 141–42.

People's Commissars. (*b*) The Committee to Fight Pogroms attached to the Central Executive Committee of Soviets of Workers, Soldiers' and Peasants' Deputies.

All complaints dealing with wrong actions and mistakes made by the above commissions are to be directed to the institutions which control these commissions and also to the People's Commissariat of Justice.

I. STEINBERG
People's Commissariat of Justice

REVOLUTIONARY TRIBUNALS

[Decree of January 1, 1918][21]

1. The Revolutionary Tribunal will have jurisdiction in cases of persons (*a*) who organize uprisings against the authority of the Workers' and Peasants' Government, who actively oppose the latter or do not obey it, or who call upon other persons to oppose or disobey it; (*b*) who take advantage of their position as government or public servants to disturb or hamper the regular progress of work in the institutions or enterprises in which they are or have been serving (sabotage, concealing or destroying documents or property, etc.); (*c*) who stop or curtail the production of articles of general use without actual necessity for doing so . . . . ; (*e*) who violate the decrees, orders, binding ordinances, and other published acts of the organs of the Workers' and Peasants' Government, if the violation of such acts calls for a trial by the Revolutionary Tribunal.

2. . . . . In fixing the penalty, the Revolutionary Tribunal shall be guided by the circumstances of the case and the dictates of the revolutionary conscience.

3. (*a*) The Revolutionary Tribunal is to be elected by the Soviets of Workers', Soldiers', and Peasants' Deputies and is to include one permanent chairman, two permanent substitutes, one permanent secretary and two substitutes, and forty jurors. All persons, except the jurors, are elected for three months and may be recalled by the Soviets before the expiration of the term. (*b*) The jurors are elected for one month. . . . . Lists of jurors numbering six, and one or two in addition, are to be made up for each session. (*c*) The session of each successive jury of the Revolutionary Tribunal is to last no longer than one week. . . . . (*f*) An investigating commission consisting of six members

[21] *S.U.R.*, 1917, No. 12, pp. 179–81. On December 31 there had been organized a Revolutionary Tribunal of the Press to try cases in which the press was charged with publishing false or perverted information about events in public life (*S.U.R.*, 1917, No. 10, p. 155).

. . . . is to be created under the Revolutionary Tribunal for the conduct of the preliminary investigation. (*g*) Upon receiving information or complaint, the investigating commission examines it and within forty-eight hours either orders the dismissal of the case, if it does not find that a crime has been committed, or transfers it to the proper jurisdiction, or brings it up for trial at the session of the Revolutionary Tribunal. (*h*) The orders of the investigating commission about arrests, searches, seizures, and releases of detained persons are valid if issued jointly by three members. In cases which do not permit of delay such orders may be issued by any member of the investigating commission singly, on the condition that within twelve hours the measure shall be approved by the investigating commission. (*i*) The order of the investigating commission is carried out by the Red Guard, the militia, the troops, and the executive organs of the Republic. (*j*) Complaints against the decisions of the investigating commission are submitted to the Revolutionary Tribunal through its president and are considered at executive sessions of the Revolutionary Tribunal. . . . .

4. The sessions of the Revolutionary Tribunal are public.

5. The verdicts of the Revolutionary Tribunal are rendered by a majority of votes of the members of the Tribunal.

6. The legal investigation is made with the participation of the prosecution and defense.

7. (*a*) Citizens of either sex who enjoy political rights are admitted at the will of the parties as prosecutors and counsel for the defense, with the right to participate in the case; (*b*) under the Revolutionary Tribunals a collegium of persons is to be created who devote themselves to the service of the law, in the form of public prosecution as well as of public defense; (*c*) the collegium mentioned above is formed by the free registration of all persons who desire to render aid to revolutionary justice and who present recommendations from the Soviets of Workers', Soldiers', and Peasants' Deputies.

8. The Revolutionary Tribunal may invite for each case a public prosecutor from the membership of the collegium named.

9. If the accused does not for some reason use his right to invite counsel for defense, the Revolutionary Tribunal, at his request, appoints a member of the collegium for his defense.

10. Besides the above-mentioned prosecutors and defense, one prosecutor and one counsel for defense, drawn from the public present at the session, may take part in the court's proceedings.

11. The verdicts of the Revolutionary Tribunal are final. In case of violation of the form of procedure established by these instructions, or the discovery of indications of obvious injustice in the verdict, the People's Commissar of Justice has the right to address to the Central

Executive Committee of the Soviets of Workers', Soldiers', and Peasants' Deputies a request to order a second and last trial of the case.

12. The maintenance of the Revolutionary Tribunal is charged to the account of the state. The amount of compensation and the daily fees are fixed by the Soviets of Workers', Soldiers', and Peasants' Deputies. The jurors receive the difference between the daily fees and their daily earnings, if the latter are less than the daily fees; at the same time the jurors may not be deprived of their positions during the session.

I. Z. STEINBERG
People's Commissar of Justice

The old gendarmerie and the political police, the Okhrana, disappeared with the fall of the Imperial régime. Public order during the time of the Provisional Government was maintained by militia attached to the local governments or by garrison troops. The political police organization was not revived. The Bolsheviks as a part of their program of transfer of power decreed, on November 10, the organization of workers' militia by all workers' and soldiers' Soviets.[22] These militia detachments developed slowly, and in the meantime Red Guards, Military Revolutionary Committees, Commissions of Inquiry, and self-appointed bodies performed such occasional police functions as were consonant with the slogan to "expropriate the expropriators."

Of quite another character was the political police revived by the Bolsheviks when on December 20 they established the Cheka "to make war on counter-revolution and sabotage."

WHY THE CHEKA WAS CREATED

[An Account by Latsis][23]

The All-Russian Extraordinary Commission was formed on December 20, 1917, when it had its first meeting and decided to call itself the Extraordinary Commission to Fight Counter-Revolution and Sabotage.

[22] *S.U.R.*, 1917, No. 1, p. 12.

[23] M. Latsis, *Chrezvychainye Komissii po borbe s kontr-revoliutsiei*, Moscow, 1921, pp. 7–8. Latsis (Sudrabs) was a prominent member of the Cheka. For some time he was in charge of the secret section of that institution.

At this time the Soviet Government . . . . was attacked on all sides. The "officials" . . . . sabotaged in the hope of stopping the machinery of government; the cadets and the old army officers started one uprising after another with the intention of taking the power from the hands of the Soviets; Vikzhel planned a railroad strike; the Mensheviks and the Socialist-Revolutionists of the Right employed all kinds of weapons in waging a continuous war against the Soviet Government; the profiteer took advantage of the difficult situation of the country to carry on his nefarious trade. . . . . At the same time the German troops of occupation were advancing, threatening the capital. . . . . Only strong measures could save the situation and such measures were taken by the Soviet of People's Commissars.

To fight the external foe there was organized a Red Guard, which later became the Red Army. To fight the internal foe it was necessary to create an organ . . . . that would protect the rear of the Red Army and permit the peaceful development of the Soviet form of government. Such an organ was the Extraordinary Commission to Fight Counter-Revolution and Sabotage. Later on its functions were enlarged to include negligence of duty, profiteering, and banditry.

The Commission itself (composed at that time of Dzerzhinsky, Ksenofontov, Averin, Sergo, Peterson, Peters, Evseev, and Trifonov) outlined its duties as follows: *To cut off at the roots all counter-revolution and sabotage in Russia; to hand over to the revolutionary court all who are guilty of such attempts; to work out measures for dealing with such cases; and to enforce these measures without mercy.* . . . . It was necessary to make the foe feel that there was everywhere about him a seeing eye and a heavy hand ready to come down on him the moment he undertook anything against the Soviet Government.[24] . . . .

[24] In another pamphlet entitled *Dva goda borby na vnutrennem fronte, Populiarnyi obzor dvukhgodichnoi deiatelnosti Chrezvychainykh Komissii po borbe s kontr-revoliutsiei, i prestupleniem po dolzhnosti,* Moscow, 1920, Latsis describes (p. 9) the motives for instituting the Cheka thus: "The November Revolution did not destroy the class [division of society]. The bourgeoisie was removed from the position of power but was not destroyed. The victorious proletariat was of necessity obliged to retain the state, the instrument of violence, for the establishment of its dictatorship. From this everything else follows: the state was compelled to create special organs to fight the vanquished class. . . . . In order that we might not be beaten, it was necessary to crush the enemy. . . . . The Workers' and Peasants' Government rightly understood the situation and created a special organ to fight counter-revolution. . . . . The need of this organ was felt more acutely because the Soviet Government had no apparatus with which to re-educate the people in accordance with its own ideas. . . . . The masses of the people were still imbued with the old spirit. . . . . Hence the necessity of an apparatus for compulsion and purification."

LENIN ON THE ORGANIZATION OF AN EXTRAORDINARY COMMISSION TO FIGHT COUNTER-REVOLUTION[25]

[Letter to Dzerzhinsky, December 19, 1917][26]

In connection with your report today dealing with the struggle against sabotage and counter-revolution, is it not possible to issue the following decree:

Struggle against Counter-Revolution and Sabotage

The bourgeoisie, landholders, and all wealthy classes are making desperate efforts to undermine the revolution which is aiming to safeguard the interest of the toiling and exploited masses. The bourgeoisie is having recourse to the vilest crimes, bribing society's lowest elements and supplying liquor to these outcasts with the purpose of bringing on pogroms. The partisans of the bourgeoisie, especially the higher officials, bank clerks, etc., are sabotaging and organizing strikes in order to block the government's efforts to reconstruct the state on a socialistic basis. Sabotage has spread even to the food-supply organizations, and millions of people are threatened with famine. Special measures must be taken to fight counter-revolution and sabotage. Taking these factors into consideration the Soviet of People's Commissars decrees: . . . .

ESTABLISHMENT OF THE EXTRAORDINARY COMMISSION TO FIGHT COUNTER-REVOLUTION

[Decree of the Sovnarkom, December 20, 1917][27]

The Commission is to be named the All-Russian Extraordinary Commission and is to be attached to the Soviet of People's Commissars. [This commission] is to make war on counter-revolution and sabotage . . . .

The duties of the Commission will be:

1. To persecute and break up all acts of counter-revolution and sabotage all over Russia, no matter what their origin.

2. To bring before the Revolutionary Tribunal all counter-revolutionists and saboteurs and to work out a plan for fighting them.

3. To make preliminary investigation only—enough to break up [the counter-revolutionary act]. The Commission is to be divided into

[25] This commission will be referred to as the Cheka, which is the Russian abbreviation of Chrezvychainaia Komissiia. The commission was also known as Chrezvychaika.

[26] Lenin, *Sochineniia,* XXII, 126.

[27] *Pravda,* No. 290, December 18, 1927, p. 2.

sections: (*a*) the information [section], (*b*) the organization section (in charge of organizing the fight against counter-revolution all over Russia) with branches, and (*c*) the fighting section.

The Commission will be formed tomorrow. . . . . The Commission is to watch the press, saboteurs, strikers, and the Socialist-Revolutionists of the Right. Measures [to be taken against these counter-revolutionists are] confiscation, confinement, deprivation of [food] cards, publication of the names of the enemies of the people, etc.

The break-up of the old army went on rapidly during the first weeks of the Soviet régime. That army was one of the state institutions which the Bolsheviks desired to destroy or to bring under their control after purging it of its hostile elements. Bolshevik policies, particularly the land and peace decrees, were effective in winning over the soldier masses who had formerly looked to the Socialist-Revolutionists and who took a neutral position with regard to the struggle between the Bolsheviks and Kerensky. The new military authorities easily gained control of the Stavka and the headquarters of the Northern and Western groups of armies. The objectives of the dictatorship were also served by the decrees of democratization of the army of December 29 and 30, 1917.

DEMOCRATIZATION OF THE ARMY

[Decree of the Sovnarkom, December 29, 1917][28]

1. The army, as the servant of the will of the toiling people, is to be subordinate to the sovereign of that people, the Soviet of People's Commissars.

2. The full power within any army unit or combination of units is to be in the hands of its soldiers' committees and Soviets.

3. . . . . The [soldiers'] committees are to exercise control over those spheres of [the army's] activity which the committees do not handle directly.

4. The elective principle for army officers is hereby introduced. All commanders up to the regimental commander are to be elected by a general vote of the [different units] . . . . Commanders higher than regimental commanders and including the supreme commander-in-chief

[28] *S.U.R.*, 1917, No. 9, pp. 136–37.

are to be elected by a congress . . . . of committees of the army units [for which the commander is being elected]. . . . .

7. Positions of a technical nature which require special training . . . . such as physicians, engineers, aviators . . . . are to be appointed by the committees . . . . from among persons having the required special knowledge.

8. Chiefs of staff are elected . . . . from among persons with special training.

9. All other staff officers are to be appointed by the chief of staff. These appointments are to be ratified by the [soldiers'] congresses. . . . .

10. Commanders above the drafting age, ... if they are not elected to any post, and are thereby demoted to the position of privates, have a right to leave service. . . . .

V. ULIANOV (LENIN)
President of the Sovnarkom

N. KRYLENKO
People's Commissar of War and Navy

PODVOISKY
People's Commissar of War

[Decree of the Sovnarkom, December 30, 1917][29]

In fulfillment of the will of the revolutionary people which is concerned with the immediate and decisive eradication of every inequality in the army, the Sovnarkom hereby decrees:

1. To do away with all ranks and titles from the rank of corporal to that of general, inclusive. The army of the Russian Republic is henceforth to be composed of free and equal citizens bearing the honorable title of "soldier of the revolutionary army";

2. To do away with all privileges and the external marks formerly connected with the different ranks and titles;

3. To do away with saluting;

4. To do away with all decorations and other signs of distinction;

5. To do away with all officers' organizations. . . . .

6. To abolish the institution of orderlies in the army. . . . .

V. ULIANOV (LENIN)
President of the Sovnarkom

N. KRYLENKO
People's Commissar of War and Navy

PODVOISKY
People's Commissar of War

[29] *S.U.R.*, 1917, No. 9, pp. 137–38.

During the first weeks of their régime the Bolsheviks proceeded slowly and obliquely with respect to educational and religious institutions, despite the fact that it was on their program to revolutionize the one and eradicate the other. The Second Congress of Soviets created a Commissariat of Education. By decree of November 22 the Commissariat set up a Commission on People's Education to which it transferred all the functions of the old Ministry of Education. The State Committee on Education of the Provisional Government was suffered to continue in a subordinate rôle until December 5, when it was dissolved.

The Provisional Government had considerably changed the status of the Orthodox Church by reorganizing the Most Holy Synod, by abolishing the office of Ober Procurator, by establishing a Ministry of Confessions, by granting religious freedom, and by transferring state-aided schools from the jurisdiction of the Church to that of the Ministry of Education. Late in August 1917 a Sobor (Assembly) met to consider changes in the government of the Church to conform to changes in political and social organization. This Sobor was still in session in Moscow when the November overturn came. The Bolsheviks did not interfere with the Sobor, which decided on November 21 to restore the Patriarchate, to which office the Metropolitan Tikhon was elected a few days later.

The first act of the Soviet Government seriously to affect the Church was the nationalization of the land, including that of ecclesiastical and monastic institutions. A few days later, December 24, the Commissariat of Education took over the control of ecclesiastical seminaries and other church schools and their property, thus depriving the Church of the means of educating candidates for the priesthood. This decree forecast the later decree on the separation of church and state. On December 31 the government deprived the Church of some of its prerogatives by decreeing that only civil marriages would be recognized and by establishing bureaus for the registration of births and deaths.

By another decree of the same date civil divorce was established.[30]

STATE COMMISSION OF EDUCATION

[Decree of the Commissariat of Education, November 29, 1917][31]

Pending the calling of the Constituent Assembly, the general direction of work connected with people's education, in so far as that education is to remain under the control of the central governments, will be intrusted to a State Commission of People's Education, the representative and executive head of which will be the People's Commissar [of Education].

In accordance with the decision of the Sovnarkom and the procedure established by the [Second] Congress of Soviets, all functions formerly discharged by the Minister of People's Education and his assistants are now transferred to the Commission of People's Education.

The Commission of Education is to be responsible for all its acts to the [Central] Executive Committee of Workers', Soldiers', and Peasants' Deputies.

The membership of the Commission will be as follows: 1. Chairman—People's Commissar of Education. 2. Secretary of the Commission of People's Education. 3. By election: two representatives of the [Central] Executive Committee of Soviets of Workers', Soldiers', and Peasants' Deputies; two representatives of the Executive Committee of the All-Russian Congress of Peasants' Deputies . . . .; two from the All-Russian Teachers' Union; one each from the Academic Union, the Central Bureau of Trade Unions, the All-Russian Center of Factory-Shop Committees, the Central Committee of the Petrograd Proletarian Cultural-Education Organizations (pending the formation of a similar All-Russian organ), the All-Russian Union of Cities, the All-Russian Zemstvo Union, the All-Russian Organization of Artists (when such comes into existence), the All-Russian Students' Union (when it is established) and the State Commission of People's Education.[32]

[30] *S.U.R.*, 1917, No. 11, pp. 161–63; *ibid.*, 1917, No. 10, pp. 150–52. An English translation of these decrees is given in *The Nation* (New York), December 28, 1918, and in Senate Judiciary Committee, 65th Congress, 3d Session, *Bolshevik Propaganda*, Washington, 1919, pp. 1198–1200, 1260–62. Cf. M. Spinka, *The Church and the Russian Revolution*, New York, 1927, pp. 102–104; B. V. Titlinov, *Tserkov vo vremia revoliutsii*, Petrograd, 1924, pp. 95–100; W. C. Emhardt, *Religion in Soviet Russia*, Milwaukee, 1929, pp. 20–21.

[31] *Sbornik dekretov i postanovlenii Rabochego i Krestianskogo Pravitelstva po narodnomu obrazovaniiu* (S 28 oktiabria 1917 g. po 7 noiabria 1918 g.), 2 vols., Moscow, 1921, I, 5–7.

[32] This Committee functioned under the Provisional Government.

4. By appointment from the Sovnarkom: fifteen persons, who will head [the following] departments: (1) universal literacy, (2) autonomous schools of university rank, (3) schools under the charge of the Ministry of Education (pending their transfer to the municipalities), (4) municipal schools, (5) pre-school education and child welfare, (6) adult education, (7) assistance to organizations aiming to educate class-consciousness, (8) science, (9) art, (10) finance, (11) statistics and experimental pedagogy, (12) technical schools and polytechnical education, (13) training of the teaching personnel, (14) school of medicine and hygiene, (15) school buildings.

The State Commission of People's Education is not to assume the rôle of a central authority in the administration of educational institutions. On the contrary all schools must be taken charge of by local self-governments. Educational activity on the part of class-conscious workers', soldiers', and peasants' organizations must have complete autonomy in relation to both the central government and municipalities. The business of the State Commission is to serve as a link and to aid in securing material, ideological, and moral support for municipal and private educational organizations, especially those undertaken by toilers and class-conscious workers.

The State Committee of Education [which functioned] from the beginning of the [February 1917] revolution formulated a number of very valuable educational projects. That Committee was democratic in its membership and included experienced specialists. The State Commission will try to co-operate with that Committee and the Commissar of Education will call at once . . . . a joint session.[33] . . . .

A. V. LUNACHARSKY
People's Commissar of Education

V. ULIANOV (LENIN)
President of the Sovnarkom

TRANSFER OF CHURCH SCHOOLS TO THE COMMISSARIAT OF EDUCATION

[Decree of the Commissariat of Education, December 24, 1917][34]

Owing to lack of clarity in the regulations of the former Ministries [of Education] on the question of the transfer of the control over

[33] The Committee of Education was dissolved by the Sovnarkom, December 5, 1917, by a special decree which reads in part: ". . . . In view of the fact that the State Committee [of Education] is in need of greater democratization, the Sovnarkom declares: the State Committee of Education in its present membership is dissolved . . . ." (*Sbornik dekretov i postanovlenii Rabochego i Krestianskogo Pravitelstva po narodnomu obrazovaniiu,* I, 11.)

[34] *S.U.R.,* 1917, No. 9, p. 131.

church-parochial schools to the Ministry of Education (this fact is manifest in the receipt of numerous inquiries from the provinces), the Commissariat of Education (formerly the Ministry of Education), having reconsidered this question, resolved: to transfer to the control of the Commissariat of People's Education all church-parochial elementary schools, teachers' colleges, ecclesiastical schools and colleges, parochial schools for girls, missionary schools and academies, and other institutions . . . . which formerly were under the control of the Ecclesiastical Department. Together with them pass to the Commissariat of Education their personnel, grants, movable and immovable property. . . . .

The question concerning the chapels of these institutions will be settled by the decree on the separation of church and state.

VL. ULIANOV (LENIN)
President of the Soviet of People's Commissars

A. V. LUNACHARSKY
People's Commissar [of Education]

VL. GALKIN
Commissar of Elementary Schools

B. INDUSTRY AND LABOR

Among the projects relating to the status of labor which the Bolsheviks had advocated before the seizure of power were a general reduction of working hours, social insurance, and workers' control of industry. On November 11 the Commissariat of Labor established a maximum eight-hour day and forty-eight-hour week. Two days later the Commissariat laid down the general principles of social insurance which were applied in subsequent decrees.

Establishment of workers' control (November 27) was a far more drastic manifestation of the proletarian dictatorship. By legalizing seizures of factories which had been made by workers' organizations here and there during the days of the Provisional Government, it served not only to win the support of many workers who interpreted "control" as "ownership," but it was, short of nationalization, a most effective attack on the economic position of the bourgeoisie. The decree, as subsequent materials show, led to much confusion and conflict. Workers attempted to run the factories without regard to the interests of anyone but themselves; owners and managers resisted, and in retaliation the government nationalized their establishments. Foreign consuls protested against the application of the decree to concerns owned by their nationals. For the purpose of organizing national economy and drawing up plans to regulate the economic life of the country, the C.E.C., on December 14, set up the Supreme Council of National Economy with power to confiscate, requisition, and consolidate all branches of industry and commerce.

Conflicts over the status of labor organizations with respect to the government and industrial control were particularly acute during this period, as is suggested in some of the following pages. Many leaders of the trade-union organizations were Mensheviks, who opposed the single-party dictatorship of the Bolsheviks and who wished to preserve the independence or neutrality of the unions. Leaders of the factory-shop committees, more revolutionary-minded, argued for the abolition of the old unions and the transfer of their functions to the committees. The Bolshevik majority desired to bring the trade unions into line with the dictatorship and the state machinery and to curb the syndicalist tendencies of the factory-shop committees. The controversy continued for many weeks and will be referred to later. Here it is worth noting that this conflict contributed another element to the confusion of the first two months.[35]

THE HOURS OF LABOR

[Decree of the Sovnarkom, November 11, 1917][36]

1. The working time or the number of working hours in a day is the time which, according to the agreement on employment (Articles

[35] Cf. A. Lozovsky, "Trade Unions in Soviet Russia: Their Development and Present Position," in *Trade Unions in Soviet Russia, a Collection of Russian Trade Union Documents Compiled by the I[ndependent] L[abour] P[arty] Information Committee and the International Section of the Labour Research Department*, London, [1920], pp. 23–24.

[36] *Sbornik dekretov i postanovlenii po narodnomu khoziaistvu. 25 oktiabria 1917 g.–25 oktiabria 1918 g.*, Moscow, 1918, pp. 367–71 (hereafter cited as *S.D.*);

48, 60, 96, 98, 103 of the Industrial Labor Law), a workman is obliged to be in the factory for the performance of work and at the disposal of his manager.

Note 1: In underground work the time used to go down into the mine and to come up to the surface is counted as working time.

Note 2: The working time of workmen sent on tasks outside of the boundaries of the factory is determined by special agreement.

2. The working time as determined by the rules of the internal organization of the enterprise (Clause 1, Article 103 of the Industrial Labor Law) should not exceed eight working hours a day and forty-eight hours a week, including the time spent in cleaning the machinery and putting the establishment in a state of orderliness.

On the day before Christmas (December 24) and on Holy Trinity Day work stops at noon.

3. After not more than six hours of work there should be a recess of not less than an hour for food and rest. Recesses are determined by the rules of the internal organization. During the recess the workman is free to dispose of his time and may leave the boundaries of the establishment.

During the recess motors, commutators, and machines should be stopped. Exceptions to this rule may be permitted in case of overtime (as provided in Articles 18–22 of this law) in case of those machines and commutators that control ventilation, water supply, lighting, etc., and in such other cases where it is impossible to stop work for technical reasons (as, for example, unfinished casting, etc.).

Note 1: Enterprises that are recognized by law or the Main Labor Office as continuous and on a three-shift day do not conform to the rules on recesses but they must give the workman the right to take his food during work.

Note 2: If the conditions of work are such that the workman cannot leave his place of work to eat, a special room or place is to be provided for that purpose. This is obligatory in case of men who come in contact with materials (lead, mercury, etc.) which, according to the rulings of the main board of the factory and mining industries (or the organ taking its place), are injurious to health.

S.U.R., 1917, No. 1, pp. 7–10. On November 15, 1917, there appeared in *Volia Naroda,* No. 161, p. 2, the following letter signed by A. Bykov and referring to the decree on the eight-hour day:

". . . . The text of the [decree] is a verbatim reproduction . . . . of my draft of a law relating to hours of labor which was written in the spring of this year on the basis of materials supplied by the Party of People's Freedom [Cadets]. It was intended to submit the draft . . . . to the Industrial-War Committee and later to the Ministry of Trade and Industry (Section of Labor). As published the decree retained references to the 'main board of factory and mining industries' which no longer exists. . . . ."

4. The total amount of time spent in recesses should not exceed two hours a day.

5. Night work is from 9:00 P.M. to 5:00 A.M.

6. Boys and girls under sixteen years of age are not to be employed for night work.

7. For enterprises which are working on a two-shift basis night work is reckoned from 9:00 P.M. to 5:00 A.M. Recesses (Article 4) may be shortened to half an hour for each shift.

8. In cases where workers (brickmakers for example) wish to have a longer noon recess or climatic conditions make [a longer recess] desirable the main industrial board may make exceptions to Articles 4, 5, 6, and 8 of this law.

9. In addition to the rules mentioned above the following regulations apply to minors (under eighteen years of age): (*a*) those under fourteen years of age are not allowed to do hired work; (*b*) those under eighteen years of age cannot be employed for more than six hours a day.

Note: After January 1, 1919, all children under fifteen years of age and after January 1, 1920, all under twenty years of age are not permitted to be hired for work.

10. The holidays when no work is allowed (Clause 2, Article 103, Industrial Labor Law) are all Sundays and the following named days: January 1, January 6, February 27, March 25, May 1, August 15, September 14, December 25, 26, Friday and Saturday of Holy Week, Monday and Tuesday of Easter week, Ascension Day, and the second day of the Descent of the Holy Ghost.

Note 1: According to their belief non-Christians may have other days of rest in place of Sundays. They are, however, obliged to observe all the other holidays enumerated in this article except those indicated below.

Note 2: At the request of a majority of the workmen of an industry or a section of it, other free days may be substituted for January 1 and 6, August 15, September 14, December 26, Saturday of Holy Week, and Easter Monday.

11. In the case of a one-shift day the minimum duration of Sunday and holiday rest to which a worker is entitled is forty-two hours. In the case of a two- or three-shift day the minimum hours of rest are determined by agreement with the labor organizations.

12. By mutual consent of the manager of the industry and the workers, the latter may (as a departure from the schedule of holidays indicated in Article 11) work on a holiday instead of on a week day. This agreement should, however, be reported immediately to the proper authorities who supervise the execution of this law.

13. The main board of factory and mining industries (or the organ taking its place) has the right to issue rules permitting departures, as

necessity arises, from the rules enumerated in Articles 3, 4, 5, and 8 in the case of those establishments . . . . which must work at night or irregularly at different seasons of the year (such as work connected with the light and water supply for cities).

14. The working hours indicated in Articles 3, 4, 5, and 8 are to be further reduced in the case of industries and occupations particularly harmful to health and in which the workers are exposed to . . . . poisons. . . . . A list of such occupations and industries with the length of working time in each as well as other conditions of work must be prepared by the main board of the factory and mining industries (or by the organ which takes its place).

15. Women and minors (under eighteen years of age) cannot be employed for underground work.

16. By agreement with the workmen and with the approval of the workmen's organizations departures from the regulations stated in Articles 3–5 and 8–12 are permitted in case of workers engaged in supplementary work such as repair work, care of the boilers, motors, lathes, heating, water supply, lighting the premises, guard and fire duty. . . . .

17. Overtime is work done outside the regular working hours and is permitted only under the regulations stated in Articles 19–22 and is paid for at a double rate.

18. Women and minors under eighteen years of age cannot work overtime. Men over eighteen years of age may work overtime if the workmen's organizations approve [and then only in exceptional cases when failure to do so may lead to interruption and harm to the plant and workers]. . . . .

19. [A special permit from the Commissariat of Labor or the Labor Inspector is required for overtime work.]

20. All overtime work is recorded in the workmen's account books . . . . and in the office books.

21. Fifty days is the maximum overtime per year allowed for each branch of industry under the conditions enumerated in Articles 19–21. A separate record is to be kept of the overtime even if it applies to only one workman in the branch.

22. The duration of overtime of any one worker shall under no circumstance be more than four hours in two consecutive days.

23. In the near future [that is], until the end of the war, organizations engaged in the work of defense may, by agreement with the management, set aside the regulation of overtime work (Article 19–23) and in industries engaged in the work of defense recesses (Articles 4–6) may not be enforced, provided the workers and workers' organizations agree to it.

24. The present law becomes effective by telegraph.

25. This law applies to all industries and occupations regardless of size or ownership and to all persons hired to work.

26. Violation of the present law is punishable by imprisonment for a period not longer than one year.

YU. LARIN
Acting Commissar of Labor

SOCIAL INSURANCE

[Decree of the Sovnarkom, November 13, 1917][37]

The Russian proletariat has placed on its banners "Full Social Insurance for Wage Workers" as well as for the city and village poor. The tsarist government of landowners and capitalists and the coalition-reconciliation governments [Provisional Government] failed to satisfy the demands of the workers in this respect.

The Workers' and Peasants' Government, being supported by the Soviet of Workers', Soldiers', and Peasants' Deputies, announces to the working class of Russia and to the city and village poor that it will immediately prepare decrees on social insurance in accordance with the ideas of the workers.

1. Insurance for all wage workers without exception, as well as for the city and village poor.
2. Insurance to cover all forms of disability, such as illness, injury, invalidism, old age, maternity, widowhood, orphanage, as well as unemployment.
3. The total cost of the insurance to be borne by the employer.
4. Full compensation in case of disability or unemployment.
5. The insured to have full control of the insurance institutions.[38]

In the name of the Government of the Russian Republic,

A. SHLIAPNIKOV
People's Commissar of Labor

WORKERS' CONTROL

[Decree of the Sovnarkom, November 27, 1917][39]

1. In the interests of a systematic regulation of national economy, Workers' Control is introduced in all industrial, commercial, agricul-

[37] *S.U.R.*, 1917, No. 2, p. 20.

[38] During the following weeks the government issued several decrees regulating the various forms of disability and unemployment insurance. French translations of some of these decrees are given in Labry, *Une législation communiste. Recueil des lois, décrets, arrêtés principaux du gouvernement bolchéviste,* Paris, 1920, pp. 251–57. Private insurance companies were not nationalized until later.

[39] *S.U.R.*, 1917, No. 3, pp. 39–40. The decree was first published on November 29, 1917.

tural [and similar] enterprises which are hiring people to work for them in their shops or which are giving them work to take home. This control is to extend over the production, storing, buying and selling of raw materials and finished products as well as over the finances of the enterprise.

2. The workers will exercise this control through their elected organizations, such as factory and shop committees, Soviets of elders, etc. The office employees and the technical personnel are also to have representation in these committees.

3. Every large city, gubernia, and industrial area is to have its own Soviet of Workers' Control, which, being an organ of the S[oviet] of W[orkers'], S[oldiers'], and P[easants'] D[eputies], must be composed of representatives of trade-union, factory, shop and other workers' committees and workers' co-operatives.

4. Until the meeting of the Congress of the Soviets of Workers' Control an All-Russian Soviet of Workers' Control will be organized in Petrograd, made up of representatives from the following organizations: All-Russian Central Executive Committee of the Soviet of Workers' and Soldiers' Deputies (5 [representatives]); All-Russian Central Executive Committee of the Soviet of Peasant Deputies (5); All-Russian Council of Trade Unions (5); All-Russian Union of Workers' Co-operatives (2); All-Russian Bureau of Factory and Shop Committees (5); All-Russian Union of Engineers and Technicians (5); All-Russian Union of Agronomists (2); from every All-Russian union of workers having less than 100,000 members (1); from those that have more than 100,000 members (2); the Petrograd Council of Trade Unions (2).

5. Commissions of trained inspectors (technicians, accountants, etc.) will be established in connection with the higher organs of Workers' Control and will be sent out either on the initiative of these higher organs or at the request of the lower organs of Workers' Control to investigate the financial and technical side of enterprises.

6. The organs of Workers' Control have the right to supervise production, fix the minimum of output, and determine the cost of production.

7. The organs of Workers' Control have the right to control all the business correspondence of an enterprise. Owners of enterprises are legally responsible for all correspondence kept secret. Commercial secrets are abolished. The owners have to show to the organs of Workers' Control all their books and statements for the current year and for past years.

8. The rulings of the organs of Workers' Control are binding on the owners of enterprises and can be annulled only by decisions of the higher organs of Workers' Control.

9. Appeals from the lower to the higher organs must be made within three days.

10. In all enterprises the owners and the representatives of the workers and employees elected to the Committee on Workers' Control are responsible to the state for the order, discipline, and safety of the property. Persons guilty of hiding raw materials or products, of falsifying accounts, and of other similar abuses are criminally liable.

11. All regional Soviets of Workers' Control (Article 3) have the power to settle disputed points and conflicts that may arise between the lower organs of Workers' Control and to give their decision regarding the complaints of the owners. They also issue instructions (within the limits fixed by the All-Russian Soviet of Workers' Control) to meet the local conditions of production and supervise the activities of the lower organs of control.

12. The All-Russian Soviet of Workers' Control makes out a general plan for Workers' Control, issues instructions, makes binding decisions, regulates mutual relations between the different Soviets of Workers' Control, and serves as the highest authority for all business connected with Workers' Control.

13. The All-Russian Soviet of Workers' Control co-ordinates the activities of the organs of Workers' Control in their dealings with other institutions of national economy.

Special instructions will be issued later defining the relations between the All-Russian Soviet of Workers' Control and other institutions of national economy.[40]

14. All the laws and circulars restricting the work of factory, shop, and other committees or Soviets of workers and employees are hereby annulled.

V. Ulianov (Lenin)
President of the Soviet of People's Commissars

A. Shliapnikov
People's Commissar of Labor

THE ORIGIN OF THE SUPREME COUNCIL OF NATIONAL ECONOMY

[Recollections of V. Obolensky-Osinsky][41]

Upon my arrival at Petrograd early in November 1917, I was asked . . . . to start the organization of the Supreme Economic Conference.

[40] A French translation of general instruction on workers' control, published in *Izvestiia,* No. 250, December 20, 1917, is in Labry, *op. cit.,* pp. 131–36.

[41] *Narodnoe Khoziaistvo,* No. 11, November 1918, pp. 11–14.

This was the name of the institution which later developed . . . . into the Supreme Council of National Economy. We chose a more modest name at the beginning, as we were not sure what form the policy of economic regulation was bound to assume. Some of us . . . . thought that the economic dictatorship of the proletariat would be limited to Workers' Control. . . . . On the other hand, two central organizations of the working class—the Council of Trade Unions and the Center of Factory-Shop Committees . . . .—claimed the right to assume exclusive control of the economic life of the country. There was also the vague question as to the relation in which the Supreme Economic institution would stand to those commissariats which had charge of economic problems (Commissariats of Trade and Industry, Finance, Food Supply, Agriculture, Ways of Communication, etc.). For those reasons it seemed more cautious to speak of a Supreme Economic Conference and let future experience determine what permanent institution should regulate national economy.

Our work . . . . proceeded in three directions:

First, we decided to formulate a statute. . . . . For that purpose we revised the statutes of the Chief Economic Committee and the [Supreme Economic] Council which existed during the Kerensky [period] . . . . and gave them a purely proletarian character . . . . adapting them to the aims of socialist construction.

Secondly, we decided to secure a staff to do the office work. . . . . Quite naturally we "requisitioned" Kerensky's Chief Economic Committee. M. A. Savelev received an "order" to "occupy" [the offices of] that committee. . . . .

Our third task was to give to our economic conference the character of a proletarian organ by attracting to its work the "live forces" of the proletariat. . . . . At that time the trade unions could not be relied upon. They were in the hands of men whose attitude toward the social revolution was either "neutral," skeptical, or hostile. Through Comrade Skrypnik we established connections with the Center of Factory-Shop Committees which was at that time the organ of the more revolutionary trade-union movement. . . . .

After some three or five days of such work Comrade Smirnov and I were transferred to the State Bank. The bank sabotaged the Soviet Power by refusing under different pretexts to give money [to the Soviets] and finally the very day I was appointed Chief Commissar of the bank the employees went on strike. For three weeks we were completely submerged in bank affairs . . . . and early in December the new Bolshevik bank was going at top speed. Upon the completion of the "strategic plan" for the capture of private banks . . . ., I petitioned to be relieved from work in problems of finance in which I had no special knowledge and to be permitted to return to economic work of a more general character.

During my absence . . . . Comrade Bukharin was added to the organization committee. He and Comrades Savelev, Larin, and Miliutin . . . . drafted in its final form the decree on the Supreme Council of National Economy. The Left S.R.'s delayed for some time the adoption of the decree by the Central Executive Committee. They demanded that half the membership in the Supreme Economic organ be reserved for the representatives of the peasant section [of the Central Executive Committee]. . . . .

At the first plenary session of the Council [of National Economy] a bureau was elected. . . . . At the second session . . . . a statute for local councils of national economy was approved.

In the interim between plenary sessions the bureau carried on the work. It first selected a presidium (Antipov, Schmidt, Larin, Smirnov, and myself) ; then it divided the Council into sections, assigning members of the bureau to the different sections. . . . .

Meanwhile . . . . life was pressing its claims. According to the decree which established the Supreme Council of National Economy the latter was given very wide prerogatives. . . . . Every economic question fell under its jurisdiction. . . . . The bank crisis and the closing of private banks brought about a great demand for state subsidies for the conduct of industries. Very often these subsidies amounted to millions of rubles. The disorganization of industry which we inherited from Kerensky and which was intensified by sabotage and civil war called for urgent measures. We were expected to supply the industries with fuel and raw material. . . . . At the same time we were confronted with the task of socialist reconstruction, and especially with that of the revolutionary disruption of capitalism. The nationalization of industry was going on in an uncontrollable fashion and we were unable to establish even regular connections with socialized factories. . . . . The situation was difficult indeed. . . . . The sphere of our activities was enormous and absolutely undefined. Moreover, entirely new economic tasks had arisen and we lacked the technical staff to attend to those tasks. . . . . That is why the Supreme Council of National Economy was so slow in developing [its activities], so deficient in technique, and so apt to lay itself open to frequent criticisms.

There were other causes within the Supreme Council of National Economy itself, which greatly contributed to the state of general disorganization. In addition to the unavoidable confusion of the first days there were in the bureau [of the Supreme Council] a number of comrades (I speak mainly of the intellectuals) who lacked the habit of systematic work and business routine. They possessed instead great verve and initiative, and the Supreme Council of National Economy was in danger of becoming an anarchistic "Commune" in which everyone could, on his own initiative and risk, make decisions of immense importance involving at times millions of rubles. . . . . System had to be introduced into the work of the Supreme Council of National Economy in order to make it an organ of government. . . . . That is why the Central Executive Committee resolved to appoint a chairman of the Supreme Council of National Economy with the rights of People's Commissar. . . . . On December 25, 1917, ... the writer was appointed chairman. With this appointment the first period of confusion came to an end. . . . .

Comrade Shliapnikov [Commissar of Labor, Trade, and Industry] and his successor, V. Smirnov, were of the opinion . . . . that to have the Commissariat of Trade and Industry as well as the Supreme Council of National Economy was utterly illogical. They therefore undertook to transfer to the Supreme Council of National Economy those sections of the Commissariat of Trade and Industry which had charge of the different branches of production. . . . . From the very first the rule was established that every section of production which was transferred to the Council was obliged to establish connections with the corresponding trade union and to ask for officials to do the responsible work of the section. . . . .

Simultaneously with the inclusion of the sections of the Commissariat of Trade and Industry into the Council [of National Economy] other "conferences" and committees, such as fuel, metal, defense, etc., were incorporated. . . . .

I can recall the negotiations which the labor representatives of the tanning industry conducted with Lenin. The workers in the tanning industry wished to form a working agreement with the capitalists [on the following basis]: the works were not be expropriated but were to come under a joint control of a bourgeois-proletarian syndicate subsidized by the state. . . . . The plan was not realized and proved nothing but a bait by which the industrialists hoped to secure a subsidy. . . . . Comrade Lenin . . . . thought at the time that it might be interesting to try an experiment of this kind.

I also recall the first session of the bureau under my chairmanship . . . . when Lenin made one of his most interesting reports defending the draft of a decree which he had introduced to the S.C.N.E. This decree . . . . advocated the nationalization of all banks and of large-scale industry, the annulment of state loans, the introduction of labor duty, consumers' communes, and budget-labor books. The members of the bureau were extremely embarrassed when they first heard the project. With the exception of Lozovsky and Riazanov, however, no objections were made to the principles involved in the project, but there were doubts as to whether it could be realized all at once. When Lenin was asked whether it was a statement of policy or a law intended to be introduced at one time he replied that he had the latter purpose in mind. A proposal was then made to develop in detail the different parts of the decree. . . . .

As is well known, almost every part of the decree is now realized. . . . . I think that Lenin was then quite serious. Legislation by declaration is of great importance during critical revolutionary periods. Both the Mensheviks and a great number of Bolsheviks failed to appreciate this fact. [Legislation by declaration] gives a spiritual impetus to the masses, frees their hands. . . . . During the mass-assault on capital it is important to proclaim the end toward which the masses should strive and it is of little importance that the legal phrase is at variance with the revolutionary deed. . . . .

ESTABLISHMENT OF THE SUPREME COUNCIL OF NATIONAL ECONOMY

[Decree of the C.E.C., December 14, 1917][42]

1. The Supreme Council of National Economy is established [as an organ] attached to the Soviet of People's Commissars.

2. The work of the Supreme Council of National Economy is to organize the national economy and state finances. With that in view the Supreme Council of National Economy will draw up general standards and plans for the regulation of the economic life of the country, coordinating and unifying the activities of the local and central regulating organs (committees on fuel, metals, transport, food-supply committee, and others) that are attached to the People's Commissariats (trade and industry, food, agriculture, finance, war-navy, etc.), the All-Russian Soviet of Workers' Control, the factory-shop committees, and the trade unions.

3. The Supreme Council of National Economy has the right to confiscate, requisition, sequester, and consolidate various branches of industry, commerce, and other enterprises in the field of production, distribution, and state finance.

4. The Supreme Council of National Economy is to take charge of all existing institutions for the regulation of the economic life and has the right to reorganize them.

5. The Supreme Council of National Economy is to include [representatives of] (*a*) the All-Russian Soviet of Workers' Control, ... (*b*) the Commissariats, and (*c*) experts invited in an advisory capacity.

[42] *S.U.R.*, 1917, No. 5, pp. 73–74.

6. The Supreme Council of National Economy is divided into sections and departments (fuel, metal, demobilization [of industry], finance, etc.). The number of the sections and departments and their respective functions are determined at a general meeting of the Supreme Council of National Economy.

7. The different departments of the Supreme Council of National Economy occupy themselves with the regulation of specific branches of the national economy, and prepare measures for the respective commissariats.

8. The Supreme Council of National Economy selects from its own body a bureau of fifteen members to co-ordinate the work of the different sections and departments and to carry out the tasks that need immediate attention.

9. All legislative measures and important undertakings having to do with the regulation of the economic life as a whole are brought before the Sovnarkom through the Supreme Council of National Economy.

10. The Supreme Council of National Economy co-ordinates and directs the activities of the local economic departments of the Soviets of Workers', Soldiers', and Peasants' Deputies, including the local organs of Workers' Control, as well as local agencies of the Commissariats of Labor, Trades and Industry, Food, etc.

In the absence of local agencies referred to above, the Supreme Council of National Economy organizes those of its own.

All the rulings of the Supreme Council of National Economy are binding on the economic departments of the local Soviets as the agents of the Supreme Council of National Economy.

YA. SVERDLOV, Chairman of the Central Executive Committee

V. ULIANOV (LENIN), President of the Sovnarkom

L. TROTSKY, I. STALIN, AVILOV (GLEBOV), People's Commissars

EARLY NATIONALIZATION DECREE

[Decree of the Sovnarkom, December 20, 1917][43]

In view of the refusal of the management of the Stock Company of the Bogoslovsk mine region to submit to the decree of the Sovnarkom concerning workers' control over production, the Sovnarkom hereby

[43] *S.U.R.*, 1917, No. 6, p. 89. This is a single one of the many punitive decrees of nationalization of this period.

decrees that the entire property of the company be confiscated . . . . and be declared the property of the Russian Republic.

The entire administrative and technical personnel must remain on their jobs and go on with their duties. . . . .

V. ULIANOV (LENIN)
President of the Sovnarkom

L. TROTSKY, I. DZHUGASHVILI (STALIN)
People's Commissars

LENIN'S DRAFT OF AN ECONOMIC PROGRAM[44]

[Submitted to the Supreme Council of National Economy, December 1917]

. . . . To enable the toilers . . . . to undertake the regulation of the economic life of the country, the following rules are hereby decreed:

(1) All stock companies are declared to be the property of the state.

(2) Members of the boards of directors of stock companies as well as the shareholders belonging to the wealthy classes (i.e., those possessing over 5,000 rubles or having an income of over 500 rubles a month) are under obligation to continue their business in conformity with the law of Workers' Control. They are to declare to the State Bank the number of shares in their possession and make weekly statements of their activities to the local Soviets of Workers', Soldiers', and Peasants' Deputies.

(3) All state loans, external and internal, are annulled (abolished).

(4) The interests of the stock and bond holders belonging to the toiling classes of the population are to be fully safeguarded.

(5) Universal labor duty is introduced for citizens of both sexes between the ages of 16 and 55. . . . .

(6) . . . . Members of the wealthy classes (see paragraph 2) must secure labor-books, in which entries will be made of the work assigned to them. . . . .

(7) To regulate properly the distribution of food supplies and other articles of prime necessity, every citizen of the state is under obligation to join one of the consumers' societies. . . . .

(8) Railwaymen's Unions must proceed at once to formulate and to carry out *extraordinary* measures for the proper organization of transport. . . . . The Railwaymen's Unions . . . . are likewise charged with the duty of fighting without mercy the bagmen and speculators.

[44] "Proekt dekreta o sotsializatsii narodnogo khoziaistva," in *Narodnoe Khoziaistvo,* No. 11, 1918, p. 15.

(9) Trade unions as well as local Soviets are charged with the duty of taking over all industries which were either demoralized or closed [by their former owners?] and putting them to work producing articles of consumption. . . . . Local Soviets and trade unions should under no circumstances wait for orders from above. They must, however, make their activities conform to the general directions of the Supreme Council of National Economy.

(10) Members of the wealthy classes are under obligation to keep all their money in the State Bank. . . . . They will be allowed to draw from 100 to 125 rubles a week. . . . . Attempts to defraud the state will be punishable by the confiscation of the entire property of the guilty person.

(11) Violators of the above law, saboteurs, officials on strike, and speculators will have their property confiscated, will be put in jail, or sent to the front. . . . .

(12) Trade unions and other organizations of the toilers shall proceed at once to organize, in co-operation with the local Soviets . . . . controlling bodies to take charge of enforcing the above decree, ... and to bring before the revolutionary courts all those found guilty of violating it.

The Russian railways suffered from all the ills which afflicted Russian national economy—lack of materials, administrative disorganization, the absence of public order, and the syndicalist tendencies of the railway committees. The situation was further complicated by the fact that Vikzhel, which was attempting not too successfully to administer the railways, favored a democratic coalition rather than the Bolshevik dictatorship. The compromise between Vikzhel and the Bolsheviks noted above broke down under the controversy over the Constituent Assembly. The efforts of the Bolsheviks to deprive Vikzhel of its influence by an appeal to the rank and file of the railwaymen, by the use of force, and finally by the establishment of a rival union added their quota to transportation troubles throughout December and January.[45]

[45] Cf. Etienne Antonelli, *Bolshevist Russia: A Philosophical Survey,* London [1920], pp. 86–88. Piatnitsky, Zimin, and Aronshtam (editors), *Zheleznodorozhniki i revoliutsiia. Sbornik vospominanii i dokumentov o rabote zheleznodorozhnogo raiona Moskov. organ. R.K.P.,* Moscow, 1923, pp. 30–33.

C. Financial Measures

In the confusion in financial matters during the first days of the revolution the Bolsheviks were immediately concerned, first, with securing funds to meet the expenses of government, and, second, with the extension of their control over financial and credit institutions of the country. In the existing political and economic situation very little could be secured from ordinary taxation; the Bolsheviks therefore resorted to methods more immediately productive. The first method was the use of the printing press. From the seizure of power to January 14, 1918, the Soviet Government printed paper money to the extent of 6,544 million rubles. This was at the rate of approximately 3,272 millions per month, as compared with 1,083.6 millions per month by the Provisional Government and 272.6 millions per month by the Imperial Government for the period 1914–1917. The currency issued by the Soviets was in part Romanov notes, in part so-called Duma notes which were issued by the Provisional Government during its early days, and in part Kerensky notes, newly designed just before Kerensky's fall.[46] Other methods of meeting expenses employed especially by local bodies, sometimes self-appointed, were expropriation and special levies on the well-to-do collected at the points of guns.

With regard to financial institutions, these had been described by Lenin before the revolution as one of the parts of the state apparatus that must not be broken up. "It must," he said, "be forcibly freed from subjection to the capitalists; the latter must be cut off, broken, chopped away from it with the threads transmitting their influence; it must be *subjected* to the proletarian Soviets; . . . . The big banks are that 'state apparatus' which we *need* for the realization of Socialism and which we *take ready-made* from capitalism. . . . . This 'state apparatus' . . . . we can 'lay hold of' and 'set in motion' at one stroke, by one decree, for the actual work of book-

[46] Cf. S. Zagorsky, *La République des soviets. Bilan économique,* Paris, 1921, p. 309; P. N. Apostol, "The Composition of the Russian Paper Currency," in *The Russian Economist,* I, 633, 634.

keeping, control, registration, accounting, and summation is here carried out by *employees*, most of whom are themselves in a proletarian or semi-proletarian position."[47] This proved to be somewhat too optimistic. The employees opposed the dictatorship and resisted its application. The Bolsheviks had to use force to gain control of the State Bank in December. Private and semi-private banks were no more amenable to the new order, and they were nationalized and the contents of their safe deposit boxes were expropriated on December 27.

HOW WE GOT CONTROL OF THE STATE BANK

[From an Account by V. Obolensky-Osinsky][48]

The [representatives of the Paris] Commune are generally blamed for not having taken possession of the French National Bank. The Soviet Government did not repeat this mistake. Already during November 1917, the Russian State Bank, which had regulated the money circulation and which had been a pivot of the [entire] banking system [of Russia]—i.e., was the bank of all banks—was seized and made subordinate to the proletarian government.

It so happened that I was to take part in this peculiar episode during the November days. . . . .

The Soviet of People's Commissars insisted upon a complete subordination of the bank and a transfer of ten million rubles which were required for urgent operations. The personnel of the bank, together with its manager, Shipov, refused to recognize the Soviet Government; they insisted upon "autonomy" in their work and refused to transfer the money. This was the argument of these gentlemen: "In conformity with the regulations of the bank, the money of the bank cannot be used for the needs of the state. If the Soviet of People's Commissars needs money it must arrange that a special assignment be officially granted to it; that is, that a special order be issued by the State Treasury transferring ten million rubles from the treasury's account to the account of the Soviet of People's Commissars. Only then can the money be transferred. Such an order of procedure is required by the existing bank regulations and if the latter are not followed, the bank's machinery is bound to collapse."

[47] "Will the Bolsheviks Retain State Power?" in *Toward the Seizure of Power*, II, 29–30.

[48] *Ekonomicheskaia Zhizn*, No. 1, November 6, 1918.

After prolonged negotiations, Comrade Menzhinsky (then Commissar of Finance) made an attempt to seize the money from the bank and to compel the clerks by armed force to issue the ten million rubles. A detachment of sailors and soldiers accompanied by a band and headed by Muravev approached the bank. But as a result of this "parade" the minor employees and the guard of the bank, who had previously been on the side of the Soviet Government, remonstrated, fearing that the bank would be looted. In order to avoid a strike of all bank employees, it was necessary "to withdraw" the detachment.

It was then decided to change our tactics and to try to break up the sabotage from within. Shipov was dismissed and the writer was appointed commissar of the bank with the duties of manager. At the same time and upon the advice of some of the higher officials of the bank (these latter expressed a more or less conciliatory attitude toward the Soviet Government in contrast to the junior clerks, who were absolutely irreconcilable and hostile) a decree was prepared which ordered the bank authorities to transfer ten million rubles from the account of the State Treasury to the Soviet of People's Commissars *without waiting* for an official order regarding this transfer from the Department of the State Treasury. In this way it was hoped to avoid breaking the bank regulations and the accepted order of procedure.

On November 24 or 25 Comrades Menzhinsky, Axelrod (Menzhinsky's assistant), Smirnov, and I came to the bank with this decree. Shipov was not there, but mysterious whispering and exchanges of glances went on among the personnel. Menzhinsky handed over the decree to one of Shipov's assistants. The latter refused to comply with it and, pleading ill health, asked to be dismissed from his post. The second assistant also refused, without giving any ground for his refusal. Yet on the previous day these two men had recommended that we adopt this plan in order to settle the conflict. They were both dismissed on the same day.

Directly after the conversation with Shipov's assistants the directors of the various departments of the bank were called to the office of the [new] manager of the bank and were told to appear the next morning at 10:00 A.M. with their reports. This invitation was received with irony by some, and with apparent misgiving by others. In reply they read a written declaration in which they stated that they continued to refuse to recognize the Soviet Government and insisted upon noninterference in the affairs of the bank and the removal from it of "outsiders."

It was evident that the strike could not be avoided. In the evening we gathered new forces and first of all brought into our "fighting group" Comrade Piatakov, who had just arrived from Kiev. Piatakov was immediately appointed assistant manager of the bank.

When we came to the bank next morning it reminded us of a desert. All officials, except four or five men, were on strike. . . . . The junior clerks, such as accountants, ... came to work but were unable to proceed by themselves. All messengers and caretakers were at their posts also.

Our position was exceedingly difficult. There were people among us who were acquainted with the banking system from books and manuals, we had specialists in the theory of the banking system (Piatakov), and we found later former employees of private banks (Comrade Solovei), but there was not a single man among us who knew the technical procedure . . . . of the Russian State Bank.

We took possession of an enormous machinery, the working of which was practically unknown to us. How the work was carried on, where things were to be found, what were the basic parts of the business machinery—all these were a closed book to us. We entered the enormous corridors of this bank as if we were penetrating a virgin forest. . . . .

We gathered in the center of the huge, empty building, in Shipov's office, and started our preliminary and feverish work. First of all we appointed some of our number to conduct negotiations with the accountants and to find out the particular responsibility of each and every employee. Then we immediately sent messengers to workers' organizations, hospital insurance boards, etc., asking them "to lend" us their bookkeepers and other workers who were acquainted with the mechanism of banking. We also searched for workers among the Soviet and party organizations and found many.

Having acquainted ourselves with the position of the various offices in the bank, its divisions, and the staff of higher officials, we proceeded to seize the most important strategic points and "to capture" the responsible members of the personnel.

Our first task was to get hold of the cash office of the bank and, therefore, our first captives were to be the custodians of the keys of the cash office and the seals of the bank with which the locks were stamped. The first day we did not know even how many repositories there were in the bank, how many keys existed, and who took charge of them. Lenin with his typical capacity for seizing the bull by the horns told us on the first day that as long as we did not get *the keys of the vaults,* we were merely *talking* about the seizure of the bank.

On the second day of the strike we got hold of the custodians of the keys and seals from the main cash office, that is, the manager of the Petersburg Office of the bank, a wicked member of the Black Hundred (Orda); the head cashier, Zheleznov; and the head bookkeeper, Kirov. We brought these men to the bank under a guard of a special detachment of sailors whom we had at our disposal. We questioned them and offered to allow them to resume work, but received a negative answer. We then demanded the surrender of the keys and threatened the men with arrest. The keys were handed over, and on the third day of the strike the cash office was triumphantly opened in presence of its keepers both old and new. In a similar manner the officials who took charge of the main vault of the bank (the vault was even more important than the cash office) were also brought to the bank and made to surrender the keys. Some of these employees consented to work for us and rendered us considerable assistance.

On the same evening the keys to the bank's millions were brought to Smolny and solemnly emptied from a special chamois bag on the table before Lenin. Lenin, however, was not satisfied with our first step and demanded from us *money* and not the keys. . . . .

Under such difficulties we could not even think of issuing money to the Soviet of People's Commissars during the first two or three days. We had to delay this operation all the more because the accountants who worked for us were as yet far from firm in their sympathies with the Soviet Government. Some of them worked simply from the sense of professional duty; they considered the bank to be a necessary public institution, similar to that of water supply, sewerage, and so forth. We could, of course, obtain the money by force (we were now in possession of the keys), but such "expropriation" might have offended the professional feelings of the accountants and caused a strike among them.

However, three days after the opening of the cash office and less than a week after the removal of Shipov and Co., money was issued to the Soviet of People's Commissars.

As far as the formal side of the matter was concerned, we used the same method to which we had resorted when cashing the treasury orders. The decree of the Soviet of People's Commissars was put in the cash box and five million rubles were taken out. As far as *we* were concerned the operation in no way differed from the method applied to the treasury orders. But for the accountants of the main cash office and for the newly appointed "head cashier" our action appeared to be equivalent to expropriation. We had to strain our patience to the utmost in order to make the cashier enter this issue of money in the ledger and to make the accountants actually count the money in a steel room and bring it from there on a little pushcart to the cash office. I remember that during this procedure, which was accompanied by grumbling on the part of the accountants, I lost my head, ran downstairs to get the guard of Semenovsky Regiment ready "to exercise its influence." At last the money was brought [to the cash office]. Comrade Gorbunov, the Secretary of the Soviet of People's Commissars, began to count it.

The time seemed to drag on terribly. There was no guard, and angry murmurs were already heard from the accountants. Piatakov left the room to look for the guard and did not return. Our nerves were overstrained. Suddenly the door flew open and two dozen armed soldiers entered the room and lined up along the table on which the money lay. The murmurs ceased. The soldiers put the money in bags and dragged them to the car. The money was sent to Smolny.

As far as the grumbling of the accountants was concerned we quieted them down on the same day by a tactful move: we asked them to elect two cashiers among them who would take charge in Smolny of the actual distribution of this money. We said that in this way the accountants would be in a position to see for themselves that the money was being spent on public needs and was not distributed [among the Soviet workers] twenty-five rubles each, as the rumors said. . . . .

NATIONALIZATION OF BANKS

[Decree of the Central Executive Committee, December 27, 1917][49]

In the interests of a proper organization of the national economy, a thorough eradication of bank speculation and a complete emancipation of the toiling masses from exploitation by the banking capitalists, and in order to found a single unified State Bank for the Russian Republic which shall serve the interests of the people and the poorest classes, the Central Executive Committee decrees that:

1. Banking is hereby declared a state monopoly.
2. All existing private joint-stock banks and other banking houses are to become a part of the State Bank.
3. Assets and liabilities of establishments in the process of liquidation will be assumed by the State Bank.
4. The manner of the amalgamation of private banks with the State Bank will be determined by a special decree.
5. The temporary management of private banks is intrusted to the Council of the State Bank.
6. The interests of small depositors will be fully protected.

[49] *S.U.R.*, 1917, No. 10, pp. 149–50. M. P. Price listened to the debate in the Central Executive Committee on the Sovnarkom's project of nationalization. Avilov of the United Internationalists insisted that the decree was unnecessary, as the private banks would be bankrupt as soon as they had spent the sums they had drawn from the State Bank on the eve of the revolution. Why, therefore, all this talk about occupying the banks with troops; why this "Red Guard nationalization"? Apparently the Bolsheviks feared that foreign embassies might come to the aid of the banks and prolong their life, and their view prevailed. (*My Reminiscences of the Russian Revolution,* London [1921], pp. 209–11.)

SEARCH OF SAFE DEPOSIT BOXES

[Decree of the Central Executive Committee, December 27, 1917][50]

1. All moneys kept in safe deposit boxes should be transferred to the current account of the holders.

Note: Gold in coin or bullion is to be confiscated and handed over to the State Gold Reserve.

2. All holders of safe deposit boxes are under obligation to appear at the bank upon notice, bringing the keys to their safe deposit boxes, and to be present while their boxes are searched.

3. All holders of safe deposit boxes who fail to appear after three days' notice will be considered as having maliciously declined to comply with the law of search.

4. Safe deposit boxes owned by persons who maliciously decline to comply with the law will be opened by investigating commissions appointed by the Commissar of the State Bank; all property contained in those vaults will be confiscated and declared the property of the people.[51]

Opening the Boxes[52]

At the time of the opening and the sequestration, in the presence of the holders, of safe deposit boxes, in Petersburg in the spring of 1918, dramatic scenes often occurred.

Most of the holders appeared composedly with their keys allowing their safe deposit boxes to be opened and looked on with resignation at the confiscation of their property. Some did not utter a word; some excitedly endeavored to prove to the officials that this or that item was not subject to confiscation; others, amid tears, attempted to convince them that the valuables in the safe deposit boxes constituted all their property, without which they must starve. The officials themselves had

[50] *S.U.R.*, 1917, No. 10, p. 150.

[51] Up till July 1, 1918, a total of 35,493 safe deposit boxes had been searched in the Moscow banks, yielding the following:

Paper money	64,649,091 rubles
Gold in Russian coin	401,662 rubles
Gold in bullion	13 puds, 8 funts, 46 zolotniks
Silver in Russian coin	251,709 rubles
Silver in bullion	25 funts
Platinum in coins	2,241 rubles
Platinum in bullion	2 funts, 57 zolotniks, 70 dolias
State bonds	307,679,902 rubles
Private bonds	256,453,861 rubles

In addition there was a considerable sum of foreign money. *Izvestiia,* No. 158, July 27, 1918, p. 6.

[52] M. J. Larsons, *Im Sowjet-Labyrinth,* Berlin, 1931, pp. 61–66.

a difficult position; they could not show any clemency and had to adhere strictly to their instructions. Even the smallest amount of foreign currency was confiscated as hoarded property.

Russian currency was also taken from the safe deposit boxes, although, strictly speaking, it was not confiscated but credited to the bank account of the owner of the safe deposit box. If he did not have an account, one was opened in his name. From this account he could withdraw monthly the already insignificant amount of one thousand rubles. . . . .

Not all the rich and well-to-do people accepted the confiscation of their safe deposits without protest. . . . . In the spring of 1918 agents called on wealthy Petersburg citizens whose safe deposit boxes were suspected of containing especially great riches and offered to deliver the contents of the boxes safely into their hands for a remuneration of 100,000 Tsar's rubles (then about 40,000 marks). The holder had only to give his consent and deliver the key of his box to the agent. . . . .

The fact is that some people, in spite of all measures to the contrary, actually recovered the contents of their safe deposit boxes in this manner. It is also a fact, however, that some bank employees employed in the safe deposit department were shot as a result of these underhand practices.

I myself had a safe deposit box in a Petersburg bank in which in addition to my private documents I had a few valuables which belonged to my relatives. These valuables were wrapped in small individual packages each marked with the name of the owner.

At the beginning of 1918 there appeared in the Petrograd papers a proclamation to the effect that owners of safes whose family names began with such and such a letter were to appear with their keys on an appointed day at the bank. The letter came at the end of February and I appeared on that particular day at the bank with my key. Tables were set up in the vault at which employees were seated. All around stood the safe deposit boxholders whose boxes were to be opened.

The plan followed was to remove all valuables (precious metals in bars, objects of platinum, gold, silver, precious stones, pearls, foreign currency, etc.), which were subject to confiscation for the welfare of the state, and to make it impossible for the owner of any particular object later to identify his property. Therefore, all of the rings, brooches, and other jewelry which were taken from the boxes were heaped in one pile and all the individual unset precious stones in another. This method was also applied in the case of remaining valuables. In a case such as mine, where the valuables were wrapped up in packages, the wrappers were torn open and the particular object was tossed on the pile. . . . .

DISCONTINUANCE OF INTEREST AND DIVIDEND PAYMENTS

[Decree of the Sovnarkom, January 11, 1918][53]

1. Until the issuing of special rulings concerning the nationalization of industry all payments of interest on investments and dividends on shares will be discontinued.

2. All transactions in bonds are prohibited.

3. Those violating rule 2 of this decree will be criminally liable and their property will be confiscated.

D. Food Control and Distribution

Food supply for the capitals, for other industrial centers, and for the army was one of the most serious of the many acute problems of these days. It was important for the Bolsheviks, who had been very critical of the food policy of their predecessors in power, to prevent hunger among the masses upon whom they depended for support, and it was no less important for them to gain control of the food-distributing organizations in order to compel recalcitrant state employees and others to bow to the dictatorship. "The grain monopoly, the bread cards, universal labour service become, in the hands of the proletarian state, in the hands of the all-powerful Soviets, the most powerful means for accounting and control, a means which, extended to the capitalists and *the rich in general,* being applied to them by the *workers,* will give a power unheard-of in history for 'setting in motion' the state apparatus, for overcoming the resistance of the capitalists, for subjecting them to the proletarian state."[54]

It took some time, however, for Lenin's proposal actually to be realized. The first step of the Soviet Government in that field was to transfer food control to the municipal government. Later the Bolsheviks undertook to transfer the work of food supply to their own institutions attached to the Soviets of Workers' and Soldiers' Deputies.

[53] *Obzor finansovogo zakonodatelstva, 1917–1921 g.g.,* Petrograd, 1921, p. 15.

[54] Lenin, "Will the Bolsheviks Retain State Power?" in *Toward the Seizure of Power,* II, 32.

TRANSFER OF FOOD CONTROL TO MUNICIPALITIES

[Decree of the Sovnarkom, November 10, 1917][55]

1. All food supplies arriving at the city, including the supplies addressed to the Army Food Supply Service, the Red Cross, and other individuals and institutions which hitherto had the right to receive and distribute supplies independently of the city—are now placed in the charge of the city government for distribution by the food-supply organization attached to the city government.

2. All individuals and institutions which hitherto had a right to receive and distribute supplies independently of the city government are under obligation to place their distribution machinery at the disposal of the city government . . . . and take orders from the city government. . . . .

Note 1: In Petrograd and Moscow, all transit trade and all shipments of supplies to the front are to be controlled by the city government.

Note 2: In Petrograd the Central Executive Committee . . . . has a right to receive at its address at Smolny Institute the amount of supplies which the government considers necessary to satisfy the needs of specially arriving army units and other extraordinary requirements.

3. All forms of double rations or increased rations are prohibited, with the exception of those granted by the city government. . . . .

4. The city government has a right . . . . to establish its supervision and control over all or some of the commercial and industrial enterprises, such as stores, restaurants, flour mills, etc. . . . . It has a right to sequester within the city limits every commercial and industrial enterprise connected with food supply. . . . .

5. The city government has a right to confiscate, requisition, and sequester all private premises which it finds necessary in order to open supply stores or for any other need connected with the business of food supply. This right applies also to privately owned products, objects, instruments, means of transport, storehouses, etc. . . . .

6. The city has a right to conscript university students and high-school seniors to work in the food-supply organization. . . . .

7. The city government has a right to force all inhabitants of a certain house or of a group of houses to form a commune and get their supplies jointly. . . . .

8. The city government has a right to establish a general or partial centralization of cooking . . . . so that hot meals will either be procured in public dining-halls or will be sent to apartments.

[55] *S.U.R.*, 1917, No. 1, pp. 6–7.

9. The resolutions of this decree relative to food products . . . . apply also to goods of prime necessity.

10. . . . . .

11. Violators of this decree are liable to imprisonment for one year and . . . . to the confiscation of their property. . . . .

12. This decree applies to cities with a population of not less than ten thousand.

13. The decree goes into force by telegraph.

VLADIMIR ULIANOV (LENIN)
President of the Sovnarkom

FOOD SHORTAGE AT THE FRONT

[Appeal of the 12th Army, November 21, 1917][56]

The 12th Army asks that food and fodder be sent to it at once. It has not a pound of flour, not a pound of oats. During the last few days the soldiers have been living on hard-tack, their last food reserve. When that is gone the army will leave the front and go in search of food. There is no force that can stop it!

Citizens! The hungry millions of soldiers will quit the front, and sweep the country clean. Both the army and the country will perish!

Give us bread!

EXECUTIVE COMMITTEE OF THE SOVIET OF
SOLDIER'S DEPUTIES OF THE 12TH ARMY

FOOD SITUATION IN PETROGRAD

[Meeting of the Central Executive Committee, November 22, 1917, Extract][57]

. . . . Yakubov reported that the food situation in the capital was extremely serious. The city was receiving 12,000 puds of bread daily, while 48,000 puds were needed to provide one-fourth of a pound to a person. Petrograd was in danger of soon being without bread. A similar calamity confronted the Moscow, Vladimir, Kostroma, Smolensk, and other gubernias. The situation at the front was no better. The Northern front had food for two days only. The measures which were being taken to unload the freight in Petrograd might help slightly. It might be possible to supply potatoes in place of bread. . . . .

[56] *Delo Naroda,* No. 207, November 25, 1917, p. 3.

[57] *Ibid.,* No. 205, November 23, 1917, p. 3.

Agitators had been sent into the bread [-producing] gubernias but . . . . such measures would not solve the food problem. . . . . The food commission was considering a law to confiscate the grain of the large proprietors. . . . . "We cannot buy the grain, because we have no money and because it takes time. The quickest way would be to confiscate it." . . . . The speaker stated that the employees of the Ministry of Food did not recognize the new government. It was necessary to make use of the old food-supply organization, for which the co-operation of the employees was necessary. The other alternative was to get new personnel, but that was impossible because they would not possess the information which the ministry [of food] has accumulated.

Lunacharsky suggested the formation of a new all-national organ, made up of representatives of all parties, to deal with the food question. . . . .

He was followed by other speakers who laid the blame on the employees. Some of the speakers suggested that persuasion be used; others advocated stronger measures. . . . .

THE SOVIET GOVERNMENT AND THE FOOD CRISIS

[Order of the Sovnarkom, November 24, 1917][58]

To All Army Organizations, Military Revolutionary Committees, All Soldiers at the Front:

The Government of the Soviet of People's Commissars is at present occupied with two questions: food for the army and an immediate armistice.

There is no shortage of food in the country. The landowners, kulaks, and merchants have hidden away large quantities of food. The higher officials of state and employees of railways and banks are helping the bourgeoisie against the soldiers, workers, and peasants. The counter-revolutionists would rather starve the soldier to death than give up the government to the people and the land to the peasant and agree to an immediate peace. The directors of the banks refuse to grant the Soviet Government money with which to secure food. The Soviet of People's Commissars has taken very energetic measures. Commissars of the Soviet, assisted by sailors, soldiers, and Red Guards, are requisitioning food reserves in all parts of the country and sending them to the front. A merciless war has been declared on all speculators, robbers, grafters, and counter-revolutionary officials who interfere with the work of food collecting. They are being arrested and will be locked up in the Kronstadt prison. Soldiers at the front! The Soviet Government is doing

[58] *S.U.R.*, 1917, No. 3, pp. 33–34. Trotsky is the author of this order.

everything possible to provide you with food and hopes to be able in a few days to supply you with your needs. . . . .

V. LENIN
President of the Soviet of People's Commissars

L. TROTSKY
Commissar of Foreign Affairs

[Order of the Sovnarkom, November 28, 1917][59]

Disorganization of the food supply, born of war and inefficiency, is being rendered acute in the highest degree by speculators, marauders, and their accomplices on railways and steamships, in transport agencies, and in other places. In circumstances of the greatest popular calamity these criminal robbers, for the sake of personal profit, gamble with the health and the lives of millions of soldiers and workers.

Such a situation cannot be tolerated for another day.

The Soviet of People's Commissars advises the Military Revolutionary Committee to take the most rigorous steps to eradicate speculation, sabotage, concealment of food supplies, wilful delaying of freight, etc.

All persons guilty of such acts are liable under the special rulings of the Military Revolutionary Committee, *to immediate arrest and detention in the prisons of Kronstadt* until their delivery to the Military Revolutionary courts of law.

All people's organizations must be called upon to combat the food supply plunderers.

V. ULIANOV (LENIN)
President of the Soviet of People's Commissars

BAGMEN

Vikzhel has received news from Cherkassy . . . . that certain individuals who travel fourth class are buying large quantities of rice and flour. They fill the cars so full that it is difficult to determine how much they have.

At the Sukhochov Station armed soldiers load cars with bread and force the railwaymen to take them to places indicated by the soldiers. Similar stories of the doings of speculators and soldiers come from Siberia. . . . .[60]

. . . . At the present moment we are in great danger of shortly being without food. The bread-producing regions will soon be exporting their

[59] *S.U.R.*, 1917, No. 3, p. 38.

[60] *Nash Vek,* No. 4, December 16, 1917, p. 4.

products to Germany through the front. Germany will pay with manufactured goods, of which the peasants are in great need.

The so-called "bagmen"[61] also contribute to a possible famine. It is reported that in Western Siberia these bagmen are buying about thirty thousand puds of grain a day. They pay twenty or more rubles a pud as against five rubles, which is the fixed price. These bagmen fill all the passenger trains and are rather rough with both passengers and railway employees.[62]

ORGANIZATION OF LOCAL FOOD COMMISSIONS

[Decree of the Central Executive Committee, January 6, 1918][63]

In order to harmonize all the measures taken in the work of food supply, and in order to create a single . . . . supply organization at Petrograd, an All-Russian Food Committee has been organized, which includes representatives of the All-Russian Army Food Commission, of the First All-Russian Navy Congress, and of the congress of organizations working for the supply of the front.

The All-Russian Food Committee maintains close contact with the Soviet of People's Commissars, standing as it does on the platform of the Second All-Russian Congress of Soviets . . . . and being in full accord with the principle that . . . . "the reorganization of the supply service can yield positive results only on the condition that the state . . . . monopolizes all the products of both urban . . . . and rural economy; that it establishes regular exchange of goods between towns and villages, as well as Workers' Control over production; and that the supply service must be democratized and intrusted to the poorest strata of the population, eliminating those bourgeois groups which are interested in raising the price of articles of prime necessity." The All-Russian Food Committee advises all Soviets . . . . immediately to begin forming food commissions attached to the Soviets and to secure the co-operation in them of all active forces of the revolutionary democracy. These commissions shall at once assume control over local food organizations. . . . . When full unity in the work of [these] commissions . . . . and the existing food organizations has been established, all food-supply organs . . . . are to be placed under the control of the Soviets, which, in turn, must bring their own work of food supply into harmony with

[61] People carrying bags containing food which had been bought from the peasants to be sold at high price.

[62] *Delo Naroda*, No. 226, December 20, 1917, p. 3.

[63] *S.U.R.*, 1918, No. 12, p. 190.

the [activities] of the central food organs. Up to the time of their final liquidation, all supply organizations must submit entirely to the directions of the local Soviets. . . . .

Immediately after forming a food commission you are requested to submit to the All-Russian Food Committee . . . . exact data on the membership of the commission . . . . stating the methods by which the business of food supply can best be transferred to the Soviets. . . . .

In a very short time the All-Russian Food Committee will call a congress of all democratic organizations and prominent food-supply workers who are entirely devoted to the interests of the . . . . revolution.

YA. SVERDLOV
Chairman of the Central Executive Committee

A. SCHLICHTER
People's Commissar of Food

E. AGRICULTURE AND THE LAND PROBLEM

The first applications of the dictatorship to agriculture were the land decree of November 8 and the instructions to the peasants adopted by the Second Congress of Soviets a few hours after the capture of the Winter Palace. These measures were, it is true, simply appropriated by the Bolsheviks from the Socialist-Revolutionists, but they were directly in line with the Bolshevik tactics of destroying the political and economic power of the landowners and of winning over or at least neutralizing the peasants. These measures established what might be termed "peasant control" of agriculture. Peasant control of agriculture, however, was far less amenable to the dictatorship than workers' control of industry, for participating in the former were the kulaks (the well-to-do) and the "middle" peasants, who were intense individualists, hostile to any kind of socialization or regulation which affected their property. For the time being, as the following pages show, the Bolsheviks did not attempt to challenge this opposition by setting up a centralized control as in industry. The caution with which they proceeded in regard to the peasants is illustrated by the abandonment of the project to levy a tax in kind.

THE ORGANIZATION OF VOLOST LAND COMMITTEES

[Decree of the Sovnarkom, November 16, 1917][64]

1. To bring about a speedy transfer of the land . . . . to the people these present regulations, regarding the functioning of the volost land committees, as approved by the All-Russian Congress of Soviets of Workers', Soldiers', and Peasants' Deputies of July 6, 1917, shall be enforced until such a time as the Constituent Assembly makes final rulings on all details of the land reform.

2. The present law will become effective by telegraph. It is understood that the term volost refers to every territorial unit equal in size to that of a volost. . . . .

3. The formation of land committees in every volost is compulsory. In those places where the law of small zemstvo units is not yet in force, the land committees will be organized as self-governing bodies on the principle of direct, equal, and secret universal suffrage. In those places where the zemstvo units are already functioning . . . . the land committee will be organized in connection with the zemstvo. . . . .

4. Where volost zemstvos are not in existence the number of members of the land committee will be determined by the inhabitants themselves. Where zemstvos do exist the local population has the right to include in the land committee representatives from different villages, in addition to members provided by law. . . . .

5. All expenses in connection with the organization and administration of the land committees will be borne by the state.

6. Arbitration boards will be organized within the volost land committees to settle all disputed questions. . . . .

7. The volost land committees are charged with the rapid and definitive liquidation of all vestiges of serfdom preserved in the village. They must abolish all forms of bondage, such as menial service, payments in kind, etc.

8. In order that there may be more rational management of the land fund, the land committee will collect all documentary data concerning the amount of land within the boundaries of the volost . . . . showing how much there is of each kind—meadow, forest, pasture, and arable land, etc.

9. The volost land committee will make a survey of the forests within the boundaries of the volost and lay down, with the assistance of the state forester, plans for felling.

The volost land committee will give priority to supplying the national needs in fuel and building material . . . . in accordance with the orders received from a special fuel commission. . . . .

[64] *Izvestiia,* No. 215, November 16, 1917, p. 4; *S.U.R.,* 1917, No. 2, pp. 23–25.

17. The volost land committee will fix the area of land to be cultivated, distributing it between the different villages and hamlets. It will see to it that the land is properly cultivated . . . . and equitably distributed among the farmers.

18. The volost land committee will fix the rentals for fields, meadows, and pastures, determining the methods by which such rentals are to be collected. . . . .

20. The volost land committee will take complete charge of carrying through the land reform within its locality. It will determine to what extent the available land fund is capable of satisfying local needs, what branches of agriculture stand in greatest need of additional land, what order is to be observed in distributing the land among those having little or no land, newcomers, etc.

21. The volost land committee will take charge of the scientifically cultivated farms and, in agreement with the uezd and gubernia land committees, will fix the area of land to be allowed to them. . . . . It will establish those branches of rural economy that are dictated by the necessities of the state and society as a whole (breeding stations, dairies, sugar-beet plantations, vineyards, etc.).

22. The volost land committee will fix the laboring wage for day and contract workers, ... and will supervise the carrying out of the terms of employment. . . . .

24. The activities of the volost land committees should be co-ordinated with those of the uezd and the gubernia land committees. All disagreements between different volosts as well as volost land committees should be settled by the uezd land committee.[65]

In the name of the Russian Republic,

V. Miliutin
The People's Commissar of Agriculture

INSTRUCTIONS TO MESSENGERS SENT TO THE PROVINCES

[Decree of the Sovnarkom, November 16, 1917][66]

1. On arriving at the gubernia to which he is sent, the messenger should call a meeting of the [local] Executive Committee of the Soviet of Workers', Soldiers', and Peasants' Deputies, explain to them the

[65] This decree was supplemented on December 26, 1917, by a new decree transforming the land committees into a land parliament elected by universal secret and direct suffrage, and empowering the gubernia congresses of these committees "to discuss and supplement the legislative acts of the central government, adapting them to local conditions." (*S.D.*, pp. 465–70.)

[66] *Izvestiia*, No. 215, November 16, 1917, p. 4.

nature of the land decree and propose that a meeting of the uezd and gubernia Soviets of Workers', Soldiers', and Peasants' Deputies be called.

2. He should make inquiries as to the land situation in the gubernia. (*a*) Has the land of the large proprietors been taken over; where and in what uezd; and has it been recorded? (*b*) Who has charge of these lands—the land committees or the large proprietors? (*c*) What has been done with the stock and machinery?

3. Have the peasants seeded more [ground] than usual?

4. What proportion of the food that it is called upon to send is the gubernia actually sending?

5. Make it clear that having received land the peasants must hasten to send food to the city, for only in that way will famine be avoided.

6. What measures are being taken or are about to be taken to hand over the land of the large proprietors to the land committees and the Soviets of Workers', Soldiers', and Peasants' Deputies?

7. It is desirable that the estates which are well improved and plentifully supplied with tools should be handed over to the Soviet of Farm-Hands' Deputies to be worked under the supervision of agronomists.

V. ULIANOV (LENIN), President
V. MILIUTIN, People's Commissar of Agriculture

LENIN TO THE PEASANTS

[A Letter, November 18, 1917][67]

In reply to many questions of the peasants it should be said that from now on the government is wholly in the hands of the Soviets of Workers', Soldiers', and Peasants' Deputies. The workers' revolution has triumphed in Petrograd and Moscow, and it will triumph everywhere in Russia. The Workers' and Peasants' Government works to achieve the union of the peasant masses, the poorest peasants, and the majority of the peasants with the workers against the landholders and capitalists.

Therefore, the Soviets of Peasants' Deputies, first in the uezd and then in the gubernia, are from now on and until the meeting of the Constituent Assembly the authorized organs of government. The Second All-Russian Congress of Soviets has done away with private ownership of land by the landlords. The law has already been issued by the present Provisional Workers' and Peasants' Government. In accordance with this law all the land of the landlords now goes wholly

[67] *Izvestiia*, No. 219, November 21, 1917, p. 4.

to the Soviets of Peasants' Deputies. The Volost Land Committees should take charge of this land, and keep a strict account of it, making sure that no harm comes to the property of the former landlord, which from now on is the people's property and is to be guarded by them. All the orders of the Volost Land Committees when issued in agreement with the Uezd Soviet of Peasants' Deputies and in accordance with the decrees of the revolutionary government are legal and are to be carried out unconditionally and immediately.

The government of the workers and peasants which has been selected by the Second All-Russian Congress of Soviets is known as the Soviet of People's Commissars.

The Soviet of People's Commissars calls on the peasants themselves to take local government into their own hands. The workers are pledged to the support of the peasants in every possible way. They will speed up the production of machinery and tools and request the peasants' help in the supply of food.

V. ULIANOV (LENIN)
President of the Sovnarkom

AGRICULTURAL TOOLS AND MACHINERY DECLARED A STATE MONOPOLY

[Decree of the Sovnarkom, December 13, 1917][68]

1. In order to provide villages with the necessary farming implements, all machinery and tools, whether already made or in the process of manufacture or importation from abroad, are declared to be a state monopoly from this time forth.

2. The distribution of machinery and tools is to be carried out in accordance with the rules to be issued separately through the Soviet organs, land committees, and other democratic organizations.

V. ULIANOV (LENIN)
President of the Sovnarkom

A. SCHLICHTER
People's Commissar of Food

HOW THE LAND DECREE WAS CARRIED OUT

[Statement by Kolegaev, Commissar of Agriculture][69]

The Land Decree[70] is very far from being a systematically devised law. It is rather of the nature of a battle cry intended to appeal to the

[68] *S.D.*, p. 244. [69] *Novaia Zhizn*, No. 214, January 13, 1918, p. 2.

[70] Passed by the Second All-Russian Congress of Soviets.

masses, and one has to admit that as a result of that battle cry the transfer of land to the peasants was accomplished in a manner that was anything but orderly and painless. . . . . There is this to be said, however. The landlords' system of agriculture is no longer in existence. . . . . All lands of the former landlords are now in the hands of the peasants. Their estates as well as the agricultural implements have passed to the peasants so completely that frequently their very houses were torn apart and the timber divided among the peasants. . . . . In general the seizure of land was accompanied with excesses . . . . but the seizure itself is an accomplished fact. To take back the land from the peasants is impossible under any condition.

FIRST ATTEMPTS TO TAX THE PEASANTRY

[Recollections of Larin][71]

[When I brought forward] a . . . . program for . . . . taxation in general, it was my intention partially to shift the burden of state expenditures to the shoulders of the peasants. . . . . In December [1917] the Sovnarkom adopted my project for a progressive agricultural tax to be collected in kind (grain, ... etc.). Furthermore, arrangements were made . . . . that 40 per cent of the crops harvested were to be turned over to the volost Soviets in order to meet local needs. . . . . The papers had already published the Sovnarkom's decisions when the peasant section of the Central Executive Committee assembled and flatly refused to accept the law. If I am not mistaken this was the only . . . . instance when a law approved by the Sovnarkom failed of passage in the Central Executive Committee. The class character of that episode is very significant.

[71] Yu. Larin, "U kolybeli," *Narodnoe Khoziaistvo,* No. 11, November 1918, p. 21.

CHAPTER VII

THE CONSTITUENT ASSEMBLY

In the days before the November uprising the Bolsheviks launched many attacks against the Provisional Government for its delay in calling a Constituent Assembly. They recognized, as did the other parties, socialist and bourgeois, the wide popularity of this project of a national democratic parliament to settle not only the form of government but also the many political and social problems of which the revolution was an expression. To many liberals and socialists the Assembly would be the authoritative expression of the national will, the consummation, in a sense, of the revolution. But to the Bolsheviks it was something quite different, for they were looking beyond this organ of democracy to the proletarian dictatorship conforming to orthodox Marxian precepts. They advocated the Assembly, therefore, largely as a matter of tactics. It provided additional ammunition with which to attack the Provisional Government; it was a popular issue to support; and, according to Bolshevik theory, it represented an advance, though inadequate, over the Provisional Government and its pre-parliaments and democratic congresses. On this basis the Bolsheviks made what capital they could of this popular project, arguing that the seizure of power by the Soviets was the best way to insure the meeting of the Constituent Assembly. But after the Bolshevik seizure of power and the formation of a Soviet government with the Bolsheviks in control the tactical situation was radically altered. The Constituent Assembly could no longer be used by the Bolsheviks against their opponents; on the contrary, it became the rallying cry of those who aimed to end the dictatorship.

The Bolsheviks were not agreed as to when the elections

should be held. According to Trotsky,[1] immediately after the November Revolution Lenin declared that the elections must be postponed, the voting age lowered to eighteen years, the electoral lists revised, and the Cadets and Kornilov supporters outlawed. Others said postponement would not do, especially since the Bolsheviks had so often reproached the Provisional Government for that very thing. Lenin answered that this was folly—the situation had changed; from the point of view of Soviet power and especially in view of the character of the old election lists, the election would be a step backward, particularly if the Assembly were controlled by Cadets, Mensheviks, and Socialist-Revolutionists. Sverdlov and others who were opposed to postponement replied that the Bolsheviks were still too weak to ignore the popular demand for the Assembly, and that the country was ignorant of the Soviet power, which, moreover, would be further weakened if the Assembly were postponed. When, however, it was decided to hold the elections, Lenin turned his attention to preparing for the meeting of the Assembly.

Stalin does not subscribe to Trotsky's interpretation of Lenin's attitude. According to Stalin, Lenin thought that in order to compromise the idea of the Constituent Assembly with the masses, in order to show them its true counter-revolutionary nature and the need for its dissolution, it was necessary to have the Assembly actually meet. A temporary combination of Soviet Republic and Constituent Assembly was merely a way of doing away with the Assembly. Stalin quotes his Lenin text, which justifies Bolshevik participation in a bourgeois-democratic parliament on the ground that such participation "makes it easier for the proletariat to prove to the backward masses why such parliaments deserve to be broken up, facilitates this break-up, and drives another nail into the coffin of bourgeois parliamentarism."[2] In any

[1] Trotsky, *Lenin,* pp. 119–20.

[2] Stalin, *Leninism,* New York, 2 vols., 1928–1933, I, 207–209. In another place in the same book (p. 153) Stalin says that the original decision of the Bolsheviks to participate in the Constituent Assembly was a mistake in tactics which was rectified when the Bolsheviks finally withdrew from the Assembly.

event the Bolsheviks permitted the elections to be held on November 25, but at the same time prepared to maintain their dictatorship regardless of the outcome of the elections and the sentiment of the delegates.

On December 11, the day on which the Constituent Assembly was to open, the parties opposing the Bolsheviks held a demonstration and about fifty of the elected representatives who had reached the capital held an unofficial meeting in the face of Bolshevik opposition. From this date until January 18, when the Assembly actually met, both sides energetically prepared for the test of strength. The Bolsheviks strengthened their hold on the government machinery, organized the Cheka to fight counter-revolution and sabotage (December 20), and summoned their followers to defend the workers' and peasants' government against the challenge of the Constituent Assembly. The opponents of the Bolsheviks, possessing a majority of the elected representatives to the Assembly, strove to rally public opinion to uphold the expressed will of the nation against the Bolshevik dictatorship. The Assembly finally met on January 18 and on the following day was dissolved by the Bolsheviks. Three days later the Third Congress of Soviets began sessions which lasted until January 31, the last three days being joint sessions with the Third Congress of Peasants' Deputies. The Congress ratified the acts of the Sovnarkom, passed the decree on land socialization, and adopted a provisional constitution for the federation of Soviet republics.

During the period covered by this chapter, the peace negotiations at Brest were in progress, Red troops were engaged with the Whites in the Don region and with the nationalists in the Ukraine, and in Finland the socialists set up a revolutionary government in Helsingfors.

A. The Elections

The weeks before the elections resounded with charges and counter-charges as to the attitudes of the parties toward the Assembly and with the promises of the rival tickets.

Shortly after the returns began to come in the Bolsheviks put through the Central Executive Committee a resolution that the Congress of Soviets had the right to call for re-elections, a threat which was not carried out. At about the same time, the Sovnarkom locked up temporarily the electoral commission appointed by the Provisional Government and appointed Uritsky, a Bolshevik, in charge of the verification of mandates.

ELECTIONS FOR THE CONSTITUENT ASSEMBLY

[Decree of the Sovnarkom, November 9, 1917][3]

In the name of the Government of the Republic, chosen by the All-Russian Congress of Workers' and Soldiers' Deputies with the participation of the Peasants' Deputies, the Soviet of People's Commissars decrees:

1. Elections to the Constituent Assembly shall be held on the day set, November 25.

2. All election committees, institutions of local self-government, Soviets of Workers', Soldiers', and Peasants' Deputies, and soldiers' organizations at the front should make every effort to insure free and legal elections. . . . .

VLADIMIR ULIANOV (LENIN)
President of the Sovnarkom

CONTROVERSY OVER THE ELECTIONS

"THEY LIE"

[From an Editorial in *Izvestiia*][4]

They lie [the papers, *Delo Naroda* and *Rabochaia Gazeta*] in saying that the seizure of the government by the Bolsheviks means the break-up of the Constituent Assembly. . . . . The Second Congress of Soviets of Workers', Peasants,' and Soldiers' Deputies has declared that the new government will proceed at once with the elections and will give all parties the right of electioneering. The legality of elections can be guaranteed only by a democratic government and not by one made up of Cadets, Kornilovists, and compromisers.

[3] *Izvestiia,* No. 209, November 10, 1917, p. 2.

[4] No. 209, November 10, 1917, p. 7.

Questions for Lenin to Answer

[Editorial in *Delo Naroda*][5]

Mr. Ulianov [*Lenin*]*!*

You signed a decree of the Soviet of People's Commissars in regard to the summoning of the Constituent Assembly on time. In this document all citizens are urged to do everything in their power to have a free and legal election on November 25. At the same time Mr. Podvoisky has declared Petrograd and its suburbs in a state of siege and has forbidden all meetings and assemblies.[6] You closed almost all the newspapers in Petrograd, seized the printing presses, introduced a censorship, and illegally arrested a number of citizens. Freedom of the press, of speech, of assembly, and personal rights which the Russian people has won with its blood, you swept away by force.

In the name of the revolution and the interests of the nation we ask you these questions: Is it not a contradiction to call for a free and legal election to the Constituent Assembly and at the same time to suppress personal freedom as well as the freedom of the press and of assembly?

By what right have you, who call yourself a Socialist, violated the law of free elections which had been prepared by the bourgeois ministers? Finally, do you not think that the system of terror which you have introduced makes any kind of election impossible?

We demand an official and clear answer to these questions, and if you should refuse to give it, we have the right to denounce the whole "Soviet of People's Commissars" . . . . as an organization aiming to break up the Constituent Assembly.

Who Breaks up the Constituent Assembly?

[From an Editorial in *Izvestiia*][7]

The Constituent Assembly is master of the Russian land. . . . . It will right the wrong against the millions of peasants and give them the land of the large landowners, not only in order to improve the condition of the peasant but also to increase the productivity of his labor.

The Constituent Assembly will have to protect the laboring classes from capitalistic exploitation by limiting the profits of the capitalists.

[5] No. 195, November 13, 1917, p. 1.

[6] "To all citizens of Petrograd: Petrograd and its suburbs are declared in a state of siege. Until special notice all gatherings and meetings in the streets are forbidden. Street-car service goes on without obstruction. N. Podvoisky, Chairman of the Military Revolutionary Committee." *Izvestiia,* No. 210, November 11, 1917, p. 2.

[7] No. 214, November 15, 1917, p. 2.

It will have to solve the financial problems left by three years of war which cost the people tremendous sums in the form of war profits which fell into the pockets . . . . of "workers" for the defense. . . . .

These questions will be brought before the Constituent . . . . Assembly. And not only these! . . . . There will be in addition the question of consolidating the economic power of . . . . workers, soldiers, and peasants and giving them the right to govern the country. . . . .

On March 15 the Miliukov-Guchkov Provisional Government declared that it would make immediate preparations for calling the Constituent Assembly. On March 26 it came out with an official statement that the Constituent Assembly would meet in Petrograd "not later than the middle of the summer," that is to say, in July. Notwithstanding these promises, it was not until June 7 that the first conference to prepare a law on elections took place. For three precious months not a thing was done to prepare for the elections. This is not all.

The Congress of Soviets of Workers' and Soldiers' Deputies that took place in June demanded an early calling of the Constituent Assembly. Yielding to this pressure the Provisional Government (this time without Miliukov and Guchkov) set September 30 as the date for the elections and October 13 as the day for the meeting of the Constituent Assembly. But even this promise was not kept. The backstairs politics of the bourgeoisie acted as a brake, and it was left for the third coalition government to change the time once more. In September the Central Executive Committee . . . . demanded that the elections to the Constituent Assembly should be held on November 11, but the Cadets insisted on a later date. The Provisional Government decided on November 25 as the date for the election and December 11 as the day for the meeting [of the Constituent Assembly].

Who interferes with the calling of the Constituent Assembly? The Bolsheviks or the Cadets . . . .? The Cadets, of course. . . . .

Proclamation on the Elections[8]

[November 20, 1917]

The All-Russian Commission on Elections having heard reports from its members on the preparations for the elections has come to the conclusion that the sad events which have taken place recently in Petrograd, Moscow, and other cities have had a demoralizing effect on the elections.

In the first place, the seizure of power by force has disorganized communications to such an extent that many parts of Russia have not the paper and envelopes [with which] to carry out the election accord-

[8] *Delo Naroda,* No. 204, November 22, 1917, p. 2.

ing to law. There is also delay in the printing of ballots, while some of the printed ballots have apparently been destroyed.

Of still greater moment is . . . . the spread of anarchy and terror which recent events have brought to certain parts of Russia. The elections will inevitably take place in an atmosphere charged with civil war. . . . .

On November 7 the work of the Commission was violently interrupted by the armed seizure of the Mariinsky Palace where the Commission was at work. As a result the Commission was forced to discontinue its regular sittings and to act only on urgent matters. For these reasons and also because of its inability to get in touch with the local election committees, it is difficult for this body to carry out its obligations of supervising and speeding up the elections. The All-Russian Commission is not in a position to yield to the demand to make certain changes in the election laws, for such power belongs only to the Provisional Government.

The Commission on Elections feels that it is its duty to explain to the nation the abnormal condition under which the elections are to be held. At the same time it has come to the conclusion that according to the law the elections must take place on the time set wherever there is a possibility of insuring legal and orderly elections.

The All-Russian Commission on Elections, being legally in charge of the elections all over the country, requests that all citizens and authorities do everything in their power to provide the necessary freedom and order for the elections. . . . .

NABOKOV
Vice-Chairman of the Commission

BOLSHEVIK COMMENTS ON THE ASSEMBLY

[Volodarsky]: . . . . We [Bolsheviks] placed the whole question [about the Constituent Assembly] not on the platform of parliamentary struggle, but on a revolutionary class platform. The soldiers and the peasants must perceive that life can be given to the revolution only if our party secures a majority. The masses have never suffered from parliamentary cretinism.[9] If the Constituent Assembly should oppose the will of the people, the question of a new uprising will arise. We do not regard the Constituent Assembly as a fetish. There might arise

[9] Commenting on the phrase, *Novaia Zhizn*, No. 186, December 6, 1917, p. 1, says: "It is difficult to argue on any matter with men of the type of Volodarsky, men who suffer from all forms of cretinism except the parliamentary variety. The only convincing argument for them is the bayonet."

a situation in which we would oppose the Constituent Assembly with the Soviets.[10] . . . .

[Zinoviev] : . . . . We [Bolsheviks] have handed over the government to the workers, soldiers, and peasants, to the Soviets, which will make the power of the Constituent Assembly look real and supreme. But the Constituent Assembly must express the actual will of the workers, soldiers, and peasants. We must see to it that the bourgeoisie do not falsify the will of the people. We must not only keep in our hands the guns which have just helped us to gain a victory over them [bourgeoisie] but we must also make use of the other gun—the ballot.[11] . . . .

LISTS

List No. 2—Cadets[12]

Citizens of Petrograd!

The day of the election to the Constituent Assembly is approaching. This body is the only true Lord of Russia. By its powerful voice, the voice of the many millions of Russians, it can determine the form of government, the organization of power, and whether we should have peace or go on with the war. Not the users of force and the grabbers of power, not the murderers, not the destroyers of the freedom of speech and the press, not the "Soviet of People's Commissars" or any other such self-appointed organizations, but the Constituent Assembly alone has the right to issue decrees of land and peace. To its decisions all the peoples of Russia must submit.

In order that the Constituent Assembly may truly express the *all-national* will, it is necessary that all citizens should vote and indicate on their ballots whom they would have as their representatives. The ballot is a powerful weapon which can be used most effectively against those who have seized the government by force and pretend to speak in the name of the Russian people. Citizens, you should make it clear that it is not for them, whose hands are soiled with the blood of their brothers, to reconstruct new Russia, but for those who are endowed with true statesmanship, who truly love their country, who are ready to free her from the foe, and who respect the people's freedom.

Remember that the Failure to Vote Helps the Bolsheviks and Is therefore a Serious Sin against the Country.

[10] Volodarsky's speech was made at a Bolshevik meeting, November 21, 1917. *Izvestiia,* No. 220, November 22, 1917, p. 5.

[11] Zinoviev's statement was made November 23, 1917. *Izvestiia,* No. 222, November 24, 1917, p. 7.

[12] Leaflet in the Hoover War Library. In Petrograd nineteen different parties had tickets in the field. The number of candidates on each ticket varied from 18 to 4.

Be Courageous in This Legal Fight against Them. Be Sure to Go to the Polls and Cast Your Ballot for the *Party of People's Freedom, the Only All-National, Non-Class, and Democratic Party.*

[On List No. 2, the following persons are named]: (1) P. N. Miliukov, (2) M. M. Vinaver, (3) N. N. Kutler, (4) F. I. Rodichev, (5) V. D. Nabokov, (6) A. I. Shingarev, (7) Countess S. V. Panina, (8) A. A. Kornilov, (9) D. D. Grimm, (10) D. S. Zernov, (11) V. I. Vernadsky, (12) A. N. Kolosov, (13) A. D. Protopopov, (14) Prince V. A. Obolensky, (15) S. F. Oldenbourg, (16) L. A. Velikhov, (17) K. N. Sokolov, (18) V. M. Hessen.

List No. 4—Bolsheviks

Workers and Soldiers:

This is the principal day[13] for the elections to the Constituent Assembly. You must all come out. Not a single worker or soldier must forget to vote. Go yourself and take along your wife and sister. Call out all toilers—domestic servant, cab driver, laundress—go to the booths and vote in accordance with the resolution of the Petrograd Soviet of Workers' and Soldiers' Deputies. *Vote for List No. 4.*

During the last eight months Kerensky's government of landowners and bourgeoisie has done all that it could to delay the elections to the Constituent Assembly. They were determined not to have it, for they knew that the Constituent Assembly would declare against them on the questions of land, peace, and on all other important matters. The only sure way of having a Constituent Assembly was to overthrow the Kerensky government and bring about a victory of the workers, soldiers, and peasants over the bourgeoisie. The elections to the Constituent Assembly are now assured and should come off on time.

The Petrograd Soviet[14]

[On List No. 4 the following persons are named]: (1) Vladimir Ilich Ulianov (Lenin), (2) Evsei Aronovich Radomyslsky (Zinoviev), (3) Lev Davydovich Bronstein (Trotsky), (4) Lev Borisovich Rosenfeld (Kamenev), (5) Alexandra Mikhailovna Kollontai, (6) Iosif Vissarionovich Dzhugashvili (Stalin), (7) Matvei Konstantinovich Muranov, (8) Mikhail Ivanovich Kalinin, (9) Iosif Stanislavovich Unschlicht, (10) Sergei Alexandrovich Cherepanov, (11) Grigorii Eremeevich Evdokimov, (12) Klavdia Ivanovna Nikolaeva, (13) Feodosy Ivanovich Krivobokov (Vladimir Nevsky), (14) Nikolai Pavlovich Avilov (Glebov), (15) Alexander Gavrilovich Shliapnikov,

[13] The elections in Petrograd lasted three days, November 25, 26, 27.

[14] *Izvestiia,* No. 223, November 25, 1917, p. 1.

(16) Nikolai Ivanovich Derbyshev, (17) Martyn Yanovich Latsis, (18) Alexander Vasilevich Shotman.[15]

LIST NO. 9—SOCIALIST-REVOLUTIONISTS

ALL POWER TO THE CONSTITUENT ASSEMBLY

If you are for "Land and Freedom," vote No. 9.

If you are for a just peace, vote No. 9.

If you are for a democratic republic, vote No. 9.

If you are for an eight-hour day, minimum wage, unemployment and accident insurance, vote No. 9.

If you are for freedom of speech, press, meeting, trade union, strike, inviolability of personal rights, vote No. 9.

ALL LAND TO ALL THE PEOPLE[16]

[On List No. 9 the following persons are named]: (1) Viktor Mikhailovich Chernov, (2) Boris Davidovich Katz (Kamkov), (3) Grigorii Ilich Schreider, (4) Maria Alexandrovna Spiridonova, (5) Isai Isaevich Milchik, (6) Anatolii Kapitonovich Boldyrev, (7) Alexander Abramovich Schreider, (8) Boris Ignatevich Kossinsky, (9) Mikhail Petrovich Kapitsa, (10) Valerian Viktorovich Lunkevich, (11) Nikolai Sergeevich Rusanov, (12) Alexandra Adolfovna Izmailovich, (13) Anastasia Alexandrovna Bitsenko, (14) Likarion Ivanovich Diasperov, (15) Nikolai Stepanovich Grigorev, (16) Makarii Fedorovich Shirokov, (17) Grigorii Ivanovich Levkin, (18) Robert Stepanovich Verbo.[17]

ELECTION RETURNS IN PETROGRAD AND MOSCOW

RESULTS IN PETROGRAD[18]

Bolshevik vote	415,587	(Delegates elected, 6)
Cadet vote	245,628	(Delegates elected, 4)
Socialist-Revolutionists' vote	149,644	(Delegates elected, 2)
All other parties' vote	117,495	(Delegates elected, 0)
Total vote	928,354	(Total delegates, 12)

[15] *Izvestiia*, No. 220, November 22, 1917, p. 1. This ticket was put into the field by the Central Committee, Military Organization and Petrograd Committee of the Bolshevik Party, and the Social-Democratic parties of Poland, Lithuania, and Latvia.

[16] *Delo Naroda*, No. 207, November 25, 1917, p. 1.

[17] Leaflet in the Hoover War Library.

[18] *Delo Naroda*, No. 211, November 29, 1917, p. 3.

Drift of Public Opinion in Petrograd Elections[19]

Leading Parties	September 2 Total	September 2 Percentage	November 25 Total	November 25 Percentage
Socialist-Revolutionists	205,665	38	149,644	16
Bolsheviks	183,694	33	415,587	45
Cadets	114,485	21	245,628	26
Others	45,534	8	117,495	13
Total vote	549,378	100	928,354	100

Vote of November 25

Leading Parties	Civilian Wards Total	Civilian Wards Percentage	Military Wards[20] Total	Military Wards[20] Percentage
Socialist-Revolutionists	139,644	16	9,980	[11] 12
Bolsheviks	347,719	[41] 43	67,868	[77] 76
Cadets	240,693	[30] 28	4,935	6
Others	112,081	13	5,414	6
Total vote	840,157	100	88,197	100

Drift of Public Opinion in Moscow Elections[21]

Leading Parties	July 8 Total	July 8 Percentage	October 3 Total	October 3 Percentage	December 2–4 Total	December 2–4 Percentage
Socialist-Revolutionists	375,000	[56] 58	54,000	14	62,000	8
Bolsheviks	75,000	[11] 12	198,000	51	366,000	[50] 48
Cadets	109,000	17	101,000	26	264,000	[36] 35
Others	108,000	[16] 13	[?]		43,000	[6] 9
Total vote	667,000		[?]		735,000	

THE RIGHT TO CALL FOR RE-ELECTIONS

[From a Decree of the Central Executive Committee, December 6, 1917][22]

The All-Russian Central Executive Committee of the Soviets of Workers', Soldiers', and Peasants' Deputies resolves that:

The Congress of Soviets of Workers' and Soldiers' Deputies . . . . has the right to call for re-elections . . . . in all representative institutions, including the Constituent Assembly. . . . .

19 *Nasha Rech,* No. 2, November 30, 1917, p. 2.

20 Wards where the barracks were situated. In this and the following tables there are errors in the percentages. Corrections are shown in brackets.

21 *Russkiia Vedomosti,* No. 257, December 7, 1917, p. 2.

22 *S.U.R.,* 1917, No. 3, pp. 47–48.

Re-elections take place in the usual manner . . . . and the newly elected persons replace at once those previously elected.

THE BOLSHEVIKS AND THE ELECTORAL COMMISSION

[Arrest of the All-Russian Commission on Elections][23]

On December 6 while the Commission was in session a Red Guard detachment appeared . . . . [and arrested the members]. . . . . When they were brought to Smolny they were asked whether or not they recognized the government of the People's Commissars; . . . . what were their relations to the Committee to Save [the Country and the Revolution]; what was their decision in regard to the meeting of the Constituent Assembly and who was to open the meeting. . . . . To the first . . . . question they answered in the negative; to the next they refused to give any reply. . . . . As to the last their answer was that the Commission was a purely technical body so that it did not consider the question who was to open the Assembly. . . . .

The Commission was locked up in Smolny until December 11. In the meantime one of the three chairmen, Vladimir Nabokov, sent out a letter in which he told of the conditions of the Commission's imprisonment, warned the public of the impending struggle over the Constituent Assembly, and charged that the appointment of Uritsky as commissar and the decision to require the presence of four hundred representatives before opening the Assembly was a scheme of the new masters of Russia to delay the meeting of the Assembly for three or four weeks.[24]

DISMISSAL OF THE ELECTORAL COMMISSION

[Decree of the Sovnarkom, December 12, 1917][25]

Because they refuse to work with the commissar appointed by the Soviet of People's Commissars, the chairman . . . . and the members of the All-Russian Commission on Elections to the Constituent Assembly . . . . are dismissed. . . . .

[23] *Delo Naroda*, No. 218, December 7, 1917, p. 4.

[24] *Novaia Rech*, No. 1, December 11, 1917, p. 2.

[25] *S.U.R.*, 1917, No. 5, p. 67.

Until the appointment of new members all matters relating to the All-Russian Commission on Elections to the Constituent Assembly will be handled by M. Uritsky.

V. ULIANOV (LENIN), President of the Sovnarkom
I. STALIN, I. STUCHKA, People's Commissars

B. THE ATTEMPT TO OPEN THE ASSEMBLY

The returns from the election came in slowly, but it was soon clear that though the Bolsheviks headed the poll in Petrograd and Moscow and a few other large towns, they would be in a minority in the Assembly even with the votes of the Socialist-Revolutionists of the Left.[26]

They were, therefore, in no hurry to have the Assembly meet. But their opponents, who now looked upon the Assembly as a means of terminating the dictatorship, were naturally anxious to have it open at the earliest possible date. On November 29 former members of the deposed Provisional Government issued a call for the first meeting of the Assembly on December 11. On December 6 the same groups that had formed the Committee to Save the Country and the Revolution organized a committee to defend the Constituent Assembly, and preparations were pushed for the opening day.

DATE SET FOR OPENING THE CONSTITUENT ASSEMBLY

[Decree of Provisional Government, November 29, 1917][27]

In accordance with the decision of the Provisional Government, the day of elections to the Constituent Assembly was set for November 25. . . . . Although not all delegates to the Constituent Assembly were elected on that date, there is sufficient evidence to indicate that by December 11 there will be about 650 members elected. . . . .

[26] Computations subsequently made by N. V. Sviatitsky show that in the elections held on November 25, December 2, and December 9, in fifty-four regions, out of a total of seventy-nine, the Bolsheviks received 9,023,963 votes out of a total of 36,262,560 ballots cast. The Socialist-Revolutionists had an absolute majority with 20,893,754 votes, while the bourgeois parties polled 4,620,000. N. V. Sviatitsky, "Itogi vyborov vo Vserossiiskoe Uchreditelnoe Sobranie," in *God russkoi revoliutsii, 1917–1918 g.g.*, Moscow, 1918, pp. 106–19.

[27] *Nasha Rech,* No. 2, November 30, 1917, p. 3.

Finding it impossible to postpone the meeting of the Constituent Assembly any longer, the Provisional Government hereby decrees: That the Constituent Assembly will open at the Taurida Palace in Petrograd on December 11, at 2:00 P.M.[28]

S. PROKOPOVICH, Acting Prime Minister
P. MALIANTOVICH, Minister of Justice

PROCLAMATION OF THE PETROGRAD UNION TO DEFEND THE CONSTITUENT ASSEMBLY[29]

[December 8, 1917]

Citizens!

The Constituent Assembly, the Sovereign of the Russian Land, is to meet in a few days. Only the Constituent Assembly can give an honorable peace to Russia. The negotiations of the Bolsheviks with the Germans have not and will not bring peace. Only the Constituent Assembly and not the Bolshevik decrees can give the land to the people, [establish] government control over industry, and bring an end to the country's ills. Only the Constituent Assembly can form a government that will be recognized by all and put an end to civil war.

It is for these reasons that the meeting of the Constituent Assembly is a national holiday—a great triumph of the revolution. Unfortunately we cannot look forward to it with joy. Threats are coming from Smolny that the Constituent Assembly will be dispersed. . . . . The Bolsheviks have closed the legally elected municipal dumas of Petrograd, Moscow, and Saratov; they are crushing the press; they are throwing hundreds of citizens into prison without trial. Knowing that the Constituent Assembly will put an end to their lawless acts, they have arrested the All-Russian Commission on Elections to the Constituent Assembly and are threatening to break up the Constituent Assembly itself.

The last hope of the Russian Revolution is in danger. . . . . [The ruin of the Constituent Assembly] is the ruin of every hope. In place of peace, land, bread, and freedom the people will get civil war, famine, reaction, demoralization, and the ruin of Russia.

Citizens! We will not allow the Constituent Assembly to be desecrated! We shall defend it to the last!

[28] *Delo Naroda,* No. 218, December 7, 1917, p. 3, carried an announcement by Kerensky that he approved this act of the Provisional Government. He also stated that he considered himself a member of the Provisional Government though he had resigned as Premier.

[29] *Ibid.,* No. 219, December 9, 1917, p. 4.

These bandits will not dare to stab the Constituent Assembly if they know that the nation stands behind it.

Representatives of various political parties (Menshevik, Socialist-Revolutionist, Socialist-Populist, and democratic organizations, ward dumas, union of workmen's co-operatives, trade unions, representatives of large industries, and some army organizations) met on December 6 and formed the "Petrograd Union to Defend the Constituent Assembly."

Citizens of Petrograd! Gather around this Union. . . . . Comrade Workers! Support the Constituent Assembly! It is not only your patriotic duty but also to your interest to do so. A "shameful" peace will surely be followed by unemployment and the break-up of the Constituent Assembly by civil war which will fall heaviest on the working class.

Comrade soldiers! Do not become an instrument of violence against the will of the whole nation. . . . .

Employees in private, public, or state institutions! Be ready to defend the Constituent Assembly with all the might of your organizations.

Let us form a united revolutionary front against these highwaymen. Let us stand as one man in defense of freedom of speech and the press! Let us all defend the Constituent Assembly!

PETROGRAD UNION TO DEFEND THE CONSTITUENT ASSEMBLY

MESSAGE FROM MEMBERS OF THE PROVISIONAL GOVERNMENT[30]

[December 9, 1917]

Citizen-President:

We, the undersigned, members of the Provisional Government, beg you to have the following read at the High Assembly.

In fulfilment of our duty toward our ruined country and in compliance with the wishes of the fully empowered organs of the revolutionary democracy, we entered the coalition government on October 8 and together with our Socialist colleagues sacredly carried out the government program which was drawn up with the collaboration of representatives of democratic organizations and proclaimed by the Provisional Government on October 8. Notwithstanding all this we were pounced upon by mutinous troops on the night of November 6–7 and dragged from the Winter Palace to the Peter and Paul Fortress, where we still are, although our Socialist colleagues have long since been set free.

[30] *Novaia Rech,* No. 1, December 11, 1917, p. 3.

Looking upon the Provisional Government as the only legal authority until the meeting of the Constituent Assembly, we have refused to have any dealings with the men who have seized the government by force and are leading the state to destruction. We have endured patiently our imprisonment and fulfilled our duty to the country to the end. Now that we are handing over our power to the Constituent Assembly—the only sovereign of the Russian Land—we pray this Honorable Body to free us and other representatives of the Provisional Government from prison, where we have been for a month.

This will make it possible for us to appear and to report to the Constituent Assembly on the work of the Provisional Government.

A. KONOVALOV A. KARTASHEV
N. KISHKIN M. BERNATSKY
M. TERESHCHENKO S. TRETIAKOV
S. SMIRNOV

PETER AND PAUL FORTRESS.

THE CADETS AND THE CONSTITUENT ASSEMBLY

[Editorial in *Novaia Rech,* December 11, 1917][31]

This day, December 11, has been awaited as the great day which is to open a new epoch in Russian history. The dream of many generations, the dream which has cost so many sacrifices and so many precious lives, the dream which has called forth so much heroism and so many beautiful examples of patriotic devotion, this dream is about to come true. . . . . When all obstacles appeared to have been overcome, a gang of criminal conspirators has appeared on the scene. Among them we recognize notorious scoundrels of the old régime, such as Kommissarov, who became famous at the time of the First Duma by issuing pogrom proclamations. These men are back at their old jobs [to help] the Bolsheviks carry out their determination to prevent the meeting of the Constituent Assembly. Look! Lenin and Trotsky are in a scramble even with their own Central Executive Committee of Workers' and Soldiers' Deputies. They would like to govern without them and in spite of them. What chance is there that these highwaymen will get along with the Constituent Assembly? They have been carrying on an active campaign against it; they have tried to show that one should not make a fetish of the Constituent Assembly; they have schemed for the re-election of deputies; they have proposed to exclude the Cadets; they have arrested the All-Russian Commission on Elections in order to disorganize its work; they have issued a decree that the Constituent Assembly cannot meet unless there are four hundred members as-

[31] No. 1, December 11, 1917, p. 1.

sembled in Petrograd—in other words they are trying to postpone it indefinitely. . . . .

Notwithstanding their clubs and their Red Guard, the Bolsheviks cannot get rid of the Constituent Assembly. No matter what tricks and deceptions Lenin and Trotsky make use of they cannot crush the will of the Russian people. As late as yesterday they were able to command enough bayonets for the criminal purpose of driving out the oldest state institution, the Senate, founded by Peter [the Great]. But the day is not far distant when these bayonets will be turned against them, and they will not dare to raise their hands against the elected of the Russian Land.

The Constituent Assembly meets in a gloomy atmosphere, quite unlike the sunny day dreamed of during the early days of the revolution. The more difficult the task the more the glory, and the more should all come to its aid.

Down with the gang of violators! Long live the Constituent Assembly!

PREPARATIONS FOR THE OPENING DAY

The Inter-Ward Conference and the Central Municipal Duma call on the population of Petrograd to greet and defend the Constituent Assembly of the Russian Land . . . . and to march with them to the Taurida Palace under the banner of "Long Live the Constituent Assembly." . . . .

On December 9–10 there were a number of meetings in Petrograd. At these meetings speakers of different parties called on those present to defend the Constituent Assembly. . . . .

December 11, the day of the opening of the Constituent Assembly, was declared a national holiday by the Red Cross. . . . .

On December 9, I. G. Tsereteli gave an address at the Chinizelli Circus on the subject of "All Power to the Constituent Assembly."[32]

Is it true that the Bolsheviks are sending out of the city the Semenovsky and Pavlovsky regiments because they can no longer depend on them and are replacing them with Lettish regiments?[33]

THE MEANING OF THE PREPARATIONS

[A Bolshevik Interpretation][34]

With the idea of breaking up the Soviet Government, the plotters, Kaledin to Tsereteli inclusive, have decided to form a bloc under the

[32] *Novaia Rech*, No. 1, December 11, 1917, p. 3.

[33] *Delo Naroda*, No. 220, December 13, 1917, p. 1.

[34] *Izvestiia*, No. 238, December 11, 1917, p. 2.

leadership of Miliukov. . . . . The plotters are preparing the ground for their counter-revolutionary plans. A number of meetings have been held lately. At these gatherings all sorts of malignant things were said against their [political enemies]. . . . . Such meetings were held yesterday [December 10] at the Chinizelli Circus . . . . where it was decided to march to the Taurida Palace. A resolution was also passed demanding the release of the All-Russian Commission on Elections. . . . .

Among the speakers was the "leader of the democracy" . . . . Tsereteli. He said that . . . . judging by the papers there was no hope of agreement between the Bolsheviks and the "democracy," and urged that the "democratic" (read "bourgeois") elements in the Constituent Assembly should unite against the Bolsheviks. . . . . "Defend the Constituent Assembly!" exclaimed the speaker. . . . .

The true democracy . . . . will show Tsereteli that it can . . . . defend the conquests of the revolution, especially the Soviet Government, peace, and land. If a majority of the Constituent Assembly will join with the toilers, with their slogans and demands . . . . then the revolutionary democracy will defend the Constituent Assembly against the Kaledins, the Miliukovs, and, if necessary, against the Avxentievs and Tseretelis.

In order to mobilize public opinion, a demonstration is planned against the revolutionary democracy. The City Duma and the Union to Defend the Constituent Assembly are behind this demonstration. . . . . The demonstration is to take place on the day of the opening of the Constituent Assembly. . . . .

It seems as if everything is being done to turn the opening day of the Constituent Assembly into a demonstration against the Workers' and Peasants' Government. . . . .

Last night . . . . there were a number of very "important" meetings. . . . . [Various questions were discussed, including that of who is to open the Constituent Assembly.] In case it should be the President of the Soviet of People's Commissars the plotters would make a great disturbance. . . . . Other schemes were also worked out by the plotters. . . . . It was decided to demand political amnesty . . . . freedom of the press . . . . and an end to "Bolshevik terror." . . . . There is also talk of forming a new government. . . . .

Kerensky is expected to be present at the opening of the Constituent Assembly . . . . accompanied perhaps by his cabinet. . . . . The question is now whether Kaledin is coming. . . . .

Conscious of its strength and the righteousness of its cause, the revolutionary democracy will wait quietly for the coming events. For the time being it will not raise a hand to interfere with this child's play.

. . . . But it would not be wise for these plotters to misunderstand our silence. Should it be necessary to defend the conquests of the revolution, the toiling masses will rise as one man. . . . .

THE GREAT DAY—DECEMBER 11[35]

The crowds made their appearance at the Taurida Palace toward one o'clock. They came to tell the members of the Constituent Assembly of their readiness to defend them with all their might. In the course of the next few hours . . . . more and more came. . . . .

It has been estimated that not less than 200,000 people passed the Taurida Palace. Each group had its own banner on which were the slogans: "All Power to the Constituent Assembly," "Long Live the Constituent Assembly," "Save Russia." . . . .

When the first group reached the Taurida Palace the Mayor of Petrograd, G. I. Schreider . . . . addressed the crowd in the following words:

"Today is a great day in Russian history. Today the people take their future into their own hands to make our country happy and great. Let us swear to allow no violence against the Constituent Assembly, the last hope of Russia! Let us swear to defend it with our last drop of blood! Long live the Constituent Assembly!"

"Long live the Constituent Assembly!" responds the crowd. . . . .

The Lettish sharpshooters . . . . let Schreider pass. . . . . Meanwhile V. V. Rudnev, the Mayor of Moscow, appeared at one of the side entrances [of the palace]. When he found the gates closed he asked the Lettish sharpshooters whether they were to disperse the Constituent Assembly.

"No," they replied, "we are here to defend the Constituent Assembly."

"In that case," said the mayor, "unload your guns and let the people pass to the palace." The soldiers obeyed. . . . .[36]

[Soon afterward other members of the Constituent Assembly began to appear. At two o'clock they assembled in private conference and decided that owing to the small number in attendance the meeting could not be regarded as formal. In order to hasten the opening of the Constituent Assembly it was agreed to hold daily meetings in the palace until enough members gathered to constitute a quorum. V. M. Chernov was elected temporary chairman.]

[35] *Nash Vek,* No. 1, December 13, 1917, p. 2; cf. Sorokin, *op. cit.,* pp. 108–10.

[36] Sorokin states that he broke in.

THE MEANING OF THE DEMONSTRATION

[According to the Socialist-Revolutionists][37]

Notwithstanding all the obstacles put in the way by the "autocrats" of Smolny, the members of the Constituent Assembly present did meet at the Taurida Palace on December 11. These men whom the toilers have elected and into whose hands they have intrusted the fate of the nation were few in number and for that reason could not declare the Constituent Assembly open. . . . . They did, however, come together and that is the *first victory*. . . . . A victory because on the evening before [the Bolsheviks] seized the Taurida Palace, locked the gates, posted guards with orders to let pass only those members of the Constituent Assembly whom they approved. But the soldiers paid no attention to these . . . . orders. When they saw thousands of people marching to the palace to greet the people's elected, the soldiers obeyed the orders of the members of the Constituent Assembly and not the orders of the usurpers.

We feel certain that the Bolsheviks will not be able to disperse the Constituent Assembly which watches over the interests of the toiling masses. We are certain of this because the Constituent Assembly will call the workers, soldiers, and peasants and they will come to its defense and support. . . . .

Of the fifty members of the Constituent Assembly who were on hand only *four* were Cadets; all the others were Socialist-Revolutionists. . . . . It is now possible to predict that the *Socialists* will have a majority in the Constituent Assembly. . . . .

Soldiers, workers, and peasants! Know that he who raises his hand or his club against the Constituent Assembly is *an enemy of the people and plays into the hands of the bourgeoisie and tsarist autocracy*. . . . . Only the Constituent Assembly can give the suffering people peace, land, and bread.

THE CADET PARTY DECLARED AN ENEMY OF THE PEOPLE

[Proclamation of the Sovnarkom, December 11, 1917][38]

To All Toilers and Exploited!

The bourgeoisie led by the Cadet Party prepared all its forces to bring about a counter-revolutionary coup d'état at the time of the Constituent Assembly. Kornilov, Kaledin, and Dutov . . . . have unfurled the flag of civil war against the Soviets of Peasants' and Workers' and Soldiers'

[37] *Delo Naroda,* No. 220, December 13, 1917, p. 1.

[38] *Izvestiia,* No. 239, December 12, 1917, p. 1.

Deputies. Bogaevsky, Kaledin's aide, has openly declared that the revolt was started at the insistence of the Cadet Party which has long since formed an alliance with the counter-revolutionary faction of the Cossacks.

On the Urals the Cadets support the counter-revolution with money and supplies. . . . . It is clear that the civil war was initiated and is led by the Cadets. The Central Committee of this party is at the present moment the headquarters of all counter-revolutionary forces in the country.

This plot, threatening as it does the cause of peace and the conquests of the revolution, is carried on under the cloak of the Constituent Assembly. The Cadet Central Electoral Commission hid from the Soviets, kept to itself the data about the elections so as not to expose the defeat of the Cadets [at the polls] before the plot of Miliukov, Kornilov, Kaledin, and Dutov had time to succeed.[39] The Soviet of People's Commissars has decided to open the Constituent Assembly just as soon as half of its members, namely 400 out of 800, are present. This decision gives the lie to those who say that the Sovnarkom . . . . is opposed to the Constituent Assembly. And that is why the bourgeoisie would not wait until the people's assembly is opened in a legal way. On the evening of December 11 a group of people calling themselves deputies, broke into the Taurida Palace without showing their certificates. They were accompanied by armed White Guards, cadets, and thousands of bourgeoisie and officials on strike.

The aim of the Cadet Party was to stage a "legal" cover for the Cadet-Kaledin counter-revolutionary uprising. They hoped to make the voices of a few bourgeois deputies sound like the voice of the Constituent Assembly.

The Sovnarkom calls this plot to the attention of the people. All the conquests of the revolution including an early peace are at stake. On the south we have Kaledin, in the east Dutov, in the center and in Petrograd the plot of the Central Committee of the Cadet Party, which directs a constant flow of Kornilov officers to Kaledin. The least hesitancy or weakness . . . . may put an end to the Soviets, peace and land reform, and bring back the mighty landlords and capitalists.

Recognizing the full responsibility that now rests on the Soviet Government for the fate of the nation and the revolution, the *Soviet of*

[39] The Commission had many Cadets among its members. Dmitriev (Socialist), representing the Northern front at the Electoral Commission, comments on the above statement in an open letter to the soldiers and workers as follows: "Is not the accusation really ridiculous? Uritsky was getting all information directly [from the provinces], while the Commission, because of the delay of the elections in many provinces, knew very little of their progress." (*Nash Vek,* No. 10, December 23, 1917, p. 2.

People's Commissars Declares the Cadet Party (as an organization of counter-revolutionary conspirators) *an Enemy of the People.*

The Sovnarkom is determined not to lay down its arms in its fight against the Cadet Party and its Kaledin forces.

The political leaders of the counter-revolutionary war will be arrested; the conspiracy of the bourgeoisie will be crushed, come what may!

In this fight the Sovnarkom counts on the support and loyalty of all workers, soldiers, peasants, sailors, Cossacks, and all other honest citizens.

Down with the bourgeoisie! There is no place in the Constituent Assembly for enemies of the people, capitalists, and landowners! The country can be saved only by the Constituent Assembly made up of representatives of the toiling and exploited classes. Long live the Revolution! Long live the Soviets! Long live peace!

SOVIET OF PEOPLE'S COMMISSARS

ARREST OF THE CADET LEADERS

[Decree of the Sovnarkom, December 11, 1917][40]

Leaders of the Cadet Party, the party of the enemy of the people, are to be arrested and handed over to the revolutionary tribunal. Local Soviets are ordered to keep a careful watch on the Cadet Party because of its connections with the Kornilov-Kaledin civil war against the revolution.

This decree goes into force as soon as it is signed.

VL. ULIANOV (LENIN)
President of the Sovnarkom

L. Trotsky, N. Avilov (Glebov), P. Stuchka, V. Menzhinsky, Dzhugashvili (Stalin), G. Petrovsky, A. Schlichter, Dybenko—People's Commissars

[As a result of the decree of December 11 the following Cadets were arrested: Countess C. V. Panina, A. I. Shingarev, F. F. Kokoshkin, Prince P. D. Dolgorukov, N. N. Kutler, M. M. Vinaver, F. I. Rodichev.][41]

[From a Speech by Trotsky, December 15, 1917][42]

We have made a modest beginning. We have arrested the Cadet leaders and have given orders that the Cadets in the provinces should

[40] *Izvestiia*, No. 239, December 12, 1917, p. 1.

[41] *Delo Naroda*, No. 220, December 13, 1917, p. 3.

[42] *Izvestiia*, No. 244, December 19, 1917, p. 8.

be carefully watched. At the time of the French Revolution more honest men than the Cadets were guillotined by the Jacobins for opposing the people. We have not executed anyone and do not intend to do so, but there are moments when the fury of the people is hard to control. The Cadets had better take warning. . . . .

C. The Struggle for Control of the Assembly

During the five weeks that elapsed between the demonstration of December 11 and the formal opening of the Assembly on January 18, the elected deputies slowly drifted into the capital. This was not a period of truce but one of intense political activity.

When the Bolshevik representatives elected from other parts of Russia arrived in the capital, they were immediately assigned, under Sverdlov's direction, to factories, industrial works, and garrison units where they worked diligently in preparing for the "Supplementary Revolution," i.e., the dispersion of the Constituent Assembly.[43] The S.R. leaders, on the other hand, counting heavily on the prestige and popular support of the Constituent Assembly, devoted great energy to drawing up projects for new laws, formulating policies on foreign relations and the land question, and preparing for debates. It was assumed that if the Assembly were attacked by the Bolsheviks it would be defended by the people who had brought it into being.

Among the ranks of the S.R.'s were some who had no faith in these assumptions. They believed that the Bolsheviks must be fought not in debate but with force, even with the old weapon of terror. Boris Sokolov, one of this group, has described the plans and the efforts made to organize this resistance.[44] They attempted to win over the Semenovsky and Preobrazhensky regiments, they published a newspaper to attack the Bolsheviks, they endeavored to organize and

[43] This is according to Trotsky, *Lenin,* p. 122.

[44] "Zashchita Vserossiiskago Uchreditelnago Sobraniia," in *A.R.R.,* XIII, 36–70. Mavor's chapter on the Constituent Assembly in *The Russian Revolution,* New York, 1928, pp. 177–200, is largely based on Sokolov's account and contains many quotations from it.

arm workers, they attempted to bring volunteers from the front ostensibly to attend a soldiers' university but actually for use against the Bolsheviks. They even worked out an elaborate plot to kidnap Lenin and Trotsky. None of these projects achieved any degree of success and the unarmed workers and intelligentsia who marched under banners to celebrate the opening of the Assembly on January 18 were driven from the streets by the fire of the Bolshevik forces.

BOLSHEVIK POLICIES AS TO THE ASSEMBLY

[Meeting of the Bolshevik Central Committee, December 12, 1917]

. . . . At the meeting of the Bolshevik Central Committee the question arose concerning the policy to be adopted toward the Constituent Assembly. . . . . Bukharin proposed to call the Constituent Assembly, expel the Cadets from it, and declare the Left section a revolutionary convention. Lomov thought that the Cadets would not appear at the Assembly anyhow, that they were more likely to go to the Ukraine and the Don, and that the Constituent Assembly would thus liquidate itself. Stalin pointed out that Bukharin's position was wrong. To bring together two sections of the Constituent Assembly which repudiate one another and to have them go through a single registration would be impossible. The fight against counter-revolution which the Sovnarkom has initiated with the decree outlawing the Cadets should be pursued relentlessly. . . . .[45]

[Meeting of the Central Executive Committee, December 14, 1917]

[At the meeting of the Central Executive Committee the question of the Constituent Assembly was raised. The Socialist-Revolutionists of the Left and the Social-Democrats (Internationalists) protested against the decrees outlawing the Cadets. Lenin and Trotsky replied to the opposition speakers.]

[Lenin]: . . . . If the Constituent Assembly is considered [in the abstract] and apart from the atmosphere of class struggle which has reached the point of civil war, then there is no institution expressing more perfectly the will of the people. But to do that is to live in a dream-world. The Constituent Assembly will have to act in the midst of civil war.

We are asked to call the Constituent Assembly as originally conceived. This will never happen. It was conceived against the people

[45] Liubimov, *Revoliutsiia 1917 goda,* p. 233.

and we carried out the insurrection to make certain that it will not be used against the people. . . . . When a revolutionary class is struggling against the propertied classes which offer resistance, that resistance has to be suppressed, and we shall suppress it by the same methods by which the propertied classes suppressed the proletariat. New methods have not been invented yet. . . . .[46]

Trotsky: . . . . You protest against the mild terror which we are directing against our class enemies. But you should know that not later than in a month's time that terror will assume very violent forms after the example of the great French revolutionaries. The guillotine will be ready for our enemies and not merely the jail. . . . .[47]

[In Karelin's account of the same speech Trotsky is credited with the statement that since the bourgeoisie as a class is passing away from the scene of history, the measures of violence used by the Bolsheviks are for the good of the bourgeoisie, since they help the latter to disappear more rapidly.][48]

[Meeting of the Second Congress of Peasants' Deputies, December 15, 1917]

[In the course of a speech at the Second Congress of Peasants' Deputies Lenin said]: The Soviets are higher than any parliament in the world, higher than the Constituent Assembly. . . . . With regard to the latter it is appropriate to recall the ancient saying: "Man does not exist for the Sabbath, but the Sabbath for man." . . . . The Constituent Assembly might have been the high assembly, indeed it should be, were it not for the fact that since the elections the masses have changed their views . . . . especially their attitude toward the Socialist-Revolutionists. That party is no longer united and that means that the deputies belonging to that party no longer represent the will of the people. . . . . Yes, the people elected those who do not defend its actual interests and we were forced to pass the law of recall. . . . .[49]

[Editorial in *Izvestiia*]

Counter-revolutionists of every shade have raised a howl about the Constituent Assembly. . . . . On a number of occasions the *Izvestiia* exposed the counter-revolutionary purpose of these outcries. . . . .

We cited historical facts and proved conclusively that democracies never bow before representative assemblies . . . . from which it fol-

[46] Liubimov, *Revoliutsiia 1917 goda,* p. 250.

[47] *Delo Naroda,* No. 223, December 16, 1917, p. 4.

[48] *Izvestiia,* No. 249, December 19, 1917, p. 7.

[49] *Nash Vek,* No. 4, December 16, 1917, p. 3; also *Delo Naroda,* No. 223, December 16, 1917, p. 3, and *Izvestiia,* No. 244, December 19, 1917, p. 6.

lows that the Russian laboring classes cannot and will not hand over their rights and powers into the hands of any parliament even if it be a Constituent Assembly. The "Sovereign of the Russian Land" is not the Assembly but the toiler himself, and he will recognize the Assembly only in so far as it carries out his will and works for his interest. . . . . Those who would help the workers, soldiers, and peasants . . . . should support the revolutionary government . . . . and not work against it. . . . .[50]

[Meeting of the Bolshevik Central Committee, December 24]

The Central Committee of the Bolsheviks met . . . . to consider the attitude of the [Bolshevik] group in the Constituent Assembly in view of the fact that that attitude deviates from the policy of the Central Committee in that it is dominated by moderate tendencies. Lenin made [the following] proposals: (1) To remove the bureau of the [Bolshevik] group;[51] (2) to state the attitude of the Central Committee toward the Constituent Assembly in the form of theses and present them to the group;[52] (3) to remind the group of the party constitution requiring complete subordination of all representative bodies to the Central Committee; (4) to appoint a member of the Central Committee to lead the group. . . . .[53]

THE SOCIALIST-REVOLUTIONISTS' ATTITUDE TOWARD THE ASSEMBLY

[From a Resolution of the Fourth Party Congress, December 17, 1917][54]

The Socialist-Revolutionists will endeavor first of all to bring up at the Constituent Assembly the land and peace questions, the problem of control over production, and the reorganization of Russia along federal lines. . . . .

It is the duty of the party to make every effort to provide a sufficient defense for . . . . the Constituent Assembly and, if necessary, to oppose by force the criminal attempts against the sovereign will of the people. . . . .

[50] *Izvestiia*, No. 242, December 15, 1917, p. 1.

[51] The bureau, i.e., the steering committee, included the following: Miliutin, Larin, Stalin, Kamenev, Riazanov, Sapronov, Rabchinsky, and others. Liubimov, *Revoliutsiia 1917 goda*, p. 257.

[52] These theses were formulated by Lenin the next day and appeared in *Pravda*, No. 213, December 26, 1917, p. 3.

[53] Liubimov, *Revoliutsiia 1917 goda*, pp. 322–23.

[54] *Delo Naroda*, No. 224, December 18, 1917, p. 3. The resolution contains seventeen paragraphs touching a great number of current political problems. We quote paragraphs 13 and 16.

[From the Socialist-Revolutionists' Appeal to the People, December 21][55]

We were elected by the people and therefore we belong to the people. To the people are we responsible and to the people alone are we accountable for what we do. We shall, therefore, address ourselves to the people so that they will know and judge us. In this first letter we wish to bring to the attention of the people the kind of problems that have been confronting us and the first steps we have taken at Petrograd.

We consider some of the principal tasks of the Constituent Assembly the speediest possible conclusion of peace, the transfer (without compensation) of the land to the toilers, and the safe-guarding of the liberties won by the people.

"Peace, Land, and Liberty"—these we must secure at the behest of the people and these we shall inscribe on our banner. Under this banner we shall live and work. Under it we shall fight all hostile forces. We believe that in this struggle we shall not be alone . . . . that the toiling masses—the army, the peasants, and the workers—will be with us.

When these questions are solved we shall take up the problem of labor, the question of fixed prices in commodities, of government control over industry and, finally, the question of the rights of the various nationalities which make up the Russian Republic.

"Peace, Land, and Liberty"—first in our slogan— . . . . Under it we shall fight, ready to die rather than surrender. . . . .

And we are apparently facing no small battle. There are those who do not wish to recognize our right to supreme authority. . . . . Not all are ready to submit to the will of the people who have elected and sent us to wage the great struggle for "Peace, Land, and Liberty." . . . .

By now it must be clear to everyone [that] the talk of the Bolsheviks regarding the speediest convocation of the Constituent Assembly was false and deceptive. Such talk was then necessary in order to usurp governmental power. They said one thing but were aiming at another. They talked about the rule of the people, but in reality they were striving to rule over the people. They have usurped power by falsehood and bloodshed and they are grasping it convulsively. It is quite plain that we are bound for a collision between the representatives of the people and the usurpers.

We are not afraid of this coming struggle. When a sufficient number of us comes together, we shall go again to the Taurida Palace and begin the work of the Constituent Assembly. We will not yield to violence! Alone, however, we have not the power to win. We need the support of the whole people and we are waiting for it. We call upon

[55] *Nash Vek,* No. 8, December 20, 1917, pp. 2–3.

the people to support their representatives in every possible way. We call upon everyone to fight the usurpers of the people's will. Otherwise we shall have no peace, no land, no liberty; in their stead poverty, oppression, and hunger are bound to come.

Be ready to come out in the defense of the Constituent Assembly when it calls upon you. . . . .

[Signatures follow]

In the meantime non-Bolshevik delegates to the Assembly were trying under difficulties to hold sessions of those members who had reached the capital. Despite the heavy guards posted near the Taurida Palace, about fifty members held a brief informal meeting on December 12. The following day Blagonravov, a Bolshevik, ordered the delegates meeting in the palace library to leave. When they refused he summoned a guard of fifty sailors, whereupon the delegates left protesting. Daily meetings were then abandoned and it was left for Chernov, the temporary chairman, to call the Assembly together when enough members had arrived in the capital.[56]

THE PETROGRAD GARRISON AND THE ASSEMBLY[57]

[December 27, 1917]

[At a meeting of the Petrograd garrison the following resolution introduced by Zinoviev was passed]:

1. The garrison considers as the principal conquest of the revolution the fact that the government passed to the Soviets and that the Soviet Government entered upon a decisive and relentless struggle against the bourgeoisie and landlords, has started peace negotiations, and has transferred the land to the peasants.

2. The workers, soldiers, and peasants can recognize the Constituent Assembly, provided the latter recognizes the Soviet Government, supports the program of the Second Congress of Soviets. . . . .

3. The garrison wishes to make clear to all soldiers that the slogan of the Constituent Assembly was adopted by the Kaledinists and Kornilovists and is used as a shield of counter-revolution. . . . .

[56] *Nash Vek,* No. 2, December 14, 1917, p. 2; *ibid.,* No. 3, December 15, 1917, p. 3.

[57] *Izvestiia,* No. 253, December 29, 1917, p. 8.

ARREST OF THE SOCIALIST-REVOLUTIONIST LEADERS

[December 30–31]

N. D. Avxentiev, formerly President of the Council of the Russian Republic, member of the Constituent Assembly, prominent Socialist-Revolutionist, was . . . . arrested on December 30 and locked up in Peter and Paul Fortress.[58]

Why Avxentiev Was Arrested

You [Socialist-Revolutionists] know as well as we do that Avxentiev was arrested not as a member of the Constituent Assembly but because of his connection with the armed uprising of the cadets against the workers and soldiers . . . . against the people's revolution. For this same reason orders have been issued for the arrest of Gotz and not at all because he was elected to the Constituent Assembly. . . . .[59]

Order of the Cheka for the Arrest of Chernov and Others

The following are to be arrested at once and handed over to the Revolutionary Tribunal: I. G. Tsereteli, V. M. Chernov, F. I. Dan (Gurevich), M. M. Bramson, M. I. Skobelev, A. R. Gotz, V. N. Rozanov, M. Binasik, G. Vengerov, V. V. Ivanovsky, P. Gamburov, V. Herman-Kamensky.

V. Dzerzhinsky
Chairman of the All-Russian Extraordinary Commission
to Fight Counter-Revolution and Sabotage[60]

Petrograd, December 31, 1917

THE LEFT SOCIALIST-REVOLUTIONISTS AND THE BOLSHEVIKS[61]

[January 2, 1918]

V. A. Karelin, a leader of the Socialist-Revolutionists of the Left and a recently appointed member of the Sovnarkom . . . . gave an interview . . . . on the questions of the moment. He pointed out that the Sovnarkom has not enough authority to solve such questions as the land question. The sanction of the Constituent Assembly is required here,

[58] *Nash Vek,* No. 17, January 1, 1918, p. 3.

[59] *Izvestiia,* No. 258, January 4, 1918, p. 1.

[60] *Nash Vek,* No. 21, January 5, 1918, p. 3.

[61] *Novaia Zhizn,* No. 206, January 2, 1918, p. 2.

though . . . . the chances that the latter will adopt a proper attitude are very slight. The Socialist-Revolutionists of the Left are doing their best to form a bloc . . . . with the S.R.'s of the Center headed by Chernov. . . . . If this is attained the Constituent Assembly is saved. . . . . I doubt, however, that a common language can be found. The S.R.'s of the Right and the Center are too blinded by their hatred of the November Revolution. . . . . In any case [the Constituent Assembly] should be opened with its present composition. . . . . It should be given a chance to pass the test before the people.

What if it does not pass the test?

In that case the problem of forming a revolutionary convention will come up. . . . .

There will be between sixty and seventy [members of our party]; we shall, therefore, be unable to form a majority with the Bolsheviks. On the other hand, if the Ukrainian S.R.'s join us, which is quite possible, ... then a government bloc . . . . will be formed with about 350 members. . . . .

Our relations [to the Bolsheviks] are quite cordial. Our only point of disagreement is the question of terror which the S.R.'s of the Left absolutely condemn. We also think that certain measures [taken by the Bolsheviks] though theoretically sound are too daring in practice. On the whole, our party performs the function of regulating and tempering the excessive boldness of the Bolsheviks.

In what did that regulating activity find its expression? . . . . In the first place, owing to our efforts, the calling of the Constituent Assembly is assured. [In the second place], we made it impossible to use the decree on recall as a means to suppress the Constituent Assembly. . . . .

THE CENTRAL EXECUTIVE COMMITTEE ON THE CONSTITUENT ASSEMBLY

[Meeting and Resolution of January 4, 1918]

[At a meeting of the Central Executive Committee on January 4] a decree was introduced to open the Constituent Assembly on January 18. . . . . Zinoviev declared that: . . . . the Constituent Assembly can be recognized only if it adopts the program of the Second Congress of the Soviets of Workers' and Soldiers' Deputies and recognizes the Soviet Government. If it should not do that, it would be a stone in the path of the social revolution and the Soviet Government will have to remove it. The Constituent Assembly can carry out its own program only over the dead body of the Soviets. . . . . In calling the Constituent Assembly the C.E.C. calls at the same time a Congress of Soviets on

January 21 and a peasant congress on January 28 in order that the oppressed people may pass sentence on the Constituent Assembly.[62]

[The C.E.C. then adopted the following resolution]:

The Constituent Assembly will open on the eighteenth of January. The parties of concealed and open counter-revolution, the Mensheviks, Socialist-Revolutionists of the Right, Kornilovists, and the sabotaging bureaucracy, are prepared to make a determined stand against the Soviet Government of Workers and Peasants. All counter-revolutionary elements without exception have rallied under the banner, "All power to the Constituent Assembly." In reality, however, the enemies of the workers' and peasants' revolution are united by the watchword, "Down with the Soviets," and that means down with all those gains which have been conquered at the price of great sacrifices. . . . .

The Central Executive Committee considers it its duty to resist in the most energetic manner the above counter-revolutionary attempts. . . . . It therefore decrees:

To call a Third All-Russian Congress of Soviets of Workers' and Soldiers' Deputies on January 21, and a Third Congress of Peasants' Deputies on January 28. . . . .[63]

PARTY AFFILIATIONS OF THE ELECTED DELEGATES

The All-Russian Commission on Elections had registered 520 members of the Constituent Assembly by January 12, 1918. The party affiliations of the members are as follows: Socialist-Revolutionist, 267; Bolshevik, 161; Representatives of the Soviet of Peasants' Deputies, 5; Menshevik, 3; Mussulman Socialist-Revolutionist, 5; Ukrainian Socialist-Revolutionist and Social-Democrat, 41; Esthonian Democratic Party, 2; Bashkir, 1; Latvian, 1; Mussulman Nationalist, 6; Jewish Nationalist, 3; Esthonian Labor Party, 3; Socialist-Populist, 1; Cadets, 15; Chuvash, 3. . . . .[64]

According to the information of the Socialist-Revolutionists there were 603 members by January 12, among them 270 Socialist-Revolutionists of the Right, 36 Socialist-Revolutionists of the Left, 53 Ukrainian Socialists, 167 Bolsheviks, and 25 Mussulmans, the majority of whom adhere to the Socialist-Revolutionists.[65]

62 *Nash Vek,* No. 22, January 6, 1918, p. 5.

63 *Vestnik Otdela Mestnago Upravleniia Komissariata Vnutrennikh Del,* December 27, 1917 [January 9, 1918], No. 1, pp. 1–2.

64 *Utro Rossii,* No. 1, January 16, 1918, p. 3. The Chuvash are a Finno-Ugrian people inhabiting parts of Kazan and Simbirsk gubernias.

65 *Russkiia Vedomosti,* No. 278, January 12, 1917, p. 3.

ON THE SUPREMACY OF SOVIET INSTITUTIONS

[Decree of the Central Executive Committee, January 16][66]

On the basis of the conquests of the November Revolution and the Declaration of the Rights of the Toiling and Exploited Masses adopted by the Central Executive Committee on January 16,[67] all power in the Russian Republic is vested with the Soviets and Soviet institutions. Every attempt on the part of any person or institution to usurp governmental authority will be considered as a counter-revolutionary act . . . . and will be suppressed by the Soviet Government by every available means, including armed force.

THE DEMONSTRATION OF JANUARY 18

The Petrograd Union to Defend the Constituent Assembly has called on all the population of the city to take part in the demonstration in honor of the opening of the Constituent Assembly.

In the . . . . City Duma a resolution was adopted to appeal to the population to take part in the demonstration. . . . . The demonstration is to be peaceful in character and under the following slogans: "All Power to the Constituent Assembly," "Down with the Fratricidal Civil War," etc. . . . .

The Sovnarkom has called out from Viborg and Helsingfors two thousand sailors, who are expected at Petrograd on January 17 . . . . to guard the Taurida Palace and the streets leading to it. . . . .[68]

[The Petrograd Soviet has passed a resolution that] not a single honest worker, not a single conscientious soldier, should join in the demonstration of the enemies of the people . . . . and that all workers should remain at their tasks and all soldiers stay in their barracks.[69]

"Demonstration or plot?" asked . . . . *Pravda*. . . . . The Sovnarkom has asked the same question . . . . and has answered . . . . by saying that it was a plot "against Socialism, against the Republic of Soviets" and has taken the necessary measures. It has put up barricades before the entrance to the Taurida Palace, machine guns at the entrance, machine guns on roofs . . . . on Smolny . . . .[70]

About 11:30 some two hundred men bearing a flag with the words, "All Power to the Constituent Assembly," came across the Liteiny Bridge. As they approached the Liteiny, armed soldiers and Red Guards

[66] *Izvestiia*, No. 2, January 17, 1918, p. 1.

[67] Text of the Declaration is given on pp. 372–74, below.

[68] *Novaia Zhizn*, No. 3, January 18, 1918, p. 2.

[69] *Ibid.*, p. 4.

[70] *Ibid.*, No. 4, January 19, 1918, p. 1.

appeared from behind the barricades .... and demanded that the crowd disperse. When no attention was paid to the order, a volley was fired. The crowd ran, the soldiers grabbed the flags .... and burned them. ....

At 12:30 two columns of paraders came together on the square in front of the Winter Palace and united. .... Some of the soldiers and workers called them names: "saboteurs, burzhui" [bourgeoisie]. .... The parade continued up to the Liteiny .... but when it attempted to turn .... toward the Taurida Palace it was met by a volley of fire. The firing lasted about fifteen minutes, after which the crowd fell back. ....

In the course of the day several were killed and many wounded.[71]

To the Inhabitants of Petrograd

The enemies of the people, counter-revolutionists and saboteurs, are spreading the reports that the revolutionary workers and soldiers shot peaceful laborers who were in the procession on January 18. This is done for the purpose of alarming the toiling masses and arousing them to attack .... the leaders of the revolution. ....

The Executive Committee asks the inhabitants not to believe these reports. ....

Executive Committee of the Petrograd Soviet of Workers' and Soldiers' Deputies[72]

D. The Suppression of the Constituent Assembly

On the afternoon of the 18th the elected deputies and the curious found the approaches and doors of the Taurida Palace, where the Assembly was to meet, heavily guarded by sailors and Red Guards. Only those with passes were allowed to enter. Gradually the deputies, except the Bolsheviks, who were said to be holding a preliminary meeting in another room of the palace, took their places. Some of the deputies brought candles and sandwiches with them in case the Bolsheviks should cut off the lights and deny them food. "Thus," says Trotsky contemptuously, "democracy entered upon the struggle with dictatorship heavily armed with sandwiches and candles."[73] A crowd of workers, sailors, and soldiers who had received cards of admission from the Bol-

[71] *Novaia Zhizn*, No. 4, January 19, 1918, p. 3.

[72] *Izvestiia*, No. 5, January 20, 1918, p. 1.

[73] *Lenin*, p. 123.

shevik commander of the palace occupied the galleries and revealed their sentiments in remarks addressed to the deputies below.[74]

THE OPENING OF THE CONSTITUENT ASSEMBLY

[From the Stenographic Report of the Session of January 18, 1918][75]

[At four o'clock] . . . . Lordkipanidze [Socialist-Revolutionist] got up and said: Comrades, it is now four o'clock, and I propose that the oldest person present take the chair and open the Constituent Assembly. Sergei Petrovich Shvetsov is the oldest person. . . . .

Shvetsov (*rings the bell*): The Constituent Assembly is now open. (*Noise from the Left* [*Bolsheviks*]: *"Get down, you self-appointed." Cheers from the Right.*) "I declare a recess." (*Just then Sverdlov, Bolshevik and chairman of the Central Executive Committee went up to the Speaker's table.*)

Sverdlov: The Executive Committee of the Soviet of Workers' and Peasants' Deputies authorized me to open the Constituent Assembly. (*Voices from the Center and the Right: "Wash your bloody hands; enough blood." Cheers from the Left.*) The Central Executive Committee of the Soviet of Workers', Soldiers', and Peasants' Deputies . . . . expresses the hope that the Constituent Assembly will accept all the decrees and ordinances of the Soviet of People's Commissars. The November Revolution has kindled the fire of the Socialist revolution not only in Russia but in all countries. (*Laughter on the Right.*) We are certain that the sparks of our conflagration will be blown all over the world . . . . and that the day is not far off when the toilers of all countries will rise against their exploiters just as the Russians . . . . did against their oppressors. (*Shouts of applause on the Left.*) We have no doubt that the true representatives of the toiling people in the Constituent Assembly will help the Soviets to put an end to class privileges. . . . .

[74] The total membership of the Constituent Assembly has not as yet been definitely determined. The computations of Sviatitsky referred to on p. 350 n. 26, above, embrace only fifty-four electoral regions of a total of seventy-nine. The Tsentrarkhiv, in its edition of the stenographic records of the Constituent Assembly which appeared in 1930 under the title *Vserossiiskoe Uchreditelnoe Sobranie*, gives a list of 707 deputies. Of these 370 were Socialist-Revolutionists of the Right, 40 S.R.'s of the Left, 175 Bolsheviks, 16 Mensheviks, 17 Cadets, 2 Socialist-Populists. The party affiliations of the rest have not been determined. But this list is also incomplete, as it does not contain the deputies from Turkestan, Northern Caucasus, Kuban, Terek, and Dagestan. (*Vserossiiskoe Uchreditelnoe Sobranie*, pp. 115–38; also M. Vishniak, *Vserossiiskoe Uchreditelnoe Sobranie*, Paris, 1932, pp. 90–91.)

[75] *Uchreditelnoe Sobranie. Stenograficheskii otchet*, Petrograd, 1918, pp. 1–9.

Just as in the days of the French bourgeois revolution . . . . there was proclaimed a Declaration of the Rights of Man and of the Citizen . . . . so today our Russian Socialist Revolution should likewise make its own declaration. . . . . It is the hope of the Central Executive Committee that the Constituent Assembly . . . . will also accept the declaration which I have the honor to read.

[Having read the declaration, Sverdlov continued]:

By the authority of the Central Executive Committee of the Soviet of Workers', Soldiers', and Peasants' Deputies I declare the Constituent Assembly open. I move that a chairman be elected. . . . . (*Shouts on the Left: Comrades! [Let us sing] the "Internationale." The Assembly sings the "Internationale."*) . . . .

Lordkipanidze: The Socialist-Revolutionists are of the opinion . . . . that we should have elected a chairman the very first thing. . . . . No other power than the Constituent Assembly can open the meeting. (*Whistling from the Left.*) . . . .

The Socialist-Revolutionists propose the name of Victor M. Chernov for chairman. . . . .

Skvortsov: . . . . The Bolsheviks propose the name of Maria A. Spiridonova.[76] . . . .

[Sverdlov]: . . . . Victor Chernov has been elected by a vote of 244 to 151. . . . . Will he please take the chair? (*Loud applause in the Center and on the Right.*)

DECLARATION OF THE RIGHTS OF THE TOILING AND EXPLOITED PEOPLES[77]

Part I

[chapter one]

[1] Russia is proclaimed a Republic of Soviets of Workers', Soldiers', and Peasants' Deputies. All central and local authority is vested in these Soviets.

[76] A Left Socialist-Revolutionist.

[77] According to Trotsky, Lenin was the author of the "Declaration." (Trotsky, *Lenin,* p. 151.) The Declaration was adopted by the Central Executive Committee on January 16 and published in *Izvestiia,* No. 2, January 17, 1918, p. 1. The version here given having been rejected by the Constituent Assembly, the Declaration was brought up before the Third Congress of Soviets (January 23–31, 1918) and accepted (January 23). In addition to substituting the words "Third All-Russian Congress of Soviets" for "Constituent Assembly," the Third Congress (and later the Fifth Congress when it embodied the Declaration in the Constitution) left out Articles 1 and 3 in Chapter Four, and made Article 3 of Chapter Three a part of Article 2, Chapter Two. (*Tretii Vserossiiskii Sezd Sovetov Rabochikh, Soldatskikh i Krestianskikh Deputatov,* Petrograd, 1918, pp. 90–92. Hereafter cited as *T.V.S.S.*)

[2] The Russian Soviet Republic is established on the basis of a free union of free nations, a federation of National Soviet Republics.

[CHAPTER TWO]

The Constituent Assembly sets for itself as a fundamental task the suppression of all forms of exploitation of man by man and the complete abolition of class distinctions in society. It aims to crush unmercifully the exploiter, to reorganize society on a socialistic basis, and to bring about the triumph of Socialism throughout the world. It further resolves:

[1] In order to bring about the socialization of land, private ownership of land is abolished. The entire land fund is declared the property of the nation and turned over free of cost to the toilers on the basis of equal right to its use.

All forests, subsoil resources, and waters of national importance as well as all live stock and machinery, model farms, and agricultural enterprises are declared to be national property.

[2] As a first step to the complete transfer of the factories, shops, mines, railroads, and other means of production and transportation to the Soviet Republic of Workers and Peasants, and in order to insure the supremacy of the toiling masses over the exploiters, the Constituent Assembly ratifies the Soviet law on workers' control and that on the Supreme Council of National Economy.

[3] The Constituent Assembly ratifies the transfer of all banks to the ownership of the workers' and peasants' government as one of the conditions for the emancipation of the toiling masses from the yoke of capitalism.

[4] In order to do away with the parasitic classes of society and organize the economic life of the country, universal labor duty is introduced.

[5] In order to give all the power to the toiling masses and to make impossible the restoration of the power of the exploiters, it is decreed to arm the toilers, to establish a Socialist Red Army, and to disarm completely the propertied classes.

[CHAPTER THREE]

[1] The Constituent Assembly expresses its firm determination to snatch mankind from the claws of capitalism and imperialism which have brought on this most criminal of all wars and have drenched the world with blood. It approves whole-heartedly the policy of the Soviet Government in breaking with the secret treaties, in organizing extensive fraternization between the workers and peasants in the ranks of the opposing armies and in its efforts to bring about, at all costs, by revolu-

tionary means, a democratic peace between nations on the principle of no annexation, no indemnity, and free self-determination of nations.

[2] With the same purpose in mind the Constituent Assembly demands a complete break with the barbarous policy of bourgeois civilization which enriches the exploiters in a few chosen nations at the expense of hundreds of millions of the toiling population in Asia, in the colonies, and in the small countries.

The Constituent Assembly welcomes the policy of the Soviet of People's Commissars in granting complete independence to Finland, of removing the troops from Persia and allowing Armenia the right of self-determination.

The Constituent Assembly considers the Soviet law repudiating the debts contracted by the government of the Tsar, landholders, and the bourgeoisie a first blow to international banking and finance-capital. The Constituent Assembly expresses its confidence that the Soviet Government will follow this course firmly until the complete victory of the international labor revolt against the yoke of capital.

[CHAPTER FOUR]

[1] Having been elected on party lists made up before the November Revolution, when the people were not yet in a position to rebel against the exploiters whose powers of opposition in defense of their class privileges were not yet known, and when the people had not yet done anything practical to organize a socialistic society, the Constituent Assembly feels that it would be quite wrong even technically to set itself up in opposition to the Soviet.

[2] The Constituent Assembly believes that at this present moment of decisive struggle of the proletariat against the exploiters there is no place for the exploiters in any organ of government. The government belongs wholly to the toiling masses and their fully empowered representatives, the Soviets of Workers', Soldiers', and Peasants' Deputies.

[3] In supporting the Soviet and the decrees of the Soviet of People's Commissars, the Constituent Assembly admits that it has no power beyond working out some of the fundamental problems of reorganizing society on a socialistic basis.

[4] At the same time, desiring to bring about a really free and voluntary, and consequently more complete and lasting, union of the toiling classes of all nations in Russia, the Constituent Assembly confines itself to the formulation of the fundamental principles of a federation of the Soviet Republics of Russia, leaving to the workers and peasants of each nation to decide independently at their own plenipotentiary Soviet Congresses whether or not they desire, and if so on what conditions, to take part in the federated government and other federal Soviet institutions.

Upon taking the chair Chernov delivered a long speech emphasizing the importance of the Constituent Assembly, what it could and would do for Russia, peace, and socialism. He was interrupted frequently by the Bolsheviks. At the end of his speech Chernov suggested that a secretary be chosen. After much noise and a little talk Vishniak was made secretary. Then Bukharin got the floor.

Bukharin criticized Chernov and abstract socialism. He said that when the Bolsheviks talked of the dictatorship of the proletariat, of workers' control, of nationalization and socialization, they had in mind bringing these changes to pass now and not two hundred years hence. Bukharin accused the moderate Socialists of standing in the way of real socialism. He concluded by calling on the world proletariat to unite.

Tsereteli accused the Bolsheviks (who were beginning to call themselves Communists) of talking a great deal about what they were going to do, without, however, producing any evidence that they could do anything constructive. There was no reason, no good argument, said Tsereteli, why the Constituent Assembly should approve everything that the Commissars had done. Since the Bolsheviks had taken control of the government the situation in the country had gone from bad to worse. He ended by proposing a Social-Democratic program which made the Constituent Assembly the highest power in the land for the time being.

Skvortsov, Kovarsky, Zenzinov, Severov-Odoevsky, Grigorev, Tsalikov, and Sorokin followed Tsereteli. After Sorokin had finished, a vote was taken on the question whether to make the Bolshevik Declaration of the Rights of Toiling and Exploited Peoples or the program of the Socialist-Revolutionists the order of the day. The vote showed 237 for the Socialist-Revolutionist program and 136 for the Bolshevik declaration. After several others had spoken a recess of half an hour was declared.

The chairman called the meeting to order about one in the morning. Skobelev, Antipin, Mamkin, Timofeev, and

Severov-Odoevsky attacked the Bolsheviks. Raskolnikov (Bolshevik) made the following statement and announced the withdrawal of the Bolsheviks from the Constituent Assembly.

BOLSHEVIK STATEMENT[78]

The great majority of the Russian toilers, workers, peasants, and soldiers, have demanded that the Constituent Assembly recognize the conquests of the November Revolution, the Soviet decrees on land, peace, and workers' control and, above all, the Government of the Soviet of Workers', Soldiers', and Peasants' Deputies. (*Applause from the public.*)

In its endeavor to carry out the will of the great majority of Russia's laboring classes, the All-Russian Central Executive Committee has recommended to the Constituent Assembly that it accept the expression of this will as law. This, however, the majority of the Constituent Assembly, influenced by the bourgeoisie, has refused to do and has thereby challenged the Russian toilers. (*Applause from the public.*) A majority of the Constituent Assembly are Socialist-Revolutionists of the Right, that is to say, the party of Kerensky, Avxentiev, and Chernov. . . . . This party, which calls itself Socialist and revolutionary, directs the fight of the bourgeois forces against the revolution of the workers and peasants and is really a bourgeois and counter-revolutionary party. (*Applause from the public.*)

The present composition of the Constituent Assembly is largely due to the interrelation of political forces at work before the great November Revolution. The counter-revolutionary majority of the Constituent Assembly . . . . (*shouts and protests on the Right*) was elected on the basis of antiquated party lists and represents yesterday's point of view. [That majority] is attempting, nevertheless, to block the progress of the workers' and peasants' movement. (*Voices from the Right: "Nonsense!" Applause from the public.*) Today's proceedings have made it quite clear that the Socialist-Revolutionists of the Right follow the tactics of Kerensky and feed the people on words, openly promising this and that but underhandedly fighting against the Soviets of Workers, Peasants, and Soldiers, against socialistic measures, against the transfer, without compensation, of the land and implements to the peasants (*shouts: "It is a lie!" Applause from the public*), against the nationalization of banks, against repudiation of state debts. (*Shouts: "Idiot!" Applause from the public.*) . . . .

[78] *Uchreditelnoe Sobranie,* pp. 87–88.

We do not intend to shield the enemies of the people in their criminal acts, and we hereby . . . . withdraw from this Constituent Assembly (*shouts of applause from the public*) so as to leave it to the Soviet Government to decide finally what attitude it shall take toward the counter-revolutionary section of the Constituent Assembly. (*Shouts: "Pogrom makers!" Applause from the public.*)

During and immediately after the reading there was such a noise, such a display of bitter feeling that the session appeared on the verge of breaking up in a free-for-all fight.

Steinberg, Socialist-Revolutionist of the Left, accused the Constituent Assembly of dodging the issues by refusing to vote on the Bolshevik declaration. This was denied by the Socialist-Revolutionists of the Right. The reply did not satisfy the Socialist-Revolutionists of the Left, and they withdrew from the Assembly.

After their departure the chairman read the Socialist-Revolutionists' proposal for a land law.

PROPOSED LAND LAW OF THE SOCIALIST-REVOLUTIONISTS[79]

1. The right to private ownership of land within the boundaries of the Russian Republic is hereby abolished forever.

2. All the land within the boundaries of the Russian Republic, with its subsoil resources, forests, and waters, is hereby declared the property of the nation.

3. The Republic has the right through the central and local organs of government, in accordance with the regulations provided by the present law, to control all the land, with all its subsoil resources, forests, and waters.

4. The autonomous provinces of the Russian Republic have title to land on the basis of the present law and in agreement with the Federal Constitution.

5. The tasks of the government as regards the administration of land, subsoil resources, forests, and waters are: (*a*) The creation of conditions conducive to the best possible utilization of the country's natural resources and the highest possible development of its productive forces; (*b*) a fair distribution of all the natural resources among the people.

[79] *Uchreditelnoe Sobranie*, pp. 108–109.

6. The rights of individuals and institutions in relation to the land, subsoil resources, forests, and waters are limited to use only.

7. The use of all land, subsoil resources, forests, and waters is free to all citizens of the Russian Republic, regardless of nationality and creed, or to associations and state and public institutions.

8. The right to use the land is acquired and lost on the basis prescribed by this fundamental law.

9. All titles to land at present held by individuals, associations, and institutions are abolished in so far as they contradict this law.

10. All land, subsoil resources, forests, and waters, at present owned by or otherwise in the possession of individuals, associations, and institutions, become the property of the people without compensation.

[At the conclusion of the reading a sailor walked up to the chairman, put a hand on his shoulder and said]:

Citizen Sailor: I have instructions to inform you that all those present should leave the hall because the guard is tired. . . . .

Chairman: What instructions? From whom?

Citizen Sailor: I am at the head of the guard of the Taurida Palace, and I have instructions from Commissar Dybenko.

Chairman: All the members of the Constituent Assembly are also very tired, but that must not stand in the way of going ahead with the land law for which Russia waits. . . . .

Citizen Sailor: I ask you to leave the hall at once. . . . .

Chairman: [temporarily ignores the sailor and reads the peace declaration].

PEACE DECLARATION OF THE SOCIALIST-REVOLUTIONISTS[80]

In the name of the peoples of the Russian Republic, the All-Russian Constituent Assembly, expressing the firm will of the people immediately to discontinue the war and conclude a just and general peace, addresses itself to the Allies with a proposal to define jointly the exact terms of a democratic peace acceptable to all the belligerent nations, in order to present these terms, on behalf of the Coalition [Allies], to the states fighting against the Russian Republic and her Allies.

The Constituent Assembly firmly believes that the attempts of the peoples of Russia to end the ruinous war will meet with a unanimous response on the part of the peoples and governments of the Allied countries and that by common efforts a speedy peace will be attained

[80] *Uchreditelnoe Sobranie*, pp. 110–11.

which will safeguard the well-being and dignity of all the belligerent countries.

Expressing, in the name of the peoples of Russia, its regret that the negotiations with Germany, which were started without a preliminary agreement with the Allied democracies, have assumed the character of negotiations for a separate peace, the Constituent Assembly, in the name of the peoples of the Russian Federative Republic, will prolong the armistice and continue the negotiations . . . . with the idea of securing a universal democratic peace and at the same time defending the interests of Russia.

The Constituent Assembly declares that it will do everything in its power to help the Socialist parties of the Russian Republic in their efforts to call an International Socialist Conference for the purpose of bringing about a general democratic peace.

The Constituent Assembly resolves to select from its body a plenipotentiary delegation to carry on negotiations with representatives of the Allies . . . . on the question of bringing the war to an early end and of carrying out the decisions of the Constituent Assembly in regard to peace negotiations with the states warring against us.

This delegation . . . . is to proceed immediately to carry out the obligations which are laid upon it by the Constituent Assembly.

The delegation is to be made up proportionately of representatives of the different parties.

All the proposals were voted upon and approved. It was moved to accept the following resolution on the form of government:

In the name of the peoples composing the Russian State, the Constituent Assembly resolves that: The Russian State is proclaimed a Russian Democratic Federative Republic and an indissoluble union of peoples and territories, each sovereign within the limits laid down by the federal constitution.

This resolution was passed. . [The motion to adjourn until five o'clock in the afternoon of January 19 was carried. The session came to an end at 4:40 A.M., January 19.]

After the withdrawal of the Bolsheviks and the Socialist-Revolutionists of the Left, the Sovnarkom met to consider what should be done with the Constituent Assembly. The S.R. members of the Sovnarkom[81] insisted either that there should be new elections to the Constituent Assembly or that

[81] Since December 23, there had been eight Socialist-Revolutionists of the Left in the Sovnarkom. (*Izvestiia,* No. 249, December 25, 1917, p. 6.)

a revolutionary convention should be formed, after the precedent of the French Revolution, to include the Left elements of the Assembly and the delegates of the Workers' and Peasants' Soviets. The Bolsheviks demanded that a decree be issued at once dissolving the Assembly without further reference to new elections or a revolutionary convention. The disagreement was referred to the C.E.C., which held a special session to consider the question.[82]

THE CENTRAL EXECUTIVE COMMITTEE VOTES THE DISSOLUTION OF THE CONSTITUENT ASSEMBLY

[Meeting of January 19, 1918][83]

Sverdlov opened the session with the statement that the Sovnarkom had introduced a decree to dissolve the Constituent Assembly and a proposal to include the Socialist-Revolutionists of the Left and the Bolshevik members of the Constituent Assembly in the Central Executive Committee. . . . .

Greeted by applause from the majority in the hall and cries of "Dictator" from the Left, Lenin began his two-hour speech defending the dissolution of the Constituent Assembly.

[Lenin's Speech][84]

Comrades! The collision between the Soviet Government and the Constituent Assembly has been prepared by the entire history of the Russian Revolution, which has been confronted with the unheard-of task of a socialist reconstruction of society. After the events of 1905 there was no longer any doubt that tsarism was doomed, and that it succeeded in rescuing itself from the abyss only through the backwardness and ignorance of the village. The revolution of 1917 has caused, on the one hand, the transformation of the bourgeois-imperialist party, which under the pressure of events became a republican party, and, on the other hand, the emergence of democratic organizations, Soviets, dating from 1905. Even at that early date Socialists understood that by organizing those Soviets something great would be created, something new and unprecedented in the history of the world revolution. The Soviets, which the people themselves created, are a form of democ-

[82] *Novaia Zhizn,* No. 5, January 20, 1918, p. 2.

[83] *Ibid.,* No. 6, January 22, 1918, p. 4.

[84] *Izvestiia,* No. 5, January 20, 1918, p. 4. *Sochineniia,* XXII, 184–87.

racy of which there is no equal in any other country. . . . . When I hear the opponents of the November Revolution shouting about the unpractical and utopian ideas of socialism, I usually ask them a simple and plain question: How about the Soviets? What are the facts that gave birth to these organizations of the people unknown in the whole history of the world revolution? To these questions I have not been able yet to get a definite answer. In their stubborn defense of the bourgeois system, the [opponents of the November Revolution] oppose these mighty organizations which not one of the revolutions of the world has ever witnessed before. But those who fight the landlords go to the Soviets of peasants' deputies. The Soviets receive one and all, anyone who, not wishing to remain inactive, is ready to enter upon the path of creative work. The entire country is covered with their network, and the tighter this net of people's Soviets is drawn the less will be the exploitation of the toiling masses, because the existence of the Soviets is incompatible with the flourishing of the bourgeois system; therein lies the source of all the contradictions of the representatives of the bourgeoisie who are fighting against our Soviets in the name of their interests.

The transition from a capitalistic to a socialistic structure of society must necessarily be accompanied by a long and stubborn struggle. The Russian Revolution, having overthrown tsarism, could not stop at the stage of a bourgeois revolution; it had to go further because the war with its resulting unheard-of suffering of the exhausted nations produced the soil for the outbreak of the social revolution. There is, therefore, nothing more ridiculous than to say that the further course of the revolution and the wrath of the masses have been brought about by any one party, by a single individual, or, as they lament, by the will of a dictator. The revolutionary conflagration burst forth only because of the ignorance and the incredible sufferings of Russia and because the conditions created by the war confronted the toiling masses in a decisive way with the alternatives either to take a bold, audacious, and fearless step or to perish and die of hunger. (*Shouts of applause.*)

This revolutionary fire manifested itself in the fact that the Soviets, this prop of the workers' revolution, were established. The Russian people accomplished a tremendous leap, a jump from tsarism to the Soviets. This is an undeniable and hitherto unparalleled fact. And while the bourgeois parliaments of all nations and states within the confines of capitalism and private property have nowhere and at no time given any support to the revolutionary movement, the Soviets, fanning the flame of revolution, imperatively command the people: Fight, take everything into your own hands, organize yourselves!

There is no doubt that in the process of revolutionary development called forth by the power of the Soviets, there will be all sorts of errors and blunders, but it is no secret to anyone that any revolutionary movement inevitably and always is accompanied by a temporary chaos, destruction, and disorder. Bourgeois society . . . . is synonymous with war and throat-cutting, a fact which brought about and sharpened the conflict between the Constituent Assembly and the Soviets. Those who remind us of the time when we also stood for the Constituent Assembly and rebuke us for now "dispersing" it simply show that they have not a single idea in their minds and are using pompous and empty phrases. For as compared with the ill-fated institutions of tsarism and the Kerensky republic the Constituent Assembly seemed to us then a step forward. But with their establishment the Soviets, being revolutionary mass organizations, naturally became immeasurably superior to any other parliament in the world, a fact which I emphasized as early as April [last year]. The Soviets, in undertaking to break up the bourgeois and the landlords' world of private property, thus aiding in the triumph of the social revolution which will sweep away all remnants of bourgeois society, have started us on a road which is leading the people to the building of a new life. We have already taken up this great constructive task, and we have done well to take it up. There is no doubt that the socialist revolution cannot be presented to the people in its pristine, smooth, and flawless perfection; it cannot help leading to civil war, sabotage, and opposition. Those who would teach us the opposite are either liars or men living in a casket.[85] (*Shouts of applause.*) . . . .

The people at large have not as yet realized all the implications of the November Revolution. This Revolution has shown in fact how the people must proceed to take over the land, the national wealth, and the means of production and transport and place them in the hands of the workers' and peasants' government.

All power to the Soviets we said then, and for this we are fighting. The people desired to call the Constituent Assembly, and we called it. But it [the people] soon realized what this vaunted Constituent Assembly really represents. And now, once more, we are fulfilling the will of the people, which declared: All power to the Soviets! And we shall crush the *saboteurs*. . . . .

The transfer of all power to the Constituent Assembly is nothing but the old policy of "conciliation" with the malevolent bourgeoisie. The Russian Soviets place the interests of the toiling masses much higher that the interests of the treasonable conciliators clad in a new garb. . . . . As long as Kaledin exists, and as long as the slogan, "All power to the Constituent Assembly" is used as a cloak to the slogan, "Down with the Soviet power," so long will there be no escape from

[85] "A Man in a Casket" is a story by A. Chekhov depicting the life of a schoolteacher, banal and pedantic.

civil war, for we will not give up the Soviet power for anything in the world! (*Shouts of applause.*) . . . . The Constituent Assembly, which failed to recognize the power of the people, is now dispersed by the will of the Soviet power. . . . . The Soviet Republic will triumph, no matter what happens.[86]

[Stroev's Speech][87]

Stroev, a representative of the United Internationalists, takes the floor. . . . .

I know, he says, that my speech will remain a voice crying in the wilderness. When people are making a desperate plunge it is useless to appeal to their reason. . . . . Lenin has been telling us that the people are disillusioned about the Constituent Assembly. All that Lenin has to go on are his observations of the representatives of the "poor peasantry," the Socialist-Revolutionists of the Left, who showed themselves to be very clever fellows. . . . . They managed to lose their faith in the Constituent Assembly in about an hour and a half, but do they really think that that time is sufficient for the people to do the same? For many years . . . . the Socialist-Revolutionists and the Social-Democrats have been instilling in the people faith in the Constituent Assembly, and now you wish to make a headlong plunge.

Yesterday red banners were being snatched from the hands of workers. One more illusion is being done away with. The respect for Socialist banners reddened with proletarian blood (*Cries, "Enough!" The tumult drowns the words from the speaker*). . . . . I am used to speaking against noises like these. I talked against the cries of the Black Hundred and wild vociferations of the mob. I should like to think that I am now under the protection of the red flag. (*A tremendous uproar fills the hall. The chairman calls upon the speaker to refrain from such comparisons.*)

The Bolsheviks who control the government failed to carry out the wishes of the Second Congress of Soviets . . . . which resolved to call the Constituent Assembly and not to disperse it. . . . . (*Cries and hisses in the hall.*)

[Stroev was not allowed to go on with his speech, and he concluded by reading a resolution of his party which ended as follows]:

The Constituent Assembly alone is capable of uniting all parts of Russia to put an end to the civil war which is speeding up the economic

[86] In chapter v of his pamphlet, *The Proletarian Revolution and Kautsky the Renegade*, London [1920], Lenin gives a further justification of the dissolution of the Assembly. See also his article, *The Elections to the Constituent Assembly and the Dictatorship of the Proletariat*, New York, 1920.

[87] *Novaia Zhizn*, No. 6, January 22, 1918, p. 4.

ruin of the country, and to solve all essential questions raised by the revolution. . . . In view of this the C.E.C. resolves that the Sovnarkom make it possible for the Constituent Assembly to go on with its work uninterruptedly, and that a new government be formed in agreement with the Socialist majority of the Constituent Assembly.

[Other Speeches]

. . . . Riazanov [Bolshevik] took the floor. He said that the Constituent Assembly was never a fetish to him, yet once it was called it should be given a chance to show what it could do. This had not been done. The people could not form an idea of its possibilities in one day. Under the circumstances Riazanov announced that he would vote against the [Bolshevik] resolution.[88]

Avilov [United-Internationalist] pointed out that Lenin talked exclusively about the superiority of the Soviet form of organization but failed to say why the Constituent Assembly did not reflect the will of the people. . . . .

Sukhanov [United-Internationalist] . . . . said that the reasons for dispersion indicated in the resolution were known prior to the calling of the Assembly. There is one additional reason, viz., that the people have no more faith in the Constituent Assembly; but this is a lie. Neither is it true that the Constituent Assembly refused to recognize the Soviet Government. That question was never brought up. Sukhanov, therefore, proposed that the concluding part of the [Bolshevik] resolution be deleted. . . . .

The decree to dissolve the Constituent Assembly is put to a vote and is accepted. . . . . Lozovsky and Riazanov voted against. . . . . [89]

THE CONSTITUENT ASSEMBLY IS DISSOLVED

[Decree of the C.E.C., January 19, 1918][90]

From the very beginning of the Russian Revolution the Soviets of Workers', Soldiers', and Peasants' Deputies came to the front as a mass organization. It brought the toiling and exploited classes together and led them in the fight for full political and economic freedom. During the first period of the revolution the Soviets increased, developed, and grew strong. They learned by experience the futility of compromising with the bourgeoisie, the deception of the bourgeois-democratic-parliamentarism, and came to the conclusion that it is not possible to free the

[88] *Pravda,* No. 7, January 24, 1918, p. 2.

[89] *Novaia Zhizn,* No. 6, January 22, 1918, p. 4.

[90] *Izvestiia,* No. 5, January 20, 1918, p. 1.

downtrodden classes without completely breaking with these forms and compromises. The November Revolution and the taking over of all power by the Soviets constituted such a break.

The Constituent Assembly which was elected on the lists made out before the November Revolution represents the old order when the compromisers and Cadets were in power.

At the time of voting for the Socialist-Revolutionists the people were not in a position to decide between the Right Wing—partisans of the bourgeoisie—and the Left Wing—partisans of socialism. This accounts for the fact that the Constituent Assembly, the crown of the bourgeois-parliamentary republic, stands in the way of the November Revolution and the Soviet Government. Naturally enough the November Revolution, which gave the power to the Soviets and through them to the exploited classes, has called forth the opposition of the exploiters. . . . .

The laboring classes have learned by experience that the old bourgeois parliament has outlived its usefulness, that it is quite incompatible with the task of establishing socialism, and that the task of overcoming the propertied classes and of laying the basis of a socialistic society cannot be undertaken by a national institution but only by one representing a class such as the Soviet. To deny full power to the Soviets . . . . in favor of a bourgeois parliamentarism or the Constituent Assembly would be a step backward and the deathblow of the November workers'-peasants' revolution.

The Constituent Assembly which opened on January 18 has . . . . a majority of Socialist-Revolutionists of the Right, the party of Kerensky, Avxentiev, and Chernov. It is natural that this party should refuse to consider the . . . . recommendation of the sovereign organ of the Soviet Government and should refuse to recognize the "Declaration of the Rights of the Toiling and Exploited People," the November Revolution, and the Government of the Soviet. By these very acts the Constituent Assembly has cut every tie that bound it to the Soviet of the Russian Republic. Under the circumstances the Bolsheviks and Socialist-Revolutionists of the Left . . . . had no choice but to withdraw from the Constituent Assembly.

The majority parties of the Constituent Assembly—the Socialist-Revolutionists and Mensheviks—are carrying on an open war against the Soviet, calling . . . . for its overthrow, and in this way helping the exploiters in their efforts to block the transfer of the land and the factories to the toilers.

It is clear that this part of the Constituent Assembly can be of help only to the bourgeois counter-revolution in its efforts to crush the power of the Soviets.

In view of the above the Central Executive Committee hereby decrees: The Constituent Assembly is dissolved.

[The Deputies Are Excluded from the Taurida Palace][91]

The second session of the Constituent Assembly scheduled for January 19 did not take place. . . . . No one except Bolshevik officials was allowed to enter the Taurida Palace. Toward five o'clock some of the members came to the palace . . . . but the guard would not let them in. . . . .

THE ASSASSINATION OF SHINGAREV AND KOKOSHKIN

[A. S. Izgoev's Account][92]

I went out for a walk early in the morning [January 20] . . . . and unexpectedly ran into the editor, M. I. Ganfman. He said to me: "Come along; a terrible thing has happened . . . . the watchman from the Mariinsky hospital has just come to say that in the course of the night the sailors killed . . . . the Cadets [A. I. Shingarev and F. I. Kokoshkin]." . . . . We hurried to the hospital and learned from the nurse that . . . . the two men were asleep when several armed men entered the room of the patients and shot them in cold blood. . . . . The murder of these two members of the Constituent Assembly completed, as it were, the death of the Assembly itself. . . . . On the street in front of the hospital a large crowd had gathered. [One could hear such remarks as]: . . . . "What is there to weep about! The death of two burzhui. They should all be killed. They helped Kerensky to plunder Russia. . . . . Shingarev, as Minister of Finance, stole twelve millions. . . . . "

When someone tried to tell the sailor that all these reports were lies, that the murdered men were poor, that Shingarev with his large family lived in a small fifth-floor four-room apartment, he would not believe it and cried out: . . . . "We know . . . . who you are. You, who defend the capitalist ministers. . . . . You, Cadets, ... were declared outside the law of the proletarian government, and there must have been a good reason for that. Those at the head of our affairs are as clever as you are."

It was clear that some of his auditors were on his side. It was not safe to argue with him. . . . . I could not help but think of the . . . . dead men who worked all their lives to enlighten these ignorant men and how they had been recompensed for their efforts. . . . .

91 *Nash Vek,* No. 5, January 20, 1918, p. 4.

92 A. Izgoev, "Piat let Sovetskoi Rossii," in *A.R.R.,* X, 1923, 25–26.

[From *Izvestiia*'s Comment on the Assassination][93]

The death of Shingarev and Kokoshkin is terrible. . . . . It is hard to believe . . . . [that there are people so low] as to attack and kill in a hospital two defenseless sick men. . . . . This murder is a blot on the honor of the revolution. . . . . It helps only the enemies of the revolution, the Black Hundred. Involuntarily the idea comes into one's mind that they conceived the idea. We do not say (for we have as yet no information) that the assassins were of the Black Hundred. Even if we might admit that the men who did the actual killing were (perhaps it would be more accurate to say regarded themselves as) revolutionists, it is yet possible that they were driven to it by the Black Hundred. . . . . These ignorant people did not realize that in killing Shingarev and Kokoshkin they were working in the interests of the enemies of the revolution. . . . . Whatever the facts are, the murderers must be found and brought before the revolutionary court. There must be no stain on the revolution.

[Dybenko's Statement, January 20, 1918][94]

During the night of January 19–20 Shingarev and Kokoshkin were murdered in the Mariinsky hospital. . . . . According to the information of hospital attendants the murder was committed by men wearing sailors' uniforms. The affair must be thoroughly investigated. The honor of the revolutionary fleet must not bear the stain of an accusation of revolutionary sailors having murdered their helpless enemies, rendered harmless by imprisonment.

I call upon all who took part in the murder . . . . to appear of their own accord before the revolutionary tribunal. . . . .

JANUARY 22, 1905, AND JANUARY 18, 1918

[Gorky on the Attack on the Constituent Assembly][95]

When on January 22, 1905, the . . . . soldiers, in obedience to the orders of the Tsar's government, fired on the defenseless and peaceful crowd of workers . . . . members of the intelligentsia and laborers rushed up to the soldiers shouting: "What are you doing . . . . ? Whom are you killing? They are your brothers; they are without arms; they bear you no malice; they are on the way to ask the Tsar to look into their needs. They are not demanding but merely petitioning. . . . . Think what you are doing, you idiots!" . . . . But the reply of the soldiers was: "We have orders. We don't know anything. We have orders."

93 *Izvestiia,* No. 6, January 22, 1918, p. 1.

94 *Novaia Zhizn,* No. 6, January 22, 1918, p. 3.

95 *Ibid.,* p. 1.

And like machines they fired . . . ., perhaps unwillingly, but they fired nevertheless.

On January 18, 1918, the unarmed Petersburg democracy, workers and employees, came out to celebrate in honor of the Constituent Assembly. For nearly a century the best of the Russians have dreamed of this day. They visualized the Constituent Assembly as a political organ capable of giving the Russian democracy an opportunity of freely expressing its will. Thousands of the intelligentsia, tens of thousands of workers and peasants have died in prison and in exile, have been hanged and shot for this dream. Rivers of blood have been shed for this sacred idea. And now that this goal has been reached and the democracy has come out to rejoice, the "People's Commissars" have given orders to shoot. It should not be forgotten that in the course of their lives some of these "People's Commissars" have impressed upon the toiling masses the necessity of fighting for the Constituent Assembly.

Pravda lies when it says that the demonstration of January 18 was organized by the bourgeoisie, by the bankers . . . . and that those who marched to the Taurida Palace were "burzhui" and "Kaledins." *Pravda* lied, for it knows that the "burzhui" have no reason for celebrating the opening of the Constituent Assembly. What is there for them to do among 246 Socialists [-Revolutionists] and 140 Bolsheviks? *Pravda* knows that those in line were workers of . . . . factories and that these workers were shot. No matter how much *Pravda* lies, the disgraceful facts remain.

It is possible that the "burzhui" rejoiced to see the soldiers and Red Guards snatch the revolutionary banners from the hands of workers, and drag them through the mud and burn them. But it is also possible that this picture made the "burzhui" sad, for among them are honest men who truly love their country and the people. One of these was Andrei Ivanovich Shingarev, foully murdered by some kind of savages. . . . .

Just as on January 22, 1905, so on January 18, 1918, there are people who . . . . ask those who fired: "Idiots, what are you doing? These are your own brothers. Can't you see the red banners? There is not a single banner hostile to the working class, or to you!"

Now, just as then, the soldiers reply: "We have orders to shoot." . . . .

I ask the "People's Commissars," among whom there should be honest and sensible men, if they understand that in putting the halter on their necks they are crushing the Russian democracy, destroying the conquests of the revolution?

Do they understand this? Or do they think: Ourselves or no one, even if it leads to destruction?

M. Gorky

E. The Third Congress of Soviets

The stated purpose of calling a congress of workers' and soldiers' deputies on January 21 and of peasant deputies a week later was to combat the alleged counter-revolutionary designs of the Constituent Assembly or, as Zinoviev put it, in order that "the oppressed people may pass sentence on the Constituent Assembly."[96] That sentence had, however, already been passed before the Congress assembled. The Constituent Assembly had been swept away, and the Congress of Soviets, meeting in the same hall in the Taurida Palace in which the Assembly had expired, ratified the policies of the Sovnarkom, approved Trotsky's report on the Brest negotiations, and adopted a provisional constitution. At the sessions which began on January 23 there were 942 active members, mostly Bolsheviks and Left S.R.'s, and only 54 opposition members.[97] Subsequently between two and three hundred peasant deputies took part in the sessions, which were finally concluded on January 31.

FIRST SESSION, JANUARY 23, 1918

[From the Stenographic Report of the Meeting][98]

The first session of the Congress opened with Comrade Sverdlov as chairman.

[Sverdlov]: . . . . Comrades! I take the liberty of saying a few words about the chief tasks which the Third All-Russian Congress of Soviets is confronted with. As a result of the conditions brought about by the events of the last few days we shall have to make a number of important and far-reaching decisions. The dissolution of the Constituent Assembly must be counterbalanced by the Third All-Russian Congress of Soviets—the sole sovereign organ which represents truly the interests of the workers and peasants. . . . . We are facing one of the most important questions—the building of a new order of life and the creation of an All-Russian government. We must decide here finally whether that government shall retain some sort of connection with the bourgeois

[96] See his speech in the C.E.C. on January 4 and the resolution of the same date, pp. 367–68, above.

[97] *T.V.S.S.*, p. 87; *Nash Vek*, No. 7, January 25, 1918, p. 3.

[98] *T.V.S.S.*, pp. 4–16.

order or whether a dictatorship of workers and peasants shall be finally and irrevocably established.

The Central Executive Committee and the Soviet of People's Commissars have definitely taken the stand for a dictatorship of the toiling elements. As the sovereign people's organ you will have to say the last and the decisive word. We are of the opinion that during the period of socialist construction there should be a dictatorship . . . . to insure the victory of socialism.

The second important question is that of war and peace. . . . . The solution of that important question must fully depend on your will. . . . . In addition we have to solve the . . . . question of nationalities. . . . .

I hope that the All-Russian Congress of Soviets will approve of the work which the Soviet government has done . . . . and will indicate further steps for the development of the revolutionary upbuilding of our new life. . . . . There is no doubt that our socialist republic will start a revolutionary conflagration in every country of the world and we shall arrive in the end at universal brotherhood where there is no war and no exploitation of man by man. (*Shouts of applause.*)

[After Platten, Swiss Socialist, had spoken the chairman called on Chicherin, who had recently returned from England.]

[Chicherin]: Comrades! The proletarian-peasant government of Russia has freed me and my comrades from the prison into which we were thrown by the English imperialists, leaders of world reaction, leaders of the war of world imperialism against the social revolution. . . . . (*Shouts of applause.*) These English imperialists, who are accustomed to decide the fate of peoples, were the first to yield to the demand of the proletarian government to free us.[99]

From what I have seen . . . . in England I can state that English imperialism is on the brink of ruin and that in the very near future . . . . the Socialist revolution will break out. (*Shouts of applause.*) . . . .

[Chicherin was followed by Petrov; Rakovsky, representing the Rumanian Social-Democrats; representatives of Norway and Sweden; and three Americans, Reinstein, John Reed, and Albert Rhys Williams.]

Comrade Williams said that he represented the proletariat of a country which has reached a high stage of capitalistic development, but the proletariat of which is very conservative. He has come, therefore, not to teach the Russian comrades, but to tell them how the Russian lessons are being received across the sea and to learn from the Russian [workers] who are the advance guard of the proletariat.

[99] Sir George Buchanan states that Trotsky refused to allow British subjects to leave Russia and threatened to arrest members of the British colony unless Chicherin and Petrov were released by the British Government. *Op. cit.,* II, 226–31. Trotsky tells the same story in *My Life,* p. 348.

[He said]: I shall carry away from Russia two lessons. The first lesson is the conviction that when the time arrives for the proletariat to achieve its liberation the bourgeoisie will have to vanish, for there is no force capable of resisting the onslaught of labor. The second lesson tells me that the forms of contemporary bourgeois parliamentarism have outlived themselves and are being replaced by . . . . the Soviets of Workers', Soldiers', and Peasants' Deputies. (*Applause.*)

We shall adopt the same forms [Soviets] when the American proletariat hardens its will for the revolutionary struggle and begins its fight against the bourgeoisie. It is as clear as day that revolution is the only method by which they can free themselves.

Long live revolutionary Russia!

Hail the International Revolution!

[Trotsky replied to the foreign representatives. The Declaration of Rights of the Toiling and Exploited Peoples was read and unanimously adopted.][100]

LENIN'S REPORT FOR THE SOVNARKOM

[Session of January 24, 1918][101]

Comrades! In the name of the Soviet of People's Commissars I wish to report on two and a half months of that body's activity. . . . .

Two and a half months is only five days longer than the period during which the Paris Commune of 1871 existed. . . . . The workers of Paris . . . . were shot by the French Cadets, Mensheviks, the Socialist-Revolutionists of the Right. . . . . We find ourselves in more favorable conditions, because the Russian soldiers, workers, and peasants have formed a . . . . Soviet Government . . . . which has the support of an overwhelming majority of the masses and is therefore unconquerable.

The betrayers of the revolution, ... those who doubted the possibility of a Soviet Government, strained their throats in clamoring that, alone, the proletariat could not maintain itself in power. As if we Bolsheviks . . . . ever overlooked the fact that only by forming . . . . a union of the proletariat and the poor peasants can a government maintain itself in power. . . . . This we succeeded in accomplishing immediately after November 7, and we organized a government on the basis of such a union.

. . . . When the time came to put socialism into practice the peasants were confronted with two alternatives of political association—either with the bourgeoisie or with the working class—and they soon perceived

[100] *T.V.S.S.*, pp. 16–18. The Declaration was again adopted at the closing session. *Ibid.*, p. 87.

[101] *Ibid.*, pp. 21–34.

that the party which more fully expressed the genuine aspirations and interests of the peasantry was the party of the Socialist-Revolutionists of the Left. (*Applause.*) We then concluded an alliance with that party. . . . . If the Russian peasants wish to bring about the socialization of land in alliance with the [industrial] workers who are putting into effect the nationalization of banks and workers' control of industry, they are our true allies, our most faithful and valuable allies. . . . .

Every thoughtful Socialist must admit that socialism cannot be forced on the peasants. . . . . And it is important to ascertain what the peasants themselves consider the best way of attaining socialism. . . . . They have already set out on the road and we must trust them completely.

The alliance we have entered into with the Socialist-Revolutionists of the Left thus rests on a firm foundation and is growing stronger, not daily but hourly. . . . . The experience of civil war has convinced the representatives of the peasants [Left S.R.'s] that there is no other way to socialism but the dictatorship of the proletariat. . . . .

Comrades! Every time I speak on this subject of proletarian government someone . . . . shouts "Dictator." Yet [there was a time] . . . . when everybody was in favor of the dictatorship of the proletariat. . . . . You cannot expect . . . . that socialism will be delivered on a silver platter. . . . . Not a single question pertaining to the class struggle has ever been settled except by violence. Violence when it is committed by the toiling and exploited masses is the kind of violence of which we approve. (*Shouts of applause.*) . . . .

We are told that the sabotage with which the Sovnarkom has to contend . . . . indicates opposition to socialism. It is clear, however, that all these capitalist crooks, riffraff, strikers are one and the same gang of bourgeois mercenaries opposing the government of the toilers. Who ever believed that it was possible to jump at once from capitalism to socialism? . . . . Those who understand the nature of class war and sabotage know that this cannot be done. . . . . Socialism cannot succeed unless these groups are broken up, unless the bourgeoisie—Russian and European—is crushed. . . . .

I recognize that we have not yet reached socialism. We are in the period of transition. If, however, you should say that our state is a Socialist Republic of Soviets you would be as correct as those who speak of the bourgeois Republics . . . . as democratic, when everyone knows that they are a long way from being democratic. . . . . We are not even in sight of the end of the period of transition from capitalism to socialism. We never flattered ourselves with the hope that we could reach the end without the aid of the international proletariat. . . . . The road is long and difficult. . . . . And it is our duty to say that our republic of Soviets is a Socialist Republic, because we have entered on the road leading to socialism and these words are not an empty promise. . . . .

We have done away with landholders, ... uprooted the bourgeoisie, and nationalized the banks. . . . . We did not proceed the way the conciliators would have recommended—to wait for the Constituent Assembly. . . . . We seized the banks . . . . and then discussed. . . . . The learned or quasi-learned shook their heads and prophesied [we could not run the banks]. But we replied: Let them prophesy. We know only one way of the proletarian revolution, and that is to seize the enemy's stronghold, to learn to govern by experience, by making mistakes. We do not underestimate the difficulties, but the most fundamental [changes] have already been made. The roots of capitalism . . . . have been cut. Repudiation of debts . . . . was easy. After bringing about workers' control it was not difficult to confiscate factories. . . . . This was followed by the creation of the Supreme Council of National Economy. . . . . The nationalization of railways is not far off. . . . . We shall soon be in a position to construct a socialist economy. . . . .

Of course the socialist idea cannot be attained in one country only. The workers and peasants who support the Soviet Government are only a fragment of that international workers' army which has become divided during this world war. . . . . But [the workers of the world] know that Russia is struggling for the common cause, for the cause of the . . . . international socialist revolution . . . . and we can see how the socialist revolution is ripening in every country of the world by hours and not by days. . . . .

DEBATE ON LENIN'S REPORT

[Session of January 25, 1918][102]

Avilov: . . . . I listened with great attention to Lenin's speech and must confess that it was anything but a businesslike report by the head of the government. It impressed me rather as a propaganda speech, too much like the other speeches I have heard Lenin deliver. . . . .

The November Revolution was accomplished under the banner of peace, land, and workers' control. . . . . The Constituent Assembly gave a satisfactory answer to the above questions . . . . and yet it was dispersed. . . . .

[Lenin] tells us that the November Revolution is a prelude to socialism. . . . . Let us see what forces took part in the November Revolution. [There were the] soldiers who were promised an immediate peace. Is it necessary to show that the soldiers do not care at all about socialism, their only concern being an immediate peace at any price? The Novem-

[102] *Novaia Zhizn,* No. 10, January 27, 1918, p. 2.

ber Revolution was also welcomed by those peasants who wished to seize the land. But here too it is safe to say that the seizure of land which is going on at present has not the slightest resemblance to socialism. Next there is the proletariat. But that class is not ready for socialism, since the objective conditions [for the new order] are absent. . . . .

We are now witnessing a sobering up of the masses; . . . . during the last few days quite a number of . . . . factories and mills have adopted resolutions hostile to policies of the People's Commissars. . . . . [Avilov was not allowed to continue. Other speakers—Martov, Sukhanov, Abramovich—criticized Lenin; Zinoviev, Rivkin, and Lenin replied to the criticisms. At the end of the session the Congress adopted a resolution approving all the policies of the Sovnarkom and recommending that the Declaration of Rights of the Toiling and Exploited Peoples be posted in every mill and factory, volost and village, and read in every unit of the army and navy.]

LIMITATION OF SELF-DETERMINATION

[Session of January 28, 1918][103]

Stalin: The nationality question . . . . is among those which greatly agitate Russia at the present time. Its seriousness is aggravated by the fact that Great Russians do not form a majority of the total population and are surrounded by a chain of non-sovereign nationalities. . . . . The Tsarist Government . . . . forced Russification on the nationalities by prohibiting the use of the native languages, by encouraging pogroms, and by other persecutions. The coalition government put an end to many of these evils but did not fully settle the question. . . . . It is only the Soviet Government that came out openly for self-determination of peoples even to the point of separation from Russia. In this respect it [the Soviet Government] has gone beyond some of the nationalistic leaders. Nevertheless certain conflicts developed between the Sovnarkom and the borderlands. The conflicts are political in their character. . . . .

The principle of self-determination should be limited in such a way as to make it applicable only to the toilers and not to the bourgeoisie. Self-determination must be a means of attaining socialism. . . . .

Martov: . . . . Each nationality . . . . should be allowed to settle its own affairs . . . . without any outside interference. You [Bolsheviks] insist . . . . that the nationalities of Russia should have a Soviet form of government and not a democratic one. Why not let each nationality have what it likes? . . . .

Preobrazhensky [Bolshevik] says that nationalistic movements are

[103] *T.V.S.S.*, pp. 72–78.

historically progressive only when they are directed against imperialism . . . . reaction . . . . and in so far as they assume the character of a revolutionary struggle.

A national movement usually has for its object the creation of a geographically independent state. . . . . When the object is attained, the soil . . . . is ready for planting the seeds of class conflict. . . . . [During the old régime] the nationalist movement . . . . was anti-tsarist and . . . . revolutionary. . . . . The Bolsheviks supported the Ukrainian nationalist movement [in the time of Kerensky] . . . . because it was against the bourgeois Provisional Government. . . . . But now that the Ukrainian bourgeoisie . . . ., sailing under the flag of socialism, is attempting to use self-determination as a means to fight the Soviet Government, both at home and abroad, a civil war, with a revolutionary object, is inevitable. In general it may be said that in so far as the bourgeoisie gives a chauvinistic and imperialistic interpretation of the principle of self-determination and uses it to mislead the ignorant masses of the border nationalities in order to turn them from class war, to that extent will the Soviet Government do all in its power . . . . to prevent this application of the principle of self-determination.

We are being reproached [with the fact] . . . . that by forcing the Soviet form of government on the territorially organized nationalities . . . . we are contradicting our own principles. Comrade Martov wonders why we demand a referendum in Poland, Courland, and Lithuania, et cetera . . . . and at the same time insist that at home (that is to say, in the Ukraine, the Caucasus, Finland, et cetera) . . . . the right to vote should be given to the toilers only. . . . . The facts are as stated. But those who see in them duplicity and contradictions . . . . do not take into consideration . . . . other factors. The Ukraine, the Caucasus, et cetera, have passed the political stage of bourgeois parliamentarism; but Poland, Courland, and Lithuania have not yet shaken off the autocratic yoke, have not yet reached the democratic stage.

Each region has to go through two stages of political development. As long as the regions on the western frontier of Russia have not thrown off the chains of monarchical slavery, it is out of the question to ask them to adopt the Soviet organization. They must first go through a purely democratic revolution and get rid of autocracy.

Selivanov said that . . . . the bourgeoisie exploits the principle of self-determination to carry on counter-revolutionary propaganda and build up a White Guard. . . . . The nationalist movement threatens the very existence of the Soviet Government. . . . . Now that Russia is a Socialist Republic and the champion of the great ideal of freeing the oppressed classes all over the world, there is no longer any reason for separating from Great Russia. . . . . Cultural self-determination . . . .

should be encouraged . . . . but not the old nationalistic point of view.[104] . . . .

[After a brief recess Stalin introduced the following resolution on the Federal Constitution of the Russian Republic]:

THE FEDERATION OF SOVIET REPUBLICS

[Resolution of the Congress, January 28, 1918][105]

1. The Russian Socialist Soviet Republic is a federation of Soviet republics founded on the principle of a free union of the peoples of Russia.

2. The highest organ of government in the federation is the All-Russian Congress of Soviets of Workers', Soldiers', Peasants', and Cossacks' Deputies, meeting at least once every three months.

3. The All-Russian Congress of Soviets of Workers', Soldiers', Peasants', and Cossacks' Deputies selects the All-Russian Central Executive Committee. In the interim between the Congresses the All-Russian Central Executive Committee is the highest organ of government.

4. The government of the federation, the Soviet of People's Commissars, is elected or dismissed in whole or in part by the All-Russian Congress of Soviets or the All-Russian Central Executive Committee.

5. The manner in which separate Soviet Republics and particular territories having peculiar customs and national organizations may participate in the federal government, as well as the delimitation of the respective spheres of federal and regional administration within the Russian Republic, shall be determined immediately upon the formation of regional Soviet republics by the All-Russian Central Executive Committee and the Central Executive Committees of these republics.

6. All local matters[106] are settled exclusively by the local Soviets. Higher Soviets have the right to regulate affairs between the lower Soviets and to settle differences that may arise between them. The Central Soviet Government sees to it that the fundamental principles of the federation are not violated and represents the Russian Soviet Federation as a whole. The central government looks after matters that concern the

[104] At a meeting of the Bolshevik group of the Congress the point of view was stressed that the principle of self-determination is now "antiquated as most of the democratic dogmas . . . . that it is necessary to oppose the decentralizing tendencies which would make an independent republic out of every gubernia." (*Izvestiia*, No. 11, January 29, 1918, p. 3.)

[105] *T.V.S.S.*, pp. 93–94.

[106] Sections 6 and 7 were introduced at the insistence of the Socialist-Revolutionists of the Left. The Bolsheviks objected but the Congress accepted them in spite of the opposition. (*Novaia Zhizn*, No. 13, February 1, 1918, p. 3, and *T.V.S.S.*, p. 81.)

states as a whole, but it must not encroach on the rights of the separate regions that make up the federation.

7. The Central Executive Committee of the Soviets is charged with the drafting of a constitution for the Russian Federated Soviet Republic [to be] submitted at the next Congress of Soviets.

RESOLUTION ON NATIONALITIES[107]

The All-Russian Congress of Soviets of Workers', Soldiers', and Peasants' Deputies whole-heartedly approves the policy of the People's Commissars in regard to nationalities based on the principle of self-determination of nations in the sense of self-determination of the toiling masses of all nationalities living in Russia. The Congress of Soviets of Workers', Soldiers', and Peasants' Deputies confirms, in particular, the decrees passed by the Sovnarkom and the C.E.C. in regard to Finland and Armenia.

The Congress expresses its firm conviction that all subsequent steps taken by the Soviet Government in this field will help to transform the former Russian Empire, which kept the different nationalities within its borders by means of oppression and force, into a brotherly union of Russian Soviet Republics freely united on federative principles.

THE CLOSING SESSION

[January 31, 1918][108]

[Changing the Name of the Government]

Comrade Sverdlov: . . . . Until now we have referred to the supreme power as the *Provisional Workers' and Peasants' Government.* But now when the revolution of the toiling masses is making headway not only in Russia but all over the world, when we are called upon to solidify the new state by means of new fundamental laws and to organize society on a new social basis, we should discard the term "provisional," and henceforth refer to the supreme power as the *Workers' and Peasants' Government of the Russian Soviet Republic.* . . . . (*Long applause.*)

The proposal is unanimously accepted.

[Fundamental Law of Land Socialization]

Comrade Kolegaev: Before reading the land law I should like to make a few general remarks on our internal conditions. . . . . Events have fully justified all our expectations. The revolution is securing a

107 *T.V.S.S.*, p. 94.

108 *Ibid.*, pp. 85–90.

new life for the toiling masses, a life that is based on the principles of socialist justice. . . . . The land will never become an instrument of exploitation. Henceforth all property rights in land are abolished. . . . . The new land law is based on the eternal ideals of the toilers, the ideals, namely, that the land can belong only to him who works it and that no one has a right by means of hired labor to make the land an instrument of exploitation. . . . . (*Shouts of applause.*)

Kolegaev then went on reading the land law.[109]

Comrade Lenin: Comrades! Before closing this Third Congress of Soviets . . . . it is well to view it . . . . historically and to determine its place in the international revolution and in the history of mankind. One may say without fear of contradiction that the Third Congress of Soviets has opened a new era in the history of the world. . . . . It has solidified the organization of the new state . . . . and has pointed the way toward the socialist order for . . . . the toilers of all countries.

We, in Russia, have finally accepted . . . . the new type of state, this Socialist Soviet Republic, as a federation of free republics of the different nationalities inhabiting Russia. . . . . Even our enemies must now concede that the Soviet Government . . . . is a result of various factors developed by the world revolution. Please recall that all great revolutions have had for their object . . . . not only to secure political rights but also to tear the very machinery of government out of the hands of the ruling classes and exploiters . . . . and to put an end, once for all, to all kinds of exploitation and oppression. . . . . Until the present time it has not been possible to reach this goal. But now, owing to peculiar political and economic conditions, Russia is the first country to hand over the machinery of government to the toilers. Now that the road is cleared of all historical lumber we shall build a mighty and sublime edifice—a new socialistic society. A new type of state, unknown to history, is now being formed which, in obedience to the will of the revolution, will assume the task to cleanse the earth of all exploitation, violence, and slavery. . . . .

The obstacles in the way . . . . are tremendous. . . . . But from now on we need not fear, because we have our own government machinery. . . . . The victorious proletariat . . . . will succeed in organizing production and consumption on socialist principles. Formerly, all human genius and efforts were occupied with providing some people with all the blessings of technology and culture while depriving others of . . . . education. But from this time forth all the wonders of technology and all the attainments of culture are for the people as a whole. . . . . Is it not worth while to give all one's strength to attain this high ideal . . . .?

We are not alone. During the last few days great events have oc-

[109] The text of the land law is given on pp. 673–78, below.

curred not only in the Ukraine and the Don . . . . but also in Western Europe.[110] You have read the news of the revolution in Germany. The flames of the revolution are drawing nearer and nearer to the old . . . . order. It was not a theory . . . . an idea of cloistered people . . . . that we, who formed the Soviet, inspired other countries to make similar attempts. The toilers had no other way of putting an end to this butchery. . . . .

We close this historical Congress of Soviets when everything seems to indicate that the world revolution is growing and that the time is not far distant when the toilers of all lands will unite in one state and together build a new socialist edifice. The way to this goal is through the Soviets. . . . .

The delegates rose and greeted Lenin with a storm of applause. When order was somewhat restored Sverdlov declared the Third Congress closed. The orchestra played the "Internationale." The delegates lingered, sang revolutionary hymns, and rejoiced in the glad news of the approaching triumph of the international revolution.

[110] At this time there were reports of Soviet victories in the Ukraine and the Don and of strikes in Germany.

CHAPTER VIII

THE BEGINNINGS OF CIVIL WAR

When at the closing session of the Third Congress of Soviets the Bolsheviks discarded the name "Provisional Workers' and Peasants' Government" and confidently proclaimed the establishment of the Russian Socialist Federated Soviet Republic, they were actually in control of only a considerable fragment of the former empire. They held the two capitals, the central and northern provinces of European Russia, and, more precariously, a few towns in Siberia and Central Asia. In the west the armies of the Central Powers occupied a vast area stretching from the Dniester to beyond the Gulf of Riga. Farther north, in Finland, a bourgeois government recently recognized by the Sovnarkom was fighting for its life against a revolt of the Social-Democrats, who were aided and abetted by the Bolsheviks. In the south, the Caucasus, and the Trans-Volga regions, improvised nationalist governments claiming the right of self-determination disputed with varying degrees of success the extension of the Bolshevik dictatorship. In the southeast officers of the old Imperial Army and politicians who had been active under the Provisional Government were organizing a movement under the banner of "Russia One and Indivisible," which opposed equally the proletarian dictatorship and the separatism of the national minorities and the règionalists. The dispersion of the Constituent Assembly, ending all hope of a compromise between the Bolsheviks and the moderate socialists, gave impetus to still a third type of opposition to the dictatorship. This movement, led principally by Socialist-Revolutionists, relying on peasant support and aiming to re-establish the Constituent Assembly as the master of the

Russian land, did not actually take the field against the Bolsheviks until several months later, but during the early months of 1918 it contributed another hostile element to the forces opposing the new régime. These opposition movements and their variants had only one thing in common, hostility to the Bolshevik dictatorship. They were incapable of joint action because of their conflicting aims; they were weakened by internal dissensions, and they were continually harassed by the undermining activities of Bolshevik partisans within their own lines.

There were sufficient political reasons for the Bolsheviks to send expeditions of Red Guards against the Don Cossacks and the Ukrainians. But aside from these political factors, to which the following documents relate, the fact that the Ukraine and the Don Basin and the Caucasian region beyond contained some of the most productive agricultural and metallurgical areas of all Russia undeniably had considerable influence on the policies pursued by the Russian parties, the Central Powers, and the Entente in these territories.

A. The Don Cossacks and the Volunteer Army

The Cossacks constituted a separate estate in the social organization of the Russian Empire. Cossack settlements came into existence in the middle of the fifteenth century in the disputed areas north of the Black Sea and the Sea of Azov, which lay between the lands of the Poles, the Tartars, and the Muscovites. In the course of the following century these communities of frontiersmen, who lived by hunting and fishing and, especially, by extensive and successful brigandage, became sufficiently merged to form two independent republics: the Zaporozhie Cossacks of the Ukraine, who derived their name from their stronghold below the rapids of the Dnieper; and the Cossacks of the Don, whose settlements were near the river of that name. At the head of the Cossack Voisko (army or host—the term included civil as well as military institutions) was the hetman or ataman, elected by the whole population as the executive of the popular council known as the Rada (council) or the Krug (circle). In time of war the ataman had dictatorial power, but he was accountable to the Krug and to the Voisko, in which there were no class distinctions and no private property in land.

In the course of time the Cossacks lost their independence and many of their democratic institutions. In the seventeenth century they became vassals of Moscow, and during the period of consolidation and expansion of the empire they were a source of trouble as well as of strength. The great popular risings of 1670–71 and 1773–75 led by Stenka Razin and Pugachev, respectively, spread from the Cossacks of the Don and the Volga. Zaporozhians fought with Charles XII against Peter in 1708–1709, but their stronghold was destroyed by Catherine in 1775 and these Cossacks were settled in the Kuban. As the Russian power moved east the Cossacks were the spearhead of advance and new communities were formed, until by the end of the nineteenth century there were eleven Cossack voiskos—Don, Kuban, Terek, Astrakhan, Ural, Orenburg, Siberia, Transbaikal, Semirechie, Amur, and Ussuri. By this time, however, although the Cossack communities had more land and greater privileges than the peasants and retained their military organization, they had lost most of their ancient rights and their social organization had been completely altered. Moreover, acute complications had arisen from the influx of landless peasants who became renters of or laborers on Cossack lands and from the growth of the proletariat in the towns and industrial areas. The situation was particularly acute in the Don, where these "outsiders" actually outnumbered the Cossacks.

During the period of the Provisional Government the Don Cossacks resumed the control of their internal affairs, summoned the Krug, which met in June, elected General Kaledin ataman, and passed various resolutions, including one on the land question which provided for the retention by the Cossacks of the lands held by the stanitsas (villages) and the voisko and the distribution with compensation of the privately owned land among the old peasant settlers in the Don.[1]

This program confirmed the hostility of the peasants, the "outsiders," and the Socialist-Revolutionists, who resented their exclusion from the government and tended to favor the Soviets. Returning soldiers (*frontoviks*) and the Bolsheviks were particularly aroused by Kaledin's outspoken advocacy of continuation of the war, his support of Kornilov, and the Cossacks' alliance with the Cadets in the elections to the Constituent Assembly. On the day of the Bolshevik seizure of power in the capital, Kaledin announced that the Voisko Government assumed full power in the Don.[2]

Similar declarations were made by Dutov, Karaulov, and Filimonov, the atamans of the Orenburg, Terek, and Kuban Cossacks. To co-ordinate activities in the southeast, the Don, Kuban, and the Terek Cossacks and the Union of the North Caucasus and Daghestan agreed on November 14 to form a Union of the Southeast. A union government was formed, with Kharlamov as president and Novocherkassk the capital.[3] The Union Government had no chance to establish itself, for each Cossack voisko was immediately engaged with all its energies in defense against the revolutionary tide which arose within its own area and which was swollen by the return of "bolshevized" soldiers from the Western and Turkish fronts. The struggle was especially severe in the Don region, where the situation was further complicated by the presence of the newly organized Volunteer Army of Generals Alexeev and Kornilov.

[1] Colonel Dobrynine, *La Lutte contre le bolchevisme dans la Russie meridionale, participation des Cassaques du Don à la lutte* (Mars 1917–Mars 1920), Prague, 1920, pp. 30–31. The author was chief of the Intelligence Division and the Operations Section of the Don army.

[2] An All-Cossack Congress in session at Kiev on the same day passed a resolution violently condemning the Bolsheviks and pledging its support to the Provisional Government. (*Novaia Zhizn,* No. 164, November 9, 1917, p. 4.)

[3] *Novaia Zhizn,* No. 183, November 30, 1917, p. 4. *Donskaia Letopis,* II, 284–92, gives a brief history of the Union.

GENERAL KALEDIN ASSUMES CONTROL OF THE DON REGION

[Declaration of November 7, 1917][4]

In view of the fact that the Bolsheviks are attempting to overthrow the Provisional Government and to seize power in Petrograd and other places, the Voisko Government of the Don considers the above attempt of the Bolsheviks to be unwarranted and criminal and will offer, in close contact with other Cossack governments, its entire support to the existing Provisional Government.

Taking into consideration the extraordinary conditions of the moment and the lack of contact with the central authorities, the Voisko Government assumes, this November 7 [1917], full executive power in the region of the Don. The assumption of power is temporary and will last only until the Provisional Government and order in Russia are reestablished.

KALEDIN
President of the Voisko Government

THE KUBAN REPUBLIC[5]

The Voisko Rada of Kuban is now engaged in the organization of a government of the Kuban region. Eight ministers have thus far been appointed. . . . . L. L. Bych was elected president of the Voisko Government. . . . . The new government proclaimed an independent Kuban Republic.

THE BEGINNING OF THE VOLUNTEER ARMY

[General Denikin's Account][6]

On November 12 [1917] General Alexeev, without abandoning the hope of a change in the political situation in Petrograd . . . . agreed to go to the Don. Accompanied by his adjutant, Captain Shapron, he arrived in Novocherkassk on November 15, and on the same day set to work organizing the armed forces which were destined to play a significant rôle in the history of the Russian turmoil.

[4] *Novaia Zhizn,* No. 165, November 10, 1917, p. 3.

[5] *Vlast Naroda,* No. 164, December 1, 1917, p. 6.

[6] General A. I. Denikin, *Ocherki russkoi smuty* (5 vols.), Berlin, 1924–1926, II, 156–57. A condensed English version of this work has been published in two volumes, *The Russian Turmoil,* London [1922], and *The White Army,* London [1930].

Alexeev's intentions were to utilize the southeastern region, the rich Don, in particular, as a base, protected by its own armed forces, to enable him to gather there the remaining loyal elements—officers, cadets, shock troops, and possibly some old soldiers—organizing these into an army, indispensable for the task of restoring order in Russia. He knew that the Cossacks did not want to be the vanguard in the execution of this great national undertaking. But he hoped that "the Cossacks would defend their own heritage and territory."

However, the situation on the Don developed unusual complications. Ataman Kaledin, when he had learned of Alexeev's plan and had listened to his request "to give shelter to Russian officers," replied sympathetically in principle. But considering the conditions which existed in the region, he begged Alexeev not to remain in Novocherkassk longer than a week, and to transfer his activities somewhere outside the boundaries of the [Don] region—to Stavropol or Kamyshin.

Not disheartened by this reception, and completely lacking the financial means, Alexeev vigorously set to work. A telegram was sent to Petrograd . . . . calling for the dispatch of officers to Novocherkassk; a building on Barochnaia Street, belonging to a hospital, was converted into officers' quarters, thus becoming the cradle of volunteers, and soon the first good-will offering for "Alexeev's organization" was received—400 rubles. This is all that Russian society allotted to its defenders in November. A charitable society gave some aid. . . . . It was touching, and to many might have appeared a little amusing, to see how the former Supreme Commander-in-Chief, who had directed armies of millions and had controlled a war budget of many billions . . . . was now exerting himself to get a few beds, a few puds of sugar, and some money, to shelter, warm, and feed homeless, persecuted people.

For they continued to increase—officers, cadets, and a few old soldiers—at first by ones and then by whole groups. They came from Soviet prisons, from shattered military detachments, away from the "freedom" of the Bolsheviks and the intolerance of [Ukrainian] self-determination. Some were able to break through the obstructing Bolshevik cordons, others landed in prison, or were taken as hostages and sometimes . . . . went to their graves. They were all going to the Don, having no idea of what awaited them—groping in the darkness through the thick Bolshevik sea—to where, like a bright beacon light, gleamed the century-old traditions of Cossack liberty, and the names of leaders who, in the people's mind, were inseparably connected with the Don. They arrived suffering, bedraggled, starving, but with spirits unbroken. A small cadre of the Georgievsky regiment arrived from Kiev, and here, at the end of December, the Slaviansky shock troops took again their former name, "Kornilovsky."

On December 2, General Kornilov and a number of officers, including Generals Denikin, Markov, Lukomsky, and Romanovsky, who had been imprisoned at Bykov for their participation in the Kornilov affair, escaped from their confinement and started for the Don. Denikin, Markov, Romanovsky, and Lukomsky variously disguised left by train,[7] but Kornilov rode off at the head of a mounted detachment of four hundred Cossacks of the Tekhintsy Regiment (troops recruited from a Turkoman tribe of Transcaspia). After several days of forced marches the Tekhintsy were surprised by a Bolshevik detachment from Minsk and an armored train near Unechi station on the Moscow-Brest railway line. The Tekhintsy suffered heavily and part of the detachment was separated from the main body and captured. Those who escaped were badly shaken and talked of surrender until Kornilov warned them that they would have to shoot him first, as he preferred death at the hands of his own men to capture by the Bolsheviks. The next day, however, Kornilov released the Tekhintsy from obligation to him and continued the journey with a small group of Cossacks and officers. Disguised as a peasant, Kornilov reached Novocherkassk on December 19.[8]

The escape of the generals, the open defiance of Kaledin and the Ukrainian Rada,[9] and the activities of Alexeev in organizing an anti-Bolshevik army naturally caused serious apprehensions among the Bolsheviks. The armistice on the German front enabled the Sovnarkom to divert considerable forces against their enemies in the south and southeast. The Stavka, now controlled by the Bolsheviks, sent a special expeditionary force to attack Kaledin from the north and northwest, and sailors from the Black Sea fleet were ordered to enter the Sea of Azov to aid the workers of the industrial and coal-mining centers of the Don Basin who had organized

[7] Lukomsky, *Memoirs of the Russian Revolution*, pp. 128–39, contains an account of the escape.

[8] Denikin, *Ocherki russkoi smuty*, II, 151–55; V. A. Antonov-Ovseenko, *Zapiski o grazhdanskoi voine* (4 vols.), Moscow, 1924–1933, I, 29, 301.

[9] See pp. 440–41, below.

Red Guards and gained control of Taganrog, Rostov, and several nearby mining centers.[10]

TROTSKY ORDERS AN ADVANCE AGAINST THE COSSACKS

[Direct-Wire Communication between Trotsky and Krylenko, December 7, 1917][11]

[Krylenko]: The Supreme Commander-in-Chief is at the apparatus.

[Trotsky]: Comrade Supreme Commander-in-Chief. . . . . Kaledin has declared the Don in a state of siege. . . . . Supported by the Cadets, the followers of Kaledin . . . . terrorize Rostov on the Don. . . . . Our investigation commissar possesses documents which prove beyond doubt that there is a close connection between Kaledin and the monarchist plot of Purishkevich.[12] In view of these facts the Soviet Government has taken measures to put an end with one stroke to the criminal acts of the Kaledinists and the Kornilovists. . . . . We are also taking measures to put an end to the counter-revolutionary rebellion of Dutov in the Urals. Supported by Cadet money he [Dutov] arrested the Orenburg Executive Committee, the Military Revolutionary Committee, and the Strike Committee, and is perpetrating hideous acts of violence over revolutionary citizens, not sparing women. . . . . Comrade Supreme Commander-in-Chief, you are requested to move to . . . . Rostov on the Don and Orenburg military forces . . . . sufficiently strong to be able in the shortest possible time to wipe off the face of the earth the counter-revolutionary rebellion of the Cossack generals and the Cadet bourgeoisie. . . . .

THE SOVNARKOM DECLARES WAR ON THE COSSACK CHIEFS

[Proclamation, December 9, 1917][13]

To All the Population:

At the very time that the Government of the Workers, Soldiers, and Peasants has undertaken to conclude a worthy peace for the suffering country, the enemies of the people—imperialists, landowners, bankers and their allies, the Cossack generals—have made a last desperate attempt to break up the negotiations, to snatch the authority from the

[10] Antonov-Ovseenko, *op. cit.*, I, 26–62. This is the same Antonov who led the Petrograd soldiers when the Provisional Government was arrested on November 8. He was afterward in charge of all operations in the south against the Cossacks and the Ukrainians.

[11] *Izvestiia*, No. 235, December 8, 1917, p. 3.

[12] See Reed, *op. cit.*, pp. 278; 362.

[13] *Izvestiia*, No. 236, December 9, 1917, pp. 1–2.

Soviets, the land from the peasants, and to force the soldiers, sailors, and Cossacks to shed their blood for the Russian and Allied imperialists. Kaledin on the Don and Dutov in the Urals have raised the flag of revolt, and the Cadet bourgeoisie gives them the needed material backing. . . . . The Rodziankos, Guchkovs, Miliukovs, and Konovalovs are trying to get back into power and, with the help of the Kaledins, Kornilovs, and Dutovs, to use the toiling Cossacks for their own criminal purposes. Kaledin has made the Don a war zone, he interferes with the transportation of food to the front, and is mobilizing forces to attack Ekaterinoslav, Kharkov, and Moscow. He has the assistance of the escaped General Kornilov, the same man who in July enforced the death penalty on the soldiers[14] and marched on revolutionary Petrograd. Dutov, in Orenburg, arrested the executive and military revolutionary committees, disarmed the soldiers, and is now working to get possession of Cheliabinsk, so as to cut off the front and the cities from the Siberian granaries. Karaulov is attacking the natives of the Caucasus.

The Central Committee of the Cadet Party is the ringleader of this uprising. The bourgeoisie is supplying tens of millions [of rubles] to counter-revolutionary generals in this conspiracy against the people and its government. The bourgeois Central Rada of the Ukrainian Republic while fighting the Ukrainian Soviets is helping Kaledin to collect troops on the Don, and interferes in the attempts of the Soviet Government to send the necessary troops against Kaledin across the territory of the brotherly Ukrainian people.[15]

The Cadets, those vile enemies of the people, who together with the capitalists of all the countries brought about this world butchery, hope through the Constituent Assembly to assist Kaledin, Kornilov, and Dutov and with them crush the people.

Workers, soldiers, and peasants! The revolution is in danger! We must fight to the finish for the cause of the people; we must exterminate the vile enemies of the people. We must give the counter-revolutionary plotters—Cossack generals, and their Cadet inspirers—a taste of the iron hand of the revolutionary people. The Soviet of People's Commissars has taken measures to move the necessary troops against the enemy. The counter-revolutionary revolt will be suppressed and the guilty will be punished in accordance with their guilt.

The Soviet of People's Commissars declares that:

1. The Ural, Don, and other areas where counter-revolution has raised its head are in a state of war.

[14] When he was appointed by the Provisional Government Commander-in-Chief, Kornilov, as a means of reviving discipline, restored the death penalty in the army. It had been abolished in the early weeks of the revolution.

[15] See below, pp. 439–40.

2. Local revolutionary garrisons should proceed at once against the enemy of the people without waiting for orders from above.

3. All negotiations with these counter-revolutionary plotters . . . . are forbidden.

4. Any support given to the counter-revolutionists by the local population or the railway personnel will be punished with all the severity of the revolutionary laws.

5. The leaders of the conspiracy are outlawed.

6. Every toiling Cossack who will throw off the yoke of the Kaledins, Kornilovs, and Dutovs will be greeted as a brother and will be given the necessary support by the Soviet Government.

THE SOVIET OF PEOPLE'S COMMISSARS

ORDER OF THE MILITARY REVOLUTIONARY COMMITTEE AT THE STAVKA[16]

Comrades!

It is clear as day that the counter-revolutionists are doing their best to destroy the rights won by the revolution. Kornilov is on the Don and with him are the dark forces of the bloody tsarist régime. A diabolical plot is being hatched to betray the revolution and the people's cause. . . . . The bands of Kaledin have begun a civil war. The Military Revolutionary Committees . . . . are to take decisive measures against the counter-revolutionists who came out against peace. The army must fight for the rule of the people which is embodied in the Soviet of People's Commissars. . . . . Loyal revolutionary regiments have been sent to aid the Black Sea sailors.

Military Revolutionary Committee at the Stavka
BOIARSKY, Chairman

SUMMONS TO THE BLACK SEA SAILORS[17]

Kaledin has formed a union with the Allied Imperialists and declared a civil war. He hopes to drown the conquests of the revolution in the blood of soldiers, workers, sailors, and toiling Cossacks. . . . . We received calls to send all Black Sea detachments, with lots of machine guns. . . . .

ROMENETS
Chief Commissar of the Black Sea Fleet

[16] *Izvestiia,* No. 240, December 12, 1917, p. 3.
[17] *Ibid.*

On December 11 Kaledin took the offensive against the Bolsheviks who had seized Rostov, and after four days of fighting, in which the Cossacks were aided by Alexeev's men, he took that city, which presently became the headquarters of the Volunteer Army. This outcome of the struggle was due to the weakness of the Bolsheviks rather than to the strength of Kaledin's forces. The young Cossacks returning from the front were out of the control of their officers, refused to fight the Bolsheviks, and declared their neutrality in the struggle. To replace these troops, partisan detachments were formed to wage guerrilla war against the Reds, and on December 15 Kaledin called a new meeting of the Krug to confirm the Voisko Government in power and to decide whether the Cossacks should fight or surrender to the Bolsheviks. The Krug re-elected Kaledin as ataman, voted confidence in his government and by way of removing internal dissensions offered half the seats to the non-Cossacks, or "outsiders." Early in January a congress of workers and peasants met and, though hostile to the Voisko Government, favorably considered participation in it.[18]

In the meantime Kornilov's arrival at Novocherkassk on December 19 had created a difficult situation with respect to the command of the Volunteer Army. Relations between Alexeev and Kornilov were by no means cordial as a result in part of incompatibility of temperament and in part of the fact that Alexeev had accepted an appointment by Kerensky as Chief-of-Staff after the dismissal and arrest of Kornilov in September. Kornilov believed that the political and administrative control of the Volunteer Army should rest in the hands of one man and offered to go to Siberia to organize the anti-Bolshevik forces there. Both generals had strong partisans among the officers and politicians at Novocherkassk and after long discussions, in which representatives of the Moscow political organization of the Right Center took part, an understanding was reached whereby Alexeev was given control of financial and political matters

[18] Dobrynine, *op. cit.*, pp. 41–45.

and Kornilov assumed command of the Volunteer Army. Kaledin, as the third member of the Triumvirate, was responsible for the internal affairs of the Don Cossack territory. An attempt was also made to broaden the base of the movement by setting up a Civil Council which included very diverse and antagonistic political elements. The anticipated friction developed immediately, and, according to Miliukov, who was present, Kornilov, supported by the generals, came to take precedence over Alexeev, with the result that the military prevailed over civilian and political elements in determining the policies of the army.[19]

THE ORGANIZATION OF THE ANTI-BOLSHEVIK MOVEMENT IN THE SOUTHEAST

[Extracts from a Report by U.S. Consul Dewitt Poole, January 26, 1918][20]

Report to the Ambassador Respecting the Movement in the Don Country for the Restoration of Order in Russia, the Holding of a Constitutional Assembly, and the Continuance of the War.

PETROGRAD, January 26, 1918

MY DEAR MR. AMBASSADOR:

Having arrived in Rostov-on-Don December 18, new style, to investigate the question of the establishment of an American Consulate in that city, I took occasion, on the 21st, to go to Novocherkassk and call upon General Kaledin, who is the chief executive of the Don Province, and also upon General Alexeev and certain others who are now in that region unofficially engaged with the movement described above. . . . .

Colonel Hucher of the French Military Mission for the provisioning of Rumania arrived at Novocherkassk on December 23. On December 27 he informed General Alexeev that the French Government had granted him (Alexeev) a credit of 100,000,000 rubles for the purpose of restoring order in Russia and continuing the war against the Central powers. . . . .

General Alexeev at once communicated to the French representative his desire that a financial commission be created to control the expenditure of this money, as well as a bureau of organization for the army, in both of which he asked that French officers be included.

At this juncture, military questions gave way to political, due to the

[19] Denikin, *op. cit.*, II, 187–89; Lukomsky, *op. cit.*, pp. 139–41; Miliukov, *Russia Today and Tomorrow*, New York, 1922, pp. 138–39.

[20] *U.S. Foreign Relations, 1918, Russia,* II, 609–15.

attitude of Boris Savinkov, former terrorist, and later member of the Kerensky government. When I first saw General Alexeev he took particular pains to say that Mr. Savinkov had endeavored to become associated with him but that his advances had not been encouraged. General Alexeev said it had been his first endeavor to bring together in the Don country what remained of the old Provisional Government, but this proving quite impossible he had appealed to certain persons in Moscow who brought about meetings in that city resulting in the choice of two delegates each by the Cadet Party, the nationalist patriotic group, the industrials, the landowners, and the right wing of the Socialist Revolutionary Party. This group was the nucleus, General Alexeev said, of an organization which would sooner or later proclaim itself to be the Provisional Government of Russia. He said that the principles of this government would be in substance as follows: (1) As to internal affairs, to create such a situation of order in Russia that elections might be held for a Constitutional Assembly in which every citizen might vote according to his wish without fear or molestation; and, a Constitutional Assembly having been so elected, to place the existing military forces at its disposal. (2) As to foreign affairs, to keep Russia's engagements with the Allies.

Mr. Savinkov persisted in his efforts to be admitted to the Alexeev group. He threatened, by intimation, to attack Alexeev before the people as a counter-revolutionary and pro-monarchist.[21] Let me say at this point that I am personally absolutely convinced of General Alexeev's high patriotic purpose. I am sure that he does not seek to carry out a partisan program. Savinkov's threat had some validity, however, because there had naturally rallied about General Alexeev certain elements which have been designated, for purposes of political propaganda, as counter-revolutionaries.

At the same time another group was forming about General Kornilov. It appeared toward the end of December (new style) that the whole movement might miscarry for want of agreement among these different groups. In part, I believe, as a result of pressure brought to bear by the French representative, the following results were obtained: (1) An agreement was signed January 7 among Generals Alexeev, Kornilov, and Kaledin, by which the first named undertook the leadership on the political side and such duties as pertained to a Minister of War; the second, the organization of the Volunteer Army and chief command of all forces

[21] Denikin confirms that the generals had no stomach for Savinkov's proposal and agreed to it only after Kaledin had said that without concessions to the democracy it would be impossible for the Volunteer Army to remain in the Don territory (*Ocherki russkoi smuty,* II, 190). Savinkov in his testimony before the Soviet court some years later complains of the hostility he encountered on the Don and describes the agreement as a "paper victory" (*Delo Borisa Savinkova; so statiei B. Savinkova, "Pochemu ia priznal sovetskuiu vlast,"* Moscow, 1924, p. 31).

whenever operations might be pushed beyond the Don; and the third, the command of the Cossacks and of all defensive operations within the Don; (2) A council was formed about General Alexeev, in which Mr. Savinkov was included.

As conditions precedent to joining, Mr. Savinkov demanded and General Alexeev conceded: (1) The admission to the council also of Mr. Ageev, Mr. Vinderzgolski [Vendziagolsky], Mr. Mazurienko, a representative of the central organization of the employees of the railways of the Caucasus and the southeast, and a representative of the armies of the Caucasus front; (2) An immediate proclamation of the purposes of the movement.

Mr. Ageev is the leader of the left wing of the Don Cossacks and president of the parliament, or so-called "krug," of the Don government.[22] Mr. Vinderzgolski is former commissar of the Eighth Army and former president of the Committee of the First Army. Mr. Mazurienko is a member of the All-Russian Peasants' Union and president of the Peasants' Union of the Don. At the time of my leaving Rostov the representatives of the other organizations mentioned above had not yet been chosen.

Negotiations are in progress for the admission to the council of three representative Social Democrats, namely, Chaikovski, Kuskova, and Plekhanov; and two Social Revolutionaries, namely, Argunov and Potresov.

On the conservative side the council, as now constituted, includes, besides the three generals (Alexeev, Kornilov, and Kaledin), Mr. Milyukov; Prince Gregory Trubetskoi; Professor Struve; Mr. Fedorov, representing the banking and other larger commercial interests of Moscow; two other Cadets or nationalist patriots yet to be chosen; Mr. Bogaevski, the vice ataman of the Don Cossacks; and Mr. Paramonov, a rich Cossack. The council will undoubtedly undergo changes in personnel, but a framework of an equal number of conservatives and radicals, not counting the three generals, appears to have been adopted.

In pursuance of the agreement with Mr. Savinkov, a proclamation to the Russian people has been drafted. At the last report it had been sent to Moscow for discussion there. The proclamation, which has been read to me, appeals to the people on the ground that the Bolshevik government has failed to provide them with the chief things promised, that is, peace with liberty and bread. It refers to the suppression of the Constitutional Assembly and asks for the support of the people in defending that institution. It is sound on the subject of the continuance of the war. The proclamation will be issued in the name of the league, unsigned, because it is frankly admitted that it has not yet been possible to obtain

[22] Ageev joined the Bolsheviks in 1920.

the names of persons who, it is thought, would be thoroughly acceptable to the people at large. For example, Alexeev's signature would be politically helpful, but Milyukov, one of the other ablest men in the movement, is known as the father of the Cadet Party which has been a special butt of radical attack. Among the "left" members the most prominent is Savinkov and to his name not a little distrust attaches, owing to his part in the Kornilov affair of last September and to his record as a terrorist. These are difficulties natural at the inception of a movement of this kind and it is believed that later a further signed proclamation can be issued revealing adhesion to the movement by a good proportion of the substantial political leaders of Russia. . . . .

You are aware that France and Great Britain are already committed to the movement. According to the information given by the French representative at Novocherkassk, France has taken under its particular care the Ukraine, the Crimea, Bessarabia, and Rumania; Great Britain has taken the Caucasus and the Cossack country.

In conclusion, I respectfully recommend that the attention of the Department be drawn at the earliest opportunity to the fact that the league[23] is not such a sectional movement as the Department has very naturally instructed us not to support. Of necessity its organization base is now in a particular section of the country but the activities of the league have already extended throughout Russia and reach into Siberia as well. In contrast to those of the Ukrainian government, the aims of the league are nationalist in the broadest Russian sense.

THE AIMS OF THE VOLUNTEER ARMY

[Proclamation of January 9, 1918][24]

1. The Volunteer Army is aiming to organize a military force capable of resisting the approaching anarchy and the invasion of Germany and the Bolsheviks. The volunteer movement is an all-national movement. Once again, as in the historic days of three hundred years ago, all Russia must rise in defense of her polluted sanctuaries and her suppressed rights.

2. The immediate aim of the Volunteer Army is to check the armed attack against the south and the southeast. Hand in hand with the valiant Kazachestvo and at the first call of the Krug and the Voisko ataman working in contact with all regions and peoples of Russia that

[23] Mr. Poole in his report refers to the organization formed about the triumvirate and the Civil Council as the "League for the Defense of Our Native Land and Liberty." The League had been organized in Moscow mainly by Cadets in November 1917.

[24] Denikin, *op. cit.*, II, 198–99.

have risen against the Bolsheviks and the Germans, the Russians who have come to the Don from every corner of the land will defend to their last drop of blood the independence of the regions which gave them shelter and which are the last hope for the restoration of a free and great Russia.

3. Along with the above the Volunteer Army will pursue another aim. The army will strive to become that active force by means of which Russian citizens can carry through the political reconstruction of free Russia. . . . . The new army will defend the civil liberties in order to enable the master of the Russian land—the Russian people—to express through the elected Constituent Assembly their sovereign will. All classes, parties, and groups of the population must accept that will. The army and those taking part in its formation will absolutely submit to the legal power appointed by the Constituent Assembly. . . . .

There was no general response to the call to join the Volunteer Army, and enlistments were far below expectations. Army officers, military cadets, and students enlisted, but the other classes remained indifferent if not actively hostile. "The volunteer movement," says General Denikin, "did not become a national movement . . . . At its very inception . . . . the army acquired a distinct class character."[25]

The formation of a union government of the Cossacks and non-Cossacks did not appreciably strengthen the resistance to the Bolsheviks, whose adherents, meanwhile, grew steadily. The young Cossacks returning from the front did not differ much from the other elements in the army which was now either pro-Bolshevik or "neutral" in sentiment.[26] Some of the more radical of the young Cossacks who desired to depose Kaledin and the Don Voisko Government called a congress of "frontovik" Cossacks which met at the Kamenskaia stanitsa on January 23 and formed a Military Revolutionary Committee for the purpose of setting up a Soviet government.[27]

[25] Denikin, *op. cit.*, II, 199. Even among the officers only a relatively small number of those in Novocherkassk, Rostov, and other large towns of the Don and Northern Caucasus responded.

[26] A Bolshevik authority states that about 50 per cent of the soldiers who voted in the elections to the Constituent Assembly supported the Bolshevik nominees. (Liubimov, *op. cit.*, p. 475.)

[27] *Proletarskaia Revoliutsiia na Donu,* IV, 115–24, 154–59.

DECLARATION OF THE UNITED GOVERNMENT OF THE DON[28]

[January 23, 1918]

On January 18 of this year an important event took place which will have a great significance in the life of our region. Two parts of the population of the region, the Cossacks and the non-Cossacks, formed a United Government for the purpose of jointly administering the region.

From now on the entire population of the region—Cossacks, native peasants, city dwellers and workers—will participate through their representatives in the regional government of the Don.

In fulfilling the wishes of the entire population, the United Government considers it necessary to establish a regional legislative organ to deliberate on all matters which concern the Cossack and the non-Cossack population of the region. The preliminary statute for this legislative organ will be presented for ratification to the Voisko Krug and the Congress of the non-Cossack population which meet at the same time in February. Pending the meeting of the Krug and the Congress, the United Regional Government of the Don [will pursue the following policies]:

(1) It will safeguard freedom of speech, press, assembly, unions. . . . . . .

(2) In its endeavor to stop civil war . . . . the United Government . . . . will send a delegation . . . . to the Bolshevik detachment . . . . with the proposal to stop the advance into the Don region. . . . . The United Government . . . . is engaged in reconstructing the life of the region on democratic principles and is convinced that this reconstruction must be undertaken by the local population alone without any interference of outside forces. The United Government therefore declares that it will oppose in the most energetic way the attempts of the Soviet of People's Commissars to force its will on the population of the Don region.

(3) In accordance with the agreement made between the non-Cossack Congress and the Voisko Government, the United Government issued an order . . . . to release all political prisoners and those held for agrarian disorders. . . . .

(4) To safeguard civil liberties the United Government revoked the state of martial law, which [however] remains effective along the railway lines. . . . .

(5) The Volunteer Army, which exists for the purpose of defending the Don region against the Bolsheviks who declared war against the Don and which also aims to defend the Constituent Assembly, will be under the strict supervision of the United Government and, in case

[28] *Novoe Slovo,* No. 2, January 30, 1918, p. 4.

counter-revolutionary elements make their appearance in that army, [these elements] will be removed from the territory of the region. . . . .

FORMATION OF THE COSSACK MILITARY REVOLUTIONARY COMMITTEE[29]

[January 23, 1918]

The Congress of the Cossacks from the front, having considered the existing situation in the Don, decided to take the revolutionary initiative in liberating the toiling Cossacks from the yoke of the counter-revolutionists of the Voisko Government—the generals, the landlords, the bloodsucking capitalists, and speculators.

The Congress is now appointing a military revolutionary committee which will enter into the history of the glorious Don and which from this date will assume power in the Don region.

The Congress and the Military Revolutionary Committee call upon every Cossack unit, all the toiling Cossacks, and the rest of the toiling population of the Don to have confidence in . . . . and support the Military Revolutionary Committee which is reviving the most glorious pages in the history of the freedom-loving Don. . . . .

PODTELKOV
Chairman of the Military Revolutionary Committee

ULTIMATUM OF THE MILITARY REVOLUTIONARY COMMITTEE OF THE DON TO KALEDIN[30]

[January 28, 1918]

1. All authority within the region of the Don Voisko . . . . is to pass from the Ataman to the Military Revolutionary Committee of the Don Cossacks.

2. All partisan troops fighting against the revolutionary armies and the Volunteer Army and the cadets are to be disbanded and disarmed. . . . .

3. Novocherkassk is to be occupied by Cossack regiments appointed for that purpose by the Military Revolutionary Committee.

4. The Voisko Krug is to be dissolved on January 28, 1918.

5. The Voisko Government is to recall its police from the mines and the factories of the Don region.

29 *Proletarskaia Revoliutsiia na Donu,* IV, 217.

30 *Donskaia Letopis,* II, 307; *Proletarskaia Revoliutsiia na Donu,* IV, 219–20.

6. To avoid bloodshed the Voisko Government is to announce to all stanitsas that it voluntarily resigns in favor of the Military Revolutionary Committee. . . . .

PODTELKOV
Chairman of the Military Revolutionary Committee

Members of the Voisko Government tried to negotiate with the Military Revolutionary Committee and called attention to the fact that in two weeks a new Krug and an assembly of non-Cossacks were to meet, when the question of a new government would be taken up. The Military Revolutionary Committee, however, insisted on an immediate answer. The government then went into private session and after a few hours' deliberation[31] made the following reply:

REPLY OF THE DON VOISKO GOVERNMENT[32]

[January 28, 1918]

The Don Voisko Government having considered the ultimatum of the Military Revolutionary Committee . . . . decided that, having been elected by the people, it had no right to surrender its authority until a new Voisko Krug is called. . . . . This new Krug . . . . will assemble February 17, together with the congress of the entire non-Cossack population. The Krug alone . . . . will have the right to dismiss the government and elect a new one. . . . .

The Military Revolutionary Committee is to be dissolved. . . . . All those arrested by the Committee should be released. . . . .

The government condemns the dealings which the Committee is having with the Soviet of People's Commissars, from which it receives money. It means that the Soviet is extending its influence on the Don at a time when the Cossack Krug and the Congress of the non-Cossack population unanimously rejected the Soviet Government. . . . .

ASSOCIATE VOISKO ATAMAN BOGAEVSKY
President of the Don Voisko Government

ELATONTSEV, POLIAKOV, MELNIKOV, ULANOV, AGEEV
Starshinas of the Don Voisko

[31] *Donskaia Letopis,* II, 308–14.

[32] *Ibid.,* 315–17; *Proletarskaia Revoliutsiia na Donu,* IV, 220–21.

DISINTEGRATION OF THE COSSACK FORCES

[The Last Appeal of A. M. Kaledin, February 10, 1918][33]

Citizens-Cossacks!

In the midst of the disorganization . . . . which is threatening the Cossacks with ruin, I, your Voisko Ataman, appeal to you, perhaps for the last time.

You undoubtedly know that the government of Lenin and Trotsky is moving its Red Army of mercenaries, Latvians, and German prisoners against the Don.

That army is approaching Taganrog, where the workers incited by the Bolsheviks have raised a mutiny. . . . . Our Cossack regiments stationed in the Donetz region have revolted and, together with the Red bands who had invaded the Donetz region, have attacked the detachment of Colonel Chernetsov operating against the Red soldiers and partly destroyed it. Having accomplished this base and foul deed, most of them dispersed . . . . leaving behind guns and stealing the regimental funds, horses, and other property. . . . .

The disintegration of the line units has reached its limit; thus facts have been established that in some regiments of the Donetz region the Cossacks actually handed their officers over to the Bolsheviks and received money for it.

The majority of the field units which are still intact refused to follow orders to defend the Don territory.

In such circumstances . . . . the Voisko Government was forced . . . . to form volunteer Cossack units and to accept the offer made . . . . mostly by students, to organize partisan detachments.

Owing to the effort of these units and thanks mainly to the help of our brave youth who have been sacrificing their lives with supreme fidelity in our struggle against anarchy and the Bolshevik bands, the Don territory is now being defended and order is maintained in towns and on the railway line. Rostov is being protected by a special volunteer organization.

The task which the Voisko Government has set itself, namely, to carry on the administration of the region until the meeting on February 17 of the Voisko Krug and of the Congress of the "outsiders," is made possible thanks to the help of these detachments. But these forces are small and the situation is certain to become exceedingly dangerous if the Cossacks do not join immediately these volunteer units. . . . .

Time does not wait; the danger is near. If you, Cossacks, cherish your independence, if you do not wish to see Novocherkassk fall into the

[33] *Proletarskaia Revoliutsiia na Donu,* IV, 229–30; *Donskaia Letopis,* II, 186–87.

hands of alien Bolsheviks and their Cossack sympathizers, who are traitors to the Don, you must hasten to help the Don Government and send volunteers to the army.

In appealing to you I am not pursuing personal aims. Atamanship is for me a heavy duty and I remain at my post only because I strongly believe that under the present conditions I may lay down my power only before the Krug.

A. M. KALEDIN, Voisko Ataman

SUICIDE OF GENERAL KALEDIN

[From a Memoir by Melnikov, Member of the Voisko Government][34]

On February 12, 1918, I was awakened early in the morning. A messenger of the Ataman arrived asking me to come to a special session of the government. When we [the members of the government] assembled, A. M. Kaledin asked the Field Ataman, A. M. Nazarov, to describe the situation on the front. General Nazarov . . . . drew a very gloomy picture: "The enemy is only a few miles from Novocherkassk, the Cossacks do not wish to fight, ... not more than 150 of our men and two companies of the Volunteer Army are defending the Don territory." . . . . Alexei Maximovich [Kaledin] followed . . . . and read a telegram from General Kornilov announcing that, in view of the critical situation, the Volunteer Army had decided to leave the Don and go to the Kuban. . . . . He then added in a low voice, ... "The struggle is now hopeless. The government must decide the question of its own existence. Personally, I think that it would be better to resign and hand over the power to the city government." . . . .

M. P. Bogaevsky attempted to speak . . . . but [Kaledin] interrupted him and said in an irritated voice: "Enough talk, Russia has been ruined by grandiloquence. Let us finish. I have decided for myself; I resign, I am no longer Ataman."

. . . . [We] decided to transfer the government to the city council . . . . and agreed to meet at 4:00 P.M. to sign an act of transfer. . . . .

About 2:00 P.M. we left the Ataman and in half an hour he was no more. . . . . Having destroyed a number of documents . . . . he had entered a small room adjoining his office, removed his uniform . . . . and shot himself through the heart.

On February 17, members of the Krug in Novocherkassk, organized as the Little Krug, elected General Nazarov ata-

[34] N. M. Melnikov, "Alexei Maximovich Kaledin (Lichnost i deiatelnost). Vospominaniia," in *Donskaia Letopis,* I, 39–40.

man. After sending an appeal for aid to Alexeev and Kornilov, who had withdrawn the Volunteer Army to the south, the Krug decided to attempt negotiations with the Bolshevik forces which were closing in on the city. On the 23d a Cossack delegation arrived at Bolshevik headquarters with the following statement:

STATEMENT OF THE DON VOISKO DELEGATION[35]

[February 23, 1918]

We have learned from authentic sources that the Soviet of People's Commissars is sending a punitive expedition to the Don for the following reasons: (1) The Voisko Krug is a non-democratic institution. . . . . (2) The non-Cossack population has no share in the administration of the region. (3) General Kaledin is at the head of the Don Voisko Government. . . . . (4) There are in the Don certain political leaders who have not the confidence of the democratic masses.

Recently the conditions . . . . in the Don have changed radically: (1) . . . . The Germans are advancing into the interior of Russia, threatening her independence and the safety of the revolution. (2) The former Voisko Krug is dissolved and a new one assembled February 17. . . . . A congress of the non-Cossack population has likewise been summoned. . . . . (3) General Kaledin is no longer with us and the former government has surrendered its prerogatives. (4) The political leaders who have not the confidence of the democratic masses are not with us. The agreement between the Krug and the Cadets[36] has been broken off. . . . .

In view of the above circumstances the Don Voisko Krug wishes to know: (1) Why the Soviet of People's Commissars wages war on the Don? (2) What aim the Soviet pursues? (3) Who ordered the attacks on the Don? (4) Why German and Austrian war prisoners are among the Soviet troops? . . . .

FROM THE REPLY OF THE SOVIET COMMANDER[37]

[February 25, 1918]

1. [We fight you] because you do not recognize the Soviet Government, i.e., the People's Commissars in the person of Lenin, Trotsky, and

[35] *Donskaia Letopis,* II, 320–21.

[36] The Don Cossacks and the Cadets formed a bloc during the elections to the Constituent Assembly.

[37] *Donskaia Letopis,* II, 321–22.

others; as soon as you recognize that government military operations will cease.

2. . . . . All class privileges of the Cossacks must be abolished. . . . .

3. . . . . The Germans and Austrians are in our ranks . . . . because they are internationalists.

4. . . . . The Volunteer Army and the partisan troops should be disarmed. Rodzianko, Miliukov, Alexeev, Kornilov, and others should be banished from the Don. No resistance should be offered when we enter Novocherkassk.

[*Signed*] YU. SABLIN
Commander-in-Chief of the Northern Detachment of Revolutionary Troops
ERSHOV, IVANOVSKY, MARKOV, PETROV

On the day on which the reply was made, Bolshevik forces occupied Novocherkassk. General Popov at the head of a few loyal Cossack troops made his escape, but the Ataman, Nazarov, and Voloshinov, chairman of the Krug, were arrested by insurgent Cossacks and shot. A Soviet government was set up in Novocherkassk and most of the stanitsas passed into Bolshevik control. Trouble soon broke out, however, between the Cossacks who had participated in the overturn and the Red Guards, and between the rival Soviets of Rostov and Novocherkassk. This internal dissension in the revolutionary forces, the growing hostility to the "outsiders," who had ridden into power in the Don on the Bolshevik tide, and the terrorism and exactions of the new rulers combined to revive the Cossack spirit of resistance. In April, as the German forces moved eastward across the Ukraine, blocking the Bolshevik lines of communication to the northeast, and as the Volunteer Army moved north from the first Kuban campaign, the reorganized Cossacks recovered the greater part of their territories.

The Cossacks of the North Caucasus, the Trans-Volga, and Siberia in general followed the tactics of their brothers of the Don in conformity with the resolutions of the All-Cossack Congress of November 7, 1917, and of the Council of the General Cossack League of December 8.[38] They de-

[38] English translation of this resolution in *U.S. Foreign Relations, 1918, Russia*, I, 309.

manded the right to manage their own affairs, repudiated the negotiations with the Germans, refused to recognize the Soviet Government, and resisted the attempts of the Bolsheviks to penetrate the Cossack areas. The Orenburg Cossacks under their recently elected Ataman, General Dutov, began their campaign against the new government in November. The following month the Bolsheviks took the offensive, occupying the city of Orenburg on January 19 and forcing Dutov's forces to retire to Verkhne-Uralsk. Dutov returned to the attack in February but was again unsuccessful. Red Guards captured Verkhne-Uralsk on March 26, the Ataman and his followers escaping into the Turgai steppes.

Like the Don and Orenburg Cossacks those of the Ural Voisko had dissension between the young men returning from the war with new and radical ideas and their fathers who upheld Cossack traditions. But thanks to the remoteness of the Ural Cossack territory from the center and to lack of communications, the Krug maintained tolerable relations with the Bolsheviks and was able to preserve its autonomy for several months. On March 10, however, a Red force fought its way into the area, seized the town of Ilek, and carried on a reign of terror which lasted for several days. The invaders were presently expelled and the Uralsk Cossacks remained masters of most of their territory throughout the summer of 1918.[39]

While the Cossacks, weakened by internal dissensions, resisted as best they could the growing pressure of the Red Guards and their allies, the leaders of the Volunteer Army endeavored to strengthen their forces by an appeal to the political groups to unite in a patriotic resistance to the Bolsheviks and the Germans. An appeal was also made to the Allies for aid.

[39] Podshivalov, *Grazhdanskaia borba na Urale 1917–1918* (*Opyt voenno-istoricheskogo issledovaniia*), Moscow, 1925, p. 114; G. V. Enborisov, *Ot Urala do Kharbina. Pamiatka o perezhitom,* Shanghai, 1932, p. 43; *Grazhdanskaia voina na Volge v 1918 g.*, Prague, 1930, pp. 172 ff.; *Kazachii sbornik,* Paris, 1930, pp. 100 ff.

KORNILOV'S POLITICAL PROGRAM[40]

. . . . Russia has fallen into the hands of political adventurers who under the guise of a social revolution are carrying out the Pan-Germanic design for the destruction of the military strength of our country. Playing, on the one hand, on the low instincts of the rabble and, on the other, on the moral and physical exhaustion of the Russian people caused by . . . . the war, the so-called "Soviet of People's Commissars" succeeded in establishing a despotic dictatorship of the mob which threatens to ruin the historical and cultural attainments of the country.

The sad experience of the revolution has demonstrated the total inadequacy of a government consisting of representatives of the different political parties completely bound in their activities by the dead letter of their respective programs. . . . .

Now that General Kornilov has entered once more the arena of political life in the hope of saving Russia and her national honor, he will strive, first of all, to destroy the Bolshevik autocracy and to substitute for it a form of government which will restore order in the country, re-establish the rights of citizenship and other worth-while conquests of the revolution, and lead Russia along the sublime path of freedom to a lasting and honorable peace which is so essential to the cultural and economic progress of the state. . . . .

The general principles of Kornilov's political program are as follows:

(1) To re-establish the rights of citizens: All Russian citizens without distinction of sex or nationality shall be equal before the law. All class privileges are to be abolished and the inviolability of home and person, freedom of travel, and of choosing one's residence will be safeguarded, etc.

(2) To re-establish full freedom of speech and of the press.

(3) To re-establish freedom of industry and commerce and to abolish nationalization of private financial enterprises.

(4) To re-establish private property.

(5) To re-establish the Russian Army on the basis of strict military discipline. The army should be formed on a volunteer basis (after the British model) without committees, commissars, or elective officers.

[40] *A.R.R.*, IX, 285–86. According to Lembich, a close associate of Kornilov, this program was composed by General Kornilov and dictated to him (Lembich) on February 5 in Rostov. As it stands the program is but an expression of the political credo of its author at that time. It was not officially acted upon by the other leaders of the volunteer movement on account of military reverses which soon compelled the volunteer forces to retreat from the Don. Lembich also states that it was Kornilov's intention to form a "Union for the Regeneration of Russia" to help carry out the program, but Kornilov was killed shortly afterward (April 15) in the unsuccessful attack on Ekaterinodar. (*Belyi Arkhiv,* II–III, 173–82.)

(6) Russia must assume all obligations arising from the treaties with the Allies. The war must be brought to an end in close co-operation with the Allies; peace must be general, honorable, and on democratic principles, i.e., with the right of self-determination for oppressed nations.

(7) Universal compulsory education will be introduced and the schools will be given extensive local autonomy.

(8) The Constituent Assembly dissolved by the Bolsheviks should be restored. . . . .

(9) The government established by General Kornilov is responsible only to the Constituent Assembly. . . . . The Constituent Assembly, as the only sovereign of the Russian land, will determine the fundamental laws of the Russian constitution and will give final form to the organization of the state.

(10) The church is to have complete autonomy in religious affairs. . . . . Complete religious freedom will be introduced.

(11) The solution of the complicated land question will be left to the Constituent Assembly. Pending that solution . . . . no anarchical seizures [of land] by individual citizens will be tolerated.

(12) All citizens shall be equal before the law. The death penalty shall remain in force, but its application shall be limited to extreme cases of treason against the state.

(13) Workers shall retain all the political and economic gains of the revolution relating to the regulation of labor, freedom of trade unions, meetings, and strikes. Forcible socialization of enterprises and workers' control, which have proved to lead to the ruin of national industry, will not be permitted.

(14) General Kornilov recognizes the right of the different nationalities composing Russia to have extensive local autonomy, provided that the unity of the state is preserved. . . . .

General Kornilov

ALEXEEV APPEALS FOR ALLIED AID

[Communication to the Chief of the French Mission in Kiev, February 9, 1918][41]

Dear General:

The Chief of the French Mission in Novocherkassk . . . . has, no doubt, informed you of the situation existing in the Don as well as of my request in connection with that situation.

I am General Alexeev. I selected the Don region as the place to form the Volunteer Army because it seemed to be a territory well supplied with bread and because it formed a part of a rich and powerful union

[41] *Proletarskaia Revoliutsiia na Donu,* IV, 227–29.

of the southeast. It seemed that that powerful political organization would easily manage to defend its independence against Bolshevism and that with the aid of the Cossacks we might succeed in forming a new and strong army to restore order in Russia and to resume [the struggle on] the front. The Don was thus selected by me as a base of operations against the Bolsheviks. I knew, moreover, that the Cossacks were not willing to undertake by themselves the difficult political task of restoring order in Russia; but I believed that they would defend their own heritage and territory, thus giving us time and security for the formation of an army. In this I was mistaken. The Cossack regiments coming from the front are in a state of complete moral dissolution. Bolshevik ideas have found a great many followers among the Cossacks, with the result that they refuse to fight even in defense of their own territory. They are firmly convinced that Bolshevism is directed solely against the wealthy classes . . . . and not against the region as a whole, where there is still order, bread, coal, iron, and oil.

On December 7 we were forced to send four hundred of our men to take Rostov, and since January 25 all our forces have been engaged [locally]. As the Cossacks do not wish to fight, the whole burden of the defense of the Don region falls upon the shoulders of the numerically small Volunteer Army. We have no opportunity, therefore, to form new units and to train them. We are in no position to receive war supplies, being cut off from the Rumanian and southwestern fronts by superior Bolshevik forces. We could go to the Kuban, but the Kuban territory, too, is managing to resist the Bolshevik attack only with the aid of a few detachments of the Volunteer Army. The Kuban Cossacks are also in a state of moral dissolution.

A mere glance at the map will show that the Kuban territory cannot be used as a base for future operations. By going there, we shall be forced to postpone for some time the beginning of the active fight against Bolshevism. . . . . That is why we persist in the unequal struggle to save the Don. But our forces are small and without some aid we shall be forced to abandon the politically and strategically important region of the Don, with dire consequences both for Russia and for the Allies.

In anticipation of that outcome I have been endeavoring for some time, but without success, to secure permission to divert at least one division of the Czechoslovak Corps to the Don. This would enable us to go on with the fight and to continue organizing the Volunteer Army. To my regret the [Czechoslovak] Corps continues to stay idly around Kiev and Poltava, while we are losing the Don. . . . . [With its aid] the Don region could be freed from the [Bolshevik] attack, ... Bolshevism would receive a decisive blow, and the local struggle would end in our favor. . . . .

Knowing your influence with General Maxa[42] and the Czechs in general, I appeal to you to adopt my plan. It may not now be too late, but a few days' delay will irrevocably change the situation to the disadvantage of the Don and Russia. The departure of the volunteer forces from the Don is certain to lessen our chances to overcome the Bolsheviks. . . . .

General A. Alexeev

Alexeev's efforts to secure foreign aid were as unproductive as the appeals for recruits, although the Allies were willing to provide funds. During December the British Government had instructed its agents to offer £20,000,000 to two groups in South Russia, the French had appropriated 100,000,000 rubles for Alexeev, and the Allied Supreme War Council on December 23 had declared it necessary to support "by all means in their power the [Russian] national groups which are resolved to continue the struggle [against Germany]." Less welcome to the anti-Bolshevik groups was the decision of the French and British to divide the Black Sea–Caspian region into "spheres," the French to direct political moves in Rumania and the Ukraine, the British in the Caucasus and Persia, and the two jointly in the Don. All these policies gave little real aid to the anti-Bolshevik groups, since the Allies found it practically impossible to deliver funds in South Russia.[43]

Faced by superior Red forces moving against Rostov and Novocherkassk, threatened by risings in the rear, and with no hope of support from the Cossacks, the four thousand men of the Volunteer Army abandoned Rostov on February 22 and marched into the Kuban steppes, hoping to unite with other anti-Bolshevik detachments which were defending Ekaterinodar, the Kuban capital.

42 Not a general, but Dr. Prokop Maxa, member of the Russian Branch of the Czechoslovak National Council.

43 *U.S. Foreign Relations, 1918, Russia,* II, 591–92, 596–600. The agreement between France and England on activities in Southern Russia is translated from the French original in Louis Fischer, *The Soviets in World Affairs: A History of Relations between the Soviet Union and the Rest of the World,* 2 vols., London, 1930, II, 836.

On March 13, when the Volunteer Army was seventy versts from Ekaterinodar, the Kuban detachments were forced to give up the city to the Bolsheviks. The Kuban Government escaped with a few troops and two weeks later joined the Volunteer Army. After some bickering over the question of the command and of the status of the Kuban Government, a protocol was finally drawn up, and under Kornilov's command the united forces moved to attack Ekaterinodar. On April 8–9 the attack began; by the 11th it was definitely repulsed. Against the advice of his staff Kornilov ordered another attack. The next day Kornilov was killed in his headquarters by a Bolshevik shell and Alexeev appointed Denikin his successor. The new commander ordered a withdrawal from Ekaterinodar, and on hearing the news of the successful rising of the Don Cossacks the Volunteer Army turned north, reaching the Trans-Don region early in May.[44]

Some evidence of the bitterness of this warfare between the Red Guards and sailors and the officer detachments which formed the nucleus of the White forces is given in the following pages. Colonel Drozdovsky, from whose diary excerpts are taken, in the spring of 1918 led a detachment of officers from the Rumanian front across the Ukraine to the Don, where he arrived in time to take part in the expulsion of the Red forces.

SCENES FROM THE CIVIL WAR

[Excerpts from the Diary of Colonel Drozdovsky, March–April, 1918][45]

March 11

At Novopavlovsk we arrested six Bolshevik leaders, the list of which Colonel Leslie received from the Ananiev officer organization. We are keeping them under arrest. Some, however, we could not capture—they fled in good time. Respectable peasants are much pleased over these ar-

[44] Accounts in English of the first Kuban campaign are given by Denikin, *The White Army,* pp. 46–124, and Prince P. A. Volkonsky, *The Volunteer Army of Alexeev and Denikin,* London, [1919], pp. 9–23.

[45] M. G. Drozdovsky, *Dnevnik,* Berlin, 1923, pp. 47, 53, 57, 66, 70, 88, 108, 118.

rests. The farther east we advance, the stronger is felt the spirit of Bolshevism; the population does not welcome us so heartily, at times there is open hostility: "Those bourgeois, kept by landowners' money, come to take away our land." . . . .

March 15, Domashevka

On the road my thoughts are continually reverting to the past, the present, and the days to come; now and then it seems that misery seizes my heart as in a vise; cultural instincts oppose the impulse to avenge oneself upon a vanquished enemy, but let the reason, the clear and logical reason, triumph over the heart's dark urges. What can we say to the murderer of three officers or to the man who personally had sentenced an officer to be executed "for bourgeois and counter-revolutionary tendencies." What can we do to one who is a spiritual leader of crimes, robberies, murders, insults, their instigator, their brain, who had been poisoning human souls with the poison of crime? We live in horrible times of brute force, of depreciation of human lives. Be still, my heart, be hardened, my will, for with these wild, depraved hooligans there is but one law that is still respected: "An eye for an eye," and, I shall add: "Two eyes for an eye, all teeth for a tooth." He who has taken the sword . . . .

In this merciless fight for life I shall be equal to this terrible animal law. If one has to live with wolves, one has to howl like one. . . . . We are surrounded, like an island by the sea, by the Bolsheviks, the Ukrainians, the Austrians, and the Germans. Snarling at the one, making politics to the right and left, we march on along this road of blood and perfidy toward one ray of light, one true faith; but how long this road, how thorny. . . . .

March 18, Elanets

The Bolsheviks are nowhere to be seen; it is said that they flee at our approach and have long left this district; all together, there are the wildest rumors concerning us; we are reported to be a corps, a division, 40,000 strong; we are bourgeoisie hired by landowners, supporters of the old régime. The local population has a hazy understanding of the situation. Often they ask: "Are you Ukrainians?" "No." "Austrians, then?" "No." "Bolsheviks?" "No." "Then who are you?" "We are Russians." "Then you must be Bolsheviks—all Russians are Bolsheviks."

In general, the masses are friendly. They ask for safety, for the establishment of order; the anarchy, the disorganization had exhausted everybody but a few rascals. They tell us that there is no one to complain to, no protection whatever, no assurance for the next day. The population of Elanets asks us to establish order and, if we lack actual means, to "give a scare." Continual raids, robberies, murders have terrorized the population, and they fear to name the culprits out of fear of vengeance. Our landlord, a Jew, who was robbed yesterday of 900 rubles, met us very hospitably: "At last we shall be at peace if even for one day."

The population brought three carloads of bread to our provisioner and they all were surprised that he paid them. The bread had been sent as a sort of bribe, so used have they become to having all passing troops loot and take things away without payment. This is the famed deepening of the revolution conducted after the Bolshevik upheaval by visitors to the villages, these sackings of estates and farms under the menace of the machine guns; at times, however, there happen to be cases of resistance, when the population tries to protect their landowners (Domanevka, Trikraty). The worst evil are the sailors and the soldiers of the Red Guard. . . . .

March 22, Vladimirovka

The head of the column arrived at Vladimirovka about 5:00 P.M. The first squadron of cavalry, which had arrived much earlier, upon obtaining from the local population the information as to the happenings at Dolgorukovka and that some armed men were moving from there to Vladimirovka, pushed on there with the mounted platoon under the command of Voinalovich. Having surrounded the village they placed the platoon in position, cut off the ford with machine guns, fired a couple of volleys in the direction of the village, and everybody there took to cover. Then the mounted platoon entered the village, met the Bolshevik committee, and put the members to death, after which they demanded the surrender of the murderers and the instigators in the torturing of the four Shirvan men (according to detailed information, there were two officers, one Shirvan private, one army clerk, and one soldier that had joined them on the way and was traveling with them). Our charge was so speedy and unexpected that no culprit had time to escape. . . . . They were delivered to us and executed on the spot. The two officers concealed by the people of Vladimirovka were guides and witnesses. After the execution, the houses of the culprits were burned and the whole male population under forty-five whipped soundly, the whipping being done by the old men. The people of this village are so brutal that when these officers had been arrested the Red Guards themselves were not thinking of murdering them, but the peasants, their women, and even children insistently demanded their death. It is characteristic that some women were anxious to save their relatives from whipping at the price of their own bodies—what more! . . . . Then the population was ordered to deliver without pay the best cattle, pigs, fowl, forage, and bread for the whole detachment, as well as the best horses. All this they kept bringing over until nightfall. . . . . "An eye for an eye." The whole village set up a howl. . . . .

March 24, Vladimirovka . . . .

Anyway, what a horror, this civil war. What beastliness it introduces into the hearts; what mortal hatred and vengefulness it brings into souls. Gruesome are our cruel punishments, gruesome is this joy, this exhilaration with murder that is familiar to some of our Volunteers. My heart is in anguish, but the reason demands cruelty. We must understand these men; many of them have lost their friends, their relatives, murdered by the rabble, their families and lives broken, their possessions either destroyed or stolen, and there is no man but was at some time or other submitted to insults and humiliations. Over all of them hatred and a will for vengeance has full sway; the time of peace and forgiveness has not yet arrived. What can one demand of Turkul, who lost three brothers killed and tortured to death by sailors, or from Kudriashev, whose entire family was massacred by the Red Guards not long ago? And how many more are there like these? . . . .

March 30, Liubimovka

There have been several cases of unauthorized arrests; the majority have been freed, but the next time I shall court-martial them. Gave orders to warn them for the last time. One of the Jews brought to us tried to escape and was shot. This is an unauthorized act, but all evidence proves that he is a great rogue, although all Jews as one man stand up for him. They all turned out to be innocent lambs. The evidence of witnesses not Jewish and of the two victims was damning. After all, serves him right, but the officers must be taught to stop this practice. . . . .

April 7, Konstantinovka

In Melitopol, with the help of the population, there have been captured and liquidated forty-two Bolsheviks.

What odd relations there exist between ourselves and the Germans; we behave like acknowledged allies, collaborate, treat each other in a severely correct manner, and in all cases of clashes between ourselves and the Ukrainians they are always taking our side. At the same time one German remarked that those officers who do not recognize our peace are our enemies. Probably, the Germans do not understand our forced alliance against the Bolsheviks, do not guess at our hidden aims or consider their realization impossible. We respond with meticulous civility. One German officer said: "We try to assist the Russian officers in every way, we feel strongly for them, while they keep away from us, behave like strangers."

With the Ukrainians, on the other hand, the relations are terrible. They are all the time after us with some demand, such as that we take off our shoulder-straps; they are afraid to fight openly—a demoralized band trying to strike from behind. They do not recognize the division of the military spoils, a principle acknowledged by the Germans. Their commandant issues severe orders not to insult us—they do not mind these. Some of them were beaten up—this made them keep their peace, the slaves, the rascals. When we left, they pulled down the railway station flag (not even strictly national), tore it into pieces, trampled it underfoot. . . . .

The Germans are our enemies, we hate them but we have some respect for them. For the Ukrainians we have nothing but contempt, as for renegades and demoralized bandits.

The Germans treat the Ukrainians with open disdain, treat them meanly, order them about. They call them bandits, rabble; when the Ukrainians attempted to take our automobile at the station the German commander shouted at the Ukrainian officer: "Let me have nothing of the sort any more!" The difference in treating us—their hidden enemies—and the Ukrainians—their allies—is tremendous.

April 11, near Berdiansk . . . .

Before I returned to Kutzaia I was met by an Austrian captain; according to an order of the Rada, all Bolshevik officials must be arrested and sent to Odessa to be tried there by a special court. We cannot execute them. As an officer he realizes that they ought to be executed, but as the executor of the orders of his superiors he is obliged to declare insistently that we must transfer all commissars not yet executed to him. We had a friendly talk, and since all that ought to have been executed have already passed to another world, I have agreed to fulfil all these obligations to the letter. . . . .

B. The Ukraine

In southwestern Russia, as elsewhere at the time of the November Revolution, the defenders of the Provisional Government were neither very numerous nor very determined. But here the situation was complicated by the existence of a regional government, the Ukrainian Central Rada, which represented the aspiration of the Ukrainian nationalism. This national movement, which had gathered considerable headway in intellectual circles in the nineteenth century, had during the early years of the present century developed various political tendencies which ranged from cultural and political autonomy within the Russian Empire—as was advocated by the Ukrainian deputies in the Imperial Duma—to the re-establishment of an independent Ukrainian state embracing not only the ten or twelve southwestern gubernias of Russia but eastern Galicia and Ruthenia as well. During the war Ukrainian separatism received encouragement from Germany and Austria-Hungary, greatly to the annoyance of Russian conservatives, who violently denied the existence of a Ukrainian nationality. The vast economic resources of the Ukraine gave the movement an especial significance to the Central Powers as well as to the successive Russian governments.

Immediately after the March Revolution the Ukrainians formed a national council which they called the Central Rada, the name of the governing body of the Ukrainian Cossack states of the seventeenth century. At the same time Jewish and Polish national councils were formed to champion the national interests of the minorities of the region. An executive committee which had been appointed by the Provisional Government and on which these bodies were represented supervised the political administration of the region. At first the Ukrainians were modest in their program and the first All-Ukrainian Army conference, while pledging its support to the Rada, sent friendly greetings to Kerensky. Presently, however, more radical nationalists gained control of the Rada, which began to press for political and economic autonomy and for the segregation of Ukrainian soldiers in the Russian army into Ukrainian national units.

A crisis arose when in June the Provisional Government refused the Rada's demands for greater power of self-government and attempted to prevent the meeting of the second All-Ukrainian Army Conference. But the conference met despite the opposition of Petrograd and enthusiastically adopted a manifesto, the "First Universal" of the Rada. "Without separating from Russia and without breaking away from the Russian State," said the manifesto, "let the Ukrainian people on its own territory have the right to dispose of its life . . . . no one knows better than ourselves what we want and what are the best laws for us. No one knows better than do our own peasants how to manage our own land." A peasants' congress meeting in June gave general approval to the Rada program, as did a workers' congress later in July. The Provisional Government urged the Ukrainians to await the meeting of the Constituent Assembly for the satisfaction of their national aspirations, but the Rada replied with the appointment of a general secretariat to work out the statute of national autonomy. Direct negotiations between Tsereteli, Tereshchenko, Kerensky, and the Rada reached a compromise agreement which recognized the General Secretariat as the governing body in Ukrainian affairs. This agreement, which caused the withdrawal of the Cadets from the Provisional Government, was confirmed by a Second Universal published by the Rada, July 16. Although the agreement remained in at least nominal effect until the November uprising, the Ukrainians tended more and more to act without reference to Petrograd.[46]

When the news of the insurrection in Petrograd reached Kiev, local Bolsheviks attempted to seize power with the aid of Red Guards and units of the local garrison. Detachments of Cossacks and military cadets offered some resistance, but the Rada remained neutral. After a few days the supporters of the Provisional Government gave up the fight, and, as the Bolsheviks lacked the strength to set up their own authority, control passed into the hands of the Rada, which, on November 20, issued a Third Universal proclaiming the Ukrainian People's Republic with the General Secretariat as the executive organ.[47]

[46] Golder, pp. 436–43. V. Vinnichenko, *Vidrodzhennia natsii,* Kiev, 1920, I, II. V. Stankevich, *Sudby narodov Rossii,* Berlin, 1920, pp. 82–84. *Bulletin periodique de la presse russe,* No. 50, p. 4; No. 51, p. 3; No. 52, pp. 1–2; No. 59, p. 2. Miliukov, *Istoriia vtoroi russkoi revoliutsii,* I, 159. I. Kulik, "Revoliutsionnoe dvizhenie na Ukraine za 1917–1918 g.," in *Zhizn Natsionalnostei,* 1918, Nos. 1–6 and 10–12.

[47] A. A. Goldenweiser, "Iz kievskikh vospominanii (1917–1921 gg.)," in *A.R.R.,* VI (1922), 194–95.

PROCLAMATION OF THE UKRAINIAN PEOPLE'S REPUBLIC

[The Third Universal of Ukrainian Rada, November 20, 1917][48]

UKRAINIAN PEOPLE AND ALL PEOPLES OF THE UKRAINE!

An hour of trial and stress has come for the Russian Republic. In the capitals, in the north, a bloody civil war is in progress. There is no central government, and anarchy, disorder, and destruction are spreading throughout the state.

Our land likewise is in danger. Without a strong, united government the Ukraine, too, may fall into the abyss of civil war and destruction.

Ukrainians, and you, brother-peoples of the Ukraine! You have appointed us to protect your hard-won rights, to keep order, and to build a new life in our land.

In order to maintain peace in our country and to save the whole of Russia, we, the Ukrainian Central Rada, carrying out the will of our people, announce that henceforth the Ukraine is the Ukrainian People's Republic.

Without separating from the Russian Republic and destroying its unity, we shall firmly establish ourselves on our own land in order that with our strength we may help the rest of Russia . . . . to become a federation of free and equal peoples.

Until the Ukrainian Constituent Assembly meets, the whole power of keeping order in our land, of issuing laws, and of ruling belongs to us—the Ukrainian Central Rada and its government, the General Secretariat of the Ukraine.

Having strength and power in our native land, we shall defend the rights of the revolution not only in our own territory but in the rest of Russia as well.

We therefore announce: To the territory of the Ukrainian People's Republic belong all lands where the majority of the population is Ukrainian, viz., Kiev, Podolia, Volyn, Chernigov, Poltava, Kharkov, Ekaterinoslav, Kherson, Taurida (excepting Crimea). The further delimitation of the frontiers of the Ukrainian People's Republic, involving the addition of parts of Kursk, Voronezh, Kholm, and other neighboring provinces where the majority of the population is Ukrainian, is to be settled in accordance with the organized wishes of the peoples.

To all citizens of the above territories we announce that within the territories of the Ukrainian People's Republic all existing rights of ownership in land belonging to pomeshchiks and other estates capitalisti-

[48] S. A. Piontkovsky, *Grazhdanskaia voina v Rossii (1918–1921 gg.); khrestomatiia*, Moscow, 1925, pp. 344–46; hereafter cited as *G.V.R.*

cally cultivated, as well as udel, monastery, cabinet, and church lands, are abolished. Recognizing that the land is the property of the whole working people and that it must pass to the people without compensation, the Ukrainian Central Rada hereby instructs the General Secretariat of Agriculture to work out immediately a law for the administration of these lands by land committees chosen by the people and to be in force until the meeting of the Ukrainian Constituent Assembly.

The labor problem in the Ukrainian People's Republic will be regulated immediately. For the present an eight-hour working day is established in the territories of the Ukrainian People's Republic.

The hour of trial through which all Russia and our Ukraine are now passing makes it necessary to regulate industry in order to distribute food supplies fairly and to organize labor. We therefore instruct the General Secretariat of Labor to establish, from this date, with the assistance of labor representatives, state control of industry all over the Ukraine. The interests both of Russia and of the Ukraine must be taken into consideration.

This is the fourth year that blood is being shed on the front, and the strength of all peoples is being wasted. By the wishes and in the name of the Ukrainian People's Republic, the Ukrainian Central Rada will take a firm stand in bringing about a speedy peace. It will make a resolute effort to compel, through the central government, both allies and enemies to begin peace negotiations at once. We shall insist that at the Peace Congress the rights of the Ukrainian people both within and without Russia are fully recognized. But until peace is concluded every citizen of the Ukrainian People's Republic together with the citizens of all the peoples of the Russian Republic must stand firmly in his position both at the front and in the rear.

Quite recently the splendid gains of the revolution have been clouded by the restoration of the death penalty. We announce that henceforth in the lands of the Ukrainian People's Republic the death penalty is abolished. To all who are imprisoned or have been arrested for political offenses committed prior to this date . . . . full amnesty is given. A law to this effect will be passed immediately.

The courts in the Ukraine must be just and in accordance with the spirit of the people. With this in mind we order the General Secretariat of Justice to make every effort to regulate the courts and administer justice according to rules understood by the people.

The General Secretariat of the Interior is hereby instructed to make every effort to strengthen and to extend the rights of local self-government . . . . which is the best foundation for a free democratic life.

All liberties won by the Russian Revolution, namely, freedom of the press, speech, religion, assembly, union, strikes, inviolability of person and habitation, and freedom to use local dialects, will be safeguarded within the Ukrainian People's Republic.

The Ukrainian people, who have fought for years to gain their national freedom and have now won it, will firmly protect the freedom of national development of all peoples living in the Ukraine. We therefore announce that the Great Russian, Jewish, Polish, and other peoples of the Ukraine have a right to that national-personal autonomy[49] which will guarantee their freedom of self-government in matters affecting their national life. The General Secretariat of Nationalities will shortly introduce a law concerning national-personal autonomy.

The food problem at this difficult and trying moment is the key to the power of the state. The Ukrainian People's Republic must make every effort to save both herself and the front as well as those parts of the Russian Republic which will need her help.

Citizens! In the name of the Ukrainian People's Republic in Federal Russia, the Ukrainian Central Rada calls upon you to fight all forms of anarchy and disorder and to help in the great constructive work of building up new government institutions which will give to the great but weakened republic of Russia new strength and power. The framing of those new government institutions is the task of the Ukrainian and the All-Russian Constituent Assemblies.

Elections to the Ukrainian Constituent Assembly will take place January 9, 1918; the opening date is January 22, 1918. A law will be published immediately concerning the calling of the Ukrainian Constituent Assembly.

KIEV, November 20, 1917

The General Secretariat as constituted included the following members: President, Vinnichenko (Social-Demo-

[49] The idea of "national-personal autonomy" received much currency at the beginning of the twentieth century in Eastern Europe in connection with the complicated question of nationalities and the impossibility of finding an adequate solution in terms of geographical adjustments. It contemplates the organization of the national minorities within a certain geographical area into autonomous unions with complete self-government in matters affecting their internal life, such as education, culture, mutual aid, emigration, etc. Membership in a nation, according to this theory, is determined not by the fact that a person lives in a certain geographical area but by the circumstance of his sharing a certain complex of beliefs and customs characteristic of the particular group or nation. Hence the expression "national-personal autonomy." The idea is worked out in great detail by the Austrian Socialist Karl Renner, in *Das Selbstbestimmungsrecht der Nationen in besonderer Anwendung auf Oesterreich* (Leipzig, Wien, 1918), whose ideas had undoubtedly an influence on the Russian Socialists. A translation of the Ukrainian law on national-personal autonomy is given in *Eastern Europe,* Paris, 1919, No. 7, 214–15.

crat); War, Petliura (Social-Democrat); Labor, Porsh (Social-Democrat); Finance, Tugan-Baranovsky (Socialist-Federalist); Foreign Affairs, Shulgin (Socialist-Federalist); Post and Telegraph, Zarubin (Socialist-Revolutionist); State Comptroller, Zolotarev (Bund); and three ministers of nationalities, Zilberfarb (Jewist Socialist), Mickiewicz (Polish Democrat), and Odinets (Socialist-Populist).[50] The action of the Rada caused considerable dissension among the political groups in the Ukrainian capital. The Kiev City Duma devoted a special session to the question and after a long and stormy debate voted on four resolutions, none of which received a majority.

RESOLUTIONS OF THE KIEV CITY DUMA

[Session of November 27, 1917][51]

The following four motions came up for the vote of the Kiev City Duma:

1. Member of the Duma Levin, in the name of the Social-Democrats and Socialist-Revolutionists, moved as follows: The Kiev City Duma is of the opinion that the establishment of new relations between the peoples of Russia can come only as the result of an expression of the popular will made in the All-Russian and the local Constituent assemblies. The declaration of the Ukrainian Central Rada thus requires the sanction of the people. In view of the fact, however, that Russia is at present torn by civil war, the administration of the Ukraine is to be taken over by the Ukrainian Central Rada and its government, the General Secretariat. . . . .

2. Member of the Duma Davidson, in the name of the Social-Democrats (Defensists), moved as follows: Having considered the declaration of the Central Ukrainian Rada of November 20, 1917, the Kiev City Duma considers it to be an act hostile to the interests of the revolution and therefore unacceptable to the revolutionary democracy.

3. The Cadets moved as follows: Having considered the declaration of the Central Rada of November 20, 1917, the Duma resolves that from the point of view of both content and origin the act cannot be considered as having any political significance or as carrying any constitutional force.

[50] *A.R.R.*, VI (1922), 195–96.

[51] *Yuzhnaia Gazeta,* No. 2456, November 28, 1917, p. 4.

4. Member of the Duma Rafes, in the name of the faction "Bund,"[52] moved: The Duma resolves to accept the declaration of the Ukrainian Central Rada.

Since by the decree of November 15, 1917,[53] the Sovnarkom had acknowledged the right of nationalities to self-determination, including the right of separation from Russia, the Bolsheviks could not formally object to the proclamation of the Ukrainian People's Republic. Although the Ukrainian government was Socialist in composition, the Bolsheviks maintained that it did not express the will of the "toiling masses" and that thus, by inference, true self-determination would be realized only when the toiling masses led by the Bolsheviks deposed the Rada and established a Soviet government. Particularly the Sovnarkom objected to the General Secretariat's recall of Ukrainian units from the front, its claim to exclusive control of the southwestern and Rumanian fronts, its embargo on food exports, its independent attitude toward foreign relations,[54] and, finally, its refusal, on the ground of neutrality, to allow Soviet units to pass through Ukrainian territory to attack the Don Cossacks. On December 17 the Sovnarkom gave the Rada forty-eight hours in which to give a satisfactory reply to a series of demands or take the consequences.

SOVIET ULTIMATUM TO THE UKRAINIAN RADA

[Decree of the Sovnarkom, December 17, 1917][55]

Taking our stand on the principle of the solidarity of the exploited masses and of the brotherly union of all workers in their struggle for socialism . . . . we, the Soviet of People's Commissars, have recognized the complete independence of the Ukrainian Republic. . . . . All that concerns national rights and national independence of the

[52] Jewish Social-Democrats.

[53] See pp. 382–83, above.

[54] The General Secretariat on December 12 notified the Entente Powers that, while the Ukraine considered itself always the ally of the powers fighting against the Central Empire, it was compelled, by the negotiations undertaken by the Russians, to begin armistice negotiations on the Ukrainian front. (*U.S. Foreign Relations, 1918, Russia,* II, 650–51.)

[55] *S.U.R.,* 1917, No. 6, pp. 82–83.

Ukrainian people we . . . . are ready to acknowledge unconditionally and without hesitation. . . . .

We accuse the Rada of playing, under the guise of nationalism, a double game, a game which for some time expressed itself in the Rada's refusal to recognize the Soviets and the Soviet power in the Ukraine (among other things, the Rada refused to call . . . . a regional congress of Soviets). This double game, which is the chief reason why we cannot recognize the Rada as the plenipotentiary representative of the toiling and exploited masses of the Ukrainian Republic, has of late led the Rada to undertake a number of steps which preclude the possibility of any agreement.

In the first place, the Rada is disorganizing the front . . . . by moving about and recalling the Ukrainian units. . . . .

In the second place, the Rada is disarming the Soviet troops stationed in the Ukraine.

In the third place, the Rada is supporting the Cadet-Kaledin plot. . . . .

Having embarked upon this policy of unheard-of treachery to the revolution, a policy of helping the bitterest enemies of . . . . the Soviets and of the toiling and exploited masses, the Rada fully deserves that we at once declare war upon her . . . . [Instead] the Soviet of People's Commissars asks the Rada . . . . the following questions:

(1) Will the Rada stop disorganizing the front?

(2) Will the Rada prevent the movement of troops[56] to the Don, the Urals, or any other place unless such movements are authorized by the Supreme Commander-in-Chief?

(3) Will the Rada assist the revolutionary troops in their fight against the counter-revolutionary plots of the Cadets and Kaledin?

(4) Will the Rada stop disarming the Soviet regiments and the workers' Red Guards in the Ukraine? . . . .

In case no satisfactory reply to the above questions is received within forty-eight hours, the Soviet of People's Commissars will consider the Rada in a state of open warfare against the Soviet Government in Russia and in the Ukraine.

THE SOVIET OF PEOPLE'S COMMISSARS

THE REPLY OF THE RADA[57]

[December 19, 1917]

The declaration of the Sovnarkom, in which the independence of the Ukrainian People's Republic is recognized, lacks either sincerity or

[56] I.e., recruits for the anti-Bolshevik forces.

[57] *Izvestiia*, No. 246, December 21, 1917, p. 2.

logic. It is not possible simultaneously to recognize the right of a people to self-determination including separation and at the same time to infringe roughly on that right by imposing on the people in question a certain type of government. . . . . The General Secretariat categorically repudiates all attempts on the part of the People's Commissars to interfere in the political life of the Ukrainian People's Republic. The pretensions of the People's Commissars to guide the Ukrainian democracy are the less justifiable since the political organization which they wish to impose on the Ukraine has led to unenviable results in the territory which is under their own control. Great Russia is more and more becoming the prey of anarchy and economic and political disruption, while the most arbitrary rule and the abuse of all liberties gained by the revolution . . . . reign supreme in your land. The General Secretariat does not wish to repeat that sad experiment in the Ukraine. . . . . The Ukrainian democracy . . . . is quite satisfied [with its government]. The only elements which are not satisfied with the composition of the Rada are those of Great Russian extraction, viz., the Black Hundred, the Cadets, and the Bolsheviks. . . . . The General Secretariat will facilitate in every way their return to Great Russia where their sentiments will receive the desired satisfaction. It is with this in mind that the anarchistically inclined soldiers of Great Russian extraction were disarmed . . . . and given a chance to return to their homeland. . . . .

The General Secretariat is doing its best to avoid bloody methods of settling political questions. But if the People's Commissars of Great Russia . . . . will force it to accept the challenge, the General Secretariat has no doubt that the Ukrainian soldiers, workers, and peasants will give an adequate reply to the People's Commissars.

VINNICHENKO
President of the General Secretariat

PETLIURA
General Secretary [of War]

In Kiev, meanwhile, an all-Ukrainian Congress of Soviets had opened on December 18. At the second session the Congress split on the policies of the Rada; the Bolsheviks and Socialist-Revolutionists of the Left, who were in a minority, bolted to Kharkov, where a more radical congress of Donetz coal miners was in session. This Kharkov Soviet Congress elected a Central Executive Committee of the Ukraine, which on December 27 proclaimed itself the sole authority of the region.[58] Two days later the Sovnarkom in a resolution welcomed the formation of the new government and promised it unconditional support.[59] An expeditionary force, formed at the Stavka with Colonel Muravev in command, soon began moving against the Ukrainian capital.

During January the Ukrainians were compensated to some extent for military losses by diplomatic gains. Early in the month France instructed its High Commissioners at Kiev to accord de facto recognition of Ukrainian independence. The British also appointed a High Commissioner and Vinnichenko announced that the Western Powers were withholding formal recognition only until the most expedient moment.[60] On January 12 the representatives of the Central Powers at Brest-Litovsk gave de facto recognition to the Rada and promised formal recognition in the peace treaty. The complete independence of the Ukraine and its separation from Russia was proclaimed by the Rada in the "Fourth Universal" of January 22.

FORMATION OF A SOVIET GOVERNMENT OF THE UKRAINE

[Declaration of the Ukrainian Central Executive Committee, December 27, 1917][61]

To All Workers, Peasants, and Soldiers of the Ukraine:

The consolidated effort of the workers, soldiers, and peasants of Russia succeeded in overthrowing the hypocritical government of Kerensky. The All-Russian Congress of Workers', Soldiers', and Peasants' Deputies, in which the Soviets of the Ukraine took part, created a new government—the Soviet of People's Commissars—which is the government of workers and peasants of the Russian Federal Republic.

With the appointment of this government the aspirations of the workers and the poorest peasants became a reality. At once a decree was issued by which the land with all agricultural implements was transferred to the peasants without any compensation [to the former hold-

[58] Liubimov, p. 297.

[59] *Izvestiia*, No. 254, December 30, 1917, p. 5.

[60] Vinnichenko, II, 232–44, gives an account of the diplomatic correspondence between the French and British agents and the Ukrainian government. (*U.S. Foreign Relations, 1918, Russia*, II, 655.)

[61] S. A. Piontkovsky, *G.V.R.*, pp. 349–52.

ers] and without waiting for the [meeting of the] Constituent Assembly. [Next were issued decrees] on workers' control, the eight-hour working day, and the peace decree, which demonstrated that only a government of the people is capable of leading the country to a peace acceptable to the revolutionary democracy. The government also introduced the elective principle into the army, thus making it democratic through and through.

The above steps of the Soviet Government have met with the warmest response on the part of the working classes . . . . and all peoples composing the Russian Federal Republic; the Soviets of Workers', Soldiers', and Peasants' Deputies are everywhere supporting the Soviet of People's Commissars.

The capitalists, on the other hand, the pomeshchiks, and other bloodsuckers have begun a bitter fight against the workers' and peasants' revolution. They found support first on the front, and subsequently on the Don and in the Ukraine. The Stavka raised its head on the front, Kaledin on the Don, and the General Secretariat of the Central Rada in the Ukraine.

The Ukrainian Central Rada was elected without the participation of the Soviet of Workers' and Soldiers' Deputies, and the leadership in it belongs to Socialists of the Kerensky type. . . . . Russian Mensheviks and Socialist-Revolutionists of the Right constitute one-third of the membership of the Central Rada. They decided to form a bourgeois republic in the Ukraine and to defend, under the guise of self-determination, the interests of the capitalists and bureaucrats of Russia and of the Ukraine, whom the workers' and peasants' revolution is threatening with final destruction and annihilation. . . . .

The bourgeois leaders of the Rada were not merely aiming to defend the Ukrainian and non-Ukrainian bourgeoisie against the attack of the working classes. They committed a much more serious crime by entering into alliance with General Kaledin, that hireling of the bourgeoisie and of the Cadets. . . . .

Under such circumstances the First All-Ukrainian Congress of Soviets of Workers', Soldiers', and Peasants' Deputies was to meet in Kiev on the 16th of December. . . . . The bourgeois Central Rada, through deceit and violence, interfered in the work of the Congress. The majority of the deputies . . . . left for Kharkov where . . . . the work of the Congress was brought to completion.

The Congress of the Ukrainian Soviets was compelled to bring to an end the criminal politics of the Central Rada . . . . and to take the government of the Ukrainian People's Republic into its own hands. The Central Executive Committee elected by the Congress was instructed to form a new government—a government of workers and peasants. By the decision of the Congress of Soviets of the Ukraine, the Central Rada was deprived of all the rights it had usurped; at the same time the General Secretariat lost all its prerogatives. From now on the only government of the Ukraine is the People's Secretariat appointed by the Central Executive Committee of the All-Ukrainian Soviet of Workers', Soldiers', and Peasants' Deputies. . . . .

Comrades, Workers, and Soldiers! Support the government of your Soviets in the cities and fight against everyone opposing that government.

Peasants! If you wish to get the land at once . . . . and have your interests protected . . . . help the . . . . Soviet Government. Remember that only a union of workers, soldiers, and peasants will be able to overcome the propertied classes. . . . .

Long live the government of Soviets of Workers', Soldiers', and Peasants' Deputies! . . . .

THE CENTRAL EXECUTIVE COMMITTEE OF THE UKRAINIAN SOVIETS OF WORKERS', SOLDIERS', AND PEASANTS' DEPUTIES

FOURTH UNIVERSAL OF THE UKRAINIAN CENTRAL RADA

[Proclamation of January 22, 1918][62]

PEOPLE OF THE UKRAINE!

By your power, will, and word a free Ukrainian People's Republic has been established in the land of the Ukraine. The old dream of your fathers who fought for freedom and the rights of the working people has come true!

But this Ukrainian freedom was born in an hour of trial. Four years of cruel war have weakened our country and our people. Factories are not producing goods, business is slackening, the railways have deteriorated, money is depreciating. The supply of bread is decreasing and famine is at hand. Bands of robbers and murderers have increased in number, especially since the Russian troops began to rush from the front, spreading bloody massacre, disorder, and ruin in our land.

In view of all this, the elections to the Ukrainian Constituent Assembly could not take place at the time announced in our preceding Universal and the Assembly was unable to convene today as previously planned in order to take over from us the provisional sovereign revolutionary authority in the Ukraine, to establish order in our People's Republic, and to organize a new government.

[62] V. Vinnichenko, *Vidrodzhennia natsii,* II, 244–52.

In the meantime the Petrograd Government of People's Commissars declared war on the Ukraine in order to put the free Ukrainian People's Republic under its domination, and is sending its troops into our territory—Red Guards and Bolsheviks who loot grain from our peasants and send it to Russia without paying for it; they do not even spare the seeds prepared for the next planting. They kill innocent people and spread anarchy, murder, and ruin wherever they go.

We, the Ukrainian Central Rada, made every effort to prevent this fratricidal war between the two neighboring peoples, but the Petrograd Government refused to meet us halfway and continues the bloody struggle against our people and our republic.

Furthermore, the same Petrograd Government of People's Commissars is delaying intentionally the conclusion of peace and is proclaiming a new war, calling it a "holy" [war]. Blood will be shed once more and the unfortunate working masses will again be sacrificed.

We, the Ukrainian Central Rada, elected by Ukrainian congresses of peasants, workers, and soldiers, can never agree to it; we do not favor any war, because the Ukrainian people long for peace and peace must come as soon as possible.

But in order that the Russian or any other government may not impede in any way the establishment of the longed-for peace in the Ukraine, and with a view to giving our country order, productive work, and to consolidating the revolution and our liberties, we, the Ukrainian Central Rada, announce to all citizens of the Ukraine that *from this date the Ukrainian People's Republic becomes a self-sufficient, independent, and free sovereign state of the Ukrainian people.*

We greatly desire to live in peace and maintain friendship with all neighboring states such as Russia, Poland, Austria, Rumania, Turkey, and others, but none of these states must interfere with the independence of the Ukrainian Republic.

The power in the Ukraine will belong to the people of the Ukraine only, in whose name, until a Ukrainian Constituent Assembly convenes, we, the Ukrainian Central Rada representing the toiling people—peasants, workers, and soldiers—and the executive organ, to be known as *the Rada of People's Ministers,* shall rule.

And so, first of all, we instruct the government of our Republic, the Rada of People's Ministers, to take charge from this day of the peace negotiations with the Central Powers already in progress, [conducting them] quite independently and endeavoring to bring them to a successful conclusion, disregarding any interference on the part of any section of the former Russian Empire, and to re-establish peace so that our country may resume an orderly and peaceful life.

As for the so-called Bolsheviks and other offenders who plunder and destroy our country, we instruct the government of the Ukrainian

People's Republic to take firm and decisive measures against them, and we call upon all citizens of our Republic to defend at the cost of their lives the well-being and liberties of our people. The territory of the Ukrainian People's Republic must be cleared of the mercenaries sent from Petrograd who are violating the rights of the Ukrainian People's Republic.

The frightful war begun by the bourgeois governments inflicted great suffering upon our people, impoverished our country, and destroyed our well-being. All this must now be ended.

At the same time, we instruct our government to start demobilizing the soldiers . . . . and after the ratification of the peace treaties to disband the remaining army altogether. In place of the regular army, a people's militia will be established so that our troops may be used for the defense of our working people and not [to minister] to the desires of the ruling classes.

The localities which were impoverished by the war and demobilization must be reconstructed with the help of the state treasury.

When our fighters return home, all [local] radas and city dumas must be re-elected on a date set for the purpose, so that the soldiers will have a voice in [these institutions]. In the meantime, with a view to establishing a government that will enjoy confidence and be supported by all the revolutionary-democratic elements, radas of workers', peasants', and soldiers' deputies elected from the local population must be added to the local self-governments to assist the latter.

The commission for the settlement of the land question elected at the last session of the Central Rada has already worked out a law for the transfer of land to the toiling people without compensation; this law is based on the principle of the abolition of the right of ownership and of socialization of land in accord with the resolution we took at the seventh session.

This law is going to be examined in a few days at the plenary session of the Central Rada and the Rada of Ministers, and every effort will be made to enable the land committees to transfer the land to the toiling peasants before spring work begins.

Forests, waters, and other natural resources, being the property of the Ukrainian toiling people, pass to the jurisdiction of the Ukrainian People's Republic.

The war has absorbed all of our country's productive forces. The greater part of business establishments, factories, and works have produced only the articles that were required for the war and the people remained without goods. Now the war is over.

We instruct the Rada of People's Ministers to place at once all factories and works on a peace basis and to produce the goods required by the working masses.

The same war has created hundreds of thousands of unemployed invalids. Not a single workingman should suffer in the independent People's Republic of the Ukraine. The government of the Republic is planning to raise the productivity of the country and to undertake constructive work in every branch [of life] where unemployed persons will be able to find work and apply their energies; the government will also provide for the maimed and those who suffered from the war.

Under the old régime traders and middlemen made enormous sums of money at the expense of the poor and downtrodden classes. Henceforth the Ukrainian People's Republic takes into its own hands the most important branches of trade, and all profits from these will be used for the benefit of the people.

The state will take charge of all imports and exports in order to do away with high prices from which, thanks to speculators, the poorest classes are the greatest sufferers.

To realize this we instruct the government of the Republic to draft and to submit for ratification a law dealing with this [question] as well as regarding the monopoly of iron, coal, hides, tobacco, and other products and goods the taxes on which fall chiefly as a burden on the working classes and to the benefit of the non-toilers.

In the same way we order the establishment of state control over all the banks which, by making loans to the non-working elements, aided the exploitation of the working masses. Henceforth bank credits must be applied in the first place to help the toiling population and to develop the national economy of the Ukrainian People's Republic. There must be no speculation and no . . . . exploitation by banks.

On account of the state of anarchy, disorganization of life, and food shortage, there is growing a feeling of discontent among certain elements of the population. Numerous dark forces are taking advantage of this discontent and are trying to persuade the ignorant people to support the old order. These dark anti-revolutionary forces are hoping to force the liberated peoples once more under the Russian tsarist yoke. The Rada of People's Ministers must fight mercilessly all counter-revolutionary forces and every individual who calls for an insurrection against the independent Ukrainian People's Republic and the restoration of the old régime must be punished for treason against the state.

All democratic liberties proclaimed in the Third Universal of the Ukrainian Central Rada are hereby confirmed, and, in addition, it is proclaimed that in the independent Ukrainian People's Republic all peoples are given the right of the national-personal autonomy[63] as recognized by the law of January 22.

[63] See footnote on p. 437, above.

The Ukrainian Constituent Assembly will put into effect as soon as possible all [the promises] made in the Universal which we, the Ukrainian Central Rada and our Rada of Ministers, may not have time to carry out.

We instruct all our citizens to carry out energetically the elections and to make every possible effort to have the counting of votes done as quickly as possible in order that our Constituent Assembly, the sovereign master and ruler of our land, may convene within two weeks, and to consolidate in a Constitution of our independent Ukrainian People's Republic the liberties, order, and prosperity of our toiling people for the present and the future. This supreme assembly of ours is to decide on the question of federative union with the People's Republics of the former Russian Empire. Until that time we call upon all citizens of the independent Ukrainian People's Republic to safeguard staunchly the newly acquired liberties and rights of our people and with all our might to defend our future from all the enemies of the peasant workers' Ukrainian People's Republic.

WHY THE BOLSHEVIKS FIGHT THE RADA

[A Statement by Krylenko, January 25, 1918][64]

A delegation of the Ukrainian soldiers . . . . arrived in Petrograd January 21, [1918] . . . . to find out under what conditions civil war could be stopped. . . . .

Seeing that no understanding with Smolny was to be reached, the delegates prepared to leave Petrograd. On the eve of their departure the delegates received the following statement, signed by Krylenko:

"I hereby inform the representatives of the Kiev garrison . . . . that we fight against the Rada for the establishment of the government of Soviets of Workers', Soldiers', and Peasants' Deputies over the entire territory of the Russian Federative Republic. . . . .

"As soon as the government in the Ukraine is transferred to the Ukrainian Soviet of Workers', Soldiers', and Peasants' Deputies, all military operations against the Ukraine will cease."

At the very time when the Fourth Universal declaring the Ukraine to be an independent state was being proclaimed, Soviet troops were closing in on Kiev, and, for eleven days, January 28–February 8, the city and its suburbs were under

[64] *Petrogradsky Golos,* No. 8, January 27, 1918, p. 3; also *Novaia Zhizn,* No. 10, January 27, 1918, p. 4.

fire and suffered great damage. On February 9, when their representatives at Brest were signing the treaty with the Central Powers, the General Secretariat and the Rada were refugees at Zhitomir.[65] The aid of Czechoslovak troops then in billets near Kiev was solicited by both sides, but they were kept out of the fight by Masaryk, who, on February 7 with the approval of the French Mission, declared these troops a part of the French Army. Masaryk also made a treaty with Muravev, who a few days later sent a written guaranty that the Czechoslovaks might leave for France unmolested.[66]

The Bolsheviks remained in Kiev about three weeks. On February 17 the Rada appealed to the Germans for help and with the aid of the troops of the Central Powers re-established itself in Kiev on March 1, 1918. Austro-German forces occupied Odessa on March 13; other regions were rapidly occupied until the whole Ukraine passed under the control of the Central Powers, who remained masters of South Russia until the end of the World War.[67]

THE BOLSHEVIK OCCUPATION OF KIEV

[Extract from Report of the United States Consul at Kiev, March 1, 1918][68]

The people of Kiev were stunned after the battle was over. They seemed dazed by the bombardment and the terrible events they witnessed during the closing hours of the battle. It is estimated that there were 6,000 casualties, of whom between 2,000 and 3,000 were killed, but these figures may be too low.

Before they left the city, the Ukrainians, whose forces were composed principally of so-called free Cossacks and volunteers, executed many soldiers who had deserted to the Bolsheviks and were later captured. For the first two days of Bolshevik occupation there were hundreds of executions, or more properly speaking, murders. It is esti-

[65] A vivid account of the fighting around Kiev is given by a French officer, Louis Ser, in "Un Parc d'Aviation Francaise en Russie Bolchéviste," *Revue des deux Mondes,* **46**: 764–98.

[66] Masaryk, *The Making of a State,* London, 1927, pp. 176–77, 185.

[67] A. A. Goldenweiser, "Iz kievskikh vospominanii (1917–1921 gg.)," in *A.R.R.,* VI (1922), 200–209; Antonov-Ovseenko, *Zapiski o grazhdanskoi voine,* II, 50–58.

[68] *U.S. Foreign Relations, 1918, Russia,* II, 675–76.

mated that 300 or 400 officers were shot down on the streets or taken to a park near the former residence of the governor, where they were killed. Many well-dressed civilians were also reported to have been shot down, but this is not confirmed. The Bolshevik troops were embittered against the officers found in Kiev, because they believed they had all assisted the Ukrainians, and at first seem to have made little effort to find out whether the officers had actually taken part in the fighting or not. They were simply shot or clubbed with rifle butts. Later, however, as order began to be established, this promiscuous shooting practically ceased, though whenever officers who carried Ukrainian papers were found, they were shot.[69]

Dozens of officers came to the Consul, disguised as common soldiers or peasants, and begged to be assisted to leave for America. People of means ceased to appear on the streets in good clothing. Furs were discarded to a great extent and many well-bred women appeared in peasant headdress instead of hats. There were robberies and looting of shops. In fairness to the Bolsheviks it must be said that much of the looting was done before the Ukrainians left the city. As the excitement wore off and the Bolshevik authorities began to get their troops back under control, vigorous efforts were made to re-establish order. The shooting of officers ceased, unless it could be shown that they had had some connection with the former government, and many robbers were summarily executed.

It is impossible to give any reliable estimate of the damage done to property in the city. Many houses were practically destroyed by shell fire, and several were burned. The house in which the American Consul lived was struck by a shell which passed through three rooms. The British Vice-Consul's house was also damaged by shell fire. It is reported that toward the last the Bolsheviks poured shells into the city from five different directions. Their guns were undoubtedly served by experienced artillerymen. Damage was greatest around the arsenal, at the railway station, and in the center of the city, known as the "old town." At the latter point the Ukrainians had a battery. Damage from shell fire, however, was general through the city.

Food became very scarce as the fighting continued and there was also much suffering when the water supply was cut off for two days. This shortage of food and water forced many people to go into the streets in search of supplies, even while the shelling was going on. Many casualties

[69] One of the Ukrainian Bolshevik leaders makes the following comment on these reprisals: "Much has been written about the unnecessary cruelty of the Soviet army and of the unnecessary firing, etc. Yes, the Soviet army was cruel, but it was just. Besides the punishment of the oppressor by the risen slave is just. The workers when criticized for the cruelty invariably reply: 'They had not spared us either.'" (I. Kulik, "Revoliutsionnoe dvizhenie na Ukraine za 1917–1918," in *Zhizn Natsionalnostei,* 1918, Nos. 1–6 and 8–10.)

resulted from this. Among the killed and wounded were hundreds of women and children. After the fighting the food situation gradually improved, but there was still a serious shortage up to the time the Consul left the city. The authorities were trying to force prices down, with the result that the peasants were bringing in little or nothing.

I have [etc.]

DOUGLAS JENKINS

THE RADA APPEALS TO THE GERMANS

[Note of February 17, 1918][70]

To the German People!

Animated by a sincere desire for peace toward our neighbors, we signed the peace treaty in order that the fratricidal war may be brought to an end and that we may devote ourselves to the building of an independent political life. But the happy events of February 9 . . . . did not bring peace to our land. The enemies of our freedom invaded our country and, by fire and sword, wish to enslave our people as they did two hundred and forty-five years ago. . . . . This barbaric invasion of our northern neighbors has as its aim the destruction of our freedom . . . . and the restoration of the old régime. We are firmly convinced that in its love for peace and order the German people will not refuse assistance to resist the invasion of our northern neighbors. We appeal to you at a moment of distress, convinced that you will respond to our call.

C. THE CAUCASUS

Shortly after the March Revolution the Provisional Government appointed a special Transcaucasian Committee to govern the Transcaucasian region in place of the deposed Imperial Governor-General. This committee, with a Russian chairman, included in its membership representatives of the three most important nationalities—Georgians, Armenians, and Tartars. Neither the committee nor the national councils nor yet the Soviet of Workers' and Soldiers' Deputies approved of the Bolshevik seizure of power in Petrograd,[71] and a new organ of government was formed,

[70] *Izvestiia,* No. 28, February 19, 1918, p. 2.

[71] The resolutions of the local Soviet are given in a collection of documents entitled *Dokumenty i materialy po vneshnei politike Zakavkazia i Gruzii,* Tiflis, 1919, pp. 1–3.

the Transcaucasian Commissariat, to exercise authority pending the action of the All-Russian Constituent Assembly. On November 28 the composition of the Commissariat was announced and on December 1 it issued its program. In the meantime Baku with its large industrial population had set up a pro-Bolshevik government.

FORMATION OF THE TRANSCAUCASIAN REGIONAL GOVERNMENT[72]

[November 28, 1917]

In view of the extraordinary political circumstances which brought about the dissolution of the central [All-Russian] Government, we, the undersigned members of the Transcaucasian Commissariat, are hereby assuming the prerogatives of the government of Transcaucasia. . . .

President of the Commissariat and Commissar of Labor and Foreign Affairs, E. Gegechkori; Commissar of the Interior, A. Chkhenkeli; Commissar of War and Navy, D. Donskoi; Commissar of Finance, Kh. Karchikian; Commissar of Education and Justice, Sh. V. Alexeev-Meskhiev; Commissar of Commerce, M. Dzhafarov; Commissar of Ways and Communications, Kh. Melik-Aslanov; Commissar of Agriculture, A. Neruchev; Commissar of Food, G. Ter-Gazarian; Commissar of Public Welfare, A. Ogandzhanian; State Comptroller, Kh.-b. Khas-Mamedov.

DECLARATION OF THE TRANSCAUCASIAN COMMISSARIAT[73]

[Tiflis, December 1, 1917]

To the Peoples of Transcaucasia:

For a period of over a hundred years the peoples of Transcaucasia have been bound in their historic fortunes to the Russian Empire. Now, for the first time, Transcaucasia must face single-handed an approaching economic and social catastrophe.

The future destinies of the Transcaucasian peoples largely depend on whether or not the revolutionary democracy will be able to safeguard the gains of the revolution and to guarantee to the region the requisite revolutionary order. Only under such conditions will it be possible for us to exercise an influence on Central Russia that will assist in bringing to an

[72] *Dokumenty i materialy . . . . Zakavkazia i Gruzii,* pp. 7–8.

[73] S. A. Piontkovsky, *G.V.R.,* pp. 672–74.

end the civil war and in creating a single revolutionary government acceptable to all groups.

To accomplish the above a regional government has been formed by agreement between the Socialist parties and the democratic revolutionary organizations. The government is of a provisional nature and will function only until the Constituent Assembly meets. . . . .

Being a provisional government it will attempt to solve problems only of the most urgent character [such] . . . . as finance . . . . transportation, ... army demobilization, [etc.] . . . .

Taking its stand on the principle of national self-determination proclaimed by the Russian Revolution, the Commissariat of Transcaucasia will at once devote itself to a just solution of the nationality question confronting the peoples of Transcaucasia. . . . .

The Commissariat of Transcaucasia appeals to all who have the interests of the revolution and of freedom at heart to support the regional government in its creative revolutionary work.

Peoples of Transcaucasia! Your fate is in your own hands. Let us prove ourselves worthy of the great mission! . . . .

The Commissariat faced numerous and perplexing problems. There were the vital matters of finance and food supply for which the Transcaucasus largely depended on Russia. During November and December the Transcaucasian Government repeatedly told the Allied and American representatives at Tiflis that acceptance of Bolshevik rule was inevitable unless foreign funds were provided. The British Government authorized its agents to offer financial aid to the Georgians and Armenians to continue the struggle against the Turks. The American Government did not commit itself.[74] There was the extremely complex relationship of nationalities between the Russians and the native peoples on the one hand and between the Moslem Tartars with a Turkish orientation and the Christian Georgians and Armenians, who looked to Russia, on the other. But most threatening of all were the results of the complete disintegration of the Russian Army on the Turkish front. Georgia, Armenia, and Azerbaijan were left exposed to the advance of the Turkish troops and besides were inundated by thou-

[74] *U.S. Foreign Relations, 1918, Russia,* II, 589–92.

sands of demoralized soldiers streaming north to their homes in Russia. There being no hope of restoring the front, the Commissariat on December 5 accepted the Turkish proposal for an armistice.[75] On January 14, 1918, the Turks proposed that the Commissariat begin peace negotiations as an independent government. This the Commissariat declined to do on the ground that Transcaucasia was a component part of the Russian Republic and could negotiate only on the authorization of the Russian Constituent Assembly.

TURKISH PEACE PROPOSAL

[Note of the Commander-in-Chief of the Turkish Army to the Commander of the Transcaucasian Army, January 14, 1918][76]

. . . . His Highness [Enver Pasha] would like to know under what conditions relations could be re-established with the independent government of the Caucasus and what views the independent government of the Caucasus entertains on the question of re-establishing peaceful relations between the two countries. With this object His Highness has asked me to send a peace delegation to the capital of the independent government of the Caucasus. . . . .

Informing you of the above I beg to bring this proposal of ours to the notice of the independent government of the Caucasus. . . . .

FERIK-VEKHIB-MEKHMED
Commander-in-Chief of the Turkish Armies
Caucasian Front

January 9, 1334

REPLY OF THE TRANSCAUCASIAN COMMISSARIAT[77]

[January 17, 1918]

Animated by the desire to conclude a peace acceptable to the Russian Democracy, we deem it our duty to inform you that we are a component part of the Russian Republic and can enter into peace negotiations only upon receiving necessary powers from the Constituent Assembly which is now in session. Your peace proposals will be presented [to the Constituent Assembly] . . . . and a reply forwarded to you as soon as possible.

[75] *Dokumenty i materialy . . . . Zakavkazia i Gruzii,* pp. 11–13.

[76] *Ibid.,* pp. 24–25.

[77] *Ibid.,* pp. 25–26.

After the dissolution of the Russian Constituent Assembly the Transcaucasian delegates to that body, together with other elected representatives of the Georgians, Armenians, and Tartars, formed a representative assembly called the Seim, which, together with the Commissariat, began to function as the sole authority of that region. In the domain of foreign relations the situation was complicated by the Brest-Litovsk peace, by which the Bolsheviks were forced to cede three Transcaucasian regions to Turkey. The Commissariat promptly repudiated the Brest treaty and attempted direct negotiations with the Turks.

RESOLUTION OF THE TRANSCAUCASIAN REGIONAL SOVIET ON THE CONSTITUENT ASSEMBLY[78]

[January 25, 1918]

The dispersion of the Constituent Assembly severed the last thread which held together the whole of Russia and the All-Russian revolutionary democracy. The Constituent Assembly was the symbol of Russian unity and of the triumph of the revolution. Now that the Constituent Assembly is dissolved, Transcaucasia is left once more to its own resources to face an ever-increasing chaos and disorganization. The vital interests of the region demand . . . . that a strong authoritative government be formed capable of maintaining revolutionary order and of carrying through all necessary reforms.

THE GOVERNMENT OF TRANSCAUCASIA PROTESTS AGAINST THE BREST-LITOVSK TREATY

[Radiogram of March 2, 1918][79]

. . . . The government of Transcaucasia . . . . will consider any agreement affecting Transcaucasia and its borders and reached without the knowledge and consent of the government as not binding and as having no international significance. The Transcaucasian Seim selected a peace delegation which is ready to start for Trebizond . . . . to conclude peace with Turkey.

G. Gegechkori
President of Transcaucasian Government

Chkheidze
President of the Transcaucasian Seim

[78] *Dokumenty i materialy . . . . Zakavkazia i Gruzii,* pp. 27–28.
[79] *Ibid.,* pp. 85–86.

TURKEY DEMANDS THE EVACUATION OF BATUM, KARS, AND ARDAGAN

[Turkish Commander to the Russian Commander, March 10, 1918][80]

General Lebedinsky, Commander-in-Chief of the Russian Armies in the Caucasus:

YOUR EXCELLENCY: The Russian Republic consented to the evacuation of the regions of Batum, Kars, and Ardagan, and has just signed a peace treaty to that effect. In view of that I have the honor to inform Your Excellency that I received orders from my generalissimo to urge you to evacuate the regions mentioned as soon as possible. . . . .

VEKHIB-MEKHMED

On March 14, 1918, the Transcaucasian peace delegation arrived at Trebizond to negotiate a separate treaty with the Turks. Although Turkey had previously addressed Transcaucasia as an independent state, the Turkish delegates now declared that, having failed to declare its independence, Transcaucasia was not an independent state and its repudiation of the Brest treaty was therefore null and void. On April 8 the Turkish delegation delivered an ultimatum requiring unconditional acceptance of the Brest treaty as a preliminary to negotiations. After communicating with their government the Transcaucasian delegates accepted the ultimatum on April 8. An armistice was agreed upon and the delegates left Trebizond to report to their respective governments.[81]

A Turkish army, meanwhile, had surrounded Batum and on April 12 ordered the garrison to surrender within twenty-four hours.[82] When the Seim met the next day to consider the ultimatum, feelings ran so high that war was declared, a war council formed, and an appeal issued to the people to mobilize.[83] This declaration of war did not go beyond the rhetoric of the leaders. There was no army, and the Tartar

[80] *Dokumenty i materialy . . . . Zakavkazia i Gruzii,* p. 86.

[81] *Ibid.,* pp. 117–19, 155–56.

[82] *Ibid.,* pp. 161–62.

[83] *Ibid.,* pp. 166–84.

Mussavat party had neither the will nor the power to arouse its Moslem followers against their Turkish kinsmen. Nothing was done to defend Batum, and the city fell on the 15th. At the session of the Seim on April 22 two resolutions were accepted: a proposal to the Turks to resume negotiation, and a formal declaration of the independence of Transcaucasia. The Turks accepted both resolutions on April 27 and peace discussions reopened at Batum on May 11.

The Turks now refused to accept the Brest-Litovsk treaty as a basis of the new negotiations but proposed to re-annex all the territories that had been lost to Russia by the Treaty of Adrianople of 1829. Turkey, furthermore, demanded the right to use the Alexandrople-Dzhulfa railway for the transfer of troops against the British forces in North Persia.[84] These new conditions, while vitally affecting Georgia and Armenia, were not seriously opposed by Azerbaijan, the third member of the confederation. Resistance was impossible, and under the threat of dismemberment the confederation fell apart. The Georgians turned to Germany for protection; the Tartars looked to Turkey; and the Armenians were in the familiar position of being left to look out for themselves. On May 26 the confederation was formally dissolved and Georgia issued a declaration of independence. Two days later the Azerbaijan Tartars and the Armenians made similar declarations.

THE SEIM CALLS UPON THE PEOPLES OF TRANSCAUCASIA TO RESIST THE TURKS

[Appeal of April 13, 1918][85]

CITIZENS OF TRANSCAUCASIA!

The destinies of our common fatherland are at stake. You know what the Turkish Government wants from us! It wants us to accept the Brest-Litovsk treaty, ... to surrender our best fortress, Kars, our best port, Batum, and three regions, Kars, Ardagan, and Batum. In vain

[84] *Ibid.*, pp. 269–70, 272–73, 312–16; Z. Avalov, *Nezavisimost Gruzii v mezhdunarodnoi politike 1918–1921 gg.*, Paris, 1924, pp. 40–42.

[85] *Dokumenty i materialy . . . . Zakavkazia i Gruzii*, pp. 185–86.

did we try to persuade the Turkish Government to renounce its claim. .... We were ready to make great sacrifices .... but we could not give up Batum, which is our only outlet to the sea. .... Turkey insists on her original demands .... and we are confronted with the choice: either a shameful peace and slavery, or war. .... That choice we made without hesitation. We did not sign a shameful peace, and peace negotiations were broken off. From now on the conflict must be decided by force of arms on the battlefield. ....

All to arms!
All to the front!
All to the defense of freedom and the fatherland!

Events followed a somewhat different course in the polyglot city of Baku, the great center of the oil industry on the Caspian coast of Azerbaijan. Here, because of the industrial character of the city and the relatively large number of Russian workers in its population, the Bolsheviks, in alliance with radical groups of Tartars and Persians, exercised a greater influence than elsewhere in Transcaucasia. Although a minority in the Baku Soviet, the Bolsheviks after the November Revolution dominated it and the governing commission composed of a Tartar, an Armenian, and a Russian Bolshevik.

The steady strengthening of the Bolshevik grip on affairs aroused opposition, which culminated in a revolt on March 18 led by the Mussavat (Tartar nationalist) party. Fighting continued for four days and ended in a Red victory when the Armenians, more for hatred of the Moslem Tartars than for love of the Bolsheviks, joined the Bolshevik side. For the massacres which followed, Bolshevik writers hold the Armenians responsible. The Soviet Republic of Azerbaijan was presently set up with Shaumian, an Armenian friend and disciple of Lenin, as chairman of its Sovnarkom. This government, though cut off from contact with the central Soviet government, remained somewhat precariously in power until midsummer 1918.[86]

[86] The following publications in Western European languages treat from various points of view the events referred to above: Haïdar Bammate, *Le Caucase et la révolution russe,* Paris, 1929, pp. 23–35; P. G. La Chesnais, *Les Peuples de la Transcaucasie,* Paris, 1921, pp. 38–81; Dr. Jean Loris-Melicof, *La Révolution*

To complete the picture of the confusion and resistance to the Bolsheviks during the first months of 1918, brief mention must be made of developments in regions not touched upon in the foregoing documents.

D. The Western Nationalities

In the extreme northwest, the Finns, who had enjoyed a greater degree of autonomy under the imperial régime than the other non-Russian nationalities, declared their independence on December 7 and asked the Bolsheviks to withdraw the Russian garrisons. The Finnish government was recognized by the Soviet of People's Commissars on January 2, 1918, and by France, Germany, and certain other Powers a few days later. But the Russian garrison, controlled by Bolsheviks, remained and joined the Finnish Social-Democrats when, on January 28–29, they drove the recognized government from Helsinki (Helsingfors) and set up a revolutionary régime. In the bitter civil war which followed, the Bolsheviks aided the Finnish Socialists with men and munitions as a part of their general policy to support every revolutionary movement.

By the treaty of Brest-Litovsk the Bolsheviks were forced to agree to withdraw their troops from Finland. This was in accord with the desires of many of the Russian soldiers, who were more interested in returning to their villages than in fighting a new war on foreign soil. Some, however, remained; but in April a German expeditionary force arrived in Finland and with the Finnish Whites routed the Red forces. On May 4 the bourgeois government returned to power in Helsinki.[87]

russe et les nouvelles républiques transcaucasiennes, Paris, 1920, pp. 101–46; Joseph Pomiankowski, *Der Zusammenbruch des ottomanischen Reiches; Errinnerungen an die Türkei aus der Zeit des Weltkrieges,* Zürich, Leipzig, Wien [1928], pp. 330–37, 359–63; Miliukov, "The Balkanization of Transcaucasia," in *The New Russia,* I (April 1920), 261–65, 306–10, 328–35; J. Castagne, "Le Bolchevisme et l'Islam," in *Revue du Monde Musulman,* LI (October 1922), 104–108.

[87] Cf. H. Söderhjelm, *The Red Insurrection in Finland in 1918, a study based on documentary evidence,* London, 1919; H. Ignatius and K. Soikkeli, *La Guerre d'indépendance en Finlande en 1918,* Helsingfors [1925]; S. Svechnikov, *Revoliutsiia i grazhdanskaia voina v Finliandii 1917–1918 gody,* Leningrad, 1923.

In Esthonia the November uprising produced a complicated situation. Taking advantage of the Bolshevik decree on nationalities, the Esthonian National Council proclaimed the independence of Esthonia on November 28. Immediately the adherents of the Bolsheviks among the Russian garrison and the Esthonian workers joined forces to disperse the National Council. But instead of attempting to establish their dictatorship by military strength alone, the Bolsheviks participated in the elections to the Esthonian Constituent Assembly which were held during January and February, 1918. The local German-Balt population, which was anti-Esthonian and anti-Bolshevik, boycotted this election, yet the Bolsheviks, despite their strong position, failed to poll more than 35 per cent of the total votes cast. The Esthonian labor party and the democratic agrarian coalition polled over 60 per cent of the votes.

Immediately after the election the Bolsheviks took the offensive, and a civil war began. Here, as in Finland, the German intervention was decisive, and on February 24 the Bolsheviks were driven from Tallinn (Reval). The Esthonian nationalists issued a new declaration of independence proclaiming a democratic form of government, but twenty-four hours later the Germans were masters of the capital and the national government was in flight. The German occupation continued until November 1918.[88]

On the Esthonian southern border are the lands of the Letts. After the great drive of 1915 German forces had occupied a considerable portion of these territories, and shortly before the November rising the Germans made a further advance, occupying Riga, the chief city of the region and the stronghold of the Bolshevik party in the Baltic. Representing those regions which were still on the Russian side of the front and including representatives of all political

[88] M. W. Graham, *New Governments of Eastern Europe,* New York, 1927, pp. 253–59; *Mémoire sur l'Indépendance de l'Esthonie présenté à la Conférence de la Paix* [Paris], 1919, pp. 24–26; *Bulletin de l'Esthonie,* No. 2 (May 1919), pp. 12–14; Hessen, *Okrainnye gosudarstva, Polsha, Finliandiia, Estoniia, Latviia i Litva,* Leningrad, 1926, pp. 76 ff.

parties except the Bolsheviks, the Latvian National Council met at Walk on November 16 and passed a resolution based on the right of self-determination and the Latvian desire for autonomy and protesting against the incorporation of the country into Germany. The National Council did not declare independence but, on the contrary, proposed that the status of the territory could be defined only by the Latvian Constituent Assembly and a national plebiscite. On their part, the Bolsheviks immediately began to extend the Soviet system throughout these regions and drove the Latvian National Council underground. In December 1917 the Letts on the German side of the front organized and passed resolutions similar to those of the Latvian National Council. On January 15 the National Council set up a tentative government which shortly afterward received de facto recognition from France. This government could not, of course, function during the German occupation, which became even more firmly established after the Brest peace.[89]

A considerable portion of the area inhabited by White Russians was also under German occupation after 1915. After the March revolution of 1917 the rather immature White Russian national movement became especially active in territories east of the German lines, and in March a large meeting in Minsk decided to create a National Council. In December 1917 a White Russian national congress of some two thousand delegates met in Minsk. It proclaimed the independence of White Russia and placed the supreme power in the hands of a Rada, which in turn established a provisional government until a constituent assembly could be convened. The Bolshevik Military Revolutionary Committee of Minsk dispersed the White Russian Congress and a Soviet of People's Commissars of the Western Region took control of White Russia. In January 1918, however, representatives of the White Russians under German occupation met at Vilna and adopted resolutions similar to those of the Minsk

[89] Graham, *op. cit.*, pp. 325–28; V. Mishke, "Podgotovka Oktiabria v Latvii," in *Proletarskaia Revoliutsiia*, 1928, No. 72, pp. 37–66; Hessen, *op. cit.*, pp. 100 ff.

Congress and sent their representatives to the Rada. In March the White Russian Rada succeeded in holding a new congress in Minsk and issued a new declaration proclaiming a democratic republic and protesting against the Brest-Litovsk peace. With the partitioning of the White Russian territory between the Germans and the Bolsheviks, the Rada ceased to exist.[90]

In the southwestern corner of the old empire the national movement of the Bessarabians added its quota to the complications of the summer of 1917. With the consent of the Provisional Government the Bessarabian members of the Petrograd Soviet sent fifty-two soldier delegates to Kishinev, where they organized the Moldavian Military Congress, which met on October 25. The Congress favored the establishment of a Russian federation with a local council, the Sfatul Tserii, to administer Bessarabian affairs pending the summoning of a Bessarabian constituent assembly. The Congress also voted to transfer all estate and church lands to the people without compensation to the owners. On December 2 the Sfatul Tserii proclaimed Bessarabia a Moldavian democratic republic constituting a part of the Russian federal republic. In January, Bolshevik soldiers occupied Kishinev, whereupon the Sfatul Tserii invited the Rumanians to intervene. On January 24 the Sfatul Tserii announced the separation of the Moldavian republic from Russia and explained that the Rumanian intervention was only temporary and for the purpose of guarding the grain supplies and maintaining order. A few weeks later the Rumanian Government signed an agreement with the Soviets which provided among other things for the withdrawal of Rumanian troops. In the meantime, however, the Rumanian Government had begun peace negotiations with the Central Powers. These negotiations involved ceding Rumanian territory (the Dobrudja) to the Central Powers, for which

[90] Liubimov, *op. cit.*, pp. 456–58; G. Gaillard, *Le Mouvement panrusse et les allogènes*, Paris, 1919, pp. 58–60: "xxx" in *Eastern Europe*, I, No. 2, September 16, 1919, p. 47; V. Knorin, *Revoliutsiia i kontr-revoliutsiia v Belorussii*, Smolensk, 1920, passim.

cession the annexation of Bessarabia offered compensation. For the sake of appearances it was desirable that this compensation should take the form of a voluntary union of Bessarabia with Rumania and that it be proclaimed before the conclusion of the treaty with the Central Powers. On April 9, therefore, the Sfatul Tserii voted for the union. This union, which was confirmed by a popular vote several months later, was not recognized by the Bolsheviks until 1933.[91]

AGREEMENT BETWEEN R.S.F.S.R. AND RUMANIA CONCERNING THE EVACUATION OF BESSARABIA[92]

[Ratified in Jassy, March 5, and Odessa, March 9, 1918]

Clause 1. Rumania agrees to evacuate Bessarabia within two months. . . . .

Clause 2. Immediately upon the signing of the agreement the protection of Bessarabia passes into the hands of local municipal and village militia. . . . .

Clause 3. Rumanian subjects arrested in Russia will be exchanged for Russian revolutionists, officers, and soldiers arrested in Rumania.

Clause 4. Rumania agrees not to engage in any unfriendly military or other operations against the All-Russian Federated Soviet Republic of Workers and Peasants and not to support any such undertakings by other nations.

Clause 5. Russia agrees to consign to Rumania the remainder of the grain in Bessarabia after the needs of the local population and the Russian troops have been satisfied. . . . .

Clause 7. In the event of a retreat from Rumanian soil the Rumanian army will find refuge and provisions on Russian soil.

Clause 8. In the event of combined operations against the Central Powers and their allies, contact will be established between the supreme military command of the Russian Soviet Army and the Rumanian Army.

[91] A. N. Kroupenski and A. Schmidt, *The Bessarabian "Parliament" (1917–1918)* [Paris, 1919]; Gratz and Schüller, *The Economic Policy of Austria-Hungary,* New Haven, 1928, pp. 148–51, 158–64; C. G. Rakovsky, *Roumania and Bessarabia,* London, 1925, pp. 22–38; J. S. Roucek, *Contemporary Roumania and Her Problems,* Stanford University, 1932, pp. 44–45; *U.S. Foreign Relations, 1918, Russia,* II, 707–19; *The Roumanian Occupation in Bessarabia, Documents,* Paris, 1920, passim; *L'Ukraine sovietiste,* Berlin, 1922, Part 2.

[92] Yu. Kliuchnikov and Sabanin, *Mezhdunarodnaia politika noveishego vremeni v dogovorakh, notakh i deklaratsiiakh* (3 vols.), Moscow, 1923–1928, II, 132–33.

Clause 9. For a settlement of possible difficulties between Rumania and the Russian Federated Soviet Republic of Workers and Peasants, international commissions will be established in Odessa, Kiev, Moscow, Petrograd, Jassy, and Galatz, composed of representatives of Russia and Rumania, England, France, and the United States.

Shortly after this agreement was signed Averescu was succeeded by Marghiloman, whose chief preoccupation was the completion of the treaty with the Central Powers. In these negotiations the annexation of Bessarabia by Rumania was agreed to by the Central Powers, with certain reservations in their interest. Marghiloman, therefore, repudiated Averescu's agreement with Rakovsky, and the Sfatul Tserii, surrounded by Rumanian troops, proclaimed the union of Bessarabia with Rumania.[93]

UNION OF BESSARABIA WITH RUMANIA

[Act of the Sfatul Tserii, April 9, 1918][94]

In the name of the People of Bessarabia, the Sfatul Tserii declares:

"The Moldavian Democratic Republic (Bessarabia), bounded by the Pruth, the Dniester, the Danube, the Black Sea, and the former Austrian frontier, torn by Russia more than a century ago from the body of ancient Moldavia, firm in its historic rights as well as in the right of relationship, and basing its action on the right of nations to determine their own status, reunites itself from today and forever to its Motherland, Roumania." . . . .

PROTEST AGAINST THE SEIZURE OF BESSARABIA BY RUMANIA

[Chicherin to Marghiloman, April 18, 1918][95]

Your announcement, published in the European press, that the representatives of Bessarabia have solemnly declared for the union of Bess-

[93] A. N. Kroupenski and A. Schmidt, Bessarabian delegates to the Paris Peace Conference, state that they were in possession of a record of a convention between Marghiloman and certain Bessarabian landowners in which Marghiloman stated that the Germans insisted that the Sfatul must proclaim the union of Bessarabia and Rumania before the conclusion of the treaty, otherwise Germany could not agree to the recognition of such a union in the treaty. (Kroupenski and Schmidt, *The Bessarabian "Parliament" 1917–1918*, p. 11.)

[94] *The Roumanian Occupation in Bessarabia; Documents*, pp. 64–65.

[95] Yu. Kliuchnikov and Sabanin, *Mezhdunarodnaia politika*, II, 138–39.

arabia with Rumania and that, on the basis of this, you henceforth considered Bessarabia an inalienable part of the Rumanian crown, constitutes not only a challenge to the Russian Federative Soviet Republic but also a crying violation of the agreement concluded by your predecessors with Russia providing for the evacuation of Bessarabia within two months.

This annexation, furthermore, is a violation of the will of the Bessarabian population, who openly and unanimously expressed their protest against the Rumanian occupation. The Congress of peasants of the Moldavian Republic, meeting in Kishinev from the 18th to the 22d of January, this year, notwithstanding the arrest of the chairman of the Congress, Rudiev, and the vice-chairman, Proshtitsky, and other repressive measures on the part of the Rumanian military power, voted unanimously against the Rumanian occupation and demanded the withdrawal of Rumanian troops from Bessarabia. Your attempt to make appear as the will of the Bessarabian workers and peasants the votes of the Bessarabian landowners, the exploiters, and the arch-enemies of the Bessarabian people who were holding their sessions under the protection of Rumanian troops has no justification whatever in international law. The forcible annexation of Bessarabia to Rumania does not destroy the unity and the solidarity of the working masses of Bessarabia and Russia.

E. The Moslem Peoples

Among Moslem peoples, who numbered nearly 14,000,000 in the old empire, national sentiment was naturally less developed than among Western minorities. But such a movement did exist, growing out of religious and economic grievances against the imperial régime. After the March Revolution the Moslem leaders in general supported the Provisional Government, but they also took steps to secure for their people greater national rights in the new Russian state.

In May 1917 an All-Russian Moslem Congress met in Moscow. Among the delegates two tendencies appeared. One group favored the establishment of a unified national state and cultural autonomy for the minorities. The second, a considerably larger group, favored a federal republic in which the constituent national units should be assured of the control of their own economic, cultural, and political affairs. This Congress also passed the significant resolution that all land should be turned over to the people and that the right to sell, buy, or own land should be abolished. The Provisional Government did not grant the demands of the Congress, but gradually the Moslem nationalities secured a considerable degree of local autonomy through their control of the temporary governmental institutions and by virtue of the fact that Moslem soldiers were detailed to the garrisons in Kazan, Ufa, and certain sections of the Ural, the Volga, and the Caucasus regions.

Immediately after their seizure of power the Bolsheviks announced policies which greatly favored the aspirations of the Moslem peoples. The first of these policies was the decree of November 15 granting the right of national self-determination, including the right of separation from Russia. The Bolsheviks gave further encouragement to Eastern nationalities by their proclamation of December 7, 1917, to the Moslems of Russia and the East.

Early in December the Bolsheviks ordered restored to the Regional Congress of Moslems in Petrograd the Koran of the Caliph Osman which for many years after its removal from Samarkand had been in the Imperial Public Library in Petrograd. In January the Soviet Government constituted a special commissariat for Moslem affairs under Mullah-Nur Vakhitov, a Tartar and a former member of the Constituent Assembly from Kazan. But in the actual relations between the Soviets and the Moslems the Bolsheviks appear to have followed Stalin's interpretation of self-determination — a doctrine to be used primarily as a means of attaining socialism and not to be applied to the bourgeoisie. The Moslem leaders, if not bourgeois, were at least hostile to Bolshevik ideas. Thus in territories inhabited by the Moslems, conflicts broke out between them and the forces of the Red Guards.[96]

[96] J. Castagne, "Le Bolchevisme et l'Islam," in *Revue du Monde Musulman,* LI (October 1922), 1–10.

APPEAL TO THE MOSLEMS OF RUSSIA AND THE EAST

[Proclamation of the Sovnarkom, December 7, 1917][97]

Comrades! Brothers!

Great events are taking place in Russia. The end of the bloody war, which was begun with the purpose of partitioning other lands, is drawing near. The rule of the robbers and enslavers of the peoples of the earth is about to end. Under the blows of the Russian Revolution, the old world of serfdom and slavery is crumbling. . . . . A new world is being born, a world of workers and free men. At the head of this revolution stands the Workers' and Peasants' Government of Russia, the Soviet of People's Commissars.

All Russia is sown with revolutionary Soviets of Workers', Soldiers', and Peasants' Deputies. The power in the country is in the hands of the people. The laboring people of Russia have but one burning desire—to achieve an honorable peace and to aid the oppressed peoples of the earth to fight for their freedom.

In this holy task Russia is not alone. The call to liberty sounded by the Russian Revolution is reaching all workers of the East and the West. The exhausted, warring peoples of Europe already stretch out their hands to us, who are making peace. The workers and soldiers of the West already gather under the banner of socialism, storming the stronghold of imperialism. And far-off India, which for centuries has been oppressed by the "enlightened" plunderers of Europe, is already raising the banner of revolt, organizing its Soviets of Deputies, casting the hated slavery from its shoulders, and summoning the peoples of the East to the struggle of liberation. . . . .

In the face of these great events we turn to you, toiling and disinherited Moslems of Russia and the East.

Moslems of Russia, Tartars of the Volga and the Crimea, Kirghiz, and Sarts of Siberia and Turkestan, Turks and Tartars of Transcaucasia, Chechens and Mountaineers of the Caucasus—all those whose mosques and chapels have been destroyed, whose beliefs and customs have been trampled under foot by the tsars and oppressors of Russia!

Henceforth your beliefs and customs, your national and cultural institutions, are free and inviolable. Build your national life freely and unhindered. You have a right to do so. Know that your rights, as well as the rights of all peoples of Russia, are protected by the Soviets of Workers', Soldiers', and Peasants' Deputies.

[97] Kliuchnikov and Sabanin, *Mezhdunarodnaia politika,* II, 94–96; *Izvestiia,* No. 232, December 7, 1917, pp. 1–2.

Defend this revolution and its plenipotentiary government!

Moslems of the East, Persians, Turks, Arabs, and Hindus, all those for whose lives and property, liberty and land, the greedy robbers of Europe have bartered for centuries—all those whose countries the plunderers who started the war wish to divide!

We declare that the secret treaties of the dethroned Tsar regarding the seizure of Constantinople, which were confirmed by the overthrown Kerensky government, are null and void. The Russian Republic and her government, the Soviet of People's Commissars, is opposed to the seizure of foreign territory; Constantinople must remain in the hands of the Moslems.

We declare that the treaty regarding the partition of Persia is null and void. As soon as military operations are brought to an end, the troops will be withdrawn from Persia and Persians will be guaranteed the right to choose freely their own destiny.

We declare that the treaty regarding the partition of Turkey and wresting from her of Armenia is null and void. As soon as military operations are brought to an end, the Armenians will be guaranteed the right to decide freely their political destiny.

Not at the hands of Russia and her revolutionary government does slavery await you, but at the hands of the marauders of European imperialism, of those who converted your fatherland into their ravished and plundered "colony."

Throw off these ravishers and enslavers of your country. Now that war and desolation are tearing down the structure of the old world, when all the world is aflame with wrathful indignation against the imperialist plunderers, when every spark of revolt kindles into a mighty flame of revolution, when even the Indian Moslems, worn out and suffering under the foreign yoke, are starting a rebellion against their oppressors—now it is impossible to be silent. Do not waste any time in throwing from your shoulders the age-long enslavers of your land. Do not permit them longer to rob you of your native homes. You yourselves must be the masters of your country. You yourselves must build your life in your own way and according to your own desires. You have this right, for your fate is in your own hands.

Comrades! Brothers!

Firmly and decisively let us strive for an honorable, democratic peace.

On our banners we proclaim the liberation of oppressed peoples of the world.

Moslems of Russia!

Moslems of the East!

We await your sympathy and support in this cause of building a new world.

DZHUGASHVILI (STALIN)
People's Commissar of Nationalities
V. ULIANOV (LENIN)
President of the Soviet of People's Commissars

The Tartars of the Crimea held a national assembly in May 1917 and adopted a program of national autonomy in the Russian federation. In November a new national assembly, the Kurultai, met at Bakhchisarai in the ancient palace of the Khans of the Crimea, declared the independence of the Crimean Tartar Republic, and in December adopted a constitution and set up a directory of five as the government. An interesting provision of the constitution gave women political equality with men. During the same period, however, workers in the ports and Russian soldiers and sailors were in control of the Soviets in Feodosia and Sevastopol. Presently, with the aid of sailors from the Black Sea Fleet, the Bolsheviks defeated the Tartar forces, and, by the end of January, they had established Soviet control over the peninsula. This lasted until April, when the troops of the Central Powers arrived on the scene.[98]

The Turco-Tartars of the Kazan region, in conformity with the resolutions of the Pan-Moslem Congress, held a national congress at Ufa in October 1917, where they adopted a program which provided for the establishment of an autonomous Volga-Ural state as a member of a Russian federated republic in which the Turco-Tartars of European Russia, regardless of the provinces in which they lived, should enjoy national cultural autonomy. The assembly also set up a National Council as a governing body for the Kazan region pending the decision of the Russian Constituent Assembly.

While the national congress of the Kazan Tartars was still in session, the Bolshevik revolution occurred, and al-

[98] J. Castagne, *op. cit.*, pp. 141–47; *Zhizn Natsionalnostei,* No. 21, October 10, 1921, pp. 1 ff.

though a minority of the convention took a sympathetic attitude toward the overturn, the majority opposed submission to the new government and voted to take measures to protect the Moslem regions against the Bolsheviks. For this purpose the Tartar regiments organized during the time of the Provisional Government were utilized. In the meantime in Kazan, Ufa, and other cities having a considerable proletarian population, regional revolutionary committees had taken over the power in the name of the Soviets. The project of a new national congress could not be carried out as soldiers returning from the front under Bolshevik leadership attacked the Tartar detachments and by the end of March 1918 the Bolsheviks had succeeded in bringing about the dissolution of these Tartar units. A decree of the Commissar for Nationalities, on March 22, 1918, organized a Tartar-Bashkir Soviet Republic of the Russian Soviet Federation. The territories of the republic, delimited according to a project of the Tartar and Bashkir revolutionary organization, included all of Ufa Gubernia, most of Kazan, and those parts of Orenburg, Perm, Viatka, and Simbirsk inhabited by Moslems. By a decree of April 13, 1918, the Bolsheviks dissolved the Central National Council and the existing Moslem regional organizations. A majority of the national and religious leaders were arrested and thrown into prison.[99]

To the south and east of the Turco-Tartars the nomadic Kirghiz people undertook to organize their national life in a somewhat similar fashion. A Pan-Kirghiz Congress met at Orenburg early in 1917 and established a national council charged with the duty of organizing the Kirghiz regions and establishing contact with the neighboring peoples of Bashkiria, Siberia, and Turkestan. During the summer of 1917 the national council, which took the name Alash Orda, attempted to organize the administration of the great area over which the Kirghiz people roamed. Because of the vast-

[99] Castagne, *op. cit.*, pp. 125–31; Batsell, *op. cit.*, p. 139; *Proletarskaia Revoliutsiia,* 1922, No. 10, pp. 337–48.

ness of this territory, it was decided to divide the administration into two sections, the Alash Orda of the West and the Alash Orda of the East. The effect of the Bolshevik revolution on the Kirghiz is described by a Bolshevik writer in these words:

"With what joy they greeted the first [March] revolution and with what horror the second [November]! This attitude of the Kirghiz can be easily understood by those who know the Kirghiz people. The first revolution was correctly comprehended and joyously received, first, because it liberated the Kirghiz from the unbearable burden of the Tsarist Government; secondly, it increased their long-cherished hopes of independence. The principles of the second revolution were incomprehensible to the Kirghiz because neither capitalism nor class differentiation existed among them; even the idea of property was different; for example, many common objects of daily use were considered in Kirghizia as common property. At the same time the October Revolution horrified the Kirghiz by its outward manifestation. The forms which the Bolshevik movement took in the central part of Russia were unknown to the Kirghiz, while in the borderlands it was followed by violence, plundering, and abuses, as well as by a very peculiar form of dictatorship. Thus in actuality the movement in the borderlands was often not a revolution (as it is generally understood) but pure anarchy."[100]

As in other Moslem areas Soviet organizations seized the power in the towns, including Semipalatinsk, the Kirghiz capital. "The members of these organizations were simply adventurers who took the name of Bolsheviks, and they often behaved in a hideous manner."[101] The Kirghiz naturally turned toward anti-Bolshevik groups.

The Alash Orda of the West joined with the Bashkirs and the Orenburg Cossacks in opposing the Red forces. The Alash Orda of the East established contact with the autono-

[100] *Zhizn Natsionalnostei*, No. 29, August 1919, pp. 1 ff.

[101] *Ibid.*

mous government of Siberia, which was also anti-Bolshevik. Early in March the Soviet Government ordered the dissolution of the Alash Orda as a bourgeois institution and instructed the Soviet agents to form the poorer Kirghiz into a political organization.[102]

The Bashkirs, near neighbors of the Kazan Tartars and the Kirghiz, also sent their delegates to the All-Russian Moslem Congress in Moscow in May 1917. They did not, however, accept the resolution abolishing private ownership of land, and when their own national congress met at Orenburg the delegates demanded that the government should return to the Bashkirs the land which had been alienated by the Russian policy of colonization. This Congress also granted equal political rights to women, demanded the organization of a separate Bashkir army, and elected a national council.

A second Bashkir national congress met at Ufa on August 25, 1917. It re-elected the National Council, prepared for the elections to the All-Russian Constituent Assembly, and took steps to set up an autonomous administration without waiting for the meeting of the Constituent Assembly. The Bolshevik revolution caused a split in the national movement. One group, consisting of frontovik soldiers and workers, favored the Bolsheviks, with a program of abolition of private property and nationalization of the land. Another group, which controlled the National Assembly (Kurultai) which met at Orenburg between December 8 and 30, 1917, was anti-Bolshevik and followed the program of the preceding national congress. During December and January Red forces advanced into the Bashkir territory, carried on successful operations against both the Bashkirs and the Orenburg Cossacks, and in March, as has been noted, decreed that Bashkiria should become a part of the Tartar-Bashkir Soviet Republic. In this conflict between Reds and Whites, the Bashkirs, who were not in full sympathy with either side, fought in both armies and saw their territories

102 Castagne, *op. cit.*, pp. 172–75; *Zhizn Natsionalnostei,* No. 20, October 3, 1921, pp. 1–2.

overrun by both forces and their Bashkir national organization dispersed.[103]

In Turkestan the Provisional Government placed the direction of affairs in the hands of a Turkestan Committee of eight members, five of whom, greatly to the displeasure of the Moslems, were not members of that faith. Moreover, this committee's principal rival for power, the Tashkent Workers' and Soldiers' Soviet, was also made up chiefly of non-Moslem followers of the Mensheviks, Bolsheviks, and Socialist-Revolutionists. The Moslems on their part formed a regional Pan-Moslem Council of Turkestan, which claimed many adherents but lacked the military strength of the Soviet. In September, after many weeks of agitation against the Turkestan Committee, the Tashkent Soviet attempted to seize power but was defeated by the intervention of troops still loyal to the Provisional Government. In October, however, the forces of the Soviets were victorious and on November 15 organized the Tashkent Council of People's Commissars, which called on all Soviets of the region to take the power into their own hands. At about the same time an All-Moslem Congress met. A majority of the Congress voted against recognition of the Bolshevik power, but a minority favored acceptance of the revolution. A later Moslem congress held at Kokand set up a government which subsequently entered into relations with the Southeastern Union. On January 30, 1918, the Bolshevik troops from Tashkent appeared before Kokand. According to the Bolsheviks the Moslems, calling to their aid a well-known bandit, intrusted to him the command of their army. According to the Moslems, although lacking arms, their soldiers made a gallant defense of the city, which was bombarded, and subsequently captured, pillaged, and burned by the Reds. In any event, in the spring of 1918 the Bolsheviks and their allies were in the ascendancy in Turkestan.[104]

[103] Cf. M. L. Murtazin, *Bashkiriia i bashkirskie voiska v grazhdanskuiu voinu*, Leningrad, 1927, pp. 51 ff.

[104] Castagne, *op. cit.*, pp. 233–35; *Proletarskaia Revoliutsiia*, 1924, No. 33, p. 138; *Zhizn Natsionalnostei*, No. 3, November 24, 1918, pp. 2 ff.

In the North Caucasus the Moslem peoples, who had resisted Russian conquest so valiantly and long, in May 1917 sent their delegates to a conference in Vladikavkaz which formed a Union of the Peoples of the North Caucasus and Daghestan and set up a Central Committee as its executive body.

The Union later refused to recognize the legitimacy of the Bolshevik government and at a congress early in December declared the independence of the North Caucasus pending the meeting of the All-Russian Constituent Assembly. The Union immediately became involved in war, first with the neighboring Cossacks and then with the Bolsheviks, who, early in March 1918, drove the local troops out of Vladikavkaz. Representatives of the Union attended the Trebizond Peace Conference and later journeyed to Constantinople, where the Sublime Porte agreed to recognize the independence of the North Caucasus and to urge its recognition by the Central Powers. On May 11, 1918, the republic of the North Caucasus declared its independence.[105]

Siberia

Beyond the Urals events moved more slowly than in European Russia. There was no November revolution comparable to what occurred in the West. Siberian regionalists, dominated by Socialist-Revolutionists, directed affairs in Western Siberia until February. In Central Siberia the Bolsheviks gained control of Krasnoiarsk soon after the seizure of power in Petrograd and early in 1918 overcame their opponents in Irkutsk. Trans-Baikalia, the stronghold of Ataman Semenov, was an active anti-Bolshevik center throughout the period under consideration. In the Far East a zemstvo government, in which the Socialist-Revolutionists had

[105] Haïdar Bammate, *Le Caucase et la révolution russe*, pp. 36–39, and "Le Problème du Caucase," in *La Revue Politique Internationale*, No. 35, November-December, 1918, pp. 193–224. J. B., "The Republic of North Caucasia: History of Its Formation," in *Eastern Europe*, Paris, I, 39–42.

a majority, managed affairs in harmony with a mildly Bolshevik Soviet in Khabarovsk.[106]

The Kalmucks, a nomadic Mongol people, Buddhist in faith, living on the steppes on the right bank of the lower Volga and the northwestern shore of the Caspian, reacted to the Bolshevik revolution in very much the same manner as the Kirghiz. Such Bolshevik ideas as they could understand violated their most sacred traditions and beliefs. They were ready, therefore, to join the Astrakhan Cossacks in a struggle with the Bolsheviks for the control of Astrakhan.

In January 1918 the Bolsheviks established their rule in this city and the Kalmucks retired into the steppes, where they continued their opposition to the dictatorship.

[106] A volume of documents relating to events in Siberia and the Russian Far East during this period is in preparation.

CHAPTER IX

BREST-LITOVSK

The conference to draft a treaty between the governments of Soviet Russia and the four Central Powers held its first meeting at Brest-Litovsk on December 22, 1917. The sessions continued with interruptions until February 10, when the Soviet delegation refused to sign the treaty or continue the negotiations. The Germans thereupon declared the armistice ended and began an advance toward Petrograd. In the face of this threat and against the strong opposition of some of their own leaders and of the Socialist-Revolutionists of the Left, the Bolshevik Central Committee decided on February 18 to sign the treaty. The Central Powers, however, now demanded the acceptance of more severe terms, to which after further debate the Sovnarkom agreed, and the revised treaty was signed on March 3, 1918. The Seventh Bolshevik Party Congress meeting March 6–8 voted for ratification, as did the Extraordinary Congress of Soviets held on March 14–18. The Socialist-Revolutionists of the Left refused to accept this decision and recalled their members from the Sovnarkom.

A. The Soviet Peace Terms

The principal representatives of the five powers assembled in Brest-Litovsk to begin formal negotiations of a peace treaty were: For Germany—Kühlmann, Secretary of State for Foreign Affairs; Rosenberg, of the Foreign Office; Kriege, legal adviser; and General Hoffmann and Major Brinckmann, representing the General Staff. For Austria-Hungary—Count Czernin, Foreign Minister; Merey, Wiesner, Count Colleredo, Count Csaky of the Foreign Office; and Lieutenant-Field-Marshal Csicserics, Lieutenant-Colonel Pokorny, and Major Glaise of the Army. For Bulgaria —Popov, Minister of Justice; Kossov, Stoianovich, Colonel Gantchev, and Dr. Anastassov. For Turkey—Grand Vizier Talaat Pasha; Ahmed Nessimy Bey, Foreign Minister; Ibrahim Hakki Pasha, Reshad Hikmed Bey, and General Zekki Pasha. For Russia—A. A. Joffe, chairman; L. B. Kamenev, Madame A. A. Bitsenko, Professor M. N. Pokrovsky, L. M. Karakhan, N. M. Lubinsky, M. P. Weltmann-Pavlovich, Vice-Admiral V. M. Altvater, General A. A. Samoilo, Colonel Fokke, Colonel I. Ya. Tseplit, and Captain V. Lipsky.

The first session took place at 4:24 P.M., December 22, 1917. Prince Leopold of Bavaria opened the conference with a speech of welcome and suggested Hakki Pasha as presiding officer. Hakki Pasha in a short speech greeted the representatives of the Russian Government "which had the courage to declare to the entire world its humanitarian principles." In conclusion he asked Kühlmann to preside at the first session. After stating a number of preliminaries for the conduct of the negotiations, Kühlmann invited the Russian delegation to state the principles on which it hoped to conclude peace.[1]

THE RUSSIAN CONDITIONS OF PEACE

[Joffe's Statement of the "Six Points," December 22, 1917][2]

[After reading the larger part of the Decree of Peace of November 8, Joffe said]:

In accordance with the principles [of the decree] the Russian delegation proposes the following six points as a basis for peace discussion:

1. No forcible annexation of territories seized during the war. Troops in occupation of such areas to be withdrawn in the shortest time possible.

[1] *Die Friedensverhandlungen in Brest-Litowsk,* p. 21; *Mirnye peregovory v Brest-Litovske, s 22/9 dekabria 1917 g. po 3 marta (18 fevralia) 1918 g.,* Moscow, 1920, I, 1–5; J. L. Magnes, *Russia and Germany at Brest-Litovsk, a Documentary History of the Peace Negotiations,* New York [1919], p. 30; Louis Fischer, *The Soviets in World Affairs,* I, 34 ff.

[2] *Mirnye peregovory v Brest-Litovske,* I, 7–8. This statement also appears in *The Soviet Union and Peace,* pp. 33–35.

2. Full political independence to be restored to those peoples who have lost it during the war.

3. Nationalities which did not enjoy political independence before the war to be assured the opportunity of deciding for themselves by a referendum whether to be a part of a particular state or to be an independent state. The referendum to be organized in such a way as to assure the fullest freedom of voting to the population of the territory in question, including emigrants and refugees.

4. In territories that are inhabited by several nationalities the rights of minorities are protected by special laws guaranteeing full cultural independence and, as far as is practicable, administrative autonomy.

5. No belligerent to pay any other so-called "war indemnities." Contributions already levied to be returned. Private individuals who have incurred losses during the war to be indemnified from a special fund to which all the warring nations should contribute proportionately.

6. Colonial questions to be decided in accordance with the principles laid down in points 1, 2, 3, and 4.

As a supplement to these points the Russian delegation proposed that the negotiating Powers should condemn the attempts of strong nations to oppress weaker nations by such indirect methods as economic boycotts, economic subjection by imposing commercial treaties, separate tariff agreements interfering with the freedom of commerce of a third country, and sea blockade having no direct military aim. These are the fundamental principles which can be accepted by all, and without which the Russian delegation does not see how it is possible to conclude a general peace.

[After hearing this declaration the conference adjourned to give the Central Powers time to prepare a reply.]

When it came to formulating a reply to the Soviets' Six Points the representatives of the Quadruple Alliance ran into difficulties. Kühlmann and Czernin agreed to a public acceptance of the Soviet formula of "no annexations" on the important condition that the Entente should also accept the formula and with the unexpressed reservation that this did not apply to Poland, Lithuania, and Courland, which, according to the German view, had decided to separate from Russia and place their fate in the hands of the Central Powers. Hoffmann objected to such an answer because it went against his feelings and because "at bottom it was a lie." The Turks wanted a provision for an immediate evacuation of the Caucasus, to which the Germans could not agree, since they might be asked to evacuate the Baltic territories. But the Bulgarians were the most difficult. They had been promised Serbian and Rumanian territory, and Popov demanded a clause stating that the acquisition of these territories should not be regarded as annexation. The Bulgarians were not brought into line until the 24th and the reply of the Central Powers to Joffe's statement could not be made until the 25th.[3]

CZERNIN'S REPLY FOR THE QUADRUPLE ALLIANCE[4]

[December 25, 1917]

The Conference opened at 10: 11 P.M.

Kühlmann:[5] Gentlemen! At the last meeting the chairman of the Russian delegation outlined, in a general way, certain principles the acceptance of which he thought would make it possible to start peace negotiations. The Allied Powers . . . . are ready to make the following reply to those proposals:

The delegations of the Allied Powers take their stand on the clearly expressed will of their governments and peoples to conclude a just and general peace as soon as possible . . . . and are of the opinion that the principles laid down by the Russian delegation form the basis for the discussion of such a peace.

The delegations of the Quadruple Alliance are prepared to conclude immediately a general peace without forcible annexations or indemnities. They agree with the Russian delegation, which condemned the continuation of the war for the purpose of conquest. The statesmen of the Allied Governments have stressed again and again in their political declarations that the Quadruple Alliance will not prolong for a single day the war for the sake of conquest. To this point of view the Allied Governments have consistently adhered and they solemnly declare their resolution to end it by signing without delay a treaty of peace equally just to all belligerents without exception.

It is necessary, however, to make it quite clear that the proposals of

[3] Hoffmann, pp. 206–207; Count Ottokar Czernin, *In the World War,* New York [1920], pp. 247–49.

[4] *Mirnye peregovory v Brest-Litovske,* I, 9–11.

[5] It was Czernin and not Kühlmann who replied to the Russians. (Czernin, p. 249; also *Die Friedensverhandlungen in Brest-Litowsk,* p. 23.)

the Russian delegation can be accepted only in case all belligerents without exception pledge themselves to accept by a certain time and without reservations the terms binding on all nations. The Powers of the Quadruple Alliance now negotiating with Russia cannot, therefore, make unconditional promises to carry out these conditions without having any guaranty that the Allies of Russia on their part will honestly and without reservations live up to these conditions in regard to the Quadruple Alliance.

Taking these principles into consideration we are ready to make the following statement in regard to the six points which the Russian delegation proposed as the basis for negotiations:

1. The Powers of the Alliance have no intention to annex by force the territories seized during the war. The conditions for evacuating the occupied territories are to be determined by the peace treaty unless some understanding is reached before that time to remove the troops from certain places.

2. The members of the Alliance have no intention of denying political independence to those nations that have lost it during the war.

3. In regard to the question of self-determination for nationalities that have not had political independence, it is the opinion of the Powers of the Quadruple Alliance that this question does not admit of international settlement. It must, in any given case, be solved by each state together with the nationalities concerned and in accordance with the constitution of that state.

4. In the same manner the protection of the rights of minorities appears to the statesmen of the Quadruple Alliance to form an essential part of the right of the peoples to self-determination which can be realized only in a constitutional way. The governments of the Alliance apply this principle everywhere, in so far as it seems practicable.

5. The Powers of the Alliance have referred again and again to the possibility for both sides to renounce not only war costs but also war losses. If this principle were adopted, each nation would have to bear merely the cost of the support of its prisoners of war and of damages suffered on its territory by the enemy subjects provided those damages are caused in violation of International Law. The proposal of the Russian Government to create a special fund for these payments is worthy of consideration provided that by a certain time all the belligerents take part in the peace discussions.

6. Of the four Powers in the Alliance Germany alone has colonies. In full agreement with the Russian proposals the German delegation would like to make the following declaration: Germany will never renounce and now demands the restoration of her colonies seized by force during the war. The Russian proposals for the enemy to evacuate imme-

diately the occupied colonial territories is in harmony with Germany's point of view. Considering the nature of the German colonies it is not now possible to carry out the principle of the right of self-determination as laid down by the Russian delegation. Notwithstanding the enormous difficulties and the insignificant chances of success against a much stronger enemy that has access to the sea, the natives of the German colonies have remained the true friends of Germany even unto death. This shows how loyal and determined they are to remain with Germany. The weight and significance of such a proof are worth more than any "expression of popular will."

The supplementary proposals of the Russian delegation in regard to economic matters meet with the hearty approval of the Powers of the Alliance. They condemn all violence in economic life, and they regard the restoration and regulation of economic relations which would satisfy the interests of all the peoples concerned as one of the most important steps leading to friendly relations between the Powers now engaged in war.

I should like to add that, taking the above principles as a basis, we are ready to enter at once into peace discussions with our enemies. In order not to lose time the Allies are willing to begin without delay to discuss the questions which appear most important both from the standpoint of the Russians and the Powers of the Quadruple Alliance.

Joffe expressed the satisfaction of the Russian delegation that the Quadruple Alliance did not aim at territorial annexation or the destruction of the independence of any people. However, he called attention to the fact that the Central Powers do not apply the principle of self-determination to the national minorities within their own borders, and he insisted that these nationalities be protected in the treaty. He further pointed out that upkeep of prisoners of war is part of war expenditure and the stipulation for the payment of such upkeep might be interpreted as payment of war indemnities. He considered, however, that the declaration of the Quadruple Alliance formed a suitable basis upon which to negotiate a general peace, and he suggested that a recess of ten days be announced to allow the governments not represented to acquaint themselves with the principles enunciated. In conclusion he expressed the willingness of the Russian delegation to proceed immediately with the discussion of such special questions as would have to be considered between Russia and the Central Powers.

On December 26 and 27 the principal bases of the peace were discussed. Questions relating to the resumption of commercial and diplomatic relations and the indemnification of private persons who had suffered from the war were taken up, and provisional drafts of corresponding articles of the future treaty were considered.[6]

Toward the end of the session Joffe proposed that before any other question was taken up, the status of the occupied territories should be decided upon and included as the first article of the treaty. Kühlmann replied that the question could not be considered that day as "the attention of those present is too strained . . . . and the interpreters are tired." Kamenev suggested that the status of the occupied regions had already been determined by the declaration of the Quadruple Alliance of December 25. To this Kühlmann replied that he preferred not to raise a question which would require a special session and which he was not yet prepared to consider.[7]

One can understand Kühlmann's reluctance to raise the crucial problem of evacuating the conquered territories at a time when he was trying to turn the Brest negotiations into a general peace conference, and when the attitude of France, England, and the United States was not yet known. General Hoffmann, on the other hand, favored an independent peace policy for the East, and insisted on plain talk with the Russians; he undertook the task of making it clear to them what the Germans understood by the principle of "no annexations." On December 27, at luncheon, he said to Joffe that the Germans could not withdraw from the Baltic territories and Poland on the conclusion of peace. Poland, Lithuania,

[6] Gratz and Schüller, *The Economic Policy of Austria-Hungary during the War in Its External Relations,* pp. 84–86, gives an account of the proceedings of December 26–27. The authors of this book were members of the Austro-Hungarian delegation.

[7] *Mirnye peregovory v Brest-Litovske,* I, 28; D. G. Fokke, "Na stsene i za kulisami brestskoi tragikomedii," in *A.R.R.*, XX (1930), 114.

and Courland, in accordance with the principle of self-determination, had withdrawn from the Russian state, and if these territories decided ultimately to unite with Germany that did not, according to the Central Powers, constitute annexation. "Joffe looked as if he had received a blow on the head." There followed long and heated arguments between Kühlmann, Czernin, and Hoffmann, and Joffe, Kamenev, and Pokrovsky, which lasted through the 27th, when the conflicting proposals for the first article of the treaty were officially presented.[8]

THE STATUS OF THE OCCUPIED TERRITORIES

[Proposals of the Russians and the Germans, December 27, 1917][9]

The conference opened at 5:05 P.M.

Joffe: . . . . We suggest the following draft of the first article [of the future treaty]:

In full agreement with the public declarations of both contracting parties that they cherish no designs of conquest and that they desire to conclude peace without annexations, Russia is ready to withdraw her troops from all parts of Austria-Hungary, Turkey, and Persia, while the Powers of the Quadruple Alliance are likewise ready to withdraw [their troops] from Poland, Lithuania, Courland, and other regions of Russia.

In accordance with the principles of the Russian Government which has proclaimed the right of all peoples without exception living in Russia to self-determination, including even separation, the populations in these districts will be given in the near future the opportunity of deciding freely the question of their union with one or the other states or of forming independent states. The presence of any troops apart from national and local militia in the territories where a plebiscite is being held shall not be permitted. Until this question is settled, the government of these regions must remain in the hands of representatives of the local population elected on a democratic basis. The date of evacuation, depending on the question of the demobilization of the army, shall be determined by a special military commission. . . . .

[8] Hoffmann, *op. cit.*, pp. 209–11; Fokke, *op. cit.*, p. 130. On Hoffmann's status at the conference see Kühlmann's statement in the Reichstag, February 20, 1918, in Lutz, *The Fall of the German Empire, 1914–1918*, I, 770–72.

[9] *Mirnye peregovory v Brest-Litovske*, I, 28–30.

[German Counter-Proposal]

Kühlmann: . . . .

Our project reads as follows:

Article 1. Russia and Germany hereby declare the state of war at an end. The two states are resolved to live in the future in peace and amity.

On condition of complete reciprocity toward her allies, Germany is ready as soon as peace is concluded and the demobilization of the Russian Army has been completed, to evacuate her present positions in Russian territory in so far as this does not conflict with the provisions of Article 2.

Article 2. The Russian Government having, in accordance with its principles, proclaimed for all peoples, without exception, living within the Russian Empire, the right of self-determination, including complete separation, takes cognizance of the decisions expressing the will of the peoples inhabiting Poland, Lithuania, Courland, and portions of Esthonia and Livonia demanding full state independence and separation from the Russian Federation.

The Russian Government recognizes that in the present circumstances the above decisions must be regarded as the expression of the will of the people and is ready to act accordingly. In view of the fact that the question of the evacuation of the districts mentioned is different from that mentioned in Article 1, a special commission shall be appointed to fix, in accordance with the Russian plan, the time and the methods of a plebiscite to ratify the will already expressed.

The German counter-proposal was telegraphed to Smolny immediately after the close of the conference at 5:45 P.M., December 27.[10] Late that night Trotsky reported to the Central Executive Committee the initial success of Soviet diplomacy. "The Germans and Austrians," he said, "have agreed to return what they have taken during the war, but they asked us not to insist on the restitution of the booty they had appropriated in the past. Even our enemies, who only recently predicted that the Germans would not even talk to us . . . . must now admit that our diplomacy has met with great success." He went on to explain that "Germany gives in not merely to the force of truth but to the fear of revolution which menaces the very existence of the bourgeois

[10] Fokke, *op. cit.*, p. 118.

régime. From the moment when we threw into the face of our 'Allies' the treaties of brigandage they had made with the Tsarist Government, we have shown that we recognize only one contract, sacred though unwritten, the contract of the international solidarity of the proletariat. By these tactics we have given to the Russian Revolution that immense force which hypnotizes more and more the proletarian masses of the West."[11]

When questioned as to how he interpreted that part of the declaration of the Central Powers in which their obligations are conditioned upon the acceptance by the Allied Powers of the invitation to come to the peace conference, Trotsky replied that this part of the declaration "admits of no two interpretations. It means that if Russia concludes a separate peace with Germany then the German obligations vis à vis our Allies will not apply to the future peace [with the Allies]."[12]

On the 29th Trotsky sent out another message to the "Peoples and Governments of the Allied Countries" announcing that the negotiations at Brest had been adjourned to give the Allies the last opportunity to take part in further discussions.

In this message[13] he contended that since the Central Powers had agreed to evacuate Belgium, Northern France, Serbia, Montenegro, Rumania, Poland, Lithuania, and Courland on the conclusion of a general peace, the Allies could no longer claim that the war was being fought for the liberation of these territories. The Allies, however, had shown no inclination to join in a genuine democratic peace. "Their attitude toward the principle of national self-determination is as full of suspicion and hostility as the attitude of the German and Austro-Hungarian governments." The Allies had ten days in which to decide whether or not they would

[11] Trotsky, *Sochineniia*, III, Book 2, 226–28.

[12] *Pravda*, No. 218, January 1, 1918, p. 3.

[13] *Izvestiia*, No. 254, December 30, 1917, p. 7. A translation is given in *The Soviet Union and Peace*, pp. 35–39.

participate in the negotiations. If they decided affirmatively the negotiations would be conducted openly in a neutral country. "If, on the other hand, the Allied governments in their stubbornness, which is characteristic of decadent classes, still refuse to participate in the negotiations, the working class will be compelled by an iron necessity to seize the power from those who cannot or will not give the people peace." This, he warned, was the last proposal to be made to the Allies, and at the same time it was a promise of support "to the working class of every country that will rise against the imperialists of their own nations. . . ."

A great soldiers' and workers' demonstration was held in Petrograd on the 30th to celebrate the success of the Soviet delegation at Brest. But on the 31st Kamenev, reviewing the course of the negotiations at a joint session of the C.E.C., the Petrograd Soviet, and army representatives, criticized the German proposal with regard to the occupied territories as "an attempt to crush the liberty of Poland, Lithuania, and a number of other countries."[14] This, he confidently predicted, would inevitably lead to the downfall of German imperialism and to a peace with revolutionary Germany. On the motion of the Socialist-Revolutionists of the Left, a resolution was adopted denouncing the Germans and calling on the peoples of the Quadruple Alliance to prevent an imperialist war against revolutionary Russia for the subjugation of the border regions.[15]

On instructions of the C.E.C., Joffe sent the following telegram:

THE RUSSIAN GOVERNMENT ON THE CONTINUATION OF NEGOTIATIONS

[Note to the Central Powers, January 2, 1918][16]

The Government of the Russian Republic considers it necessary to conduct further negotiations on neutral ground and proposes to transfer

[14] *Izvestiia,* No. 256, January 2, 1918, p. 2.

[15] *Ibid.*

[16] *Ibid.,* No. 257, January 3, 1918, p. 1.

the meetings to Stockholm. Your answer to this proposal will be awaited in Petrograd.

As regards our attitude to the proposals of the German and Austrian delegation of December 25 formulated in Articles 1 and 2, the Government of the Russian Republic and the Central Executive Committee of the Soviets of Workers', Soldiers', and Peasants' Deputies are in entire agreement with the view expressed by our delegation, considering these proposals to be contrary to the principle of national self-determination, even in the restricted form in which it appears in point 3 of the declaration [of December 25] of the Quadruple Alliance.

A. A. JOFFE

The German reply to Joffe's telegram arrived the following day, containing a flat refusal to transfer the negotiations to Stockholm.[17] On January 4 Hertling announced in the Reichstag that a peace delegation of the Ukrainian Rada had arrived at Brest-Litovsk and that separate negotiations with the Ukrainians were under way.[18] On the 5th, Petrograd received another telegram, signed by Kühlmann and Czernin, stating that since Russia's allies had failed to join the negotiations for a general peace, the declaration of the Quadruple Alliance of December 25 was no longer valid.[19] There could no longer be any doubt of the intention of the Central Powers to reject the Soviet terms as a basis of negotiations. They could not be deterred from their intention by threats of the Russians to resume the war but only by rapid revolutionary developments in Germany and Austria which might force the acceptance of the Soviet terms. To drag out the discussions at Brest would give more time for these developments to take effect and even promote them by revealing the imperialistic aims of the Central Powers. Trotsky writes: " 'To delay negotiations, there must be someone to do the delaying,' said Lenin. At his insistence I set off for Brest-Litovsk."[20]

[17] *Protokoly sezdov i konferentsii vsesoiuznoi Kommunisticheskoi Partii (b). Sedmoi sezd. Mart 1918 goda,* Moscow, Leningrad, 1928, p. 278.

[18] *Berliner Tageblatt* (evening edition), No. 7, January 4, 1918, p. 1.

[19] *Mirnye peregovory v Brest-Litovske,* I, 245.

[20] Trotsky, *My Life,* p. 363.

In view of these developments, it was no longer possible to play off the Central Powers' willingness to negotiate against the Allies' refusal. The Bolsheviks accordingly revised their tactics toward the Allies. While continuing to denounce the Entente governments in public,[21] they at the same time negotiated privately with the Entente agents for a commitment to support the Soviets in case they broke off negotiations at Brest and renewed the war. These informal negotiations through the medium of Robins, Sadoul, and later of Lockhart were continued until the Brest treaty was finally ratified. On January 2, 1918, the American Ambassador stated in writing to Robins that on being informed that the Soviet Government had broken off negotiations and had decided to prosecute the war against Germany he would recommend that the American Government render all aid and assistance possible.[22] The recommendation was, of course, never sent, since the war was not resumed. Sadoul, who was endeavoring to bring the French Ambassador to make a similar declaration, was informed by Trotsky on January 4 that the Bolsheviks were convinced that the Allies had given up hope of victory in the West and were secretly negotiating a peace with Germany at the expense of Russia.[23] Two days later *Izvestiia* and *Pravda* accused the Allies of betraying Poland, Lithuania, and Courland in order to get concessions from Germany in the West.

As for the Allied governments, the revelation of the German terms at Brest gave an opportunity to pay back the score made against them by the publication of the secret treaties, by calling attention to the imperialistic aims of their ene-

[21] On December 21, on the basis of papers seized in the apartment of an officer of the Russian Red Cross, Trotsky had charged the American Ambassador and the American Red Cross with furnishing aid to Kaledin. Mr. Francis hotly denied the charge and gave evidence in support of this denial. (*U.S. Foreign Relations, 1918, Russia,* I, 321–22, 326–30; Andrew Kalpashnikoff, *A Prisoner of Trotsky's,* New York, 1920, 18–49; David R. Francis, "Foreword," in *A Prisoner of Trotsky's,* pp. vii–xiii.)

[22] This communication was drafted by Robins and initialed by Francis and is given in *R.A.R.,* pp. 65–67.

[23] Sadoul, *op. cit.,* p. 176. He reports a similar statement by Lenin a week later, p. 191.

mies and by emphasizing their own unselfish objectives. Lloyd George's speech to the British labor leaders and Wilson's Fourteen Points address specifically referred to the Brest negotiations. The President particularly emphasized his approval of the Soviet formula and asserted the desire of America to help the Russian people "attain their utmost hope of liberty and ordered peace." At the same time the fact that the Soviet Government, in the face of the German terms, did not break off negotiations and continued to denounce the Allies tended to confirm the suspicion in many quarters that the Bolsheviks were the dupes or the agents of the Central Powers. The suspicions of the Allies were not by any means allayed by the arrival in Petrograd of the Austro-German naval and economic missions which began discussions with the Russians on December 31.

In Vienna and Berlin also, the Brest negotiations were the subject of discussion in high places. The opinion in Vienna was that "peace *must* be arranged but a separate peace without Germany is *impossible*."[24]

In Berlin Ludendorff did not conceal his lack of faith in Kühlmann's diplomacy and declared that because of the plan for the drive in the West peace in the East was necessary on military grounds and that all attempts to drag out negotiations must be prevented.[25] But Kühlmann, supported by the Kaiser, left for Brest, authorized to continue his attempts to secure the border regions under the guise of self-determination.[26]

B. The Stalemate

The Soviet delegation arrived at Brest on the 7th. The German officer who accompanied the delegation from Dvinsk reported that the Russian trenches were practically deserted and at many stations deputations came to demand peace.

[24] Czernin, *op. cit.*, p. 256.

[25] *Ludendorff's Own Story, August 1914–November 1918*, 2 vols., New York [1919], II, 170.

[26] Hoffmann, *op. cit.*, pp. 214–15.

The Soviets must accept a bad peace or no peace at all, and in either case, according to the Germans, the Bolsheviks would be swept away. Kühlmann observed, "Ils n'ont que le choix à quelle sauce ils se feront manger." And Czernin added, "Tout comme chez nous."[27] On the 8th there was a preliminary meeting of the heads of the delegations, Kühlmann, Czernin, Trotsky, Talaat Pasha, Popov, and Golubovich, the last-named representing the Ukrainian Rada. Trotsky immediately put an end to the fraternization between the Soviet delegates and the representatives of the other Powers and asked to have the Russians' meals served in their own quarters; he declined to meet Prince Leopold, and in general put the proceedings on a more formal basis.

At the first plenary session on the 9th, Kühlmann led off with a long speech reviewing the whole course of negotiations and making the following points: (1) Since the Entente Powers had failed to respond to the invitation to join the discussions, the declaration of the Central Powers of December 25 was void. (2) The Central Powers would continue the negotiations only at Brest-Litovsk. (3) Events had occurred during the suspension of negotiations which caused the Central Powers to doubt the candid intentions of the Russians, particularly the wireless report of Joffe's statement on December 28, which was invented in every particular.

Czernin followed, emphasizing the determination of the Central Powers to negotiate only at Brest, and adding that all four Powers were agreed to negotiate on the territorial question on the basis of Kühlmann's and his own statements of December 27, which the Russians had accepted. If the Russians now declined to go on, the responsibility for war would fall exclusively on the Russian delegation. The Bulgarian and Turkish representatives associated themselves with this statement. Hoffmann then took up the attack, charging that wireless messages and appeals signed by rep-

[27] Czernin, *op. cit.,* p. 259. Trotsky admits that the state of mind of the soldiers did not permit of talk of renewing the war. (*Lenin,* pp. 103–104.)

resentatives of the Russian Government and army and containing abuse of the German army constituted a violation of the spirit of the armistice. The Austrian, Bulgarian, and Turkish military representatives joined this protest. Trotsky then moved that the session be adjourned.

When the session was resumed the following day, the chairman of the Ukrainian delegation made the following declaration:[28]

DECLARATION OF THE UKRAINIAN DELEGATION[29]

[January 10, 1918]

The government of the Ukrainian People's Republic, known as the General Secretariat, hereby informs all belligerent and neutral powers that:

The Ukrainian People's Republic has been proclaimed by the third Universal of the Ukrainian Central Rada on November 20, 1917,[30] by which act its international status has been determined.

Endeavoring to create a confederation of all republics which have arisen on the territory of the former Russian Empire, and awaiting the formation of a federal government in Russia which will distribute the sphere of foreign relations between the two republics, the Ukrainian People's Republic, through its General Secretariat, is entering upon a course of independent international relations. . . . .

In the name of the Ukrainian People's Republic the General Secretariat declares. . . . . [31]

7. The Ukrainian People's Republic, which at the present time is holding its own front and is appearing independently in international relations . . . . must participate in all peace negotiations, conferences, and congresses on an equal basis with other Powers.

8. The government of the Soviet of People's Commissars does not extend over the whole of Russia and is not recognized by the Ukrainian People's Republic. Therefore, the peace which may eventually result from the negotiations with the Powers at war with Russia can be binding for the Ukraine only when the conditions of such a peace are

[28] *Mirnye peregovory v Brest-Litovske*, I, 44–48.

[29] *Ibid.*, pp. 49–51.

[30] See pp. 435–37, above.

[31] The first six paragraphs deal with the principles of a general peace.

accepted and ratified by the government of the Ukrainian People's Republic.

9. Peace can be concluded in the name of Russia as a whole only by a government . . . . which has been recognized by all republics and all provinces of Russia. Should the formation of such a government become impossible in the near future, the conclusion of peace will have to be intrusted to the united representatives of these republics and provinces. . . . .

Kühlmann immediately inquired of Trotsky whether or not, in view of the Ukrainian declaration, the Russian delegation must still be considered as the sole representative of all Russia. Trotsky replied that, having recognized the Ukraine's right to self-determination, the Russian delegation found no objection to the participation of the Ukrainian delegation in the peace conference. Kühlmann was not satisfied with the answer and pressed Trotsky to state whether he regarded the Ukrainian delegation as subordinate to the Russian or independent of it. Trotsky replied that, since the Ukraine entered the negotiations independently and since the Russian delegation in its recognition of the right of the Ukrainian delegation to participate in the negotiations imposed no limitations on that participation, the question raised by Kühlmann did not call for a reply. Kühlmann then proposed to return to the issues raised at the plenary session on January 9 and asked Trotsky to state the attitude of the Russians.

Trotsky began by saying that the Russian delegation was ignorant of the telegram sent out from Petrograd and answered Hoffmann by stating that neither the armistice nor the character of the negotiations limited the freedom of speech or of the press. He took cognizance of Kühlmann's statement that the bases for general negotiations as formulated on December 25 were void, but added that . . . . "the principles of a democratic peace . . . . which we shall continue to defend, cannot lose their validity in ten days or during any other length of time, since they constitute the only conceivable basis for the peaceful co-operation of peoples." With regard to the continuation of the negotiations at Brest, Trotsky said: "We are confronted with an ultimatum either to negotiate at Brest-Litovsk or not to negotiate at all. The ultimatum is good proof that the governments of the Quadruple Alliance . . . . would rather wreck the negotiations on technical grounds than settle the future of Poland, Lithuania, Courland, and Armenia. . . . . We declare before the entire world . . . . that we accept the ultimatum. We remain here at Brest-Litovsk so that the slightest possibility of peace may not remain unexhausted. Notwithstanding the extraordinary attitude of the delegates of the Quadruple Alliance, we think it our duty to the peoples and armies of all countries to make a fresh effort to establish clearly and distinctly here at the Headquarters of the Eastern front whether immediate peace with the Quadruple Alliance is possible without violence to the Poles, Lithuanians, Letts, Esthonians, Armenians, and other nationalities to whom the Russian Revolution, on its part, assures the full right to free development without reservation, restriction, or *arrière pensée.*"[32]

During the remainder of the session an agreement was reached to set up a special commission on political and territorial questions composed of representatives of Germany, Austria-Hungary, and Russia, and to form a committee of experts for preliminary discussions of economic and legal questions. The political commission held sessions on the 11th and 12th, but made no progress in the matter of self-determination for Poland and the Baltic provinces. The Russians demanded immediate evacuation of German troops as a preliminary to a plebiscite, while the Germans maintained that self-determination had already taken place in the action of various public bodies which had declared for separation from Russia.[33] In the afternoon session on January 12 Kamenev made the following statement:

[32] *Mirnye peregovory v Brest-Litovske,* I, 52–59.

[33] *Ibid.,* pp. 61–87.

THE RUSSIAN PROPOSAL REGARDING SELF-DETERMINATION OF OCCUPIED TERRITORIES

[From Kamenev's Statement in the Special Commission on Political Questions, January 12, 1918][34]

The [Russian] delegation calls attention to the fact that during the [German] occupation of Poland, Lithuania, and Courland no democratically elected organ was created which could be considered as expressing the will of the majority of the population. . . . . As regards the claim . . . . that [the territories mentioned] are striving toward complete state independence, the Russian delegation considers it its duty to state:

1. From the fact that the occupied territories belonged to the former Russian Empire the Russian Government draws no conclusion which would impose any constitutional obligation on the population of these regions in relation to the Russian Republic. The old frontiers of the former Russian Empire . . . . have vanished with tsarism. The new frontiers of the fraternal union of peoples of the Russian Republic and the peoples which desire to remain outside its borders must be defined by a free resolution of the peoples concerned.

2. In the present negotiations the Russian Government is aiming primarily . . . . to safeguard real freedom of self-determination for the territories mentioned as regards both their internal organization and their international relations.

3. The problem thus understood implies a previous understanding . . . . on four fundamental points:

I. The extent of territory over which the population will be called upon to exercise the right of self-determination.

II. The general political principles that will govern the destinies of the territories and nations included.

III. The nature of the provisional régime that will exist pending the final constitution of the governments of the regions in question.

IV. The ways and means by which the population of these regions will be called upon to express their will.

The answers to these points must replace Article 2 of the German proposal of December 27, 1917.

On its part the Russian delegation proposes the following solution of the above questions:

I. Territorial. The right to self-determination belongs to nations as such and not merely to those territories lying within the area of occupation, as is contemplated by Article 2 of the German proposal. . . . .

[34] *Mirnye peregovory v Brest-Litovske,* I, 92–94.

Accordingly, the Russian Government, on its own initiative, grants the right of self-determination to those territories of the nations concerned which lie outside the zone of occupation.

Russia binds herself not to exercise direct or indirect pressure on these territories to accept a particular form of government, and not to restrict their independence by any tariff or military conventions concluded before these regions are finally established on the basis of their right to political self-determination.

The governments of Germany and Austria-Hungary, on their part, categorically confirm the absence of any claims either to annex the territories of the former Russian Empire now occupied by their armies, or the so-called frontier "rectifications" at the expense of these regions. They further undertake not to compel these regions, in a direct or indirect way, to accept a particular form of government, nor to restrict their independence by any tariff or military convention concluded before these regions are finally established on the basis of their right to political self-determination.

II. The solution of the question of the future destiny of the peoples in the self-determining regions can be undertaken only under conditions of complete political freedom and the absence of all constraint. The plebiscite must, therefore, take place after the withdrawal of foreign armies and the return of all refugees. . . . .

The maintenance of law and order in the plebiscite regions will be handed over to the national armies and local militia. All refugees should be given the opportunity and material aid to return to the regions which they were forced to abandon during the war.

III. From the moment when peace is signed until the final constitution of the governments of the above provinces, the internal administration, such as the direction of local affairs, finances, etc., shall pass into the hands of provisional organs formed by agreement between those political parties which have proved their vitality both before and during the war. These provisional organs . . . . will undertake the organization of the plebiscite.

IV. The final solution of the question of the [international?] status of the provinces named as well as their political forms of government shall be left to a general referendum.

HOFFMANN'S REPLY[35]

[January 12, 1918]

I must first of all protest against the tone of these proposals. The Russian delegation talks as if it stood victorious on our soil. I should

[35] *Mirnye peregovory v Brest-Litovske*, I, 94–95.

like to point out that the facts are just the reverse: the victorious German armies are on Russian territory. I should further like to emphasize the fact that the Russian delegation is asking that the right of self-determination of peoples be applied to the occupied territories in a form and to an extent which its government does not apply to its own country. Its government is based purely on violence, ruthlessly suppressing all who think differently. Anyone with different ideas is regarded as a counter-revolutionary and bourgeois and is declared outside the law.

I shall substantiate my statement by just two examples. During the night of December 30–31 the first White Russian Congress at Minsk, which insisted on the right of White Russians to self-determination, was broken up by the Bolsheviks with bayonets and machine guns.

When the Ukrainians claimed their right of self-determination the Petrograd Government sent an ultimatum and endeavored to carry through its will by force of arms. As far as I can make out from wireless messages lying before me, civil war has not yet come to an end. This is how the Bolshevik Government applies the principle of self-determination in practice.

The German Supreme Command therefore considers it necessary to prevent any attempt to interfere in the affairs of the occupied provinces. To us it is obvious that the peoples in the occupied provinces have already expressed their will to separate from Russia in a way that leaves no doubt whatever as to their wishes. . . . .

Also, for reasons of a technical and administrative nature, the German Supreme Command must refuse to evacuate Courland, Lithuania, Riga, and the islands of the Gulf of Riga. None of these regions had administrative organs, courts, railways, post, and telegraph. All these have been created and are administered by Germany. Neither will these peoples be able to establish in a short time an army and a militia of their own. . . . .

Hoffmann's speech won the congratulations of Ludendorff, distressed Kühlmann and Czernin,[36] inspired the legend of his militant table-thumping, and so furnished excellent propaganda material for Trotsky and the Entente. The Quadruple Alliance replied to Kamenev's proposals with a written statement presented by Wiesner on January 14. After characterizing the Russian proposals as unacceptable, the Central Powers set forth their position on the four

[36] Czernin writes in his diary: "Hoffmann has made his unfortunate speech . . . . Kühlmann and I did not conceal from him that he gained nothing by it beyond exciting the people at home against us," p. 264.

fundamental points stated by Kamenev: (1) The Central Powers did not intend to annex the occupied territories nor to compel them to accept one or another form of state institutions but reserved for themselves as well as for these territories the right to make agreements of every kind. (2) Troops of occupation could not be withdrawn during the war, but under favorable conditions they might be reduced. (3) The internal administration will gradually be placed in the hands of the local population. (4) The Central Powers agreed in principle to a popular referendum to determine the state to which the people wished to adhere. Such a referendum was, however, held to be then impracticable. Later (on the 18th) Kühlmann emphasized this reservation, saying that the people of these territories were not sufficiently experienced politically for such a referendum and that the institutions already in existence should be extended to settle this question.

In the discussions of the next three days no progress was made in adjusting the divergent points of view, but a significant event occurred. The Central Powers had begun private, separate negotiations with the Ukrainians.[37] At the session of the Political Commission on the 18th Trotsky asked Kühlmann to state exactly what territories would come under the German scheme of self-determination. Hoffmann answered the question by spreading out a map on which a blue line had been drawn. To a Russian question regarding the occupied territories south of Brest, Hoffmann said this would be discussed with the Ukrainian Republic. Trotsky then said that the status of these territories would require an agreement between Soviet Russia and the Ukraine, and to a further question he declared that his government did not recognize the right of the Ukrainian delegation to take up this matter independently.[38]

[37] Kreppel, *Der Friede im Osten*, Vienna, 1918, p. 127; Gratz and Schüller, *The Economic Policy of Austria-Hungary during the War in Its External Relations*, pp. 100–102.

[38] *Mirnye peregovory v Brest-Litovske*, I, 97–127.

At the resumption of the session at 5:49 P.M. after an adjournment to enable the Russians to study the map, Trotsky made the following statement:

EXTRACT FROM TROTSKY'S STATEMENT[39]

[January 18, 1918]

The position of our opponents . . . . is now absolutely clear. . . . . Germany and Austria wish to cut off from the possessions of the former Russian Empire a territory comprising over 150,000 square versts. That territory includes the former Kingdom of Poland, Lithuania, and large areas inhabited by Ukrainians and White Russians. Furthermore, the line drawn on the map cuts in two the territory inhabited by the Letts and separates the Esthonians on the islands of the Baltic from the same people on the mainland. Within these regions Germany and Austria are to maintain a régime of military occupation to last not only until the conclusion of peace with Russia but also after the conclusion of a general peace. At the same time the Powers mentioned refuse to make any definite statement regarding the time and the conditions of evacuation. Thus the internal life of these provinces will remain for an indefinite period of time in the hand of the occupying Powers and the political development of these regions will follow a course prescribed for it by these Powers. It is clear that under such conditions the free expression of will by the Poles, Lithuanians, and Letts will prove illusory, and that means that the governments of Austria and Germany take into their own hands the destiny of these nations. . . . .

At the end of the session Trotsky announced that it was necessary for him to return to Petrograd, and it was agreed to suspend the sessions of the Political Commission until the 29th. Trotsky left, taking with him Hoffmann's map as further evidence of German intentions.

The Brest negotiations had reached the point where the Bolshevik leaders had to decide whether to accept the annexation peace or to fight. On Trotsky's return to the capital the party debates began, debates which continued intermittently for a month and a half and which, like the earlier crises, nearly split the party. On January 21 a group of

[39] *Mirnye peregovory v Brest-Litovske,* I, 130.

party leaders met to consider the situation. Lenin, insisting that the issue was revolutionary war or acceptance of the peace, came out for acceptance with the statement which is given below but which was not published until February 24. Bukharin and others called for revolutionary war and Trotsky favored breaking off negotiations and accepting the peace only in the face of an obvious use of force by the Germans. When the vote was taken Lenin's proposal received 15, Trotsky's 16, and the revolutionary program 32.[40] At this time, according to Trotsky, over two hundred local Soviets were asked for their views on this question and only two voted for peace, Petrograd and Sevastopol, the latter with reservations.[41] Lenin's program very likely was closer to the desires of the masses of peasants and soldiers than either of the others, but it ran directly counter to the slogans and official party propaganda on the subject of peace. For a long time party workers had been summoned to oppose unceasingly a surrender such as now proposed, and they had been told over and over again of the triumphs of Bolshevik diplomacy and (as in the quotation from *Pravda* given below) of the rising tide of revolution in the West which soon would sweep away the capitalist governments. Why, if "the triumph of international socialism is near," if "the victory of an honest peace is assured," should they surrender to the crumbling capitalist powers?

On January 22 the Central Committee of the party voted on the question. The proposal for revolutionary war was lost by 11 to 2. Lenin's motion to continue the negotiations was carried 12 to 1 and Trotsky's project of "no peace no war" was affirmed by the close vote of 9 to 7.[42] This vote did not dispose of the question of accepting the German terms. It merely instructed the delegates to go back and kill time in the hope that a revolution would break out in Ger-

[40] *Protokoly sezdov i konferentsii vsesoiuznoi Kommunisticheskoi Partii* (*b*). *Sedmoi sezd. Mart 1918 goda,* pp. xxvi–xxvii.

[41] Trotsky, *My Life,* p. 383.

[42] *Protokoly sezdov i konferentsii vsesoiuznoi Kommunisticheskoi Partii* (*b*). *Sedmoi sezd. Mart 1918 goda,* p. xxvii. Trotsky, *My Life,* pp. 383–84.

many. Before returning to Brest, Trotsky delivered his long report on the international situation to the Third Congress of Soviets on the 26th. Two extracts from that report are given below because of their bearing on the Soviet negotiations with the Allies and the Central Powers.

REVOLUTIONARY WAR OR GERMAN PEACE

[Lenin's Argument for Peace, January 20, 1918][43]

1. The condition of the Russian Revolution at the present moment is such that practically all the workers and a large majority of the peasants are on the side of the Soviet Government and the social revolution. In that respect the success of the Socialist Revolution in Russia seems assured.

2. At the same time the civil war which was caused by the furious resistance of the propertied classes, who realize full well that this is their last and final fight for private property in land and instruments of production, has not reached its highest point. In the end the Soviet Government will win the fight, but it will take much time and a good deal of energy, and a certain period of disorganization and chaos incidental to every war and especially civil war is inevitable before the bourgeoisie is finally crushed.

3. Furthermore, the resistance [of the bourgeoisie] in its less active and non-military forms such as sabotage, bribing tramps and other hirelings of the bourgeoisie to join the Socialist ranks with the purpose of undermining their cause, etc., etc., this resistance has proved to be so obstinate and capable of assuming such varying forms that it will take time, several months perhaps to put it down. Without a decisive victory over this passive and veiled resistance of the bourgeoisie and its adherents the success of the Socialist Revolution is impossible.

4. Finally, the task of organizing Russia on a socialistic basis is so huge and difficult that its solution, owing to the abundance of the petit-bourgeois in the midst of the Socialist proletariat and on account of the low cultural level of the latter, will take a considerable time.

5. All these factors taken together show clearly that to make a success of socialism in Russia a certain time, some months at least, is necessary during which the Socialist Government can have a free hand, first to overcome the bourgeoisie of its own country and then to lay the basis for extensive and deep-rooted organizational work.

6. The situation in which the Socialist Revolution in Russia finds itself is to be taken as the point of departure for every definition of the

[43] *Pravda,* No. 34, February 24, 1918, pp. 2–3; *Sochineniia,* XXII, 193–99.

international task confronting the new Soviet Government, because the international situation as it stands during the fourth year of war precludes the possibility of predicting the time of the outbreak of revolutions and the overthrow of the imperialistic governments of Europe (including the German Government). That there will be a Socialist revolution in Europe there is no doubt. All our hopes in the final triumph of socialism are based on this certainty, which is in the nature of a scientific prediction. Our propaganda work in general and our fraternization in particular should be strengthened and developed [in order to help bring about the Socialist revolution]. But it would be a mistake for the Socialist Government in Russia to formulate its policy on the supposition that within the next six months (or thereabouts) there will be a European, to be more specific, a German Socialist revolution. It is impossible to make such predictions, and every attempt to do so is a blind gamble.

7. The Brest-Litovsk negotiations have made it clear by now (January 20, 1918) that the war party in Germany has the upper hand and has sent us what amounts to an ultimatum . . . . either to continue the war or to accept a peace of annexation, that is to say, that we give up all the territory we have seized, while the Germans retain all that they have seized. In addition they impose on us an indemnity in the (concealed) form of paying for the support of the prisoners. This amounts to about three billion rubles and is to be paid over a period of several years.

8. The Russian Socialist Government is confronted with a question which requires an immediate solution, either to accept the annexation peace or to start at once a revolutionary war. No other solution is in fact possible. We cannot put off the decision; we have already done everything possible and impossible to drag out the negotiations.

9. When we consider the arguments for an immediate revolutionary war we find first of all the argument that a separate peace now is virtually an understanding with German imperialists, an imperialistic transaction, etc., and that, therefore, such a peace would signify a complete break with the fundamental principles of proletarian internationalism.

This reasoning is fallacious. Workmen who lose a strike and accept conditions not favorable to themselves but favorable for the capitalist do not thereby betray socialism. They betray socialism who bargain with the capitalists, accepting favors for part of the workmen in exchange [for conditions] that are favorable to the capitalists. Agreements of this kind are inacceptable.

He betrays socialism who calls the war against German imperialism a defensive and righteous war and who, at the same time, accepts the help of Anglo-French imperialists and conceals from the people the secret agreements concluded with these imperialists. But he who hides nothing from the people, makes no secret agreements with imperialists, but agrees, because of temporary inability to go on with the war, to sign a peace treaty unfavorable to the weak nation and favorable to one group of imperialists does not in any way betray socialism.

10. Another argument for an immediate war is that by concluding peace we become agents of German imperialism because we free German troops on our front in addition to millions of prisoners, etc. This argument is equally fallacious. A revolutionary war at this time would place us in the position of agents of Anglo-French imperialism in so far as we should be aiding the cause of the latter. The English have offered our Supreme Commander Krylenko one hundred rubles a month for every one of our soldiers if we continue to fight. Even if we do not accept a penny from them, we should still be helping them by detaining German troops. No matter which way we turn we cannot wholly escape this or that imperialistic group. That is impossible without the complete destruction of world imperialism. The only true inference to be drawn from this is that from the time a socialist government is established in any one country questions must be determined not with reference to preferability of any one imperialistic group but solely from the point of view of what is best for the development and the consolidation of the socialist revolution which has already begun. In other words our tactics must be based not on the consideration of whether it is more expedient to help one or the other of the imperialist groups but solely on the question of safeguarding the socialist revolution in one country until the others are ready to join.

11. It is said that the German Social-Democrats who are opposed to the war have become "defeatists" and beg us not to give in to German imperialism. [To this our reply is that] we accepted "defeatism" only with reference to our own imperialistic bourgeoisie but we always opposed a victory over the imperialism of other countries if that victory had to be obtained through a union, real or formal, with a "friendly" imperialistic power. The argument is thus a repetition of the preceding one. If the German Left-Wing Socialists should make us a proposal to delay a separate peace for a definite period and guarantee to us that during that time Germany would have a revolution, then we should have a different situation. But they have no such proposition to make. On the contrary, they say this: "Resist as long as you can and then decide in accordance with the best interests of the Russian Socialist Revolution, because at present it is impossible to say anything positive about the German revolution."

12. It is said that in our party declaration we "promised" that we should wage a revolutionary war and that the conclusion of a separate peace is therefore a failure to keep our word. This is not true. We talked of the necessity for a Socialist government during the period of

imperialism "to prepare to wage" a revolutionary war. We advocated this in opposition to the theory of abstract pacifism, against the theory which absolutely rejects the "defense of the fatherland," and, finally, against the selfish instincts of certain groups of soldiers, but we never assumed the obligation to wage a revolutionary war regardless of whether time and conditions were favorable for such a war.

We should by all means prepare now for a revolutionary war. We live up to our promises now as we have in the past whenever it is possible to carry them out immediately. We have abrogated the secret treaties, we have offered all nations a just peace, and we have prolonged in various ways the peace negotiations so as to give other nations a chance to join.

The question whether it is possible to undertake at once a revolutionary war must be answered solely from the point of view of actual conditions and the interest of the Socialist Revolution which has already begun.

13. If we summarize the arguments for an immediate revolutionary war we shall find that the policy advocated in them is capable of giving satisfaction to those who crave the romantic and the beautiful but who fail completely to take into consideration the objective correlation of class forces, and the real conditions within which the Socialist Revolution is developing.

14. There is no doubt that at the present time (and probably during the next few weeks and months) our army is in no condition to stop a German offensive. In the first place, it is very tired and very hungry, owing to the unprecedented disruption of the army supplies, etc.; secondly, on account of the shortage of horses our artillery is absolutely doomed; thirdly, in view of the impossibility of protecting the coast from Reval to Riga which gives the enemy a good chance to get possession of what remains of Livonia, then Esthonia, to attack our troops in the rear, and to occupy Petrograd.

15. There is no doubt whatsoever that, were the question put to a vote peasants, who constitute the majority in the army, would come out for a peace of annexation rather than for an immediate revolutionary war. The formation of a Socialist army, with the Red Guard as its nucleus, has only just begun. To attempt now, with the present democratization of the army, to force a war against the wishes of a majority of the soldiers would be hazardous. It will take months and months to create an army imbued with socialist principles.

16. The poorest peasantry in Russia would support a socialist revolution led by the working class, but it is not in a position now to wage a revolutionary war. It would be a fatal blunder to overlook the actual strength of the different classes.

17. The question of revolutionary war, therefore, stands as follows: If a revolution should break out in Germany during the next three or four months, then perhaps the tactics of an immediate revolutionary war would not ruin our Socialist Revolution. If [on the other hand] the German revolution does not take place and we go on with the war, Russia would be so badly defeated that she would be forced to sign an even worse separate peace; such a peace would be signed not by a socialist government but by some other, by some kind of coalition between the bourgeois Rada and the followers of Chernov or some similar government, for after the first shock of defeat the peasant army which is so badly worn out by the war would overthrow the Workers' Socialist Government in a few weeks.

18. Under the circumstances it would be very bad policy to risk the fate of the Socialist Revolution on the chance that a revolution might break out in Germany by a certain date. Such a policy would be adventurous. We have no right to take such chances.

19. The German revolution will in no way suffer objectively if we conclude a separate peace. It is probable that the triumph of chauvinism will weaken it [the revolution] for a time, but the position of Germany will remain very critical. The war with England and America will go on for a long time; the aggressive imperialism of both groups has unmasked itself finally and completely. Under such conditions a Socialist Soviet Republic in Russia will be a model for all other peoples and excellent material for propaganda purposes. On the one side there will be the bourgeois system engaged in a strife between two coalitions of confessed plunderers, and on the other side a Socialist Soviet Republic living in peace.

20. In concluding a separate peace now we rid ourselves as far as present circumstances permit of both imperialistic groups fighting each other. We can take advantage of their strife, which makes it difficult for them to reach an agreement at our expense, and use that period when our hands are free to develop and strengthen the Socialist Revolution. We can reorganize Russia on the basis of the dictatorship of the proletariat, nationalize the banks and large industries, bring about a moneyless exchange of products between the city and the small peasant co-operatives in the village. All these are economically feasible provided we have a few months peace to work out these projects. Such a reorganization would make socialism unconquerable in Russia and in the whole world and would at the same time lay the basis for the formation of a powerful workers' and peasants' Red Army.

21. A truly revolutionary war at this moment would be a war between a socialist republic and the bourgeois countries. Such a war would have to be fully approved by the socialist army and have as its object the

overthrow of the bourgeoisie in other countries. For the time being, however, we cannot make this our object. In reality we should be fighting now for the liberation of Poland, Lithuania, and Courland. There is not a single Marxist who, while adhering to the foundations of Marxism and socialism, would not say that the interests of socialism are above the right of nations to self-determination. Our Socialist Republic has done and is doing everything possible to give real self-determination to Finland, the Ukraine, etc. But if the concrete circumstances are such that the safety of the Socialist Republic is being endangered in order to [prevent] the violation of the right of self-determination of a few nations (Poland, Lithuania, and Courland), there is no question but that the interests of the Socialist Republic must predominate. If that is true, then he who says "we cannot sign a shameful and humiliating peace; we cannot hand over Poland, etc.," fails to perceive that if we make peace on condition of the liberation of Poland we are only strengthening German imperialism against England, Belgium, Serbia, and the other countries. Peace on condition of the liberation of Poland, Lithuania, and Courland would be a "patriotic" peace from the Russian point of view, but it would be none the less a peace with annexationists and with the German imperialists.

PRAVDA HAILS THE INTERNATIONAL REVOLUTION

[January 22–February 1, 1918]

The flow of the social conflagration has spread over Austria. Vienna is on the eve of important events. The triumph of the international socialist revolution is near.[44]

The red flag of the communist revolution is raised in Europe. Soviets of workers' deputies have been set up in Vienna and Budapest. At Warsaw there is about to begin a general strike of the socialist proletariat. Here, too, the revolution has formed Soviets of workers. In Berlin *Vorwärts* has been suppressed. Long live the international revolution! Long live the International Soviet of Workers' and Soldiers' Deputies![45]

Revolutionary disturbances in Austria continue. In England revolutionary strikes are about to begin. The Paris workers are ready to greet the new international. In Spain there are new troubles. In Finland the laborers are storming the citadel of capitalism.

The international workers' revolution is going forward. Its path is lighted by the beacon of the Great Socialist Soviet Republic in Russia.

[44] No. 6, January 22, 1918, p. 1.

[45] No. 8, January 25, 1918, p. 1.

Long live the world revolt of the proletariat!

Long live the Soviets of Workers', Soldiers', and Peasants![46]

The conflagration of the world proletarian revolution is spreading. *The German proletariat has risen. Berlin has a Soviet of workers' deputies.* The destruction of capitalism is inevitable. The sun of socialism is rising. The victory of an honest peace is assured. Hail the International Proletarian Revolution! Hail the International Workers' Republic of Soviets! Proletarians of all countries unite![47]

TROTSKY ON THE PEACE TERMS

[Extracts from His Report to the Third Congress, January 26, 1918]

The Allied Governments are responsible for these [peace terms]. . . . . London gave its tacit approval of Kühlmann's terms; I declare this most emphatically. England is ready to compromise with Germany at the expense of Russia. The peace terms which Germany offers us are also the terms of America, France, and England; they [these terms] are the account which the imperialists of the world are making with the Russian Revolution. . . . .[48]

We are leaving tonight for Brest-Litovsk . . . . we make no triumphant boasts . . . . but we will fight together with you for an honest democratic peace. We will fight against them and they cannot scare us by their threats of an offensive. They have no assurance that the German soldiers will follow them. We shall proceed with our program of demobilizing the old army and forming a socialist Red Guard. If German imperialists attempt to crush us with the war machine . . . . we shall call to our brothers in the West, "Do you hear?" and they will answer, "We hear."[49]

Members of the Third All-Russian Congress of Soviets discussed Trotsky's report on the 27th, but they were not

[46] No. 10, January 27, 1918, p. 1. [47] No. 14, February 1, 1918, p. 1.

[48] *Novaia Zhizn*, No. 11, January 30, 1918, p. 6. Sadoul (*op. cit.*, p. 204) writes on January 24 that Trotsky gave him Hoffmann's map and asked him to show it to Noulens and General Niessel. Trotsky is alleged to have said, "We shall not sign that peace, but what can we do? The Holy War? Yes, we shall declare it, but what will be the result? The moment has come for the Allies to decide." On January 29 Sadoul writes (p. 210) that Lenin and Trotsky, especially the latter, were ready to accept the collaboration of the Allies without which they will be forced to accept a peace humiliating for Russia and fatal to the revolution. Trotsky also sent for Robins and asked him what the United States was going to do about recognizing the Bolsheviks. The Ambassador sent word he had no instructions. (*U.S. Foreign Relations, 1918, Russia*, I, 358–59.)

[49] *T.V.S.S.*, pp. 70–71.

given an opportunity to vote on the formula which had been adopted for the Sovnarkom by the party Central Committee. The advocates of revolutionary war had, however, by no means given up the fight and they demanded that the question be referred to a party conference to be held within a week. On February 1 the Central Executive Committee discussed the matter and Lenin urged that instead of a conference those who favored a revolutionary war should go to the front and see for themselves if it was possible to fight. It was, however, finally agreed that a conference should be called on March 5.[50]

In the meantime Trotsky had returned to Brest and negotiations were resumed on January 30. The position of the Bolsheviks vis-à-vis the Central Powers had not improved during the interval. It is true that the Finnish Social-Democrats, aided by Russian soldiers, had seized Helsingfors and were setting up a revolutionary government in close association with the Russian Soviets, that Red Guards were victorious over the slender forces of the Ukrainian Rada, and that there were strikes in Germany and Austria; but this was only one side of the medal. Internal conditions in Russia were anything but encouraging, the old army had completely disintegrated, the Red Guards were of little value against disciplined troops and had their hands full in opposing the Whites who were mobilizing in the southeast. The party was divided on the question of peace, and although it had strengthened its hold on the government by the dissolution of the Constituent Assembly it had by this act weakened its international position. The Germans interpreted the break-up of the Assembly as an indication that the Bolsheviks would not make terms with the patriotic groups and would accept peace at almost any price. To workers and Socialists in the West recent events seemed to confirm the rumors that the Bolsheviks had been bought by the Germans and had broken up the Assembly in order to make a sepa-

[50] *Protokoly sezdov i konferentsii vsesoiuznoi Kommunisticheskoi Partii (b). Sedmoi sezd. Mart 1918 goda*, pp. xxvii–xxviii.

rate peace.[51] The Allied governments, of course, had the same suspicions and were wary of Trotsky's angling for their support. On February 8 Francis telegraphed to Washington that he had "absolutely reliable evidence that Lenin, Trotsky accepted German money from June to October professedly for peace propaganda and army demoralization . . . ." Five days later the Ambassador sent a summary of the documents which with subsequent additions were acquired by Edgar Sisson and made public September 15, 1918. The authenticity of the documents has been seriously questioned, but they undoubtedly influenced Western official and public opinion against the Bolsheviks.[52]

The arrest and imprisonment on January 13 of the Rumanian Minister and the seizure of Rumanian gold in Russia by the Bolsheviks in retaliation for hostile Rumanian activities in Bessarabia did not improve relations between the Allied diplomats in Petrograd and Trotsky. The entire diplomatic corps protested to Lenin, and Count Diamandi was released and expelled from Russia. Not so the gold.[53] The Western Allies and the United States had further cause for hostility to the Bolsheviks when on February 10 the Soviet Government issued a decree annulling all foreign loans.[54]

51 Cf. Trotsky, *Lenin,* p. 105. *Novaia Zhizn,* No. 7, January 24, 1918, p. 2, published an article by Eduard Bernstein, the German Socialist, in which he said that German army circles openly explained the success of negotiations with the Russians by the fact that all whom it had been necessary to oil had been oiled. Bernstein says that German Socialists do not doubt the personal honesty of Lenin and Trotsky and they can explain the situation only on the theory that the Bolsheviks had for business reasons accepted German money to further their propaganda and have now become slaves by this heedless step. Quoted by A. L. P. Dennis, *The Foreign Policies of Soviet Russia,* New York [1924], pp. 27–28. See also Trotsky's reference to these rumors in *Lenin,* pp. 106–107.

52 The capture by Allied forces in the Second World War of the archives of the German Ministry of Foreign Affairs has thrown a light on the much debated question of whether the Bolsheviks received money from the German government. The documents published in 1958 raise a strong probability that substantial sums of money from official German sources reached the Bolsheviks after March 1917. See *Germany and the Revolution in Russia 1915–1918. Documents from the Archives of the German Ministry of Foreign Affairs.* Edited by Zeman, London, 1958.

53 *U.S. Foreign Relations, 1918, Russia,* I, 477–82; Francis, *op. cit.,* pp. 216–22; C. Anet, *op. cit.,* III, 226–34; Sadoul, *op. cit.,* pp. 195–96; Noulens, *op. cit.,* I, 182–93.

54 See below, p. 602.

In spite of the importunities of Ludendorff, in spite of their knowledge that Russia could not effectively resume the war, Kühlmann and Czernin did not deliver the expected ultimatum, and negotiations dragged on until February 10, when they were broken off not by the Central Powers but by the Russians. Kühlmann and Czernin had good political reasons for their policy of endeavoring to force the Russians to sign with the threat of the separate peace with the Ukrainian Rada. Trotsky countered by declaring that Soviet forces had gained control of the Ukraine and that the Rada's delegates represented nothing. He produced two delegates of the Ukrainian Soviets who insisted they were alone entitled to speak for that territory. The Central Powers refused to acknowledge that this was the situation, one of the Rada delegates delivered a long and violent denunciation of the Bolsheviks, and on February 3 negotiations were suspended while Kühlmann and Czernin went to Berlin.

The Germans and Austrians were back in Brest on the 6th and Schüller and later Czernin and Gratz of the Austro-Hungarian delegation began private discussions with Trotsky, who objected to the territorial demands of the Germans and the separate negotiations with the Rada. As the German military refused to make territorial concessions and the Austrians were under pressure from home to make a "bread peace" with the Ukraine, these discussions were futile.[55] Thereupon the Central Powers concluded their negotiations with the Rada, and the Ukrainian peace treaty was signed on February 8.[56] Negotiations continued until the 10th, when Trotsky stated that while Russia declined to sign a formal peace treaty the state of war with Germany, Austria-Hungary, and Turkey was at an end.

[55] Gratz and Schüller, *op. cit.*, pp. 103–107; Czernin, *op. cit.*, pp. 276–77.

[56] The German and Russian text of the treaty is given in *Reichsgesetzblatt*, No. 107, Berlin, 1918, pp. 1009 ff. English translations are given in *Texts of the Ukrainian "Peace,"* Washington, 1918, and Lutz, *The Fall of the German Empire 1914–1918*, I, 802–809. This last-named work (pp. 810–27) contains translations of German discussions in the Reichstag of the treaty.

NO PEACE AND NO WAR

[From the Declaration of the Russian Delegation, February 10, 1918][57]

We declare to all peoples and governments that we are dropping out of the war. We are issuing orders for full demobilization of all troops that now face the armies of Germany, Austria-Hungary, Turkey, and Bulgaria. We wait and trust that all nations will soon follow in our steps.

We announce at the same time that the conditions of peace offered us by Germany and Austria-Hungary are basically against the interests of all peoples. . . . . The peoples of Poland, Ukraine, Lithuania, Courland, and Esthonia regard these conditions as a violation of their will, while for Russia they constitute a perpetual menace. The peoples of the world, guided by their political convictions and moral instincts, are condemning these conditions and are awaiting the day when the working classes of all countries will establish their own forms of peaceful co-operation of peoples. We refuse to sanction those conditions which the sword of German and Austro-Hungarian imperialism is ready to inscribe on the living bodies of the peoples involved. We cannot enter the signature of the Russian Revolution under conditions which carry oppression, sorrow, and suffering to millions of human beings. . . . .

In connection with the above declaration I wish to deliver to the Quadruple Alliance the following written statement:

"In the name of the Soviet of People's Commissars, the Government of the Russian Federated Republic hereby informs the governments and peoples warring against it, as well as the Allies and neutrals, that in refusing to sign the annexation peace Russia at the same time declares the war with Germany, Austria-Hungary, Bulgaria, and Turkey at an end. Orders for general demobilization have already been issued."

L. TROTSKY A. BITSENKO
A. JOFFE V. KARELIN
M. POKROVSKY

C. ACCEPTANCE OF THE GERMAN TERMS

Trotsky's statement produced an overwhelming impression. "The whole Congress," says Hoffmann, "sat speechless when Trotsky had finished his declaration. We were all dumfounded."[58] When the delegates of the Quadruple Alliance

[57] *Mirnye peregovory v Brest-Litovske,* I, 207–208.

[58] Hoffmann, *op. cit.,* p. 226.

met later in the evening to consider the situation, Hoffmann was the only one who advocated the resumption of war against Russia. Kühlmann and Czernin objected, fearing the unfavorable reaction that such a course might produce at home and abroad. But General Headquarters supported Hoffmann, and at a conference of the Kaiser and the highest military and civil officials on February 13, in Bad Homburg, the soldiers overcame the civilian opposition and it was agreed to denounce the armistice.[59]

The Russians left Brest-Litovsk on the 10th, apparently well satisfied and in the comforting belief that the Germans would not resume hostilities.[60] On February 13 Trotsky and Karelin reported to the Central Executive Committee and Sverdlov moved a resolution affirming the action of the Brest delegation.[61] Three days later General Samoilov telegraphed the following:

END OF THE ARMISTICE

[General Samoilov's Telegram][62]

BREST-LITOVSK, February 16, 1918

General Hoffmann today gave . . . . official notice that the armistice concluded with the Russian Republic comes to an end on February 18, at 12 o'clock, and that war will be resumed on that day. . . . .

GENERAL SAMOILOV

When the Central Committee of the Bolsheviks met on the 17th to consider the situation, Lenin moved that a telegram accepting the peace terms should be sent to the Germans. The motion was lost 5 to 6. Trotsky's motion to delay the resumption of negotiations until the German offensive had actually started and its effect on the masses could be

59 Ludendorff, *op. cit.*, II, 181–82, 185–86.

60 Fokke, *op. cit.*, p. 207.

61 *Protokoly sezdov i konferentsii vsesoiuznoi Kommunisticheskoi Partii* (*b*). *Sedmoi sezd. Mart 1918 goda,* p. 284.

62 *Pravda,* No. 29, February 19, 1918, p. 3.

judged was carried 6 to 5. Lenin then put the question: "Should the German offensive become a fact and no revolutionary upheaval take place in Germany and Austria, are we then to sign peace?" Bukharin and the revolutionary war advocates and Krestinsky did not vote. Joffe alone voted "No"; the majority, including Trotsky, voted for peace.[63]

German aëroplanes appeared over the Russian front on the 17th and the offensive was started on the 18th. A proclamation to the Russian people was issued by the German Command explaining that the offensive was in the interests of civilization and against the Bolshevik Government which "has raised its bloody hand against your best people, as well as against the Poles, Letts, and Esthonians."[64] At the meeting of the Central Committee on the 18th Lenin once more moved that a telegram accepting the peace terms be sent to the Germans at once, but the motion was lost again by one vote, 7 to 6, Trotsky voting against the motion.[65]

In the course of the day news reached Petrograd that the Germans had occupied Dvinsk and were seizing Russian supplies and moving into the Ukraine. The Central Committee met a second time and Trotsky proposed that a telegram be sent asking the Central Powers to state their terms. Lenin was for immediate acceptance of the terms offered. "We cannot," he said, "joke with war. . . . . The people will not understand what we are trying to do. . . . . If we meant war, we had no right to demobilize. . . . . The revolution will surely crash if we pursue a half-way policy. To delay is to betray the revolution. Had the Germans said that they demanded the overthrow of the Bolsheviks [as a condition of peace], then we should have had to fight. . . . . To write notes to the Germans now is to waste paper. . . . . While we

63 Lenin, *Sochineniia,* XXII, 557. A 1928 reprinting of the same document places Trotsky among those who did not vote on the last question. *Protokoly sezdov i konferentsii vsesoiuznoi Kommunisticheskoi Partii* (*b*). *Sedmoi sezd. Mart 1918 goda,* p. 194. In 1928 Trotsky was excommunicated for his heresies.

64 *Pravda,* No. 39, March 2, 1918, p. 1.

65 *Protokoly sezdov i konferentsii vsesoiuznoi Kommunisticheskoi Partii* (*b*). *Sedmoi sezd. Mart 1918 goda,* pp. 195–96.

write they go on seizing warehouses and railway cars. . . . . History will condemn us for betraying the revolution when we had the choice of signing the peace. . . . . This is no time to exchange notes. . . . . It is too late to send out 'feelers.' . . . . The revolution in Germany has not begun, and we know that it takes time for a revolution to triumph. If the Germans should seize Latvia and Esthonia we shall have to surrender them in the name of the revolution. . . . . They may have revolutionary Finland too. All these sacrifices will not ruin the revolution. . . . . All the Germans are after is the grain [from the Ukraine]. After they have taken that they will depart. . . . . I move that we notify the Germans that we are ready to accept their peace."

On this motion, Trotsky shifted from opposition to support and it was carried 7 to 6 with Lenin, Smilga, Stalin, Sverdlov, Sokolnikov, Zinoviev, and Trotsky for and Uritsky, Joffe, Lomov, Bukharin, Krestinsky, and Dzerzhinsky against. Lenin and Trotsky were authorized to communicate with the German Government.[66]

THE SOVNARKOM ACCEPTS THE PEACE TERMS

[Radiogram, February 18–19, 1918][67]

To the German Government, Berlin:

The Soviet of People's Commissars protests against the action of the German Government in moving troops against the Russian Soviet Republic, which has declared war ended and has begun the demobilization of troops on all fronts. The Workers' and Peasants' Government hardly expected such a move in view of the fact that neither directly nor indirectly has either of the parties given the other the seven days' notice required by the agreement of December 15, 1917.

Under the circumstances the Soviet of People's Commissars finds itself forced to sign the treaty and to accept the conditions of the Four-Power Delegation at Brest-Litovsk.

[66] *Protokoly sezdov i konferentsii vsesoiuznoi Kommunisticheskoi Partii (b). Sedmoi sezd. Mart 1918 goda*, pp. 197–201.

[67] *Pravda*, No. 30, February 20, 1918, p. 3.

The Soviet of People's Commissars declares that it will furnish without delay a detailed reply to the terms of peace offered by the German Government.

THE SOVIET OF PEOPLE'S COMMISSARS
V. ULIANOV (LENIN)
President of the Soviet of People's Commissars
L. TROTSKY
People's Commissar of Foreign Affairs

The Germans took their time about acknowledging the Soviet surrender and continued their advance, encountering no opposition and capturing large quantities of stores. Petrograd was alarmed. There was no certainty that the Germans would accept the belated surrender, and dissatisfaction with the radiogram of the Sovnarkom of February 18–19 was growing more pronounced.

On February 20 a group of leading Moscow Bolsheviks protested against the actions of the party Central Committee, resigned from their posts, and declared themselves free to agitate for revolutionary war both in and outside of the party. Their protest, however, was not made public and the resignations were not accepted. Even Lenin was beginning to waver. Trotsky says that "All of us, including Lenin, were of the impression that the Germans had come to an agreement with the Allies about crushing the Soviets and that a peace on the Western front was to be built on the bones of the Russian revolution."[68]

Under such circumstances Lenin thought there was nothing to do but to fight. On the 21st the Sovnarkom issued a long appeal to the toiling people of all Russia in which it defended its policy, accused the Allies of having sabotaged the Soviet peace efforts by aiding Dukhonin, Kaledin, Alexeev, the Rada, and Rumania, charged the bourgeoisie with rejoicing at the advance of the Germans and with commencing a campaign against the Soviets, and urged the greatest effort by local Soviets to organize a disciplined Red

[68] Trotsky, *My Life*, pp. 388–89.

Army. Petrograd was declared in a state of siege, and a revolutionary mobilization was decreed in a statement given below. A number of hostile newspapers were suspended and the revolutionary Committee for the Defense of Petrograd forbade all meetings and assemblies.[69]

Still no reply came from Berlin, but there were disturbing reports of the progress of the Germans toward Petrograd. The party Central Committee met on the 22d and discussed, among other things, Trotsky's report of an offer of aid from the Allies.

True, the Allies had not changed their attitude toward the Bolsheviks nor had the Bolsheviks made any attempt to conciliate the Allies. In fact they had done just the opposite by the decree on February 10 annulling the loans made to Russia before the November Revolution.[70] Against this decree the Allied and neutral representatives protested on the 12th. *Izvestiia* answered (February 17) with the assertion that there was not a counter-revolutionary act or conspiracy in which the agents or military missions of the Allies had not taken part, and *Pravda,* on the same day, recalling that the publication of the secret treaties had dealt capitalism a blow, declared that the cancellation of loans was no less of a blow to the Entente powers than German victories on the Western front. The objectives of the Bolsheviks and the Allies were too far apart for any lasting collaboration, but the advance of the Germans and the talk of a holy war offered a possibility of co-operation of a sort against a common enemy. Sadoul, who had been working for weeks to secure this co-operation, after explaining its possibilities to Trotsky, persuaded the French Ambassador to give a conditional assent. Noulens telephoned to Trotsky, "In your resistance against Germany, you can count on the military and financial aid of France," and the other Allied and American diplomatic representatives "agreed to support resistance if offered" and to meet Trotsky for conference at the French

[69] *Izvestiia,* No. 31, February 22, 1918, p. 1.

[70] The sums involved are given on p. 603 note 72.

or American embassies but not at the Foreign Office.[71] Trotsky favored accepting Allied aid, Bukharin opposed, and Lenin, who was absent, sent a note stating that he agreed to accept the aid "of the imperialist robbers of the Anglo-French coalition," and this was approved by a vote of 6 to 5. It was at this meeting that the party leaders referred to above agreed to withdraw their resignations. Trotsky meanwhile offered his resignation as People's Commissar for Foreign Affairs.[72]

THE SOCIALIST FATHERLAND IS IN DANGER

[Proclamation of the Sovnarkom, February 21, 1918][73]

In order to save the exhausted and depleted country from new war miseries we made the supreme sacrifice and notified the Germans of our readiness to accept their peace conditions. Our delegates left Rezhitsa for Dvinsk on the evening of February 20, but as yet we have no news. The German Government is apparently delaying an answer. It appears that it does not desire peace. German militarism is carrying out the orders of the capitalists of all countries and is aiming *to crush the Russian and Ukrainian workers and peasants, to give back the land to the landlords, factories and banks to the bankers and to restore the monarchy*. The German generals plan to establish "order" in Petrograd and Kiev. *The Socialist Republic of the Soviets is in the greatest danger.* Until the time when the German proletariat rises and conquers, it is the sacred duty of the workers and peasants of Russia to defend the Republic of the Soviets against the hordes of the bourgeois-imperialistic Germany.

The Soviet of People's Commissars has decreed that:

1. *All the forces and resources of the country shall be devoted wholly to the revolutionary defense.*

[71] Sadoul, *op. cit.*, pp. 241–43; *U.S. Foreign Relations, 1918, Russia,* I, 386. Noulens states that he promised French aid immediately and without restriction and put the French military mission at the disposal of the Soviet Government. (*Op. cit.*, I, 223.)

[72] *Protokoly sezdov i konferentsii vsesoiuznoi Kommunisticheskoi Partii* (*b*). *Sedmoi sezd. Mart 1918 goda,* pp. 202–204; Trotsky, *My Life,* p. 389. Trotsky says that he told Lenin privately that he proposed to resign in order to suggest to the Germans that the Bolsheviks were ready to sign the treaty. Trotsky also says that after the meeting in which the negotiations with the Allies were discussed, Bukharin wept on his neck and exclaimed, "We are turning the party into a dung-heap."

[73] *Pravda,* No. 32, February 22, 1918, p. 1.

2. *All Soviets and revolutionary organizations shall defend every position to the last drop of blood.*

3. Railway organizations and their Soviets must in every possible way prevent the enemy from making use of the railway machinery. As the Russians fall back they should destroy the line, blow up or burn the buildings, and send all the cars and locomotives eastward into the interior.

4. All food stores and other valuable property which might fall into the hands of the enemy should be destroyed. The responsibility for carrying out these orders falls on local Soviets and their chairmen, who are held personally responsible.

5. The workers and peasants of Petrograd, Kiev, and all cities, villages, and hamlets on the line of the new front shall mobilize battalions to dig trenches under the supervision of military specialists.

6. *All able-bodied persons of the bourgeoisie, both men and women, should be included in the battalions and should work under the eyes of the Red Guard. In case of refusal or opposition, shoot them down.*

7. All publications opposing the revolutionary defense, siding with the German bourgeoisie, or hoping to make use of the invasion of the imperialistic hordes to overthrow the Soviet Government should be closed and their able-bodied editors and collaborators put to work digging ditches and other such work.

8. *Enemy agents, profiteers, thieves, vagabonds, counter-revolutionary agitators, and German spies should be shot on the spot.*

The Socialist Fatherland is in danger!

Long live the Socialist Fatherland!

Long live the International Socialist Revolution!

SOVIET OF PEOPLE'S COMMISSARS

GERMANY'S NEW PEACE TERMS

[Kühlmann's Ultimatum, February 21, 1918][74]

PETROGRAD

To the Soviet of People's Commissars:

Reply of the German Government to the communication of the Russian Government of February 19, 1918. Germany is willing to resume peace negotiations with Russia and conclude peace on the following conditions:

1. Germany and Russia declare the state of war at an end. Both nations are resolved to live in peace and friendship in the future.

[74] *Pravda,* No. 34, February 24, 1918, p. 3; also cited in *U.S. Foreign Relations, 1918, Russia,* I, 432–33.

2. The territories lying to the west of the line indicated to the Russian representatives at Brest-Litovsk and which formerly belonged to Russia will no longer be under a Russian protectorate. In the Dvinsk district this line must be moved toward the eastern frontier of Courland. No obligation whatsoever toward Russia shall devolve upon the territories referred to because of their former relations to the Russian Empire. Russia renounces every kind of interference in the internal affairs of these countries. Germany and Austria-Hungary intend to determine the future destiny of these territories in agreement with their inhabitants. Germany is ready after the conclusion of a general peace and the completion of the Russian demobilization to evacuate all territories east of the designated line, in so far as Article 3 does not determine otherwise.

3. Livonia and Esthonia are immediately cleared from Russian troops and Red Guards who will be replaced by German police until such time as the reconstruction of the country will guarantee safety and governmental order. All inhabitants arrested on political grounds must be immediately released.

4. Russia concludes peace immediately with the Ukraine People's Republic. The Ukraine and Finland must immediately be cleared of Russian troops and Red Guards.

5. Russia will do everything in her power to secure for Turkey the orderly restoration of her eastern Anatolian provinces and to recognize the abolition of Turkish capitulations.

6. (*a*) A full demobilization of the Russian Army, including the units recently organized by the present government, must take place immediately. (*b*) Russian warships in the Black Sea, the Baltic Sea, and the Arctic Ocean must be immediately brought to Russian ports and interned there until the conclusion of a general peace or be disarmed. Warships of the Entente under Russian control are to be treated as Russian ships. (*c*) Commercial navigation in the Black Sea and the Baltic Sea is to be resumed as provided in the armistice agreement; the removal of mines is to begin at once; the blockade of the Arctic Ocean is to continue until the conclusion of a general peace.

7. The Russo-German commercial treaty of 1904 goes into force. . . . .

8. [This article deals with the re-establishment of legal and political relations, prisoners, etc.] . . . .

9. Russia obliges herself to stop all agitation and propaganda, carried on by the government or by organizations supported by the government, against the governments of the Quadruple Alliance, their civil and military institutions, including the territories occupied by the Central Powers.

10. The terms mentioned above are to be accepted within forty-eight hours. Russian plenipotentiaries are to start immediately for Brest-

Litovsk and there within three days sign the peace agreement, which should be ratified within two weeks.

BERLIN

VON KÜHLMANN
Minister of Foreign Affairs

The new German peace terms reached Petrograd February 23. When the Central Committee of the party met to decide whether or not to accept the German terms, Bukharin and others were still waving the war flag and firing off revolutionary speeches. Lenin had no patience with these arguments. "It is time," he said, "to put an end to revolutionary phrases and get down to real work. If this is not done I resign from the government. To carry on a revolutionary war, an army, which we do not have, is needed. Under the circumstances there is nothing to do but to accept the terms."

Trotsky pointed out that it was impossible to wage a revolutionary war with a divided party, particularly with Lenin in opposition, and he was, therefore, for submitting to German force. Bukharin remained unconvinced.

Lenin again took the floor and declared he was tired of words. "It is a question," he said, "of signing the German terms now or signing the death sentence of the Soviet Government three weeks later. These terms do not interfere with the Soviets. . . . . The German revolution is not yet ripe. It will take months. We must accept the terms."

Lenin's position was attacked and defended, and finally the question was called for. Of the fifteen present, seven—Lenin, Stasova, Zinoviev, Sverdlov, Stalin, Sokolnikov, and Smilga—voted to accept the terms. Four—Bubnov, Uritsky, Bukharin, and Lomov—voted against; and the remaining four—Trotsky, Krestinsky, Dzerzhinsky, Joffe—did not vote. Although Lenin did not have a majority, the plurality vote was interpreted as binding on all members of the party at least until the party congress. The four who voted for war—the "left-wing communists"—handed in their resignations.[75]

[75] *Protokoly sezdov i konferentsii vsesoiuznoi Kommunisticheskoi Partii (b). Sedmoi sezd. Mart 1918 goda,* pp. 204–209. Trotsky claims (*My Life,* p. 389) that

This vote of the party Central Committee settled the matter of the reply to be made to Kühlmann, but it was put before the Central Executive Committee on the night of February 23–24. The Central Executive Committee voted for acceptance 116 to 85, with 26 not voting.[76]

THE SOVNARKOM ACCEPTS THE ULTIMATUM

[Telegram of February 24, 1918]

In accordance with the decision of the Central Executive Committee of the Soviet of Workers', Soldiers', and Peasants' Deputies taken on February 23–24 (4:30 A.M.) the Soviet of People's Commissars has agreed to the terms proposed by the German Government and is sending a delegation to Brest-Litovsk.

VL. ULIANOV (LENIN)
President of the Sovnarkom
L. TROTSKY
People's Commissar of Foreign Affairs[77]

In reply to the message of the People's Commissars to renew negotiations with the Quadruple Alliance, the German Government proposed new conditions of peace, demanding control over Courland, Esthonia, Dvinsk. These proposals, dated February 21, at Berlin, ask that the Russian Federated Republic answer within forty-eight hours, but do not indicate from what time.[78] The proposals were handed in a sealed envelope to our man at Dvinsk on February 22. They came to the hands of the Soviet of People's Commissars at 10:30 A.M., February 23. The Central Executive Committee accepted them on February 24, 4:30 A.M., and immediately made its decision known to the Soviet of People's Commissars, which passed it on to Berlin, where it was received 7:32 A.M., February 24. In addition the Supreme Commander-in-Chief Krylenko sent the following message to the headquarters of the German commander-in-chief:

---

the decision at this meeting depended on his vote and that he abstained from voting to insure a majority for Lenin. He might, of course, have given Lenin a real majority by voting for his motion.

[76] *Pravda,* No. 35, February 26, 1918, p. 3; *Nash Vek,* No. 34, February 26, 1918, pp. 2–3.

[77] *Pravda,* No. 35, February 26, 1918, p. 3.

[78] At the meeting of the Central Committee on February 23 Trotsky said that the "forty-eight hours expire on February 24, 7:00 A.M." (Lenin, *Sobranie sochinenii,* first edition, 1922, XV, 632.)

"I take for granted that from the moment that the Soviet of People's Commissars has accepted the German terms of peace all reasons for continuing the war have come to an end. I should like to know whether the German high command also believes that from the moment that the German Government received the reply of the Soviet of People's Commissars a state of armistice was restored as before February 18 when the war was renewed by the Germans."

The above message was received by the Germans on February 24, 1:35 P.M. But so far neither Krylenko nor the Soviet of People's Commissars has received any reply, and the German advance continues. . . . .[79]

THE GERMANS REFUSE TO STOP THE ADVANCE

[Hoffmann to Krylenko, February 24, 1918][80]

In reply to telegrams No. 95, 6, 24, 2, signed by the Supreme Commander-in-Chief Krylenko, the German high command replies . . . . that the old armistice is dead and that it cannot be revived. According to Article 10 of the German terms submitted on February 21 peace must be concluded within three days after the arrival of the Russians at Brest-Litovsk. Until then the war is to go on . . . . for the protection of Finland, Esthonia, Livonia, and the Ukraine.

MAJOR-GENERAL HOFFMANN

SIGNING THE TREATY

ARRIVAL OF SOVIET DELEGATION AT BREST

[Karakhan to the Sovnarkom, March 1, 1918][81]

We arrived at Brest on February 28, 3:00 P.M.[82] We had a conference in regard to the order of the day for tomorrow. We insisted that war activities should end in view of our acceptance of the ultimatum and our arrival. Our opponents, however, replied that this could be done only after the peace treaty had been signed. The three days begin with the first session on March 1, 11:00 A.M.

KARAKHAN

[79] *Pravda,* No. 35, February 26, 1918, p. 2.

[80] *Ibid.,* No. 37, February 28, 1918, p. 3.

[81] *Ibid.,* No. 39, March 2, 1918, p. 3.

[82] The peace delegation left for Brest-Litovsk on February 24, 10:00 P.M. Its membership was as follows: G. Ya. Sokolnikov, G. I. Petrovsky, G. V. Chicherin, L. M. Karakhan, A. A. Joffe, Vice-Admiral V. M. Altvater, Captain V. Lipsky, General Danilov, and Professor Andogsky. (*Mirnye peregovory v Brest-Litovske,* I, 211.)

The Germans Make New Demands

[Karakhan to the Sovnarkom, March 2, 1918][83]

As we expected, it was absolutely useless to discuss the peace terms. They are worse than the ultimatum of February 21 and have the character of an ultimatum.

In view of this, and owing to the fact that the Germans have refused to stop war activities until the treaty is signed, we have decided to sign without discussion and leave at once. We have asked for a train, expecting to sign and leave tomorrow.

The worst part of the new treaty as compared with the ultimatum of February 21 is the taking of the region of Ardahan, Kars, and Batum from Russia under the guise of self-determination.

Karakhan

The Treaty Is Signed

[Karakhan to the Sovnarkom, March 3, 1918][84]

Today, March 3, 5:00 P.M., central European time, the treaty was signed. General Hoffmann . . . . reported that war activities came to an end at one o'clock today. Issue orders at once to stop hostilities by our troops.

Karakhan

Statement of the Russian Delegation

[Before signing the treaty the Russian delegation issued the following statement] :[85]

The Workers' and Peasants' Government of the Russian Republic, which has announced the cessation of war and has demobilized its army, was compelled by the attack of the German troops to accept, February 24, the ultimatum presented by Germany and has delegated us to sign these terms, which are being imposed on us by force.

The previous negotiations at Brest-Litovsk . . . . made it sufficiently evident that the so-called "peace by agreement" is in fact an imperialistic and annexationist peace . . . . a peace dictated at the point of the gun . . . . and which revolutionary Russia is compelled to accept with its teeth clenched. Under the pretext of "liberating" the Russian frontier districts, the latter are in reality turned into German provinces and deprived of the right of free self-determination. . . . . Germany is furthermore occupying by force of arms regions with a purely Russian

[83] *Pravda,* No. 40, March 3, 1918, p. 2.

[84] *Izvestiia,* No. 40, March 5, 1918, p. 1.

[85] *Mirnye peregovory v Brest-Litovske,* I, 229–31.

population, is establishing there a régime of military occupation, and is restoring the pre-revolutionary order. In the Ukraine and in Finland, Germany demands non-interference of revolutionary Russia and at the same time actively assists the counter-revolutionary forces against the revolutionary workers and peasants. In the Caucasus . . . . Germany tears away for the benefit of Turkey the districts of Ardahan, Kars, and Batum, which were not conquered even once by the Turkish armies. This unconcealed . . . . annexation of important strategic points can have only one end in view: to prepare a new invasion of Russia and to defend the interests of capitalists against the workers' and peasants' revolution. . . . .

Under the circumstances Russia has no freedom of choice. . . . . The German proletariat is as yet not strong enough to stop the attack [of German imperialism]. We have no doubt that the triumph of imperialism and militarism over the international proletarian revolution will prove to be temporary and ephemeral. Meanwhile the Soviet Government . . . . unable to resist the armed offensive of German imperialism, is forced to accept the peace terms so as to save revolutionary Russia. . . . .[86]

The treaty signed on March 3 included, in addition to the paragraphs of the ultimatum already given, a stipulation that Russia would evacuate the districts of Ardahan, Kars, and Batum in the Caucasus and "not interfere in the reorganization of the national and international relations of these districts." By this treaty it was estimated that Russia lost territories and resources approximately as follows: 1,267,000 square miles, with over 62,000,000 population, or one-fourth of her territory and 44 per cent of her population; one-third of her crops and 27 per cent of her state income; 80 per cent of her sugar factories; 73 per cent of her

[86] In defending the treaty in the Reichstag, von dem Bussche made the following comment on the tactics of the Soviet representatives: ". . . . The negotiators, who, this time without Trotsky, again arrived at Brest-Litovsk, realized the justice of our action in raising our demands. Our negotiators gained the impression that the Russians expected far more severe demands after they had, by their conduct, forced us to a fresh appeal to arms and to further considerable expenditure. If during the negotiations between March 1 and March 3 the Russians protested against our action and also made a further protest at their conclusion . . . . that was assuredly done more to save their own faces than from any real conviction. . . . ." (Lutz, *op. cit.*, I, 778.) Other speeches attacking and defending the treaty are given in the same work, I, 766–95.

iron and 75 per cent of her coal. Of the total of 16,000 industrial undertakings, 9,000 were situated on the lost territories.[87]

Kühlmann and Czernin, who were at Bucharest negotiating a treaty with Rumania, signed the document on March 7. The Brest treaty was to come into effect upon ratification and the Russian Government agreed at the desire of the Quadruple Alliance to exchange ratifications in Berlin within two weeks. Ratifications were exchanged in Berlin, March 29, 1918.

According to Article I the four Central Powers and Russia intended to live in peace and amity henceforth.

Article II prohibited agitation or propaganda against the state and military institutions of either party.

Article III provided that the territories separated from Russia should have no obligations toward that country because of past connections and, further, that Russia should refrain from all interference in the internal affairs of these territories, whose future status was to be determined by Germany and Austria-Hungary.

Under Article IV Germany agreed to evacuate the alienated Russian territory as soon as a general peace was concluded, and Russia agreed to evacuate immediately the districts of eastern Anatolia, which were to be returned to Turkey, and the regions of Ardahan, Kars, and Batum.

Russia agreed in Article V to demobilize its army immediately and to detain its warships and those of its allies in port until peace was concluded.

Article VI obligated Russia to conclude peace with the Ukraine Rada, to recognize the treaty between the Rada and the Quadruple Alliance, to evacuate Russian troops from the Ukraine, and to stop all agitation and propaganda against that country. Esthonia, Livonia, Finland, and the

[87] Report by S. Zagorsky, published in *Novaia Zhizn*, No. 80, April 30, 1918, p. 2. Consul-General Summers estimated the losses: of population, 34 per cent; of agricultural land, 32 per cent; of beet-sugar land, 85 per cent; of industrial undertakings, 54 per cent; of coal mines, 89 per cent. (*U.S. Foreign Relations, 1918, Russia,* I, 490.)

Aaland Islands were to be evacuated by the Russians immediately and the Aaland fortresses dismantled.

Both parties agreed in Article VII to recognize the political and economic independence and the territorial integrity of Persia and Afghanistan.

Article VIII provided for the return of war prisoners.

Under Article IX both parties renounced compensation for any expenditures made during the war.

Diplomatic and consular relations were to be resumed under Article X.

Article XI provided for the economic regulations between the contracting parties according to appendices attached to the treaty.

Article XII stated that public and private legal relations, exchange of war prisoners, amnesties, and merchant ships will be regulated by separate treaties.

Article XIII provided that the various language texts were authoritative for the interpretation of the treaty.

Article XIV provided for the exchange of documents in Berlin as soon as possible.[88]

The Seventh Bolshevik Party Congress, where Lenin and his peace group were to fight it out with Bukharin and the partisans of revolutionary war, took place in Petrograd, March 6–8, 1918. On March 5, the day before the meeting opened, a new paper, the *Kommunist,* appeared, edited by Bukharin, Uritsky, and a score of other well-known Bolsheviks. They attacked Lenin, his policies, and his followers. Lenin replied in *Pravda,*[89] treated his "Left" opponents like a lot of schoolboys, and read them lessons from history: ". . . . He who wishes to learn lessons from history," said

[88] The official German and Russian text of the treaty is in the *Reichsgesetzblatt,* No. 77, June 11, 1918, pp. 479 ff., and an English translation is in Lutz, *op. cit.,* I, 796–801. German texts are also given in *Die Friedensverhandlungen in Brest-Litowsk,* pp. 176–80, and Kreppel, pp. 228–32. Other English versions are given in Magnes, pp. 168–71, in *Texts of the Russian "Peace,"* pp. 14–21, and in *U.S. Foreign Relations, 1918, Russia,* I, 442–75.

[89] No. 42, March 6, 1918, p. 2.

Lenin, "should read about the wars of Napoleon. . . . . At different times Prussia and Germany concluded treaties with France, treaties ten times more humiliating and more oppressive than the one we just made with Germany. . . . . We have concluded a Tilsit peace, just as the Germans did . . . . and just as the Germans freed themselves from Napoleon . . . . so will we get our freedom. It will probably not take us so long, because history now moves faster than at that time. Let's cease the blowing of trumpets and get down to serious work."

There were only forty-six active delegates present at the Congress.[90] Care was obviously taken to keep away the Bolsheviks of the "November crop," as Lenin ironically called his most recent converts, who, in his judgment, were not likely to fall in line with a "consistent policy." The debate in the Congress was none the less very stormy. One side blamed the other for the unfortunate situation in which they all found themselves. ". . . . That which I have predicted," exclaimed Lenin, "has come to pass. In place of the Brest-Litovsk peace we have one that is far more crushing. The blame falls on those who refused it [Brest peace]. By this refusal you [opposition] are helping German imperialism by handing over to them millions of our resources—guns, ammunition, food. . . . . We must do it [sign peace] nevertheless . . . . to gain a breathing spell. . . . . But the *Kommunist* makes light of the 'breathing spell'."[91]

At the conclusion of the debates each side introduced resolutions. The Leninists passed their resolution by a vote of 30 to 12.[92]

[90] *Protokoly sezdov i konferentsii vsesoiuznoi Kommunisticheskoi Partii (b). Sedmoi sezd. Mart 1918 goda,* pp. 187–88.

[91] *Ibid.,* pp. 20–21.

[92] *Ibid.,* p. 133.

THE SEVENTH BOLSHEVIK PARTY CONGRESS AND PEACE

[March 8, 1918]

Majority Resolution for Peace[93]

In view of the fact that we have no army, that our troops at the front are in a most demoralized condition, and that we must make use of every possible breathing spell to retard imperialist attacks on the Soviet Socialist Republic, the Congress resolves to accept the most onerous and humiliating peace treaty which the Soviet Government signed with Germany.

At this stage of the social revolution it is historically inevitable that the imperialistic states (west and east) should make frequent attacks on Soviet Russia. Both the internal conditions arising from the class struggle within each country and the international situation are almost certain to bring about at any time, even within the next few days, an imperialistic offensive against the socialist movement in general and against the Russian Socialist Republic in particular.

Under the circumstances this Congress declares that the first and most fundamental task of our party, of the whole advance guard of the class-conscious proletariat, and of the Soviet Government is to make the most energetic and ruthlessly resolute steps to raise the discipline and self-discipline of the workers and peasants of Russia, to explain to them that it was historically inevitable that Russia should have to face in the near future this patriotic and socialist war of liberation, to unite the masses into organizations possessing an iron will and capable of acting together at all times and especially at critical moments in the life of the nation, and, finally, to give systematic military drill and training to the entire adult population, both men and women.

The Congress perceives that the only hope for success of the Socialist Revolution, which so far has been victorious only in Russia, is by turning it into an international workers' revolution.

The Congress believes that from the point of view of the international revolution the step taken by the Soviet Government [signing the treaty] was unavoidable and inevitable under the present correlation of international forces.

Believing that the workers' revolution is steadily growing in all belligerent countries and is preparing the inevitable and complete defeat of capitalism, the Congress declares that the socialist proletariat of Russia will do everything within its power and will use all its resources to help the proletarian revolutionary movement in all countries.

[93] *Protokoly sezdov i konferentsii vsesoiuznoi Kommunisticheskoi Partii (b). Sedmoi sezd. Mart 1918 goda*, pp. 180–81.

Minority Resolution for Revolutionary War[94]

1. The imperialistic war is everywhere disorganizing capitalistic productive relations, creating sharp social conflicts, breaking up capitalistic groupings, and putting whole countries (Austria) out of the capitalistic world. The above facts form the matrix within which the Socialist Revolution is being formed. Its first signs in the West are the strikes and risings in Austria and Germany.

2. The war of the imperialist coalitions may now be viewed from two standpoints: either the coalitions have arrived at a silent temporary understanding among themselves at the expense of Russia, or they are determined to continue the war. In either case we shall have to face the attempts on the part of international capital to partition Russia. . . . . [If] the second alternative [is true], Germany will do her best to crush the Soviet Government, since she can continue the war only if she can have Russian food and raw materials.

3. It would seem then that from the point of view both of class struggle and of imperialistic exploitation it is impossible for Soviet Russia for the present to live in peace with the imperialistic coalition of the Central Powers.

4. This is clearly brought out in the peace terms laid down by Germany, which completely cripple the Soviet Government in its external and internal policies.

5. The treaty cuts off Russia's revolutionary center from the producing regions which feed her industry, divides the labor movement by ruining a number of important centers (Latvia, Ukraine), hinders the socialist economic policy on the question of the annulment of debts, socialization of industry, etc.,[95] nullifies the international importance of the Russian Revolution (prohibition of international propaganda), converts the Soviet Republic into a tool of imperialistic politics (Persia, Afghanistan), and, finally, disarms her (demobilization of old and new units). These terms not only give no breathing spell, but place the proletarian struggle in a worse position than before.

6. The signing of the peace, so far from giving us a breathing spell, demoralizes the revolutionary will of the proletariat and retards the development of the international revolution. Under the circumstances the only proper course to pursue is to wage revolutionary war on imperialism.

7. In view of the fact that the old army is demoralized . . . . a revo-

[94] *Protokoly sezdov i konferentsii vsesoiuznoi Kommunisticheskoi Partii* (*b*). *Sedmoi sezd. Mart 1918 goda*, pp. 226–29.

[95] Article IV, Clause 7, of additional treaty provides for compensation of property confiscated by the Russian Government and owned by nationals of the Quadruple Alliance.

lutionary war will have to be carried on, at least at first, in a guerrilla manner, gradually drawing in the city proletariat and the poor peasant until the struggle becomes a civil war between the toiling classes and international capital. Such a war, in spite of its initial disadvantages, is bound in the end to exhaust the strength of capitalism.

8. Under the present conditions of unemployment and general economic disorganization, the proletariat tends to break up. A proletarian army would keep it together . . . . as soldiers of the proletarian revolution.

9. The fundamental task of the party is to wage war on imperialism and, at the same time, to organize its own military forces. . . . . In the very course of fighting a strong Socialist army will be developed.

10. The policy of the party leaders has been one of vacillation and compromise, a policy which not only interfered with the preparation for the defense of the revolution but also demoralized . . . . the enthusiasm of those . . . . who wished to fight.

11. The social basis for such a policy may be explained by the transformation of our party from a purely proletarian to an "all-national" party, which was bound to happen because of its gigantic growth. The soldier-masses, who were determined to have peace at all costs, ... exerted their influence and the party, instead of raising the peasant [soldier] masses to its standard, was dragged down to the peasant level. . . . .

12. As the struggle with international imperialism continues, the peasant too is bound to be dragged into it for fear of losing his land.

13. Under such conditions the aims of the party and the Soviet Government are: (*a*) to refuse to accept the peace treaty; (*b*) to increase the propaganda and agitation against international capital, aiming to clarify the meaning of this new civil war; (*c*) to create a fighting Red Army, arm the proletariat and the peasants, and train them in the technique of war; (*d*) to adopt energetic measures which will destroy the bourgeoisie economically, unite the proletariat, and raise the enthusiasm of the masses; (*e*) to wage ruthless war on the counter-revolutionists and compromisers; (*f*) to carry on a most active international revolutionary propaganda and call for volunteers from all nationalities and states to join the Red Army.

D. Ratification of the Treaty

After the Communist Party had agreed to accept the German Treaty, the question of ratification was brought before an Extraordinary Congress of Soviets which met

March 14 to 18 in Moscow, which on March 12 had become the seat of the central government.

The question of transferring the capital was voted upon at the Extraordinary Congress, but had been determined shortly before that in Petrograd. The official reasons for the removal were stated by Zinoviev, March 16, at the Congress, as follows: "The German imperialists are now in Pskov and Narva, and are marching on Petrograd through Finland. .... Petrograd cannot be our capital now."[96] Lenin is reported to have said, "If the Germans .... take possession of Petersburg with us in it, the revolution is lost. If on the other hand the government is in Moscow, then the fall of Petersburg would only mean a serious part blow."[97]

There were 1,172 active members at the Congress and 80 members with no votes.[98] The Socialist-Revolutionists of the Left, who until now had been somewhat uneasy partners of the Bolsheviks, turned against them on the peace question and led the opposition. In the documents that follow brief summaries are given of the more pertinent arguments presented by both sides.

THE FOURTH CONGRESS OF SOVIETS RATIFIES THE TREATY

Summary of Lenin's Argument for Ratification[99]

[March 1918]

Comrades! The question that confronts us is the most crucial in the development of the Russian Revolution and the world revolution. To understand fully the reasons why the Soviet Government signed this humiliating peace and why it now offers it for your ratification, it is necessary to realize the meaning of the November Revolution, the main phases in its development and the causes of the present defeat.

96 *Stenograficheskii otchet 4-go Chrezvychainogo Sezda Sovetov Raboch., Sold., Krestiansk. i Kazachikh Deputatov,* Moscow, 1920, p. 69. Hereafter cited as *S.O. 4 Ch. S.S.*

97 Trotsky, *Lenin,* p. 141.

98 *S.O. 4 Ch. S.S.,* p. 83. According to the figures of the Mandate Commissar published in *Izvestiia,* No. 150, March 17, 1918, p. 2, the number of active delegates was 1,204.

99 *S.O. 4 Ch. S.S.,* pp. 13–22.

The main source of disagreement among the Soviet parties is to be found in the fact that our opponents are completely overwhelmed by a feeling of justified indignation and cannot analyze the facts objectively.

Until now our revolution enjoyed a period of comparative independence. It was a period of great triumphs. We conquered the bourgeoisie, the landlords, and established the dictatorship of the proletariat. This we were able to accomplish because we were left unmolested by the beasts of international imperialism. But now we are entering upon a new period of defeats and trials. We have to give way to forces stronger than ourselves, to forces of international capitalism which are attacking us. The proletariat of the world has not given its assistance in time. We had to face the enemy single-handed and we suffered defeat. The thing for us to do now is to retreat and hold at least part of our position while waiting for a more favorable international situation and allowing the proletariat of the world to gather more strength in order to defeat the enemy. For a European revolution has to face an enemy which is well organized and, therefore, more difficult to overcome.

This is where the Socialist-Revolutionists of the Left go wrong. Instead of analyzing the international situation and the conditions of the class struggle, they point to the humiliating character of the treaty and use revolutionary phrases to appeal to our emotions and feelings of indignation. But revolutionary phrases will not do. We have no army; we could not keep the army at the front. We need peace to gain a breathing spell to give the masses a chance to create new forms of life. In all probability that breathing spell will be of short duration. The period of imperialistic wars is over, and we are entering a new period of revolutionary wars on an international scale. We must prepare for the struggle. Victory is certain. The proletariat of the world understands that Russia is fighting its cause. It is our true ally. After we have rested, then, together with the international proletariat, we shall start a new November revolution, but this time on a world scale.

Summary of Kamkov's Argument against Ratification[100]

By this peace Russia becomes a tool of German-Austrian imperialism. A refusal to ratify would bring us the support of the international proletariat. As long as we stand by the internationalist point of view, it matters little how much territory Germany grabs. Sooner or later the international proletariat is bound to come to our aid. By ratifying this robber treaty we admit that we are traitors to those parts of Russia that are being handed over to the Germans in order to save other parts.

[100] *S.O. 4 Ch. S.S.*, pp. 23–30.

"We must have a breathing spell," says Lenin. We have heard this hundreds of times. It is nothing but words, words, words. What does he really mean by it? Who is going to benefit by it? We or the Germans? By the time we get our breath the revolutionary proletariat will be dead and Russia, cut off from her economic resources and loaded down with indemnity, will have no chance to recuperate and offer any resistance in the future.

We should at least face the situation squarely. Do you mean to carry out the treaty honestly or have you mental reservations? Do you really think you can fool the Germans? If the latter is the case, we should be honest with the peasants and the proletariat and tell them that the war is to continue. On the other hand, if you intend to carry out honestly the peace terms, and there is every reason to suppose that you will have to, you become the tools of German imperialism. Does not the commercial treaty deal a deathblow to the main conquests of the revolution? How can you nationalize the banks when a definite portion of the capital is exempt by treaty from nationalization? You know very well that there is going on an unprecedented transfer of shares and bonds to neutral countries and from there to Germany. We shall have to pay them all. We refuse to pay the French and agree to pay the Germans. Why this discrimination? Are you not deceiving yourselves? You may rest assured that if you pay to one group you will have to pay to the other. It is only a question of time. The German and Austrian capitalists are threatening Petrograd, but on the east Japan is guarding the interests of the Allied capitalists. The same thing is happening to the land: it is being sold to capitalists abroad and in the end the peasants will have to pay for it.

Summary of Martov's Argument against Ratification[101]

Comrades! We are asked to ratify a treaty the text of which some of us have not seen, at least neither I nor my comrades have seen it. Do you know what you are signing? I do not. You Bolsheviks, of course, know everything. The most complicated things are simple in your eyes. Talk about secret diplomacy! During the last two weeks all the free press has been closed. The Russian Socialist proletariat cannot be held responsible for what is being done here. If this treaty is signed, the Russian proletariat will make war on the government that signed it. This treaty is the first partition of Russia; Japan is preparing for the second; and the third will not be long in coming. By this treaty we obligate ourselves not to carry on propaganda against the governments of the Quadruple Alliance. In return these governments obligate themselves not to do anything against the Soviet Government. I con-

[101] *S.O. 4 Ch. S.S.*, pp. 30–33.

gratulate Lenin. From now on he is under the protection not only of the Red Guard but also of Kaiser Wilhelm.

Our Social-Democratic Party asks this Congress not to ratify the treaty. The Soviet of People's Commissars had no right to conclude it, and should, therefore, resign in favor of a government capable of tearing up this document and carrying on the war against imperialism.

Excerpts from the Resolutions of the Bolsheviks and of the Socialist-Revolutionists of the Left[102]

Resolution of the Bolsheviks: The Congress ratifies the peace treaty concluded by our representatives on March 3, 1918, at Brest-Litovsk. . . . .

Resolution of the Socialist-Revolutionists of the Left: . . . . The Congress . . . . spurns the terms of the treaty and regards them as the deathblow for Russia and the international revolution. . . . .

In addition to the above resolutions five others opposing ratification were introduced. In the vote, however, the Bolshevik resolution for ratification received 784 votes to 261 against it. The Left-Wing Bolsheviks, who also opposed ratification, did not vote. After the Congress had ratified the treaty, the Socialist-Revolutionists of the Left issued the following declaration:

THE SOCIALIST-REVOLUTIONISTS OF THE LEFT REPUDIATE THE RATIFICATION[103]

[March 16, 1918]

The Socialist-Revolutionists of the Left regard the ratification of the peace treaty with Germany as a betrayal of the international program and of the Socialist Revolution begun in Russia. . . . . The party . . . . declares to the toilers of Russia that it is not bound by the terms of this treaty . . . . and that it is its duty to organize the toiling masses to fight this encroaching international imperialism with all their might. The situation brought about by the ratification of the treaty compels the party to recall its representatives from the Soviet of People's Commissars. At the same time the Socialist-Revolutionists of the Left wish to say that they are ready to support the Sovnarkom in so far as it will carry through the program of the November Revolution.

[102] *S.O. 4 Ch. S.S.*, pp. 56–57.

[103] *Ibid.*, p. 67.

[Statement in *Pravda,* March 19, 1918][104]

Disagreeing with the peace policy of the Fourth Congress of Soviets the Socialist-Revolutionists of the Left have resigned from the Soviet of People's Commissars. The more prominent seceders have gone to different parts of Russia to organize an "uprising." . . . .

This move is an insurrection of the leaders of the intelligentsia against the masses. It is about the only way that we can explain this step. . . . . The policy of washing your hands and walking off is an easy one. . . . . It is not likely that the masses will give their approval. . . . . Where have they gone? To organize an "uprising"? This is childish. What can they hope to accomplish against an enemy who is splendidly armed? . . . .

During the last stages of the negotiations and prior to the final ratification of the treaty, agents of Great Britain, France, and the United States worked busily to arrange some kind of co-operation between the Allied powers and the Soviets in order to prevent the definite conclusion of peace on the Eastern front. Five days after the Bolshevik Central Committee had agreed to accept the German ultimatum, Ambassador Francis cabled Washington that the Sovnarkom and the C.E.C. had decided to resist the Germans and that the five Allied Ambassadors had agreed to support this resistance if offered. As has been noted, however, the C.E.C. on February 23–24 accepted the German terms and signed the treaty on March 3. In the meantime German troops leisurely advanced on Petrograd, from which the Allied embassies and legations departed February 27–28.[105]

These events did not end Allied-Soviet negotiations. Lenin told Lockhart on February 29 that so long as the German danger existed he was prepared to risk co-operation with the Allies but that he doubted if the Allies would see things in that light. To Lockhart's report the British Government replied on March 4 that it was willing to aid the

[104] No. 52, p. 1.

[105] *U.S. Foreign Relations, 1918, Russia,* I, 386, 388–89. The American, Siamese, and Japanese diplomatic missions went to Vologda. The British, French, Italian, Belgian, and Portuguese left for Finland; the British got through the Finnish lines to Sweden, but the other missions were turned back and went to Vologda.

Bolsheviks in resisting the Germans but that thus far the Soviet Government had done nothing but issue proclamations which had not caused the "Germans to withdraw nor the Russians to fight."[106] On the following day Trotsky made a new proposal of which Raymond Robins gives the following account:

PROPOSAL FOR ALLIED SUPPORT OF SOVIETS

[Robins' Account of Interview with Lenin and Trotsky, March 5, 1918][107]

[Mr. Robins] : . . . . On the 5th of March I am in Petrograd. I am going up to see about some of our stores. We have now something like 400,000 cans of condensed milk, which I have kept through a number of weeks of want and misery—kept even when children were dying for want of milk—because I knew that between March and May when the new supply would come would be the real strain, and Bolshevik rifle and machine-gun men had prevented riots of mothers from getting that milk. That was the kind of power they exercised in Petrograd, and they did what they said they would do. We had the milk. I am going up there to Smolny to see about the change of guards. Trotsky said to me, "Do you want to prevent the Brest peace from being ratified?" I said, "There is nothing that I wanted so much to do as that." He said, "You can do it." I laughed and said, "You have always been against the Brest peace, but Lenine is the other way; and frankly, Commissioner, Lenine is running this show." He says, "You are mistaken. Lenine realizes that the threat of the German advance is so great that if he can get economic cooperation and military support from the allies he will refuse the Brest peace, retire, if necessary, from both Petrograd and Moscow to Ekaterinberg, reestablish the front in the Urals, and fight with allied support against the Germans."

Senator Sterling: This was Trotsky stating what Lenine would do?

Mr. Robins: Yes; and he in agreement with it. That was in entire agreement with my representation made to him through the ambassador on the 1st or 2d of January, better than two months before, that if they got to the place where they would really fight, we would help. I said to him, "Commissioner, that is the most important statement that has been made to me in this situation. Will you put that in writing?" He said, "You want me to give you my life, don't you?" I said, "No; but I want

[106] R. H. Bruce Lockhart, *British Agent*, pp. 236–37; *U.S. Foreign Relations, 1918, Russia*, I, 390–91.

[107] *U.S. Senate Documents, 66th Congress, 1st Session*, 1919, IV, 800–801.

something specific. I do not ask you to sign it. You make a written statement of your specific inquiry, interrogatories to the American Government, and that with affirmative response these things will take place, and after writing arrange that Lenine will see me and that he will agree to this, which is counter to what I have had in mind as Lenine's position, arrange that a fourth person, my confidential Russian secretary, whom you know and I know, Mr. Alexander Gumberg, shall be with me, and I will act on that." I go back at 4 o'clock. In Trotsky's office is handed me this original document in Russian. We then go down to Lenine's office. We then hold a conference upon this document. It is explained, translated, stated what will be done. I am satisfied for the hour of the genuineness of the position, that they will act in this way, or am sufficiently satisfied to act, and I leave there and go to the British commissioner, R. H. Bruce Lockhart. . . . .

[Note from the Soviet Government to the American Government, March 5, 1918][108]

In case (a) the all-Russian congress of the Soviets will refuse to ratify the peace treaty with Germany, or (b) if the German government, breaking the peace treaty, will renew the offensive in order to continue its robbers' raid, or (c) if the Soviet government will be forced by the actions of Germany to renounce the peace treaty—before or after its ratification—and to renew hostilities—

In all these cases it is very important for the military and political plans of the Soviet power for replies to be given to the following questions:

1. Can the Soviet government rely on the support of the United States of North America, Great Britain, and France in its struggle against Germany?

2. What kind of support could be furnished in the nearest future, and on what conditions—military equipment, transportation supplies, living necessities?

3. What kind of support would be furnished particularly and especially by the United States?

Should Japan—in consequence of an open or tacit understanding with Germany or without such an understanding—attempt to seize Vladivostok and the Eastern-Siberian Railway, which would threaten to cut off Russia from the Pacific Ocean and would greatly impede the concentration of Soviet troops toward the East about the Urals—in such case what steps would be taken by the other allies, particularly and especially by the United States, to prevent a Japanese landing on our Far East,

[108] *Congressional Record,* January 29, 1919, p. 2263.

and to insure uninterrupted communications with Russia through the Siberian route?

In the opinion of the Government of the United States, to what extent—under the above-mentioned circumstances—would aid be assured from Great Britain through Murmansk and Archangel? What steps could the Government of Great Britain undertake in order to assure this aid and thereby to undermine the foundation of the rumors of the hostile plans against Russia on the part of Great Britain in the nearest future?

All these questions are conditioned with the self-understood assumption that the internal and foreign policies of the Soviet government will continue to be directed in accord with the principles of international socialism and that the Soviet government retains its complete independence of all non-socialist governments.

On the same day Lockhart also talked with Trotsky and wired his government: "I had a long interview with Trotsky this morning. He informed me that in a few days the Government will go to Moscow to prepare for the Congress [of Soviets] on the 12th. At the Congress holy war will probably be declared or rather such action will be taken as will make a declaration of war on Germany's part inevitable.

"For the success of this policy, however, it is necessary that there should be at least some semblance of support from the Allies. He could not say friendly relations because that would be hypocritical on both sides, but suggested some working arrangement such as he has already outlined to me in previous conversations. If, however, the Allies are to allow Japan to enter Siberia, the whole position is hopeless. . . . ."[109]

On the day following Trotsky's conversation with Robins and Lockhart the Seventh Bolshevik Party Congress declared for ratification by a vote of 30 to 12. As for the Allies, the British Foreign Office on March 6 expressed its doubt of the effectiveness of a holy war; "an army cannot be made by fine words, though they can easily destroy it. The Bolsheviks have with complete success endeavored to shat-

[109] *R.A.R.*, p. 82. The Bolsheviks—and for that matter the other parties as well—were considerably exercised by the rumors of an impending Japanese intervention in Vladivostok. Lenin and Trotsky sent Sadoul to interview Francis in Vologda on this matter and on possible allied co-operation against the Germans. (Sadoul, *op. cit.*, pp. 251–59; *U.S. Foreign Relations, 1918, Russia,* I, 392.)

ter the fighting spirit of Russia, and they can hardly revive it the same way." The Bolsheviks were advised to appeal for aid to the Rumanians (with whom they were at war) and to make a "working agreement" with the Japanese (whom the Russians wished to keep out of Siberia at all costs). The American State Department did not receive Trotsky's note of March 5 until the 12th. In the meantime it had sent, apparently at Colonel House's suggestion, President Wilson's message to the Soviet Congress. This message, Lansing wired on March 19, was a sufficient answer to Trotsky.[110]

WILSON'S MESSAGE TO THE CONGRESS OF SOVIETS

May I not take advantage of the meeting of the Congress of the Soviets to express the sincere sympathy which the people of the United States feel for the Russian people at this moment when the German power has been thrust in to interrupt and turn back the whole struggle for freedom and substitute the wishes of Germany for the purposes of the people of Russia. Although the Government of the United States is unhappily not now in a position to render the direct and effective aid it would wish to render, I beg to assure the people of Russia through the Congress that it will avail itself of every opportunity to secure for Russia once more complete sovereignty and independence in her own affairs and full restoration to her great rôle in the life of Europe and the modern world. The whole heart of the people of the United States is with the people of Russia in the attempt to free themselves forever from autocratic government and become the masters of their own life.

WOODROW WILSON.[111]

[The Soviet Reply]

The Congress expresses its gratitude to the American people, above all the laboring and exploited classes of the United States, for the sympathy expressed to the Russian people by President Wilson through the Congress of Soviets in the days of severe trials.

The Russian Socialistic Federative Republic of Soviets takes advantage of President Wilson's communication to express to all peoples perishing and suffering from the horrors of imperialistic war its warm sympathy and firm belief that the happy time is not far distant when the

[110] *U.S. Foreign Relations, 1918, Russia,* I, 397–98, 402; *The Intimate Papers of Colonel House,* III, 399.

[111] *U.S. Foreign Relations, 1918, Russia,* I, pp. 395–96.

laboring masses of all countries will throw off the yoke of capitalism and will establish a socialistic state of society, which alone is capable of securing just and lasting peace as well as the culture and well-being of all laboring people. (*Applause.*) . . . .[112]

The ratification of the Brest treaty by the Soviet Congress was discussed at a meeting of the Allied Supreme War Council in London on March 16 where the French representatives urged that the Allies and the United States consent to Japanese intervention.[113] The British and American governments, particularly the American, hesitated, hoping that the Sovnarkom would request intervention. Trotsky went to the extent of asking that American and Allied officers in Russia be assigned to advise on the reorganization of the Russian Army. This request was granted. Francis explained to Washington that while the new army was ostensibly for defense he believed its real purpose was "resistance to all existing governments and promotion of socialism throughout the whole world." He considered, however, that an army so organized might be taken from Bolshevik control and used against Germany or its creators if they proved to be German allies.[114] Later (April 3) Allied diplomatic and military representatives agreed that collaboration in the organization of the Red Army should continue on condition that the Soviets consent to Japanese intervention and grant to Allied nationals the same treatment granted Germans in the Brest treaty. Francis states that he prevailed on his colleagues to withdraw these conditions and to advise against Japanese intervention. Noulens says that the American Ambassador was the only one of the Allied representatives to change his mind.[115] In any event nothing came of the projected military co-operation nor of various plans for economic collaboration. The landing of Japanese and Brit-

[112] *Ibid.*, pp. 399–400. Francis reported that Zinoviev had boasted that this reply was a slap in the face of the president of the bosses' republic. (*Ibid.*, p. 486.)

[113] *The Intimate Papers of Colonel House*, III, 400.

[114] *U.S. Foreign Relations, 1918, Russia*, I, 487–88.

[115] *Ibid.*, I, 493; Noulens, *op. cit.*, II, 57–58.

ish troops at Vladivostok on April 5 produced violent protests from the Soviet Government. Count Mirbach arrived in Moscow on April 23 and as Soviet-German relations improved the Allies abandoned the idea that the Red Army would ever resume the war against the Central Powers. Thereafter Allied support was given openly to those movements in Russia which were both anti-German and anti-Bolshevik.[116]

[116] The development of this policy will be treated in a subsequent volume of this series.

CHAPTER X

CONSOLIDATING THE DICTATORSHIP

The signing of the Brest-Litovsk treaty did not bring peace to Russia nor did it end the controversies within the Bolshevik Party and between that party and its allies, the Socialist-Revolutionists of the Left. But peace with the Central Powers removed, at the cost of large territorial losses including the Ukraine and its enormous economic resources, the immediate menace of an exceedingly efficient military machine. It gave to the Bolsheviks a brief "breathing spell" during which they could turn their energies from external questions to the no less pressing problems of the internal front. During the period covered by this and the following chapter—from the middle of January until the first of May 1918—the dictatorship endeavored to modify its tactics; transferred the capital from Petrograd to Moscow; began the formation of a workers' and peasants' Red Army; developed the efficiency of the machinery of terror, the Cheka; decreed the separation of church and state; promoted the disruption of the old educational system; annulled state loans; attempted to check the anarchical confiscation of industries and to work out a compromise with owners, managers, and technicians; gained partial control of the co-operatives; and nationalized foreign trade. This was a period of utter confusion in finance and industry, bringing with it widespread unemployment and a shortage of food so acute that many regions lived in the shadow of famine.

A. The Program of the Communist Party

On March 12, 1918, the government and the party headquarters were moved from Petrograd to Moscow.[1] According-

[1] Yu. Kliuchnikov and A. Sabanin, *Mezhdunarodnaia politika,* Book II, 134; *Izvestiia,* No. 46, March 12, 1918, p. 1.

ing to the Bolshevik interpretation this move, taken for purposes of security, marked the end of the first—"the Smolny"—phase of the revolution. The seizure of power had been accomplished, the opposition had been defeated, and now, according to Lenin and the party majority, the problem was the consolidation of the dictatorship in the political and economic life of the country.

A week before the transfer of the capital, March 6–8, the Seventh Bolshevik Party Congress met in Petrograd. As has been noted in the preceding chapter, the Congress voted to accept the Brest-Litovsk peace, and, further, that in view of an anticipated military attack on Russia by "imperialist states" it was the duty of the party to take the most energetic, decisive, and ruthless measures to revive the discipline among the workers and peasants of Russia and to explain the inevitable historical march of Russia toward a war of national liberation, toward a socialist war. It then voted to adopt the name "Communist" and authorized a revision of the party program along the lines advocated by Lenin and the majority. Representatives of the party minority, the "Left Communists," who had opposed acceptance of the Brest peace, continued their opposition to the internal program of the majority after the removal to Moscow, notably in the papers *Kommunist, Spartak,* and *Uralskii Rabochii.*[2]

"LOOT THE LOOTERS"

[Lenin's Advice to Workers and Peasants][3]

You . . . . have before you the very difficult and noble task . . . . of organizing the new economic order in the provinces and of establishing on a firm foundation the power of the Soviets. In doing this you will be helped . . . . by all workers and peasants . . . . who are coming more and more to see that apart from the Soviet Government there is no escape from famine and death. . . . .

[2] Cf. E. Yaroslavski, *Histoire du parti communiste de l'U.R.S.S.* (*Parti Bolchévik*), Paris, 1931, pp. 304–305.

[3] Lenin, *Sochineniia,* XXII, 249–51. This appeared in *Pravda,* No. 18, February 6, 1918, p. 3.

The bourgeoisie . . . . and the saboteurs are . . . . conspiring against us. They know that they will be completely ruined . . . . if the people succeed in dividing the national wealth which is now in the exclusive possession of the rich. . . . .

That is where your function begins. You must organize and consolidate the Soviet power in the villages. You will encounter there the village-bourgeoisie—the kulaks—who will hinder your work in every way. But to fight them will be an easy matter. The masses will be with you. . . . .

Make it clear to the peasant that the kulaks and the bloodsuckers must be expropriated in order to bring about a just and equitable distribution of goods. . . . . The bourgeoisie are concealing in their coffers the riches which they have plundered, and are saying, "We shall sit tight for a while." We must catch the plunderers and compel them to return the spoils.

Your chief business will be this: do not let the brigands get away with their riches, otherwise we shall perish. . . . .

That Bolshevik was right who in reply to a question whether or not it was true that the Bolsheviks are looters, said, "Yes, we loot the looters."

CONDITION OF THE BOLSHEVIK PARTY

[Sverdlov's Report to the Seventh Party Congress, March 6, 1918][4]

. . . . At the Sixth Party Congress[5] about 180,000 members were represented. . . . . During the last seven or eight months the party has grown enormously. Many organizations have increased their membership two or three times. . . . . In Petrograd there are 36,000 members. . . . . In Moscow [the membership] increased from 14,000 to 20,000 . . . . in the Urals from 18,000 to 40,000. . . . .

Altogether there are at least 300,000 members.

There were times, particularly in July and August [1917], when the Central Committee . . . . suffered many hardships. Then we had only one paper [*Pravda*] in Petrograd, and that did not appear regularly. It was very difficult to send it by mail. At times we had to conceal it in bourgeois papers. . . . . The circulation of the *Pravda* during October rose to 220,000. . . . . Lately it has fallen to 85,000 . . . . owing to the disorganization of transport. . . . . The treasury of the Central Committee contained about 650,000 rubles made up exclusively of receipts from the undertakings [newspapers] and membership dues. . . . . As yet the Soviet Government has given nothing to the party. It is true

[4] *Protokoly sezdov i konferentsii vsesoiuznoi Kommunisticheskoi Partii (b). Sedmoi sezd,* pp. 4–7.

[5] August 1917.

that the Soviet of People's Commissars had approved the appropriation of 250,000 rubles, but there was no money in the [state] treasury and the appropriation could not be realized. . . . .

CHANGING THE NAME AND PROGRAM OF THE PARTY

[Lenin's Statement at the Seventh Party Congress, March 8, 1918][6]

Comrades! The question of changing the name of the party has been before us ever since April 1917 and has brought forth a great deal of discussion . . . . leading to almost complete unanimity. . . . . The Central Committee now proposes to change the name . . . . to Russian Communist Party (Bolshevik). The word "Bolshevik" is necessary . . . . because it has acquired a certain political significance both in Russia and abroad. . . . . The term "Social-Democratic Party" is scientifically inaccurate and our press has already called attention to that fact.

When the workers formed their own government they came to see that in the process of revolutionary development the old conception of democracy, bourgeois democracy, has been left behind. We have arrived at a democracy which existed nowhere in Western Europe. The nearest thing to it was the Paris Commune, which, according to Engels, was not a state in the proper sense of that term. In so far as the toiling masses themselves undertake to govern a state and to organize military force for the support of that state, to that extent the special government machinery . . . . and the state compulsion apparatus disappears. We cannot therefore stand for a democracy in its old form. On the other hand, in undertaking socialist reforms, we should clearly formulate the object toward which these reforms are aiming. That object is to create a communistic society and not merely to expropriate factories, shops, land, and other means of production or to introduce strict accounting and control over production and distribution. We must go beyond that and realize the principle: *from each one according to his ability and to each one according to his needs.* That is why the name—Communist Party—is the only scientifically correct name. . . . . The most important reason for changing the name of the party is the fact that the old official socialist parties in the leading European countries have not yet broken away from the spirit of chauvinism and patriotism which has led to the complete crash of European socialism. . . . . Now almost all official socialist parties stand in the way of the workers' revolutionary socialist movement. . . . . Our party, which at the present time has without doubt and in an extraordinary measure the good will of the toiling masses of all

[6] *Protokoly sezdov i konferentsii vsesoiuznoi Kommunisticheskoi Partii* (*b*). *Sedmoi sezd,* pp. 144–50.

countries, ... should come out with a . . . . clear and straightforward statement that it has broken with the old official socialism. The change of name of the party will serve as the best means of attaining that end.

The most difficult question is the theoretical part of our program. . . . . Two points of view are in evidence. . . . . One, of which I am the protagonist, maintains that there is no reason to discard the old theoretical part of our program. . . . . All that is necessary is to add a description of imperialism as the highest stage in the development of capitalism, and then—a description of the era of the socialist revolution, which is now in progress. . . . .

The second point of view . . . . that of Comrade Bukharin . . . . and Comrade V. Smirnov . . . . maintains that it is necessary to remove part of the old program which deals with the evolution of industrialism and capitalism . . . . and substitute the later stages of capitalism, viz., imperialism, emphasizing at the same time the impending transition to the social revolution.

I do not think that the two standpoints are so radically divergent, but I shall insist on my own point of view. . . . .

Our next task must be to describe the Soviet type of state. . . . . I believe that the . . . . official socialists of Western Europe have perverted completely the Marxian conception of the state. The experience of the Soviet Revolution and the formation of Soviets in Russia are remarkable proofs of this fact. There is no doubt that much in our Soviets is of a primitive and unfinished character . . . . but, from the point of view of the historical development toward socialism, the important thing is that we have here an entirely new type of state. . . . .

We have made only a start in Russia and our start may be a bad one. . . . . We must show the European workers concrete evidence of the kind of job we have undertaken. . . . . They will see [a concrete plan for achieving socialism and they will say to themselves]: "The Russians are doing a splendid thing, they are doing it badly, so let us do it better." . . . .

[Resolution of the Seventh Party Congress, March 8, 1918][7]

1. The Congress resolves that henceforth the name of the Russian Social-Democratic Labor Party ("Bolshevik") is changed to Russian Communist Party with the addition of the word "Bolshevik" in parentheses.

2. The Congress resolves to change the program of our party either by revising the theoretical part or supplementing it with material relating to the epoch of imperialism and the new era of the international socialist revolution.

[7] *Ibid.*, pp. 181–82.

3. The political sections of our program should be changed so as to bring out in relief the peculiar characteristics of the new type of state, the Republic of Soviets, which embodies the dictatorship of the proletariat and which takes up the work of the international workers' revolution begun by the Paris Commune.

4. The program should indicate that, in case . . . . of a setback, ... our party will not refuse to make temporary use of bourgeois parliamentarism. In any case and under all circumstances the party will work for a Soviet Republic as the highest type of democratic government and as the most appropriate form of the dictatorship of the proletariat by means of which the yoke of the exploiters can be broken and their opposition crushed.

5. The economic, agrarian, educational, and other parts of our program should be gone over in the same spirit. Stress should be laid . . . . on the tasks already begun . . . ., the immediate problem facing the Soviet Government and the consequences of the measures already undertaken toward the expropriation of the expropriators.

6. The Congress authorizes a committee of seven (Lenin, Bukharin, Zinoviev, Trotsky, Stalin, Sokolnikov, and V. Smirnov) to undertake without delay the formulation of our new program in accordance with the above suggestions and to adopt it as the party program.

[Bukharin on Why the Name of the Party Was Changed][8]

Until the last [seventh] congress our party was called the Social-Democratic Party. Throughout the world all parties of the working classes bore this name. The war, however, created a split in the ranks of the Social-Democratic parties and now we find three distinct groups—an extreme Right, a Center, and an extreme Left.

The Social-Democrats of the Right are real traitors to the working classes. They lick . . . . the boots of generals stained with workingmen's blood. . . . . Of these gentlemen there is a large number in France and England. . . . .

The second group is the Center. It agitates against [existing] governments but is incapable of carrying on a revolutionary struggle. It cannot make up its mind to call the workers into the streets. It fears like fire the armed struggle which alone can decide the question.

Finally there is the third group—that of the Extreme Left. In Germany this group is represented by Liebknecht and his friends. . . . .

In Russia where in November the revolutionary struggle . . . . set at stake the establishment of socialism and the overthrow of the bourgeois power, the struggle between the socialist-traitors and the protago-

[8] N. Bukharin, *Programma kommunistov (bolshevikov)*, Moscow, 1918, pp. 61–62.

nists of socialism had to be decided by force of arms. The Socialist-Revolutionists of the Right and the Mensheviks were on one side of the barricades with all the counter-revolutionary swine; the Bolsheviks were on the other side with the workers and the soldiers. Blood has created a gulf between us. This is not and never will be forgotten. It is why we had to give our party another name, to distinguish us from these traitors of socialism. . . . .

LENIN'S DRAFT OF A NEW PROGRAM

[Presented to the Seventh Party Congress][9]

The Revolution of November 7, 1917, established in Russia the dictatorship of the proletariat, which is now supported by the poorer peasants or the semi-proletariat.

That dictatorship places before the Russian Communist Party the following tasks:

[1] To continue . . . . and bring to completion the expropriation of the landlords and the bourgeoisie and to transfer to the ownership of the Soviet Republic all factories, mills, railroads, banks, and other means of production and exchange.

[2] To utilize the solidarity of the city workers and the poorer peasants . . . . in the interest of a gradual and resolute transition to communal methods of tilling the land and to large-scale socialistic agriculture.

[3] To consolidate and develop the Federative Republic of Soviets as a form of democracy immeasurably higher and more progressive than bourgeois parliamentarism, and as the only type of state which the experiments of the Paris Commune of 1871 and the Russian Revolutions of 1905 and 1917–18 have shown to be the appropriate form of government for the period of transition from capitalism to socialism, i.e., the period of the dictatorship of the proletariat.

[4] To make every use of the torch of the world socialist revolution first kindled in Russia to paralyze the attempts of the imperialistic bourgeois governments to interfere in Russia's internal affairs . . . . and then to carry the revolution into all other countries.

Ten Theses on the Nature of the Soviet Power

The Solidification and Development of the Soviet Power

[We are concerned with] the solidification and development of the Soviet power as a form of the dictatorship of the proletariat and the

[9] *Protokoly sezdov i konferentsii vsesoiuznoi Kommunisticheskoi Partii (b). Sedmoi sezd,* pp. 182–86.

poorer peasantry (semi-proletariat) which has been tested in experience and brought forth by the mass movement and the revolutionary struggle. This solidification and the development must aim toward the realization . . . . of these tasks which history had imposed on this form of state power, this new type of state. [These tasks are as follows]:

(1) To unite and organize only the workers who are oppressed by capitalists and the exploited masses, i.e., only workers and poorer peasants (semi-proletariat) excluding . . . . the exploiting classes and the well-to-do representatives of the petty bourgeoisie.

(2) To unite the most active, energetic, and class-conscious sections of the oppressed classes—their advance guard—[and have them] educate the entire toiling population to take an independent part in the government of the state, not theoretically but practically.

(3) To do away with parliamentarism, to unite the legislative and executive functions of government. Amalgamate executive power with legislation.

(4) [To establish] more intimate connection between government institutions and the masses . . . . than [existed] in the old forms of democracy.

(5) To form an armed force of workers and peasants. . . . .

(6) [To set up] more complete democracy by lessening formalism and providing greater facility for election and recall.

(7) [To establish] close (immediate) contact with trade unions and producing economic units (elections in factories and in districts inhabited by peasant farmers and craftsmen). This close contact will make it possible to introduce far-reaching socialist reforms.

(8) . . . . To remove bureaucracy . . . . as completely as possible.

(9) To shift the main emphasis in questions of democracy from mere formal equality between the bourgeoisie and the proletariat, poor and rich, to the practical use of freedom (democracy) by the toiling and exploited masses of the population.

(10) Further development of the Soviet organization of the state must proceed along the lines of compulsory participation by every Soviet member in the government. [As time goes on] the entire population must be called upon to take part in Soviet organizations (under condition that the Soviets are under control of workers' organizations) and to assume the duties of government.

How the Task Can Be Realized

A. In the sphere of politics—by developing the Soviet Republic. . . . . Six points.

[1] [By] extending the Soviet Constitution to include the entire population, in proportion as the resistance of the exploiters breaks down.

[2] [By using] the [Soviet] federation of nations as a transition to a more enlightened and closer union between the toilers, who will have learned to rise above national differences.

[3] [By using methods of] compulsory and merciless suppression of exploiters. . . . .

[4] [By granting] "liberties" and democracy not to all, but only to the toiling and exploited masses in the interests of their emancipation. . . . .

[5] [By] arming the workers and disarming the bourgeoisie.

[6] [By using] the Soviet state as a transition period to a gradual abolition of government by systematically enlisting an ever greater number, and finally all of the citizens in a direct and daily discharge of their share in the management of the state.

B. In the economic sphere.

[By introducing] socialist organization of production on a national scale, managed by workers' organizations (trade unions, factory-shop committees, etc.) under the general supervision of the Soviet Government as the only sovereign.

[By organizing] on a similar basis transport and distribution (first, a state monopoly of "trade," then complete and final abolition of "trade" in favor of a planned organization of distribution through trade and industrial unions) under the leadership of the Soviet Government, and by compelling the population to join consuming-producing communes.

By making it legally compulsory for all transactions of buying and selling to be made through the consuming communes but without abolishing money (for the time being) or prohibiting such transactions by individual families.

By introducing universal labor duty at once and by extending it gradually to small peasants who live on their own farms and do not hire outside labor.

By compelling all wealthy people with an income exceeding five hundred rubles a month, all owners of enterprises that hire labor, and all families employing domestic servants to keep consuming-labor (account) books. [This is necessary] as a first measure, ... toward the establishment of universal labor duty.

By allowing buying and selling outside the commune (during one's journey) provided the transaction exceeding a definite sum is entered in the consumers' labor book.

By concentrating all banking business and bank capital in the hands of the state. By introducing current accounts for all. By having all money deposited in banks and all money-transfers made through the banks.

By keeping a universal account and control over the production and distribution of all goods. This account and control should be exercised first by workers' organizations and later by the entire population.

By organizing competition between the various (all) consuming-producing communes with the aim of increasing discipline and the production of labor, of adopting higher technique, of economizing labor and material, of shortening the labor day to six hours, and of equalizing by degrees the wages in all professions and categories. By adopting steadfastly and systematically measures aiming to replace individual housekeeping by separate families by communal feeding of large groups of families. . . . .

C. In the financial sphere.

By replacing indirect taxes by progressive-income and property taxes and by deducting a certain proportion of profit from state monopolies. In this connection it is desirable that the wages of certain categories of workers employed by the state should be paid in kind—bread rations and other products.

D. In international politics.

By supporting in the first instance the revolutionary movement of the socialist proletariat in the advanced countries.

By propaganda, agitation, fraternization.

By mercilessly struggling with opportunism and chauvinism. By supporting the democratic revolutionary movement in all countries in general, and in colonies and dependencies in particular.

By freeing all colonial peoples. [By advocating] federation as a form of transition to voluntary union.

THE AIMS OF THE PARTY

[Concluding Words of Sverdlov Delivered at the Seventh Party Congress, March 8, 1918][10]

I wish to say a few words first about the present aims of our party and, secondly, about the internal crisis within our ranks. . . . . I consider it important to emphasize that from now on greater attention will have to be paid to party organization and activity than has hitherto been the case. Till now the greatest attention has been paid to the organization of Soviets through which all the conquests of the November Revolution were consolidated. . . . . But now the party is facing new objectives. It has to undertake certain tasks which previously were performed by the Soviets.

We shall not be able, for example, to continue our international propaganda . . . . after we ratify the [peace] treaty. But this does not mean that we intend to give up in the least that propaganda. What we

[10] *Protokoly sezdov i konferentsii vsesoiuznoi Kommunisticheskoi Partii (b). Sedmoi sezd,* pp. 178–79.

shall have to do is to carry on propaganda in the name not of the Sovnarkom but of the Central Committee of our party. We shall have to carry on in the provinces a whole series of undertakings which Soviet organizations have hitherto performed but which our party will be compelled to assume. In calling the attention of our comrades to these new tasks I wish to emphasize at the same time the fact that it will be necessary to increase the efforts of the party organizations . . . . and when you go back home you will have to explain to your comrades the new situation. Take the question of arming the masses, for example. The party organizations have, no doubt, taken an active part in arming the workers, but in the future the party organizations will have to take a greater part in this activity. There will be other tasks also which the party must take upon itself . . . . continuing at the same time its work in the Soviets.

As regards the crisis through which our party is passing just now[11] there appear to be two possibilities. Either the differences will disappear shortly by virtue of changed objective conditions, in which case there will be no ground for disagreement, or the breathing spell, about which we have talked so much here, ... may force us to forge new weapons with which to continue the struggle, in which case the disagreement will remain. . . . . When viewed from this angle . . . . we must remember that the interests of the party are higher than those of individual members, and I should like to express my assurance that the party masses will not approve of a split . . . . and that at the next congress we shall meet as a united family. . . . .

During the winter months of 1918, as has been shown above, the Soviet Government considerably extended the area under its control, particularly in the larger towns of the southeast, the Trans-Volga, and Central Asia. There were in this period no fundamental changes in the structure of the Soviet Government as set up by the Second and Third Congresses of Soviets. The Communists were concerned in applying the basic principle of the Soviet state which was defined in Bukharin's "Programme of the Communists (Bolsheviks)":[12]

[11] Sverdlov makes reference here to the Left opposition in connection with the Brest-Litovsk peace treaty. See above, pp. 525–29.

[12] Published May 1918 in Russian (*Programma kommunistov*) and later in English by "The Group of English-Speaking Communists in Russia" and reprinted in *Revolutionary Radicalism, Its History, Purposes, and Tactics with an Exposition and Discussion of the Steps Being Taken and Required to Curb It*, Albany, 1920, otherwise known as "The Lusk Report," II, 1677–1762.

". . . . in a Soviet republic the non-working elements are deprived of the franchise and take no part in administrative affairs. The country is governed by Soviets which are elected by the toilers in the places where they work, as factories, works, workshops, mines, and in villages and hamlets. The bourgeoisie, ex-landowners, bankers, speculating traders, merchants, shopkeepers, usurers, the Korniloff intellectuals, priests and bishops—in short, the whole of the black host have no right to vote, no fundamental political rights."[13]

In the meantime, throughout the Soviet territory most of the old local governmental institutions disappeared. The zemstvos, however, showed a rather remarkable power to survive. The Zemstvo Union held a congress in Moscow in January 1918, and despite the nationalization of its property and unceasing conflicts with the Government, continued to exist for nearly a year.[14] Phillips Price writes of attending sessions of the Vologda Zemstvo in March 1918, where, under the chairmanship of a local landlord, the zemstvo discussed the application of regulations on the land question issued by the Provisional Government with no mention of the Soviets or their land decrees. But a few days later, the Vologda Soviet interrupted a meeting of the zemstvo and arrested and expelled from town all its members.[15]

The extension and stabilization of Soviet power did not contribute much to bringing order out of the chaos induced in economic life by the revolutionary upheaval; it did not produce food or jobs for hungry, unemployed workers, whose numbers rapidly grew. In the face of these conditions Lenin began to advocate a less violent policy in the economic field. Where "loot the looters" had held the foremost place in Bolshevik policy, now the organization of accounting and control was the first necessity. He now wished to proceed

[13] *Revolutionary Radicalism,* II, 1696.

[14] T. J. Polnar, Prince V. A. Obolensky, S. P. Turin, Prince G. E. Lvov, *Russian Local Government during the War and the Union of Zemstvos,* London, 1930, p. 306.

[15] *Op. cit.,* p. 263.

slowly toward socialism and to set up during the transition period a type of state capitalism which should include private as well as socialist economy and state enterprises with private capitalist participation. He also desired to utilize the technical experience of the former industrial managers and institute a system which was in effect workers' control with capitalist management. These proposals aroused the strong opposition of the Left-Wing Communists, who had also opposed Lenin's policy at Brest.

On April 4, 1918, the party leaders met to discuss the divergent points of view. Lenin presented his "theses" on the current tasks of the Soviet powers, and the Left Communists stated their own program. Though, as usual, Lenin carried a majority of the party Central Committee with him, the actual course of events shaped itself more in accordance with the program of the Left Communists, who condemned all compromises with the bourgeoisie and demanded the thorough socialization of industrial production.

LENIN AND THE "BREATHING SPELL"

[Theses Presented at the Conference of Bolshevik Leaders, April 4, 1918][16]

Now that peace has been attained, even though it is of a burdensome character and is unstable, the Russian Soviet Republic has the opportunity to concentrate its powers for a certain period of time on the most important and difficult aspect of the socialist revolution—the task of organization. . . . .

Our real guaranty of peace lies exclusively in the strife between the imperialist powers . . . . and the sharp imperialist rivalry between Japan and America for ascendency in the Pacific. . . . . We must make use of this breathing spell, which circumstance has given us, to heal the wounds which the war has inflicted on the social organism of Russia and to raise the economic level of the country. . . . . In so far as we solve the problem of organization, so far shall we be in a position to assist the socialist revolution in the West, which is late in arriving. . . . .

The development of the Bolshevik Party, which is now the governing party in Russia, clearly indicates . . . . the nature of the historic

[16] *Sochineniia,* XXII, 439–68; first published in a supplement to *Izvestiia,* No. 85, April 28, 1918.

turning-point and the uniqueness of the political moment, both of which require a new orientation on the part of the Soviet power, i.e., a new formulation of new tasks.

The first task of every . . . . party is to convince the majority of the people of the truth of its program and tactics. . . . . The second task of our party was to seize political power and to put down the opposition of the exploiters. . . . . The third task [of our party] is to organize the administration of Russia. . . . . We, the Bolshevik Party, *convinced* Russia. We *snatched* Russia from the rich for the poor, from the exploiters for the toilers. We must now *govern* Russia. But the uniqueness of the present moment and the whole difficulty is to understand the peculiarities connected with the transition from the tasks of convincing the people and of suppressing the exploiters by military force to the task of *government,* which is the principal one. . . . . The order of the day is to restore the country economically . . . . to maintain elementary order. . . . . Keep an accurate and honest account of money, be an economical manager, do not loaf, do not steal, maintain rigid discipline in labor—these are the slogans which, though rightly ridiculed by revolutionary proletarians when by similar speeches the bourgeoisie disguised its overlordship as an exploiting class, are now, after the overthrow of the bourgeoisie, becoming the current and principal slogans. . . . .

The bourgeoisie is conquered, but not yet rooted out. . . . . There is in the order of the day a new task, a superior form of struggle against the bourgeoisie, a transition from the simple problem of expropriating the capitalists to a much more complex and difficult task of introducing conditions under which the bourgeoisie could not rise into being again. . . . .

Of decided importance is the organization of the strictest accounting and control over the production and distribution of goods on a national scale. And yet in these undertakings . . . . which we took away from the bourgeoisie, this has not been achieved. Yet without this there can be no question of increasing . . . . the productivity of labor. It would, therefore, be inaccurate to define the task of the present moment in the simple formula: continue the offensive against capital. In spite of the fact that we have not delivered the final blow to capital and that the continuation of the offensive by the toilers against capital is unquestionably necessary . . . . we shall fail to grasp the uniqueness of the present moment unless we recognize that in order that that offensive may eventually be continued, we must "stop" that offensive now. . . . .

Of course, we speak of the "stopping" in a metaphorical sense only. In ordinary warfare a general order can be issued to stop an offensive, to stop the advance. In the war against capital this cannot be done. . . . .

What is in question here is the shifting of the *center of gravity* of our economic and political work. Up till now measures connected with the expropriation of expropriators occupied the foremost place, but now the organization of accounting and control must take precedence. . . . . If we were to continue the expropriation of capital at the previous tempo we should be certain to suffer defeat, because our work of organizing proletarian accounting and control . . . . lags behind that of "expropriating the expropriators." . . . .

Very often we are accused by the lackeys of the bourgeoisie of having conducted a "Red Guard" attack on capital. This accusation is nonsensical, worthy only of the flunkies at the money bag. The "Red Guard" attack on capital was in its time dictated absolutely by circumstances . . . . and in freeing the toilers and the exploited from the yoke of the exploiters the Red Guards were doing the noblest and, from a historical point of view, the most important thing. . . . . At that time we could not use administrative methods in place of repressive measures, because the art of administration is not inborn in man but is gained by experience. Then we lacked the experience. Now we have it. . . . . The "Red Guard" attack on capital was successful because we triumphed over the armed resistance of capital and the sabotage of capital.

Does this mean that the "Red Guard" attack on capital is always and under any circumstances the only suitable method of attack, and that we lack other means of fighting capital? To think thus is puerile. We conquered with light cavalry, but we have heavy artillery also. We conquered by methods of suppression, but we shall also be able to conquer by methods of administration. One has to know how to change his methods of combating an enemy when conditions change. We shall not hesitate one moment in using "Red Guard" attacks on gentlemen like Savinkov and Gegechkori. . . . . But we are not so foolish as to use "Red Guard" methods at a time when . . . . the opportunity has arrived for the proletarian state to use the bourgeois specialists so to plow through the soil that no bourgeois class can ever grow on it again. . . . .

Without the guidance of specialists in the different branches of science, technology, and experience, no transition to socialism is possible, because as compared with capitalism socialism requires a deliberate and forward mass movement toward higher productivity of labor. . . . . But the majority of the specialists are bourgeois. . . . . Many of these saboteurs "go to their jobs," but the best organizers and the biggest specialists can be utilized by the state either in the old, bourgeois way (i.e., for high salaries) or in the new, proletarian way (i.e., by instituting a régime of all-inclusive accounting and control which would inevitably subordinate and attract the specialists).

For the present we shall have to adopt the old bourgeois method and agree to pay very high salaries for the "services" of the biggest bourgeois specialists. All who are familiar with the situation see the necessity of such a measure, though not all understand its significance for the proletarian state. Clearly, it is a compromise measure, a departure from the principles of the Paris Commune. . . . .

History knows of no successful military campaign during which the victor made no mistakes, suffered no partial defeats, or was not compelled to retreat. . . . . Our campaign against capitalism is a million times more difficult than the hardest of military campaigns. . . . .

Let us consider the question from a practical point of view. Suppose the Russian Soviet Republic needs a thousand first-class scientists and specialists in the different branches of science, technology, and practical experience to lead the people toward a rapid economic advance of the country. Suppose that we have to pay to each of these "stars of the first magnitude" twenty-five thousand rubles a year, because the more demoralized the majority of them are by bourgeois customs the greater they cry about the demoralization of the workers. Suppose that this sum (twenty-five million rubles) has to be doubled . . . . or quadrupled . . . . Is it too high a price to pay . . . . for the reorganization of the national economy in accordance with the last word of science and technology? Certainly not! . . . . The problem has another aspect, to be sure. The demoralizing influence of high salaries upon the Soviet power . . . . and the working masses is indisputable.

. . . . But if in a year's time the workers and poorer peasants can learn how to get organized . . . . and to create a mighty workers' discipline, then we shall free ourselves from that "tribute." . . . . The sooner we ourselves—workers and peasants—learn a better labor discipline and a higher technique of labor, using for that purpose bourgeois specialists, the sooner we shall free ourselves from every tribute to bourgeois specialists.

Our work in organizing [a system of] . . . . accounting and control over production and distribution of goods lags far behind that of expropriating the expropriators. This situation is fundamental for an understanding of the peculiarities of the present moment. . . . . Everything hinges . . . . on the organization of that accounting and control. . . . . Even the measures that have already been decreed are far from being carried into effect. . . . . In order to continue further the nationalization of banks and to transform the banks into centers of public accounting under a socialist system, it is necessary first of all to increase the number of branches of the People's Bank, to attract deposits . . . . to catch all acceptors of bribes and shoot down scoundrels, etc. [It is necessary] to solidify and bring order into those state monopolies (bread, leather, etc.) which have already been introduced and thus pave the way for the monopoly of foreign trade by the state; without such monopoly we shall not be able to free ourselves from foreign capital. . . . . The whole possibility of socialist reconstruction depends on whether or not we shall be able, during a definite transition period in which we shall pay a certain contribution to foreign capital, to safeguard the independence of our home economy.

With the collection of taxes in general, and of property and income tax in particular, we are very far behind. The imposition of contributions on the bourgeoisie, a measure which is no doubt acceptable and deserving of the approbation of the proletariat, indicates that we are still closer to the methods of conquest . . . . than to those of administration. But in order to grow stronger . . . . we must adopt the latter methods . . . . which would yield greater revenues to the proletarian state. . . . .

Our failure to introduce labor duty shows once more that the order of the day is organization work . . . . which will prepare the ground for an operation [to achieve] the complete encirclement . . . . and surrender of capital. . . . . The introduction of labor duty must start immediately . . . . and gradually . . . . and in the first instance must be applied to the rich. . . . .

The state, which for centuries existed as the instrument of oppression and plunder of the people, left us as a legacy a very great hatred and suspicion on the part of the masses for everything that emanates from government. To overcome this is a difficult task which only the Soviet power can possibly accomplish but which will require considerable time and perseverance. The baneful influence of that "legacy" is especially noticeable in the problem of accounting and control. . . . . It will take considerable time for the masses . . . . to perceive that without government accounting and control over production and distribution of goods the power and freedom of the toilers cannot be maintained and that a return to the yoke of capitalism is imminent.

All the habits and traditions of the bourgeoisie, and especially of the small bourgeoisie, are opposed to state control and at the same time in favor of the inviolability of the "sanctity of private property," the "sanctity" of private enterprise. Now we can see particularly well the truth of the Marxian assertion that anarchism and anarcho-syndicalism are bourgeois movements, and in what irreconcilable opposition they stand toward socialism, the proletarian dictatorship, and communism. The struggle to inculcate into the masses the idea of Soviet or government control and accounting, to put that idea into effect and to break with the damnable past which accustomed people to look upon the earning of bread and clothing as a "private" affair, on buying and selling as a transaction "which concerns myself only," this struggle is of the greatest universal historical significance—it is the struggle of socialist rationality against bourgeois-anarchic chaos. Workers' control was introduced as a law, but as yet it has hardly begun to penetrate the life or the consciousness of the great masses of the proletariat. . . . . But until workers' control does become a fact . . . . the second step toward socialism cannot be attempted and it is impossible to pass to workers' regulation of production.

The socialist state can come into being only in the form of producers' and consumers' communes keeping an honest account of their production and consumption, economizing labor, steadily increasing its productivity, and thus making it possible to lower the working day to seven, six, or fewer hours. It is impossible to go on without the organization on a national scale of the strictest accounting and control over bread and the production of bread (and other necessary products). Capitalism left us an inheritance in the form of . . . . consumers' societies which should facilitate the transition to mass accounting and control over the distribution of goods. In Russia they are less developed than in the advanced countries, but they do comprise more than ten million members. The recently published decree on consumers' societies is an extremely significant event which clearly illustrates the uniqueness of the present situation and the present aim of the Socialist Soviet Republic. The decree represents a compromise with the bourgeois co-operatives and the workers' co-operatives which are still imbued with bourgeois ideas. . . . . If the proletariat acting through the Soviet government could have organized control or even the beginnings of control over production and distribution throughout the country, it would not have been necessary to resort to this kind of compromise. . . . . In concluding this agreement with the bourgeois co-operatives the Soviet power deliberately adopted tactical aims and particular methods of action that were suitable for this particular phase of development. By keeping a hand on the bourgeois sections of the population, by using them and making special concessions to them, we are creating conditions necessary for the advance, and though that advance will progress more slowly than we originally supposed, it will be more solid, the base of communication will be safer, and the position already gained will be better fortified. . . . .

In every socialist revolution, as soon as the proletariat has completed the task of seizing power and in proportion as the problem of the expropriation of the expropriators is solved in its essentials and fundamentals, there inevitably comes into the foreground the radical problem of establishing a social order which is superior to capitalism, viz., increasing the productivity of labor and . . . . the superior organization of labor. Our Soviet power is precisely in this situation now that the victory over the exploiters from Kerensky to Kornilov makes it possible to approach the problem directly. But it should be clear that . . . . the task will take several years.

To raise the productivity of labor it is necessary first of all to safeguard the material bases of large-scale industry. . . . . So far the Russian Soviet Republic is happily situated in that it commands, even after the Brest peace, enormous supplies of minerals, coal, oil . . . . the development of which will lay the foundation for the unprecedented progress of productive forces. The other condition for increasing the productivity of labor is, first, the raising of the educational and cultural level of the masses. This process is going on even now with enormous rapidity . . . . owing to Soviet organizations. Secondly, ... it is the raising of workers' discipline, the ability to work, to hustle. . . . .

The Russians are bad workers as compared with the advanced nations. It could not have been otherwise under the tsarist régime with the system of slavery still alive. To learn how to work is a problem which the Soviet power must place before the people in all its significance. The last word of capitalism in that respect—the Taylor system—is, like every other capitalist improvement, a combination of the most refined brutality of capitalist exploitation with the richest scientific gains. This is achieved by analyzing the mechanical movements of a worker at his task, by eliminating superfluous awkward motions, by elaborating the best processes of work, by introducing the best system of accounting, control, etc.

The Soviet Republic must at any cost adopt everything that is valuable in the conquests of science and technology. . . . . The realization of socialism will be determined precisely by our success in combining the Soviet power and Soviet organization of administration with the most up-to-date progress of capitalism. It is necessary to introduce into Russia the study and teaching of the Taylor system. . . . . At the same time it is necessary . . . . to lay the foundations for a socialist organization of competition and to use compulsion in order that the dictatorship of the proletariat may not in practice degenerate into a jelly-like condition.

Among the absurdities which the bourgeoisie is eagerly spreading about socialism is the statement that the socialists deny the importance of competition. In reality, however, socialism alone, in so far as it annihilates classes and consequently the enslavement of the masses, is able, for the first time, to pave the way to competition on a mass scale. . . . .

As yet we have hardly begun the enormous, difficult, and noble task of organizing competition in the commune. . . . . The model communes should serve as educators, teachers . . . . to the more backward communes. The press should become an instrument of socialist rebuilding, giving detailed accounts of the success of the model communes . . . . and putting on the black list those which obstinately adhere to "capitalist traditions," i.e., anarchy, laziness, disorder, speculation. . . . . Statistics . . . . should be brought down to the masses and made popular in order that the workers may learn to understand in what way and how much work should be done. . . . .

[The last section of the report deals with the function of the dictatorship in the realization of the tasks listed above. It is foolishness, Lenin maintains, to suppose that the transition from capitalism to socialism can be effected without compulsion and a dictatorship. Time and an iron hand are needed to subdue the bourgeoisie. But so far the dictatorship had resembled jelly more than iron. The greater the progress made in suppressing the bourgeoisie, the more dangerous will the numerically greater class of the petty bourgeoisie become. Compulsion is the only method of dealing with this anarchic elemental force. There is no contradiction between the principle of Soviet democracy and the exercise of dictatorial power by separate individuals in so far as that exercise is in the interests of the large masses.]

PROGRAM OF THE LEFT-WING COMMUNISTS

[Theses Presented at the Conference of Bolshevik Leaders, April 4, 1918][17]

10. Two ways are now open to the party of the proletariat. One way is to defend and consolidate the remaining territories of the Soviet state. From an economic standpoint and in view of the incompleteness of the revolutionary process [the present Soviet state] is merely a transitory stage toward socialism. [It is characterized by] the incomplete nationalization of banks, capitalistic forms of financing industry, the partial nationalization of enterprises, the prevalence of small-scale agriculture in the village and the tendency of peasants to solve the agrarian problem by dividing the land. From the political point of view it [the Soviet state] can be transformed from a dictatorship of the proletariat supported by the poorer peasantry into a tool for the political ascendency of the semi-proletarian–petty-bourgeois masses and in the end can prove

[17] Lenin, *Sochineniia,* XXII, 567–71. The program was published April 20, 1918, in the weekly organ of the Left Wing, the *Kommunist,* No. 1, pp. 4–9. The first nine points deal with the consequences of the Brest-Litovsk peace and restate on the whole the position taken by the group during the Seventh Party Congress on March 8, 1918, and cited above, pp. 528–29.

a transition stage to the complete victory of finance capital. This course can be justified—in words only—by the desire at all costs to preserve revolutionary force and the Soviet state within the confines of Great Russia for the international revolution. If this is done, all energies will have to be directed toward consolidating and developing the forces of production and toward an "organic reconstruction" that will lead to a refusal to continue the destruction of capitalistic relationships in production and will be accompanied by a partial restoration of the latter.

11. The following is the economic and political program which may possibly be anticipated if the above course, which in part has already been recommended by certain representatives of the Right Wing of the party, is consistently realized.

In foreign policy the aggressive tactics for the unmasking of imperialism would be succeeded by the diplomatic maneuvering of the Russian Government with imperialist powers. The Soviet Republic not only would make trade agreements with them, but also would form more organic connections, economic and political, and would solicit military and political support (by inviting military instructors, by contracting loans with the permission of internal control, by joint political action, etc.).

The economic policy of such a course would aim to form agreements with capitalist business men, both native and foreign, as well as with the "solid" groups in the village ("co-operators"). The denationalization of banks, even though in a concealed form, would logically be bound up with such agreements. Such denationalization could be effected through the formation of special (semi-private and semi-state) banks for separate branches of industry (the by-laws for the flour-mill banks have already been approved), by giving to the so-called "co-operative" bank rights of extraterritoriality, by refusing to adopt the system of centralized public accounting, and by establishing a capitalistic system of credit, partially controlled by the state.

Instead of leading from partial nationalization to complete socialization of large-scale industry, agreements with "captains of industry" would lead to the formation of large trusts controlled by the latter and embracing all basic branches of industry. The trusts, to be sure, would be given the appearance of government undertakings. Such a system of organizing production would provide a social basis for evolution toward state capitalism and would be but a transition to it.

The policy of organizing the management of [industrial] enterprises on a centralized and semi-bureaucratic basis and of permitting capitalists to participate widely in that management would naturally be bound up with the labor policy, which would aim to introduce among workers discipline under the guise of "self-discipline," labor duty for workers (such a project had already been proposed by the Right-Wing Bolsheviks), a piecework system of wages, longer hours of labor, etc.

Government would have to become more bureaucratic and centralized, and individual commissars more dominant. Local Soviets would have to be deprived of their independence and the type of "commune-state" governed from below would have to be abandoned. Numerous facts go to indicate that there is already a definite tendency in this direction (the decree relating to the management of railroads, the papers of Latsis, etc.).

In the domain of military policy a tendency toward the re-establishment of military duty on an all-national scale (including the bourgeoisie) would assert itself; this tendency is already manifesting itself (appeals of Trotsky and Podvoisky). . . . .

12. The course described above, when considered as a whole, as well as the spirit prompting its adoption, appears extremely dangerous to the cause of the Russian and the international proletariat. It would perpetrate the attempt initiated by the Brest peace to separate the "Great Russian" Soviet Republic from the All-Russian and international revolutionary movement and to confine it to the limits of a national state with a transitional economic and petty-bourgeois political order.

In foreign affairs, considering the weakness of Soviet diplomacy and Soviet influence in the arena of the international imperialist struggle, this course would subordinate the Soviet Republic to imperialist connections and sever all ties with the revolutionary proletariat of all countries. Thus the international revolutionary significance of the Soviet power and the Russian Revolution would be greatly diminished.

Within the country it would increase the economic and political influence of the Russian and international bourgeoisie and thus strengthen both the forces of counter-revolution and those groups of the intelligentsia that sabotaged the Soviet Government. In view of the decline of the world productive forces, concessions to the bourgeoisie must fail to produce a rapid improvement in the national economy conducted according to capitalistic forms. At the same time these [concessions] would preclude the possibility of a more economical and better-planned utilization of the remaining means of production feasible only under a system of thoroughgoing socialization.

The introduction of labor discipline in connection with the restoration of capitalist leadership in production could not materially increase the output of labor, but it would diminish the class initiative, the activity and the organization of the proletariat. . . . . To put that system into effect . . . . the Communist Party would have to lean for support on the small bourgeoisie against the workers and would thereby ruin itself as the party of the proletariat. . . . .

Attempts to re-establish universal military service, in so far as they are not condemned to failure, would lead in the end to the arming of the petty-bourgeois and bourgeois counter-revolutionists. This is especially clear with regard to the re-establishment of the officer corps of the old régime. . . . .

The line of policy described above is bound to increase the influence of foreign and domestic counter-revolutionary forces in Russia, to shatter the revolutionary might of the working class and, by tearing apart the Russian and the international revolutions, to contribute to the ruin of both.

13. The proletarian communists find it necessary to pursue a different line of policy. They repudiate the policy which urges the safeguarding of the Soviet oasis in the north of Russia by making concessions which tend to transform [that oasis] into a petty-bourgeois state. They reject the call to "organic internal work" [a call] which is fortified by the consideration that "the critical period" of civil war has come to an end.

The critical period of civil war is past only in the sense that no longer is there objective necessity for applying everywhere extreme physical methods of revolutionary violence. Once the bourgeoisie is beaten and is incapable of open combat, "military" methods become mostly unnecessary. But the pungency of class opposition between the proletariat and the bourgeoisie cannot diminish. As before, the position of the proletariat in relation to the bourgeois is reduced to one of absolute negation [aiming] at the extermination of the [bourgeoisie] as a class. The termination of the critical period of civil war must not mean that [the proletariat] may bargain with the remnants of the bourgeoisie. The "organic construction" of socialism, which is undoubtedly the most urgent question of the moment, can be carried on, not by some sort of co-operation with the "propertied elements" as such, but only by the energies of the proletariat aided by qualified technicians and administrators.

The Russian workers' revolution cannot "save itself" by departing from the road of the international revolution or by avoiding an open struggle and retreating before the onset of international capital by making concessions to "native capital."

From this point of view the following [policies] appear to be necessary: a fearless foreign policy which is based on class principles, which unites international revolutionary propaganda both in word and in deed, and which aims to establish organic connection with international socialism (and not with the international bourgeoisie); a determined resistance to every interference of imperialists in the internal affairs of the Soviet Republic; a refusal to form political and military agreements which would make the Soviet Republic a tool of imperialist camps.

In international economic policy only trade bargains, loans, and securing a supply of technical aid should be allowed, care being taken that Russian capital is not subordinated to the control of foreign finance capital.

The nationalization of banks both extensively (socialization of the so-called "co-operative banks") and intensively (organization of socialized public accounting and doing away with capitalist forms of financing) must be completed. The nationalization of banks must be linked with the socialization of industrial production, and the remnants of capitalistic and feudal relationships in production which hinder its organization on a large and well-planned scale must be completely removed. The management of [industrial] enterprises should be handed over to united collegiums of workers and technical personnel and placed under the control and leadership of local Soviets of people's economy. The entire economic life should be subordinated to the organizing influence of these Soviets which are to be elected by workers, excluding the "propertied elements" but including the unions of the technical personnel and other employees of the undertakings.

[There must be] no capitulation before the bourgeois and petty-bourgeois intellectual flunkies; rather [must we seek] the complete ruination of the bourgeoisie and the final defeat of sabotage. The counter-revolutionary press and counter-revolutionary bourgeois organizations must be liquidated; labor duty for qualified specialists and the intelligentsia must be introduced; consumers' communes must be organized; the [food] consumption of the well-to-do classes must be curtailed and the remnants of their property confiscated. A war of poor peasants against the rich must be organized in the village, and large-scale communal farming must be developed. . . . .

In place of piecework wages and the lengthening of working hours, which are absurd measures in a situation where unemployment increases steadily, [we advocate] the introduction of production norms by local councils of national economy and the shortening of the working day by trade unions. . . . .

In granting wide initiative to local Soviets and in making it impossible for commissars appointed by the central government to interfere with their activity, the Soviet authority and the party of the proletariat must look for support in the class initiative of the large masses, to the development of which every effort should be directed. . . . .

15. The proletarian communists define their relation to the party majority as that of the Left Wing of the party and of the advance guard of the Russian proletariat. At the same time they claim to pre-

serve complete unity with the rest of the party provided that the policies of the majority do not create an irreparable breach within the ranks of the proletariat . . . . and do not deviate on to the ruinous path of petty-bourgeois politics. In case of such a deviation the Left Wing of the party will be forced to take up the position of a businesslike and responsible proletarian opposition.

THE NECESSITY OF ACCOUNTING AND CONTROL

[Resolution of the C.E.C., April 29, 1918][18]

4. As far as the economic aspects of socialist construction are concerned, the most urgent question is the tendency of our work in organizing a nation-wide and all-embracing system of accounting and control over the production and distribution of goods to lag considerably behind [our] work of directly expropriating the expropriators—the landlords and capitalists. This is the basic fact which defines our future policy.

As a result of this situation . . . . the struggle with the bourgeoisie enters a new phase—in other words, organization of accounting and of control become the central points in our program. It is only in this way that [our] economic victories over capitalism which have been won since November can be made permanent; and it is, likewise, only in this way that a successful ending of the struggle with the bourgeoisie, i.e., the establishment of socialism on a firm and durable basis, can be achieved.

The above fact may also explain why the Soviet Government was forced in certain cases to take a step backward or to compromise with bourgeois tendencies. An example of . . . . such deviations from the principles of the Paris Commune was the introduction of high salaries for a number of bourgeois specialists. Another example was the agreement with the bourgeois co-operatives regarding measures . . . . to be taken for drawing the entire population into these organizations.

Until the proletarian government definitely establishes a system of nation-wide accounting and control, such types of compromise are necessary. [Therefore], without concealing . . . . the shortcomings [of these new policies] we must make every possible effort to improve [state] accounting and control as the only means toward eliminating the necessity of such compromises. At the present moment these compromises are essential, since, owing to our delay in establishing a system of accounting and control, they are the only guaranty of slow but steady progress. When such accounting and control over the production and distribution of goods is fully established, the need for such compromises will disappear.

[18] *Vserossiiskii Tsentralnyi Ispolnitalnyi Komitet 4 sozyva*, pp. 16–17.

5. Among the first tasks to be performed is legislation aiming at an increase in labor discipline and productivity. Measures which have already been taken—especially by the trade unions—with this end in view must be energetically supported, strengthened, and reinforced. As examples of such measures, we can point to the introduction of piecework, the use of many of the most scientific and progressive features of the Taylor system, and the regulating of wages on the basis either of factory output or the results achieved in railway and water transportation, etc. In this connection we can also point to the organization of competition between separate industrial and consumers' communes, to the selection of organizers [of such work], and similar measures. . . . .

6. A dictatorship of the proletariat is absolutely necessary for the transition from capitalism to socialism, and our revolution has fully justified this truth. . . . .

Iron discipline and the dictatorship of the proletariat pressed to the bitter end against petty-bourgeois wavering—these are the outstanding slogans of the moment.

B. The Red Army

Although the Red Guards and some of the surviving fragments of the democratized old army gained victories over the national minorities, the Cossacks, and the officer detachments, this was due less to the efficiency of the Soviet forces than to the lack of cohesion of their opponents. Early in 1918 the Bolsheviks took steps to create a fighting force on the theory, as expressed by Trotsky, that "Revolutionary violence is the means of attaining the freedom of the toilers. From the moment of assuming power revolutionary violence assumes the form of an organized army."[19] The first attempt to build an army of volunteers was a failure. Then new methods were adopted. In March Trotsky resigned his office as Commissar of Foreign Affairs and became Commissar of War and Chairman of the Supreme War Council.[20] In line with the new policies advocated by Lenin and the party majority in economic affairs, discipline and control were to be

[19] Trotsky, *Kak vooruzhalas revoliutsiia* (*na voennoi rabote*), 3 vols., Moscow, 1923–1925, I, 13; hereafter cited as Trotsky, *K.V.R.*

[20] He says that he undertook these military responsibilities with some hesitancy and at the insistence of Lenin and Sverdlov (*My Life,* pp. 348–49).

re-established and former officers employed as specialists. These policies again added their quota to the friction within the ranks of the government.

THE DISSOLUTION OF THE OLD ARMY

[Part of a Letter from the Front, February 2, 1918][21]

In December [1917] elections of army officers took place. The attitude of the [old] officers varied. Some tried to fight "democratization" by abstaining altogether from the elections . . . . others . . . . submitted to the orders of the new power. . . . A private . . . . was elected commander of our [artillery] brigade. . . . . He understands next to nothing about problems relating to field service and very little about what concerns the everyday life of the brigade. The brigade is run by a committee . . . . in which there is not a single officer. Things are in great confusion and every battery lives as it pleases.

The divisional commander is also a private . . . . a youngster about twenty years old. . . . . In four batteries former officers were re-elected. The attitude toward officers who were not re-elected is on the whole good . . . . but many of these officers left the army under various pretexts. . . . . Out of forty-two officers only fourteen remained in our brigade. . . . . In some of the batteries not a single officer was left.

Prior to the Bolshevik overturn there were very few deserters among the artillery soldiers. During December and January, in connection with the conflicting rumors of a final conclusion of peace and of a break in the [peace] negotiations, desertion assumed enormous proportions. Very few batteries retained half of their personnel. In some only forty men remained in place of 219. . . . . On account of this "demobilization" the food situation became greatly improved . . . . though this cannot be said about the feeding of horses . . . . the situation in that respect was very alarming. . . . . About half or three-fourths of the horses either starved to death or else were given away to the inhabitants [in the neighborhood]. . . . . The soldiers are chiefly occupied with sleep, card-playing, and drinking and tediously wait . . . . for the time when it will be possible to divide the property of the battery. . . . . The bold [soldiers] insist on dividing the money belonging to the battery, [the hope of getting their share] being the only thing which keeps them at the front. . . . . One company decided to send a special delegation to Lenin to ask his permission to divide the money. . . . . The first line trenches are deserted. . . . . Our unit is completely cut off . . . . from other parts [of the army]. . . . . The news of the dissolution of the Constituent Assembly . . . .

[21] *Novaia Zhizn*, No. 24, February 14, 1918, p. 2.

was received with utter indifference. Not a single soldier joined the Red Army. . . . .

KRYLENKO CALLS THE WORKERS AND PEASANTS TO ARMS[22]

[January 11, 1918]

Comrades: . . . . Before the Russian workers and peasants stands the question of defending the conquests of the Revolution and carrying on a holy war against . . . . the bourgeoisie of Russia, Germany, England, and France. . . . . The bourgeoisie will never forgive the [Russian] people for making the revolution. . . . . The bourgeoisie is a most cruel beast. . . . . The problem is to form an army of defense. . . . . The old army is not fit for this task. We must have a new army . . . . of the workers. I call on all men to whom freedom is dear to help form such an army. . . . . Everyone who joins this Socialist, worker-peasant guard, should know that he is entering the ranks of those who are ready to fight and die for the cause. . . . . The strictest discipline will be enforced. . . . .

KRYLENKO
Supreme Commander-in-Chief

FORMATION OF THE WORKER-PEASANT RED ARMY

[Decree of the Sovnarkom, January 28, 1918][23]

I

The Soviet of People's Commissars hereby resolves to organize on the following principles a new army to be known as the *Worker-Peasant Red Army:*

1. The Worker-Peasant Army is to be made up of the more class-conscious and organized elements of the toiling masses.

2. Admission to the army is open to all Russian citizens of eighteen years and over. Admission is by recommendation of the army committees or democratic organizations, standing on the platform of the Soviet Government, party and labor organizations, or at least by two members of such organizations. . . . .

II

1. Soldiers of the Worker-Peasant Army are fully provided for by the state and receive in addition fifty rubles a month.

[22] *S.U.R.*, 1918, No. 13, pp. 202–203.

[23] *Ibid.*, No. 17, p. 259.

2. Dependents of Red Army soldiers will be provided for according to the local standards as worked out by the local organs of the Soviet Government.

III

The Supreme Commanding organ of the Worker-Peasant Army is the Soviet of People's Commissars. The direct command and administration of the army is concentrated in the Commissariat of War and its specially created All-Russian Collegium.

V. Ulianov (Lenin)
President of the Sovnarkom
N. Krylenko
Supreme Commander-in-Chief
Dybenko, Podvoisky
People's Commissars of War and Navy

THE ORGANIZATION OF THE RED ARMY

[Excerpts from an Account by Trotsky][24]

In the beginning we could not resort to conscription. We had neither political nor other machinery for drafting the recently demobilized peasants. We called for volunteers and .... although we got a number of self-sacrificing young workmen, the majority of those who enlisted were vagabonds of the worst kind. ....

The political difficulties and the problem of organization were exceedingly great. The psychological break from the decay of the old army to the formation of the new led to constant internal frictions and conflicts. ....

A real army cannot be run by elected committees and elected officers who may be dismissed at any moment by their subordinates. But the army did not even intend to fight. It was carrying on a social revolution within itself by overthrowing its bourgeois officers and forming .... Soviets of Soldiers' Deputies. These [changes] were desirable .... from the point of view of destroying the old army, but they did not create a new one. The tsarist regiments that survived the Kerensky régime broke up after November and then vanished entirely. .... [We were not going to introduce the same system of committees and elective officers]. .... The Red Army was an institution built from the top on the principle of the dictatorship of the working class, with officers selected and controlled by the Soviet Government and the Communist

[24] Trotsky, *K.V.R.*, I, 14–21.

Party. . . . . [But] the Socialist-Revolutionists of the Left wished to carry the pseudo-democratic principle to an absurdity. They demanded that each regiment should be allowed to decide for itself whether it would comply with the terms of the German armistice or would go on fighting. In this way the Socialist-Revolutionists of the Left attempted to stir up the army against its organizer, the Soviet Government.

The old officers who remained in our service were either idealists, who understood the meaning of the new epoch (they were, of course, an insignificant minority), or time-servers, men without initiative, without principles, and without even enough energy to join the Whites. A great many active counter-revolutionists . . . . also remained with us.

We had to consider these tsarist officers for reasons of their professional training. . . . . Without them we should have had to begin from the beginning, and it was not likely that our enemies would have given us the time needed to carry our self-education to the necessary level. We could not build up a centralized army . . . . without making use of the . . . . old officers; they were to come in, however, not as representatives of the old ruling class but as appointees of the new revolutionary class. It is true that many of them betrayed us and went over to the enemy . . . . but it is equally true that the backbone of their class resistance was broken. Nevertheless they were hated by the common masses and that explains one of the reasons for the spread of the partisan movement. In small . . . . detachments there was no need of qualified military leaders. While [with one hand] we crushed . . . . the resistance of the counter-revolutionary officers, [with the other] we made it possible for the loyal ones to work with the Red Army. . . . .

The institution of [military] commissars played a most important part in the formation of the commanding staff. It was made up of revolutionary workers, Communists, and, in part . . . . of Socialist-Revolutionists of the Left (up to July 1918). . . . . The commander occupied himself with purely military matters and the commissar with political-educational work. The important thing, however, was that the commissar functioned as the direct representative of the Soviet Government in the army. A commissar was not in any way to interfere with nor to do anything to lower the authority of the commander but was to strive to bring about a state of affairs that would make it impossible for the commander to use his authority against the revolution. The working class gave its best sons to this office. Hundreds and thousands of them died performing the duties of commissar and many of them rose to the rank of commander.

Military academies were organized at the very beginning. They were at first quite inadequate, reflecting as they did the general weakness of the military organization. A short course of several months did not produce commanders. . . . . But considering the fact that many in the army did not even know how to handle a rifle, these four-month short-course men [stood out and] were made . . . . officers. We invited the former non-commissioned officers of the old army to join our ranks. As you know the majority of them came from the well-to-do families of the city and village, most of them being educated sons of kulaks. Between these non-commissioned officers and their superiors (the wearers of the gold epaulets, the nobility-intelligentsia) there was always a feeling of hostility. From the former group we secured many leaders, the most brilliant of whom was Budeny. This group also gave not a few commanders to the counter-revolution. . . . .

The technical equipment of the Red Army reflected and still reflects the general economic condition of the country. During the first period of revolution we had at our disposal the vast material inherited from the imperialistic war. . . . . We had too much of one kind of material and too little of another. As a matter of fact, we did not know what we had and those who did know kept the secret to themselves. The "local governments" held on to everything that happened to be in their territory and the revolutionary partisan leaders grabbed what they could lay their hands on. Railway authorities sidetracked or misdirected ammunition trains. During the first period of the revolution the imperialistic war supplies were shamefully wasted. Quite often detachments and regiments were equipped with armored cars and aircraft while lacking cartridges and bayonets. . . . .

In the beginning both peasants and workers refused to join the army and the fighting forces of the Soviet Republic were formed of a small number of self-sacrificing proletarians. . . . . The peasant regiments, politically ignorant and militarily untrained, could not be depended upon. They surrendered without any resistance to the Whites and when lined up against the Reds went over to them. To show their complete independence some peasant groups deserted both Whites and Reds . . . . and became Green, that is to say, formed units of their own. But their lack of a common object and their political helplessness doomed their efforts to failure. . . . . The peasant masses . . . . wavered between the bourgeoisie and the proletariat but in the end joined the workers against the landholders. In backward regions such as Kursk and Voronezh . . . . thousands refused to enlist in our ranks until the White generals invaded their territory. The appearance [of these generals] brought about a change in the attitude of the population and caused the deserters of yesterday to flock to the Red Army. This social phenomenon is the principal explanation for our victories. . . . .

COMPULSORY MILITARY TRAINING

[Decree of the Central Executive Committee, April 22, 1918][25]

One of the principal aims of socialism is to free mankind from the burdens of militarism and of bloody international war, to bring about universal disarmament and to establish a fraternal co-operation of all the races on earth. But this cannot be achieved until state authority and the means of production pass from the exploiters to the workers, who will use them for the welfare of the toilers and for the formation of a communistic society,[25a] which is the only firm foundation for the solidarity of mankind.

At the present time Russia is the only country where the workers are in possession of the government. Everywhere else the imperialistic bourgeoisie is at the head of affairs, and it aims to crush the communistic revolution and to enslave all weak nations. Being surrounded by enemies on all sides the Russian Soviet Republic must have a mighty army under the protection of which the reorganization of society on a communistic basis can take place.

The Workers' and Peasants' Government has for its immediate object the bringing about of universal labor and military service. The

[25] *S.U.R.*, 1918, No. 33, pp. 419–20.

[25a] "We ask the workers to join the Red Army and say to them: 'Arm, unite, learn to shoot! . . . . Is not that a contradiction of our principles? . . . . In the past there were socialists who had different methods to achieve their aims. Instead of appealing to the oppressed 'to unite and to arm' they called on the oppressor, exploiter, and violator . . . . 'to disarm, to stop killing one another, to cease oppressing.' Naïve! It is like asking the wolf to take out his teeth. The teachings of these early socialists and communists were extremely naïve . . . . and for that reason scientific socialism speaks of them as Utopians. . . . . The mention of the name brings to mind our own great man and writer, Lev Nikolaevich Tolstoy. He worked to bring about a better order on earth and thought that he could do so by the conversion of the oppressor. Is that possible? . . . . The experience of mankind, the history of the human race, goes to disprove the politics of the Utopians and the pacifism of Tolstoy. The desire to oppress is inherited, handed down from generation to generation. . . . . The oppressor feels that the toiling masses are created for no other purpose than to make it possible for a small lordly group . . . . to dominate. . . . .

"We are trying to create a communistic society . . . . in which there will be no conflicts, because there will be no classes, no international wars, because nations will not be separated by state fences but will live together and work for a common cause. As far as the main object is concerned we see eye to eye with the Utopians, but we differ from them as to the means to be employed to attain the object. . . . . We believe in the use of force, because we cannot trust the ruling classes . . . . they will not yield an inch without a struggle. . . . . There can be no change in the social relations without a bloody war. . . . ." (From a speech, April 21, 1918, Trotsky, *K.V.R.*, I, 46–47.)

effort is opposed by the bourgeoisie, which is not willing to renounce its economic privileges. Through traitorous schemes and wicked plots with foreign imperialists it hopes to get back into power.

To arm the bourgeoisie would mean to introduce strife within the army and thereby weaken it in the fight against the external foes. The parasitic and exploiting elements of society are not willing, like others, to assume obligations and rights and cannot, therefore, be permitted to bear arms. The Workers' and Peasants' Government will find a way to make the bourgeoisie bear part of the burden of the defense of the republic which they have thrown into great adversity and distress by their criminal acts. During this approaching transitional period military training and bearing of arms will be only for the workers and those peasants who do not exploit the labor of others.

Citizens between the ages of 18 and 40, having passed the course of compulsory study, will be put on the service list. At the first call of the Workers' and Peasants' Government it will be their duty to take up arms and fill the ranks of the Red Army, which is made up of the more loyal and self-sacrificing fighters for the freedom and independence of the Russian Soviet Republic and the International Socialist revolution.

1. Military training is compulsory for citizens of the Russian Soviet Federated Republic of the following ages: (*a*) School period—lower grades as determined by the People's Commissariat of Education. (*b*) Preparatory period—ages 16 to 18. (*c*) Military service period—18 to 40. Women, if they wish, may take this course on the same terms as others.

Note: Citizens who for religious reasons are opposed to bearing arms are expected to take up the study of other phases of military life.

2. The preparatory and military service periods of training are in charge of the Commissar of War; the school period is in charge of the Commissar of Education with the close co-operation of the Commissar of War.

3. Workers in factories, shops, mills, villages, and peasants who do not exploit others are subject to military training.

4. The organization of compulsory military training in the provinces falls on the (regional, gubernia, uezd, and volost) war commissars.

5. No pay is allowed for the period of training, and the schedule of studies should be arranged so as not to interfere with regular occupation.

6. The course of training should be continuous for eight weeks and not less than twelve hours per week. . . . .

7. Persons who were formerly in the regular army may be excused from the military course after having passed successful examinations. In such cases they are given the same certificates as those who have taken the regular course.

8. Instructions should be given by qualified teachers and in accordance with the program approved by the Commissar of War.

9. Those who refuse to take the course and who are negligent in their work will be held legally responsible.

YA. SVERDLOV
Chairman of the Central Executive Committee

OATH OF THE RED WARRIOR

[Decree of the Central Executive Committee, April 22, 1918][26]

1. I, son of the toiling people, citizen of the Soviet Republic, take upon myself the name of warrior in the Worker-Peasant Army.

2. In the presence of the laboring classes of Russia and of the whole world, I bind myself to uphold honorably this title, to study conscientiously military science, and to protect as I would the apple of my eye, national and military property from destruction and depredation.

3. I bind myself to observe strictest revolutionary discipline and to carry out the orders of the commanders appointed by the authority of the Workers' and Peasants' Government.

4. I bind myself to restrain myself and to restrain my comrades from all criminal acts unworthy of a citizen of the Soviet Republic and to have ever before me the great idea of freeing the toilers of the world.

5. At the first call of the Workers' and Peasants' Government I bind myself to defend the Soviet Republic from all dangers and against all her enemies, to fight for socialism, and for the brotherhood of man. For these causes I bind myself to give my whole strength and life itself.

6. If, owing to evil influence, I fail to keep all my solemn promises, may my acts be looked upon with general contempt and may the heavy hand of the revolutionary law deal with me.

C. THE CHEKA AND THE COURTS

The Cheka during this period did not acquire the sanguinary reputation later attributed to it,[27] but it spread its net far beyond the two capitals and made considerable progress

[26] *S.U.R.*, 1918, No. 33, p. 422.

[27] M. Latsis, in *Chrezvychainaia komissiia po borbe s kontr-revoliutsiei*, p. 9, states that during the first half-year of its existence the Cheka shot twenty-two persons. S. P. Melgunov in his investigation of the Red Terror challenges this statement. He writes that on the basis of information from casual sources he compiled a list of 884 names of persons executed by the Cheka during this period. (Melgunov, *The Red Terror in Russia*, London, 1926, pp. 27–28.)

in repopulating the prisons, which had been emptied by the revolution. It was, perhaps, the most efficient agency of force and terror in the defense of the dictatorship. Its function was to enforce the restriction or outright denial of civil liberties to the opponents of the dictatorship. The "Programme of the Communists" states the party position on this issue:

"Since we have a dictatorship of workers and peasants whose aim is to crush the bourgeoisie completely and to put down any attempt of reviving the bourgeois government, it is plain that there can be no question of freedom, in the wide sense of the word, for the bourgeoisie, just as there can be no question of allowing the bourgeoisie the right of franchise nor of transforming the Soviet Government into a republican bourgeois parliament. . . . ."[28] "The party of the Communists not only allows no freedom (such as liberty of the press, speech, meetings, unions, etc.) for the bourgeois enemies of the people, but goes still further, and demands of the government to be always ready to close the bourgeois press, to break up gatherings of the enemies of the people, to forbid their lying and libeling, and sowing panic; the party must mercilessly suppress all attempts of the bourgeoisie to return to power. And this is what is meant by a dictatorship of the proletariat."[29]

The bourgeoisie did not suffer alone. Anyone—Socialist, worker, or peasant—who opposed the Communist dictatorship, was stigmatized with the usual epithets as an ally of the class enemy. "It follows," says the "Programme," "that when the socialist traitors and socialist-traitors' organs begin to serve the bourgeois too fervently, or when they cease to differ in their line of action from the Black Hundred Cadet organizers of pogroms—then they should and must be treated in the same way as their beloved teachers and benefactors."[30]

[28] *Revolutionary Radicalism*, II, 1701–1702.
[29] *Ibid.*, p. 1703.
[30] *Ibid.*, p. 1705.

Under these policies most of the non-socialist press was closed and bourgeois organizations were driven underground. Socialist and workers' periodicals and organizations opposed to the Communists continued a precarious life harassed by the Cheka and other organs of revolutionary violence.

It was inevitable that the Cheka, in the execution of its very broad mandate, should come into frequent collision with the newly organized courts which interpreted their mission also as the defense of the revolution.

THE CHEKA ORDERS THE ARREST AND SHOOTING OF COUNTER-REVOLUTIONISTS

[Order of February 22, 1918][31]

To All Soviets

.... The All-Russian Extraordinary Commission to Fight Counter-Revolution, Sabotage, and Speculation asks the [local] Soviets to proceed at once to seek out, arrest, and shoot immediately all members .... connected in one form or another with counter-revolutionary organizations .... (1) agents of enemy spies, (2) counter-revolutionary agitators, (3) speculators, (4) organizers of revolts .... against the Soviet Government, (5) those going to the Don to join the Kaledin-Kornilov band and the Polish counter-revolutionary legions, (6) buyers and sellers of arms to be used by the counter-revolutionary bourgeoisie —all these are to be shot on the spot .... when caught red-handed in the act.

THE ALL-RUSSIAN CHEKA

[Order of March 27, 1918][32]

The All-Russian Extraordinary Commission to Fight Counter-Revolution .... request all members of the House of Romanov living in Moscow to appear before the Commission at Lubianka No. 11, on March 29, 1918, for the purpose of registration.

Those who fail to appear will be declared counter-revolutionists, arrested, and handed over to the court.

ALEXANDROVICH
Chairman of the Commission

[31] *Pravda,* No. 33, February 23, 1918, p. 1.

[32] *Izvestiia,* No. 58, March 27, 1918, p. 3.

EXECUTIONS[33]

Executions continue. Not a day, not a night passes without several persons being executed. Last night a group of soldiers escorted four prisoners: V. Alexeev, A. Weis, D. Lebedev, and A. Smorchkov. Near Basseinaia Street all four were shot. The soldiers claim that the prisoners attempted to escape.

Another execution took place in the Viborg side (Petrograd). Some time ago the Viborg side Soviet arrested Likhanin for belonging to the organization, "The Black Automobile." Last night Likhanin was being transferred from the investigation commission to the house of detention. On the way he was shot "for attempting to escape."

In March 1918 the government issued a decree creating a people's circuit court having jurisdiction over all offenses not within the authority of the local courts. The judges, elected by Soviets, were subject to recall. In criminal cases the courts consisted of not more than twelve people's co-judges and two substitutes with the power to decide matters of fact, of law, and of the punishment to be inflicted. The presiding judge could only advise. Defense counsel was permitted to participate even in the preliminary investigations. The procedure was in accord with the judiciary statutes of 1864 "in so far as not repealed . . . . and not contradictory to the socialist conception of law." This statute, later repealed, virtually set up trial by jury in line with Western traditions and for this the law was later roundly denounced by Communist legal authorities.[34]

JUSTICE IN THE PROLETARIAN STATE

[Report of Professor M. A. Reisner, an Authority on Bolshevik Jurisprudence, Delivered at the First All-Russian Conference of Commissars of Justice, April 22, 1918][35]

The principle of the separation of powers, so prominent in most states, including some democratic republics, is wholly absent in the Soviet Republic. The reasons for this are as follows:

[33] *Novaia Zhizn,* No. 71, April 19, 1918, p. 3.

[34] *S.U.R.,* 1918, No. 26, pp. 401–404. Cf. J. Zelitch, *Soviet Administration of Criminal Law,* Philadelphia, 1931, pp. 18–20.

[35] *Materialy Narodnogo Komissariata Iustitsii,* 1918, No. 1, pp. 49–50.

a) The separation of powers into legislative, executive, and judicial is primarily a political matter. It corresponds to the structure of the bourgeois state where the principal task is the balancing of the main political forces, viz., the possessing classes on the one hand and the toiling masses on the other. Being by nature an inevitable compromise between exploiters and exploited, the bourgeois state has to balance and divide power. . . . . This balancing and dividing tempers the ferocity of class domination, and the arrangement is cherished by all states which exist for the purpose of continued oppression.

The separation of the judicial power . . . . has an additional advantage in that it tends to subordinate the administrative power to the judiciary in the interest of the bourgeois class, at the same time giving the character of impartiality and objectivity to what is, in fact, class justice. . . . .

b) It is well known that in order to secure the above-mentioned impartiality of the judiciary power all bourgeois states adopt a series of measures intended to secure the independence of the judges' conscience. Among such measures are non-recall, appointment for life, high salaries, etc. Even in a democratic republic, where, by virtue of popular sovereignty, concessions had to be made to the masses, we encounter, alongside the practice of electing judges, certain remnants of the past in the form of non-recall and life tenure for members of superior courts. But the principle of non-recall never guaranteed the independence of the judges and the inviolability of the judicial conscience. On the contrary, judges appointed for life had always tended to form a special caste beyond the reach of the uninitiated and separated from the needs of the people by a high impenetrable wall, thus making them narrower and more intolerant defenders of the dominant class. One can say without exaggeration that in a bourgeois society the jurists are the most determined defenders of capitalism.

c) The Russian Socialist Republic has no interest in any division or balancing of political forces, for the simple reason that it bases itself on the domination of one all-embracing force, i.e., the Russian proletariat and the peasant masses. This political force is engaged in the realization of a single end, the establishment of a socialist order, and this heroic struggle requires unity and concentration of power rather than division. Furthermore, our Republic stands in no need of hiding or camouflaging its purposes, and, in so far as it leads an active fight against counter-revolutionary forces, it comes out openly with its Revolutionary Tribunals as a weapon of revolutionary struggle. Finally, our Republic is based on the sense of justice possessed by the masses and not on the justice of the oppressors, so that the thing we need is not an artificial system of rights and laws imposed from above but a system of rights emerging from the masses. In the same way our Republic does not need a caste of trained and cunning jurists who, under the guise of the law, defend the narrow interests of a propertied minority; we need judges able to understand and interpret the sense of right inherent in the masses. We need a people's court, elective, subject to recall, and amalgamated with the Soviet Government by an identity of purpose and the revolutionary struggle. . . . .

ACCUSATIONS AGAINST THE CHEKA

[Hearing of the Petrograd Revolutionary Tribunal, April 18, 1918][36]

. . . . The Revolutionary Tribunal considered the case of the newspaper *Petrogradskoe Ekho*,[37] which had been closed and brought before the Tribunal for violating the order of the Extraordinary Commission to Fight Counter-Revolution . . . . prohibiting the publication of news relating to the activities of the Commission not released under the signature of one of the members of the presidium of the Commission. . . . .

The incriminatory article of the *Petrogradskoe Ekho* stated that Zekin, a commissar of the Extraordinary Commission to Fight Counter-Revolution . . . . , came to search the premises of Balson, a merchant. Unable to find any stock of shoes . . . . he took thirty-seven thousand rubles and several thousand Finnish marks. Balson was arrested and brought to the Commission. . . . . The article further states that Zekin —the Commissar—takes advantage of his position, makes searches, and arrests for personal gain.

Only one witness, a newspaper reporter, appeared at the court. He gave the Tribunal interesting information relating to the activities of the Commissar Zekin, and of the Extraordinary Commission. It transpired that they were looking for stocks of shoes at Balson's place and that the search warrant stated that Balson's arrest would depend on the results of the search. Zekin found no stocks of shoes at Balson's, but took the money and twelve dozen [decks?] of playing-cards. Balson was arrested . . . . but on the following day was set free by Uritsky. When Balson came again to recover the confiscated money he was received not by Uritsky but by Zoff. . . . . Zoff inquired from Balson who set him free. Balson replied that Uritsky did that. Zoff then said: "This does not satisfy me, I shall arrest you again for the simple reason that you have money . . . . while my hands are calloused. . . . ." Balson was taken to jail, where he was kept about a week and then released.

[36] *Novaia Zhizn,* No. 71, April 19, 1918, p. 3.

[37] During the period of its existence from December 1917 to May 1918 this paper was several times closed or brought before the revolutionary courts.

The thirty-seven thousand rubles he received back, but the Finnish marks and the playing-cards disappeared. . . . .

Uritsky came to the defense of Zekin. He charged *Petrogradskoe Ekho* with spreading false information about Zekin. While it is true that Zekin was placed under arrest, this was done not for abuses during arrests but because Zekin and two other commissars drank some wine which they confiscated . . . . instead of bringing that wine to the Commission as is the custom. . . . .

[The Tribunal dismissed the case.]

THE CHEKA AND THE COMMISSARIAT OF JUSTICE

[From the Minutes of the Second All-Russian Conference of Commissars of Justice, Moscow, July 2–6, 1918][38]

Comrade Lebedev said that the Extraordinary Commissions made pretentions to the administration of justice. They have their own investigating committees, existing by appointment and not by election. Those committees function side by side with the investigating committees of the Revolutionary Tribunals and spread [exercise] their activity even on such cases as drunkenness. . . . . One has to acknowledge that they tend to control all institutions of justice.

The speaker further pointed out that granting the necessity for the existence of the Extraordinary Commissions, it was nevertheless important to delimit their sphere of activity. . . . . Otherwise we shall have a state within a state, with the former tending to widen its jurisdiction more and more.

Comrade Krestinsky pointed out that the Extraordinary Commissions are under the control not of the Commissariat of Justice but of the Commissariat of the Interior. . . . . There is, there has been, and there will be friction between the Cheka and the Commissariat of Justice. And this is natural enough. The Cheka is an administrative organ and the experience of the past has amply demonstrated the inevitability of friction between institutions of justice and administrative organs. . . . . In the end one has to acknowledge that the work of the [Commissariat] of Justice is essentially of a post-revolutionary character, a kind of Red Cross work, aiming to heal the wounds. It is altogether different with the Cheka, which is called upon to fight counter-revolution. So long as the Cheka functions, the work of justice must take a secondary place, and its sphere of activity must be considerably curtailed. . . . .

Comrade Terastvatsaturov said that the question about the Extraordinary Commissions was raised not because the Commissars of Justice wish to extend their control over the former. In the provinces the ques-

[38] *Materialy Narodnogo Komissariata Iustitsii,* 1918, No. 3, pp. 13–17.

tion of the activities of the Extraordinary Commissions is a very acute one. The Commissions do everything they please. The Presidium of our Central Committee instructed me to find out what the jurisdiction of the Extraordinary Commission is. The president of our Cheka in Orel said: "I am responsible to no one; my powers are such that I can shoot anybody." . . . .

Comrade Malykhin said: "We were told here that the [Commissariat] of Justice has nothing to do with the Extraordinary Commission. Yet the two institutions touch each other at a number of points. Take the jails, for example. The Extraordinary Commission is busy in filling the jails and keeping people there indefinitely, while the Commissariat of Justice has a decree limiting the period of detention to 48 hours. The Extraordinary Commission ignores completely that decree, saying that it does not apply to it. Those who suffer come to us, the Commissars of Justice, and we are helpless to interfere; we do not know what to say." . . . .

[At the end of the debate a resolution was passed recommending that the Cheka be placed under control of the Executive Committees of the Soviets.]

Among the most active in applying the Bolshevik slogan, "Loot the looters," were the so-called anarchist clubs which had established themselves in expropriated premises in Moscow, Petrograd, and elsewhere. Some of these clubs were made up of real anarchists, others contained looters pure and simple, and still others were composed of officers who adopted the anarchist name as a camouflage for anti-Bolshevik activity. Early in April anarchists expropriated Colonel Robins' automobile. Robins went to the Cheka and Dzerzhinsky promised to recover the car but did not do so. Robins then went to Trotsky and later to Lenin. Trotsky explained that Robins would have to wait a few days for his car, as elections were then being held and the Communists did not wish to use force while the elections were in progress, since such an action would be interpreted as another evidence of Bolshevik rule by the bayonet. The elections being over, the anarchist clubs were raided on the night of April 11–12.[39]

[39] W. Hard, *Raymond Robins' Own Story,* New York [1920], pp. 76–81. Cf. Robins' testimony before the Senate Judiciary Committee given in *Bolshevik Propaganda,* pp. 822–24.

THE CHEKA AND THE ANARCHISTS

[Communiqué of the Extraordinary Commission][40]

On the night of April 11–12 the All-Russian Extraordinary Commission proceeded to disarm the bands which call themselves anarchists. This operation . . . . was continued the next day. At some places there was resistance. Particulars regarding the development and results of the operation will be given when it has been completed.

[Action against the Anarchists][41]

The Moscow Soviet authority, together with the All-Russian Extraordinary Commission to Fight Counter-Revolution, Sabotage, and Speculation, decided to disarm the criminal elements which have crowded Moscow and which have been concealing their criminal activity under the flag of anarchism.

On April 11 there was a special meeting of the Extraordinary Commission to which the representatives of several departments and of all city wards were invited. It was decided . . . . at this meeting to proceed immediately to disarm the robber bands. . . . . A detailed plan was worked out for liquidating the centers of "anarchists." . . . . Detachments of the Cheka and Soviet troops took part in the liquidation.

The . . . . regional Soviets were informed of the planned action on the evening of April 11. Certain districts were surrounded by Soviet troops and machine guns placed at definite points. On the same evening a number of arrests were made without any excesses.

At midnight . . . . the operation commenced. Armored cars were placed opposite the houses [occupied by anarchists]. The anarchists were asked to surrender their arms immediately. Five minutes were given for reflection. The majority of the [anarchists] surrendered their arms without any resistance. . . . . Serious resistance was offered by only three groups: (1) the house [called] "Anarchia" in M. Dmitrievka Street; (2) the house of Tseitlin, in Povarskaia Street; and (3) one in Donskaia Street.

[Press Comments]

The newspapers contain a great many comments on the "liquidation" of anarchists carried out with such energy by the Soviet Government. While the Soviet press . . . . justifies the resoluteness of [the Soviet] actions and the anarchist *Golos Truda* indignantly threatens "Woe to the victors," the rest of the press is simply puzzled.

"Why," asks *Narodnoe Slovo,* "was there used a method of clearing

[40] *Izvestiia,* No. 73, April 13, 1918, p. 3. [41] *Ibid.*

the town that resulted in street fighting and the employment of machine guns and artillery? Was it not possible to purge the houses that had been seized by 'anarchists' without this fighting?

"In place of conducting battles for the return of the houses seized [by the anarchists] it would have been much simpler to have prevented their seizure in the first place. For a long time [these seizures] had been tolerated. For a long time something incomprehensible has been taking place in Moscow and elsewhere. Private individuals calling themselves anarchists would come to a certain house, evict its inhabitants, settle down in it, making themselves at home and appropriating the furniture and whatever other property they found. There was no protection from such 'anarchists' anywhere to be found. What is more, 'Soviet authorities' often supplied the anarchists with permits for the seizure of certain buildings . . . . or houses."

Vpered speaks still more frankly and entitles its article on the events of the night of April 11–12, "The Fathers of Anarchy against Anarchists." [It says]: "Who was it that called upon the assistance of armed anarchists to fight the so-called counter-revolutionists and allowed [the anarchists] to arm themselves with rifles, machine guns, bombs, and even artillery, while peaceful citizens under the threat of capital punishment were deprived of every single revolver which they needed for self-defense from the bandits in the streets? Who has allowed the anarchists to seize printing offices [in order to print these appeals] inciting to pogroms and expropriations? Who was it that tacitly approved the occupation of private and public buildings by anarchists . . . . while ordinary citizens were put out of their apartments in order to provide room for the officials of the Bolshevik Government?"

Zemlia i Volia in like manner reminds [its readers] of the not distant past when in collaboration with anarchists the Bolsheviks deposed the "counter-revolutionary government" of "Kerensky" and worked toward the "solidification and deepening of the conquests of the November revolution." . . . .[42]

The fight with anarchists in Moscow is the center of public attention. *Pravda* gives an official reason for Moscow's "action":

"Since the November Revolution, which transferred complete authority to the workers and poorer peasants, the anarchists have played a double game. On the one hand, they seemed to express a readiness to support the policies of the Soviet Government; on the other hand, they tried to put a spoke in the [government's] wheel.

"The struggle with the bourgeoisie, the expropriation of the expropriators, must be carried on on a national scale; [only under condition of] proletarian centralism can the victory of socialism be made secure.

[42] *Svoboda Rossii,* No. 4, April 14, 1918, p. 1.

"Sporadic expropriations and arbitrary actions of separate groups of workers can only play into the hands of the enemies of the working class; they disorganize and demoralize the masses. . . . ."

Novaia Zhizn . . . . asks a number of rhetorical questions:

"Do they [the Bolsheviks] not demoralize by their demagogy 'the immediate socialists,' do they not encourage different adventurers, crooks, and hooligans to adopt arbitrary 'revolutionary' acts?

"Until now the Bolsheviks have made advances to their 'Left' friends, until now the Bleikhmans, the Gays, and others were welcome guests in Soviet organizations and in the Red Army. It is exactly on account of the Bolsheviks' toleration of anarchists that the latter were in a position to seize houses and to take possession of artillery and machine guns. . . . . Will not the anarchists call the people to a new November coup, this time against the Bolsheviks as traitors and betrayers of the working class, for having entered . . . . into agreement with the bourgeoisie in order to re-establish law and order and quiet? . . . ."

Delo Naroda emphasizes that "it is not anarchism but anarchy that is dangerous and it is the latter that is spreading in the country and is weakening all creative efforts toward regeneration. This anarchy is inevitable as long as the Soviet Government continues upon the course which it has adopted.

"It is not difficult, of course, with the help of bayonets, to clear the Moscow houses and to destroy by artillery the anarchist clubs. But this police measure is not sufficient to overcome the more radical evils of our life, i.e., the economic anarchy and political disorder."

Den sees in the Bolsheviks' action against anarchists an inevitable phase in the development of the Revolution: "The coalition between the proletarians of maximalist tendencies, the poorest peasants, as represented by the soldiers who have lost their previous class standing and the desperate petty-bourgeois elements in the cities, including even criminals—this coalition of Bolsheviks, Left Socialist-Revolutionists, and anarchists could last only as long as the struggle for power continued. Adventurism and anarcho-syndicalism united forces. But the moment of victory was also the moment of rupture. Now they are devouring each other. . . . ."

Burevestnik, the organ of the "federation of anarchist groups," published on the first page and in large letters a proclamation which says:

"We have come to the limit! Bolsheviks having lost their senses have betrayed the proletariat and have attacked the anarchists. They have joined the Black Hundred generals, the counter-revolutionary bourgeoisie, and have declared war on revolutionary anarchism.

"Bolsheviks wish to purchase the good will of the bourgeoisie with the heads of anarchists.

"The anarchists did not desire any clash. We considered you [Bolsheviks] as our brothers in the revolution, but you proved to be traitors. You are Cains, you have killed your brothers. You are also Judases, the betrayers. Lenin has built his November throne on our bones. Now he is resting and is arranging for 'breathing spells' on our dead bodies, the bodies of anarchists. You say anarchists are suppressed. But this is only your July 16–18.[43]

"Our November is still ahead.

"There can be no peace with the traitors of the working class. The executioners of the revolution wish to become the executioners of anarchism."[44]

D. The Attack on the Church

The moderation of the Bolsheviks toward the Orthodox Church during the first weeks of their rule came to an end in January. Various church properties were requisitioned, state support of religious institutions and offices was withdrawn, chaplains were discharged from the armies, printing presses were occupied. The Church replied with protests, appeals, excommunications, and anathemas. Throughout the country where church seizures were made conflicts occurred between the faithful and those who desecrated their shrines. On their part the Bolsheviks on February 5, 1918, decreed the separation of church and state, reaffirmed the right of freedom of conscience, and encouraged their followers to repudiate religion in all its forms.

The position of the Bolsheviks with respect to religion and the church is stated in the "Programme of the Communists":

"In nearly all capitalist countries the church is just as much a state institution as is the police; and the priest is as much a state official as is the executioner, the gendarme, or the detective. He receives a government salary for administering his poison to the masses. This is the most dangerous part of the whole affair. Were it not for this monstrously firm and strong organization of the plundering capitalist

[43] This is an allusion to the victory which the Provisional Government gained during the "July Days."

[44] *Nash Vek,* No. 73, April 14, 1918, p. 2.

state, there would be no room for a single priest. Their bankruptcy would be swift enough. But the trouble is that the bourgeois states support the whole church institution, which in return staunchly supports the bourgeois government. At the time of the Tsar the Russian priests not only deceived the masses, but even made use of the confession to find out what ideas or intentions their victims entertained toward the government; they acted as spies whilst discharging their 'sacred duties.' The government not only supported them but even persecuted, by imprisonment and exile and all other means, all so-called 'blasphemers' of the Greek Orthodox Church.

"All these considerations explain the program of the Communists with regard to their attitude to religion and to the church. Religion should be fought, if not by violence at all events by argument; the church must be separated from the state. That means that the priests may remain, but should be maintained by those who wish to accept their poison from them or by those who are interested in their existence. . . . .

"Let the believers, if they wish it, feed the holy fathers at their own expense on the fat of the land, a thing which they, the priests, greatly appreciate.

"On the other hand, freedom of thought must be guaranteed. Hence the axiom that religion is a private affair. This does not mean that we should not struggle against it by freedom of argument. It means that the state should support no church organization. As regards this question the program of the Bolshevik Communists has been carried out all over Russia. Priests of all creeds have been deprived of state subsidy. And that is the reason why they have become so furious and have twice anathematized the present government, i.e., the government of the workers, by excommunicating all workers from the church."[45]

[45] *Revolutionary Radicalism,* II, 1745–46.

REQUISITIONING OF CHURCH PROPERTY

[Order of the Commissariat of Social Welfare, January 26, 1918][46]

In view of the decision of the People's Commissar to requisition all . . . . buildings, inventories, and valuables of the Alexandro-Nevskaia Lavra[47] you are hereby ordered to surrender to the representative of the Ministry of Social Welfare all papers relating to the administration of properties and capital of the Lavra. . . . .

A. KOLLONTAI
People's Commissar

THE PATRIARCH ANATHEMATIZES THE BOLSHEVIKS

[A Pastoral Letter, February 1, 1918][48]

THE HUMBLE TIKHON,
by the Grace of God Patriarch of Moscow and of All Russia,

To all God's beloved, prelates, priests, and all faithful children of the Orthodox Russian Church.

. . . . "He might deliver us from this present evil world." . . . . (Gal. 1:4.)

The Holy Orthodox Christian Church is passing through a period of stress. The open and concealed enemies of the truth of Christ have started to persecute that truth and are aiming a mortal blow at the cause of Christ. In place of Christian love they are sowing seeds of malice, envy, and fratricidal war.

Christ's precept to love our neighbor is forgotten and trampled under foot. Every day we learn that innocent people, not excluding those lying sick in bed, are being frightfully and brutally murdered for the sole offense that they have honestly discharged their duty to the country and have devoted all their energies to serve the welfare of the

[46] A. I. Vvedensky, *Tserkov i gosudarstvo. (Ocherk vzaimootnoshenii tserkvi i gosudarstva v Rossii 1918–1922 g.)*, Moscow, 1923, p. 123.

[47] A monastery on the Neva in Petrograd founded by Peter the Great in honor of the Novgorod Prince Alexander Nevsky. The monastery contained an ecclesiastical academy, a seminary, and a valuable library and was a place of pilgrimage.

[48] A. I. Vvedensky, *Tserkov i gosudarstvo,* pp. 114–16. This letter was first read in Moscow at the All-Russian Church Sobor, February 2, 1918. It was intended that one million copies should be printed, but the printers refused to do the work. Multigraphed copies were circulated throughout Russia and read during church services.

people. These crimes are committed . . . . in broad daylight with unprecedented effrontery and outrageous brutality . . . . in almost every city of our native land. . . . .

These crimes fill our heart with deep sorrow and compel us to denounce sharply these monsters of the human race . . . . in accordance with the precept of the Holy Apostle: "Them that sin reprove in the sight of all, that the rest also may be in fear." (I Tim. 5: 20.)

Think what you are doing, you madmen! Stop your bloody reprisals. Your acts are not merely cruel, they are the works of Satan for which you will burn in Hell fire in the life hereafter and be cursed by future generations in this life.

By the authority given me by God I forbid you to partake of the Christian Mysteries. I anathematize you if you still bear a Christian name and belong by birth to the Orthodox Church.

And you, faithful children of the Orthodox Christian Church, I beseech you to have nothing to do with this scourge of the human race: "Put away the wicked man from among yourselves." (I Cor. 5: 13.)

Violent outrages are being committed against the Orthodox Christian Church. The blessed mysteries, which sanctify the birth of man or the union of husband and wife in a Christian family, are openly declared unnecessary and superfluous. Holy Churches are being destroyed by gunfire (churches of the Moscow Kremlin) or looted and desecrated (the chapel of Our Saviour in Petrograd); monasteries most revered by the faithful, such as Alexandro-Nevskaia and Pochaevskaia Lavras, have been seized by the godless rulers of darkness under the pretext that they are the people's property. Schools maintained by the Orthodox Church for the training of ministers and religious teachers have been declared useless and turned either into schools of atheism or into nurseries of immorality.

Church and monastery properties are being confiscated under the pretext that they are the property of the people, but the legitimate will of the people is never taken into consideration. And, finally, the government which promised to give Russia justice and truth and safeguard freedom and order acts everywhere and toward everyone, including the Holy Orthodox Church, with unrestrained arbitrariness and violence.

Is there no limit to this insolence . . . . ? Is there no way of stopping the aggressiveness of the enemies of the Christian Church?

I summon you, faithful and loyal children of the Church. Come to the defense of your outraged and oppressed Holy Mother! . . . . I summon you, beloved children of the Church, even if you should have to suffer for the cause of Christ, ... for the Apostle has said: "Who shall separate us from the love of Christ? Shall tribulation, or anguish, or persecution, or famine, or nakedness, or peril, or sword?" (Rom. 8: 35.)

And you, fellow prelates and priests, sound the call . . . . for the defense of . . . . the Orthodox Church, without an hour's delay. Organize unions of crusaders of the spirit . . . . who can resist external force with the zeal of the faithful, and I firmly believe that the enemies of the Church . . . . will be vanquished by the Cross of Christ, because the edifice of the Divine Crusader cannot be demolished: " . . . . I will build My Church; and the gates of Hell shall not prevail against it." (Matt. 16: 18.)

TIKHON
The Patriarch of Moscow and of All Russia

RESISTANCE TO THE SEIZURE OF CHURCH PROPERTY

[Resolution by the Church Sobor, February 4, 1918][49]

Of late reports have frequently arrived from different dioceses . . . . concerning the looting of churches and monasteries and the forcible seizures of church and monastery lands . . . . by peasants and persons styling themselves representatives of the government.

In view of the fact that all real and movable church property is common church property . . . . held by the parishes and monasteries as the inheritance from the Holy Fathers to be preserved and handed over intact to the future generation of the faithful, the Holy Sobor recommends that the Holy Synod issue the following instructions for the guidance of the . . . . parochial priests, parishioners, monasteries, and their pilgrims:

(1) Not to surrender voluntarily any belongings of the Holy Church . . . .

(2) When the demand for the surrender of church or monastery property is accompanied by threats of violence the Father Superior must refuse the demand and address the violators, calling them to reason.

(3) When the names of the plunderers and robbers of church and monastery property are known they should be sent to the Archbishop, who may excommunicate [the guilty] from the church. . . . . .

(4) If acts of sacrilege are committed by a whole village the Archbishop may order that all acts of sanctification be suspended (except baptism and the administration to the sick of the Holy Mysteries of Christ's Flesh and Blood), and the churches closed until the guilty repent . . . . and return everything they have seized.

(5) If violence is committed against a priest the measures mentioned [in 4] shall be adopted.

(6) To organize Orthodox brotherhoods in connection with

[49] A. I. Vvedensky, *Tserkov i gosudarstvo,* pp. 148–49.

churches and monasteries for the defense of church and monastery property.

(7) In their sermons the priests shall . . . . try to interpret the meaning of passing events from the Christian point of view.

A WARNING BY THE METROPOLITAN OF PETROGRAD[50]

Veniamin, Metropolitan of Petrograd, has sent the following letter to the Soviet of People's Commissars:

"In the *Delo Naroda* of January 13 and in other papers there was a statement that the Soviet of People's Commissars is considering the question of separating church and state. If such a thing were done it would bring much grief and suffering to the Orthodox Russian population.

"As soon as the inhabitants of Petrograd heard of this, they became greatly excited. This excitement may develop into elemental movements . . . . may bring on an uprising with serious consequences. No power will be in a position to control the movement.

"Of course, I am quite certain that every government in Russia is working for the good of the Russian people and would do nothing to bring grief and misery on that section of the people which forms the great majority. I feel it to be my duty, however, to warn those who are at present at the head of the government not to put into force a decree that would deprive the church of its property. The Orthodox Russian population will never permit encroachments on its holy places. We have enough miseries already without adding new ones.

"I trust that my warning will be heeded and that the rights of the Orthodox Church will not be violated.

"VENIAMIN
"Metropolitan of Petrograd and Gdov"

On this letter the President of the Soviet of People's Commissars wrote the following: "I should like it very much if the collegium of the Commissariat of Justice would hurry up the decree separating the church from the state."

SEPARATION OF CHURCH AND STATE

[Decree of the Sovnarkom, February 5, 1918][51]

1. The church is separated from the state.

2. Within the territory of the Republic the passing of any local laws or regulations limiting or interfering with freedom of conscience or

[50] *Novaia Zhizn,* No. 18, February 7, 1918, p. 4.

[51] *S.U.R.,* 1918, No. 18, pp. 272–73.

granting special rights or privileges to citizens because they belong to a certain faith is forbidden.

3. Every citizen has a right to adopt any religion or not to adopt any at all. Every legal restriction connected with the profession of certain faiths or with the non-profession of any faith is now abolished.

Note: Official acts shall make no mention of a citizen's faith.

4. State or semi-official public functions are not to be accompanied by religious ceremonies or rituals.

5. Religious performances may be carried on freely in so far as they do not disturb the public order or encroach upon the rights of citizens of the Russian Republic. Local authorities have the right to take the necessary measures to preserve order and safeguard the rights of citizens.

6. No one can decline to carry out his civic duties on the ground of his religious views. Exception to this ruling may be made by special decisions of the people's court provided one civic duty is substituted for another.

7. Religious oaths are abolished. In case of necessity a solemn promise will suffice.

8. All civil acts are performed exclusively by the civic authorities [in charge of] the department for the registration of marriages and births.

9. The school is separated from the church. The teaching of religion in state and public schools, as well as in private schools where general subjects are taught, is forbidden. Citizens may study or teach religious subjects privately.

10. Church and religious societies are subject to the same laws and regulations as private societies and unions. They do not enjoy any special privileges or subsidies from the state or from local institutions.

11. The levying of obligatory collections or imposition for the benefit of church or religious societies is forbidden. These organizations are forbidden also to coerce or punish their members.

12. Church and religious societies have no right to own property. They do not have the rights of a legal person.

13. All property in Russia now owned by churches and religious organizations is henceforth the property of the people. Buildings and objects that are needed for religious services revert to the free use of religious organizations by special arrangement with the central or local [Soviet] authorities.

ULIANOV (LENIN)
President of the Sovnarkom

PODVOISKY, ALGASOV, TRUTOVSKY, SCHLICHTER,
PROSHIAN, MENZHINSKY, SHLIAPNIKOV, PETROVSKY
People's Commissars

TO THE RUSSIAN ORTHODOX PEOPLE[52]

On February 14 the following proclamation was posted on the walls of the city [Petrograd] : . . . .

"Orthodox Christians . . . . what have we come to? The Orthodox faith is being persecuted. . . . . Some of our churches are closed . . . . others are desecrated. . . . . The holy relics are being removed. . . . . Priests are forbidden to baptize, bury, or marry people without permission of the commissar. The Winter Palace church was looted. . . . . Our printing presses are taken from us . . . . and we are no longer able to print prayer books . . . . and issue the official organ of the church. . . . .

Orthodox soldiers, Cossacks, workers, and all the Orthodox people of Russia! Raise your mighty voices in protest. . . . .

You ungodly ones, stop . . . . ! Consider well before you raise your hands against the Holy Cross! Know that no Christian soldiers will . . . . pierce the side of the Saviour. Hands off from the Holy Mother Church and the Orthodox faith! . . . . Do not arouse the anger of God. . . . . You say you are not afraid of God because you do not believe in Him. . . . . But you are terribly mistaken . . . . for the hour is not far off when the wrath of the Almighty will descend upon you.

You, soldiers and Cossacks, stand for the Orthodox faith just as your ancestors did in days of old. . . . .

CONFLICTS OVER CHURCH PROPERTY

[Seizure of the Synod's Building and Funds][53]

On February 11, a representative of the Commissariat of the Interior . . . . appeared at the building of the Synod and demanded . . . . the surrender of the building and all capital belonging to the Synod. The vice-director of the Synod . . . . objected . . . . but the representative of the Commissariat was supported by the junior clerks and messengers. The vice-director then announced that he submitted to force, led the representative of the Commissariat to the Synod treasury, and handed over forty-eight and one-half million rubles. . . . . The same day the offices of the former Minister of Religious Cults were seized.

[In Voronezh, February 6, 1918][54]

On February 6 a Bolshevik, ... accompanied by Red Guards, came to the . . . . monastery and put a seal on some of the doors. . . . . Some

[52] *Novaia Zhizn,* No. 28, February 19, 1918, p. 4.

[53] *Ibid.,* No. 23, February 13, 1918, p. 4.

[54] *Ibid.,* No. 24, February 14, 1918, p. 4.

of the women who watched him tore off the seals. . . . . A man who tried to defend the Bolshevik . . . . was slapped in the face by one of the women. He hit back and in a short time there was a free-for-all fight. . . . . Late in the evening the Bolshevik returned, and this time he barely escaped with his life. . . . . On the day following, special services were held in the churches . . . . and the city was greatly aroused. . . . . Thousands of people stood in the streets. . . . . Here and there one could hear the statement:

"They [the Bolsheviks] have done away with God." In the minds of the dark masses there is an urge to find who is to blame. . . . . Some accuse the Jews, others the Baptists. Several lynchings occurred during the day.

A young Jewish girl mounted the steps of the Smolensky Cathedral and protested against the accusation that the Jews were responsible for the desecration of the holy places. She spoke with great feeling of the great betrayal of what was best in Russia's traditions. . . . .

A seminary student asked her what her nationality was.

"I am Jewish," she replied.

The mob . . . . dragged her down and began to beat her. Mounted guards arrived in time to save her life. . . . .

[In Omsk, February 19, 1918][55]

. . . . The Alliance of Orthodox Christians [of Omsk] issued an appeal to Cossacks and soldiers urging resistance to commissars who desecrate churches. The Bishop was arrested last night. On that occasion the priests aroused the whole city with the ringing of church bells. There was shooting in which soldiers and Red Guards took part. There are some wounded. The city has been declared in a state of siege.

[In Novo-Nikolaevsk][56]

From the provinces reports come of conflicts between the Soviet authorities and the masses in consequence of the attempts to introduce the decree of the Separation of Church and State.

At Novo-Nikolaevsk there was almost bloodshed. When a number of the faithful were meeting in the church . . . . to deliberate on the decree . . . . a man walked in and, without taking off his hat, called out: "Down with the priests, the bloodsuckers! We don't need churches! . . . . " Before he had finished, the women made a rush for him, chased him out of the church. . . . .

A few minutes later an officer with a Red Guard detachment sur-

[55] *Utro Rossii,* No. 23, February 22, 1918, p. 4.

[56] *Novaia Zhizn,* No. 41, March 14, 1918, p. 4.

rounded the church. A commissar of the Soviet walked in, revolver in hand, and without removing his hat ordered that no one should leave the building, because a search would be made. . . . . "Antichrists, bandits, take off your hats," were hurled back at them. The Red Guards . . . . did not know what to do. It looked as if there would be a general fight. Just then, however, the commissar retreated. . . . .

On the same day in another church a man walked in shouting, "Pull down the ikons! Burn them!" He was killed. . . . .

E. Education

In the educational field the teachers, who for the most part favored democratic institutions and were unpaid and hungry, resented and opposed the Bolshevik policies, which encouraged the students to defy their instructors and put the management of the schools in the hands of commissars responsible to the manual workers on the school premises. Little could be accomplished in the atmosphere of conflict of the Smolny period, nor could much be achieved because of economic and other factors during the succeeding months in applying the Communist principles as stated by Bukharin:

"In order to construct life on new principles it is necessary that a man should be accustomed from childhood to honest toil. For this purpose school children should be taught all kinds of manual labor in the schools. The doors of the high schools should be open to all. The priests should be turned out of the schools; let them, if they wish to, fool the children anywhere they like but not in a government institution; schools should be secular and not religious. The organs of local government of the workers have control over the schools and should not be parsimonious where public instruction and the supply of all the requisites for successful teaching for girls and boys is concerned.

"At present in some of the villages and provincial towns, some idiotic schoolmasters aided by the 'kulaks' (or rather the 'kulaks' aided by these idiots) are carrying on a propaganda, saying that the Bolsheviks are aiming at destroying science, abolishing education, and so on. This is of course a most despicable lie. The Communist Bolsheviks have quite different intentions; they wish to liberate science from the yoke of capitalism and to make all science accessible to the laboring masses. . . . ."[57]

TEACHERS' STRIKE[58]

On December 28, the teachers of the city [of Petrograd] went on strike. . . . . The committee in charge of the strike represents more than thirty thousand teachers.

Employees of the Committee of Education, of public libraries, and of people's houses have joined the strike.

STATE PUBLISHING HOUSE

[Decree of the C.E.C., January 11, 1918][59]

Taking into consideration . . . . the widespread unemployment among printers and the book hunger in the country the library publication section of the People's Commission on education is authorized to proceed with publishing at once and on a large scale. This work is to be done with the co-operation of the following institutions and bureaus: adult education, school departments, arts and sciences, printers' union, and other organizations concerned, as well as experts especially invited by the Commission.

First of all, cheap popular editions of Russian classics should be published. Books on which the copyright has expired should be brought out in new editions. The writings of all authors which in this way cease to be private property . . . . should in each case be declared by the State Commission on Education a state monopoly for a period of not more than five years. The Commission is to use this right especially in relation to great works of literature, which, according to the present decree, are made the property of the people. These works are to be published in two series: As a complete scientific edition which should be handed over for editing to the section of Russian language and literature of the Academy of Sciences (after that institution has been democratized to correspond with the new form of government and social order of Russia) and as an abridged, compact, one-volume edition of selected works. In making the selections the editor should have in mind, among

[57] "Programme of the Communists (Bolsheviks)," in *Revolutionary Radicalism,* II, 1747–48.

[58] *Delo Naroda,* No. 235, December 30, 1917, p. 4.

[59] *S.D.,* pp. 243–44.

other things, the degree of appeal which a book has to the toiling people for whom the popular editions are issued. Each collection and each single volume should have an introduction by a competent critic or historian of literature, etc. There should be created a special editorial collegium of representatives of educational, literary, and learned societies, as well as of especially invited experts and representatives of labor organizations. The editors chosen by the collegium must submit their plans and editorial notes to this body for approval.

Popular editions of classics should be sold at cost or, if finances permit, below cost or free through the libraries that serve the toiling democracy.

The state publishing house should bring out textbooks in large numbers. The revision and correction of old texts and the compilation of new ones shall rest with a special commission on texts, including representatives of educational, learned, and democratic organizations and especially invited experts. The state publishing house may subsidize publications, such as periodicals and books, undertaken by societies and individuals and recognized as being generally useful, provided that if such publications are profitable the state will be compensated first of all.

In order to proceed at once with this important public work the Soviet of People's Commissars proposes to place a million and a half rubles to the credit of the State Commission on Education.

All printing orders will be distributed in accordance with the decision of the printers' union. . . . .

A. V. Lunacharsky
People's Commissar [of Education]

SELF-DETERMINATION FOR STUDENTS

[Announcement of the Commissariat of Education][60]

Quite a number of anonymous letters have been arriving at the Division of High Schools [of the Commissariat of Education] . . . . containing complaints by high-school students against the inhuman treatment they receive at the hands of teachers and school authorities. . . .

In its desire to defend the rights and interests of student youth the People's Commissariat of Education . . . . urges the students to cast aside their fear and come out openly and courageously in defense of their interests. The students need not fear punishment from their [school] "authorities"; they [the students] should remember that the Worker-Peasants' Government is always ready to come to their defense against any oppression. . . . .

[60] *Izvestiia,* No. 9, January 26, 1918, p. 4.

The [Commissariat] calls the attention of the students to the Union of Teacher-Internationalists and also to the Union of Socialist Student Youth [as organizations] around which students should rally in defense of their needs and demands.

PROBLEMS OF SCHOOL MANAGEMENT

The Provisional Government did nothing to reconstruct the schools. . . . . The "New Government" . . . . has attempted to democratize the schools, and so far the result has been rather chaotic. . . . . For example, the old institution of rectors and directors is dead and the administration of higher schools has been handed over to commissars who are either elected or appointed by the employees [of the schools] without the participation of faculty or students, as was the case in the Petrograd Polytechnic Institute. . . . . The higher schools are becoming a battleground between faculty and students on the one side and employees on the other. . . . .[61]

According to the regulations of the Women's Polytechnic School the decisions of the pedagogic council have to be confirmed by the council of porters, doorkeepers, and messengers. A few days ago the pedagogic council voted to buy certain electrical apparatus needed for the laboratory, and when the matter came before the council of porters they voted it down. This aroused the young women students. They had a meeting and petitioned the pedagogic council to dismiss the porters and others . . . . whose manual work they offered to do. The pedagogic council agreed and told the porters to give up their positions, offering to pay them their salaries for the next three months. The latter complained to Lunacharsky. He replied that . . . . he could do nothing.[62]

INSTITUTIONS OF LEARNING ARE PLACED UNDER JURISDICTION OF THE PEOPLE'S COMMISSARIAT OF EDUCATION

[Decree of the Commissariat of Education, February 23, 1918][63]

In order to reorganize education in Russia . . . . on the basis of the principles of the new pedagogy and socialism, all institutions of learning, ... general and special, under different ministries are transferred with all their buildings and resources . . . . to the Commissariat of Education.

[61] *Novaia Zhizn,* No. 21, February 10, 1918, p. 1.

[62] *Ibid.,* p. 2.

[63] *S.U.R.,* 1918, No. 28, p. 353.

For the purpose of carrying out this decree an inter-departmental committee will be formed, including representatives of the People's Commissariat of Education and the different ministries in charge of such schools.

A. V. LUNACHARSKY
People's Commissar of Education

ELECTION OF TEACHERS AND OFFICERS OF SCHOOL ADMINISTRATION

[Resolution of the State Commission on Education, February 27, 1918][64]

1. In view of the fact that we recognize the principle of school autonomy and believe that only schools in which the teaching personnel enjoys the confidence of the democracy can properly use the principle of autonomy, the State Commission on Education hereby advises all Soviets of Public Education to organize elections within the next few months, by the end of July 1918 at the latest.

At these elections persons would be chosen to fill all teaching and administrative positions. . . . .

Note: The principles of school autonomy will be published later.

2. All those wishing to take the post of teacher, educator, or school physician must send in an application to the Soviet of Public Education or . . . . to the Soviet of Workers', Soldiers', and Peasants' Deputies. . . . .

Note 2: The lack of a teacher's certificate or diploma will not be considered an absolute hindrance to the occupation of a teaching position. . . . .

A. V. LUNACHARSKY
People's Commissar of Education

EDUCATIONAL REFORMS[65]

The Commissar of Education of Vladimir issued the following order . . . . .

"With a view to doing away with barrack discipline and spirit in the schools, the following school regulations are abolished: (1) to stand for recitation; (2) to assign lessons for home work; (3) to memorize; (4) to make curtsies to teachers. The pupils also have the right to talk back to the teachers."

[64] *Sbornik dekretov i postanovlenii rabochego i krestianskogo pravitelstva po narodnomu obrazovaniiu (s 28 oktiabria 1917 g. po 7 noiabria 1918 g.)*, I, 82–83.

[65] *Novaia Zhizn,* No. 38, March 9, 1918, p. 4.

EDUCATIONAL PROBLEMS AND PROJECTS

[Excerpts from a Speech by Lunacharsky at the Congress of Local Commissars of Education, April 10, 1918][66]

The Congress of Gubernia and Uezd Commissars of Education opened yesterday. . . . . After the report of the organization committee, A. V. Lunacharsky, Commissar of Education, spoke. . . . . He indicated the conditions under which the Commissariat of Education had had to work since the November Revolution, when the intelligentsia adopted a policy of sabotage. He said, however, that in spite of that, a good deal had been accomplished during that time. . . . . Lunacharsky thinks that the time has arrived when the whole system of education has to be reorganized and that this can be accomplished without the elements which deserted the people. The greatest difficulty arising out of the financial crisis has been overcome. The Soviet of People's Commissars has approved the [education] budget of 1,200,000,000 rubles.

In the first place, the elementary schools will be reorganized. . . . . Education must be conducted in the spirit of socialist citizenship. . . . . The high school . . . . as we understand it, is [at present] a nursery of counter-revolution. Even the more liberal elements are infected with the spirit of the reactionary Black Hundred. The majority of our high-school teachers are conformists . . . . and are utterly useless to us. First of all, the proper high-school teachers must be selected. . . . .

Passing on to the universities, A. V. Lunacharsky said . . . . that in their present state . . . . they are of no value whatever, being nothing but "diploma factories." Professors were selected for the sole purpose of educating bureaucrats to support the Romanov dynasty. . . . . The university should be an institution of learning where every member of the toiling class, irrespective of his previous training, can acquire knowledge. For special sciences special schools should be established. University lectures should deal with the general theory of the sciences and everybody should have a right to attend these lectures as he does a museum. . . . .

[Session of April 11, 1918][67]

Representatives of Vladimir, Kaluga, Riazan, Orel, Kostroma, and other gubernias reported on the [school] situation in the provinces. They painted a dark picture of the condition of the schools, especially the lower schools. The local schools have lost all contact with the center [of administration]. . . . . The schools are suffering from the financial

[66] *Svoboda Rossii,* No. 1, April 11, 1918, p. 3.

[67] *Ibid.,* No. 2, April 12, 1918, p. 4.

crisis. Teachers have not been paid for three months. Teachers' salaries have been raised to 150 rubles, but the increase was only on paper, since the teachers will receive nothing. . . . . This causes frequent conflicts between teachers and the Soviet authorities. High-school teachers have, up to now, refused to make peace with the Bolsheviks. . . . .

F. Financial Policies

On February 10 the Soviet Government annulled all state loans, thus putting into effect a measure which had been discussed for several weeks. The Entente Powers particularly resented this repudiation, since their governments and citizens were heavy creditors of Russia. Their resentment was not mitigated by the fact that the subsequently signed supplementary agreement to the Brest Treaty protected the Germans from losses of this kind. During the same month the Soviets made another thrust against the "principal economic fortresses of capitalism" by the confiscation on February 8 of the capital assets of private banks. Under the "breathing-spell" policy the bank policies of the government were relaxed somewhat, without, however, accomplishing any noticeable amelioration of the crisis in finance.

The fiscal problems of the government as a result of the "loot the looters" policy are gloomily described by Gukovsky in the quotation given below. The only productive sources of revenue were the printing press and expropriations, and the more these were used the less they produced. According to the Communist program the time was coming when taxation would become obsolete, money would become unnecessary, and finance would become extinct: "Society is being transformed into one huge labor organization or company to produce and distribute what is already produced without the agency of gold coinage or paper money. The end of the power of money is imminent."[68] In the meantime the government needed money very badly, and there appeared to be only one way to get it. "In the time of revolution," says the Communist "Programme," "the imposition of contributions on

[68] *Revolutionary Radicalism,* II, 1738.

the bourgeoisie is justifiable. It is certainly not at all advisable for one local Soviet to tax the bourgeoisie according to one system, whilst the other does so in accordance with another system, and a third according to a third. This would be as bad as if there were varying forms of levying taxes in a given locality.

"We must strive toward a uniform system of taxation, suitable for the whole Soviet Republic. But if in the meantime we have not been able to build up such machinery, contributions are admissible. There is a Russian proverb which says: 'When you can't get fish, a lobster will do.' We must bear in mind that the duty of the party and of the Soviets as well as that of the working class and the poorest peasantry consists in uniting and centralizing, on one definite plan, the collection of taxes, thereby systematically driving the bourgeoisie out of their economic stronghold."[69]

CONFISCATION OF CAPITAL STOCK OF PRIVATE BANKS

[Decree of the Sovnarkom, February 8, 1918][70]

1. Capital stocks which belonged to private banks are hereby transferred without reserve to the State Bank of the Russian Republic.
2. All bank shares are annulled and all payment of dividends is absolutely discontinued.
3. Present holders of bank shares are to deliver these shares to the local branches of the State Bank.
4. Owners of bank shares who do not have their shares on hand are to submit . . . . memoranda indicating the exact place where these shares may be found.
5. Owners of bank shares who fail to deliver their shares or to submit memoranda within two weeks from the day of publication of this decree will have all their property confiscated.
6. All transactions and transfers of bank shares are absolutely forbidden. Those guilty of such acts will be punished by three years imprisonment.

V. Ulianov (Lenin)
President of the Sovnarkom

[69] *Ibid.*, II, 1736.

[70] *S.U.R.*, 1918, No. 19, pp. 286–87.

ANNULMENT OF STATE LOANS

[Decree of the Central Executive Committee, February 10, 1918][71]

1. All state loans made by the governments of the Russian landowners and bourgeoisie . . . . are hereby annulled (abolished) as from December 1917. The December coupons of these loans are not subject to payment.

2. Guaranties given by the said governments on loans made by different enterprises and institutions are likewise annulled.

3. All foreign loans without exception are unconditionally annulled.

4. Short term notes and State Treasury bonds retain their value. Interest on them will not be paid, but the bonds themselves are to circulate as legal tender.

5. Citizens of small means who hold certificates of not more than 10,000 rubles (nominal value) of annulled internal state loans are to receive in exchange certificates of the new loan of the Russian Socialist Federated Soviet Republic up to but not exceeding 10,000 rubles. There will be a special announcement of the terms of the loan.

6. Deposits made in the state savings banks and interest on them are not disturbed. All bonds of the annulled loans belonging to savings banks are transferred to the debit books of the Russian Federated Soviet Republic.

7. Co-operatives, municipalities, and other democratic and public service institutions which own bonds of the annulled loans will be indemnified in accordance with the rules to be determined by the Supreme Council of National Economy in co-operation with representatives of the above institutions, provided it can be proved that the bonds were acquired prior to the publication of the present decree.

Note: Local organs of the Supreme Council of National Economy shall determine whether the institutions presenting a claim are of a democratic or public service character.

8. The general liquidation of the state loans is in the hands of the Supreme Council of National Economy.

9. All detailed matters of liquidation are handled by the State Bank, which is to proceed at once to register all state bonds in the hands of different owners and other interest-bearing securities, irrespective of whether or not they are subject to annulment.

10. The local Soviets of Workers', Soldiers', and Peasants' Deputies, in agreement with the local councils of national economy, are to form commissions to determine what citizens fall within the category of [those having] small means.

[71] *S.D.*, p. 875.

The commissions have the right to annul completely unearned savings, even if the sum does not exceed 5,000 rubles.

YA. SVERDLOV
Chairman of the All-Russian Central
Executive Committee[72]

A draft of a decree annulling state loans had been published early in December, and a decree was officially adopted by the Sovnarkom on January 14, 1918. It was not acted upon, however, by the C.E.C. until February 3 and was published some days later.[73] Raymond Robins states that when he learned that this decree was under consideration he went to Trotsky and urged that it be withheld because of the effect it would have on the efforts then being made to work out some form of co-operation of the Allies and the Soviets against Germany. Colonel Robins attributes the delay in issuing the decree to his intervention.[74]

The Allied and neutral diplomats in Petrograd immediately issued the following notification signed by the United States, Japan, France, Spain, Italy, England, Sweden, Switzerland, Holland, Norway, Belgium, Persia, Denmark, Siam,

[72] "According to official data the general state indebtedness . . . . at the close of 1917 was sixty billion rubles. A considerable portion of that debt was in the form of short term treasury notes. . . . . Of the sixty billion rubles about one-fourth were foreign loans, distributed as follows (in million rubles):

England	7,500
France	5,500
Germany	1,250
Holland	750
U.S.A.	500
Japan	200
Switzerland	200
Italy	100
Total	16,000

(From an article by Bronsky in *Pravda,* No. 28, February 17, 1918, p. 1.) Pasvolsky and Moulton place the foreign indebtedness at 13,823 millions of rubles and give the following figures as to the distribution of the debt by countries: pre-war government debt, France 80 per cent, Great Britain 14 per cent; industrial securities, France 32 per cent, Great Britain 25 per cent, Germany 16 per cent, Belgium 15 per cent, United States 6 per cent; war debt, Great Britain 70 per cent, France 19 per cent, United States 7 per cent. (*Russian Debts and Russian Reconstruction,* New York, 1924, pp. 20–22.)

[73] *U.S. Foreign Relations, 1918, Russia,* III, 29–33.

[74] *Bolshevik Propaganda,* p. 812.

China, Serbia, Portugal, Brazil, Argentina, and Greece. The Inter-Allied Council on War Purchases and Finance also adopted a resolution that the obligations of Imperial Russia could not be repudiated by any succeeding authority "without shaking the very foundations of the law of nations."[75] *Pravda* retorted with the declaration that the decree would be a blow to the Entente Powers no less severe than the German victories on the Western front and that as soon as the French people discovered how they had been deceived into buying tsarist bonds the hour of punishment for the Clemenceaus and the Poincarés would sound.[76]

PROTEST OF FOREIGN DIPLOMATS[77]

The Diplomatic Corps addressed the following note to the Soviet of People's Commissars:

All Allied and neutral ambassadors and ministers accredited to Petrograd herewith inform the Commissariat of Foreign Affairs that they consider as non-existent all decrees of the Workers' and Peasants' Government regarding the repudiation of state loans, confiscation of property, etc., in so far as these decrees affect the interests of foreign subjects. At the same time the ambassadors and ministers make it known that their governments reserve the right to demand firmly, whenever they consider it necessary, that . . . . compensation be rendered for all damage and all losses which the operation of these decrees may cause to foreign states in general and to their subjects living in Russia in particular.

FISCAL DIFFICULTIES DURING THE EARLY SPRING OF 1918

[From Report of the Commissar of Finance, Gukovsky, to the Central Executive Committee, April 15, 1918][78]

The project for an estimate for 1918 cannot, as yet, be worked out; . . . . and it will scarcely be possible in the near future to have anything like a definite budget. Attempts are being made in this direction and many institutions are bringing in their estimates. I have before me a

[75] *U.S. Foreign Relations, 1918, Russia,* III, 33–34.

[76] *Pravda,* No. 28, February 17, 1918, p. 1.

[77] *Izvestiia,* No. 26, February 15, 1918, p. 3.

[78] *Protokoly zasedanii Vserossiiskogo Tsentralnogo Ispolnitelnogo Komiteta 4-go sozyva.* (*Stenograficheskii otchet*), Moscow, 1920, pp. 130–32.

list of those estimates which have been submitted to the Commissariat and which are being considered. I must tell you that these estimates are extremely discomfiting. The expenditures amount to 20,480,237,000 rubles and over; and, even then, they do not include the upkeep of all the Commissariats. . . . . We must take into consideration that the railways will require about 10,000,000,000 rubles for a half-year, and water transport will require about 1,500,000,[000] more. I do not as yet know the sum which the Commissariat of Food Supply will require, but in any case it will amount to billions of rubles. The Supreme Council of National Economy has [also] failed to submit an estimate of its running expenses.

Naturally no sources of revenue, in view of the present condition of our productive forces, will yield any such amounts. . . . . For the first half-year I estimate the receipts at 3,294,000,000 rubles. . . . . In view of the fact that . . . . loans have succeeded only with great difficulty, even before the November Revolution, it is hardly possible to hope that this huge deficit can in any way be covered by loans, especially since we have repudiated the loans we now owe. It is difficult to suppose that anyone would give us money after we had become insolvent debtors. Likewise, I fail to see such sources of income as could really reduce this deficit to any material degree. It is clear that we must [instead] look for a way of cutting down [our] expenditures. . . . .

Before the war our budget . . . . was made up [of revenues] from the drink monopoly, the railroads, ... and other indirect taxes. . . . . It is an open secret that the principal source of revenue to cover state expenditures came from agriculture. . . . . [Now, however] all our efforts to induce the peasant to give us his foodstuffs have been rather fruitless, because in exchange for his produce we offer him paper money which cannot buy anything. We have no means now of inducing the peasant to sell food to the cities. . . . . If we want to get food from the villages we have to organize the production of city goods in such a way as to make them suitable for exchange with the villages. I am sorry to say that the expenses connected with economic [industrial] organization are so high and our [state] economy so poorly organized that success in the near future seems to me highly problematical. . . . .

Our railroads . . . . are in a shocking condition. Their carrying capacity has fallen off 70 per cent and the expense of operating them has probably risen as high as 150 per cent. As an example let me quote the following figures: Before the war the cost of maintaining and operating the railroads was 11,579 rubles per verst. According to present estimates, the wages paid to railroad workers alone amount to 80,000 rubles per verst. In view of the fact that the total operating expenses of our [railroads] . . . . were equally divided between wages and other expenditures, such as fuel, oil, spare parts, etc., we must assume that the relation [between wages and total expenses] continues to hold. . . . . At any rate[79] the total expenditure must be estimated to be at least 120,000 [rubles] in place of eleven and a half thousand. . . . . I do not know from what sources this sum can be covered. It is clear, however, that the exploitation of our railroads has to be reorganized on different principles . . . . if we are to emerge from the difficult financial situation in which we find ourselves. . . . .

A similar situation exists in the factories of the large cities. Work has either stopped altogether or else goes on only part time. The productivity of the factories is very low. . . . . The Sormovo shops which used to turn out eighteen locomotives a month now produce only two. . . . . Every locomotive costs 600,000 rubles. . . . . The same situation exists in other branches of industry. . . . Masses of workers remain idle [while continuing to be on the payroll].

Our administrative machinery is in an equally sad situation. The machinery of the old régime is almost intact . . . . and its running expenses have increased. . . . . At the same time new [administrative] machinery (local Soviets, Sovnarkoms, Central Executive Committees) . . . . function . . . . and these have to be kept up from the same sources. . . . .

How large these expenses are I do not know . . . . I can only judge from the daily telegrams and letters which ask protection against "contributions" [which the local Soviets impose] to secure funds. . . . . These "contributions" reach enormous sums. . . . . At the same time the [local] Soviets ask for financial assistance [from the Central Government]. If these "contributions" continue, from what sources will the Central Government obtain its funds? . . . .

We have nationalized the banks, but we have not as yet created anything new to take the place of the old credit machinery. . . . . Before the war we had 1,600,000,000 rubles in circulation . . . . now we have about 30,000,000,000. . . . . The more [money] we issue the more we seem to need. . . . .

It seems to me that we have lost our sense of perspective owing to the ease with which we seized the power. We have formed the idea that the savings of the country were very large and that they would enable us to exist for a very long time. We adopted the line of least resistance and began to expropriate the expropriators. However, our savings are so negligible that we shall not be able to exist on them so very long. . . . . No country can exist without creating new values. . . . .

We need a clear and firm realization that we cannot go on without work. . . . .

[79] *Protokoly . . . . Tsentralnogo Ispolnitelnogo Komiteta 4-go sozyva,* pp. 112 ff.

THE FINANCIAL SITUATION AS VIEWED BY LENIN

[Speech at the Central Executive Committee, April 18, 1918][80]

For the present one thing seems to be clear, and that is that we shall not be able to solve the financial problem in the near future. . . . . It is quite obvious to me that even the best plan in the domain of finance cannot be realized at present because we have not yet organized the machinery to carry out a plan. Any attempt on our part to try any system of taxation would be defeated by the fact that separate regions are imposing their own taxes in whatever way they see fit. . . . . In this respect the Soviets, as local organs of government, are at present wholly devoid of any connection with one another . . . . and with the Central Government. . . . . I had occasion to visit Soviets which not only lack the ability to adopt the financial plan we are now trying to formulate but also are unable to assert as they should the authority which belongs to them. Very often, owing to the general situation in which we find ourselves, the Soviets make no use of their authority and are not in a position to use it, because authority is often assumed by separate groups which compete with the Soviets and which have armed force at their disposal. . . . . Let me cite an example: not very far from Moscow, in Riazan Gubernia, I witnessed the following situation: They have a Soviet there, but there is also a Military Revolutionary Committee. The Military Revolutionary Committee regards itself as independent of the Soviet and collects taxes without giving any account of them to the Soviet. The Soviet, too, has a taxation policy of its own. You can see, then, that if under these conditions we attempt to formulate a plan here [in the center] nothing will come out of it, ... because local revolutionary committees do not wish to submit to the [local] Soviets and the [local] Soviets cannot do a thing for the Central Authority. Something must be done. A new organization must be formed [to make sure] that the decrees which we issue do not remain mere decrees but are put into effect. . . . .

PAPER MONEY

[From an Article by S. Katzenellenbaum][81]

In our Socialist fatherland balance sheets of the State Bank are no longer published. . . . . Since November 5, 1917, not a single balance

[80] *Sochineniia*, XXII, 428–29.

[81] *Svoboda Rossii*, No. 7, April 19, 1918, p. 5. Katzenellenbaum was Professor of Economics at the University of Moscow. See also his book *Russian Currency and Banking 1914–1924*, London, 1925, pp. 55–60. Similar figures are given by Larin in *Izvestiia*, No. 88, May 3, 1918, p. 1.

sheet has appeared and we have no exact data as to the amount of credit notes put in circulation since the November Revolution. Of late, however, representatives of the Soviet Government are beginning . . . . to quote official figures which enable us to draw certain conclusions relating to this domain [of finance].

In an article published some time ago in *Pravda* . . . . the following figures were quoted as the average daily issue from July till December, 1917, inclusive.

July	34.5 million rubles
August	41.0 million rubles
September	63.0 million rubles
October	77.0 million rubles
November	71.5 million rubles
December	72.5 million rubles

The same article states that "the January [1918] issue was about equal to that of December, in February it was higher . . . ., while in March there was a considerable drop."

The "considerable drop" in March was apparently . . . . due to hindrances in the "productivity" of the printing press caused by the evacuation [to Moscow]. In fact the tempo of issue soon increased. It is safe to say that the monthly issue of credit notes since November 1917 has been about two and one-quarter billion rubles.[82]

According to the balance sheet of the State Bank for November 5, 1917, the Provisional Government left us an inheritance of 18,917 billion rubles in credit notes. From the end of October [1917] till the middle of April [1918] the Soviet Government added about eleven billion rubles. By that time the issues of paper money in circulation totaled thirty billion rubles. This coincides with the figures quoted by the Commissar of Finance, Gukovsky, in his speech at the Central Executive Committee on April 15. The printing of paper money has not been stopped and we are now being fed the thirty-first or thirty-second billion.

These eleven or twelve billion rubles do not exhaust the addition which the Bolsheviks contributed to the total amount of money in circulation. The Soviet Government declared the short-term treasury notes and the 100-ruble coupons of the Liberty Loan to be legal tender.[83] . . . . This substitute money amounted to four or five billion rubles. . . . . In this way the new authorities have "donated" to the people during the past five months fifteen or sixteen billion rubles, so that the total paper money in circulation is about thirty-five billion rubles. . . . .

[82] Zagorsky, *op. cit.*, p. 309, gives the average monthly issue from January 1 to April 1, 1918, as 1,513 million, and that from April 1 to May 20 as 4,474.8 million.

[83] See decree on the annulment of debts above, and the decree of the Sovnarkom, February 14, 1918, Labry, *op. cit.*, p. 273.

ALL HAIL THE PRINTING PRESS![84]

The revolutionary government of France managed to exist and to wage war thanks to the issue of paper money. The *assignats* saved the Great French Revolution. The paper money of the Soviet Republic has sustained the Soviet Government during the most difficult period when there was no possibility of paying for civil war out of direct taxation. All hail the printing press! Its days, to be sure, are numbered now, but it has accomplished three-fourths of its task. In the archives of the great proletarian revolution, along with the guns and rifles which mowed down the enemies of the proletariat, an honorary place will be occupied by the machine gun of the People's Commissariat of Finance which attacked the bourgeois régime from the rear by delivering a blow against its monetary system. In this way it utilized the bourgeois economic law of money circulation as a weapon for the destruction of the bourgeois régime.

G. The Management of Industry

Through the early weeks of 1918 the expropriation of industry went on under varied forms and names and without effective guidance or control by the central Soviet authorities. To check this anarchical procedure the Supreme Council of National Economy on February 16 issued regulations forbidding confiscation of enterprises except by the orders of the Supreme Council or the Sovnarkom. These regulations, however, appear to have had little effect.

The application of workers' control had equally disastrous effects, partly because of the tendency of the workers to use the resources of the enterprises to satisfy their own immediate needs without regard to the interests of the state. As Larin puts it: "During the first months there prevailed the slogan: 'The Ural for the Ural Workers,' 'The Volga for the Volga Workers,' and so on. . . . . Simultaneously there was a general ejection of the technical personnel from the management."[85] Another cause of the catastrophic fall of production was the cumbersomeness and incompetence of the management by workers' committees, and another was the

[84] E. Preobrazhensky, *Bumazhnye dengi v epokhu proletarskoi diktatury,* Moscow, 1920, p. 4.

[85] *Narodnoe Khoziaistvo,* 1918, No. 11, p. 22.

decline of labor productivity. Factories closed because of the inability to secure credits or raw materials, unemployment grew rapidly and was increased by the demobilization and evacuation of war industries in Petrograd. All these factors contributed to the Bolsheviks' decision to attempt to check the destructive spirit whipped up by appeals to loot the looters and to persuade the workers to take the orders of the dictatorship set up in their name. As the Communist program explained it: ". . . . There can be no question whatever of a labor discipline when the whip of the capitalist is brandished over the workman's head and the whip of the landowner over that of the peasant and the farm laborer. Things are different now. These whips have been destroyed. The working class is now working for itself."[86]

By way of bringing some kind of order out of the anarchical procedure of workers' control there were created under the Supreme Council of National Economy control bodies called *Glavki* or *Tsentry* (e.g., *Glavsakhar* for sugar; *Glavbumaga* for paper, *Tsentrochai* for tea, etc.), for the purpose of directing the administration, financing, technical consolidation, and conditions of labor of the industries concerned. By March 1918 there were fifteen of these controls.[87]

These measures, but especially the efforts to restore production by the employment of specialists, the adoption of the Taylor system, and other concessions to capitalist technique, aroused opposition not only among the workers' committees but among the Left Communists, who foresaw the destruction of the creative forces of the revolution.

NATIONALIZATION OF A PLANT UNABLE TO CONTINUE OPERATIONS

[Decree of the Supreme Council of National Economy, January 24, 1918][88]

Because of the company's inability to continue operating its plant and in view of the importance [of the latter] to the government, all

[86] *Revolutionary Radicalism,* II, 1732–33.

[87] Cf. Zagorsky, *op. cit.,* pp. 22–23, citing Larin in *Izvestiia,* No. 208, 1918.

[88] *S.D.,* pp. 270–71.

establishments of the Novorossiisk Company producing coal, iron and steel, and rails in Yuzovka are to become the property of the state.

A member of the Supreme Council of National Economy's finance council acting as commissar is to assume temporary control over the Novorossiisk Company's Petrograd office.

All clerical and technical employees are required to remain at their posts and to continue their work under the direction of a provisional committee [of control]. Those guilty of wilfully abandoning their regular duties will be handed over to the revolutionary court.

All institutions which have been doing business with the company or which have accounts with it are required to maintain such relationships by dealing with the above-mentioned . . . . commissar.

[*Signed*] For the Presidium of the Supreme Council of National Economy:
SMIRNOV, LOMOV, LARIN

NATIONALIZATION OF THE MERCHANT MARINE

[Decree of the Sovnarkom, February 8, 1918][89]

1. . . . . All navigation companies, with all their movable and immovable property, assets, and liabilities, all river and ocean freight and passenger boats owned by stock companies, partnerships, commercial houses, and large private firms are declared to be the . . . . property of the Soviet Republic.

2. The following are not taken over by the Soviet Republic: (*a*) Boats used . . . . as a means of making a living (minimum standard); boats owned by small companies, organized as labor partnerships. (*b*) Whaling and fishing boats; pilot-association vessels; boats belonging to cities and villages; boats not used for freight and passenger service, except those belonging to stock companies.

3. In co-operation with seamen's unions and branches of the All-Russian Soviet of Sailors and in agreement with the Soviet economic organizations (regional councils of national economy, economic committees, etc.), the local Soviets should take immediate steps to safeguard vessels and other property which now become the property of the Soviet Republic. . . . .

4. The institutions and organizations mentioned above are authorized to appoint temporary commissars to take charge of the offices of the steamship companies. They must see to it that the offices and agencies continue their business and that the repairing of boats does not stop. The above is to be enforced even to the point of threatening to hand over the employees to the revolutionary court. The commissars

[89] *S.U.R.*, 1918, No. 19, pp. 284–85.

who are appointed to take charge of these offices have control of all the company's money, pay the workers their wages promptly and at the old scale, appropriate money for repairs, etc.

5. More detailed instructions regarding the nationalization of shipping enterprises will be issued in a special decree.

6. This decree becomes effective by telegraph.

V. ULIANOV (LENIN)
President of the Sovnarkom

V. OBOLENSKY, V. ALGASOV, A. SHLIAPNIKOV
People's Commissars

REGULATIONS FOR THE CONFISCATION OF INDUSTRIAL ENTERPRISES

[Resolution of the Supreme Council of National Economy, February 16, 1918][90]

1. The confiscation of industrial and other enterprises is to be conducted according to a well-defined state plan of economy by: (*a*) the Supreme Council of National Economy, and (*b*) the Soviet of People's Commissars.

2. From now on no institution other than those indicated in Article 1 has a right to confiscate enterprises. Institutions that have already made confiscations should report all these to the Supreme Council of National Economy.

3. Proposals to the Soviet of People's Commissars from any department, institution, or person, suggesting that some enterprise be confiscated, must be accompanied by a statement of the Supreme Council of National Economy.

4. All questions concerning the confiscation of enterprises are to be forwarded to that bureau of the Supreme Council of National Economy which deals with the organization of production, and the decisions of the bureau are to be submitted for approval to the presidium.[91]

[90] *S.D.*, 1917–1918, p. 203.

[91] On April 27, 1918, the Supreme Council of National Economy issued the following announcement to all local Soviets and local Councils of National Economy:

"In view of the fact that the local Sovdeps and the local Councils of National Economy continue to confiscate and nationalize enterprises without the knowledge of the Supreme Council of National Economy, attention is called to the resolution of the Supreme Council of National Economy made on February 16, 1918. [Text of the resolution follows.]

"If the illegal confiscation of enterprises continues, the presidium of the Supreme Council of National Economy will not appropriate any money for the confiscated enterprises." (*Ibid.*, pp. 203–204.)

THE RESULTS OF NATIONALIZATION OF INDUSTRY (TO MAY 1918)

[From Miliutin's Report of the First All-Russian Congress of Councils of National Economy, May 21, 1918][92]

According to statistical investigations which have been conducted by one of the departments of the Supreme Council of National Economy but which have not been completed, nationalization has been brought about not only by the central government but also by regional and local Soviets. According to data received, 304 enterprises were "nationalized" or "sequestered" before May 15, 1918, and these enterprises [may be divided] among the following branches of industry:

"NATIONALIZED" AND "SEQUESTERED" ENTERPRISES UP TO MAY 15, 1918

Nos.	Branch of Industry	"Nationalized"	"Sequestered"
I.	Mining and metallurgy	90	6
II.	Manufacture of metal products	41	12
III.	Electro-technical industry	6	3
IV.	Miscellaneous mineral products	2	1
V.	Chemical products	11	6
VI.	Food products	19	18
VII.	Animal products	6	5
VIII.	Wood-working and wood-pulp production	13	7
IX.	Paper manufacturing and printing	16	2
X.	Textile manufacturing	12	10
XI.	Miscellaneous	18	..
	Total	284 [*sic*]	70

You can see from this table that nationalization chiefly affected the so-called heavy industries—namely, mining and metallurgy and metal manufacturing. In these, 50 per cent of the establishments were nationalized. If we study the problem by regions, we can state that nationalization has chiefly affected the Ural district, where 80 per cent of all mining and metallurgical enterprises were nationalized. . . . .

We are being blamed because we nationalized [only] individual establishments and because we introduced nationalization without adequate preparation. When people make such statements they forget the atmosphere of class struggle in which we were obliged to take over the administration of economic life. There is no doubt that nationalization must be planned in advance; and such planning requires preliminary work. But in the atmosphere of public strife in which we were obliged to take over the government, and carry on a political and economic

[92] V. P. Miliutin, *Istoriia ekonomicheskogo razvitiia SSSR, 1917–1927,* Moscow and Leningrad, 1929, pp. 95–96.

struggle, nationalization assumed the aspect, ... of a *punitive* measure. It often grew out of the revolutionary clashes between the capitalists and the proletariat, and, therefore, was directed toward the seizure of individual establishments rather than of separate branches of industry. . . . . [93]

HOW NATIONALIZATION WAS CARRIED OUT

[From an Account by Gurovich, an Official in the Supreme Council of National Economy in 1918][94]

There existed in theory a plan for the nationalization of production. It was supposed that those branches of production which had come under the control of a few large companies would be nationalized first of all; and that in other branches of production nationalization was to take place only after compulsory trustification and other . . . . measures leading to centralization had been introduced. In practice, however, there was no system in carrying out these measures. Everyone who wished to "nationalize" did so: local "sovnarkhozes,"[95] "ispolkoms" [executive committees], "voenrevkoms" [military revolutionary committees], [and] even the Chekas. . . . . Such action was generally prompted by some special motive in each individual case and was not due to any kind of a plan. Sometimes an "ispolkom" became angry with the factory owner, sometimes a person's fancy was caught by the supply of fuel of a certain factory, sometimes a competing [factory owner] would pay a special visit to the presidium of the "gubsovnarkhoz" [Gubernia Council of National Economy] bringing the necessary presents, and sometimes an engineer employed by the Supreme Council of National Economy would come to the conclusion that he could demonstrate his as yet unrecognized ability in a certain establishment. A nationalized [enterprise] was first swept by a wave of looting on the part of various local authorities; and it was only after a considerable interval that the Supreme Council of National Economy gained control . . . . of the enterprise, taking it over in an already completely ruined state. Some day the archives of the Supreme Council of National Economy will reveal to the historian the whole tragic story of the period of [this type] of "socialization." . . . . .

[93] T. Weinberg, of the Supreme Council of National Economy, estimated that 513 industrial enterprises were confiscated, nationalized, or sequestered up to June 15, 1918. He admits that the exact number cannot be determined but that it is probably far larger than the figure which he gives. (*Narodnoe Khoziaistvo*, No. 4, June 1918, pp. 45–56.)

[94] Gurovich, *A.R.R.*, VI (1922), 310–11.

[95] Councils of National Economy—Sovety Narodnago Khoziaistva.

ADMINISTRATION OF NATIONALIZED INDUSTRY

[Resolution of the Supreme Council of National Economy, March 3, 1918][96]

Part I

1. The central administration of nationalized enterprises of a given branch of industry is to appoint for every large nationalized enterprise [in that branch of industry] a technical and an administrative director to take complete charge and direction of the enterprise. Such directors will be responsible to the central administration and its appointed commissar.

2. The technical director is to appoint the technical personnel and issue all orders relating to the technical management of the enterprise. The shop committee will have the right to lodge complaints with the commissar of the central administration relative to the appointments and orders of the technical director, but the appointments and orders may be canceled only by the commissar or the central administration.

3. The administrative director will work in connection with an economic-administrative Soviet consisting of representatives of workers, employees, and engineers of the enterprise. The Soviet will examine the estimates, plans of work, internal regulations, complaints, material, and moral conditions of the work and life of the workers and employees and other questions relating to the life of the enterprise.

4. In questions of technical administration the Soviet will have consultative powers only, but in other questions it will have power to make decisions. . . . .

5. The decisions of the economic - administrative Soviet will be enacted by the administrative director.

6. The Soviet of the enterprise may petition the central administration to remove the director and recommend its own candidate. . . . .

10. Workers' control over nationalized enterprises will be effected through the factory-shop committees . . . . which will send in their findings to the economic-administrative Soviet. . . . .

12. In those branches of industry where no central administrative department exists all [administrative] rights will belong to the regional councils of national economy. . . . .

13. Estimates and plans of work in the nationalized enterprises must be prepared every three months. . . . .

Part II

17. The central administration (Glavnyi Komitet) of each branch of industry which had been nationalized will be attached to the Supreme

[96] *S.D.*, pp. 311–15.

Council of National Economy and will consist of representatives of workers and employees of the given industry (one-third), representatives of the general proletarian, state, political, and economic organizations, and institutions such as the Supreme Council of National Economy, the People's Commissariats, the All-Russian Council of Trade Unions, the All-Russian Council of Workers' Co-operatives, the Central Executive Committee of Soviets (one-third), and the representatives of scientific, technical, and All-Russian democratic organizations . . . . (one-third).

18. The central administration is to elect a bureau . . . . to do current business. . . . . .

19. The central administration is to organize regional and local administrations of the given branch of industry. . . . .

20. The rights and duties of every central administration (Glavnyi Komitet) will be defined in each case by the ordinance which brings it into existence, but in every case the central administration will take charge of: (*a*) the administration of the enterprises of the given branch of industry, (*b*) the financing [of these enterprises], (*c*) their technical consolidation and reform, (*d*) the conditions of labor in the given industry.

21. Every central administrative body must abide by the decisions of the Supreme Council of National Economy. . . . .

23. The central administration will have a monopoly of export and import of goods . . . . and will co-operate with the all-national organization for foreign trade. . . . .

Yu. Larin

RESTRICTIONS ON COMMERCIAL AND INDUSTRIAL ENTERPRISES

[Decree of the Commissariat of Trade, April 20, 1918][97]

Until the issue of a new law . . . . it is forbidden without the special authorization of the Commissariat of Commerce and Industry:

1. To sell, buy, lease, mortgage, transfer, wholly or in part, commercial and industrial enterprises.

2. To form or open new enterprises.

3. To combine enterprises owned by separate individuals into partnerships . . . . and stock companies.

4. To change the membership of partnerships or of stock companies.

Enterprises affected by this regulation are those which are classed (according to the payment of the principal industrial tax) as com-

[97] *S.U.R.*, 1918, No. 32, pp. 397–98.

mercial enterprises of the 1st and 2d degrees (*razriada*) and industrial enterprises of the first four degrees (*razriadov*).

Persons violating this decree are to be punished by having their enterprises closed and their property confiscated.

M. BRONSKY
Acting Commissar of Trade and Industry

NATIONALIZATION OF FOREIGN TRADE

[Decree of the Sovnarkom, April 22, 1918][98]

I

All foreign trade is to be nationalized. Contracts with foreign countries and foreign commercial houses for buying and selling all kinds of products (raw, industrial, agricultural, etc.) are to be made in the name of the Russian Republic by specially authorized organs. Aside from these organs all export and import agreements are forbidden.

Note: Regulations for the import and export of packages and travelers' baggage will be published separately.

II

The People's Commissariat of Trade and Industry is the organ in charge of nationalized foreign trade.

III

In connection with the People's Commissariat of Trade and Industry a Council of Foreign Trade is to be formed to organize exporting and importing. The Council is to be composed of representatives of the following departments, institutions, and organizations: (*a*) the departments of war, navy, agriculture, food, transportation, foreign affairs, and finance; (*b*) the central organs for the regulation and administration of the different branches of industry (central committees of the tea, sugar, textile industries, etc.) and all branches of the Supreme Council of National Economy; (*c*) the central organizations of co-operatives; (*d*) the central organizations of trade, industry, and agriculture; (*e*) the central organs of trade unions and unions of employees; and (*f*) the central organs of commercial enterprises for the export and import of important products.

Note: The People's Commissariat of Trade and Industry has the right to include in the Council of Foreign Trade representatives of other organizations not mentioned in this decree.

[98] *S.D.*, pp. 235–36.

IV

The Council of Foreign Trade will act upon the plans of foreign trade approved by the People's Commissariat of Trade and Industry.

The aims of the Council of Foreign Trade include: (*a*) keeping account of supply and demand of exports and imports; (*b*) collecting goods for export, using the respective central bureaus of the different industries (sugar center, oil center, etc.), co-operatives or agencies established for that purpose; (*c*) organization of buying abroad through state buying commissions and agencies, co-operative organizations and commercial firms; (*d*) fixing of prices on exports and imports.

V

1. The Council of Foreign Trade is to be divided into sections corresponding to each branch of industry and principal item of export and import. The chairman of each of these sections must be a representative of the People's Commissariat of Trade and Industry.

2. The chairman of the general meeting of the Council of Foreign Trade and of its presidium, which is elected at the general meeting, must be a representative of the People's Commissariat of Trade and Industry.

Note: The internal organization of the Council of Foreign Trade, the number of sections, their duties, rights, and scope of their activities will be determined later.

3. The presidium of the Council will submit the decisions of the sections to the People's Commissariat of Trade and Industry for approval.

VI

The present decree will become effective from the moment of its publication.

V. Ulianov (Lenin)
President of the Soviet of People's Commissars

Gukovsky, Bronsky, Stalin, Chicherin
People's Commissars

RESULTS OF WORKERS' CONTROL

[Statement by Arsky, a Bolshevik Economist][99]

The revolution created a chaos in the minds of certain people. The ideas of socialism were quite often . . . . interpreted in the spirit of the middle classes and the small bourgeoisie . . . . as an opportunity to

[99] *Izvestiia,* No. 58, March 27, 1918, pp. 1–2.

divide property. . . . . The peasants divide the land . . . . and agricultural implements . . . ., the soldiers divide the army supplies . . . . and now the workers carry away the machines . . . . from the factories . . . . considering these objects as their own property. . . . .

[From an Editorial in *Izvestiia*][100]

What has Workers' Control given us up to the present? We must have the courage to admit that its results are not always satisfactory. Often—it may be observed in many enterprises—in place of the former owner of the business, another proprietor came who was just as individualistic and anti-social as the previous one. The name of this new proprietor is "Control Commission." It was no accident that in the Donetz basin the metal works and the mines refused to deliver to each other coal and iron, respectively, on credit, and were selling the iron to the peasants without taking into consideration the interests of the state. And this was taking place under the banner of Workers' Control over production! In quite a number of enterprises the Control Commission asks the state for subsidies for *their* works. In other instances a number of smaller and technically backward concerns had to be nationalized at the insistence of the Control Commissions, with the result that they became a heavy charge on the national budget. . . . .

[From a Statement by A. Pinkevich][101]

Workers' control was among the slogans of the November Revolution. . . . . The future of the working class under workers' control was pictured in such rosy colors that the workers seized upon this idea as their only way of salvation.

Six months have now passed and it is possible to estimate the results of [the] control.

In the first place it should be said that the majority of workers, especially in the provinces, owing to their ignorance of market conditions, functions of the banks, etc., were quite sincere in their belief that as soon as "control" started there would come to the surface lots of money which the sabotaging entrepreneurs were supposed to be hiding away. Naturally, their expectations were not justified by the facts. A communist worker . . . . gives the following account of this search for money: "I arrived at the factory and began to exercise control. I broke open the safety vault . . . . but could take no account of the money. There was none to be found there." It is with some such naïve faith and understanding of the rôle of industrial capital that a

[100] *Ibid.*, No. 84, April 27, 1918, p. 1.

[101] *Novaia Zhizn*, No. 95, May 21, 1918, p. 1.

great number of workers undertook the "accounting and control" of Russian industry.

Let us see what . . . . results the control had.

Two general tendencies have been noticeable during this period. Either workers have shown a tendency toward "nationalization," meaning by this the taking of the enterprise into their own hands, or they have entered "into contract" with the entrepreneurs, soliciting [from the government] money, raw material . . . . for the enterprise.

Control, nationalization, and seizure [of factories] have proved in the majority of cases to be synonymous terms. Ordinarily the Control Commission begins its activity by assuming complete control of a factory or shop, as if that factory or shop belonged to the workers. It [the Control Commission] interferes with the acts of the administration, annuls its orders, and upsets the entire economic plans of the factory. . . . .

As a result of the insistent pressure of a number of factory-shop committees, many enterprises, utterly useless to the state, have been nationalized. Now these enterprises have become a heavy burden on the state budget, a fact which is fully recognized by Communists such as Holtzman. . . . . The other extreme is the alliance . . . . between the factory-shop committee and the administration. . . . .

The two extremes just noted reflect the same fundamental tendency, viz., the feeling of property which leads to the desire [on the part of the workers] to secure favors for their factories and to compete with other factories. . . . . So far we can see only one result of the workings of workers' control, and that is the disappearance of class unity among the workers and the acquisition by workers of the habits of small proprietors. Small wonder that among the most active members of the Control Commission we find mostly ex-soldiers who have become declassed, while regular workers are thrown out [of the commissions]. . . . .

Some [of the leaders] are beginning to sober up from the orgy of the November demagogy. Frequently one hears voices urging the establishment of control not only over the bourgeoisie but also over the workers. . . . . The state is now appearing in the capacity of an entrepreneur who has invested large money in business and is afraid that his "money went begging." . . . . But this must lead to failure. . . . . The masses of workers will not grasp the double policies of the state capitalists. Primitive communism is more to the taste of the workers than is the complex theory of the ingression of socialism into capitalism. . . . .

THE DECLINE IN INDUSTRIAL PRODUCTIVITY

[From a Summary by Professor Grinevetsky][102]

At the present moment industry is in a state of collapse as a result of

1. *A completely disorganized system of supplying raw materials and fuel,* caused [in turn] by the decline in their production and by the paralysis of transportation.

2. *A crisis in the labor [market]*, due to the disintegrating effects of the revolution and the class struggle; and a decline in labor productivity, due to various causes.

3. *Technological disorganization,* affecting both physical plant and administrative control, and growing more serious because of the relative weakness in technical [efficiency] of Russia's pre-revolutionary industries.

4. *The extreme instability or [even] the dying-out of the market* . . . . despite a shortage of most of the necessary articles of consumption.

5. *The catastrophic nature of demobilization,* as revealed in the violent and unexpected interruption of war-time production at a moment when no adequate preparations [had been made] for the transition to peace-time market relationships. . . .

6. *The financial collapse of industry,* due to a rise in wages and a decline in labor productivity, as well as to the complete disintegration of the distributive system, the nationalization of banking, etc.

One feature of the "breathing-spell" policy which came to nothing was an attempt to form mixed companies in which the Soviet state and Russian and foreign capitalists were to participate. During March and April, Meshchersky, a Moscow business man, negotiated with the government for the consolidation of a number of enterprises into a great metallurgical trust under state ownership with former owners participating in the management and profits. The Stakhaev Company proposed a similar arrangement for the creation of a Ural metallurgical trust, and another group of financiers and public men advanced a scheme for the formation of international trading companies—Russo-French, Russo-American, Russo-Japanese, etc.—to develop foreign trade on the

[102] V. I. Grinevetsky, *Poslevoennye perspektivy russkoi promyshlennosti,* 2d ed., Moscow, 1922, p. 31. The first edition of this work was written early in 1918.

basis of an exchange of goods.[103] About this time the Export Trade Council of the S.C.N.E. prepared a memorandum on Russian-American commercial relations in which American capital was invited to participate in the exploitation of fishing, mining, construction, and agricultural resources of Siberia and Northern Russia.[104]

These and similar projects designed to produce a kind of state capitalism as a stage of transition to socialism aroused no great enthusiasm among the business men and experts and they aroused much opposition among many Communists. A few weeks later the projects were abandoned when the civil war took on a new and more serious aspect. The "breathing spell" came to an end, a general nationalization policy was adopted, and Soviet Russia entered the period of War Communism.

ATTITUDE OF CAPITALISTS TOWARD SOVIET ECONOMIC POLICIES

[Editorial in *Novaia Zhizn*][105]

It is extraordinarily interesting to note that during the whole period from the November Revolution our industrialists abstained from adopting any political resolution. Even during the [recent] Congress of the All-Russian Union of Factory and Mine Owners . . . . the industrialists adopted a resolution only concerning workers' control, without making any reference to the [question of] government. . . . . Even the resolution on workers' control is far from being hostile. It recognizes the necessity of state control [over industry] for the duration of the war and while protesting against the seizure of enterprises under the guise of [workers'] control, it accepts workers' control in so far as the latter does not interfere with the management of the enterprise.

To be sure, the true attitude of the industrialists toward workers' control is not as simple as this, and it is obvious that from "diplomatic" consideration the industrialists prefer not to touch upon . . . . political questions.

[103] K. Leites, *Recent Economic Developments in Russia,* London, 1922, pp. 84–86; Zagorsky, *op. cit.,* p. 37.

[104] *R.A.R.,* pp. 204–12. The memorandum was sent May 14 by Lenin to Robins for presentation to the State Department and American export specialists.

[105] No. 20, February 9, 1918, p. 1.

The resolutions of local unions of industrialists are of a more pronounced character. . . . . But in so far as it is possible to judge from scattered information of the press the capitalists very seldom close their enterprises on account of workers' control. On the contrary, they let the workers find out for themselves the grave situation in which industry finds itself at present. The industrialists know too well that by themselves the workers will not be able to cope with the enormous task involved in the reconstruction of the national economy. . . . .

During the last few days two political resolutions were issued by the industrialists. The Council of Representatives of Trade and Industry issued a protest against the favored treatment of German imports, while the Moscow trade and industry organization issued an appeal [protesting] against . . . . workers' interference in the life of undertakings and against the nationalization of banks, which deprives industry of the necessary credits. These are the first open "declarations of war" against the "workers' government" on the part of organized capital. . . . .

EARLY ATTEMPTS AT CO-OPERATION BETWEEN SOVIET OFFICIALS AND RUSSIAN INDUSTRIALISTS

[V. A. Auerbach's Memoirs][106]

The Council and Board of Directors of the Union of Representatives of Metal and Iron Works . . . . had its headquarters in Petrograd . . . . but the overwhelming majority of the metal, iron, and coal works was . . . . in the south of Russia. There was every reason why the board of directors should move to Kharkov after the November coup d'état when all connections with the government were broken off and when all banks were nationalized. Kharkov was the headquarters of the workers' trade union council, of [numerous other workers' organizations], and of the government of the Krivdonbas[107] Republic . . . . which was interfering in the industrial life of the region to a far greater extent than was the Central Petrograd Government. [However, the Council did not move to Kharkov. No one believed that the Bolsheviks could maintain power for any length of time, and, therefore, the author as member of the board of directors had to make frequent visits to Kharkov.] . . . .

One day[108] early in 1918, ... a young man entered the office of our union in Kharkov and said that he was the secretary of Savelev and that the People's Commissar would like to have an interview with

[106] "Revoliutsionnoe obshchestvo no lichnym vospominaniiam," in *A.R.R.*, XVI (1925), 58–73. The narrative relates to the period of February and March, 1918.

[107] Krivoi Rog and Donetz Basin.

[108] *A.R.R.*, XVI (1925), 68.

the officials of the Union. . . . . We . . . . replied that the office of the Union was open until 11:00 A.M., and then the young man left.

Next day Savelev himself appeared and the following conversation took place:

"I beg your pardon; maybe you are busy and I am disturbing you?" he said in a low and bashful voice. . . . .

"I have come in accordance with the instruction of the Soviet of People's Commissars in the interests of heavy and especially of metal industries. . . . . I should like to get information on the conditions of the metal industry . . . . and I hope that those who for many years have taken charge of that industry will help me."

"What is your position in the Soviet of People's Commissars?"

"I am the temporary chairman of the newly organized Supreme Council of National Economy."

"Who will be the permanent chairman?"

"Most likely Lurie (Larin). . . . . "

"What are your plans? Do you intend to nationalize the industry?"

At these words Savelev began to smile.

"No, the question of nationalizing industry is a very complicated one and no decision has as yet been taken with respect to it. Before doing anything it is necessary to weigh all circumstances and to consider all difficulties. For that purpose I should like to consult with the [industrial] leaders. I understand that all directors of the metal works have arrived at Kharkov. Would it be possible to talk to them?"

The politeness and modesty with which Savelev said this made a very favorable impression and we invited him to come to the next session of the conference of the directors of the metal works.

There were eighteen metallurgical works in the south of Russia. . . . . Representatives of the coal industry also asked permission to be present [at the conference] so that when Savelev entered the conference room he found there about thirty people, most of them engineers. We were drawn to this refined man [Savelev] by a common level of mental development and of culture; our only difference with him was in understanding the nature of social organization and of the conditions of labor required for the well-being of the country and the successful working of national economy . . . . He pointed out that the existence and the development of industry was due to the skill, knowledge, energy, and labor of the directors . . . . the administrators . . . . and their technical personnel. . . . . [He said that] the question of the ownership of the works would be solved only after a careful study. Nationalization can be attempted only if the present directors of the metal works remain in their places. . . . .

Savelev's speech further implied that the question of nationalization was a purely technical one, depending largely on the relative efficiency of the state, or of private capital in financing industry. The real issue lay in the necessity of preserving the vital forces of industry; and it was to this question that he wished to have our answer.

Had this question been presented to us in March 1917 . . . . the answer would have been in the negative. But early in 1918, after the introduction of workers' control, when the real masters of the situation were not the owners but the working masses whose main endeavor was to undermine the established order, to destroy both works and production and to terrorize the administration, many of us thought that nationalization was both inevitable and welcome as a measure capable of re-establishing the equilibrium in industrial life and of removing the antagonism between the administration ("the flunkies of capitalism") and the workers. . . . . Besides, many of us thought that all this would be temporary, that the Soviet Government would not be able to manage the nationalized works, and that nationalization would merely enable industry to pass intact through the period of turmoil. . . . .

Knowing this general attitude of the directors I preferred not to answer Savelev's question directly. . . . . Instead I called his attention to the fact that nationalization would do away with freedom of initiative . . . . transform all workers from top to bottom into bureaucrats, and, what is worse, into state parasites. I pointed out that the important thing for the present was not the curtailment of the owners' profits, of which there were none, nor was it to limit the arbitrary power of the exploiters, since they have lost all power. Rather was it a question of bringing the workers back to productive labor . . . . which was necessary for the salvation of industry. . . . .

Another speaker who followed me pointed out that under existing conditions nationalization was a desirable measure from the point of view of the owners since it would save them from losses and would relieve the administration from being terrorized by workers. As for the engineers, who have given all their energies to the industry, most of them have identified themselves with the works to such an extent that they were not likely to leave them even if conditions changed. The main thing was to preserve plant equipment intact. Savelev seemed to be no more in favor of nationalization after this statement had been made. It was too clear that this mode of reasoning reflected merely the recognition of the inevitability of nationalization as a temporary measure for the period of distress.

We also called Savelev's attention to the fact that, while the People's Commissars were debating the question of the nationalization of industry, nationalization or socialization . . . . was taking place at the initiative of workers' meetings, local Soviets . . . .; furthermore, the Soviet of the Krivdonbas Republic was preparing for the general nationalization of the mines of the Donetz Basin. . . . . Savelev definitely condemned local nationalizations. He said that he had had no time to discuss with the leaders of the new republic the matter of the intentions of the Soviet of Krivdonbas Republic, but that he thought that a question of such general importance could be solved only by the central authorities. . . . .

So far as I was able to find out, the leaders of the [Krivdonbas] Republic received Savelev with utter independence and complete disregard, while the Soviet of that Republic refused to listen to him. . . . .

This[109] indecision with regard to the nationalization of industry was characteristic not of Savelev alone but of a number of other prominent leaders. Fearing that general nationalization would deprive industry of expert leadership, the Soviet Government attacked [private industry] in a sporadic fashion and offered very moderate and enticing conditions [to those establishments that were willing to submit]. The board of directors [of such establishments] was asked to work under the control of a commissar appointed for the purpose, or under a workers' control commission, or to include representatives of workers on the board. In case of refusal the board was placed under arrest, while the establishments were "sequestered" or "nationalized" (either of the terms was applied with equal consequences). . . . . A different policy directed against the industrialists consisted in the organization of trusts in which the directors were compelled to take part. . . . . All attempts in this direction, however, failed and all industries were subsequently nationalized.

The Soviet Government viewed nationalization as the compulsory alienation in the interests of the state of property rights over plants and mines. The workers, on the other hand, tended to look upon nationalization as well as upon workers' control, which preceded nationalization, as a means for personal and immediate enrichment at the expense of industrial capital. . . . .

It is remarkable that in the majority of cases the initiative in the seizure of plants came from workers who arrived from other places. Local workers very often resisted [that seizure] and a considerable period of time was needed to bring about the general expropriation of works. . . . .

The order in which [different industries] were nationalized as well as the form of management instituted after they had been nationalized varied widely with local conditions. . . . . [The process of] nationalization took on wild and chaotic aspects in the mines, where the level of

[109] *A.R.R.*, XVI (1925), 72.

the workers' mental development was very low. In a good many shops, on the other hand, it was carried out in very orderly fashion, of which the Briansk Metallurgical Company is an especially remarkable example. The Alexandrovsky plant continued under the management of its former director and mining engineer . . . . who worked in close co-operation with the workers' control commission. . . . . In the Briansk plant of the same company a coalition management of representatives of former managers, workers, and the Soviet Government was organized. . . . .

H. The Co-operatives

All the disturbing factors of the winter of 1917–18—expropriations, contributions, the lack of money and credit, transport troubles, made private trade always difficult and hazardous and often impossible. The co-operatives, although they suffered from these same troubles, were by comparison in a much better position and expanded their membership as private trade declined. Thus they came to play an increasingly necessary rôle in the chaotic system of distribution. Because of the importance of the co-operatives and because of the neutral or hostile position of the leading co-operators, it was important for the Communists to extend their control over these organizations. But it was important also not to push that control to the point of forcing the co-operators into open revolt. The compromise which is described below did not conform to the idea either of the co-operators who stood for complete autonomy or of the Communists who favored complete subordination of the co-operatives as a part of the state machine. The agreement, however, was characteristic of the general policy of the period.

THE CO-OPERATIVE MOVEMENT DURING THE FIRST MONTHS OF SOVIET RULE

[From an Article of V. Totomianz][110]

When the Bolsheviks came into power, Central Russia soon found itself isolated from other parts of the country, and the central co-oper-

[110] "The Co-operative Movement in Russia in 1918," in *Struggling Russia*, 1919, No. 26, I, 413–14. Professor Totomianz, who had been closely associated with the Russian co-operative movement, remained in Russia until October 1918.

ative organizations could only with great difficulty communicate with their branches in the Ukraine, Siberia, and other provinces of Russia.

The Industrial Department of the Central Union of Consumers' Societies, and co-operative production in general, experienced great difficulties owing to the scarcity of raw materials, as well as of labor, workmen who would work without presenting exorbitant demands being practically absent. Generally speaking, the very spirit of enterprise was lacking. However, ... the number of co-operative productive undertakings increased considerably, owing to the fact that the co-operative organizations acquired a great number of works and factories from private manufacturers.

The Moscow Narodny Bank suffered a great deal of hardship; . . . . both the head office and the numerous branches in the provinces had to exert much effort in order to prevent the nationalization of the bank. On the other hand, the bank gained considerably because the nationalization of banking left it in a position of practical monopoly as the only bank coexisting with the State Bank. The Moscow Narodny Bank drew to itself many millions of deposits from the late depositors of the nationalized banks. Similarly many unions of credit societies also gained considerably through the nationalization of banking. . . . . The Union of Credit Societies of Nizhni-Novgorod, a large co-operative banking institution of that province, acquired the premises of many branches of the nationalized banks, retaining also the services of their former staffs. . . . .

The All-Russian Union of Consumers' Societies, otherwise the "Centrosouz," during 1917 had a turnover of 200 million rubles. . . . .

Notwithstanding highly unfavorable conditions, ... the turnover of the Union for the first four months of 1918 grew to enormous figures. The turnover of the Central Office of the Union, i.e., not counting that of the branch offices, amounted to 70.5 million rubles, the largest part of this amount, about 23 million rubles, being due to the operations of the fish and grocery departments of the Union. . . . .

It is possible to give only some more or less approximate figures about the turnover of some of the largest co-operative organizations. In a paper read at a meeting of the co-operative unions and combinations of the province of Moscow, held in January 1918, the total value of the purchasing operations of the co-operative societies of the ten provinces adjoining Moscow was put at 800 million rubles. To this may be added that the total value of the sale operations of the whole of distributive co-operation in Russia is estimated by some authorities to reach 5,000 million rubles. . . . .

THE GOVERNMENT AND THE CO-OPERATIVE SOCIETIES

[An Official Statement of Negotiations, March 21–29, 1918][111]

The Supreme Council of National Economy had two conferences during the last few days with representatives of the co-operative societies.

The problem of properly adjusting the exchange of goods and of forming an adequate apparatus for that purpose occupied the attention of the Supreme Council of National Economy for some time. It was becoming apparent that the trade machinery of the consumers' co-operatives was the best available means of distributing goods among the entire population. At the same time it was equally evident that the co-operatives in their present form of organization possessed certain characteristics which made it impossible for them to function as genuine socializing agencies. It was only natural that the Soviet Government should seek to apply the socialistic policies, which they had inaugurated in every sphere of economic life, to the problem of distribution and exchange. Therefore, a conference was called on March 21, 1918, to find out whether or not it was possible to co-ordinate the activities of the co-operatives with those of the Supreme Council of National Economy.

The following points were agreed upon at this conference:

"1. Co-operative organizations will serve the interests of the entire population within a given locality. . . . .

"2. Every . . . . co-operative will serve a given locality.

"*Note:* Purely working class co-operatives may form an exception (if they so wish).

"3. Only two co-operatives may function within a given territorial unit: one for the general public and one for the working class.

"4. Members of the co-operatives will be represented on government boards of food supply (central and regional). . . . .

"5. The co-operatives will undertake the task of drawing the entire population into co-operative organizations. (There will be no payment of dividends on shares.)

"6. The carrying out of the above principles will be undertaken by the co-operatives in agreement with the government organs of food supply. . . . .

"7. . . . . The co-operatives will gradually assume the business of distributing articles of consumption among the population.

"8. In proportion as the co-operatives are supplied with commodities the attempt will be made to introduce a new wage system by which payments will be made in coupons which will entitle their holders to receive from the co-operative stores certain articles of consumption.

[111] *Narodnoe Khoziaistvo,* 1918, No. 2, pp. 12–15.

"9. Measures will be devised whereby the currency which the people receive from the state for the purchase of commodities will find its way back to the state treasury.

[*Signed*] "Khinchuk, Odnobliudov, Belousov, ...
"All-Russian Council of Workers' Co-operatives
"Miliutin, Larin
"Committee on Economic Policies of the S.C.N.E.

"March 21, 1918"

The project underwent considerable change at the Presidium of the S.C.N.E. A new conference of representatives of the co-operatives and supply organs of the S.C.N.E. was called . . . . at which Miliutin presented in the name of the S.C.N.E. the following project:

"1. Co-operative organizations will serve the interests of the entire population of a given locality. Non-members will pay an additional 5 per cent on their purchases.

"*Note:* The additional 5 per cent will go to the government.

"2. Wage-earners whose income is less than 150 rubles a month may become members of a co-operative society without paying the membership fee or acquiring a share.

"*Note:* The local Soviets will have the right to lower the above sum in accordance with the standard of living.

"3. Every co-operative . . . . must confine its business to a definite territory and will not be allowed to sell to outsiders.

"4. There will be only one co-operative within a given territory.

"5. The placing of the different co-operatives and the fixing of norms for the distribution of monopolized articles will be in the hands of the government and Soviet municipal organs of control. The co-operatives will be subject to the control of the agencies mentioned.

"6. Members of the co-operatives will be represented on government boards of food supply (central and regional). . . . .

"7. Persons hiring labor or having servants, well-to-do peasants . . . . may be on the board of directors of a co-operative society, but their number must not exceed one-third of the total membership of the board. . . . .

"8. Co-operatives which succeed in organizing the entire population within a given territory will be granted certain privileges in regard to taxes."

9. [This section is the same as point 6 of the original draft.]

10. [Same as point 8 of original draft.]

"11. The co-operatives are obliged to deposit on their current account the money which they realize in trade. Out of this money they will pay for goods on which there is a state monopoly and will pay wages to their employees."

This project caused a considerable amount of controversy, at the end of which the following declaration was made: "The representatives of the Central Union of Co-operatives, of the Union of Workers' Co-operatives, of Siberian Co-operatives, and of the food-supply organizations consider the second project of the Presidium inacceptable in view of the changes introduced in points 1, 2, 4, and 7. They consider it possible, however, by a further development of the project, to reach some general agreement. In view of this they recommend that a new conference of the Presidium of the S.C.N.E. take place in the near future. . . . .

[On March 29 a joint meeting of representatives of co-operatives, food-supply organs, and the S.C.N.E. took place to consider the relation between the co-operatives and the food-supply organizations. After a point-to-point discussion of the second project, a new draft was agreed upon which was taken as the basis for the decree on Consumers' Co-operatives of April 10.]

OBJECTIONS OF THE CO-OPERATIVES TO THE GOVERNMENT'S POLICY

[Proceedings of the Special Congress of Co-operative Societies][112]

The Second All-Russian Congress of Workers' Co-operatives took place on March 31 [1918] and continued for six days . . . .

The Congress assembled to consider chiefly the situation created by the proposed decree of the Soviet Government to establish consumers' communes. It was feared that the decree threatened to break up the co-operative societies. Furthermore, local Soviets, without waiting for the final decision of the central government . . . . have already started on a policy that tends to destroy the co-operatives.

Three points of view were brought out at the Congress: One . . . . was inclined to accept without any criticism every wish of the Soviet Government; another . . . . took an irreconcilably hostile position, maintaining that there was no way of reaching an agreement with the Soviet Government; a third view—that of compromise—strove to take the sting out of the government's project, which was directed against the consumers' co-operatives . . . . In the end, the third point of view carried the day, and after long discussion the Congress accepted the following points of a report by Khinchuk:

"1. The government's decree on consumers' communes is not acceptable to the workers' co-operatives because it tends to destroy the

[112] *Kooperativnaia Zhizn*, 1918, No. 2, pp. 24–25.

co-operative movement . . . . and to undermine the principle of co-operation: (*a*) The decree establishes only one consumers' co-operative for a given region. . . . . (*c*) It introduces the principle of compulsory membership instead of voluntary activity. . . . . (*e*) It tends to destroy local initiative by introducing a system of state grants.

"2. The government's purpose lying behind the decree could be readily accomplished by the co-operatives without the introduction of measures that oppose the principles of co-operation . . . .

"3. The consumers' co-operatives . . . . are in a position to increase the number of stores so as to serve practically the entire population . . . . thus preparing the ground for the abolition of private trade.

"4. The establishment of such new co-operative stores should be left to the discretion of the co-operative centers. Membership in a co-operative must be voluntary.

"5. Every family should be registered in a definite region where they can get their food supplies. . . . . The more specific attachment to a particular store should be left to the co-operative organizations."

THE DECREE ON CONSUMERS' CO-OPERATIVES[113]
[April 10, 1918]

1. The Consumers' Co-operatives are to serve the interests of the entire local population.

All trading houses supplying the population with articles of consumption are to be taxed by the treasury to the extent of 5 per cent of their entire turnover. Members of consumers' societies are to be exempt from that tax and are to receive a refund of 5 per cent on their yearly purchases.

2. Those without funds and wishing to join a consumers' society may do so by paying a minimum membership fee (not more than fifty kopeks). They may acquire membership shares by letting the 5 per cent refund accumulate. . . . .

3. Every region or locality is to have its separate consumers' society.

4. Only two Consumers' Co-operatives may function within any given place or territorial unit, one for the general public and one for the working class.

5. All regulations coming either from the central or from the local organs of the Soviet Government, especially those of the departments of food supply which deal with the distribution of products, etc., are applicable both to private trading concerns and to co-operative organizations.

6. Representatives of unions of consumers' societies are to take part in the work of all central and local government organs of supply, super-

[113] *S.U.R.*, 1918, No. 32, pp. 393–94.

vising private trade enterprises, and putting them under state control whenever necessary. . . . .

7. Owners or managers of private trade or industrial enterprises cannot be on the board of directors of consumers' societies.

8. Co-operatives which succeed in organizing the entire population within a given territory will be granted certain privileges in regard to taxes.

9. The carrying out of the above principles will be undertaken by the co-operatives under supervision of the government organs of food supply.

10. In proportion as the co-operatives are supplied with commodities the attempt will be made to introduce a new wage system by which payment will be made in coupons which will entitle their holders to receive from the co-operative stores certain articles of consumption. . . . .

12. The consumers' societies are to assist the Soviet Government in effecting the transfer of money belonging to private individuals and institutions to the State Bank. The consumers' societies will initiate that movement by depositing at once all their capital in the State Bank. The People's Commissariat of Finance will guarantee them complete freedom to dispose of this capital as they wish.

13. In proportion as the trade machinery and economic resources of the consumers' societies develop, these societies will be charged by the government with the business of supplying and manufacturing commodities under the supervision . . . . of the Supreme Council of National Economy.

V. Ulianov (Lenin)
President of the Soviet of People's Commissars

WHY THE CO-OPERATIVES AGREED TO WORK WITH THE SOVIET GOVERNMENT

[An Editorial in the Official Organ of the All-Russian Co-operative Union, May 1918][114]

The Soviet of People's Commissars has published recently a number of decrees relating to co-operatives. Members of the co-operative societies took part in the negotiations at which the decrees were drafted. . . . . We must ask ourselves what it all means. Does it mean that the co-operatives followed blindly the lead of the government, or were they overcome by pangs of conscience and therefore decided by way of recanting their errors to approve and welcome the policies of the present Russian Government? . . . .

The mere fact of participating in the framing of a policy for regulating one branch of the economic life does not in itself signify approval

[114] *Kooperativnaia Zhizn*, 1918, No. 2, pp. 1–3.

of the political course [of the government]. . . . . The great majority of the co-operative workers have never given such an approval . . . . they have not yet forgotten their "credo."

It is important to remember, however, that the co-operatives are not a political party but an economic organization . . . . and they should take cognizance of the actual relation of existing forces. The Soviet Government is the de facto government, and no matter what our moral judgment of it may be, a business attitude imposes the necessity of recognizing that fact, just as we were compelled to recognize the old autocratic régime. . . . . By entering into business relations [with the Soviet Government] the co-operatives will save themselves from becoming an organ of the government . . . . and will preserve their independence . . . .

Quite a number of causes contributed toward the co-ordination of the activities of the government and of the co-operatives. The economic disruption of the country, the collapse of industry, and the approaching . . . . famine were forcing the government to search for an agency that would help in regulating economic relations. The enormous development of the co-operative movement in Russia naturally attracted the government's attention. At first this attention was of a hostile nature. The government nationalized the credit institutions of the co-operative societies—the Moscow People's Bank—and advanced a project which aimed to nationalize all consumers' societies and to establish consumers' communes instead. In the provinces the situation was even worse. The properties of the co-operatives were being confiscated . . . . and the officials arrested. . . . . But the government soon perceived that this policy was certain to antagonize vast masses of peasants and workers. This the government could not afford to do, and it decided to change its policy in regard to the co-operatives.

On April 12 the Supreme Council of National Economy sent out the following telegram: "To all *Sovdeps*. . . . . The government has concluded an agreement of mutual assistance with the All-Russian Co-operative Union. In the name of the Sovnarkom you are hereby ordered to cease hostilities against the co-operatives, re-establish those that have been nationalized, and set free their officials." . . . .

The co-operative societies, on their part, could not withdraw their share of work. . . . . First of all, the very existence of the co-operatives was at stake. . . . . [Secondly] the interests of the country were deeply involved, and an attitude of mere criticism would be of little help. They decided, therefore, to participate in organizing the economic life of the country . . . . thus lessening the suffering incidental to the transition period. . . . . [115]

[115] See Lenin's statement of the reason why the Soviet Government compromised with the co-operatives, on p. 558, above.

CHAPTER XI

THE WORKERS, THE PEASANTS, AND THE GOVERNMENT

The transition from revolutionary expropriation to the breathing spell which the ruling party attempted in the spring of 1918 was affected not only by external conditions, civil strife, and the chaos in finance, industry, transport, and trade but also by the relations of the workers and peasants to the dictatorship and the acute food crisis of that time. In January 1918 the First All-Russian Congress of Trade Unions met. Here, as in the congresses of other organizations since the seizure of power, the Bolsheviks registered a victory over their Socialist opponents and passed resolutions subordinating the unions to the government and the factory-shop committees to the unions. Opposition to this aspect of Bolshevik policy did not cease but was intensified by the rapid increase of unemployment caused by the demobilization of war industries and the general economic breakdown. Despite this opposition the trade unions, during the period, became at least officially a part of the dictatorship and the factory committees lost to some degree the privileged place they had taken as the labor institutions most representative of the revolutionary program of the Bolsheviks.

Likewise in the realm of food control and distribution the Bolsheviks and their allies controlled the All-Russian Food Congress which met in January and passed resolutions subordinating the food organizations to the Soviets. This, however, did not relieve the food shortage. The peasants refused to sell grain at fixed prices in depreciated paper, and the attempts to organize barter of manufactured goods for bread failed to relieve the situation because of the shortage of goods and the inefficiency of the system. The hungry population resorted to speculators or to the more direct action of looting warehouses and the stores of the possessors of grain. Toward the end of the period under consideration the Communists adopted the strong-arm methods of a food dictatorship and a "bread war" between the towns and the villages actually began.

The bread war and the extension of the civil war to the villages, which received the official benediction of the Communists in May and are outside the scope of this volume, represented a radical change in the peasant policy of the dictatorship. During the winter and spring of 1918, as during the two preceding months, the Communists acquiesced in the agrarian program of their Left Socialist-Revolutionist allies as expressed in the early land decrees and especially in the Fundamental Law of Land Socialization of February 19, 1918. Here and there attempts were made to set up land communes and state farms more or less in line with the true Communist program for the socialization of agriculture, but for the most part the peasants were left to complete the "expropriation of the expropriators" which had been begun in the summer of 1917.

A. Labor and the Government

The First All-Russian Congress of Trade Unions met in Petrograd January 20 to 27, 1918, just after the dissolution of the Constituent Assembly. The Bolsheviks were denounced by their opponents in the Congress. The dispersion of the Assembly, the suppression of civil liberties and the use of force against the workers, and the program to subordinate the unions to the state and to transform the factory-shop committees into local units of the unions were attacked from two sides. Mensheviks, representatives of the Bund, and other Socialists who favored a social-democratic coalition and opposed the single-party dictatorship demanded that the unions retain their independence and avoid absorption in the state apparatus at all costs. Several Bolsheviks with long service in the labor movement who favored a mitigation of the dictatorship likewise defended the autonomy of the unions. Lozovsky was one of these and was excommunicated for his deviation from the party line. From another side the Bolsheviks were attacked by the anarcho-syndicalists and by some of the champions of the shop committees, who described the old unions as "living corpses" and opposed the subordination of the committees to the unions or to the state.

The Bolsheviks carried their resolutions in the Congress but, regardless of resolutions, factory-shop committees clung obstinately to their positions as the executants of workers' control; and many labor leaders and a number of unions continued to oppose the dictatorship and fight for the independence of labor organizations.

EXCOMMUNICATION OF A BOLSHEVIK LABOR LEADER

[Resolution of the Bolshevik Central Committee, January 11, 1918][1]

Taking into consideration that:

1. Since the beginning of the November Revolution Comrade Lozovsky has expressed views radically different from those of the party, views which have nothing in common with the view of the revolutionary proletariat in general but which agree in every essential with the petty-bourgeois denial of the dictatorship of the proletariat as a necessary transition to socialism.

2. By his November articles in *Novaia Zhizn,* a paper which went over to the camp of the bourgeoisie, Comrade Lozovsky called forth the general indignation not only of all party men but also of all class-conscious workers. Soon after the appearance of those articles the Central Committee of the Russian Social-Democratic Labor Party decided to expel Comrade Lozovsky from the party, but this decision was not made public or enforced solely because of the hopes which certain comrades entertained that Comrade Lozovsky's hesitations might prove a transitory phenomenon caused exclusively by his inability to grasp the significance of the historical change which had occurred with such great rapidity.

3. The hopes of the comrades who wished to give Comrade Lozovsky time to grasp fully the scope of the revolution were not justified

[1] *Novaia Zhizn,* No. 7, January 24, 1918, p. 1. The resolution was adopted on the eve of the All-Russian Trade Union Congress, where it was feared Lozovsky might have a large following among the Bolshevik delegates.

and the general political behavior of Comrade Lozovsky, especially his articles in the *Professionalnyi Vestnik,*[2] Nos. 7–8, testifies to his complete departure from the basic principles of socialism on the question of the rôle of the proletariat in the socialist revolution.

4. The membership in the party of a man who occupies an important position in the trade-union movement and spreads unheard-of corruption in that movement not only compromises the party and demoralizes all organization work among the proletariat but also is harmful to the cause of organizing socialist production through the trade unions.

5. It is impossible to work in the same party with a man who fails to grasp the necessity of the dictatorship of the proletariat, [a necessity] which our party program had accepted, who fails to realize that no socialist revolution, not even a consistently democratic revolution, is possible without such a dictatorship, i.e., without a socialistic, merciless suppression of the exploiters, a suppression which does not stop with any bourgeois-democratic formula. . . . .

6. It is impossible to work in the same party with a man who ridicules the socialist aim of the proletariat which the political authority has called into being—a man who denies that the trade unions should regard it as their duty to assume government functions and to undertake . . . . the socialist reorganization of production and distribution.

7. In view of the above the Central Committee of the Russian Social Democratic Labor Party resolved to expel Comrade Lozovsky from the R.S.D.L.P. (Bolshevik) and to publish the resolution at once.

PROGRESS OF THE TRADE-UNION MOVEMENT

[From Lozovsky's Report at the First All-Russian Congress of Trade Unions, January 21, 1918][3]

The Russian trade-union movement has during the last few months made a great stride forward. It has shown such a vitality . . . . as no other country has ever witnessed. There were 1,475,000 organized workers represented at the Third All-Russian Conference [July 1917] . . . . and now, after six months of constructive work . . . . that number . . . . has passed the 3,000,000 mark. This is a huge figure, a figure unheard of for such a short period of time.

These six months . . . . were devoted chiefly to trade-union organization, to the unification of separate industries and the formation of large industrial unions. . . . . At present we have about eighteen All-Russian unions represented at the Congress, but their total number is much larger. . . . . According to figures now at my disposal, we have

[2] Organ of the Central Council of Trade Unions.

[3] *Pervyi Vserossiiskii Sezd Professionalnykh Soiuzov,* Moscow, 1918, pp. 29–30.

twenty-eight unions of an All-Russian scope. Of these, twenty belong to the All-Russian Central Council of Trade Unions. The most important [of these unions] . . . . are the All-Russian Union of Metal Workers, which numbers now about 600,000 members; the All-Russian Union of Textile Workers, with a membership of over 500,000; the Union of employees in the sugar industry with a membership of 200,000 to 210,000. . . . . There are many other unions with as large a membership which have not as yet joined the All-Russian [Trade] Union. . . . . We started our work in a void, as it were. There were no trade unions of an All-Russian type . . . . and there existed a number of very important . . . . industries which kept aloof from the general trade-union movement, viz., the railway and the post and telegraph [unions] . . . . Lately, however, as a result of a number of conferences . . . . we ascertained that a large number of organizations comprising the railwaymen's union wish to join the All-Russian Trade Union. . . . .

In addition to the twenty-eight All-Russian [Trade] Unions, there exist . . . . about twenty-two regional unions. I am quite sure that there are many more of these regional unions all over Russia, but I have been able . . . . to ascertain only twenty-two. . . . .

SUBORDINATION OF THE TRADE UNIONS TO THE SOVIET GOVERNMENT

[Resolution of the First All-Russian Congress of Trade Unions, January 23, 1918][4]

1. The political victory of the workers and poorer peasants over the imperialists and their petty-bourgeois agents in Russia brings us at the same time a victory over capitalistic ways of production and the beginning of the international socialist revolution. The Soviets of Workers', Soldiers', and Peasants' Deputies have become government organs, the policy of the government of the workers and peasants has become the policy of socialist reconstruction of society.

2. The November Revolution, which transferred the power from the hands of the bourgeoisie into the hands of the working class and the poorer peasantry, gave rise to entirely new conditions for the activities of all workers' organizations without exception, including the trade unions.

3. Revolutionary socialists have never considered trade unions as mere instruments of the proletariat's economic struggle for bettering the conditions of the working classes within the capitalist order. Revolutionary socialists have always looked upon trade unions as organiza-

[4] *Ibid.*, pp. 119–20. This resolution was adopted.

tions called upon to fight side by side with all the other revolutionary organizations of the working class for the dictatorship of the proletariat and the realization of socialism. So much greater is the part which the trade unions are called upon to play now when the class struggle has brought the Russian proletariat face to face with the socialist revolution, with the actual realization of a number of the most important socialist projects.

4. The idea of trade-union "neutrality" has always been and remains a bourgeois idea. There is no neutrality and there can be none in the great historic strife between revolutionary socialism and its adversaries. Behind professed neutrality there is almost always concealed the support of bourgeois politics and treason to the interests of the working class. This is proved by the conflict of the two leading tendencies in the European trade-union movement during three and a half years of the World War. The "neutralists" of yesterday everywhere became defensists and servants of imperialism; true socialists should have renounced once and for all the idea of trade-union "neutrality."

5. Still less is it possible to have a "neutral" trade-union movement in Russia, a country which is living through a great revolution and is throwing off the bourgeois yoke. The questions of the Constituent Assembly, the nationalization of banks, the suppression of the bourgeois press, the annulment of loans, the fight against counter-revolution—all these questions touch in the most direct way the interests of the working class, and thereby the interests of the trade-union movement. In all these questions the trade unions must support fully and loyally the policy of the socialist Soviet Government directed by the Soviet of People's Commissars.

6. The center of gravity in the work of the trade unions must, at present, be shifted to the field of economic organization. Trade unions, being class organizations of the proletariat, must take upon themselves the task of organizing production and restoring the shattered productive forces of the country. They should aim to participate most emphatically in the work of all the centers regulating production, to organize workers' control and the registration and distribution of workers, to organize [a system of] exchange between villages and cities, to participate most actively in the demobilization of industry, to fight against sabotage, to enforce the duty of universal labor, etc. Particular attention should be given to the centralization of the trade-union movement on an All-Russian scale and to the organization of powerful unions of agricultural workers.

7. In their mature state, after they have gone through the process of the socialist revolution which is now taking place, trade unions will become instruments of state authority and as such will work in co-

ordination with other instruments of the socialist state for the realization of new principles in the organization of economic life.

8. To achieve this end and to effect the amalgamation of all economic organizations of the working classes (particularly the factory-shop committees), there should be the closest possible co-operation and an uninterrupted organizational connection between trade unions and the political organizations of the proletariat and, in the first instance, with the Soviets of Workers' and Soldiers' Deputies.

9. The Congress is convinced that as a result of the process already taking place the trade unions will inevitably become instruments of the socialist state and that the membership in them of all persons employed in a given industry will be enforced by the government.

The Russian trade-union movement will not be able to fulfil its great tasks unless it establishes the closest contact with the international trade-union movement. The Congress considers it to be its duty to assist in every possible way the rebirth of the international trade-union movement, and thinks that it would be in order to call a general international trade-union congress as well as a number of international trade-union conferences of separate branches of industry.

As a first step in this direction the Congress resolves to call an International Conference of Trade Unions to meet in Petrograd on February 15.

ON THE INDEPENDENCE OF THE TRADE UNIONS

[Menshevik Resolution in the First All-Russian Congress of Trade Unions, January 23, 1918][5]

Taking into consideration (1) that the present revolution, when viewed objectively, is not a socialist but a bourgeois one, and that all possible social attainments of the working masses, in the course of the revolution, are not capable of changing the foundations of the capitalistic order; (2) that, because of the above, all socialist experiments conducted at the present time, while powerless to shake the foundations of the capitalistic order, are in fact contributing to the complete disintegration of the national economy and thereby making very much worse the conditions of the life and struggle of the proletariat; (3) that, therefore, the Russian proletariat will in the future be forced to fight capital in all its forms in order to improve its economic conditions within the framework of bourgeois society and to achieve its final liberation through socialism; (4) that the proletariat's mightiest support in this struggle is and will continue to be the free and class-independent trade unions, which throughout the course of a systematically growing class

[5] *Pervyi Vserossiiskii Sezd Professionalnykh Soiuzov*, p. 122. This resolution was not accepted.

war will co-operate more and more with the political party of the proletarian classes—[in view of these facts] the First All-Russian Congress of Trade Unions, in confirmation of the resolution of the Third All-Russian Conference on the Aims of Trade Unions, repudiates in the most energetic fashion the attempt of the Soviet of People's Commissars to turn the trade unions into auxiliary organs of the so-called Workers' and Peasants' Government, and openly proclaims that in the future trade unions must remain free and independent associations of the class struggle of the proletariat.

SUBORDINATION OF FACTORY-SHOP COMMITTEES TO THE TRADE UNIONS

[Resolution of the First All-Russian Congress of Trade Unions, January 27, 1918][6]

1. The Great Russian Revolution, which has brought to life all the creative forces of the working class, also created—at the very outset—organs of workers' representation at the factories and shops. These organizations took upon themselves [the duty] of safeguarding the workers' interests in each industrial establishment. In this way the factory-shop committees assumed certain tasks which are usually performed by the trade unions.

2. But with the development and strengthening of the . . . . trade unions the factory-shop committees [in a given industry] must become the local branches of the corresponding trade unions.

3. In view of the fact that several complicated tasks of an economic and organizational character connected with the . . . . demobilization, control, and regulation of industry require a united effort on the part of the proletariat, and that the existence of two parallel economic organizations of the working class with overlapping functions can only hamper the process of concentrating all the proletariat's forces, the Congress considers that the most satisfactory way in which the working class can carry out all the economic and organizational tasks mentioned above is to accept the leadership of [the trade unions] which have been organized on an industrial basis. . . . .

TRADE UNIONS AND SOVIET ECONOMIC INSTITUTIONS

[A Statement by V. Schmidt, Commissar of Labor][7]

It is possible to disagree . . . . as to the precise moment in the course of the socialist revolution at which the trade unions become organs of

[6] *Pervyi Vserossiiskii Sezd Professionalnykh Soiuzov,* p. 374. This resolution was adopted.

[7] *Professionalnyi Vestnik,* Nos. 3–4, February 23, 1918, pp. 8–10.

the socialist state, but it cannot be denied that recent events have brought us closer [to this situation]. . . . . The nationalization of the largest branches of national economy . . . . has created conditions under which the trade unions can no longer play the rôle of critics . . . . but must assume economic tasks and responsibilities. It is only natural that these tasks should radically modify the policies of the [trade] unions. . . . . The industrial trade unions will have to carry the burden connected with the organization of industrial management, technical equipment, raising industrial production, regulation of labor and wages, and labor inspection. To bring these measures into effect it will be necessary to give to the industrial trade unions corresponding powers . . . . which will inevitably make [the unions] a part of the state.

Some trade unions have already undertaken the solution of the basic problems in the direction just indicated. The union of textile workers has organized "Tsentrotekstil," assuming two-thirds [of the responsibility] for the management and organization of the entire textile industry. The union of tanners does the same thing in the [tanning industry]; the union of sailors of the merchant fleet has been in charge of water transport for some time; the union of railwaymen took charge of the railroads; the union of the Ural miners is managing the nationalized Ural mines. Under these conditions, while managing an entire branch of industry, ... [the trade unions] can no longer call strikes. This is coming to be recognized by some of the industrial trade unions, and the largest of them, the Union of Metalworkers . . . . omitted in its constitution all reference to strikes. . . . . There is no need to argue that the task of safeguarding the conditions of labor has always been and still is one of the principal tasks of the trade unions. . . . . But the methods by which this task is carried into effect must now change. . . . .

From the above brief sketch it will be seen that the activities of the trade unions are, for the present, directed mainly toward the organization of national economy and the safeguarding of labor conditions. [But] these two problems constitute the chief concern of two Soviet . . . . institutions, [viz.] the Supreme Council of National Economy and the People's Commissariat of Labor. . . . .

The Supreme Council of National Economy proposes to supervise the general direction of economic policies and to organize the entire [economic life of the country] on the principle of socialization of the means of production. With this in view the Supreme Council of National Economy has undertaken steps to nationalize the largest branches of industry and to hand over their management and direction to the trade unions concerned. . . . . Of the eighty members [of the Supreme Council of National Economy], forty-five represent the trade unions.

The People's Commissariat of Labor . . . . has defined its tasks as follows:

"The Commissars of Labor . . . . aim to defend the interests of the proletariat. During the period of the social revolution all activities [of the Commissars of Labor] will be directed toward achieving the complete liberation of the proletariat as speedily as possible. . . ."[8]

Under such conditions the independent functioning of these institutions and of the centers of the trade-union movement is bound to become destructive to the cause of the great revolution. . . . . The problem is to find the most rational method of bringing about an amalgamation . . . . between the All-Russian Council of Trade Unions and the Commissariat of Labor. This is the more imperative as the two pursue similar aims. . . . . The difference lies only in the methods [employed]: . . . . strikes . . . . or government intervention. Both the [First] All-Russian Congress of Trade Unions . . . . and the majority of the Executive Committee of the All-Russian Council [of Trade Unions] favored the latter method. It would seem that from tactical considerations there are no obstacles to the amalgamation [of the trade unions and the Commissariat of Labor]. . . . .

END OF TRADE-UNION INDEPENDENCE

[Resolution of the Fourth Conference of Trade-Union Leaders, March 12–17, 1918][9]

(1) Having transformed all social-economic relationships and having placed the proletariat face to face with the most intricate problems, hitherto unknown in the experience of world history, the November Revolution sharply changed not only the meaning and character of state organs but also the aims and significance of proletarian organizations as well.

(2) During the period of coalition [Provisional Government] the Ministry of Labor played the rôle of arbitrator and peacemaker between labor and capital, but now that it has been transformed into the instrument of the Worker-Peasant Government, in which the dominant rôle is played by the industrial proletariat, it becomes the champion of the economic policy of the working class and has at its disposal the machinery and the state's entire force of compulsion.

(3) On the other hand, trade unions organized on industrial lines tend to change from purely fighting organizations to more and more economically productive associations of the proletariat. They are [there-

[8] From a resolution of the First Conference of Commissars of Labor.

[9] *Professionalnyi Vestnik,* Nos. 5–6, April 20, 1918, pp. 13–14.

fore] acquiring national significance as the organs called upon to regulate conditions of labor and production in the interests of the working class as a whole.

(4) Transacting business along the same lines but independently of one another, the trade unions and the Commissariat of Labor often solve the same question differently, thus introducing an objectionable dualism into the unified economic policy of the working class.

(5) Only in so far as the trade unions are acknowledged to be the sole authoritative representative of the industrially organized proletariat which is called upon to realize a unified economic policy in the interests of the working class as a whole can the objectionable divergence in the solutions of many questions in that sphere be removed.

(6) The above description duly defines the rôle and aims of the Commissariat of Labor as a government organ executing with authority and state compulsion the will of the industrially organized proletariat.

In this way the Commissariat of Labor will appear as the government organ of the economically organized proletariat and is responsible to the organizations [of the proletariat].

(7) From this it follows that all important decisions of the higher organs of the trade unions (congresses, conferences, etc.) are binding upon the Commissariat of Labor. . . . .

(8) As the first step toward the practical realization of this [relationship] the All-Russian and local councils of trade unions will form collegiums attached to the Commissariat of Labor . . . . to co-ordinate all practical measures.

(9) But in order to remove finally all harmful divergence in the solution of economic questions, the political organizations of the proletariat must give up, once and for all, all independent action, and abolish forever all "sections," "bureaus," "commissions," etc. . . . .

PROTESTS AGAINST THE SOVIET TRADE-UNION POLICY[10]

The workers have supported the new government which calls itself the government of the workers and peasants and promises to do our will and work for our welfare. All our organizations stood back of it and our sons and brothers shed their blood for it. We bore patiently both want and famine. . . . .

Four months have passed and we find ourselves without faith and without hope. This government which calls itself a Soviet of Workers and Peasants has done everything to oppose the will of the workers. It has blocked every attempt to hold new elections to the Soviets, it

[10] *Novaia Zhizn,* No. 46, March 20, 1918, p. 3. This protest was adopted at a meeting attended by 83 delegates representing 25 of the more important industries.

has threatened to use machine guns [against workers], and it has broken up meetings and demonstrations.

We were promised an immediate peace, a democratic peace . . . . but were given a shameful capitulation to German imperialism. The peace which we have has dealt a fatal blow to the workers' International and has condemned to death the Russian labor movement. . . . .

We were promised bread and were given hunger, civil war . . . . and economic disorganization. Under the guise of socialism our industries and finances have been thoroughly disorganized. . . . . The accumulated wealth has been plundered, and now as never before graft and profiteering reign triumphant. There is unemployment everywhere and . . . . no means of fighting it. Our trade unions are crushed, and the factory committees can do nothing for us.

The City Duma is scattered and the co-operatives are harassed in every way. The Soviet of People's Commissars has departed from Petrograd and has left us to our fate. The mills and factories are closed and we are thrown on the street without money, without food, without work, without hope.

We were promised freedom . . . . but where is freedom of speech, assembly, unions, and press? People are executed without trial by men who act as informers, provocateurs, witnesses, prosecuting attorney, and judges all in one. . . . .

[Demands for Independence of Labor Organizations][11]

On March 27 . . . . a special meeting of the delegates from Petrograd factories and workshops was held. There were present 170 representatives of 56 enterprises.

Among other [questions] the problem of fighting for the independence of workers' organizations was discussed at the meeting. . . . .

A worker [named] Kimmerwald presented a report on the struggle for independent workers' organizations. The main points of the report were that the class organizations of the workers—the factory committees and the trade unions—had been . . . . turned into bureaucratic organs of the Soviet Government and were not carrying out their fundamental tasks.

The disgraceful peace, hunger, incompetence displayed in connection with the evacuation [of industry], the complete disorganization of factory life, all these [evils] fell as a heavy burden upon the workers, ... who were deprived of their professional organizations and [thus] have to face unarmed all these misfortunes. The trade unions have lost their independence . . . . and . . . . are no longer fighting in defense of the workers' rights. . . . .

[11] *Nash Vek,* No. 59, March 28, 1918.

A number of speakers supported the position taken by [Kimmerwald] and sharply attacked the representatives of the Soviet Government for turning the workers' professional organizations into weapons for combating the workers themselves.

A resolution embodying these views . . . . was passed by an overwhelming majority.

[Statement of Minority Group of Trade-Union Leaders, April 29, 1918][12]

The trade-union movement is in danger. The fighting economic organizations of the working classes cannot flourish at a time when the revolution, in which the proletariat plays such an active rôle, is breaking down as a result of national economic disorganization and external defeat.

Every day brings a decrease of the productive forces of the country. Industry has now become a state pensioner. The majority of factories and shops subsist on grants from the state treasury. The productivity of labor is alarmingly low, the production of goods is diminishing, and the printing of paper money is increasing steadily. All this renders extremely difficult the work of the trade unions. On the shoulders of the economic organizations of the proletariat falls the heavy burden of regulating industry and introducing order into the prevailing economic chaos. . . . . But the economic organizations of the proletariat are threatened from still another quarter . . . . from the side of the Soviet Government.

The Soviet Government takes the stand that it alone expresses fully the interests of the working masses and that, therefore, all other organizations can exist only in so far as they subscribe without a murmur to the internal and external policies of the Soviet of People's Commissars. Since the November Revolution we have witnessed innumerable instances of how big, small, or even microscopic commissars have used every kind of oppression, including bayonets, in their dealings with recalcitrant proletarian organizations. Here are a few instances: the Soviet Government closed the quarters of the Union of Employees of Credit Institutions, arrested several times its board of directors, closed the co-operative store which supplied the families of the employees [of the credit institutions] in order to force the starving employees formally to recognize the Soviet Government. In Rybinsk the executive committee [of Soviets] ordered an "inspection" of the local Soviet of trade unions. . . . . To fight opposition tendencies of certain trade unions new unions of the same trade and sharing the point of view of

[12] *Novaia Zhizn,* No. 80, April 30, 1918, p. 4. Lozovsky was among those who signed the statement.

the Soviet Government are set up. The authorities then decide which union is more adequate for the interests of the workers.

Along with the persecutions of irreconcilable trade unions, other unions are being systematically subjugated and are being converted into instruments of the government. The seaman's union of the trade fleet is taking charge of the department of commercial navigation . . . . the railwaymen's unions are subsidized by the state, etc. A whole scheme for putting the different branches of national industry under the management of the trade unions is being elaborated. This will lead to greater confusion and disintegration of the political life of the country. . . . . Since its acceptance at the First Congress of Trade Unions this scheme has been enforced consistently all over the land. In a number of places [trade] unions have employed Red Guards in their economic struggle . . . . other trade unions are investing all their capital in production, organizing out of their own resources artels for home building, establishing stores for the sale of products, undertaking the management of sequestered factories. . . . . At the same time the membership of trade unions is decreasing. . . . .

The above facts cannot but rouse our deep anxiety for the future of the Russian trade-union movement. . . . . The majority of trade-union leaders seem to be under the impression that we are living after a successfully executed socialist revolution and that all capitalist relationships have been abolished in Russia. This idea was born with the successful November Revolution, which was carried through under the slogan of "land and peace" and supported by workers and peasants, the latter of which are becoming more and more the dominant social basis for political authority. But an authority dependent on two classes is least of all fitted to become a socialist authority, and that is why the attempts to identify or to merge the purely proletarian trade organizations with the Soviet organizations, which are of a mixed class composition, cannot fail to produce sad results. . . . . [The warning ends with an appeal to safeguard the independence of the trade unions and to exert pressure on the Soviet Government to force it to change its relations with German imperialism "which compromise the Russian Revolution."]

In the spring of 1918 a number of the great industries of Petrograd were transformed from a war to a peace-time basis. The machinery of many plants was evacuated to other regions; other industries closed down for lack of fuel or other causes. The stated reasons for the evacuation were the nearness of Petrograd to the new western frontier and the shortage of fuel. "Until the war," *Izvestiia* explained,[13] "Petrograd industries had cheap foreign coal. . . . . It is not likely that they will again be able to secure such fuel very soon. Our transportation service is so broken down that supplying Petrograd with coal from the Donetz or using oil to run the industries is not to be thought of. Under the circumstances Petrograd industries are doomed."

As the following materials show, the evacuation added to the confusion of the time, increased unemployment, and embittered the workers. The efforts of the government to ameliorate the situation by labor exchanges and public works were not particularly fruitful.

THE UNEMPLOYMENT CRISIS[14]

The old apparatus [Provisional Government] was able to hide the process of economic disintegration. But soon the trying days arrived. Under the pressure of the Germans who threatened to occupy Petrograd the [Soviet] government undertook the evacuation of factories, to transfer them into the interior of Russia. Then came the Brest peace and the democratization of industry. . . . . The evacuation which was undertaken in a state of panic was in itself a complete breakdown [of industry]. Orders were given to pack and remove not only valuable materials but machinery as well, and wherever the removal was impossible the factory equipment had to be destroyed. It was found out, however, ... that the task of moving a factory is in most cases unrealizable and at any rate requires a tremendous amount of preliminary work. . . . . [At the new places] the factories could not resume work . . . . and they had to be shut down. . . . .

The evacuation increased the number of unemployed to a very high degree. The panic, however, soon subsided.

The Germans stopped at the Pskov-Narva line. But the evacuation only increased the tragedy of the workers when the time came [for industry to be transferred from war] to peace production. . . . . Among the problems raised [by that transfer], that of the demobilization [of industry] was undoubtedly among the most acute. . . . .

The demobilization had to be carried out under conditions of an ever growing process of disorganization [of industry]. . . . . The oil

[13] No. 45, March 10, 1918, p. 1.

[14] L. M. Kleinbort, *Istoriia bezrabotitsy v Rossii, 1857–1919 g.g.*, Moscow, 1925, pp. 269–86.

fields of Baku, Grozny, and Emba regions came to a standstill. . . . . The coal fields were in the same condition. . . . . The production of raw materials was in no better state. The cultivation of cotton in Turkestan fell to from 10 to 15 per cent of 1917. . . . . It was transport, however, that underwent a most rapid process of disintegration. . . . . These conditions little favored a transition to peace production . . . . [and in so far as the proletariat was concerned] it spelled unemployment and nothing more. . . . .

The proletariat of Petrograd suffered most of all. . . . .

Take for example the Erikson works. When the transfer to peace production was officially decreed, ... those workers who had been paid off refused to leave. The situation was saved by the evacuation. The committee [at the factory] took measures to prevent panic among the workers. The latter, however, frightened by the unrest which had appeared in neighboring establishments, demanded that they be paid off with a six weeks' advance in wages, as had been provided by law. This demand was met and the factory was closed. . . . . Eighteen thousand workers from the "Treugolnik" plant were thrown out of work, owing to the closing of the establishment on account of lack of benzine. . . . .

The Petrograd tube works were transferred . . . . to Penza. . . . . Three freight trains loaded with work-bench and metal supplies were sent. But a complete transfer would have required twenty such trains, and consequently 20,000 workers were discharged.

At the works of Siemens and Halske, out of 1,200 men, there remained only 700, and later no more than 300. The Nevsky shipbuilding works also closed . . . . 10,000 men being dismissed. The Obukhov works . . . . closed down, due to lack of coal. All together, 14,000 men were dismissed. The same thing happened at the Putilov works, where more than 30,000 men were laid off. . . . .

In contrast with the Petrograd workers, who were being everywhere discharged, workers in the Moscow region—according to *Vestnik Promyshlennosti*—were usually able to keep their jobs, at least in the [region's] most important branch of industry, the textiles. The private market [for textiles] began to absorb everything it was offered, irrespective of the price asked; and the . . . . industry also proved itself to be in a better position as far as the supply of fuel and raw materials was concerned. Moscow factories were using peat and wood fuel and were less dependent upon Donetz coal than were the Petrograd works. Even [in the Moscow region], however, the war industries were being closed down and all their workers dismissed. The metal workers were those who suffered most. . . . . All together, 215,000 workers were discharged.

"A feeling of apprehension and sadness hovers over Moscow,"

wrote *Vecherniaia Zvezda:* "all life seems to have stopped. Ilinka, in whose dirty and narrow side streets the warehouses used to be almost bursting with goods, is now empty. . . . . Factory owners and their technical personnel are running away. . . . ."

The same news came from the provinces. The collapse which was enveloping Russia also reached Vitebsk. "Establishments are being closed one after another; the flax-mill 'Dvina,' with 1,500 workers, has been shut down; unemployment is growing and has already reached appalling figures." "A terrific growth of unemployment has been witnessed in Kiev. Privation among the unemployed is very great." In Tula out of 60,000 or 65,000 workmen, 15,000 were unemployed. In Kharkov the Southern Russian Company for the Manufacture of Rope was closed, as were the agricultural machinery works of Helferich-Sade. In the Tula arsenal the employees were dismissed en masse. . . . .

The same calamity overtook the workers of the Ural region and in Siberia. In the Bogoslovsky copper-mining region, the Bogoslovsky smelter was closed down, together with three mines. . . . . There were about 30,000 workmen in this district who lost their jobs. In Nizhni-Tagilsk—belonging to the heirs of Demidov—the same conditions prevailed. The owner surrendered his property rights; [and] the establishment was turned over to the workers (40,000 men). But having become the owners, the latter found themselves in a hopeless situation: "Unemployment in the Ural, which has been growing worse from day to day," wrote *Vecherniaia Zvezda,* "forces skilled workers to engage in any sort of labor, ... including the chopping of ice, the clearing away of rubbish, etc. There are even cases . . . . of death from starvation." . . . .

Such were the results of the fuel crisis, of the evacuation which had scattered the machinery belonging to different plants all over . . . . [the country], and of the demobilization of industry which had almost extinguished factory life. . . . . Unemployment caused terrific suffering.[15] Here, for example, is the "Treugolnik" with its enormous mass of chimneys. . . . . A meeting of the commission for closing down the factory is being held. Regret and sadness born of unfulfilled hopes penetrate your very soul. You wish to free yourself from the nightmare. But where is the way of escape for thousands of workers? Crowds of from eight to ten thousand men receive the news of dismissal with the agonized and sickening groans of those who are perishing. Tears, angry words. A drunken soldier appears on the platform. With a grimacing and distorted face he is malignantly whispering something quite incomprehensible. The displeasure and the noise increase. . . . . Wasted lives have been sacrificed to the merciless Moloch—capital. How

[15] Kleinbort, *op. cit.,* p. 282.

many of them—who can say? [And] where will [the surviving workers] go? There is no place for them. . . . .

Here is another crowd of workers who have been dismissed. Although there are thousands of them, you do not hear a word about politics, revolution, German imperialism, or other burning questions of the day. To all these men and women, these young boys and girls, and those old people who can hardly stand on their feet, such fundamental questions of the moment appear infinitely remote. Individual cries are heard from different corners: "It's a tough life—we had better lie down and die."

Here they talk about the labor exchange [in which] hundreds wait where one receives employment.

"One or two are given jobs, and that is all," says an unemployed worker. "There is no work, absolutely none. Everything is being liquidated and closed down. I have been going [to the labor exchange] for the last two months, but without results." . . . .

"Large groups of [Petrograd] workers,"[16] . . . . we read, "are leaving with their families and belongings in search of a better life in Siberia. . . . . The workers go away with the idea of becoming farmers. Skilled mechanics, such as blacksmiths, are also departing in the hope of settling in these regions." Many workers have snatched at this idea. Some go to the north, some to the Urals, others to Siberia. When they are seated in the railway cars, conversation begins: "I'm from Riazan. Where am I going? People at home are already swollen with hunger. I have news that they are eating bark." Another says: "I am going to Orel. They say that work can be found there. I have a family, a wife, and four children. The trip is expensive—my seven hundred rubles won't last long. But that's all right; I shall find work in Orel. And if I don't, then what? Jump down from the bridge into the river."

And then comes new and impromptu advice, and they are ready to turn and go to some other locality. But what can these workers expect [to find] in Siberia, in the north, or in the Ural region? . . . .

As has been noted in chapter vi, Vikzhel, the organization of the railway workers, had taken over the management of the railways but at the same time remained hostile to the Bolshevik dictatorship and its methods. At the Extraordinary All-Russian Congress of Railwaymen, held in January 1918, Vikzhel secured a small majority (273 to 261) which favored the Constituent Assembly as against the Soviets.

[16] Kleinbort, *op. cit.*, p. 286.

The minority supporting the Bolsheviks then bolted the Congress, sent representatives to the C.E.C., and formed an All-Russian Executive Committee of Railwaymen (Vikzhedor),[17] consisting of twenty-five Bolsheviks, twelve Left Socialist-Revolutionists, and three Social-Democrat Internationalists. To this organization the government confided the management of the railways, the executive body being a collegium of seven, one member of which, Rogov, was appointed Commissar of Ways and Communications. The regulation of January 23, which confirmed workers' control of the various lines and divisions and the interference of local authorities, created unlimited confusion, which the government attempted to remedy by establishing a more centralized control in the hands of the Commissariat of Ways and Communications.

WORKERS' CONTROL OVER THE RAILROADS

[Regulations of January 23, 1918][18]

1. . . . . Administrative control over the railroads . . . . is to be intrusted to Soviet railway authorities—namely, the Soviets of Railwaymen's Deputies and their executive committees.

2. . . . . The administration of each separate railway line . . . . is to be intrusted to a . . . . Soviet elected by the railwaymen of that line. . . . .

5. The Soviet of Railwaymen's Deputies of each line elects an executive committee . . . . to carry out the Soviet's instructions and to attend to all current business. . . . . The executive committee is responsible to the . . . . Soviet and may be recalled at any time. . . . .

8. Control . . . . over each traffic division of a given line . . . . is to be intrusted to a . . . . district Soviet elected by the railwaymen of that division. . . . .

9. The district Soviet . . . . elects a district executive committee to attend to all current business. . . . .

10. Local railway Soviets are to be formed at points indicated by the district Soviets. . . . . They shall be composed of representatives of the local railwaymen's committees. . . . .

[17] Vserossiiskii Ispolnitelnyi Komitet Zheleznodorozhnikov.

[18] *Vestnik putei soobshcheniia,* 1918, No. 1, pp. 2–4.

11. In order to co-ordinate the work of railroad lines in a given region . . . . regional Soviets of railwaymen's deputies shall be formed. . . . .

18. General control over the Russian railroads . . . . shall be vested in an All-Russian Congress of Soviets of Railwaymen's Deputies. . . . .

21. The All-Russian Congress is to elect an . . . . Executive Committee . . . . to carry out its resolutions and attend to current business. . . . .

CONDITION OF THE RAILWAYS UNDER WORKERS' CONTROL

[Extracts from Shliapnikov's Report to the Central Executive Committee, March 20, 1918][19]

On my way here to Moscow I decided to . . . . find out how things stood on this most important road, and I telegraphed to all the stations, asking the representatives of committees or station-masters to prepare brief reports on . . . . what is going on in their respective divisions, stations, depots, and shops. The picture which presented itself to me as a result of these reports is a very sad one. It brings us face to face with the necessity of taking the most rigorous measures for re-establishing labor discipline on the railways at any cost and before all else. For instance, trains nowadays often go unlighted, without observing any of the regulations with regard to signals, ... while the cars are never cleaned. . . . . The usual excuse is that no kerosene or candles are available. However, I have ascertained that both these commodities are available but are being pilfered in the most shameless manner. Moreover, the railway crews, being not at all interested in the exploitation of the railways, sometimes refuse to man the trains. Thus . . . . both cars and locomotives may be available, but there are no engineers and no conductors: . . . . they either pretend illness or else simply refuse to go. It sometimes happens that on a certain train . . . . a substitute has to be found for a [member of the train crew] who is really ill; but the station-master is unable to exercise his authority, for as soon as he puts someone in the place of the sick man, the substitute tells him that he will not go without the consent of the Committee, and since it is impossible to get the Committee together on the spot the train cannot be dispatched. . . . . There have been cases like the following: . . . . the station of Tver has locomotives available but . . . . for a number of days, twenty-seven engineers were sick and consequently twenty-seven locomotives were tied up. . . . . You can easily imagine what a traffic jam resulted at that junction point.

[19] *Protokoly zasedanii Vserossiiskogo Tsentralnogo Ispolnitelnogo Komiteta 4-go sozyva (Stenograficheskii otchet)*, pp. 44–45.

The disorganization and demoralization that prevail in the railway shops defy description. At the station of Klin the roundhouse has been converted into a club and the engines are being repaired in the open air. It is known that the repair shops release very few cars and locomotives. In a word, from the moment the railway employees were guaranteed a minimum wage they ceased to display any minimum degree of efficiency. . . . . Right here [in Moscow] and along all the railways, we hear from all the class-conscious elements . . . . the same complaint: we must at any price get our railwaymen interested in the exploitation of the roads. This may be done by introducing piecework [in the shops] . . . . and payment per verst for the crews. This is the only painless method to raise the efficiency of the railway employees. . . . .

END OR WORKERS' CONTROL OVER THE RAILROADS

[Decree of the Sovnarkom, March 26, 1918][20]

In view of the obvious need of preventing any further disintegration of the railway system . . . . [and of checking the well-meant but disastrous] . . . . interference of local, oblast, and central organizations in . . . . the management of the railways, the Soviet of People's Commissars decrees:

1. The People's Commissar of Ways and Communications is to be in control of the Commissariat of the same name. . . . .

2. The Collegium of Ways and Communications is to consist of the . . . . Commissar, as chairman, and members elected by the All-Russian Congress of Railroad Workers and approved by the Soviet of People's Commissars and the All-Russian Central Executive Committee. In case of any disagreement between the Collegium and the Commissar, the former may appeal to the Soviet of People's Commissars and to the All-Russian Central Executive Committee.

3. The Collegium . . . . is not to interfere . . . . with the regulations of the Commissar of Ways and Communications, who is given dictatorial powers in matters relating to railway transport.

4. The complicated network of organizations directing [railway] transport . . . . is to be simplified, and unnecessary units are to be abolished. A list of the latter is to be prepared by the People's Commissar of Ways and Communications. . . . .

6. Each local, district, and regional railway center is to select from among its members a worker who has shown himself to be the most energetic and loyal to the Soviet régime and who understands railroad

[20] *S.D.*, pp. 820–22.

business. This worker is to be made chief executive of the given railway center and is to be responsible to the People's Commissar of Ways and Communications. Within a given traffic division this official is vested with full dictatorial powers. . . . .

8. On those lines or in those localities where . . . . elected committees of railway workers, refusing to indorse the Soviet government's policy, carry on secret sabotage, the most active and revolutionary-minded railway men must organize railway military revolutionary committees which, upon [receiving] the approval of the People's Commissar of Ways and Communications, ... are to assume complete control. [Such authority] they are [then] to delegate to a single responsible individual. . . . .

[The rest of the decree deals with arrangements for guarding the railway lines, plans for increasing the railroads' technical and administrative efficiency, and penalties to be imposed in case of failure to carry out the decree.]

VL. ULIANOV (LENIN)
President of the Soviet of People's Commissars

A. ROGOV, V. NEVSKY
People's Commissars

B. THE FOOD CRISIS

Along with all the other afflictions which they endured during the winter and spring of 1918, the Russian people, particularly of the industrial centers and the consuming areas, suffered severely from an acute food shortage. Aside from the general breakdown of distribution and transport, the Bolsheviks stated that they were hampered in their efforts to relieve the situation by the neutral or hostile attitude of the officials of the food organizations. From the point of view of maintaining the dictatorship it was, of course, important for the Bolsheviks to gain control of these organizations, especially if they were to apply the measure so often urged by Lenin of using food to compel the bourgeoisie to work for the Soviet state. In January 1918 the Bolsheviks adopted their usual tactics by summoning an All-Russian Food Congress in which they and their supporters had a majority of votes. This Congress approved the policies of the government and set up an All-Russian

Council of Supply. The new Council failed to gain or exercise any authority, which remained in the hands of the Food Commissar. Nor was this official able to curb the growing activities of the bagmen or provide other ways by which food could be obtained. The government then appointed an extraordinary commission to make war on the bagmen and expedite the transport of food to the cities.

ESTABLISHMENT OF AN ALL-RUSSIAN COUNCIL OF SUPPLY

[Proceedings of the All-Russian Food Congress, January 27–29, 1918]

On January 27 there was a meeting of the All-Russian Food Congress made up of representatives of Soviets of Workers', Soldiers', and Peasants' Deputies. On the 29th the People's Commissar of Food, Schlichter, made a speech. . . . . He pointed out that the government of the People's Commissars is not to blame for the disorganization of the food supply . . . ., the situation had been critical in Kerensky's day. . . . . Schlichter further stressed the difficulties which the Soviet Government had encountered on account of the . . . . sabotage of higher officials. . . . .

Some way must be found to get food out of the village. Armed detachments should be sent to compel the peasants to give up grain. Force alone, however, will not accomplish much. An exchange of goods between the city and the country should be organized. The village should be supplied with agricultural machinery, manufactured goods, iron, etc. This can be done only if there is a monopoly of industry. Transportation must also be improved by repairing and acquiring new rolling stock and by finding a means of fighting the soldier mobs who crowd the trains and disorganize the service. Some of the men dressed as soldiers are mere speculators. . . . .[21] It is an error to suppose that the food policy can be separated from general policies. . . . . The food policy must be in line with the general revolutionary policy of the Sovnarkom. . . . . Only by revolutionary determination . . . . can we create conditions under which the food question will find its normal solution. Establishing a revolutionary order in the South and a victory over the bourgeois Rada will enable us to get supplies [from the South]. The Kaledins and Vinnichenkos . . . . will soon be swept away by revolutionary wars. . . . .[22]

[21] *Novaia Zhizn,* No. 12, January 31, 1918, p. 8.
[22] *Izvestiia,* No. 13, January 31, 1918, p. 3.

After the debates the Congress adopted a resolution which stated that the salvation of the people depends on the establishment of a Soviet Socialist Republic. . . . . As regards the organization of food supply the Congress moved that there should be established in connection with the Supreme Council of National Economy an All-Russian Council of Supply.

The Sovnarkom is to have the right of general supervision . . . . over matters relating to supply. Local organs of supply are completely subordinated to [local] Soviets. . . . .[23]

[On January 30, the All-Russian Council of Supply was elected. It includes thirteen Bolsheviks, eleven Left Socialist-Revolutionists, and three non-party men.][24]

ACTIVITIES OF THE BAGMEN

The Congress in Omsk is discussing whether or not to have a bread monopoly [in Siberia]. . . . .

The delegates from Tobolsk, Cheliabinsk . . . . tell of the waves of bagmen against whom "stringent" measures are being taken. . . . . As a whole the Congress is opposed to the harsh measures that are being taken against them . . . ., such as confiscating the grain they have bought, etc. . . . .

The Congress asked one of these bagmen, a peasant of Kostroma, to say a few words.

"I am a bagman," said he, "but I do not understand why we are being called bad names. . . . . I never would have come two thousand versts if the land committees had given us what we need. . . . . We are hungry. . . . . You have no idea how we suffer. . . . . Famine is no respecter of paper laws . . . . give us bread!"[25]

Bagmen may be divided into several classes. In the first class are peasants from the famine areas, particularly Riazan and Vladimir, who are in search of food for their hungry families. Unless they have an experienced hand with them they are easily caught. . . . . If they get away with their lives they are lucky. In the second class are profiteers who are always on the go, buying where it is cheap and selling where it is dear. They know all the tricks of the trade—where a search is likely to be made, etc. They are always on guard. The third and most pitiful class is made up of passengers who pick up a sack of flour or a few pounds of meat to take home to their families. They suspect everyone; they are always watching and never rest. . . . .

[23] *Novaia Zhizn,* No. 12, January 31, 1918, p. 6.

[24] *Ibid.,* No. 13, February 1, 1918, p. 7.

[25] *Ibid.,* No. 9, January 26, 1918, p. 4.

Some stations on the Southeastern Railway, such as Griazi and Grafsky, have a bad reputation. . . . . Voronezh and Tambov gubernias are fighting the bagmen, treating all alike. At Grafsky there is a machine gun which is turned on the train. After the gun has rained bullets on the roofs of the cars, guards enter the train and throw out the filled sacks. The bagmen look on weeping and cursing. Experienced bagmen plan to pass this station at night. This trick does not always save them, for they are likely to receive as warm a reception at Griazi or Kozlov or some other station. . . . .

It happens sometimes that a train with bagmen is sidetracked. Just the other day twenty-five freight cars filled with bagmen were sent to Voronezh. . . . . To add insult to injury the bagmen were compelled to carry their heavy sacks to the warehouses. . . . . After going through these hardships and taking these risks we can understand why the bagmen ask such high prices for their goods.[26]

FIGHTING FOR FOOD

The villages of Voronezh are engaged in a class war. In almost every village one can see two hostile camps. One is composed of the well-to-do peasants, the village intelligentsia, practically all of them Socialist-Revolutionists of the Right . . . . and the other of the poor peasants who see the need of organizing . . . . taking the government into their own hands and shaping the village life on a more just basis.

On January 30 the Bukrin Soviet of Riazan Gubernia . . . . voted to make an inventory of the grain in the township. On the day following . . . . five soldiers were sent to the village of Alabino to make an inventory of the grain and to requisition any surplus in the hands of the citizens and the pomeshchik Muratov.

The peasants refused to submit to the orders of the Soviet. They not only concealed their supplies but also seized whatever Muratov had. . . . .[27]

In one of the villages of Riazan there was a fight between the peasants and soldiers who came to requisition bread. A number were killed and wounded. The peasants rushed to the city, disarmed the local militia, seized all the guns, and put the soldiers to flight. . . . .[28]

Owing to famine and [unemployment] many people are fleeing from Petrograd. In some cases this is done in the following manner: Those wishing to go organize parties of 100 or 150, collect the neces-

[26] *Delo Naroda,* No. 19, February 8, 1918, p. 4.

[27] *Pravda,* No. 27, February 16, 1918, p. 4.

[28] *Novaia Zhizn,* No. 27, February 17, 1918, p. 4.

sary money, and reserve a car. On the appointed day they come with their baggage and guns, take possession of the car, and fight off all others who try to force their way into the car.[29]

The city of Rzhev is passing through a severe food crisis. . . . . The local Soviet passed a decree that all supplies arriving in the city through the railways should be first distributed among the soldiers, and what is left . . . . goes to the rest of the population. . . . . More recently the commissars issued another decree prohibiting [the peasants from the neighboring villages] bringing food to the city. At first the peasants attempted to ignore the decree [with the result that] all the supplies which they brought to the market were requisitioned. . . . . The peasants stopped bringing food to the market and the city population had to go to the village [to get supplies].[30]

CURBING THE SPECULATORS[31]

The Third Western Siberian Congress of Soviets . . . . has decided to do away with excess profits . . . . to close all business enterprises that functioned up to the March Revolution and which do not have a license from the gubernia food committees and to prohibit the export of the necessities of life addressed to private parties.

In regard to minor speculations . . . . the Congress has made the following recommendation to the Soviet of People's Commissars.

1. The first time goods are found in the possession of speculators . . . . such goods are to be requisitioned by paying 50 per cent of the market price.

2. In case of a second offense the goods are to be confiscated and the speculators imprisoned for six months.

3. In case of a third offense the goods are to be confiscated and the speculator imprisoned for two years.

The Congress believes that only by taking the foreign commerce into its own hands can the state put an end to speculation and improve the economic conditions of Russia. . . . .

The Reval Executive Committee of the Soviet . . . . has given orders . . . . (1) to search persons suspected of concealing bread and other foodstuffs; (2) to confiscate the concealed products . . . .; (3) to hand over the concealers to the Revolutionary Tribunal . . . . in order to put a stop to the secret exporting of food; [(4) to put guards at the stations]. . . . .

[29] *Novaia Zhizn,* No. 26, February 16, 1918, p. 3.

[30] *Ibid.,* No. 27, February 17, 1918, p. 4.

[31] *Pravda,* No. 23, February 12, 1918, p. 1.

Similar measures have been adopted in a number of other provincial cities. Searches and confiscations are being made not only in stores but also on railways. . . . . The confiscated goods are used to feed the needy population, and confiscated manufactured goods are exchanged for bread to be sent to the front. . . . .

But all these and similar measures are insufficient to put a stop to speculation. More radical steps will have to be taken. . . . .

THE EXTRAORDINARY COMMISSION ON FOOD AND TRANSPORT

[Decree of the Sovnarkom, February 15, 1918][32]

1. In order to supply the people with food and other necessities of life an All-Russian Inter-Departmental Extraordinary Commission is being organized. This Commission is to guard the railways. It is to be made up of the Commissar of Railways, the Chairman of the Central Committee on Army Supplies, and the Vice-Chairman of the Council of Supplies.

2. All the existing organizations having to do with the guarding of the railways are merged in the new Commission. . . . .

5. The Commission is to make merciless war on speculation and the transportation of food without authorization.

V. ULIANOV (LENIN)
President of the Sovnarkom

[Order of the Extraordinary Commission][33]

1. Local Soviets, railway committees, and all other organizations along the railway lines are called upon to take strong action against the "bagman," a vicious type of speculator, who demoralizes the food supply and transportation.

2. At railway junctions military units . . . . will be stationed to take from the bagmen their food and arms.

Note: Each person is allowed to have a half pud [of food] [18 pounds]. This may include not more than 10 pounds of flour, not more than 2 pounds of butter, and not more than 3 pounds of meat.

3. In case the bagmen resist, they are to be arrested and handed over to the people's courts. If they draw guns, they are to be shot on the spot.

4. All confiscated goods are to be listed and handed over to the nearest uezd or gubernia food organization, which must notify the Commissar of Food by telegraph.

[32] *Pravda,* No. 26, February 15, 1918, p. 2.

[33] *Ibid.,* No. 28, February 17, 1918, p. 1.

5. These instructions and orders are to be posted in all food institutions, railway stations, and cars. They go into force three days after their publication.

L. TROTSKY
Chairman of the Extraordinary Commission on
Food and Transport

A CRITICISM OF THE GOVERNMENT FOOD POLICIES

[From an Editorial in *Novaia Zhizn*][34]

The famine which has been foreseen . . . . is on us. . . . . We have had two food congresses since the November Revolution. . . . . The last one in December, made up in large part of representatives of the Soviets of Workers', Soldiers', and Peasants' Deputies, predicted the famine and indicated a program of action. . . . . One recommendation . . . . was to organize an exchange of goods between city and village, and the second was not to disturb too much the central and local food machinery. . . . .

Conversations with Smolny followed. . . . . Finally, on January 25, the Soviet of People's Commissars agreed to hand over the control of food to an All-Russian Food Council made up of delegates from the December congresses and representatives of the Supreme Council of National Economy. . . . . This decision was never carried out because of the opposition of the Congress of Soviet Food Commissars called by the Food Commissar Schlichter. That food congress consisted of persons selected by the Third All-Russian Congress of Soviets and they favored Soviet policies. . . . .

After two weeks of trial the Sovnarkom . . . . removed [Schlichter's organization] . . . . and appointed an extraordinary commission with Trotsky at the head. This commission was given unlimited power and was made up of nine members . . . . in part from the December Congress and in part from Schlichter's organization.

This extraordinary commission has decided to . . . . shoot the bagmen. It is agreed that the bagmen are an evil . . . . but they are the result and not the cause of the famine. . . . . [Had the exchange between city and village been well organized there would be no place for the bagmen, but for some reason or other this exchange is not effective. The famine grows apace and millions of people will perish.]

[34] No. 29, February 20, 1918, p. 1.

ATTEMPTS AT BARTER

[Kerosene for Bread][35]

A local organization . . . . in Riazan . . . . sent one of its members . . . . in search of bread. He returned the other day and reported that in certain villages he was offered a pud of rye flour for a pud of kerosene. . . . .

[Vodka for Bread][36]

Rumors spread in the town of Orsk that the local government planned to destroy about 80,000 vedros of vodka. This news aroused a great deal of discussion and the soldiers announced that they would not permit it. Someone suggested that the alcohol be sold in order to avoid possible trouble. A commission was formed to look into the matter and work out the details. . . . . After several days of deliberation the commission recommended that the vodka should be sold by cards to the townspeople at the price of 2.5 rubles per bottle and to the peasants in exchange for grain. This news spread like fire. Early in the morning there were long waiting lines in front of the vodka shops. By noon the peasants with grain began coming. In two days more than 100,000 rubles' worth of vodka was sold. After this the cards were done away with and vodka was sold to all. People came to town with baskets and bags of grain and departed with vodka. News of this free sale of vodka reached Orenburg, which issued an order to stop it, but no attention was paid to it.

Neither the Extraordinary Commission on Food and Transport nor the decree of April 2 ordering the organization of barter on a nation-wide scale were effective. Hungry people continued to "expropriate" food whenever they could find it and were strong enough to take it. Soviets, trade unions, and other privileged bodies began more and more to employ the same methods by organizing armed detachments to "requisition" grain. In this fashion the "bread war" between city and village began to replace all other methods in the struggle against hunger.

[35] *Pravda,* No. 29, February 19, 1918, p. 4.

[36] *Novaia Zhizn,* No. 38, March 9, 1918, p. 4.

"EXPROPRIATIONS AND REQUISITIONS"

The Food Commission of Ufa received a telegram from Inza that a band of hungry "partisans" had attacked a food train. They first tore up the tracks and then opened fire on the train guard. They were driven off, and the train reached Ruzaevka. . . . .[37]

In the beginning of March a small company of men was sent to the village of T—— to requisition the bread reserves. When the men arrived they were disarmed . . . . by the peasants. . . . . Another company with two machine guns was sent, and they returned without the machine guns. A third expedition was ordered out. . . . . At a given signal the peasants opened fire, killed six, and wounded others. . . . . A fourth and much better armed force was put into the field. It arrested the local Soviet, recaptured the machine guns and rifles. . . . . Investigations are being made. . . . .[38]

News is arriving of the bread war which is taking place in Voronezh, Smolensk, Tambov, Riazan, Simbirsk, Kursk, Kharkov, Ufa, Orenburg, and a number of other gubernias. Armed detachments of Red Guards and hired soldiers are roaming over villages and hamlets in quest of bread, making searches, laying traps with more or less success. Sometimes they return with bread; at other times they come back carrying the dead bodies of their comrades who fell in the fight with the peasants. . . . .

Many of the villages are now well armed, and seldom does a bread expedition end without victims. . . . . At the first report of a requisitioning expedition the whole volost is mobilized . . . . and comes to the defense of the neighboring village.

Voronezh has ten requisitioning companies, with a hundred men in each, provided with machine guns, automobiles, and bombs. . . . .

In February there was a real battle at the station Muchkala. . . . . It is reported that several thousand people participated. . . . .

At Smolensk two villages were wiped out and many peasants and Red Guards were killed and wounded. . . . .

The situation of the uezd and volost Soviets is not enviable. . . . . They are between two fires. . . . . If they take the part of the requisitioning gangs they are beaten by the peasants, and if they protect the peasants they are pounced upon by the gubernia Soviets. Recently one of the Soviets drove out the requisitioners, and immediately a punitive expedition was sent out and arrested the Soviet.

The bread requisitioned does not always reach its destination. Occasionally it is stolen on the way. . . . . Trains are held up and plun-

37 *Pravda*, No. 51, March 17, 1918, p. 4.

38 *Novaia Zhizn*, No. 51, March 26, 1918, p. 4.

dered. . . . . Sometimes it takes two or three hundred men to guard a train. . . . . Many villages have organized gangs who attack neighboring villages and waylay people with food. . . . .[39]

EXCHANGE OF COMMODITIES TO INCREASE THE SUPPLY OF GRAIN

[Decree of the Sovnarkom, April 2, 1918][40]

1. In order to increase the supply of grain and other food products, the People's Commissariat of Food is charged with the task of organizing an orderly exchange of commodities on a nation-wide scale within the limits indicated below.

2. Some of the following commodities may be used for exchange: dry goods, threads, notions, leather, harnesses, boots, galoshes, matches, soap, candles, kerosene, lubricating oil, agricultural machines, wire, sheet iron, assorted iron, horseshoes, nails, binding twine, rope, glass, utensils, tobacco, tobacco products, salt, molasses, sugar, tea, and their substitutes.

Note: This list can be supplemented and revised upon the agreement of the Commissariat of Food and the Supreme Council of National Economy.

3. The commodities listed in Article 2 are transferred to [the control of] the Commissariat of Food in the quantities necessary to carry out the plan stated above. This transference is to be made on request of the Commissariat of Food in accordance with the plan worked out by the Commissar of Food and the Chairman of the Supreme Council of National Economy. The central and local organs for distributing these commodities are to carry out the instructions of the Commissariat of Food.

Note: Some of the goods mentioned which are not listed among those to be exchanged are to be distributed by the respective organs in accordance with the plans approved by the Commissariat of Food and by the Supreme Council of National Economy.

4. The Commissariat of Food will issue special instructions to determine the procedure and rules concerning exchanging [manufactured] goods for grain and other food products. . . . . These instructions should aim: (*a*) to attract the village poor to help in the organizing of interchange of commodities by handing over to the volost or some other unit for further distribution among the needy population the goods to be exchanged for grain; (*b*) to work out a plan that will guarantee to the Soviet Republic the return of all the money spent on this inter-

[39] *Novaia Zhizn,* No. 71, April 19, 1918, p. 4.

[40] *S.U.R.,* 1918, No. 30, p. 375.

change of commodities and will draw out of the village bourgeoisie as much paper money as possible.

5. Local food organs and other authorized . . . . organizations are responsible for carrying out the interchange of goods in accordance with the instructions of the Commissariat of Trade.

6. Without the permission of the Commissariat of Food or its authorized organs no exchange of goods is allowed.

7. Persons guilty of exchanging goods for grain without authority or failing to comply with this decree are subject to arrest and trial.

V. Ulianov (Lenin)
President of the Sovnarkom
A. Tsiurupa, G. Petrovsky, V. Miliutin
People's Commissars

FOOD CRISIS IN THE SPRING OF 1918[41]

The problem of provisioning the people until the new harvest is now clearly understood. There can be no more illusion about the improvement of nourishment during the next few months.

The recently published data dealing with the crop of 1917 indicate that there was a surplus of grain in European Russia (excluding Siberia and the Caucasus) amounting to from 320 to 360 million puds. The separation of the Ukraine and the [Kuban region] reversed that surplus into a shortage of over 190 million puds. So that, in proportion as the free exchange of commodities with the south comes to a standstill, the provisioning of the gubernias which remained in the Soviet Republic is bound to become worse.

Other [places] from which grain [is usually obtained] cannot make up the lack caused by disappearing Ukrainian bread. The regions of the middle and the lower Volga and that of the Urals . . . . have a shortage of 82,000,000 puds. . . . . The Caucasus and Siberia remain as the only hope, but the civil war makes it impossible [to import their surpluses]. Furthermore, the Siberian grain is unavailable on account of transport [conditions]. Western Siberia had orders to ship . . . . by the first of May a total of 43,000,000 puds. But the Omsk [rail] road has a monthly capacity of only 4,000,000 puds. Actually only about 3,000,000 puds were shipped during the past two and a half months. To help the situation, the Sovnarkom granted the other day a sum of 10,000,000 rubles to build railways in the bread [producing] regions of Siberia.[42] But this measure can have no practical significance for the current food campaign.

[41] *Svoboda Rossii,* No. 7, April 19, 1918, p. 5.

[42] Decree of April 4, 1918. (*S.D.,* pp. 833–34.)

Under such conditions it would seem that the only way to prevent famine would be to allow free trade. But the Soviet Government holds on firmly to the bread monopoly. Stern rules are being published daily directed against "speculators" and bagmen . . . .; food "dictatorships" have been announced in Siberia and in the Ukrainian regions occupied by the Germans . . . .; an ever greater number of articles [of consumption] are being taken under control. . . . .

These socialist utopias, however, cannot stand the test of life. In a number of gubernias fixed prices have already been abolished. All measures of the central authorities suffer defeat [as soon as they are applied by local authorities]. At present not a single person will find his way in that chaos [which results from] the variety of food organs, commissars, and committees which, together with the local "Sovdeps" and "Sovnarkoms," take charge of the distribution and collection of the "monopolized" grain. Each institution of the consuming gubernia sends its messengers to investigate the situation [in the food-producing gubernias]. [Upon arrival] these messengers, invested with all sorts of extraordinary and ordinary powers, begin to negotiate with one another as well as with the local regional Soviets, Sovdeps, and other authoritative bodies. [Soon] the telegraph office becomes congested with the overflow of long-drawn-out dispatches containing complaints against the arbitrariness and "selfishness" of the local authorities. [The negotiations with the local authorities] assume the aspect of regular diplomatic negotiations in which at first "Petrograd" and now "Moscow" plays the part of mediator. Finally, an "agreement" is drawn up . . . . usually founded on the so-called "exchange of goods." In fact, the only method of getting the peasant to give up his bread voluntarily is to offer in exchange manufactured and industrial articles. But even here . . . . the business is so organized that [the exchange] amounts to a free distribution of the remaining stock of goods to the "poorest peasants" without getting back a quantity of bread of equal value. Armed force appears in the last analysis to be the most reliable method for grain "collection" by the state. . . . . But these methods encounter the organized resistance of the peasants and in the end cannot yield very much.

The grain monopoly . . . . remains a paper measure. In connection with that monopoly hundreds of thousands of members of the different committees have to be fed, and the extra expenses which this [food] organization entails fall as a heavy burden on a negligible quantity of food which the people receive. In Moscow government-controlled bread is sold at higher prices than in the provinces, where free trade has been declared. . . . . There is no prospect of alleviating the crisis so long as the [bread] monopoly continues to function. . . . . In the face of these facts the official optimism of the Soviet Government is gradually waning, and every declaration [which government officials make] relative to the food situation sounds more and more hopeless.

WHY THE SOVIET FOOD POLICIES FAILED

[From a Statement by Tsiurupa, Food Commissar, at the Fifth Congress of Soviets, July 9, 1918][43]

We were confronted with a number of circumstances which interfered with our work, ... such as local grain monopolies, the detention of grain shipments, and many other impediments. We were not informed about the loading and shipment [of grain], about the execution of our orders—in a word the business [of food supply] was dominated by chaos complete and terrifying. . . . . The railroads were completely disorganized. . . . . There was also the phenomenon known as requisition, i.e., plain plundering of grain shipments. . . . . [All these] will indicate the difficulties which interfered with our plans. . . . .

The exchange of goods [between city and village] has proved to be of little use. There have been many instances in the course of our work when the peasants, having convinced themselves that no goods were then available, said: "We shall not give away [our grain] unless we receive goods in exchange." When the goods actually arrived [in the villages], they were distributed by the peasants among themselves; but even then we received no grain. . . . .

Furthermore, owing to the fact that on their own initiative local food organs quite unjustifiably changed the prices of grain and refused to carry out the orders of the central government, pursuing instead a completely . . . . independent policy, ... and in this way disorganizing not only the territory in which they were operating but also adjacent localities (a circumstance which must also be taken into consideration), we came to the conclusion that it was necessary to reorganize the local food organs and to centralize the collection and distribution of foodstuffs. . . . .

C. The Peasants and the Government

During the winter of 1918 the peasants were busily carrying through the expropriation of the landowners, destroying the last vestiges of the old order, and quarreling among themselves over the spoils. The Bolsheviks in these months made

[43] *Piatyi Vserossiiskii Sezd Sovetov, Rabochikh, Krestianskikh, Soldatskikh i Kazachikh-Deputatov. Stenograficheskii otchet. Moskva, 4–10 iiulia 1918 g.*, Moscow, 1918, pp. 141–42.

no serious attempt to substitute their own plans of collectivization for the Socialist-Revolutionist program which had been temporarily adopted for tactical reasons. The Bolsheviks, as one of their commentators explains, were able to make their policies dominant in village Soviets and committees only in the consuming areas (i.e., the northern and central industrial gubernias, the Ural, and the lake regions, where many peasants were part-time industrial workers) and even here they had strong competition from the Left Socialist-Revolutionists. In the central agricultural region, the middle and lower Volga, the Left S.R.'s were in the ascendancy, while in the Ukraine it was the Right S.R.'s. Moreover, at the All-Russian Congress of Land Committees held in January, Spiridonova had declared that if the Bolsheviks opposed the principle of socialization of the land that opposition would be overcome by union of the S.R.'s of the Left with those of the Right.[44] In the circumstances the Bolsheviks did not press their differences with the Left S.R.'s but even accepted with slight amendment Kolegaev's draft of the Fundamental Law of Land Socialization published on February 19.

But the Bolshevik–Left S.R. alliance was not comfortable for either party. The latter group bitterly opposed the Brest peace; they opposed the subordination of the trade unions and the proposed limitations on workers' control, and they objected to the methods of the dictatorship in respect to food control and other matters. On their part the Bolsheviks prepared for the inevitable conflict with their uneasy allies by urging the community of interest of the proletariat and the poorest peasants in carrying expropriation one step farther, i.e., to expropriate the middle and well-to-do peasants who were known to be fundamentally hostile to the proletarian dictatorship. The situation was such, according to Lenin, that the Communists must control these millions of peasants or be overthrown by them.

[44] Cf. A. Shestakov, "Oktiabr v derevne," in *Proletarskaia Revoliutsiia,* 1927, No. 69, pp. 91–109.

DESTRUCTION OF ESTATES

From Danov come reports that the palace of the former governor of Riazan has been destroyed. . . . . The furniture and art objects of the palace were valued at a million rubles. . . . . Pictures of noted artists were burned. The peasant women grabbed the Sèvres vases and now use them for sour cream. . . . . The stock farm was looted and the thoroughbred stock driven off. . . . . Drunkenness and looting have spread. . . . . In some cases the peasants have begun to attack each other.[45]

From Kharkov come reports of the destruction of estates, houses, art treasures, grain, and live stock. . . . . The Kropivnitsky collection of rare books, pictures, manuscripts, and notes is no more. This is a great loss.[46]

The pogroms and destructions which began in March are still going on in Tula and Samara gubernias. Not a single estate in Tula Gubernia has escaped either partial or total destruction. . . . . The loss in machinery, live stock, and grain amounts to about thirty million rubles.

In Simbirsk Gubernia the situation is somewhat similar. Among the art treasures lost is the home of the historian Karamzin, ... the villa of Prince Kurakin, which contained a very rare collection of [eighteenth century] engravings. Thanks to Austrian war prisoners one building of the Kurakin estate was saved. . . . . In Penza Gubernia the savagery of the mob was so great that the villas and palaces were set on fire with everything in them. . . . .

In some parts, Tver and Taurida, the peasants organized themselves to protect estates. This was also true on the lands of the Cossacks. . . . .[47]

DISORDERS IN THE PROVINCES

[A Letter from Siberia][48]

Our [railway] car is wandering through Siberia. . . . . We have become used to the "communistic" régime in Petrograd, but the things that are going on in the provinces, on the railroads, and in the railway stations are simply incredible. Language is inadequate to describe the

[45] *Delo Naroda*, No. 20, February 9, 1918, p. 4.

[46] *Novaia Zhizn*, No. 27, February 17, 1918, p. 4.

[47] *Ibid.*, No. 28, February 19, 1918, p. 4.

[48] *Izvestiia*, No. 27, February 17, 1918, p. 2. The author of this letter was a Menshevik member of the Petrograd Duma who was commissioned by that institution to buy supplies in Siberia. The letter was first published in *Novyi Luch*, No. 23, February 15, and was reproduced in *Izvestiia*.

chaos, the anarchy, perpetrated by bands of cutthroats, branded criminals, and ex-convicts, now calling themselves Bolsheviks. . . . . The militia in every town is being removed and replaced by Red Guards. The appearance of these rascals . . . . is almost invariably a signal for robberies, murders, and removal of fur coats from passers-by. (The latter operation is especially popular in Siberia.)

What are the elements from which these Red Guards are being recruited? In small towns everyone is known by name and the names [of the Red Guards] are quite significant, being surnames taken from the vocabulary of criminals. Here are "Vaska" (Cain), "Mitka" (the Golden Hand), "Senka" (the Cutthroat), "Vanka" (the Chief), etc., etc. These criminal elements, formerly hidden underground . . . . have now, under the protection of the Soviet authorities, emerged to the surface. They receive arms, a fixed salary . . . . and engage in their trade with the sanction of the law. The roads leading from the railway station to the cities are especially favored by them. . . . . The term Bolshevik has become here a synonym for "robber," "thief," "murderer," etc. . . . .

The way the dark masses are being instigated against those who think differently [from the Bolsheviks] is simply monstrous. . . . . At every meeting you can hear threats against Mensheviks and Socialist-Revolutionists, who are called "bloodsuckers," "fat bourgeois," etc. In most cases it is hard to understand what these newly born Bolsheviks really want. All one hears are wild outcries calling to murder, plunder, etc.

S. Shchupak-Vladimirov

DRUNKENNESS IN THE VILLAGE

[A Letter from Volyn]

Almost all the grain is turned into vodka. Practically every village has from fifteen to twenty distilleries. Rye sells at from forty-five to fifty rubles a pud, but if turned into home brew . . . . it brings twice that amount. So much alcohol is distilled that there is enough for local consumption and for export. . . . . Everybody is engaged in this business, even some of the members of the executive committees. One hears such remarks as: "What kind of freedom is this when a man can't make a bottle of vodka for his own use?" . . . .

When under the influence of strong drink, men loot estates and destroy state and private forests. The authorities in the gubernia are quite unable to handle the situation, as is evidenced by the following: The commissar of the gubernia learned that there were a number of stills in the village of Karpovtsy and that deserters were perpetrating murders and robberies. Gathering a company of a hundred soldiers and officials he started for the place. He arrived about two in the morning, surrounded the village, and began his search. The dogs and chickens gave the alarm, the village was aroused, and the deserters hid. The search for vodka disclosed that it was the exceptional house that did not have at least a bottle or two of it. A number of stills were also located. By that time the search came to an end, the soldiers got drunk, and joined with the natives in defending "freedom" and the "frightened population."

Sixteen deserters were caught, but sixty of the soldiers disappeared. . . . .[49]

The villages are having a "big drunk." Village expeditions are sent to procure the "national wealth," as vodka is called. . . . . These expeditions go armed with guns, revolvers, and clubs. . . . . Not infrequently they run into "expeditions" from other villages and a pitched battle takes place. Wild, drunken orgies are the order of the day. Old men, young men, women, and minors drink. Even tiny children are given alcohol to put them to sleep so that their parents may drink undisturbed. Licentiousness and gambling keep company with this drunkenness. Venereal diseases are spreading fast. . . . . Typhus is an everyday visitor in the village. The sale of drugs, guaranteed to cure everything, has also made its appearance. Though their price is high, yet there are buyers. . . . .

The village is flooded with paper money . . . . and not knowing what to do with it the peasants have taken to gambling. The favorite game is "21." Thousands of rubles change hands in an evening.

This lack of law and order has brought forth bands of robbers, thieves, and the lynch law. . . . . The "burzhui" are blamed for all the evils of the village—for the lack of salt, sugar, etc. . . . .[50]

Phillips Price attended the sessions of the Land Commission at which Kolegaev's draft of the land law was discussed. He says that the Left S.R.'s objected to the Bolshevik amendment providing for the setting up of state farms on which the workers should be wage-earners as in industry. "Shall the Revolution," asked one of the S.R.'s, "set up wage-slavery again under the auspices not of landlords nor of the bourgeoisie but this time of persons with the high-sounding name of People's Commissars?"[51]

[49] *Nash Vek,* No. 20, January 4, 1918, p. 4.

[50] *Novaia Zhizn,* No. 39, March 10, 1918, p. 4.

[51] Price, *op. cit.,* pp. 254–58.

This provision for state farms and certain other amendments were adopted, but in general the Bolsheviks did not press their program and the law when published reflected the theories of the Left S.R.'s.

The publication of the law was delayed until February 19, the anniversary of the emancipation of the peasants in the reign of Alexander II.

THE FUNDAMENTAL LAW OF LAND SOCIALIZATION

[Decree of the Central Executive Committee, February 19, 1918][52]

PART I. GENERAL PROVISIONS

Article 1. All private ownership of land, minerals, waters, forests, and natural resources within the boundaries of the Russian Federated Soviet Republic is abolished forever.

Article 2. Henceforth all the land is handed over without compensation (open or secret) to the toiling masses for their use.

Article 3. With the exceptions indicated in this decree the right to the use of the land belongs to him who cultivates it with his own labor.

Article 4. The right to the use of the land cannot be limited on account of sex, religion, nationality, or citizenship.

Article 5. All minerals, forests, water, and other natural resources[53] (depending on their importance) are placed at the disposition of the uezd, gubernia, regional, or federal Soviets to be controlled by them. The methods of utilizing and managing the above resources will be determined by special decree.

Article 6. All privately owned live stock, agricultural implements, and buildings of estates that are worked by hired labor shall be taken over by the land departments of the uezd, gubernia, regional, and federal Soviets without compensation.

Article 7. All buildings referred to in Article 6 and others that are of economic value, together with the agricultural enterprises attached [to these buildings], pass without compensation to the uezd, gubernia, regional, and federal Soviets.

Article 8. All persons unable to work and who are deprived of the means of livelihood in consequence of this decree may, on presenting a certificate from the local courts and land departments of the Soviet Government, receive a pension (as long as they live or until they are of age) equivalent to that of a soldier. This will obtain until a general

[52] *S.U.R.*, 1918, No. 25, pp. 327–35.

[53] Literally, the "live forces of nature."

decree is promulgated concerning the insurance of citizens unable to work.

Article 9. The distribution of agricultural land among the toilers is in the hands of the land departments of the village, volost, uezd, gubernia, regional, and federal Soviets.

Article 10. The administration of the land reserve in each republic is in the hands of the main land departments [of the republics] and the federal Soviet.

Article 11. In addition to effecting an equitable distribution of the agricultural land among the toiling agricultural population and a more efficient utilization of the national resources, the local and federal land departments have also the following duties: (*a*) to create conditions favorable to the development of the productive forces of the country by increasing the productivity of the soil, to develop scientific farming, and to raise the general level of agricultural knowledge among the land toilers; (*b*) to create a reserve of agricultural land; (*c*) to develop agricultural enterprises such as horticulture, apiculture, market-gardening, stock raising, dairying, etc.; (*d*) to hasten in certain areas the transition from a less productive to a more productive system of land cultivation by effecting a better distribution of the agricultural population; (*e*) to encourage the collective system of agriculture at the expense of individual farming, the former being more economical and leading to socialistic economy.

Article 12. The distribution of land among the toilers should be made on an equal basis and in accordance with the ability to work it; local standards and traditions should also be taken into consideration. Care should be exercised that no one should have more than he can work or less than he needs for a comfortable existence.

Article 13. The basic right to the use of agricultural land is individual labor. The organs of the Soviet Government may, in addition, make use of a portion of the land reserve (formerly belonging to monasteries, the state, udel,[54] the cabinet,[55] and pomeshchiks) for . . . . model farms and experiment stations. In such cases hired labor may be employed under the general regulations of labor control.

Article 14. All citizens engaged in agriculture are to be insured at the expense of the state against loss of life, old age, sickness, accident, and disability.

Article 15. All incapacitated agriculturalists and members of their families who are unable to work are to be taken care of by the Soviet Government.

[54] Lands used for the support of members of the Imperial family except the immediate family of the Emperor.

[55] Lands belonging to the Tsar.

Article 16. Every farm is to be insured against fire, live-stock epidemics, poor crops, drought, hail, and other such misfortunes through Soviet mutual insurance arrangements.

Article 17. Surplus income derived from the natural fertility of the soil or from nearness to market is to be turned over to the organs of the Soviet Government, which will use it for the good of society.

Article 18. The Soviet Government has a monopoly of the trade in agricultural machinery and seeds.

Article 19. The grain trade, both foreign and domestic, is to be a state monopoly.

Part II. Who Has the Right to Use the Land?

Article 20. Within the limits of the Russian Federated Soviet Republic, separate plots of the land's surface may be used for public and private needs on the following bases:

A. For educational and cultural purposes: (1) The state in the person of the Soviet organs of government (federal, regional, gubernia, uezd, volost, and village). (2) Public organizations (with the authorization and under the control of the Soviet Government).

B. For agricultural purposes: (3) Agricultural communes. (4) Agricultural partnerships. (5) Village associations. (6) Separate families and individuals.

C. For building purposes: (7) Organs of the Soviet Government. (8) Public organizations, families, and individuals (if the construction is not undertaken with the object of making profit). (9) Commercial, industrial, and transportation enterprises (with the special authorization and under the control of the Soviet Government).

D. For transportation purposes (building roads): (10) Organs of the Soviet Government (federal, regional, gubernia, uezd, volost, and village, depending on the importance of the road in question).

Part III. Order in Which the Land Is Apportioned

Article 21. Land is given in the first place to those who wish to cultivate it not for personal profit but for the benefit of the community.

Article 22. For those who engage in agriculture for their own benefit the following order of apportioning the land will be observed:

In the first place, the land will be given to local agriculturists who have little or no land, and to hired farm laborers. The land is to be distributed in equal shares.

In the second place, it will be given to newcomers, i.e., agriculturists who arrive at a given locality after the publication of this law.

In the third place, it will be given to non-agricultural elements in the order in which they are registered by the land department of the local Soviets.

Note: In making the allotments of land, preference will be given to agricultural associations over individual farmers.

[Article 23 deals with the allotment of garden land; 24 with land going under buildings.]

Part IV. The Consumption-Labor Standard[56]

Article 25. The area of land allotted to individual farms to furnish the means of subsistence must not exceed the limits of the consumption-labor standard, which is to be calculated on the basis of the following instructions:

Instructions for Determining the Consumption-Labor Standard

1. Agricultural Russia is to be divided into as many zones as there are different systems of land cultivation (farm-fallow system, three-field system, eight-field system, many-field system, rotation of crops, etc.) in practice at the present time.

2. Each zone is to have its own standard, which, however, may vary in accordance with conditions of climate, natural fertility of the soil, and marketing facilities.

3. In order to determine the standard for each zone, an All-Russian agricultural census will be taken in the near future.

Note: Immediately after putting this law into force the land will be surveyed and topographic maps made.

4. [The distribution of land will take place gradually.]

5. In determining the consumption-labor standard for a given zone the average farm of the least thickly populated uezd will be taken as a basis. . . . . The uezd in question must be characterized by such a relation between the different branches of agriculture as is judged by the local population to be most normal, i.e., most favorable for carrying on the type of agriculture dominant in the given zone.

6. In determining the average peasant farm as it exists today, only those lands will be taken into consideration which the peasants actually cultivated prior to 1917, that is to say, the lands bought and rented by peasant societies and individuals.

[56] The corresponding Russian expression, which played an important part in the discussions of the period, is rather difficult to render into appropriate English. Russian economists were in search of what they called *potrebitelno-trudovaia norma*, literally, consuming-labor standard, and signifying an amount of land for a single farm such as would provide an adequate standard of living for the cultivator operating it without hired labor. See *Glavnyi Zemelnyi Komitet* [Proceedings of the Central Land Committee], Vol. 2, *Normy zemelnago obezpecheniia*, Petrograd, 1919.

7. Forests, minerals, and waters are not to be included in this calculation.

8. Neither will there be taken into account those privately owned lands which were under capitalistic cultivation or those which up to now belonged to the state, private banks, monasteries, udel, or pomeshchiks (cabinet and church); these lands will constitute a land reserve out of which allotments will be made to peasants who have no land or whose shares fall below the existing consumption-labor standard.

[Points nine to thirteen set forth rules for the calculation of the total amount of land available for distribution.]

14. In taking the population census the number of workers and the number of consumers [literally "bread-eaters"] will be calculated separately. The whole population is to be classified in respect to age as follows:

Having No Capacity to Work

Girls	to 12 years of age
Boys	to 12 years of age
Men	from 60 years of age
Women	from 50 years of age

Capable of Work

	Age	Worker Units
Men	18–60	1.0
Women	18–50	0.8
Boys	12–16	0.5
Girls	12–16	0.5
Boys	16–18	0.75
Girls	16–18	0.6

Note: These figures may be changed in accordance with climatic conditions and local customs by decision of the appropriate organs of the Soviet Government.

15. The amount of land per worker unit may be determined by dividing the number of desiatins by the number of worker units.

16. The number of dependents to be provided for by one worker unit may be obtained by dividing the number of non-workers by the number of "worker units."

17. It is further necessary to make an estimate of the number of cattle which can be fed on a desiatin and by one working unit.

18. In order to determine the average size of a farm in a uezd, which may be taken as typical for a given zone, the average fertility and quality of a desiatin must be ascertained. This average will be found by dividing the total crop . . . . by the number of types of soil.

19. The average thus found will be taken as the point of departure in determining the consumption-labor standard in accordance with which the equalization of all farms is to take place.

Note: In case the above average proves insufficient for a satisfactory standard of living it may be increased out of the land reserve.

20. The amount of land . . . . required for additional allotments by those whose shares fall below the normal average may be determined by multiplying the amount of land which goes to one "worker unit" in a particular uezd by the total number of worker units of that zone and subtracting from the result the number of desiatins in actual possession of the peasants.

21. Then the land reserve fund . . . . should be compared with the amount of land required for additional allotments in order to ascertain whether migration can take place within the zone in question. . . . . In case this is impossible [it is necessary to find out] how many families will have to move to another zone.

[The rest of the land law, which contains altogether some fifty-two articles, makes provision for cases of possible shortage of land resulting from overpopulation and unequal distribution of the available land fund. Regulations as to the emigration of farmers indicate such points as the selection of those who are to migrate and state provision for all expenses connected with the emigration, and aid to the new settlers.]

YA. SVERDLOV
President of the Central Executive Committee
VOLODARSKY, ZINOVIEV, KAMKOV, LANDER
MURANOV, NATANSON-BOBROV, OKULOV
PETERSON, SPIRIDONOVA, USTINOV
Members of the Presidium
V. ULIANOV (LENIN)
President of the Sovnarkom
A. KOLEGAEV
People's Commissar of Agriculture

RESULTS OF LAND SOCIALIZATION

[From Statements by B. Knipovich][57]

Socialization of land was not carried out on a national scale. The transformation of Russia into an all-embracing commune with frequent redistribution of land on the basis of equality, contemplated in the programs of the Socialist-Revolutionists, could not be realized. In practice

[57] Knipovich was a responsible official of the Commissariat of Agriculture.

the land was simply appropriated by the local peasants, and no attempt was made on their part to migrate from places where land was scarce to those having it in greater abundance. Equal distribution of land inside a village took place everywhere, but equalization between volosts was less frequent. Still less frequent were the cases of equal distribution between uezds and gubernias.[58]

Having gotten the land . . . . the well-to-do peasant class seems to have attained its aim. But the results . . . . of the partition were much less significant than was expected. The enormous amount of land, when distributed among many millions, gave most unsatisfactory results. A special investigation of the central office of the Land Department established the fact that the increase of area per capita in some places would be expressed in infinitesimal figures: tenths, and even hundredths, of a desiatin. In the majority of the gubernias that increase did not exceed half a desiatin. . . . .[59]

HOW THE PEASANTS SOCIALIZED THE LAND

[From the Recollections of "Z——"][60]

For a number of years I spent the summers and parts of the winter at the estate of my friends N——. In the neighborhood I was taken as a member of [the N——] family and I came to know practically every peasant living near by. . . . .

The estate of my friends was situated in a gubernia in the neighborhood of Moscow. . . . . There were practically no large estates there . . . . and the pomeshchiks who make their homes in the village were in direct contact with the peasants. . . . . There were no agrarian disorders in 1905.

The members of the N—— family . . . . were of a liberal trend of mind. . . . . With many of the peasant families they established the most cordial relations. They christened the [peasants'] children, attended the [peasant] weddings, received the newly-weds, etc. Such

[58] B. Knipovich, "Napravlenie i itogi agrarnoi politiki 1917–1920 gg.," in *O Zemle*, I, 24–25.

[59] B. N. Knipovich, *Ocherk deiatelnosti Narodnogo Kommissariata Zemledeliia za tri goda (1917–1920)*, Moscow, 1920, p. 9. The official figures of the results of the redistribution of land in 1917–1918 are given in *Izvestiia* for November 7, 1920, No. 250, p. 1. According to those figures over twenty million desiatins were distributed in thirty-two gubernias of European Russia. The increase of land per capita varied between 0.007 of a desiatin in Olonetsk Gubernia to 0.77 of a desiatin in Petrograd Gubernia. The average figure, however, varied between 0.09 and 0.39.

[60] "K poznaniiu proisshedshago," in *Russkaia Mysl*, III–V, 1923, 238–56.

were the personal relations [between the landlords and the peasants] in the locality which I am about to describe.

The March Revolution was received in the village with a feeling . . . . of perplexity. . . . . In April [1917], army deserters made their first appearance in the village and [the peasants] began to get excited. They began to see that the events had a greater significance than the mere "change of drivers." . . . . The first revolutionary happening on the N—— estate took place in June 1917 and fully demonstrated the direction in which the peasants' thoughts were running. . . . . The land of the N—— estate was leased to the peasants of the neighboring village of Ivanovka . . . . and not to the village of Lebiadka, the peasants of which were formerly the serfs of the pomeshchik who sold the land to N—— after emancipation . . . . When the time arrived [in 1917] to work the fields, the Ivanovka peasants went to their work as usual . . . . but were met by Lebiadka peasants [determined to prevent them working the field]. The Ivanovka peasants offered no resistance, a fact which is very characteristic of the year 1917. . . . . They notified the owner, who immediately grasped the situation, but decided to play the rôle of a progressive intellectual, loyal to the Revolution and the Provisional Government.

"What is the trouble, gentlemen?" he asked the Ivanovka peasants, with an air of astonishment.

"We will not give up our land to strangers," clamored the crowd.

"What do you mean by strangers?" replied N——. . . . . "The land should belong by right to those who are in need of it. You [have plenty of land] while the Ivanovka peasants have very little. That is not just. They are not strangers but your fellow-peasants who are in need of the land."

Then an old man from among the Lebiadka peasants came to the front . . . . [and said]:

"It is not for you, barin [nobleman], to decide who is rich and who is poor. The land belonged to our landlords. You bought it, but it is ours just the same. They [the Ivanovka peasants] have their own landlords; so let them go to them. We will not give up our land. . . . ."

It is an interesting fact that the Ivanovka peasants kept silent and made no attempt to support N——. . . . . They mounted their horses and departed. . . . . The land was leased to the Lebiadka peasants . . . . and up till November [1917] there was not a single misunderstanding. . . . .

On November 16 or 17, a group of peasants from Lebiadka and from another village (the two villages considered themselves as the former serfs of the particular estate), entered the office of the estate and proposed to the manager to leave at once, or else he would be drowned in the lake. The manager became frightened, ran to the manor house, and asked to be discharged. At the time there was no one in the house but two very young girls. . . . . The younger of the two . . . . came out to the peasants . . . . and asked them what they wanted. There were a few minutes of embarrassed silence. Finally, a peasant came forward . . . . and delivered a long speech. The gist of it was that in view of the possibility of anarchic excesses it was necessary to do everything in an "organized way." . . . . The girl . . . . then said, "Well, do as you please," and entered the house. The peasants . . . . found themselves in a difficult position. They scattered all over the estate, apparently with the intention of taking over the property, but did not seem to know where to begin. . . . . It developed, however, that the two villages were suspicious of one another, each fearing to be cheated by the other. . . . . From subsequent conversations [with the peasants] I gathered that the partition of the pomeshchik's movable property was not part of the peasants' idea of justice. Some of them were opposed to that [partition] . . . . refusing to participate in it; others took part only when threatened with death. Such compulsions were frequent (the idea of common responsibility). . . . .

[Two days later a crowd of about fifty peasants made another visit]. . . . . A young soldier . . . . stepped to the front and made a typical Bolshevik speech. Everybody listened with great attention. Among other things the speech touched on the French Revolution. . . . . One [of the N—— girls] suddenly interrupted the speaker, calling his attention to some historical error which he made. The soldier started to argue at first, but then, fearing that he might compromise himself by arguing with a mere child, silenced her by saying: "It is not a child's business to mix in." And he went on talking. . . . . When he reached that part of his speech in which he said, "All these properties are not yours but ours; you have plundered it; you've sucked enough of our blood," . . . . the older girl began to cry and ran out of the room.

[The older peasants became conscience-stricken and silenced the speaker. However, they took the keys from all the properties and went away. Two days later the children left the estate and the peasants proceeded to divide the property.]

The Lebiadka [peasants] had much land which had been bought from "outside landlords." This land they turned over without any . . . . argument . . . . to the peasants who were formerly the serfs of the landlord from whom the land was purchased. . . . .

The month of April 1918 was in a political sense . . . . the month of a miraculous transformation. . . . . For five days there was a continuous uproar in the fields. . . . . The partition of land . . . . was taking place. . . . . In a week's time everything was settled and the peasants came out to plow their new fields. It seemed almost like a miracle. The speed, the order, and the equality with which the partition was made convinced me of many things. Had the partition benefited only a minority, it is safe to say that it would not have taken place. . . . . The idea of land partition was accepted as morally just by both the gainers and the losers. . . . . When left to themselves the peasants partitioned the land . . . . peacefully . . . . and without the aid of land surveyors, relying solely on the experience gained from communal land ownership. . . . .

DIVIDING THE LAND

Many landowners of Simbirsk had everything taken from them. They have tried to become members of the peasants' organizations in order to be able to remain in the village and to receive at least something to keep them from starving. The peasants, however, take a hostile attitude toward these "bloodsuckers." They either will not admit them at all or else ask an impossible entrance fee. . . . . In a few cases these "bloodsuckers" paid their fee and were admitted, but were later expelled, losing, of course, their money.[61]

. . . . From the center come only general ideas . . . . and the villages try to carry them out . . . . each village in its own way. . . . . There is nevertheless some semblance of uniformity. . . . . Nearly every village has its land committee. . . . . The Zemstvos have practically disappeared . . . . in some cases they have been absorbed by the Soviets; in other cases they work alongside of them. . . . . At the beginning [immediately after the Revolution] land committees were formed in the volost, uezd, and gubernia. Now, however, they are giving way to the Soviets, sometimes working beside them and on their platform. . . . . There have been cases where the committees put up a fight against the Soviets but had to yield in the end.

Peculiar institutions have developed in Soligalich Uezd. . . . . Here there are a number of agricultural communes . . . . from twelve to fifteen families in each. It is a mixed crowd socially—peasants, agronomists, engineers, students, *et al.,* who believe in the communistic idea. . . . .

Occasionally there is opposition to the Soviet Government. . . . . For example in a certain part of Orel Gubernia the peasants resent Soviet interference. In this particular uezd there are valuable private estates which the peasants have plundered and are selling the plunder to speculators. They refuse to divide it [with other peasants] saying,

[61] *Novaia Zhizn,* No. 48, March 22, 1918, p. 4.

"Our lord, our property." They cannot get through their heads that the land belongs to the nation as a whole.

In a certain uezd of Samara Gubernia, two Soviets have been formed—one representing the prosperous peasants, another the poor. They had several fights . . . . and in the end the poor, being the more numerous, carried off the victory. . . . .

A similar struggle between these two elements is going on in Voronezh. The poor are organizing and forcing the kulaks from their positions. Fights are not uncommon.

In [a certain village in] Tver the kulaks declared openly that they were "White Guards" and defied the local Soviet. No open breaks have as yet taken place.

All privately owned land has been taken over by the . . . . Soviets, but by no means in a uniform manner. In a certain uezd in Samara one landowner has been allowed to retain his fifteen hundred desiatins of land by coming to an understanding with the peasants of the neighboring villages. . . . . Here and there a community, realizing the great value of having a well-cultivated estate, has refused to take it into its hands. . . . .

Until almost the end of February there existed in Samara a union of landowners. . . . . They succeeded in organizing the agricultural laborers into a kind of union claiming right over the land of the landowners and telling the Soviet to keep off. . . . .

The question of dividing the landed estates among the different villages is a very complicated one and is being variously settled [in different localities]. . . . . In Pskov Gubernia there is being organized an inter-volost committee to settle disputed claims. . . . . At times these disputes are not settled in a peaceable manner. . . . . Usually the live stock is distributed among the poor farms. The manor houses, etc., are declared to be the property of the nation. . . . . In some gubernias the land is divided up among the population, each receiving from one and a half to two and a half desiatins.[62]

PLANS FOR STATE FARMS[63]

It had always seemed to me that a . . . . fundamental food-supply measure would be the organization of large-scale agricultural enterprises . . . . by different cities or factories—or even directly by the state. . . . . Prior to the [November] Revolution, I had christened such

[62] *Izvestiia,* No. 73, April 13, 1918, p. 6.

[63] Y. Larin, "U kolybeli," in *Narodnoe Khoziaistvo,* No. 11, November 1918, p. 19.

a system with the name, "urbanization of agriculture," . . . . and had become a propagandist in its behalf. [But] the forced adoption of "socialization of land" on November 7 seemed at first to deal a fatal blow to the chances of having my plan adopted. In March, however, the Socialist-Revolutionists withdrew from the Sovnarkom; and early in April I read a report [at the meeting of] the Moscow Soviet . . . . [pointing out] the necessity of introducing state control over agricultural production on those large estates formerly run on a profit-making basis. The Sovnarkom soon adopted my suggestion in a decree which authorized the new Commissariat of Agriculture to form a separate "section for administering land under cultivation."

Gradually the working-class government of our nation of peasants acquired possession . . . . of the estates of the former landlords. . . . .

SOCIALISM AND THE PEASANTS

[A Communist Statement][64]

The Bolshevik insurrection of November 1917 overthrew the power of the bourgeoisie. The main obstacle in the way of carrying out the equal distribution of land was gone. But was it really possible to undertake in November, as an immediate task, the bringing about of socialism—the system of socialized labor on socialized land? Everybody can understand that this was not possible. . . . . The peasant masses have no idea what socialism means and want only a free additional allotment of land on egalitarian principles. We had to accept that program as it was. . . . . Though the law is a considerable improvement on the old order, there is no grain of socialism in it. . . . . The peasantry followed the city proletariat . . . . in its struggle against the immediate enemies—the Tsar, the landowner, the bourgeoisie and financiers. . . . . But no farther! As an independent factor in the struggle for socialism the peasants are of practically no importance. . . . . That is the most obvious and irrefutable fact. What is more, the peasants are frankly opposing socialism. . . . .

That class [the peasants] has nearly everything (everything except a socialistic consciousness!). Why should it then change its habits and seek a new life? Why should it strive to organize agriculture on a communal basis with its rejection of private property and its instituting of an order of complete equality even in matters of consumption . . . . ? That class is still looking up toward its immediate neighbors on the social ladder, toward the village bourgeoisie, and regards with suspicion

[64] V. Meshcheriakov, *O selsko-khoziaistvennykh kommunakh,* Moscow, 1918, pp. 11–12, 16–17, 24–25. Meshcheriakov was a member of the Commissariat of Agriculture.

our attempts to organize the village poor. . . . . For the same reason it is hostile toward the workers' struggle for grain and the food detachments. . . . . Even now we perceive signs of cleavage in the village. The well-to-do peasants begin to view with alarm the village poor raising their heads. Already differences have appeared with regard to the food policy. Where lies the cause of that cleavage? Well, precisely in the class diversity of the village. So long as the peasants had a common interest, viz., the ejection of the landowners, there was unity in the village. But now that we have come closer to the realization of socialism . . . . the possessive instincts of the well-to-do and independent farmers become affected . . . . and their petty-bourgeois prejudices reveal themselves full-fledged.

THE PEASANT VS. THE GOVERNMENT

[A Statement by Lenin][65]

The millions of small [peasant] proprietors [having saved money during the war] . . . . cling to it [as a means of getting control of public property]. They conceal that money from the "state" and reject both communism and socialism, "lying low" until the storm of the proletarian revolution blows over. Either we must bring the small bourgeoisie under *our* control (which can be done by organizing the poor . . . .) or they will overthrow . . . . [the] workers' government just as inevitably and unavoidably as the Napoleons and Cavaignacs—figures which are bound to develop in a soil permeated with small bourgeois mentality—have previously succeeded in doing. Such is the problem which confronts us. The Left Socialist-Revolutionists—with their rhetoric about the "toiling" peasantry—are the only ones who do not perceive this simple and self-evident truth. But who can take seriously a Left Socialist-Revolutionist drowned in his own oratory?

[65] Lenin, *Sochineniia,* XXII, 515.

CHRONOLOGY

1917

Feb. 13 Strikes in a number of Petrograd factories.

18 General Khabalov, Commander of Petrograd Military District, invested with special powers to maintain order.

23 M. V. Rodzianko, President of the State Duma, urges the Tsar to appoint a new ministry having "the confidence of the people."

27 The Duma resumes sessions. Spread of strikes.

March 3 Strike in Putilov factories.

8 Demonstrating workers march toward the center of capital. First clashes with the police.

10 Petrograd workers declare general strike. Troops guard streets. All schools closed. Papers cease to appear. Shooting in many parts of the city. First elections to Petrograd Soviet of Workers' Deputies. Duma passes resolution demanding freedom of speech and press. Tsar decrees dismissal of the State Duma.

11 Strikes break out in Moscow.

12 Mutinous troops occupy the arsenal and Peter and Paul Fortress. Golitsyn resigns as president of Council of Ministers. Provisional Committee of State Duma announces that it has taken into its own hands the restoration of state and public order. Petrograd Soviet of Workers' Deputies formed. Ministers and high state officials arrested.

13 Provisional Committee of Duma appoints special commissars in charge of the ministries. A Revolutionary Committee takes over authority in Moscow. Moscow Soviet formed.

14 First Provisional Government formed. Provisional Executive Committee of State Duma recognized officially by French and English ambassadors. Soviet of Workers' and Soldiers' Deputies issues "Order No. 1."

15 Nicholas II abdicates in favor of Grand Duke Michael Alexandrovich. Tsar appoints Grand Duke Nicholas Nikolaevich Supreme Commander-in-Chief and Prince Lvov president of the Council of Ministers. Ukrainian National Rada formed at Kiev.

18 Michael Alexandrovich declines to become head of state.

19 General amnesty declared. Autonomy of Finland proclaimed. Executive Committee of the Soviet appoints its own commissars to all army units. End of general strike.

20 Petrograd Committee of Bolsheviks appeals to Petrograd Soviet to introduce eight-hour day and to appeal to proletariat of the belligerent countries to support peace. Provisional Government decrees the arrest of Emperor and Empress.

21 Nicholas II arrested.

22 Provisional Government recognized *de jure* by United States.

24 Provisional Government recognized *de jure* by France, England, and Italy.

25 Provisional Government abolishes death penalty. All properties and income of Nicholas II transferred to State.

27 Petrograd Soviet appeals "to the people of the entire world" to conclude a democratic peace.

28 All properties of Imperial family nationalized. Strikes in Moscow for eight-hour day.

29 Provisional Government proclaims independence of Poland.

April 2 Government proclaims equal rights for women.

7 Government orders establishment of a grain monopoly and local food-supply organs. Buriat congress at Irkutsk, with representatives of some other Eastern Siberian natives, deliberates on local nationality affairs and administration.

11 All-Russian Conference of Soviets in Petrograd.

16 V. I. Ulianov (Lenin) and other Bolsheviks reach Petrograd.

20 Publication of Lenin's theses against continuation of the war, against the Provisional Government, and for a Soviet republic.

May 1 P. N. Miliukov, Minister of Foreign Affairs, publishes note stating that Provisional Government would adhere to agreements with Allies.

3 Demonstrations in Petrograd and Moscow against Miliukov's note. Firing in streets. Siberian Regionalist Congress at Tomsk discusses regional administration for Siberia.

4 Provisional Government orders establishment of Central Land Committee to prepare land law for approval by Constituent Assembly.

6 Government approves statute organizing factory-shop committees.

7 All-Russian Conference of Bolshevik Party opens in Petrograd.

8 Executive Committee of Soviet schedules international Socialist Conference for Stockholm.

13 A. I. Guchkov, Minister of War and Navy, resigns.

15 Miliukov resigns.

16 Transactions in land prohibited by order of Provisional Government.

17 All-Russian Soviet of Peasant Deputies established. L. D. Trotsky returns to Russia.

18 First Coalition Government formed.

19 Ukrainian Army Congress declares for Ukrainian autonomy.

June 7 Resolution of All-Russian Congress of Peasants' Deputies to transfer the land to the peasants without compensation.

12 Ukrainian Peasant Congress declares for federal republic and Ukrainian autonomy. First conference of factory-shop committees in Petrograd.

16 First All-Russian Congress of Soviets of Workers' and Soldiers' Deputies opens. Provisional Government proposes an Inter-Allied Conference to revise war aims and postpones question of Ukrainian autonomy until All-Russian Constituent Assembly.

17 Provisional Government decrees zemstvo self-government for Siberia and Far East.

24 Ukrainian Rada issues "First Universal" and proclaims Ukrainian autonomy.

27 Provisional Government sets October 13 as opening of Constituent Assembly.

July 1 Russian offensive in Galicia begins.

4 All-Russian Conference of Trade Unions meets in Petrograd.

11 Defeats of Russian Army.

15 Provisional Government declares National Autonomy for Ukraine.

16 Cadet ministers resign in protest. Riots in Petrograd under Bolshevik slogans.

17 Riots and strikes continue.

18 Bolsheviks accused of being German agents.

19 Arrest of Bolshevik leaders ordered. Russian front broken through near Tarnopol. Finnish Seim proclaims the autonomy of Finland.

20 Prince Lvov resigns. Kerensky appointed Prime Minister.

21 At Orenburg, congress of Kirghiz declares for regional autonomy.

25 Provisional Government re-establishes death penalty at the front.

Aug. 1 General Kornilov appointed Supreme Commander-in-Chief.

6 Second Coalition Government formed with Kerensky as Prime Minister.

8 Sixth Congress of Bolshevik Party opens in Petrograd.

19 Moscow Conference of Factory-Shop Committees demands transfer of power to Soviets.

25–28 State Conference at Moscow.

29 All-Russian Church Sobor opens in Moscow.

Sept. 3 Germans occupy Riga.

8–12 Kornilov affair.

9 Kornilov declared an enemy of people.

14 Russia declared republic. Directory of five formed.

27 All-Russian Democratic Conference opens in Petrograd.

Oct. 4 Democratic Conference resolves to form Provisional Council of the Republic (Pre-Parliament).

6 Strike of railway workers. C.E.C. resolves to call All-Russian Congress of Soviets for November 3.

7 Third Coalition Government formed.

8 Trotsky elected chairman of Petrograd Soviet.

18 Provisional Government decides to transfer the capital to Moscow. Kuban Cossack Rada proclaims Kuban independent republic and member of Federation of Russian Nationalities. Congress of Moslems of Orenburg demands national cultural autonomy.

20 Pre-Parliament opens. Bolsheviks withdraw from it. Kuban Cossack Rada resolves to form union of the Southeast to include Kuban, Don, Terek, and Astrakhan Cossacks, and peoples of Northern Caucasus.

23 Central Committee of Bolshevik Party declares for armed uprising against Provisional Government.

24 Congress of Soviets of Northern Region opens in Petrograd.

25 Resolution of the Executive Committee of Petrograd Soviet to form a "Military Revolutionary Committee."

30 C.E.C. postpones opening of Second Congress of Soviets to November 7.

Nov. 3 Petrograd garrison acknowledges authority of Military Revolutionary Committee and advocates transfer of power to Soviets.

4 M.R. Committee orders Petrograd garrison to disregard orders of District Military Staff.

5 M.R. Committee appoints special commissars to different units of garrison.

6 Provisional Government proclaims Petrograd in state of insurrection and summons troops from front.

7 M.R. Committee declares Provisional Government deposed. Second Congress of Soviets opens at Smolny. General Kaledin assumes control over Don region. Moldavian Military Congress proclaims Bessarabian autonomy. Military Revolutionary Committee organized in Moscow.

8 Winter Palace captured by insurgent troops and members of government arrested. Anti-Bolshevik groups organize a "Committee to Save the Country and the Revolution." Kerensky, at Northern front, organizes expedition against Petrograd. Second Congress of Soviets proclaims assumption of power by Soviets and issues peace and land decrees. New Soviet Government formed. Revolutionary troops occupy Moscow Kremlin.

11 Anti-Bolshevik uprising of cadets of Petrograd military schools. Sovnarkom decrees eight-hour working day. Inter-party negotiations to form all-Socialist government under auspices of Vikzhel. Street fighting in Moscow.

12–13 Kerensky's forces defeated at Pulkovo and retreat to Gatchina.

15 General Alexeev arrives in Novocherkassk and begins organization of Volunteer Army. Sovnarkom issues decree on rights of peoples of Russia to self-determination. Bolshevik victories in Moscow.

20 Ukrainian Rada proclaims Ukrainian National Republic. Sovnarkom orders Dukhonin to open armistice negotiations.

21 Trotsky proposes general armistice to French Ambassador.

22 Lenin appoints Krylenko commander-in-chief and urges soldiers and sailors to negotiate with enemy. Russian secret diplomatic documents published by Bolsheviks.

23 Abolition of class distinctions and civil ranks.

23–28 Special Congress of Peasants' Deputies.

25–27 Elections for Constituent Assembly in Petrograd.

27 Central Powers agree to open peace negotiations. C.E.C. issues decree on Workers' Contrŏl. Agreement reached between Bolsheviks and Left Socialist-Revolutionsts.

28 Esthonian National Council appoints committee which provisionally assumes functions of local government. Regional Government of Transcaucasia formed.

Dec. 1 Russian delegation leaves for Brest-Litovsk to negotiate armistice.

2 Moldavian National Council (Sfatul Tserii) proclaims Moldavian Democratic Republic part of Federal Russian Republic.

3 General Dukhonin murdered.

5 Agreement on suspension of hostilities signed at Brest-Litovsk.

9 Sovnarkom declares war against Cossack chiefs (Kaledin, Kornilov, Dutov, etc.). Second All-Russian Congress of Peasants' Deputies opens.

10 Tartar National Assembly (Kurultai) appoints directory of five as government of Crimean Tartar Republic.

11 Moslem Congress in Turkestan proclaims territorial autonomy of Turkestan.

14 C.E.C. establishes Supreme Council of National Economy.

15 Armistice signed at Brest-Litovsk.

17 Sovnarkom sends ultimatum to Ukrainian Rada.

20 All-Russian Extraordinary Commission (Cheka) formed and holds first meeting.

22 First session of peace conference at Brest-Litovsk. Representatives of Left Socialist-Revolutionists enter Sovnarkom. Occupation of Bessarabia by Rumanian troops.

23 Tartar National Assembly of Crimea appointed regional government.

25 First All-Ukraine Congress of Soviets at Kharkov elects a C.E.C. to take over power in Ukraine.

26 Kirghiz Congress declares autonomy of Kasak-Kirghiz and establishes government of Alash-Orda at Semipalatinsk.

27 Banks nationalized. Search of safe deposit boxes and confiscation of hoarded gold ordered.

31 Civil administration of Volunteer Army formed at Novocherkassk. Sovnarkom recognizes Finland's independence. White Russian congress dispersed by Bolsheviks.

1918

Jan. 5 Representatives of Ukrainian Rada arrive at Brest-Litovsk to negotiate peace with Central Powers. Central Committee of All-Russian Zemstvo Union dissolved by Sovnarkom.

11 Sovnarkom orders discontinuance of interest and dividend payments and prohibits all transactions in bonds.

13 Bolsheviks arrest Rumanian Minister, Diamandi, and seize Rumanian gold in retaliation for Rumanian activities in Bessarabia.

14 Commander-in-Chief of Turkish Army proposes peace with "independent" government of the Caucasus.

16 C.E.C. declares all power in Russian Republic vested in Soviets and Soviet institutions.

18 Constituent Assembly opens. Bolsheviks and Socialist-Revolutionists of Left withdraw from Constituent Assembly. Demonstrations in Petrograd broken up by Bolshevik armed forces.

19 C.E.C. dissolves the Constituent Assembly.

20 First All-Russian Congress of Trade Unions.

22 Rada declares Ukraine independent.

23 First session of Third Congress of Soviets. "Declaration of the Rights of the Toiling and Exploited People" adopted. Cossack Military Revolutionary Committee formed to fight Kaledin.

26 Third All-Russian Congress of Soviets of Peasants' Deputies opens.

28 Third All-Russian Congress of Soviets passes resolution establishing Federal Constitution of Russian Republic. Sovnarkom decrees organization of Worker-Peasant Red Army.

29 Provisional revolutionary government formed in Finland and outbreak of civil war there. Soviet troops enter Kiev. Ukrainian Rada deposed. C.E.C. of Ukrainian Soviets and People's Secretariat of Kharkov proclaimed government of Ukraine.

31 "Fundamental Law of Land Socialization" adopted by Third Congress of Soviets. Third Congress of Soviets adjourns.

Feb. 1 Patriarch anathematizes Bolsheviks.

5 Separation of church and state.

8 Czechoslovak Corps in Russia declared autonomous part of Czechoslovak forces in France. Merchant Marine nationalized by Sovnarkom.

9 Rada signs separate peace treaty with Germany.

10 At Tomsk "All-Siberian Peasant Congress" declares for Siberian Regional Duma. Russians break off negotiations at Brest-Litovsk with the "No peace no war" declaration. Annulment of state loans.

12 Death of Kaledin.

15 Sovnarkom creates Extraordinary Commission on Food and Transport.

16 Germans declare the armistice at an end at noon of February 18.

17 Rada appeals to the Germans for help to withstand invasion of Soviets.

18 Sovnarkom agrees to accept peace terms of German Government.

19 Decree on socialization of land published by C.E.C.

25 Bolsheviks occupy Novocherkassk, capital of Don region.

27 American and other foreign embassies leave Petrograd.

March 3 Brest-Litovsk Treaty signed.

5 Allies land at Murmansk.

6–8 Seventh Congress of Bolshevik Party. Name of the party changed to Russian Communist Party (Bolshevik).

8 Seventh Bolshevik Party Congress passes Majority Resolution for peace.

12 Moscow becomes seat of central government.

14–16 Fourth Congress of Soviets.

15–16 Fourth Congress of Soviets ratifies Brest-Litovsk Treaty.

16 Kiev occupied by Germans.

26 Soviet-Czech agreement for evacuation of Czechoslovak legions concluded.

April 2 Exchange of commodities for grain decreed by Sovnarkom.

5 Japanese and English forces landed at Vladivostok. Peace between Germany and Finland. Kharkov occupied by Germans.

6 Chicherin protests against Japanese intervention.

9 Union of Bessarabia and Rumania proclaimed.
10 Decree on Consumers' Co-operatives passed by Sovnarkom.
11 Anarchist clubs liquidated by Bolsheviks. Failure of Volunteer Army at Ekaterinodar.
13 Germans occupy Odessa.
15 Batum seized by Turks.
18 Chicherin protests against Rumania's seizure of Bessarabia.
20 German troops occupy Crimea.
22 Transcaucasian Republic declares independence. Foreign trade nationalized. Compulsory military training decreed by C.E.C.
23 Count Mirbach arrives in Moscow as German Ambassador.
29 Decree on Accounting and Control.

INDEX

(Including biographical and other details)

D

E

O

Q

R

Riabtsov, Colonel (district commander, Moscow, 1917), 176–77

Riazan, 599, 658, 659, 663, 664, 670

Riazanov, David Borisovich (Goldendakh) (1870–1933; active in Russian Trade Union movement, 1905–1907; editor of works of Marx and Engels; joined Bolsheviks, July 1907; active in organization of Tsentroarkhiv, Communist Academy, Marx and Engels Institute; excommunicated from the party, 1931), 3 n., 110, 154, 166, 168, 203, 313, 363 n., 384

Robins, Raymond (1875–1954; American; social-economist; social worker in Chicago, 1902–1912; active in Progressive movement; chairman Progressive National Convention, 1916; head of American Red Cross Mission in Russia, 1917–1918), 488, 488 n., 506 n., 535–36, 581, 603, 622 n.

Rodichev, Fedor Izmailovich (1856–1933; active in zemstvo work; member of Liberation League and of Cadet Party and of the 1st, 2d, 3d, and 4th Dumas; commissar, Provisional Government in Finland, 1917), 346, 359

Rodzianko, Mikhail Vladimirovich (1859–1924; Kammerherr of Imperial Court; later active in zemstvo affairs; Octobrist; member 1st, and president, 3d and 4th Dumas; chairman Provisional Committee of the Duma which organized the Provisional Government), 64, 66, 70, 408, 422

Rogov, A., People's Commissar, 653, 656

Romanovsky, General (–1920; participant in the Kornilov affair; chief-of-staff, Volunteer Army under Denikin; assassinated by a Russian officer in Constantinople, 1920), 267 n., 406

Romei, General (representative of the Italian General Staff in Russia), 265

Rosenberg, Dr. von (Privy Counsellor, German Ministry of Foreign Affairs, 1912–1918; Minister Plenipotentiary, 1918; at Brest-Litovsk), 269, 476

Roshal, Semen Grigorevich (1896–1917; joined Bolsheviks, 1914; commissar, Rumanian Front after November Revolution; shot by the Whites, 1917), 268

Ross, E. A., *The Russian Bolshevik Revolution,* 106 n.

Rostov-on-Don, 30, 407, 410, 411, 415 n., 422, 427

Roucek, J. S., *Contemporary Roumania and Her Problems,* 463 n.

Roumanian Occupation in Bessarabia; Documents, The, 463 n., 464 n.

Rozhkov, Nikolai Alexandrovich (1868–1927; historian; professor Moscow University; Bolshevik, 1905; arrested, exiled, 1908; released, 1917; joined United S.D. Internationalists, 1917; contributor to *Novaia Zhizn;* later closer to Bolsheviks), 192

R.S.D.L.P. (Bolshevik), *see* Bolshevik Party

Rudnev, Vadim Vasilevich (1874– ; S.R.; Mayor of Moscow, 1917; member Union for Regeneration of Russia; active anti-Bolshevik during civil war), 180, 356

Rumania, 243, 427, 485; and the armistice, 259; and Bessarabia, 462–65; and the Central Powers, 462–63, 464, 508, 524

Rusanov, Nikolai Sergeevich (1859– ; member Executive Committee *Narodnaia Volia;* later an S.R.; editor various S.R. papers in Russia and abroad), 347

Russian Economist, The (quarterly journal of the Russian Economic Association in London; September 1920–June 1923), 318 n.

Russian Social-Democratic Labor Party, split in, 3 n.; *see also* Menshevik Party, Bolshevik Party, Menshevik Internationalists, and Social-Democrats Internationalists (United)

Russkaia Mysl (periodical founded 1880 by V. M. Lavrov reflecting Slavophil, later liberal Narodnik, and still later Cadet ideas; closed, 1918; resumed publication abroad, edited by P. S. Struve), 679 n.

Russkaia Volia (daily, founded in Petrograd in 1916 by Protopopov with the financial assistance of large banks; discontinued in 1917), 221

Russkiia Vedomosti (daily newspaper, organ of Russian Liberals, founded in Moscow in 1863 by N. F. Pavlov; edited by N. S. Skvortsov, 1866–1882;

T

W

Y

Z